The Egyptian Heaven and Hell

E. A. Wallis Budge

THREE VOLUMES BOUND AS ONE

DOVER PUBLICATIONS, INC.
Mineola, New York

Published in Canada by General Publishing Company, Ltd., 30 Lesmill Road, Don Mills, Toronto, Ontario.

Published in the United Kingdom by Constable and Company, Ltd., 3 The Lanchesters, 162–164 Fulham Palace Road, London W6 9ER.

Bibliographical Note

This Dover edition, first published in 1996, is a republication in a single volume of the work originally published by Kegan Paul, Trench, Trübner & Co., Ltd., London, in 1905 as Volumes XX–XXII in the series "Books on Egypt and Chaldaea." The original foldout frontispiece in Volume II has been reduced and is now on pp. ii and iii in the Volume II section. In addition, two other plates have been repositioned in the present edition.

Library of Congress Cataloging-in-Publication Data

Budge, E. A. Wallis (Ernest Alfred Wallis), Sir, 1857–1934.
The Egyptian heaven and hell / E.A. Wallis Budge.
p. cm.
Originally published : London : Kegan Paul, Trench, Trübner & Co., 1905.
"Three volumes bound as one."
Includes index.
Contents : v. 1. The Book of ȧm-ṭuat—v. 2. The short form of the Book of ȧm-ṭuat and the Book of gates—v. 3. The contents of the books of the other world described and compared.
ISBN 0-486-29368-8 (pbk.)
1. Eschatology, Egyptian. I. Book of that which is in the nether world. English. 1996. II. Title.
PJ1551.B7 1996
299′.31—dc20 96-33509
CIP

Manufactured in the United States of America
Dover Publications, Inc., 31 East 2nd Street, Mineola, N.Y. 11501

The Egyptian Heaven and Hell

VOLUME I

THE BOOK ȦM-ṬUAT

NOTE

THIS volume is the first of a series of three volumes which treat of the Egyptian Heaven and Hell. It contains the complete hieroglyphic text of the BOOK ȦM-ṬUAT, with translations, and reproductions of all the illustrations. A series of Chapters dealing with the origin and contents of Books of the Other World, with prefatory remarks, and a full index to the whole work, will be found in the third volume.

CONTENTS.

ERRATA

P. 32, l. 1, for "phallus" read "Ass"; p. 60, l. 13, for "Hon" read "Hou"; *ibid.*, l. 19, for "confieh" read "coufieh"; p. 70, l. 7, for 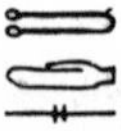 read 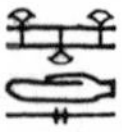; p. 81, l. 6, for 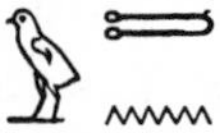 read 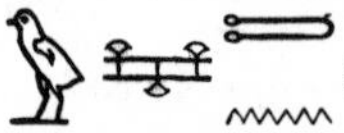; p. 139, l. 3, for "Thepḥet-Åsår" read "Thepḥet-shetat"; p. 256, l. 3, for "Then-neteru" read "Kheper-kekiu-khāu-mestu."

THE BOOK ȦM-ṬUAT

THE TITLE OF THE WORK

"The writings and the drawings of the hidden "palace which appertain to the souls, and the "gods, and the shadows, and the spirits, which "compose the Beginning of the Horn of Ȧment, "of the horizon of Ȧment, [which is] the utmost "boundary of the thick darkness of the horizon of "Ȧmentet, containing the knowledge of the Souls "of the Ṭuat, and the knowledge of the Secret "Souls, and the knowledge of the doors and "the ways through and on which the great god "journeyeth, and the knowledge of . . . ., "and the knowledge of the hours and of their "gods, and the knowledge of the journeyings of "the hours and of their gods, and the knowledge "of the formulae [which they say] to Rā, and "the knowledge of the speeches which he maketh

"TO THEM, AND THE KNOWLEDGE OF THE GODS WHO "PRAISE HIM AND OF THOSE WHO EFFECT DESTRUCTION."

[1] The duplicate text reads:— 

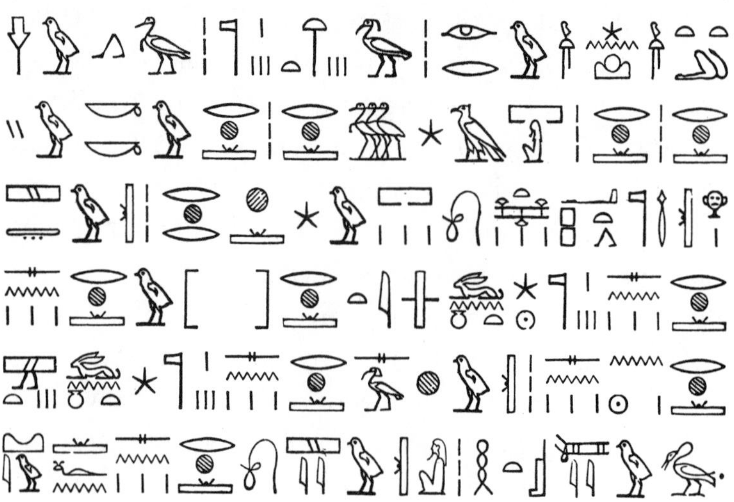

CHAPTER I.

THE FIRST DIVISION OF THE ṬUAT, WHICH IS CALLED NET-RĀ.

In the scene that illustrates the First Division of the Ṭuat, which is passed through by the Sun-god during the First Hour of the night, we see that the centre of the middle section is divided lengthwise into

The Boat of Āf, the dead Sun-god. Maāti goddesses. Neken-f.

two parts by a river which flows along it. In the upper part is the boat of the dead Sun-god Āf, [hieroglyphs], who is in the form of a ram-headed man; he wears a disk upon his head, and stands within a shrine in the Sektet boat, i.e., the boat in which the god travels from noon to sunset. In front of the shrine in the boat stand the three deities, ȦP-UAT, , SA, , and the "Lady of the Boat," , who wears on her head a disk and horns. Behind the shrine stand five gods, each having the head of a man; the names of the first four are ḤERU-ḤEKENU, , KA-SHU, , i.e., the "double of Shu," NEHES, , i.e., the "Look-out," and ḤU, , and the fifth is the Steersman KHERP, . On the high prow of the Sektet boat hangs an object which is said to be a carpet by some, and a reed mat by others, and on the side, near the curve of the prow, is an *utchat*. In front of the boat march:—

1. The two goddesses MAĀT, the one representing the South of Egypt, and the other the North.

2. The god NEKENT-F, , who holds a spear, or knife, in his left hand.

3. The god KHENTI ȦMENTET, bearded, and in mummy form, and wearing the White Crown and the Menȧt.

4. The god SEKHET, or as it is written here SEKHMET, , lioness-headed.

5. The god SEḤETCH-UR, , ram-headed.

6. Four Terms, the first of which is called UT-METU-RĀ,

, the second UT-METU-TEM, , the third UT-METU-KHEPERÀ, , and the fourth UT-METU-ÀSÀR, .

7. The leader of the company, who is called TCHA-UNNUT, ; by his side is a serpent, called SA (?), that stands on his tail.

The gods Khenti-Àmentet, Sekhet, Seḥetch-ur, the Four Terms, and Tcha-Unnut.

This scene is explained by the horizontal line of inscription written above it, and the hieroglyphic text, based on the editions of Lefébure and Champollion, reads :—

"The name of this Field is 'MAĀTI.' This god "arriveth in the SEKTET BOAT, he maketh a way "through the Court of this city, which is two hundred "and twenty measures in length, which he travelleth "through to URNES. He passeth through the water, "which is three hundred measures in extent, and he "bestoweth the fields upon the gods who follow him. "NET-RĀ is the name of this Field, ȦRNEBȦUI is the "name of the guardian [of this Field]. This god "beginneth to declare in this region the words which "perform the destinies (?) of those who are in the "Ṭuat."

In the lower part of the middle section of the scene we have another boat, in the centre of which is a beetle; on one side of the beetle is a god with his knees in the direction of the prow of the boat, but having his head turned behind him and his hands raised in adoration of the beetle, and on the other is a god who also has his hands raised in adoration of the same object. The legend reads [1], i.e., "the coming into being of Osiris"; as the boat has

[1] For  *kheper en*.

no reed mat or carpet hanging from the prow, we may assume that it is intended to represent the Āṭet or Māṭet Boat, i.e., the boat in which the Sun-god travelled over the sky from sunrise to noon.

The Boat of the Birth of Osiris, with serpents and gods.

In front of the boat glide three serpents, which are called SEK-RE, , SEFÀ, , and NEPEN, , and in front of these march four man-headed

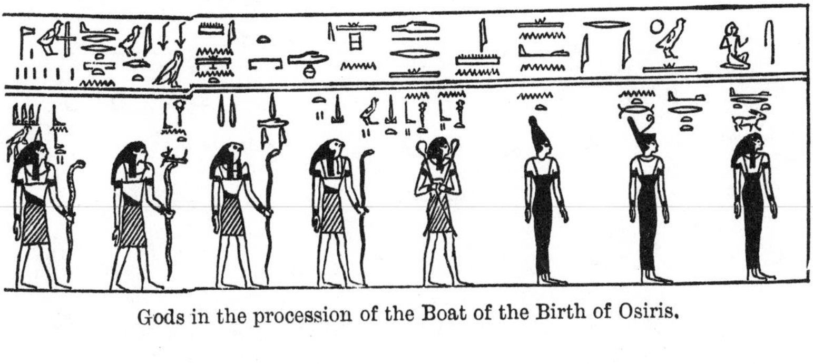

Gods in the procession of the Boat of the Birth of Osiris.

gods and two hawk-headed gods, each with a serpent in his left hand, a god called NĀBTI, , who holds a crook in each hand, NET, or NEITH, goddess of the South, NET, or NEITH, goddess of the North, and the goat goddess ĀRTET, . The two hawk-headed gods are called TCHATUI, , and METI, , and the four following gods ĀBENTI, , BENBETI, , SEKHTI, and SEKHET (?), .

The explanation of this scene is given by the horizontal line of hieroglyphic text written above it, which reads:—

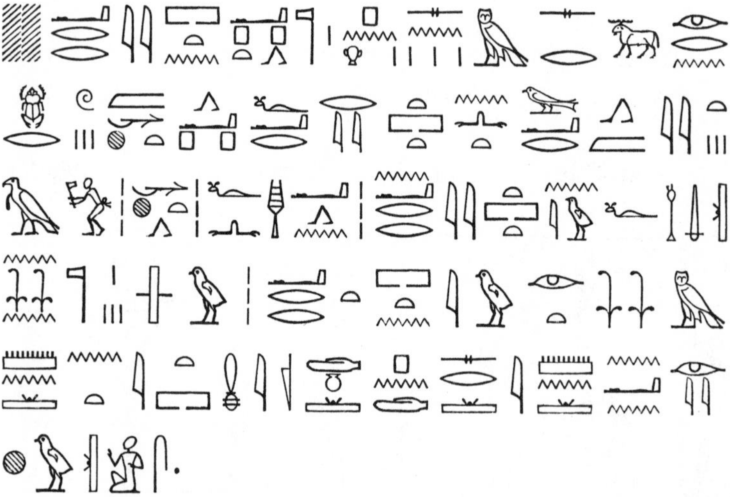

"[The god cometh to] this Court, he passeth through it "in the form of a ram, and he maketh his transformations "therein. After he hath passed through this Court, "the dead who are in his following do not [go with "him], but they remain in this Court, and he speaketh "words unto the gods who are therein. If copies of "these things be made according to the ordinances of "the hidden house, and after the manner of that which "is ordered in the hidden house, they shall act as "magical protectors to the man who maketh them."

In the upper register are the following:—

I. Nine apes, who are described as "the gods who open the gates to the Great Soul," . Their names are:—1. UN-TA, . 2. BA-TA, . 3. MAA-EN-RĀ, . 4. ÅBTA, . 5. ÅBÅBEN, . 6. ÅKEN-ÅB, . 7. BENTH, . 8. ÅFÅ, . 9. TCHEḤTCHEḤ, .[1]

II. Twelve divine beings, who are described as the "goddesses who unfold the portals in the earth," . Their names are:—1. QAT-Ā, . 2. NEBT-MEKET, . 3. SEKHIT, . 4. ÅMENT-URT, .

[1] The variants are:—1. . 2. . 3. . 4. . 5. . 6. . 9. .

5. SHEFTU, . 6. REN-THETHEN, . 7. ḤEKENT-EM-SA-S, . 8. QAT-EM-KHU-S, . 9. SEKHET-EM-KHEFTIU-S, . 10. ḤUIT, . 11. ḤUNT, . 12. NEBT-ĀNKH, .

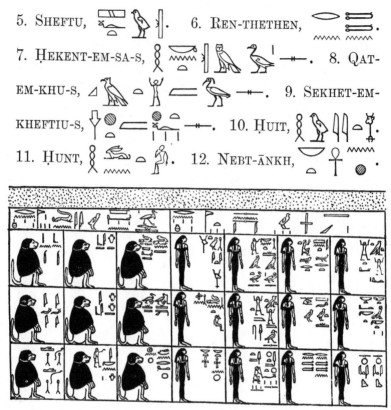

The nine Ape-warders. The twelve goddesses of the gates.

Each goddess stands with her arms hanging by her sides.[1]

[1] The variants are :—1. . 2. . 4. . 5. . 6. . 7. . 8. . 9. . 10. . 11. . 12 .

III. Nine seated gods, each with his hands raised in adoration of Rā; they are called the "gods who praise Rā," . The first three are man-headed, and are called ḤETCH-Ā, , MAA-Ā, , and ḤES-Ā, ; the second three are jackal-headed, and are called NEB-TA-ṬESHER, , ÅP-UAT, , and ÅP-SEKHEMTI, ; and the third three are crocodile-headed, and are called TCHAT-ṬUAT, , SEḲI, , and SEKHEM-ḤRÅ, .[1]

IV. Twelve divine beings, in the form of women, who are described as "the goddesses who guide the great god," . Their names are:—1. ṬENṬENIT, . 2. SBAI, . 3. MAT-NEFERU-NEB-SET, . 4. KHESEFET-SMATET, . 5. KHUAI, . 6. MĀKET-ÅRI-S, . 7. URT-ÅMT-ṬUAT, . 8. ḤER-ÅB-UÅA-

[1] The variants are:—1. . 2. . 3. . 4. . 5. . 6. . 7. . 8. . 9. .

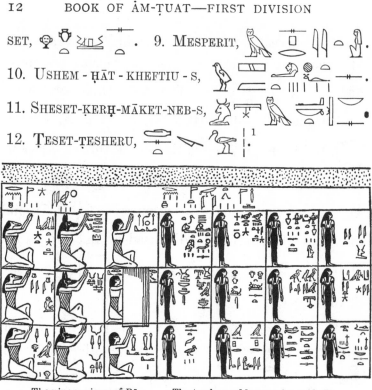

SET, . 9. MESPERIT, . 10. USHEM - ḤĀT - KHEFTIU - S, . 11. SHESET-ḲERḤ-MĀKET-NEB-S, . 12. ṬESET-ṬESHERU, .[1]

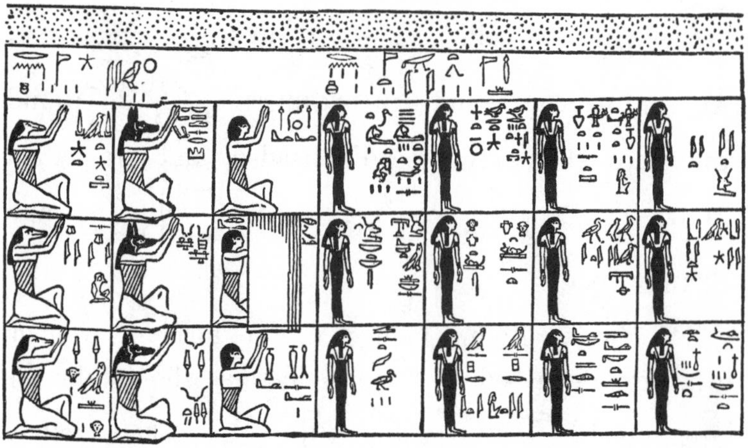

The nine praisers of Rā. The twelve goddesses who guide Rā.

In the lower register are the following:—

I. Nine seated apes, who are described as the "gods

[1] The variants are:—1. . 2. . 3. . 4. . 5. . 6. . 7. . 8. . 9. . 10. . 11. . 12. .

who sing to Rā as he entereth into the Ṭuat," . Their names are:—
1. Ȧm-kar, . 2. Khenti-she-f, . 3. . . . . ḤEN, . 4. Ḥeken-em-ben-f, . 5, 6. . . . . 7. Heththi, . 8. Pa-theth, . 9. . . . .[1]

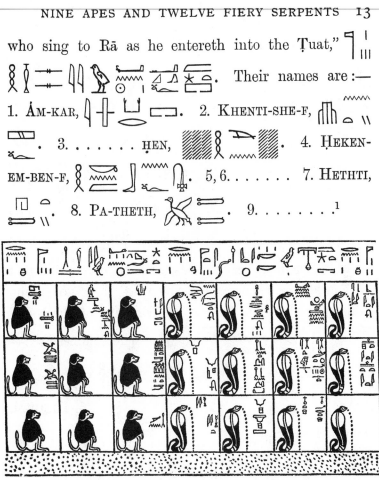

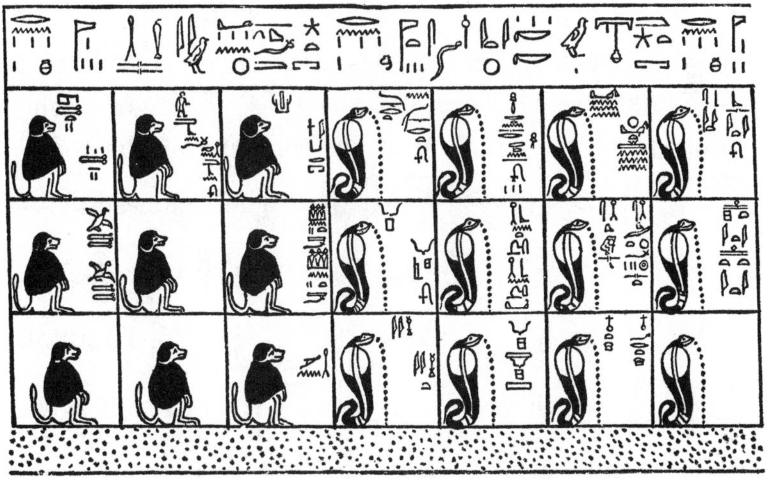

The nine singing apes. The twelve light-giving uraei.

II. Twelve serpents, who throw fire forth from their mouths, and are described as "those who make light

[1] The variants are:—1. . 4. . In Dümichen's edition (pl. iii.) three of the apes are called Besi, , Ṭuai, , and Ȧbti, .

the darkness in the Ṭuat." Their names are:—1. BESIT, . 2. ḤETEPIT, . 3. . 4. KHUT-MU, . 5. ḤESEQ-KHEFTI-SET, . 6. NEFERT-KHĀ, . 7. MERT-NESER, . 8. BEḤENT, . 9. ÅP-SHE, . 10. NESERT, . 11. ÅP-ÅST, . 12. SHENIT, .[1]

III. Nine man-headed gods, with their hands raised in adoration, who are described as the "gods who praise [Rā], . . . the lord of the company of the gods," . Their names are:—1. KA-ṬUAT, . 2. ḤETEM-ÅB, . 3. ÅRÅ, . 4. ÅAU, . 5. HEMHEM, . 6. KA-NETERU, . 7. ṬUATI, . 8. ḤEKENNU-RĀ, . 9. ĀA-ÅTER, .

[1] The variants are:—1. . 4. . 5. . 6. . 7. . 8. . 10. . 11. . 12. .

IV. Twelve goddesses, with their arms hanging by their sides, who are described as " those who give praises to Rā as he passeth over URNES," . Their names are:—1. MAA-NETER-S, . 2. ÅRT-NETER-S, . 3. ḤEKENT, . 4. NET, . 5. ĀPERT-RE,

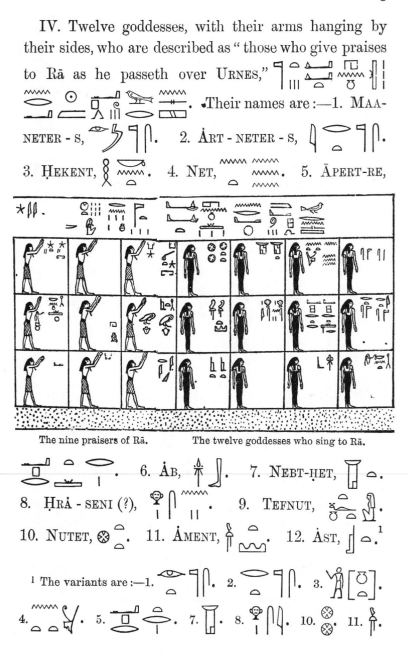

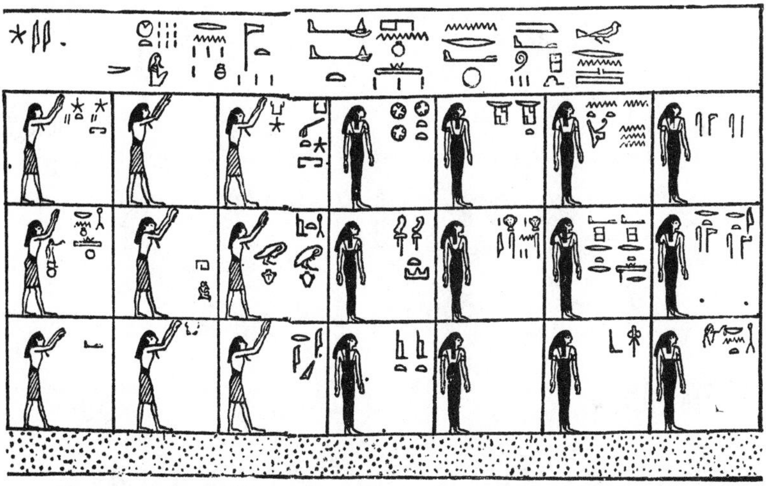

The nine praisers of Rā. The twelve goddesses who sing to Rā.

. 6. ÅB, . 7. NEBT-ḤET, . 8. ḤRÅ-SENI (?), . 9. TEFNUT, . 10. NUTET, . 11. ÅMENT, . 12. ÅST, .[1]

[1] The variants are:—1. . 2. . 3. . 4. . 5. . 7. . 8. . 10. . 11. .

The address which the Sun-god makes to the gods in the First Division of the Ṭuat reads:[1]—

[1] See Léfebure, *op. cit.*, part iv., pl. 28, and *Description de l'Égypte*, tom. v., pl. 41, no. 5.

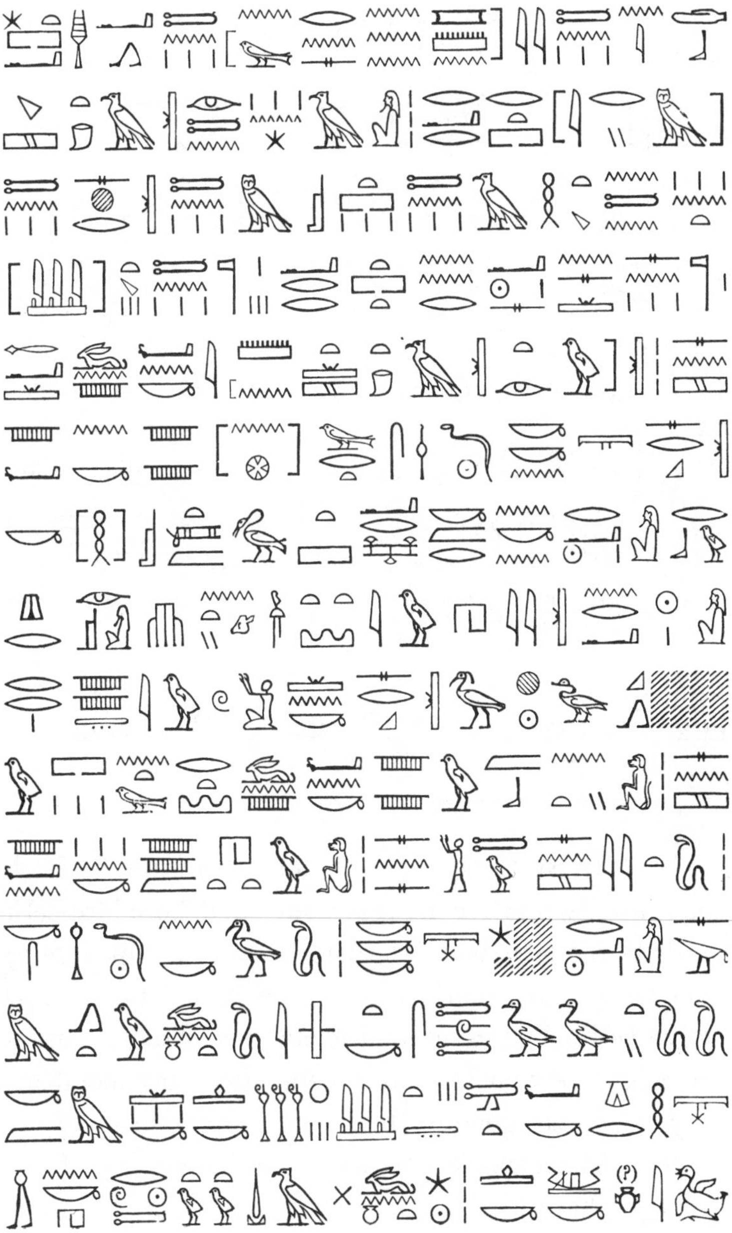

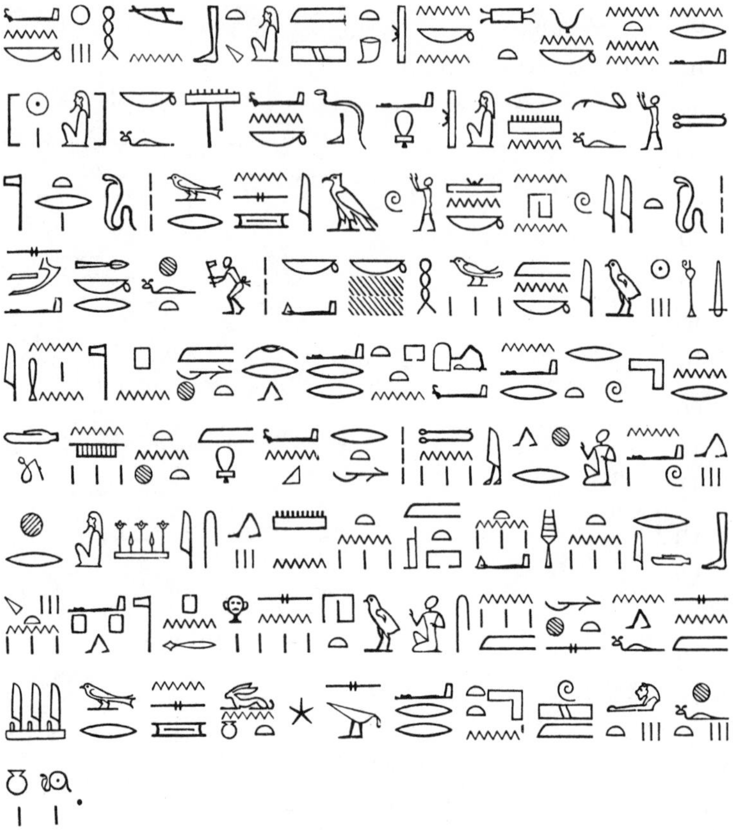

The Majesty of this god standeth up after he hath taken up his position in this Court, and he addresseth words to the gods who are therein, saying, "Open ye to "me your doors, and let me come into your Courts! "Give ye light unto me, and make ye yourselves guides "to me, O ye who came into being from my members, "my word hath gone forth to you. Ye are made of my "bodies, I have made you, having fashioned you of my "soul. I have created you, I have made you by means "of my enchantments, [and] I have come to avenge "myself the blood of my members which have risen up "against me, and I will bring to destruction that which "hath been made for it. I will make perfect with the ". . . . . . of my forms Osiris Khenti Ȧmenti. Open "to me the doors with your hands, O ye Apes, unfold "to me the portals of the Courts, O ye Apes, [and "welcome] the gods (or, goddesses) who have come "into being from my divine Souls, come ye into being, "come ye into being for (?) KHEPERȦ, O ye who have "your being at the head of the Ṭuat. Stand ye up, in "URNES, and stablish ye yourselves on the secret banks "thereof, and work ye for the gods of Ṭuat in the "Court which ye guard, possess ye your plans in your "seats, in your domains and in your fields."

The gods of this Court say unto Rā, "O great god, "[the doors] are opened to thee, and the portals of the "secret Ȧment are thrown open before thee, the doors "of Nut the great are thrown wide open, illumine "thou the darkness of night (or, thick darkness), "provide for that which is in the place of destruction, "and approach thou in thy name of Rā the place where "is OSIRIS KHENTI ȦMENTI. There is a shout of joy "to Rā at the entrance to the doors of the earth (?). "Praise be to thee and make thou perfect the light, and "enter thou [in through the habitations] of the Great "Country. The Apes (*ambenti*) open the doors to thee, "the Apes (*amhetetu*) unfold to thee the portals, the "serpents sing and exalt thee, and the divine serpents "lighten thy darkness for thee. . . . . . . O Rā, the "goddess of the hour cometh to thee, the two Soul-"Goddesses tow thee along in thy form, and thou "takest up thy position on the ground of the Field of "[this] land. Thou hast taken possession of the night, "and thou wilt bring in the day, and [thou] dost "likewise make long the hours, and thy boat cometh "to rest. Thou seizest the grain of the god Ḥenbet "in thy secret place (?) Net. Thou openest Net-Rā, "thou uncoverest the god Tchebā, the uraeus goddesses "(*neterit*) of Urnes acclaim thee, the uraeus goddesses "(*nehenuit*) ascribe praise to thee, thy word is *maāt* "against thine enemies, thou givest tribulations to "those who are condemned."

The Majesty of this god uttereth words after he hath come forth into this Court, he doeth battle at the fortifications thereof, the doors of this [Court] are strong, saying, "Shut [your doors] by your bolts. "Come ye to me, advance ye to me, make ye your way "[to me], and ye shall abide in your place; take ye up "your stand on the banks of the stream [Urnes]." This great god passeth them by, and they (i.e., the gods) wail when he hath gone by them in the Field of Urnes. [The goddess of] the hour who guideth [this great god] through this Court is "Ushem-ḥāt-kheftiu-nu-Rā."

CHAPTER II.

THE SECOND DIVISION OF THE ṬUAT, WHICH IS CALLED URNES.

In the scene that illustrates the Second Division of the Ṭuat, which is passed through by the Sun-god

The Boat of Åf in the Second Hour.

during the Second Hour of the night, the Boat of the Ram-headed god Åf is seen making its way along the stream which flows, as before, through the division lengthwise; the crew consists of the same gods, and they occupy the same positions in the boat as they did in the First Division. It is, however, important to notice that immediately in front of Ȧp-uat we see two serpents, which are called Isis and Nephthys respectively, , occupying the front of the boat. No carpet or mat hangs over the bows of the boat, and the *utchat* is not represented on its side; the boat moves over the waters by means of some power exerted either by itself or by some of the gods who stand in it. In front of the boat of ȦF the way is led by a procession of four boats, which are moved, presumably, by the same power which moves the boat of Rā.

The FIRST BOAT has ends which terminate in bearded human heads, and its celestial and solar character is attested by the sign for "heaven," , and the *utchat* , with which its sides are ornamented. The object of this boat is to support the disk of the full moon, which rests within a crescent upon a support divided into thirteen sections, each typifying a day; thus the full moon as it appears on the fourteenth day of the month is here represented. By the disk kneels a god who is "supporting Maāt," , which is symbolized by a feather, and is described by the word MAĀT, , written between it and the support of the moon's disk. In the mutilated text above the boat it is said that "this great god approacheth this "region, and he is conveyed along in the boats of the "earth, by means of their . . . . ., and he paddleth "along through this Field and uttereth words,"

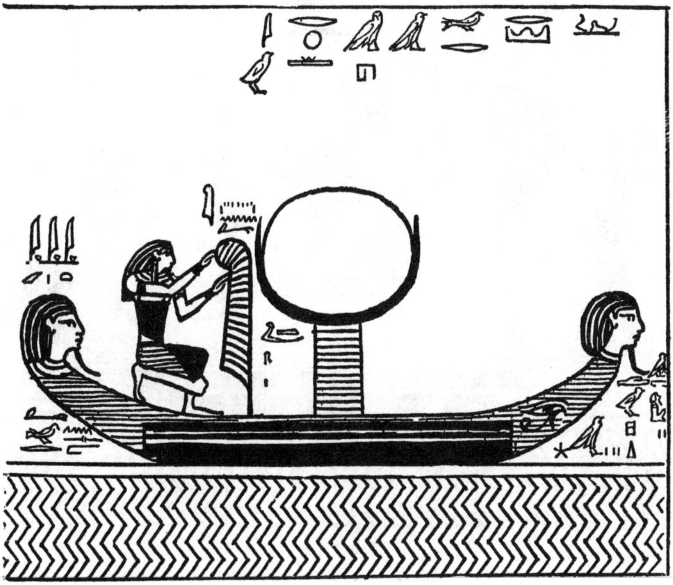

The Boat of the Full Moon.

The name of the fore part of the boat appears to be URER, 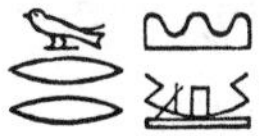, and in front of the boat is written "Chief of the gods of the Ṭuat," ;[1]

[1] Var. .

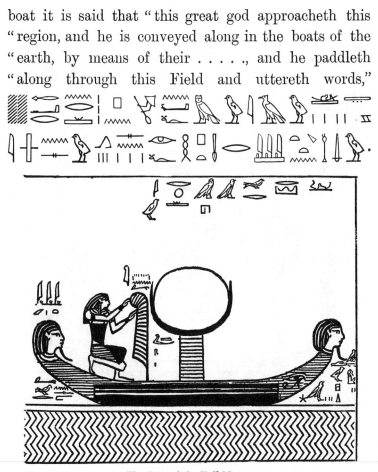

the hieroglyphics above the full moon read  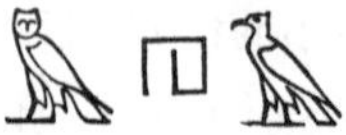, and those above the stern of the boat read, "Field of him that beareth up URNES,"  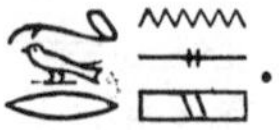.

The ends of the SECOND BOAT likewise terminate in

The Boat of the goddess Hathor.

bearded human heads, but each is surmounted by a pair of plumes. In the centre of the boat, between two goddesses, stands a huge sistrum, which is the symbol of the goddess Hathor, and indicates that the boat is that of HATHOR, or of HATHOR-ISIS. In the fore part of the boat is a beetle, which is described as "This great god NEPER," .

Above the goddess to the left of the sistrum are written the words, "their boats send forth their words," ; over the plumed head in front is written , and over that at the other end of the boat, "Osiris crieth to it,"

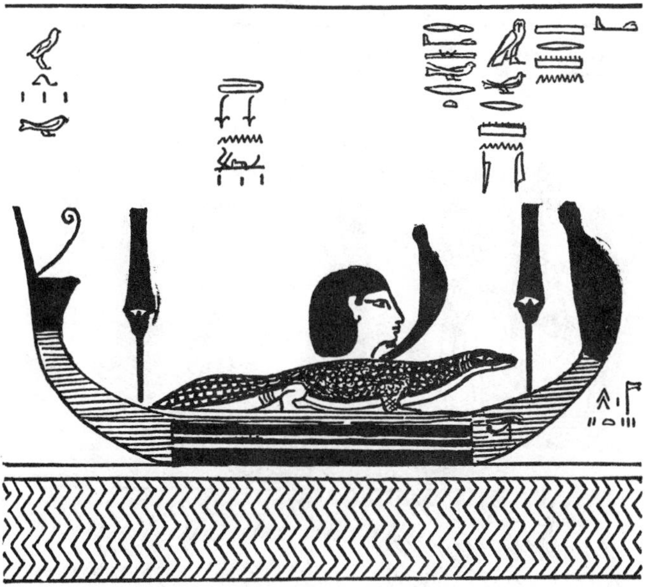

The Boat of the Lizard-god.

. On the side of the boat are the signs  and .

The prow of the THIRD BOAT is surmounted by a crown of the South, and the stern by a crown of the North, and between the two sceptres, 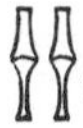, which symbolize the gods ÁNPU and ÁP-UAT, i.e., the jackal-headed gods of the South and North, is a huge lizard, from the back of which spring the head of Osiris and a White Crown. On the side of the boat are the signs and . Above the crown of the North is the legend U-UR, , which, however, probably refers to the sceptre near it; above the lizard we have

The Boat of the Grain-god Neper.

, above the foremost sceptre, , and immediately in front is , and under the front of the boat is .

The prow and stern of the FOURTH BOAT terminate in heads of uraei, each of which is turned towards the deity who is kneeling in the middle of the boat. In the centre kneels a woman without arms, and before and behind her stands a man, who is likewise without arms. At each end of the boat grows a plant or, perhaps, a large ear of wheat, which indicates that the boat is that of the form of Osiris as the god of vegetation, who is known by the name NEPER. The legend by the ear of corn in the front of the boat reads, "the boat which conveyeth Neper," 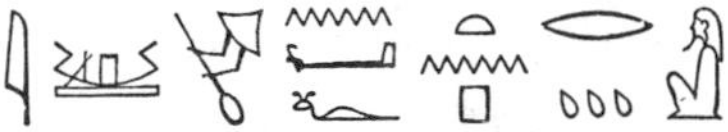, and that by the ear in the stern, "collector (?) of herbs and plants," . The deity in the boat, or the boat itself perhaps, is called ḤEPT-MENÀ-F-ṬUÀ-UÀA-F, 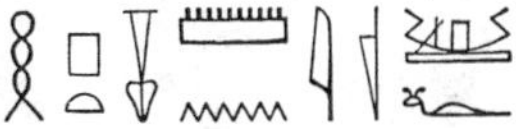 . This boat is the boat of the god NEPER, the god of grain, and a form of Osiris as the god of vegetation; it may be noted that its side has no *utchat*  upon it.

In the upper register are:—

1. A bearded god, with a phallus in the form of a knife, called ÀST NETCH-T, 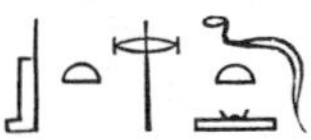, or, , i.e., "Isis, the avengeress."

2. A god of similar form and attribute called SEB-QENBETI, , i.e., "Seb of the two corners."

3. A ram-headed god, with a similar attribute, called

KHNEMU QENBETI, , i.e., "Khnemu of the two corners."

4. An ibis-headed god, with a similar attribute, called TEḤUTI-ḤER-KHENṬ-F, , i.e., "Thoth on his steps."

5. An ape-headed god, with a similar attribute, called ÅFU-ḤER-KHENṬ-F, , i.e., "Åfu on his steps."

Second Hour. Upper Register. Gods Nos. 1—7.

6. Lioness-headed deity, with a similar attribute, called KETUIT-ṬENT-BA, , i.e., "Cutter of the soul."

All the above gods are in mummied form, and occupy chairs of state.

7. A god standing upright, and holding a *kherp* sceptre or weapon, , in his left hand; he is called

SEKHEM-Ā-KHEFTIU, 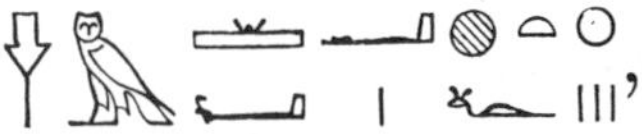, i.e., "Overcomer of the power of the enemy."

8. A hawk-headed god, with a uraeus on his head, called ḤERU-ṬUAT, , i.e., "Horus of the Ṭuat."

9. A god, who holds a knife in his left hand, and has his right raised to strike; he is called SEBEN-ḤESQ-KHAIBITU, 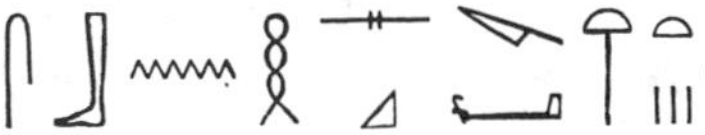.

Second Hour. Upper Register. Gods Nos. 8—15.

10, 11. Two ape-headed gods, called respectively BENTI, , and ÅĀNĀ, 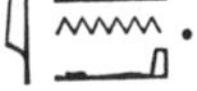.

12. A god with the head of a hawk and the head of an animal, i.e., SET and ḤERU-UR, who is here called "He of the two faces," .

13, 14. The crook of Osiris, , and the upper half of a serpent called MEṬ-EN-ÅSÅR, i.e., "staff of Osiris."

15. The term of Osiris facing a deity with the head of a lioness, who is called SESENT-KHU, , i.e., "Terrifier of spirits."

16—18. Three goddesses, each of whom has a sceptre in her left hand, and a uraeus on her head; their names

Second Hour. Upper Register. Gods Nos. 16—21.

are:—MEST-S-TCHESES, , ĀMĀMA KHEFTIU, , and ḤERT-ṬUATI, .

19—21. The goddesses SEKHET, of Thebes, , ĀM-TCHERU, , ÅMENT-NEFERT , and NET-ṬEPT-ÅNT, .

In the lower register are the following:—

1. A god, standing, called NEBÀUI, .

2—4. Three gods, each of whom has two ears of corn stuck in his hair; these are called BESUĀ, , NEPER, , and ṬEPU (?), (or, PÀN,).

5—7. Three gods, each holding an ear of wheat in

Second Hour. Lower Register. Gods Nos. 1—8.

his left hand; their names are ḤETCH-Ā, , ĀB, , and NEPEN, .

8. A god, holding a knife in his left hand, called ÀR-ÀST-NETER, .

9—11. Three gods, seated, in mummy forms. The first has the head of a horned animal, and is called ĀMU-ĀA, , i.e., "the Eater of the phallus"; the second has the head of a man, and is called , AKHABIT; and the third has the head of a jackal, and is called NEBT-TA-TCHESER, .

12. The god OSIRIS UN-NEFER, , in mummy form, wearing the crown of the South.

13. The god KHUI, , who holds in each hand a long lotus-topped sceptre surmounted by a star.

Second Hour. Lower Register. Gods Nos. 9—15.

14. The two-headed god (Horus-Set ?) called ḤRȦ-F-Ā-F, .

15. The god ḤERU-ḤEN, .

16, 17. Two gods, each holding in his left hand the sign of life inverted; their names are ḤUN, , and ḤETCHETCHTU, .

18—20. Three gods, each holding a palm branch; their names are NEḤÀ, (or, NAREḤ,), MAKHI, , and RENPITI, .

21. A god, who holds a knife in his left hand, and is called ĀFAU, .

22. A god, holding in his hand the symbol of "year," , who is called FA-ÀR-TRU, .

Second Hour. Lower Register. Gods Nos. 16—22.

The text referring to the gods in the upper register reads:—

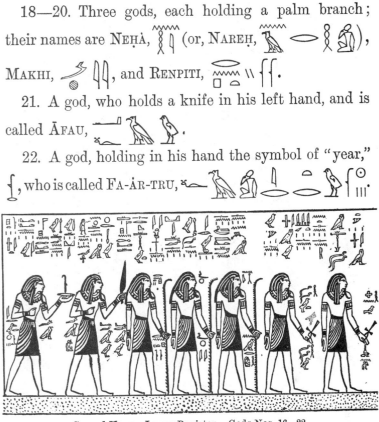

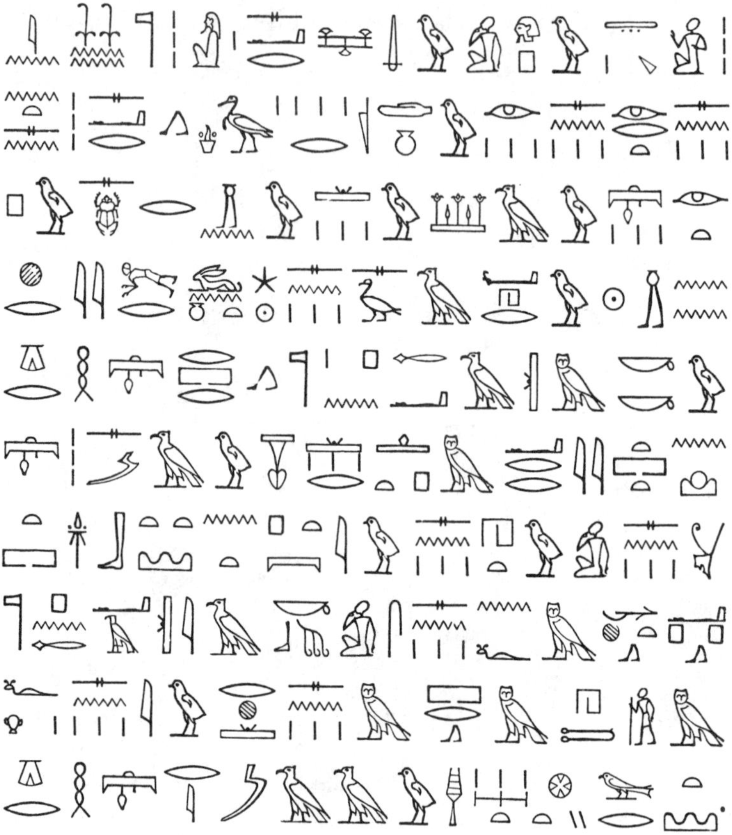

"[Those who are in this picture] praise this great "god after he hath come forth to them, and behold, it "is their words which lead him to them; they lament "when he hath passed onwards, having spoken words "to them. Behold, these gods are they who make the "words of those who are upon earth to reach [the god], "and it is they who make souls to approach their forms. "Their work consisteth in causing to come into being "the offerings of the night, and in performing the "overthrow [of enemies] at their hour. It is they who "guard the day, and who bring on the night until this "great god cometh forth from out of the thick dark-"ness to repose in this Court of the eastern horizon of "heaven. They cry out in lamentation to this great "god, and they utter wailings for him after he hath "passed by them. Those who know them shall come "forth by day, and he shall be able to journey "during the night to the divisions of the great double "city."

The texts which describe the duties of the gods in the lower register read:—

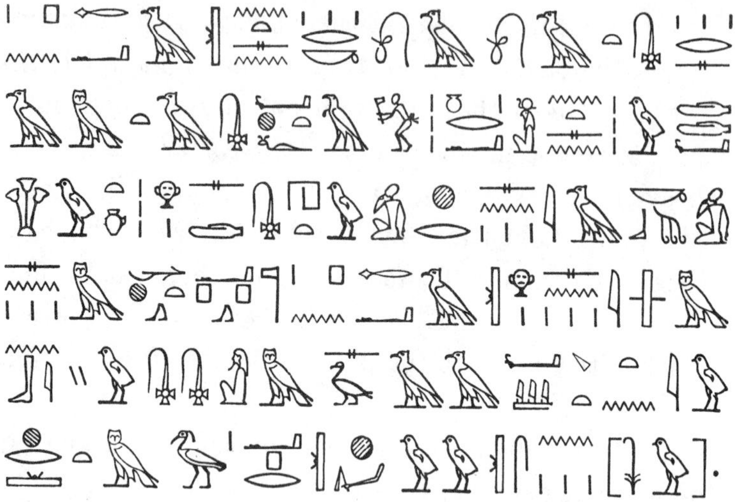

"[Those who are in this picture give unto this great "god the seasons] and the years which are in their "hands. When this great god hath made speech with "them, they answer him, and they have life through "the voice of this great god, and their throats draw in "breath, for when he crieth to them he ordereth them "what they are to do, and he appointeth to them green "herbs in abundance in their field. And they supply "with the green herbs of URNES the gods who are in "the following of Rā, and they make offerings of water "to the spirits by the command of this great god, and "they kindle flames of fire in order to burn up the "enemies of Rā, and there is wailing to them, and they "lament after this great god hath passed them by. "ȦM-NEBȦUI is the guardian of this Field; whosoever "knoweth [this] is in the condition of a spirit equipped "with [words of power], and [the gods] protect [him]."

The five lines of text which contain the address of the gods to Rā, and the answer of the god, read:—

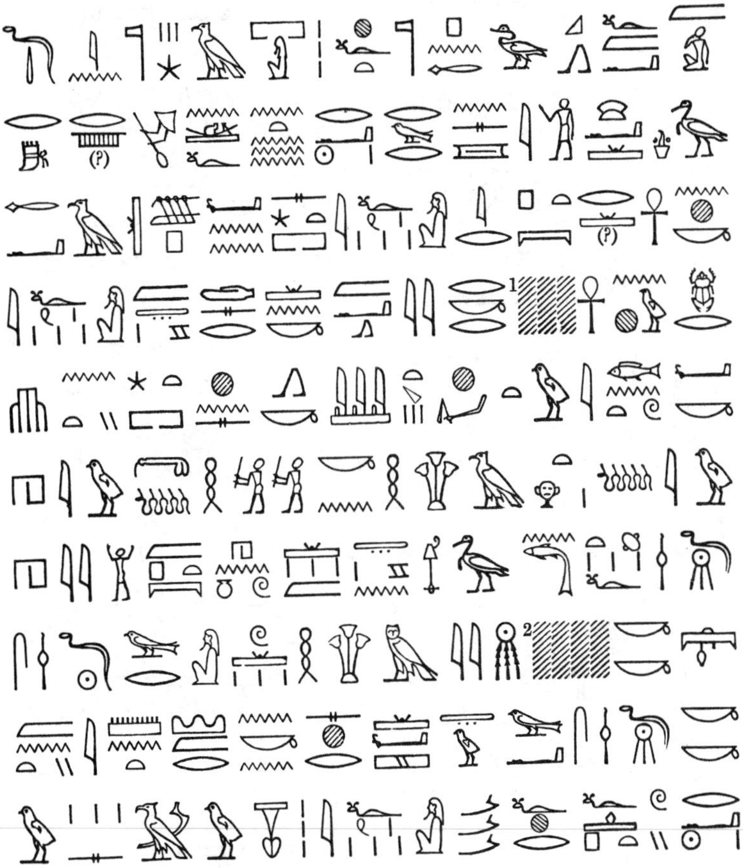

[1] The sarcophagus of Nectanebus gives 

[2] 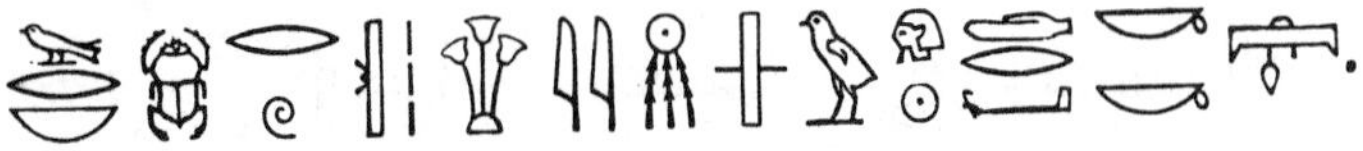 *Ibid.*

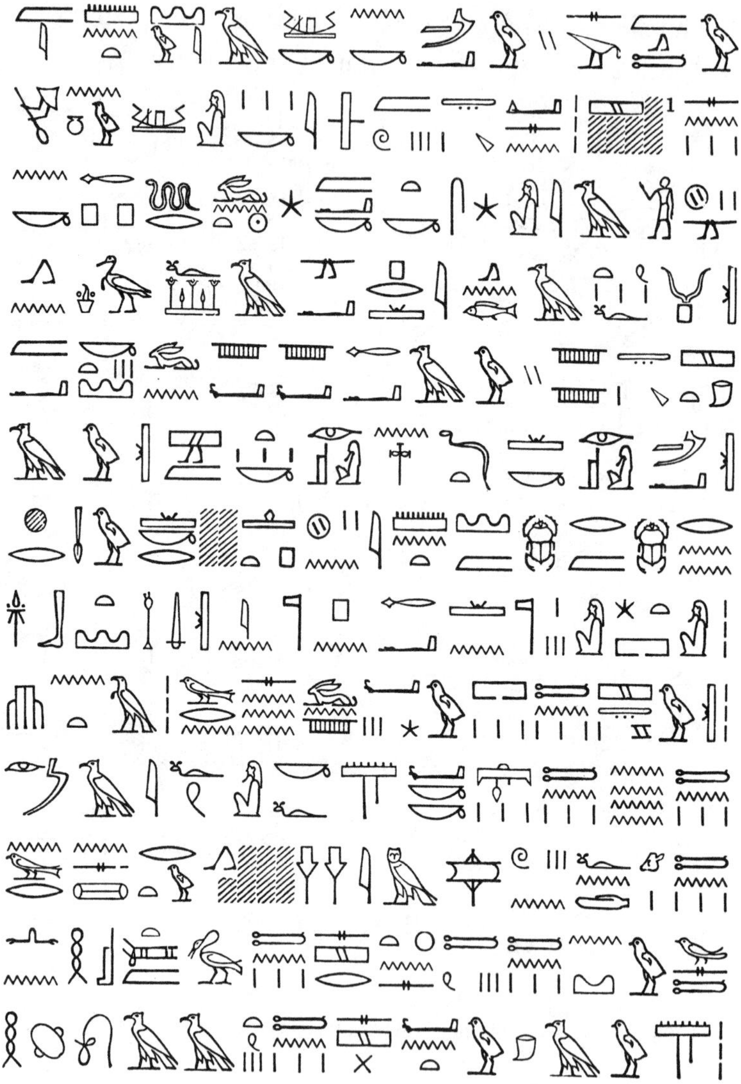

1 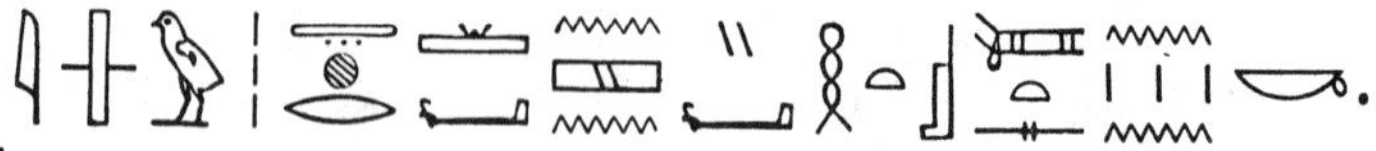
Ibid.

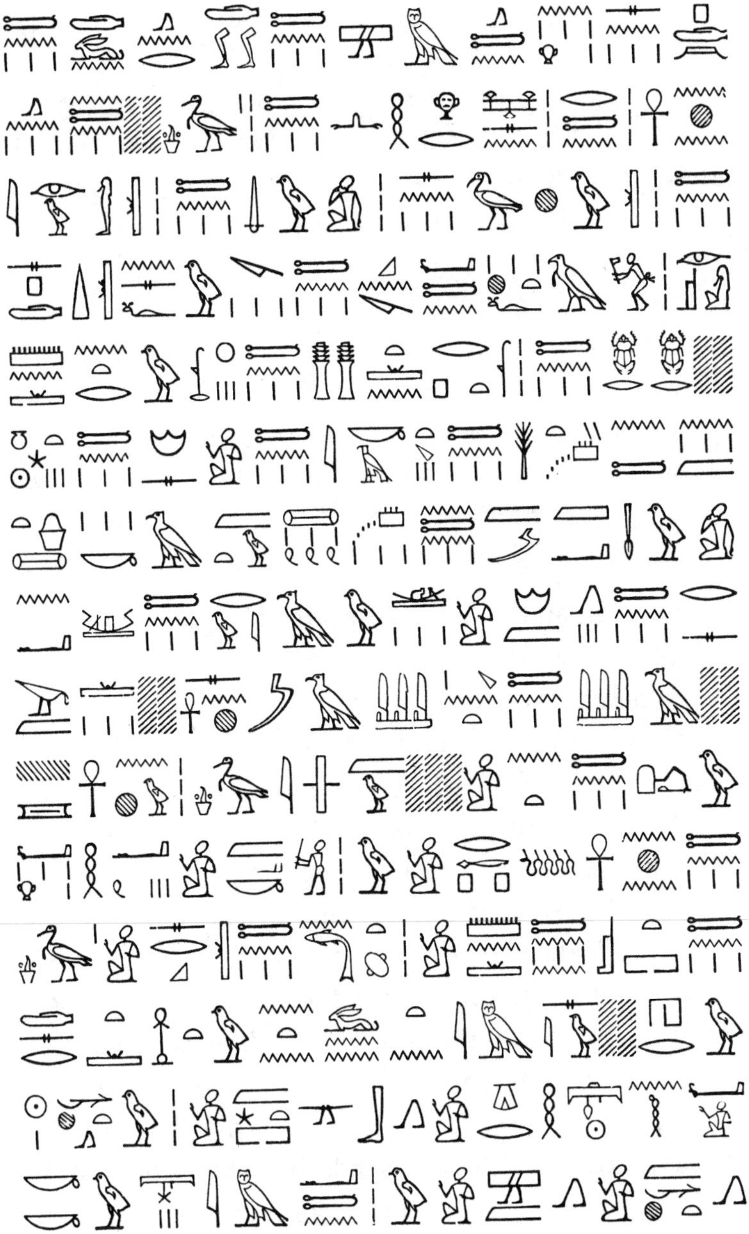

The gods of the Ṭuat speak to this great god as he entereth in with understanding to the boundary, and he is borne over NET-RĀ into URNES, saying, "Hail, "thou who risest as a Mighty Soul (KHĀ-BA-ĀA), who "hast received [the things which belong to] the Ṭuat, "ȦF, thou guardian of heaven . . . . . thou livest, O "ȦF, in TA-ṬESERT. Come thou, and cast thou thine "eye in thy name of Living One, Kheperȧ, at the head "of the Ṭuat. Traverse thou this Field, O thou who "hast might, bind thou with fetters the ḤAU serpent, "and smite thou the serpent Neḥa-ḥrȧ. There is "rejoicing in heaven, and there are shouts of gladness "upon the earth at the entrance of thy (literally, his) "body. He who shineth sendeth forth light, and the "URU gods give light [at dawn; destroy thou] the "darkness which is in ÅMENT in thy name of SEKHER-"SHETAU-UR-Ā, illumine thou the thick darkness, O ÅF. "His jawbones are to him, and Rā taketh up his "position in ÅMENT. Thy boat is to thee, and it is thy "right, thou art guided along, and those who convey "thee over the water and who dwell in the earth make "calamities to come upon ĀPEP straightway on thy "behalf. Thy protector is the Star-God (SBA), thou "art praised and adored, thy soul passeth on, thou "goest onward and thy body is equipped with power, "and the regions (?) are opened [to thee]. The doors "of the hidden land are opened [before thee], OSIRIS "cometh unto thee, OSIRIS avengeth thee, and thy "word is *maāt* against thy enemies. Thou goest to "rest, thou goest to rest in ÅMENT, and thou comest "into being in the form of KHEPERÅ in the East."

This great god sendeth forth words to the gods who dwell in the Ṭuat and to those who inhabit URNES, saying, "Open ye your hidden doors so that the god "ÅF may look [upon you] and may throw aside your "darkness, and that ye may draw your water from "URNES, and your bread from . . . . . ., and that wind "may come to your nostrils, and that ye may not be "destroyed and overcome by your own foul odour, and "that ye may not be choked by your own dung, and "that ye may untie and cast away your swathings, and "that ye may lift up your legs and walk upon them, "and that ye may stretch out your arms, and that your "souls may not be made to remove themselves from "you. O ye who live in your forms, and who utter "your words of magical power, who are provided with "your swords [whereby] ye may hack in pieces the "enemies of Osiris, whose seasons are permanent, whose "years are well established, who pass your state of "being [in] your hours, who dwell in your estates, who "have your barley in your bread cakes, who have "loaves of bread made of the grain which is yours, "whose word is *maāt*, depart from my boats, and "retreat before [my] images, [that I] may vivify "anew this your Field, the Field . . . . . . living ones. "[My] soul is among . . . . . . you who have done "battle on my behalf, who have protected me against "Āpep, who have life through my soul, who have being "through my bodies, who stablish your seats of holiness "which have been decreed to you that ye may exist "therein, [who are with your souls] by day, who are in "my following in the Ṭuat, when I make my way "through the night and when I destroy the darkness, "O grant me your help so that I may travel on in the "following of my eye, and that I may journey forwards "with those who go to my place in the East. Utter "ye cries of joy, O gods of the Ṭuat, for I avenge you, "[utter ye cries of joy,] for I order your destinies."

When they have addressed this god whilst rowing along his boat ÅM-TA, they cry out, and they bring him to rest in the Field of the NEPERTIU gods who are in the following of Osiris. If these scenes be done [in writing] according to the similitudes which are in the hidden place of the palace, and if a man hath knowledge of [these] words . . . . they shall act as magical protectors of a man upon earth, regularly, unfailingly, and eternally. The name of this hour is SESHET-MĀKET-NEB-S.

CHAPTER III.

THE THIRD DIVISION OF THE ṬUAT, WHICH IS CALLED NET-NEB-UĀ-KHEPER-ĀUT.

IN the scene which illustrates the THIRD DIVISION of the Ṭuat, which is passed through by the Sun-god

The Boat of Åf, the dead Sun-god, in the Third Hour.

during the THIRD HOUR of the night, we see the boat of the god making its way over the waters of the river in the underworld. The dead Sun-god Ȧf stands within a shrine in the form of a ram-headed man, as before, but there is a change in the composition of the crew, which now consists only of four mariners, two of whom stand before the shrine and two behind, and the goddess of the hour and a hawk-headed deity, one of

The Boat which capsizeth.

the forms of Horus, who is occupied in tying loops of rope to the elongated hawk-headed rowlocks in which the paddles may be worked. The boat of Ȧf follows in the train of three boats, which may be thus described:—

The foremost boat is called Uȧa-Penāt, ,

i.e., "The boat which capsizeth"; it contains three hawk-headed forms of the god Horus, and is steered by two male figures, who stand one in the bows and the other at the stern. In the middle of the boat stand the hawk-god BÀK, , and the hawk-goddess BÀKET, , and behind them, standing on a snake, is the

The Boat of Rest.

third form of Horus. Between the front steersman and BÀKET is the serpent TEKA-ḤRÀ, , i.e., "Fiery face," and the aft steersman bears a name of similar meaning, NÀB-ḤRÀ, .

The second boat is called UÀA-HERER, ,

i.e., "The boat of Rest," and has in the middle an Osiris god in the form of a mummy; each end of the boat terminates in the head of a cynocephalus, and it is steered by two beings, one of whom is called ṬESEM-ḤRȦ-F, , i.e., "He whose face is like a knife," and the other KHEN-EN-URṬ-F, ,

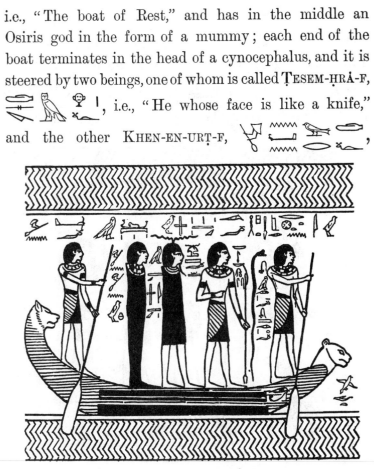

The Boat of the Branch.

i.e., "The ferryman who resteth not." The Osiris god stands between two gods, one of whom is called ĀU-MATU, , and the serpent which stands on its tail between the steersman in the bows and the first god is called SET-EM-ḤRȦ-F, .

The third boat is called PA-KHET, , i.e., "The Branch," and each end terminates in the head of a lion. In the middle of it stands the form of Osiris, who is called SHEFSHEF, , and he wears on his head a pair of ram's horns; his arms and the upper

The Four Forms of Osiris.

portion of his body are swathed. Behind him stands the mummied form called ȦM-TA, , and before him the god NEB-UAST, . Of the two steersmen, only the name of the second, KHEN, or KHENNU, , is given; the name of the serpent which stands on its tail is SET-EM-MAAT-F, 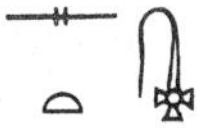 .

The procession of boats is met by four forms of Osiris, who stand with the upper portion of their bodies swathed. Their names are:—1. NEB-NET, . 2. MENI, 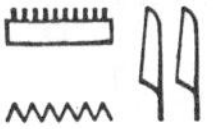. 3. ĀRI-TCHERU, . 4. MAA-TCHERU, 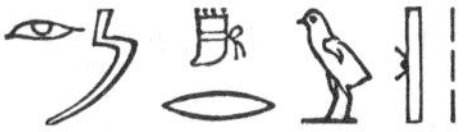.

The text written above the boats reads:—

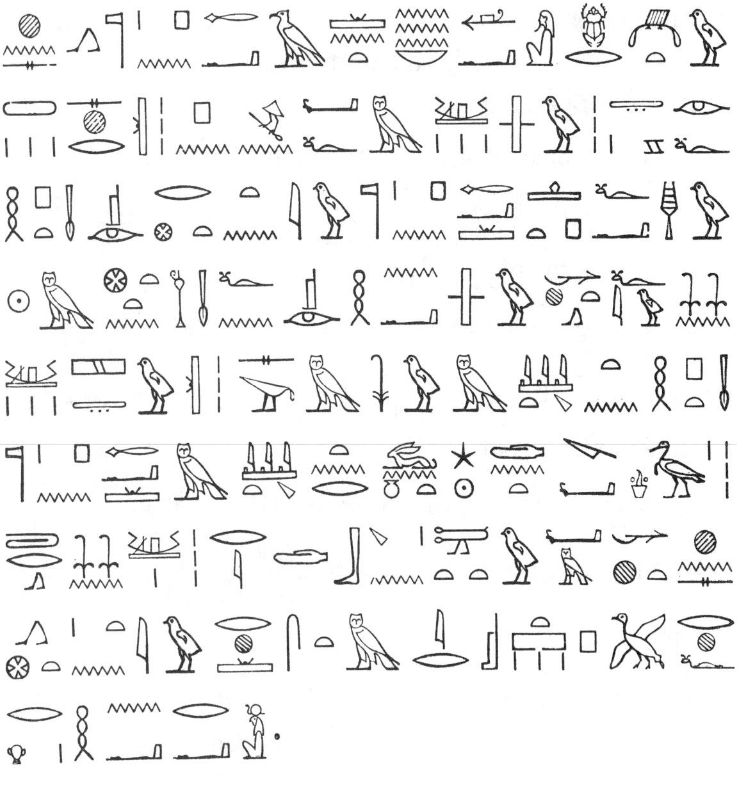

"This great god journeyeth over NET-NEB-UĀ-KHEPER-"ĀUT (i.e., the Water of the Lord One, the Creator of "food). [He who is in] this picture transporteth the "boats which are in the earth, and he paddleth Osiris "to this City. This great god resteth for a period in "this City, and he sendeth forth his voice to Osiris, "and to those who are in his following, and [then] "these hidden boats guide him into this Field. This "great god paddleth through this Field towards the "Hour ṬENT-BAIU, and these boats journey round to "the district of THETTU, after traversing this City. "Whosoever knoweth these things shall have both his "habitation and his bread with Rā."

In the upper register are the following:—

1. A dog-headed ape seated on an oval mass of sand; he is called ḤER-SHĀ-F, 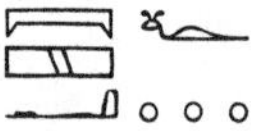, or , "He who is on his sand."

2. A dog-headed ape called TCHEB-NETER, , or ṬEBI-NETER, , seated in a coffer (?) with a vaulted roof.

3, 4. Two jackal-headed gods called ȦNPU, , and NEHEM-KHERU, , or NEHA-KHERU, .

5, 6. A man and a woman, who hold in each hand a pupil of the Eye of Horus, or Rā; the man is called

ÅNTH, , i.e., "He who brings," and the woman , ÅNTET,[1] i.e., "She who brings."

7. The ram SMA-KHEFTIU-F, .

8. A mummied form, with projecting hands, called PEṬ-ĀḤĀT, .[2]

Third Hour. Upper Register. Gods Nos. 1—6.

9. ANUBIS of Thebes, , in the form of a jackal, couchant on a pylon.

10. A kneeling man, who holds in his left hand a pupil of the Eye of Rā, and is called ÅN-MAAT-RĀ-SEḤETEP-NETERU, , i.e., "The "bringer of the Eye of Rā, who maketh content the "gods."

[1] Or, .   [2] Or, .

Third Hour. Upper Register. Gods Nos. 7—11.

11. The papyrus sceptre UR-ḤEKAU, [hieroglyphs], i.e., "Great one of words of power," surmounted by a piece of flesh, [hieroglyph].

12—15. Four gods, whose names are SĀḤ-ÅB,

Third Hour. Upper Register. Gods Nos. 12—19.

, THEMA, , ḤUN-SĀḤU,
, and THET-EM-ḲERḤ, .

16—19. Four mummied forms. The first has a pair of horns on his head, the second two curved plumes (?), the third a winged uraeus, and the head of the fourth is without ornament; their names appear to be PEBA-F,

Third Hour. Upper Register. Gods Nos. 20—26.

, KA-ĀRU, , ĀUAI, ,
and ṬEBA, .

20—23. Four goddesses, whose names are ḤAIT, , ĀKEBTIT, , MATHI, , and REMIT, ; these, as their names testify, were professional mourners.

24. The god ḤERU-KHETI, , followed by

the ḤENNU, 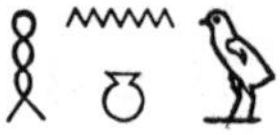, standard, i.e., the hawk of SEKER upon a standard, .

25, 26. The gods MEḤ-MĀAT, , and NETER-NEFERU, .

The text which refers to the above reads:—

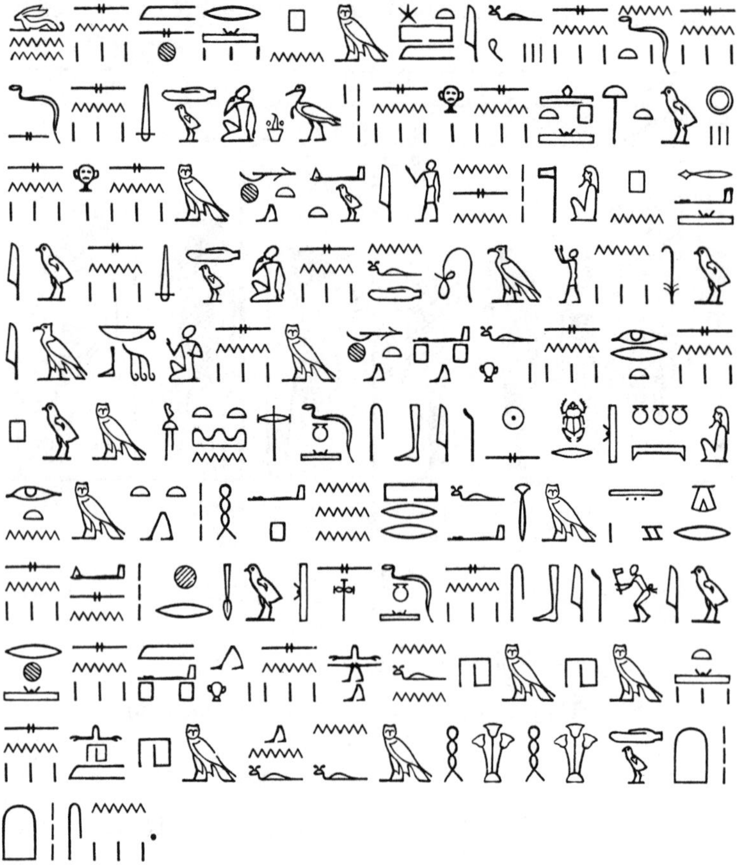

"Those who are in this picture in the ṬUAT have "the flesh of their own bodies, and their souls speak

" over them, and their shadows are united unto them, " and after this great god hath addressed them, they " speak to him, and they say words of praise to him, " and they weep after he hath passed them by. The " work which is theirs in Åmentet is to take vengeance " upon the Sebå fiend of Rā, to make Nu to come into " being, to make Ḥāp (i.e., the Nile) to flow, and when

Third Hour. Lower Register. Gods Nos. 1—6.

" he hath come forth in the earth from them, they send " forth their voice, and take vengeance upon the Sebå " fiend. Whosoever knoweth [these things] shall, when " he passeth by these beings, not be driven away by their " roarings, and he shall never fall down into their caverns."

In the lower register are:—

1. The god KHNEMU, ram-headed.

2. A bearded male figure called NERTA, , with hands raised in adoration.

3—6. Four forms of Osiris, mummified, bearded, and wearing the White Crown, and seated on chairs of state; their names are ÅSÅR-NEB-ÅMENTET, , ÅSÅR-KHENT-ÅMENTET, , ÅSÅR-ÅSTI, , and ÅSÅR-THET-ḤEḤ, that is, "Osiris, lord of

Third Hour. Lower Register. Gods Nos. 7—13.

Åmentet," "Osiris at the head of Åmentet," "Osiris of the two seats," and "Osiris, conqueror of millions of years."

7—11. Five goose-headed beings, each holding a knife in his right hand; four of their names are NEHA-ḤRÅ, ,[1] AḲEBSEN, , ÅTEMTI, ,[2] and ṬUATUI, .

[1] Or, .

[2] Or, .

12—14. A male figure called SEPAĀSHĀT, , or , who holds a knife with both hands, and stands between two women, whose names are MESKH-SET, , and ṬEPT-BES-S, , or .

15. The male bearded figure ÅMENTI, .

Third Hour. Lower Register. Gods Nos. 14—19.

16—19. Four forms of Osiris, mummified, bearded, and wearing the Red Crown, and seated on chairs of state; their names are ÅSÅR-KA-ÅMENTET, , ÅSÅR-ḤER-KHENṬU-F, , ÅSÅR-BÅTTI (?), , and ÅSÅR-KHERP-NETERU, .

20, 21. The two goddesses SEḤ, , and ĀḤĀU,

, who stand grasping the sceptre with both hands, and have their heads turned behind them.

22. The goddess BA-KHATI, , who holds in each hand one of the eyes of Horus or Rā.

23. The god KHETRȦ, , holding and .

Third Hour. Lower Register. Gods Nos. 20—26.

24—26. Three gods, with bowed backs, who touch the earth with their hands.

The text relating to the above reads:—

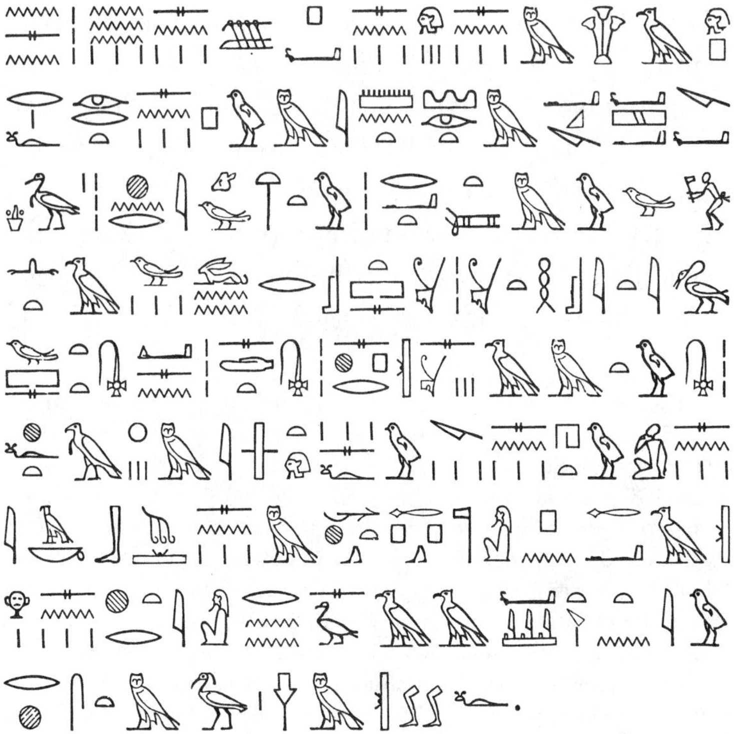

"Those who are in this picture [and those who are "in] the house of ṬEṬ praise this great god, and when "this great god hath sent forth words to them, they "come to life, for when he hath called to them and "hath sent forth his words to them [they have] their "water, and they receive their due (literally, heads) in "addition to the utterance of his mouth. The work "which they have to do in Ȧment is to hew and to "hack souls in pieces, and set restraint upon shadows, "and to destroy such doomed beings as have their "being in their place of destruction which blazeth with "fire. They send forth flames and they cause fires to "spring up, and the enemies are as those who have "their knives over (or, on) their heads. They wail "and they lament when this great god hath passed "them by. The name of the warder of this Field is "KHETRȦ. Whosoever knoweth this shall be in the "condition of a spirit who hath dominion over his legs."

M. Maspero, in his description of the THIRD HOUR,[1]

[1] The portions rendered by M. Maspero read thus:—Ce grand dieu dit aux *Biou shetiou* (âmes mystérieuses) qui suivent Osiris: "O vous dont j'ai rendu mystérieuses, dont j'ai occulté les âmes, "que j'ai mis à la suite d'Osiris pour le défendre, pour escorter ses "images, pour anéantir ceux qui l'attaquent, si bien que le dieu Hon "est à toi, ô Osiris, derrière toi, pour te défendre, pour escorter tes "images, pour anéantir ceux qui l'attaquent, si bien que Hon est à "toi, ô Osiris, que Sa est à toi, ô Khontamentit, vous dont les formes "sont stables, vous dont les rites assurent l'existence, vous qui "respirez l'air [de vos narines, qui voyez] de vos faces, qui écoutez "de vos oreilles, qui êtes coiffés de vos coufièh, qui êtes vêtus de vos "bandelettes, qui avez des revenus d'offrandes à vous sur terre par "l'office des prêtres du dieu, qui avez des champs à vous de votre "propre domaine, vous dont les âmes ne sont point renversées, dont "les corps ne sont point culbutés, ouvrez vos cercles et tenez-vous à "vos places, car je suis venu pour voir mes corps, inspecter mes "images qui sont dans l'autre monde, et vous m'avez convoyé pour "me permettre de leur apporter mon aide, si bien que je conduis à "la rame ton âme au ciel, ô Osiris, ton âme à la terre, ô Khonta-"ougrit, avec tes dieux derrière toi, tes mânes devant toi, ton être "et tes formes [sur toi ?], et alors ton mâne est enchanté, ô Osiris, "vos mânes sont enchantés, ô vous qui suivez Osiris. Je monte en "terre et le jour est derrière moi; je traverse la nuit, et mon âme "se réunit à vos formes pendant le jour, j'accomplis de nuit les "rites qui vous sont nécessaires, j'ai créé vos âmes pour moi, afin "qu'elles soient derrière moi, et ce que j'ai fait pour elles vous "empêche de tomber au lieu d'anéantissement."

includes an extract from the speech which the Sun-god Rā makes to the inhabitants of NET-NEB-UĀ-KHEPER-ĀUT; as he points out, though three copies of the speech are extant, all are mutilated (see Lefébure, *Le Tombeau de Seti Ier.*, 1re partie, pll. xv.-xvii., pll. xviii.-xx., and pl. xxii.), and it is impossible at present to reconstruct the text, although the general meaning of several sentences is clear enough.

CHAPTER IV.

THE FOURTH DIVISION OF THE ṬUAT, WHICH IS CALLED ĀNKHET-KHEPERU.

IN the scene that illustrates the FOURTH DIVISION of the Ṭuat, which is passed through by the Sun-god during the FOURTH HOUR of the night, a region which is entirely different from anything seen previously is entered. We see that the general arrangement which makes each Division to contain three sections has been followed, but the actual path of the Boat of the Sun is different. Instead of passing along the middle section as before, the god is obliged to pass *over* the region of the kingdom of Seker. The course which was usually passed over by the dead runs from one side of the section to the other diagonally, and it may be thus described:—Starting from the upper side of the topmost division, the corridor, which is called RE-STAU, 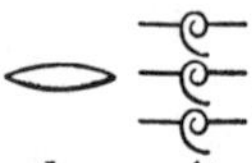, slants across to the lower side; at the point where it touches the line which divides the first and second section is a door, which is thrown open. The door is called MĀṬES-SMA-TA, 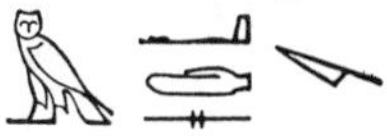 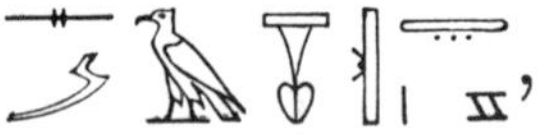, or 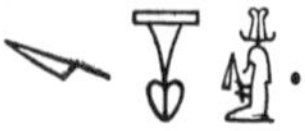. The corridor runs

The Kingdom of Seker.

parallel with the line which divides the first and second section for some distance, and is described as the "road of the secret things of Re-stau; the god doth "not pass through the leaves of the door, but they hear "his voice," 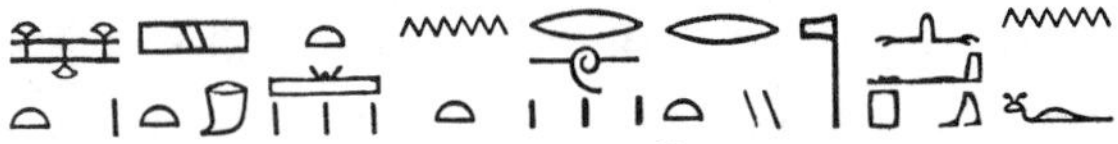 , or  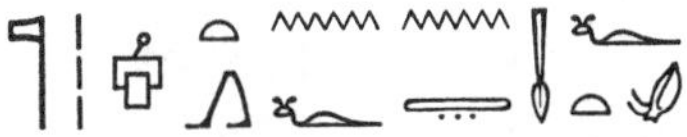. A sharp bend takes RE-STAU in a slanting direction across the middle section of the scene, and at the bottom of it is another door, which is called METES-MAU-ĀT, ; the corridor runs parallel with the line which divides the second and third section for some distance, when it crosses the section, again in a slanting direction, and at the end of it is a third door, which is called METES-EN-NEHEH, . In the second slant of the corridor is an inscription which describes it as the "road by which entereth the body of SEKER, "who is on his sand, the image which is hidden, and is "neither seen nor perceived," 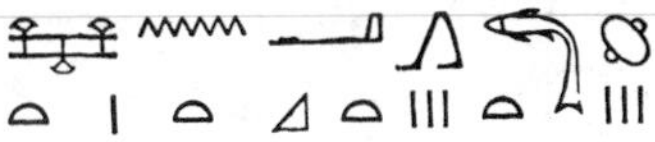 .[1]

[1] Variant,  .

As the further course of the corridor will be described under the Fifth Hour we may pass on to consider the Boat of the Sun, and the means by which the god makes his way onward.

Rā and the gods who formed his crew have left the boat in which they travelled until now, and have betaken themselves to one, each end of which terminates in the head of a serpent. This serpent-boat is drawn along by four gods, who are called ṬUN-EN-MAĀ, 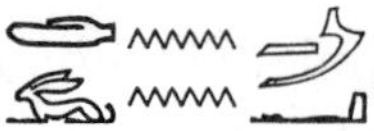,[1] ḤER-UARFU, 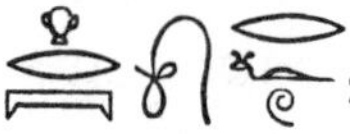,[2] ȦR-NEFERTU, 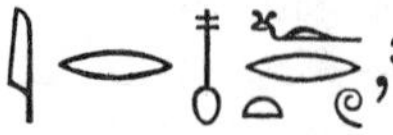,[3] and SHETAI, . Above the boat is written, "[Whilst] this great god journeyeth over "those who are in this scene the flames which the "mouth of his boat emit guide him through these "pools; he seeth not their forms, but he crieth to "them and to their places, and they hear his voice,"

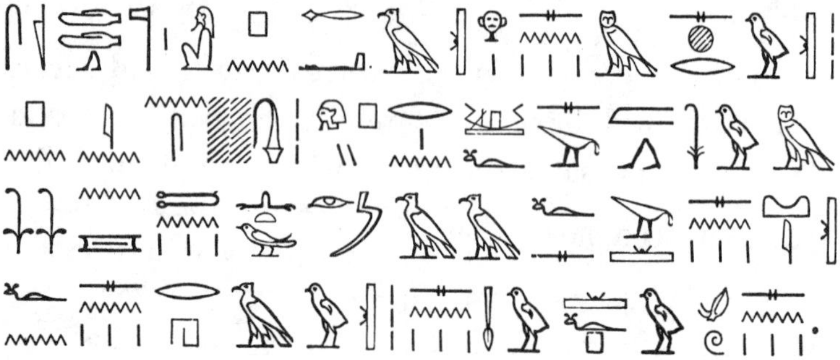

[1] Variant, . [2] Variant, 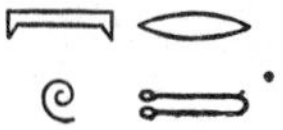.

[3] Variant, 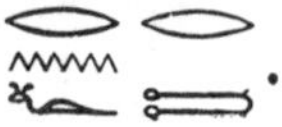.

The Kingdom of Seker.

In front of those who tow the boat of Rā are:—

1. A form of Osiris called EM-ĀNKHTI, , or 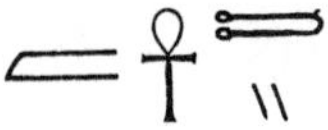 (see p. 71).

2. The crook of Osiris, 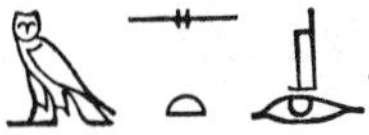, or 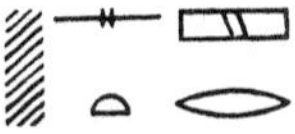 (see p. 75).

3, 4. Thoth, ibis-headed, and Horus, hawk-headed, standing facing each other, with the UTCHAT, , above their outstretched hands and arms; the title of Thoth is UTHESU, 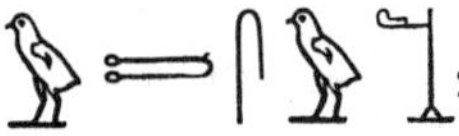, or , i.e., "the Raiser," and that of Horus is ĀU-ĀU, , or , "the wide of hands." The Utchat is called SEKRI, 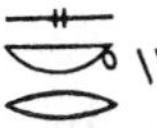.

5. The god SETHEN-ḤĀT, 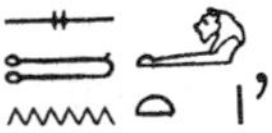, or , wearing the crown of the South.

6. The god ḤER-ṬEBAT-F, , i.e., "He who is over his place of burial," having in the place of a head two curved objects, which M. Maspero identifies with mummy bandages (see p. 79).

7. The god UATCH-ḤRÀ, , i.e., "Green Face" (see p. 79).

8. The god ḤETEP, 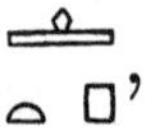, who carries the crook of Osiris mentioned above (No. 2) (see p. 79).

9—11. Three gods, each of whom carries  in his left hand, whose names are SEM-ĀNKH, , ȦN-ḤER, 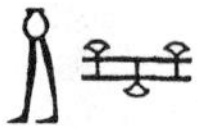, and UT-MEṬ,  (see pp. 79, 83).

12. The goddess NEBT-ĀNKH, 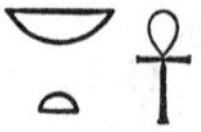 (see p. 83).

The text which refers to these beings reads:—

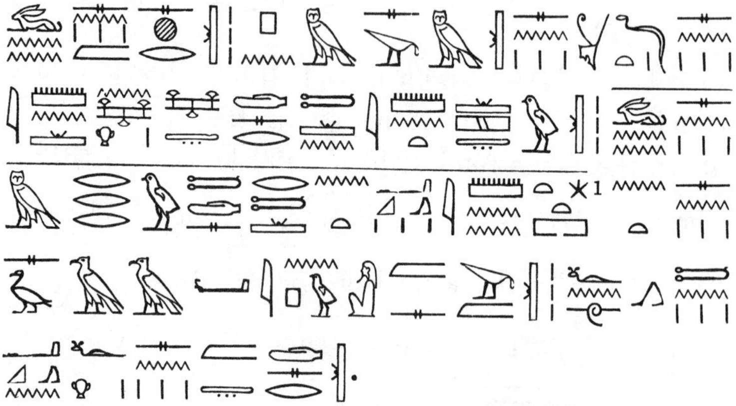

"Those who are in this picture, in their forms of "their bodies, are the hidden [travellers] upon the way "of the holy country whose secret things are hidden. "They are the guardians of the way of the holy [land] "for those who enter into the hidden place of the "Ṭuat, and they keep ward over Ȧnpu in his forms as "he tows them along, when he entereth in by them in "the holy land."

In the upper register are:—

1. A goddess, wearing the crown of the North, apparently a form of Neith (see p. 63).

[1] The words over which a line is printed are repeated inadvertently by the scribe.

The Kingdom of Seker.

2. A serpent, with a human head, and two pairs of human feet and legs (see p. 63).

3—5. Three serpents, which move side by side along the ground "upon their bellies,"  . Of them it is said, "Those who are in this "picture make their passage to every place each day,"  (see p. 67).

6. The scorpion ĀNKHET, , and a large uraeus. Of these it is said, "Those who are in this picture "stand in Re-stau at the head of the way [to guard "it]," 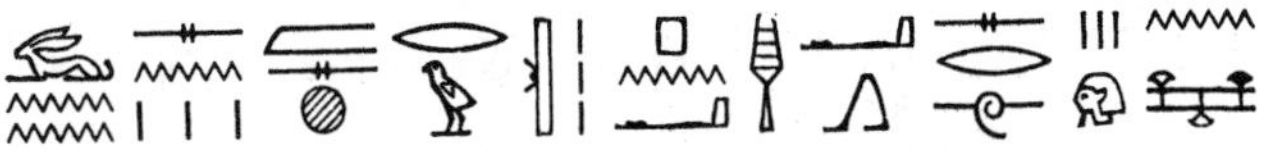.
Behind these stands a god, who appears to be making an offering of two libation vases to the serpent. Of him it is said, "He who is in this picture is the guide of the holy way,"  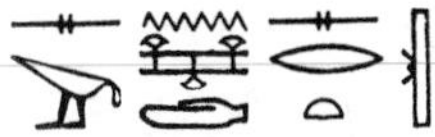 (see p. 71).

7. A three-headed serpent, with a pair of hawk's wings, and two pairs of human legs, and of him it is said, "He who is in this picture in the Ṭuat is the "warder of this holy way of Re-stau; he liveth upon "the abundance [which cometh] from his wings, his "body, [and] his heads," 

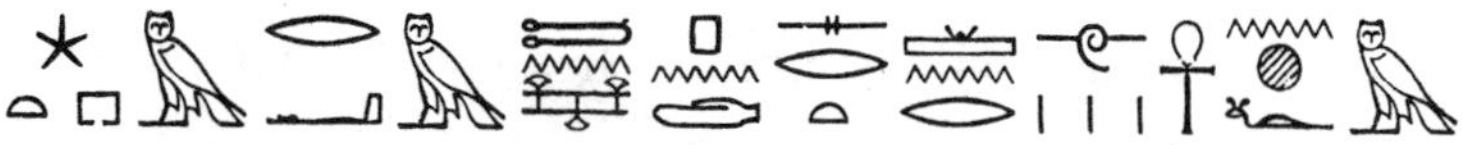

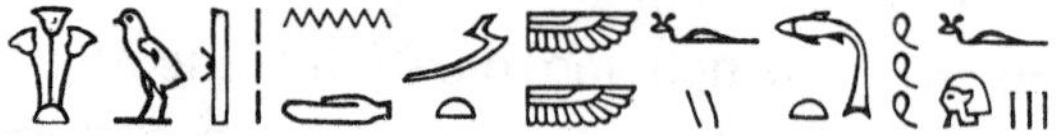 (see pp. 71, 75).

8. The god ÅP-ṬUAT, 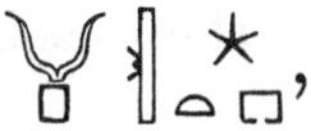, who holds a sceptre, , in his right hand, and stands before the serpent NEḤEB-KAU, 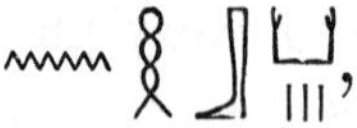, which has two heads on one end of its body, and one head, instead of a tail, at the other. Of the god ÅP-ṬUAT it is said, "He who is in "this picture is in the form which Horus made, and he "openeth [the way] for the two gods on this way,"

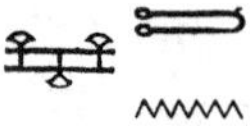. Of the serpent NEḤEB-KAU it is said, "He "who is in this picture is at his place NET-MU, by the "holy way of passage of RE-STAU, and he journeyeth "about to every place each day, and he liveth upon the "abundance of that which issueth from his mouth,"

(see pp. 75, 79).

9. A god, who grasps the third head of NEḤEB-KAU with his right hand, and a staff with a curled end in the left; facing him is a headless god called ĀB-ṬUAT  (see pp. 79, 83).

The Kingdom of Seker.

10. A goddess of the South (NEKHEBET) and a goddess of the North. Of the last group of figures it is said, "Those who are in this picture are in the form wherein "Horus hath made them; they are the warders of "the serpent NEHEPU, who guide him to the hidden "thing which is on this secret way," 

 (see p. 83).

In the lower register are:—

1. A large boat, each end of which terminates in the head of a woman; lying along the bottom of the boat is the serpent ḤETCH-NĀU, 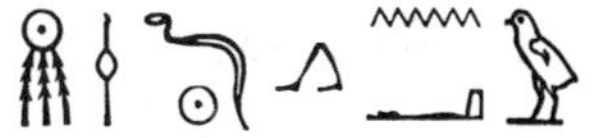 (see pp. 63, 67). Concerning him it is said, "He[1] who is in "this picture . . . . in his boat great, is the [serpent] "which guardeth the ĀḤETH chamber; he standeth up at "the mouth of the hidden passages of the ÅḤET chamber, "and he liveth upon the two voices of the heads of the "boat," 

[1] The text is in the plural.

. Under the neck of this serpent is the emblem "life," .

2. A woman called MUTHENITH, , standing (see p. 67).

3. A woman called SHATHETH, 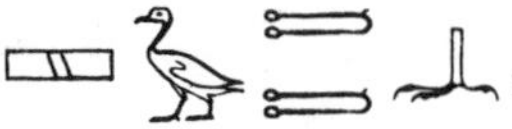, standing (see p. 67).

4. The divine mummy form BENNI, 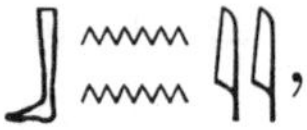, seated (see p. 71).

5. A lion-headed goddess called ḤEN-KHERTH (?), 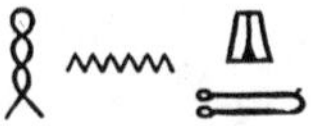 (see p. 71).

6. A goddess, with a pair of horns on her head, in a sitting position, but with no throne to sit upon; her name is THEST-ȦPT, 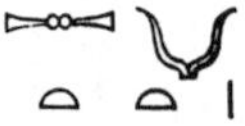 (see p. 71). Of these beings it is said, "Those who are in this picture are in "the forms wherein Horus made them, and they stand "on the ground of Re-stau in the hidden place . . . ."

7. The male serpent ȦMEN, 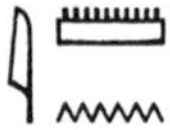 (see pp. 75, 77).

8. The female serpent ḤEKENT, 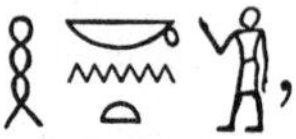, which has a human head growing out of its body, a little distance from the tip of its tail; the human head faces the serpent ȦMEN. Of the male serpent it is said, "He

The Kingdom of Seker.

"who is in this picture is the guardian of the secret "passages which lead to the ĀḤETH chamber; he "journeyeth round to every place each day, and he "liveth on the words of the gods who guard this road,"

The meaning of the legend which refers to the female serpent Ḥekent is not clear; it reads: 

9. The three-headed serpent (see p. 79) MENMENUT, 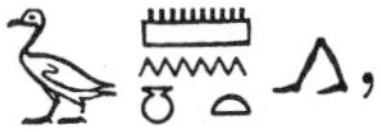, which is described as the "hidden image "of the ĀḤETH chamber [of Seker], which is illumined "daily at the birth of KHEPERÅ by that which cometh "forth from the faces of [the serpent] MENMENT,"

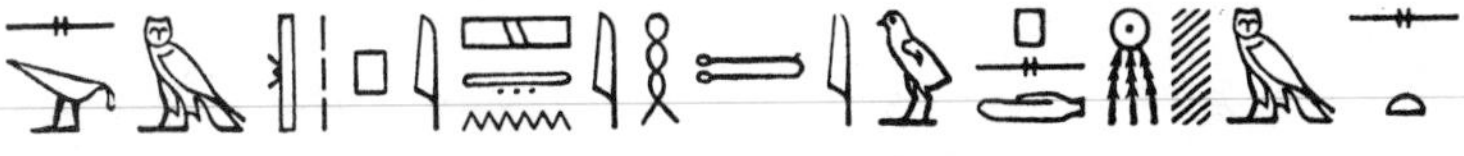

. Over the back of this serpent are six stars and fourteen human heads, each of which is surmounted by a disk. These fourteen heads represent, as M. Maspero has well shown, the gods of the first fourteen days of the month, who are being carried by the three-headed serpent to

the Utchat, which Thoth and Horus are carrying to it; they appear again in the next Division of the Ṭuat, where they are seen drawing along the boat of the sun.

10. The winged disk of the god KHEPERȦ, . Beneath stands the "envoy of heaven," 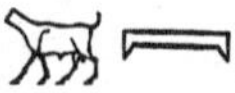, with his right hand raised, and his left stretched out, and behind him is the goddess MAĀT,  (see p. 83).

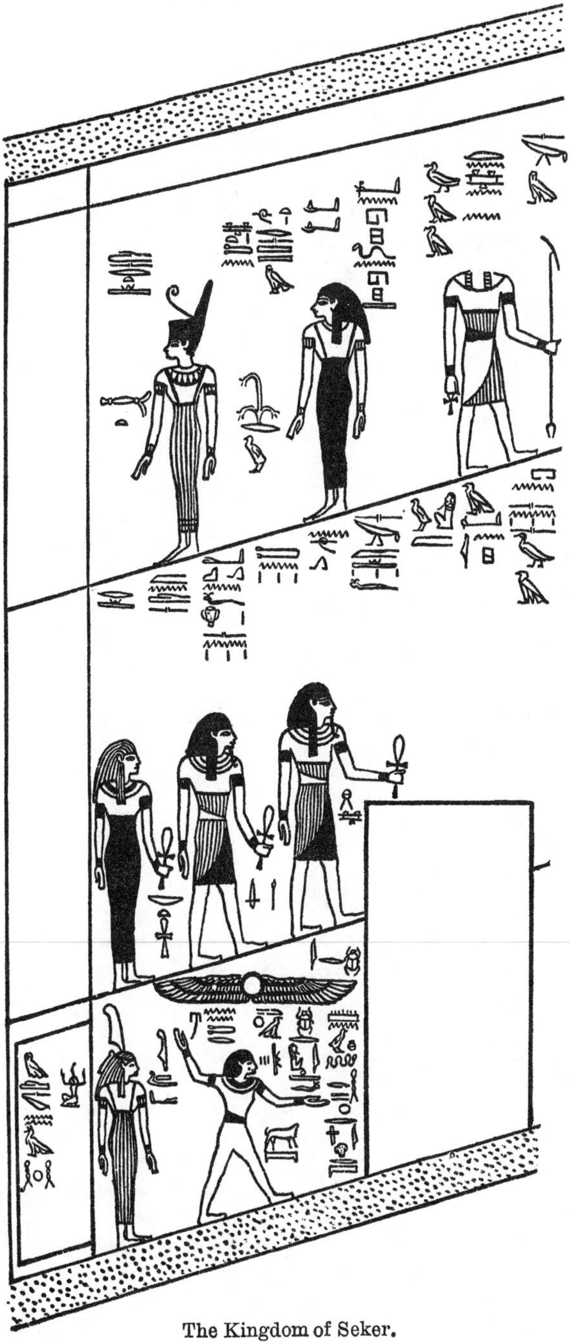

The Kingdom of Seker.

CHAPTER V.

THE FIFTH DIVISION OF THE ṬUAT, WHICH IS CALLED ÅMENT.

In the scene that illustrates the Fifth Division of the Ṭuat, which is passed through by the Sun-god during the Fifth Hour of the night, we see the boat of the sun being drawn along by seven gods and seven goddesses (see pp. 91, 95, 99, 103, 107). The legend over the seven gods is partly broken away, but what remains of it proves that it must have been similar in meaning to that which is over the heads of the goddesses, which reads, "These are the goddesses which tow Rā along in the "Ṭuat over this Circle, and they make this great god "to advance so that he may rest in Nu in the Ṭuat,"

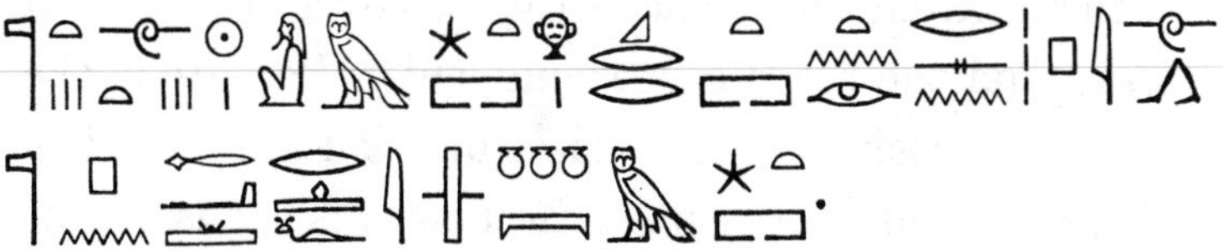

In front of the seven goddesses march four gods, who appear to be under the guidance of "Isis of Åmentet," 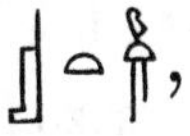, and who are described as the "great sovereign "chiefs who provide food in this Circle," 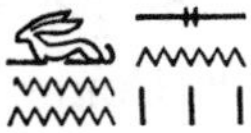

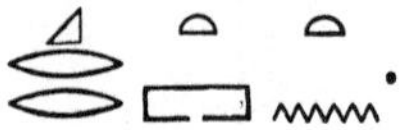 The first god is called ḤER-KHU, , and holds a staff in his hand; the second is ȦN-ḤETEP, , and holds the sceptre in his hand; the third is ḤERU-ḤEQUI, , is hawk-headed, and holds the crook in his hand; the fourth is UT-METU, , and holds a tree in his left hand.

The text containing the address of the Sun-god to the seven gods is broken away, and all that remains of it reads, "This great god maketh his journey by means "of those who tow him over this Circle in [his] boat . . . . . ." 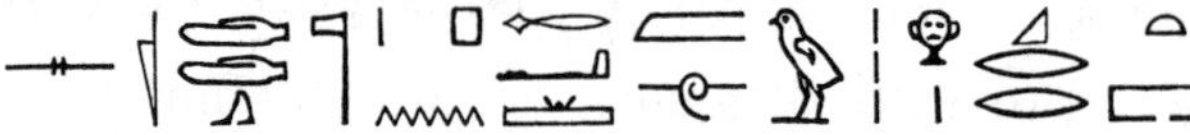

 A portion of the answer of the seven gods to him is also broken away, but what remains of it reads, "Is opened to thee the earth to "such an extent that thou hast passed over the Beautiful "Land, and the roads concerning which Rā hath spoken "to thee, O Osiris. Thou criest out, O Rā, to the Land "of Seker, and Horus hath life upon his sands. Come "to Kheperȧ, O Rā! Come to Kheperȧ! Work ye "with the cord, O ye who make Kheperȧ to advance, "so that it may give the hand (i.e., help) to Rā whilst "he passeth over the hidden ways of Rā, in the horizon. "[Come] in peace, in peace, O Rā of the Beautiful

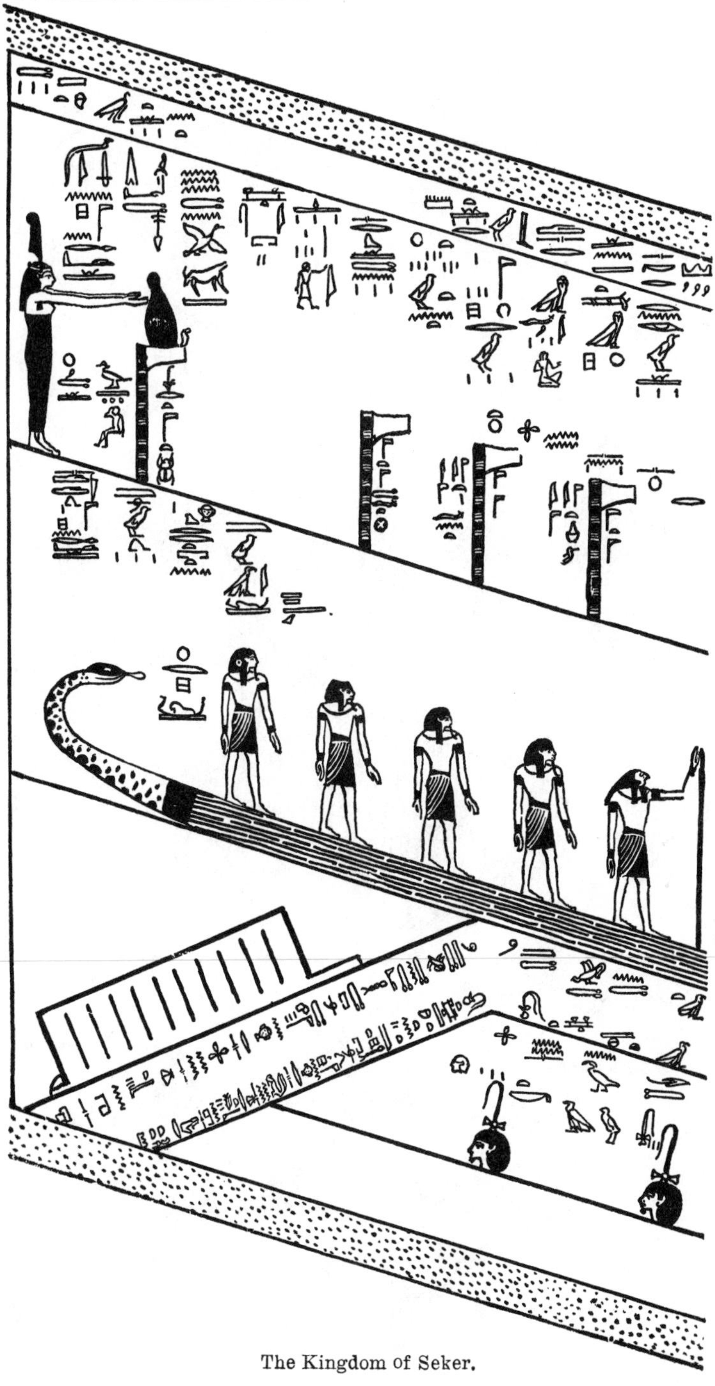

The Kingdom of Seker.

"Åment." 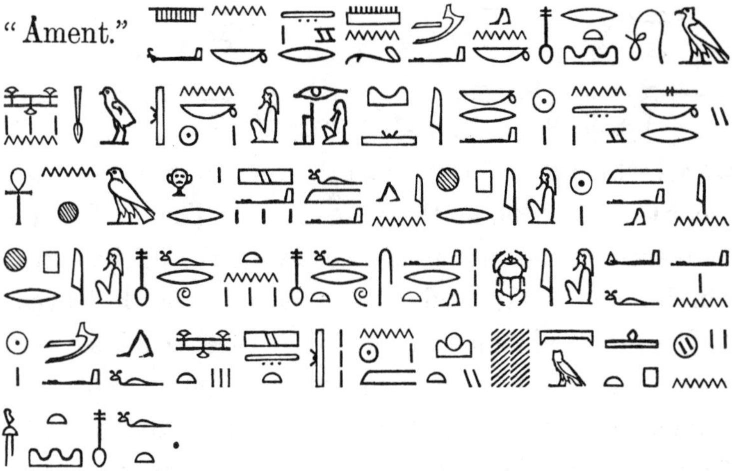

In the middle of the scene we see that the ground rises (see p. 103) and forms a kind of hollow mound, the highest point of which terminates in the head of a woman, which faces to the right; immediately above her head is a scarab which is in the act of descending, but only one half of its body is visible. Concerning the beetle it is said, "Behold Kheperå "who, immediately the [boat of Rā] is towed to the "top of this Circle, unites himself to the roads of "the Ṭuat; when this god standeth on the head of "the goddess he speaketh words to Seker every day,"

The short lines of text just above the mound read, "The majesty of this great god journeyeth on by "being towed along, and these goddesses receive him,"

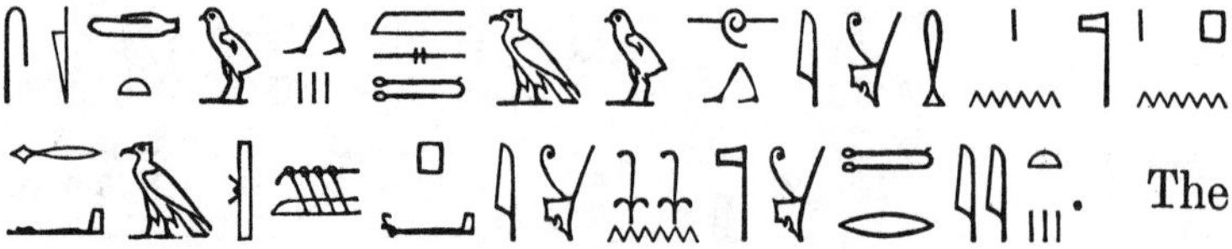 The words which are addressed to the god by the goddesses are, "Come, O Rā, in the peace of the Ṭuat! Let Rā "advance on the road in the boat which is in the earth, "in his own body, and let his enemies be destroyed. "[The goddess] Ȧment crieth (?) to thee, O Rā, so that "thou mayest join her, and mayest go forwards in "the sky as the GREAT ONE who is in the horizon, "and mayest be towed along by those who tow "thee, and, verily, mayest destroy all thine enemies,"

 To this address Rā replies, saying, "O ye who have received "your weapons, O ye who have grasped your sceptres, "O ye who shake your spears, O ye who stand by your "*tchefau* food, who sit down to your offerings, who are "the warders of food and bread and are the lords of "the provisions in Ȧment, Isis giveth herself unto you, "and Ȧment joineth herself unto you, so that I may

The Kingdom of Seker.

"stand up by you for your protection when I pass by you "in peace," 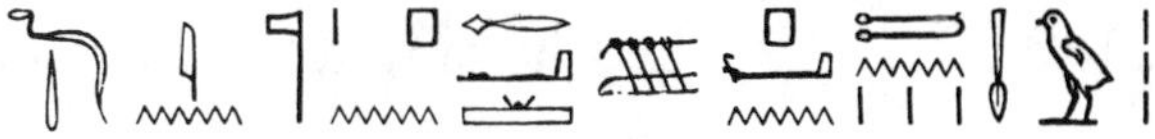

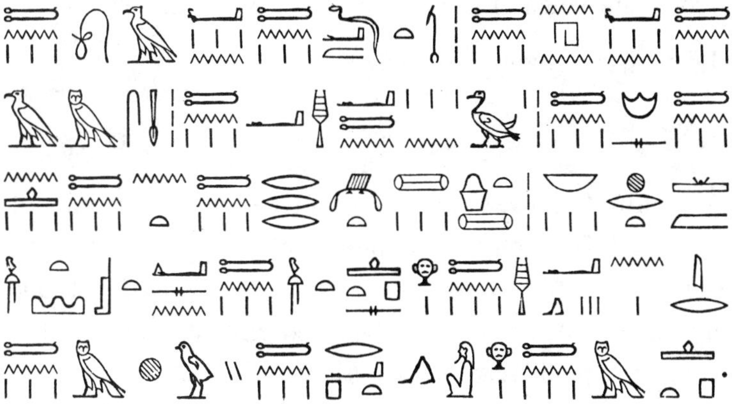

The "Land of Sekri," 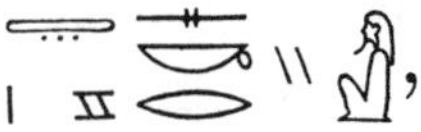, which is mentioned by the seven gods who are towing the boat of Rā, lies immediately below the mound of earth, and forms, as it were, an oval island in the river of the Ṭuat; its shape is, as M. Maspero has said, an elongated ellipse, , and it is formed wholly of sand. The "Land of Sekri" is described in the legend which is written at each end of the oval as "The horizon (?) of "the hidden country of Sekri, which guardeth the "hidden body (or, flesh)," 

This mysterious oval is supposed to rest upon the bodies of two man-headed lion sphinxes set tail to tail; of these, however, only the heads and fore quarters appear, one at each end of the oval. Each sphinx is called ȦF, 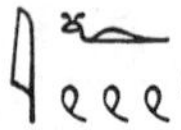, and he is said "to have his existence "from the voice of the great god," and "his work is to "keep ward over his image," 

.

Within the oval already described is stretched out at almost full length on the ground a monster serpent (see pp. 99, 103), which has two snakes' heads at one end of his body, and a bearded human head at the other (see p. 99); the text above his snakes' heads is mutilated, and all that can be made out satisfactorily are the words *neter āa,* "great god." From the middle of his body springs a pair of wings, and between them, immediately under the female head at the top of the mound, stands the god SEKRI, in the form of a hawk-headed man. Of him it is said, "His work is to "protect his own form," ; and of the serpent, "he liveth upon the magical pro-"tection which issueth from his mouth every day,"

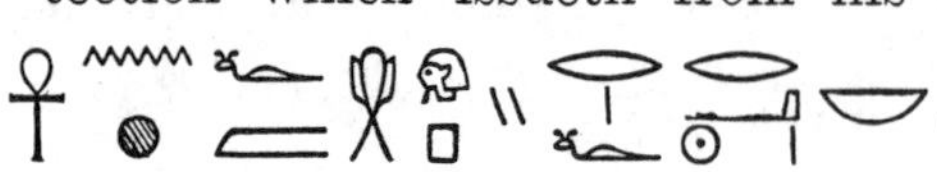.

The text which refers to the oval reads:—

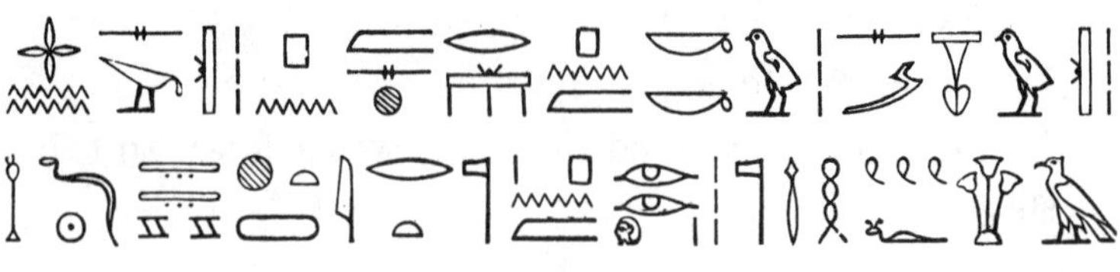

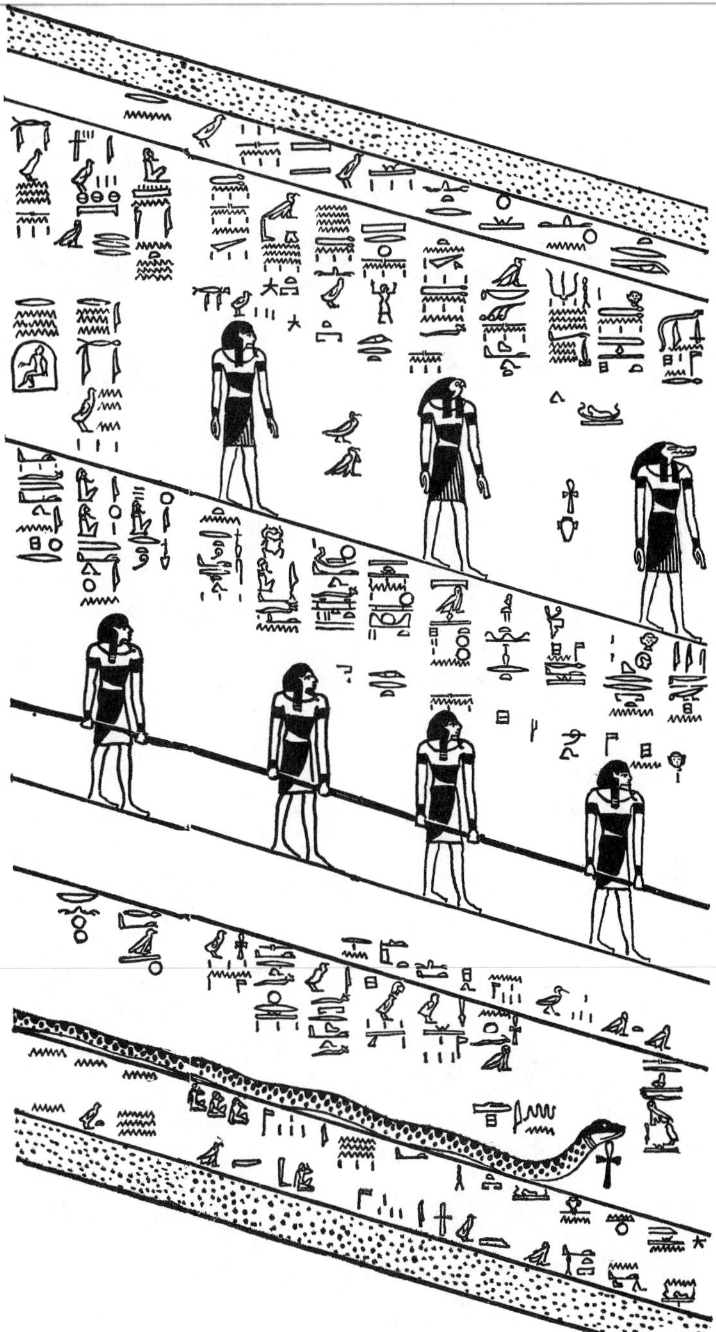

The Kingdom of Seker.

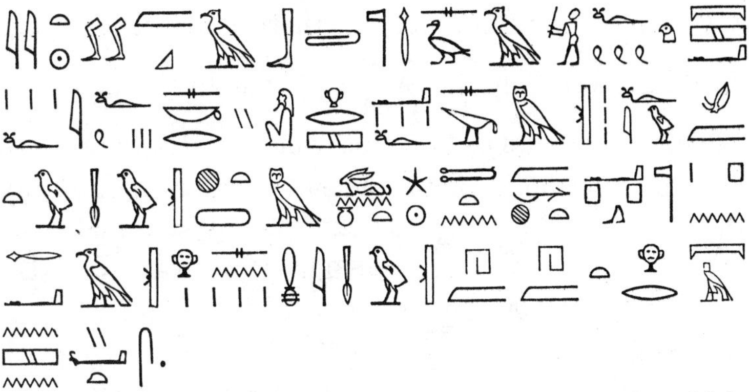

"The Image which is in this picture is in thick "darkness. The dawn in the horizon which belongs to "this god [cometh] from the eyes of the heads of the "great god, whose flesh sendeth forth light, and whose "legs are bent round, the great god who keepeth ward "over the flesh of SEKRI, who is on his sand, his own "image. The voice of this horizon is heard in this "hour after this great god hath passed them by, like "unto the sound of the roarings which are in the "heights of heaven when they are disturbed by a "storm."

On the left of the horizon (see p. 95) of SEKRI is the serpent ṬEPÅN, 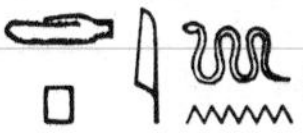, "who liveth by the voice "of the primeval gods of the earth. He cometh forth "and he goeth in, and he presenteth the offerings made "to this great god every day unseeing [and unseen],"

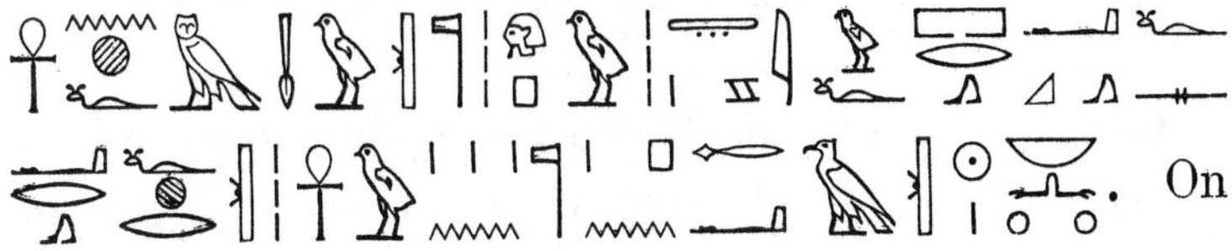 On

the right (see p. 107) of the horizon is the serpent ĀNKHȦA-PAU, , "who liveth upon the "flames which issue from his mouth. His work is to "protect the horizon, and he never entereth into any "house of the Ṭuat," 

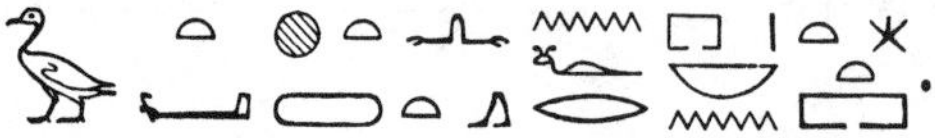

Immediately in front of this serpent are four seated gods (see p. 111), of whom the heads of two are turned behind them; they are described as the "gods who "hold the secret forms of SEKRI, who is on his sand,"  The first holds on his knees the White Crown, , the second the Red Crown, , the third the head of the ram of ḤERU-SHEFSHEFIT, and the fourth the plumes of Shu, or some other god of light and dryness. The legend above them reads, "Their forms are in the place among "them in their own bodies. They follow after this "great god unseeing and unseen," 

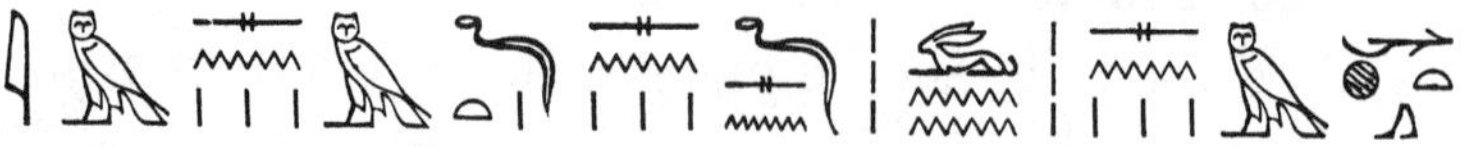

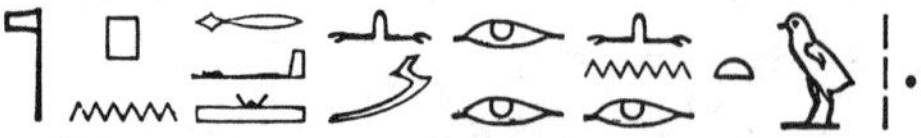

Behind the serpent ṬEPȦN (see pp. 87, 91) are four human bearded heads, each with a mass of fire upon

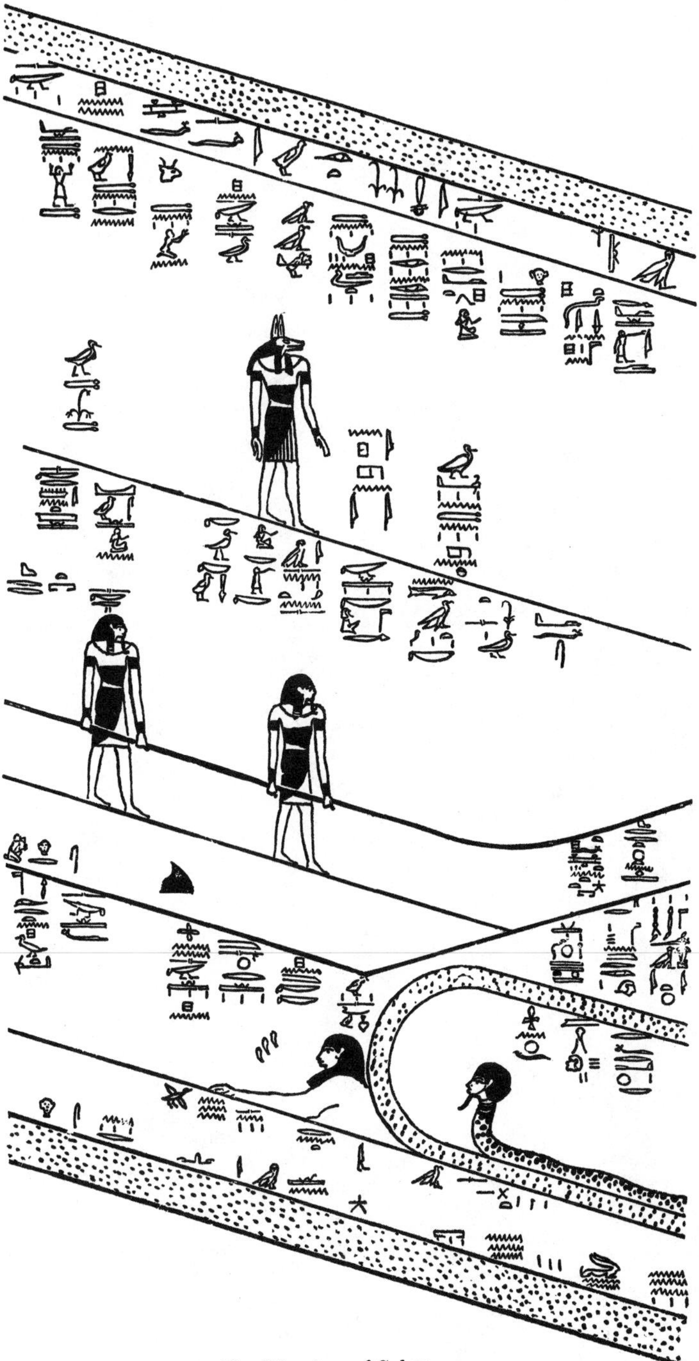

The Kingdom of Seker.

the top of it, which project from the long, narrow lake called NETU, ; these are called the "Blazing heads," . Along the lake are written, in two methods of writing, "The gods who are "in the Åmmāḥet weep when the boat hath passed "them by on its way to the . . . . . Ṭuat . . . . . "and the waters which are here are like unto fire "to those who are in them," 

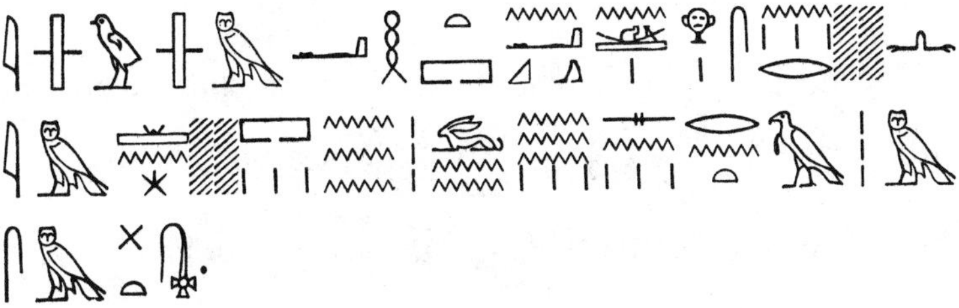.

In the upper register are:—

1. The goddess ÅMENTIT, standing with her arms stretched out in front of her at right angles to her body, and wearing the feather of Maāt on her head (see p. 87).

2. A group of nine large axes (four are broken away), the foremost surmounted by the Crown of the North, and the hindmost by the Crown of the South (see pp. 87, 91). The mutilated speech of the god written above them reads, "Give me thy hand (i.e., help me) Åmentet! "Good is this water which leadeth to the tomb [where] "rest the gods. Hail, exist ye, O nine gods who have "come into being from my flesh, and have not come

"into being from your own forms, and who are firm in "respect of your food, I avenge you, do ye avenge me."

3. The god who is the "guardian of those who are submerged,"  (see pp. 91, 95).

4. The god SATIU (?),  (see p. 95).

5. The god ĀNKH-ÅB, , hawk-headed (see p. 95).

6. The god BATH-RESTH (?) crocodile-headed,  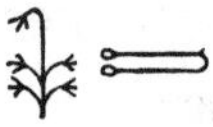 (see p. 95).

7. The god ÅNP-HENI, , jackal-headed (see p. 99). Of these five gods it is said, "They act as "guardians of Net, and of those who are submerged in "the Ṭuat, and they [protect] and make to pass on the "boat," 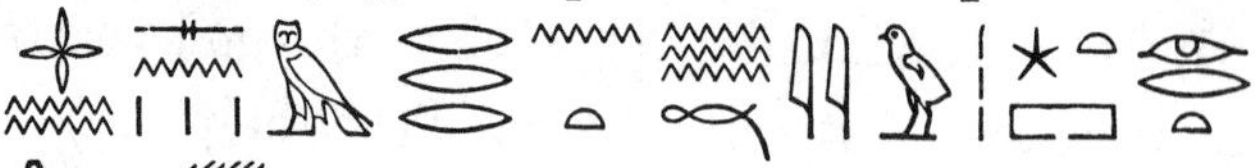 . To these the Sun-god makes an address, which reads 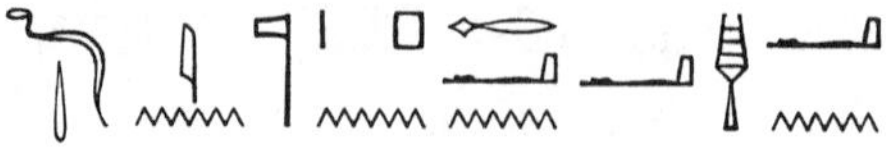

The Kingdom of Seker.

, "This great god saith, O ye who stand by "your waters, who keep ward over your lands, who go "round about in the pool of those who are submerged "in Nu, pilot ye these to the lands of the sea of the "Ṭuat, unto your waters which never dry up, and rise "ye up in your lands and let me travel over you in "peace. This great god saith, O ye, lift ye up your "weapons to your . . . . . image, and protect ye the "foreheads of your *maāt*, and perform ye your work, "in order that I may be able to pass by you in peace,"

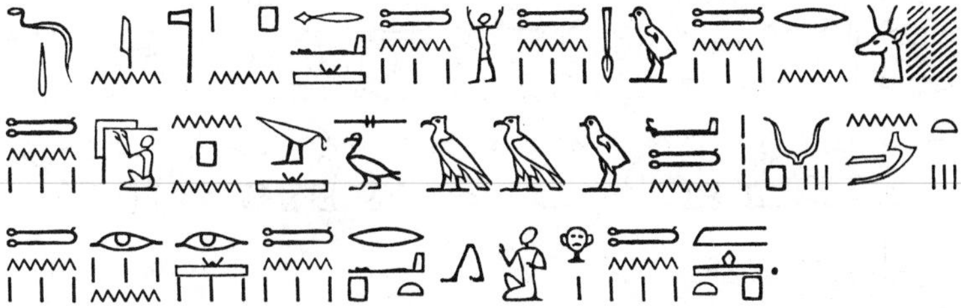

8. Immediately in front of the god ÅNP-HENI is an object which looks like a chamber with a rounded roof; but whatever it may be, it is filled with sand, and from the fact that the sign of "night" or "darkness," 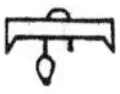, appears at the top, we may conclude that it represents

some form of the dark underworld of Seker. To each side of it a hawk clings by his claws, and from the lower part of it emerges the scarab, which has already been mentioned (see p. 103).

9. A huge serpent, the two heads facing the object described under No. 8. Of him it is said, "He liveth "by Rā every day, he travelleth over every place of "*maāt* in the Ṭuat, and it is he who setteth himself in "opposition to the scarab,"  . To this serpent Rā saith, "Hail, thou serpent ṬER, whom I myself "have fashioned, open thou to me thy folds, open thou "thy folds wherewith thou hast doubly sealed the "earth to protect me, and march thou against those "who are in my following, in order that I may pass by "thee in peace," 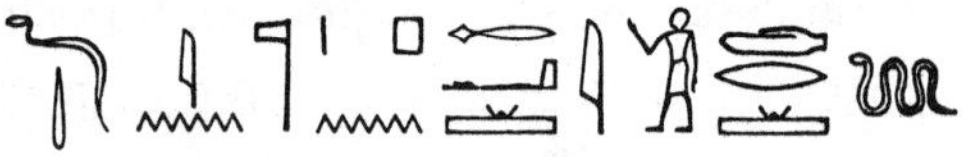  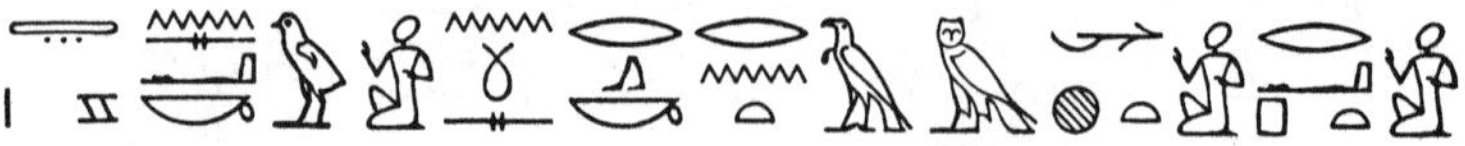 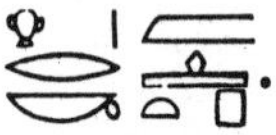.

10. The god BAFERKHEFTIU, , ram-headed (see p. 111).

11. The god IU-ḤER-ȦPTESU, , who holds a lasso in each hand (see p. 111).

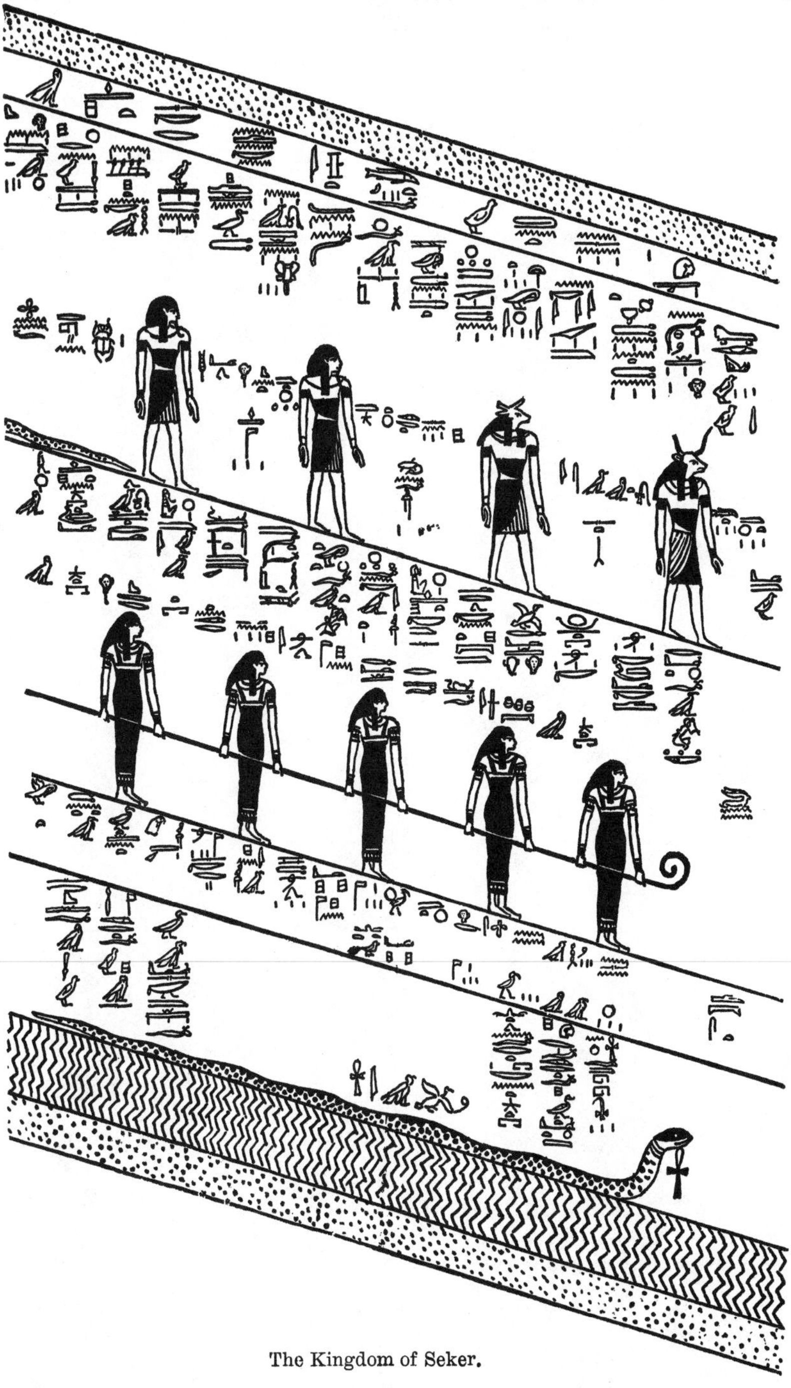

The Kingdom of Seker.

12. The god ÅN-ÅT, , wearing a feather of Maāt (see p. 111).

13. The god ĀBUI, , with his head turned behind him; he is provided with a shade,  (see p. 111).

14. The god ĀMU, bull-headed (see p. 107).

15. The god SET, bull-headed (see p. 107).

16. The god SENṬ-NEF-ÅMENTIU,  (see p. 107).

17. The god ḤETEP-NETERU, 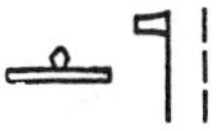 (see p. 107).

Of these eight gods it is said, "They stand by at the "annihilation of the dead in the Ṭuat, and their work "is to burn up with fire the bodies of the dead by the "flames from their mouths in the course of every day,"

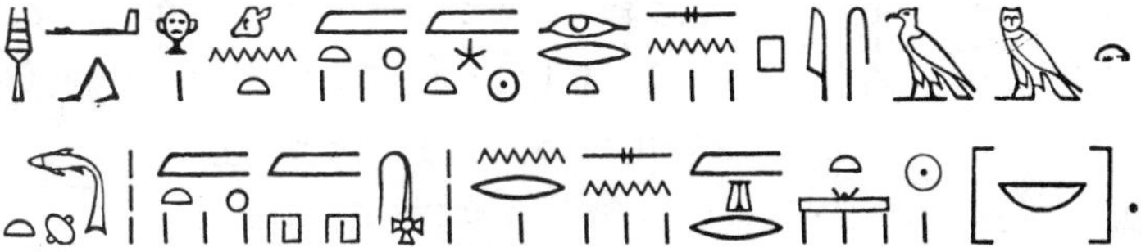.

18. A goddess, standing upright, with her hands stretched out to the top of the head of a man who is kneeling before her, and is cutting open his head with a hatchet; the goddess is called , and "lives upon the blood of the dead, and upon "that which the gods give," 

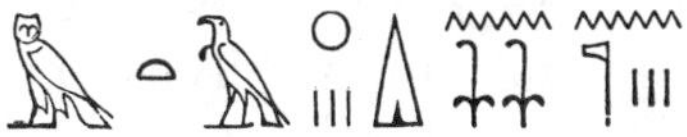 (see p. 113).

The text of the speech which the god makes to the eight gods reads :—

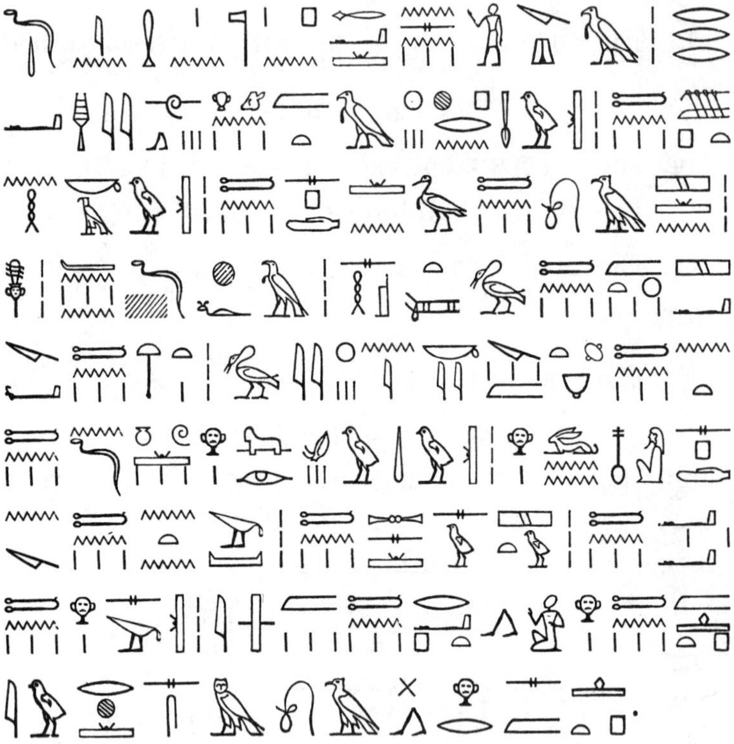

"The Majesty of this great god saith unto them, "Hail, ye who stand at the blocks of torture, and who "keep ward at the destruction of the dead, ye whose "voices have come into being for you, who have "received your words of power, who are endowed with "your souls, who sing hymns to the accompaniment of "your sistra, who take vengeance on the enemies, who "annihilate the dead, who hack in pieces shades [of "men and women], who destroy and cut in pieces the

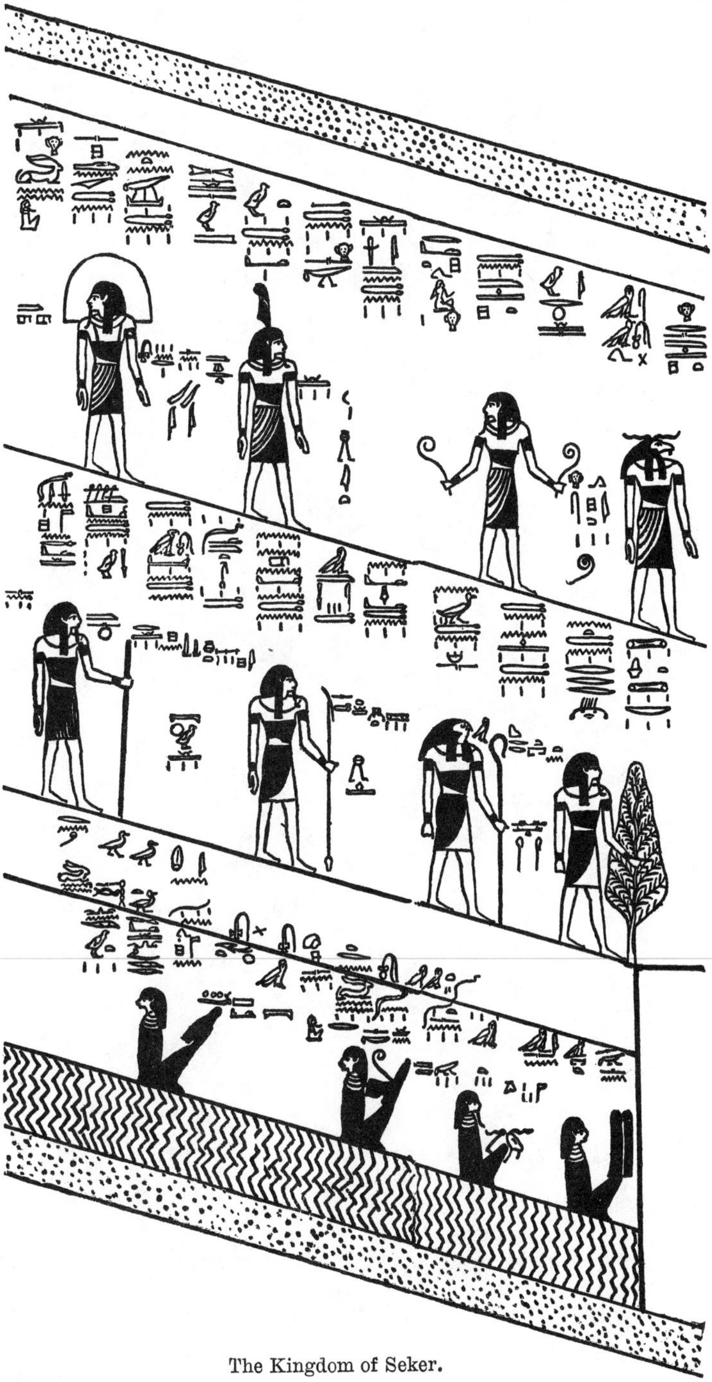

The Kingdom of Seker.

The Kingdom of Seker.

"dead, who avenge Osiris and hearken unto words near "Unnefer, provide ye yourselves with your slaughtering "knives, fetter and bind with your hands [this] figure "which is with you, so that I may journey past you in "peace. Whosoever knoweth this shall pass by the "goddess in peace."

The entrance into the Sixth Division of the Ṭuat is made through a door in the lower register, which is guarded by a serpent "who openeth it himself," 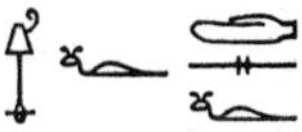; here, too, appears the large five-rayed star which is the symbol of the planet VENUS, and is described as the "living god which journeyeth, and "journeyeth, and travelleth," 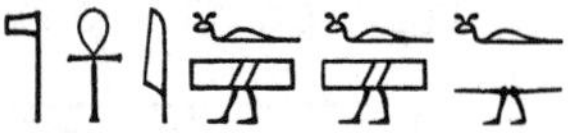.

CHAPTER VI.

THE SIXTH DIVISION OF THE ṬUAT, WHICH IS CALLED METCHET-MU-NEBT-ṬUAT.

IN the scene which illustrates the SIXTH DIVISION of the Ṭuat, which is passed through by the Sun-god during the SIXTH HOUR of the night, we see, in the middle register, the dead Sun-god ÅFU-RĀ, 𓆑𓆑𓆑 ☉,

The Boat of Åf, the dead Sun-god, in the Sixth Hour.

once again standing in his boat, under the canopy, accompanied by his usual company of gods. He is no longer in the serpent boat wherein he passed through the domain of Sekri, and he is no longer being towed along. In front of the boat are:—

1. The god Thoth, in the form of a man with the head of a cynocephalus ape, seated on a throne, and

bearing the name TEḤUTI-KHENTI-NEB-ṬUAT, 
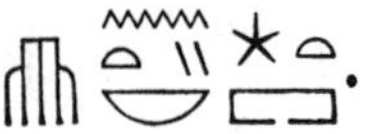.

2. A female figure, with her hands turned behind her, holding in each the pupil of an eye of Horus or Rā; she is called ÅMENT-SEMU-SET, .

The text above the boat reads: 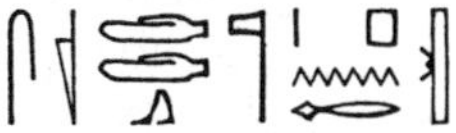

The goddess Åment-semu-set. Thoth of the Ṭuat.

, "This great god travelleth "through this city, being provided with [his] boat, on "the water; he worketh the paddle in this country "towards the place of the body of Osiris." . . . "The "Majesty of this great god [speaketh to] the gods who "are in this country when he arriveth at these houses "which are hidden, and which contain the image of "Osiris. This god crieth [to the hidden forms which

"are in them, and they hearken to the voice of this "god, and then he passeth them by," [ ]

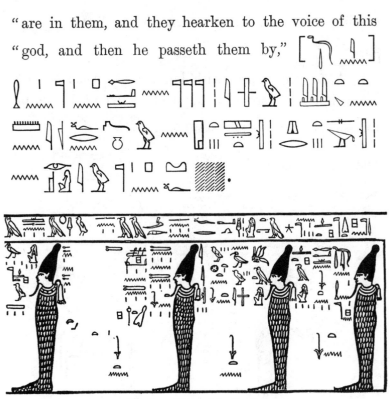

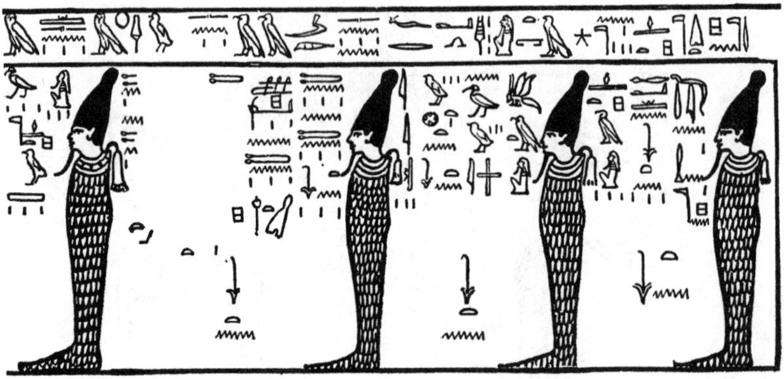

The Four Kings of the South.

In the abode of Osiris are sixteen gods in mummied forms. The first four are bearded, and wear the *menȧt* and the White Crown, and each is described by the title *suten*, , i.e., "King of the South." The second four are bearded, and are described as ḤETEPTIU, ; the third four are bearded, and wear the *menȧt* and the Red Crown, and each is described by the title *bȧt*, ; and the fourth four are bearded, and are called

The Four Ḥeteptiu gods.

The Four Kings of the North.

The Four "Spirits."

KHU, , i.e., "Spirits." Immediately in front of these gods is an enormous serpent with five heads, which is called ĀSH-ḤRȦU, , i.e., the "Many-faced." The body of this serpent is bent round to form an oval, and within it lies on his back the god ȦFU, , who is holding upon his head a beetle, which is the symbol of the god KHEPERȦ. The text written above reads:—

The Serpent Āsh-ḥrȧu.

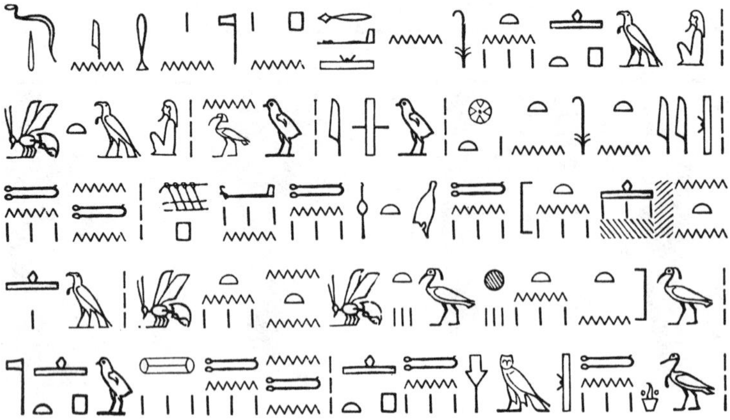

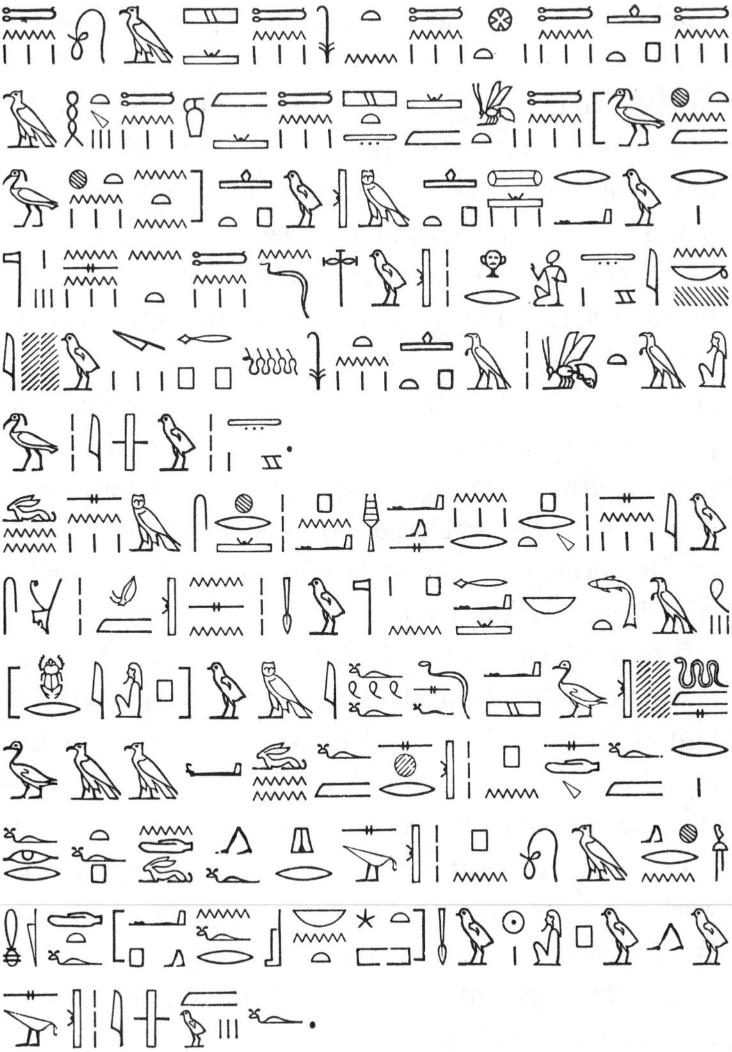

"Saith the Majesty of this great god to the kings of "the South, to the Ḥeteptiu, to the kings of the North, "and to the Spirits who are in this City:—May your "royal state and condition be with you, may ye receive "your White Crowns, and ye Ḥᴇᴛᴇᴘᴛɪᴜ [may ye receive] "your offerings, and ye kings of the North may ye "receive your Red Crowns, and ye Sᴘɪʀɪᴛs may ye "receive your appointed rites; may your offerings be "unto you, and may ye be in peace. May ye have "power over your souls, may ye be adored (?), may ye "have sovereignty over your city, may ye have peace "in your fields, may ye join yourselves to (i.e., attain "to) your secret things with your crowns (?), may your "appointed rites be paid to you, may your sacrifices of "propitiation be made to you, and give to the gods "their mouth. Avenge ye me in [this] land, and hack "in pieces the serpent Āpep, O ye kings of the South, "ye Ḥeteptiu, ye kings of the North, and ye Spirits, "who dwell in [this] land."

"Those who are in this picture stand up in their "places, and they hear the voice of the great god, the "lord of the dead body, that is to say, KʜᴇᴘᴇʀÀ in his "own flesh . . . . . . in the act of guarding."

Of the Serpent of Many Faces it is said, "Of him "who is in this picture, with his tail in his mouth, his "work is to rise up with this image, to journey to the "West in his form, and to travel to every place of the "Ṭuat. Through the voice of Rā it is that the figures "who are in him advance."

The text which runs in the border above the upper register reads:—

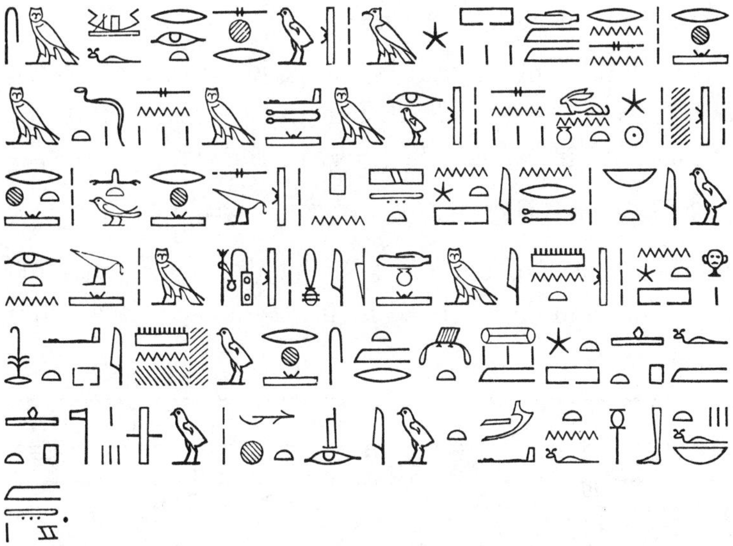

"[This is] the hidden path of Ȧmentet, on the water "of which is transported this great god in his boat to "arrange the lots (or, plans) of those who are in the "Ṭuat. If their names be uttered, if their bodies be "known, if their true forms and the knowledge of their "hours be known, and the qualities of this secret figure "of the Ṭuat (which are unknowable), by any man "whatsoever: or if an exact representation in drawing "be made of what is in the Hidden Place (Ȧment) of "the Ṭuat, which is to the south of the Āt of Ȧmentet: "whosoever knoweth this thing shall be one who is "fully provided with food in the Ṭuat, and he shall "partake in the offerings which are made to the gods "who are in the following of Osiris, and he shall have "(i.e., receive) the offerings which all his kinsfolk are "in duty bound to make to him upon earth."

In the upper register are :—

A company of nine gods and goddesses, all of whom are represented as seated, but their seats of state or thrones are invisible; they may be thus enumerated :—

1. The god Ḥetep-khenti-Ṭuat, 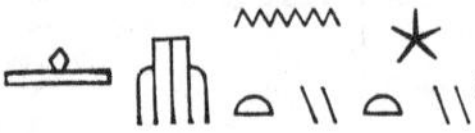, in the form of a mummy; his hands project from his bandages, and on his head he has symbols of meat and drink.

Åsår-åm-åb-neteru. Åsth-meḥit. Ḥetep-khenti-Ṭuat.

2. The goddess Åsth-meḥit, or Åst-åmḥit,  , or , with the Crown of the North on her head. The name means "Isis in the North."

3. The god Åsår-åm-åb-neteru, 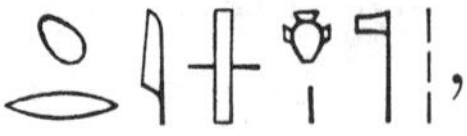, i.e., "Osiris in the heart of the gods."

4. The god ḤERU-KHENTI-ÅḤET-F, , i.e., "Horus at the head of his field," hawk-headed, with his hands projecting from his bandages.

5. The god BENTI-ÅR-ÅḤET-F, , or , ape-headed, with his hands projecting from his bandages.

6. The god MAĀ-ÅB-KHENTI-ÅḤET-F,

Ḥenbethem. Maā åb-khenti-åḥet-f. Benti-år-åḥet-f. Ḥeru-khenti-åḥet-f.

, wearing the White Crown and *menåt*, and with his hands projecting from his bandages.

7—9. Three goddesses, the first two of whom are called ḤENBETHEM (?), , and THEḤBITH, . The text which refers to this company of the gods reads:

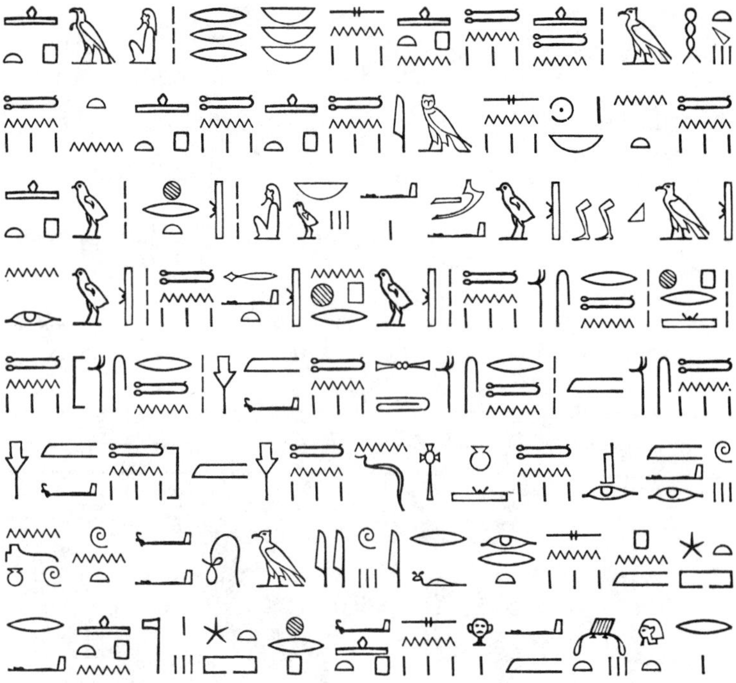

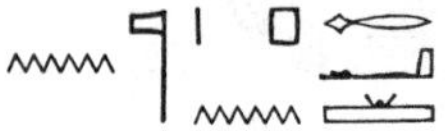, "Saith the Majesty of this great god "to the gods who are over this Field:—O ye gods who "dwell in the Ṭuat, ye Ḥeteptiu who keep ward over "your masters, ye unto whom offerings are made from "the offerings of your fields of offerings, whereon ye "take your rest each day, unite ye yourselves to the "provisions which are mine. Ye are the lords of "[your] hands, ye have right [to direct] [your] feet, ye "are exalted in your forms, ye are great in your "transformations, ye have power over what ye produce, "ye have power over what ye have possession of, ye "have possession of that over which ye have power, ye

"have power over that over which ye have possession, ye "have possession of that over which ye have dominion, "protect ye Osiris from those who would act with "violence and wrong against him. The work of these "gods in the Ṭuat is to give offerings to the gods of "the Ṭuat, who are masters of their offerings and of "the food which proceedeth forth from the mouth of "this great god."

10. Three sceptres of the form [?], each surmounted

Three Sceptres of the White Crown. .... Theḥbith.

by the WHITE CROWN; from the base of each projects a knife.

11. Three sceptres of similar form, each surmounted by the RED CROWN; from the base of each projects a knife.

12. Three sceptres, of similar form, each surmounted by a uraeus; from the base of each projects a knife. The text which refers to these reads: 

 "Saith
"the Majesty of this great god to the Majesties of the

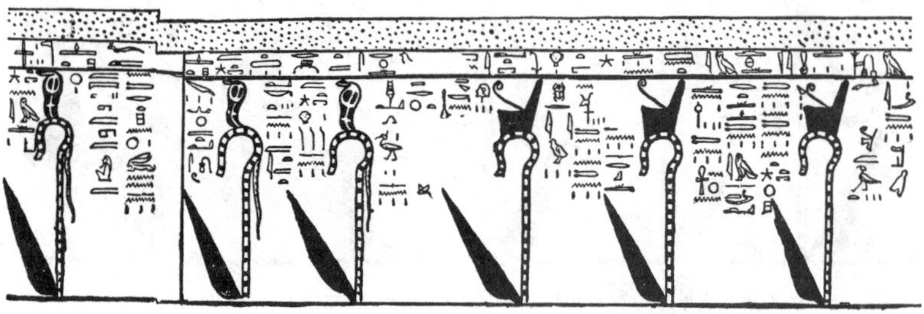

Three Sceptres of the uraei. Three Sceptres of the Red Crown.

"kings of the South and North who dwell in the Ṭuat:—
"Reap ye, O ye who wear the White Crowns, and ye
"who wear the Red Crowns like Souls [who are in]
"their lands. Ye who belong to the Ṭuat produce
"your own offerings therein. Make ye to be Maāt
"your sceptres (?), let your souls live, and let your
"throats have food to swallow, and ye shall come into
"being upon the land . . . . . . Their souls shall rise
"up in the Ṭuat on their sceptres (?), they are provided

with knives, and no violence shall be done to them . . . . . goddess . . . . ."

13. The lion KA-HEMHEMET, , couchant, and facing the two companies of the gods described above. Above his back are the two Utchats, between which is the sign .

14. A form of the goddess ISIS, , in a sitting position, but without a throne.

Thath-neteru. Ḥetchefu. Isis-Thaȧth. Ka-hemhemet.

15. The god ḤETCHEFU, .

16. The god THATH-NETERU, , in mummied form, holding a sceptre in one hand and a knife in the other.

17. A chamber, with an opening under the roof, through which a snake, which stands on its tail outside it, belches fire; under a vaulted covering is an "image," , of Rā, in the form of the hind-quarters of a lion, . The chamber is called ḤET-ṬUAU-RĀ, .

18. A similar chamber, with an "image" of Rā in the form of a hawk's wing, ; the name of the chamber is ḤET-STAU-KHER-ĀḤA, .

19. A similar chamber, with an "image" of Rā in the form of a human head; the name of the chamber is ḤET-ṬEMṬET-RĀ, 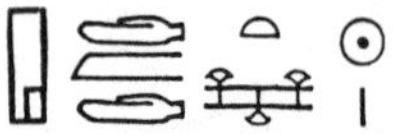. The texts read:

Ḥet-ṭemteṭ-Rā. Ḥet-stau-kher-āḥa. Ḥet-ṭuau-Rā.

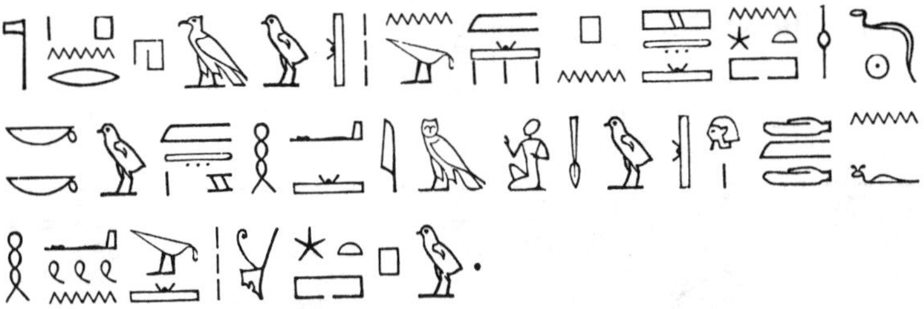

In the lower register are:—

1. The god Ḥenti (?), , crocodile-headed, and in a seated position, but without a throne.

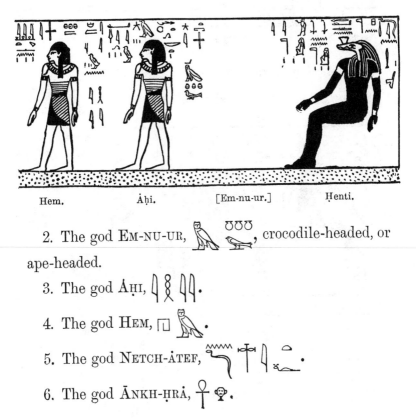

Hem. Ȧḥi. [Em-nu-ur.] Ḥenti.

2. The god Em-nu-ur, , crocodile-headed, or ape-headed.

3. The god Ȧḥi, .

4. The god Hem, .

5. The god Netch-Ȧtef, .

6. The god Ānkh-ḥrȧ, .

7. The god MEṬ-ḤRȦ, .

8. The god NETCHTI, .

Netchti. Meṭ-ḥrȧ. Ānkh-ḥrȧ. Netch-ȧtef.

9—12. Four goddesses, each in a seated position, but without a throne; the first is called ȦNTHETH, ,

Seḥith. Ḥemt. Ḥenḥenith. Ȧntheth.

the second ḤENḤENITH, , the third ḤEMT, , and the fourth SEḤITH, .

The text which refers to these reads: 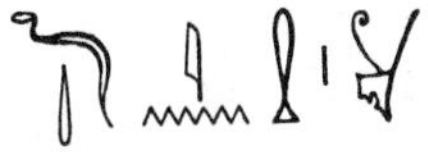

, "The Majesty of this great "god saith unto these gods:—O ye gods who dwell in "the Ṭuat, and who are in the following of the lord of "the beings who are in the Ṭuat, who stand up and sit "down in Nu, who dwell in your Field, O ye gods who

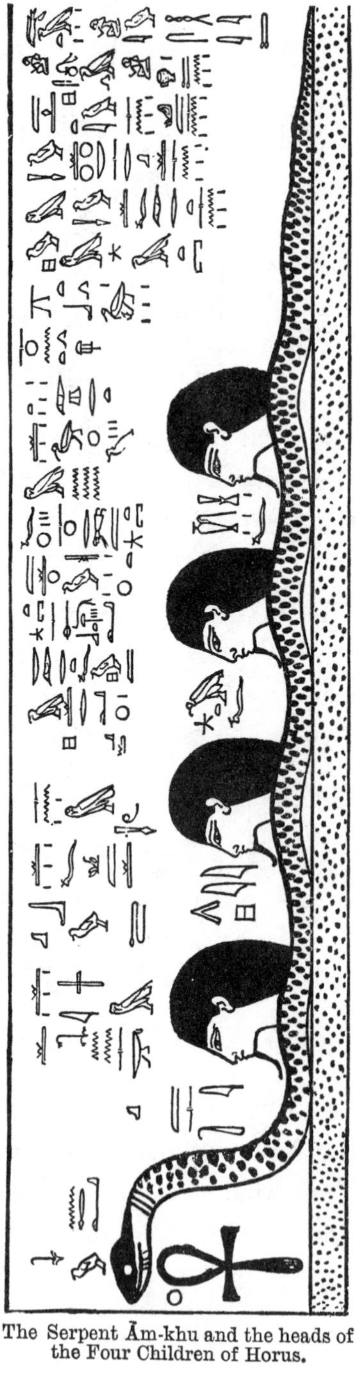

The Serpent Ām-khu and the heads of the Four Children of Horus.

"send forth light, and who "make to stand up your "bodies, and O ye goddesses "who sit down in the fol- "lowing of the SCARAB in "the place where are his "bodies in the Ṭuat, O ye "who live on your . . . . . ., "whose hearts live on their "food, who send forth light "in the darkness which sur- "roundeth you, who have "the mastery over your Red "Crowns, who partake in "content of the offerings "made to you, let them "travel in my following, let "my soul be with me, let "me rest (or, unite myself) "to my bodies, and let me "pass by you in peace. "These gods hear the voice "of Rā every day, and they "have their life through his "voice. The work which "they have to do in the "Ṭuat is to convey along "souls, and to accompany "the shades of the dead, "and to make provisions for spirits, [and to find for "them] water."

13. The monster serpent ĀM-KHU, , with his head raised from the ground, and the symbol of "life" under his head. Out of the crest of each of the four undulations of his body springs a bearded head, and the four heads are those of the children of Horus—MESTHȦ, , ḤĀPI, , ṬUAMUTEF, , and QEBḤ-SENNU-F, 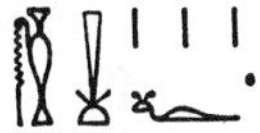. The text which refers to the serpent reads: 

, "This serpent is himself invisible "to this great god, but these forms (i.e., the heads of "the four children of Horus) have their being in his "folds, and they hear the voice of this great god every "day. The work which he doeth in the Ṭuat is to "devour the shades of the dead, and to eat up the "spirits of the enemies [of Rā], and to overthrow "[those who are hostile to him] in the Ṭuat."

14. The god ḲAI, .

15. The god MENI, .

16. The god ÅNN-REṬ, .

17. The god URṬ, . Each of these four gods is

Urṭ. Ånn-reṭ. Meni. Ḳai.

in a sitting position, but has no throne whereon to sit.

18. A company of nine serpents, each of which belches fire from its mouth and is armed with a huge

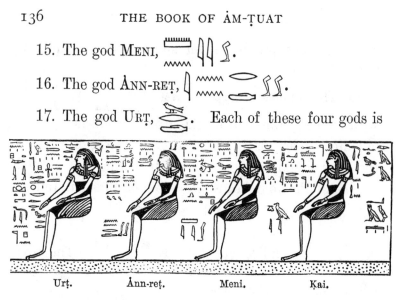

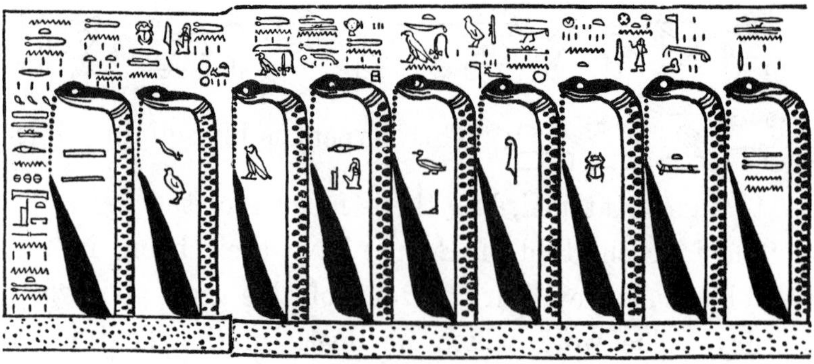

The serpents of a company of gods.

knife; only the heads and upper parts of the bodies of these serpents are visible. Their names are TA-THENEN, , TEM, , KHEPERÅ, , SHU, , SEB,

, ÅSÅR, , ḤERU, , ÅPU, , and ḤETEPIU, 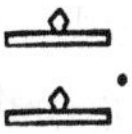. The text which refers to the four gods and the nine serpents reads:—

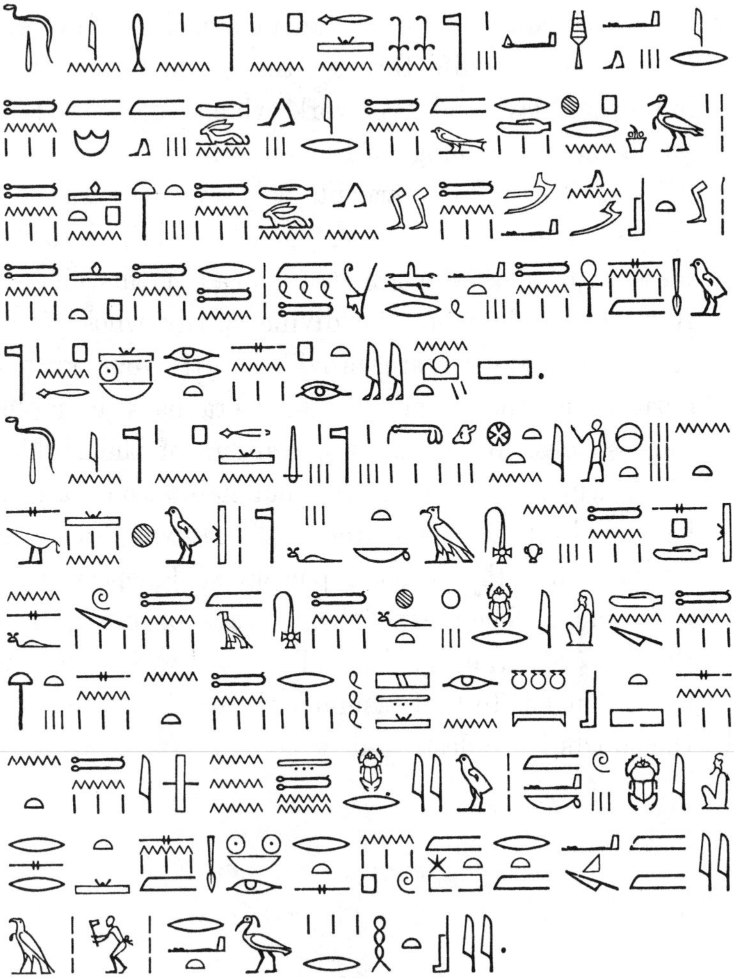

"Saith the Majesty of this great god to these gods:— "O ye who make yourselves to be standing up although "ye are seated, ye who are in motion although ye are "at rest, ye whose souls come into being, ye who are "united to your shades, who lift up your feet and who "move onwards by your thighs, unite ye yourselves to "your flesh, and let not your members be fettered. "They have their life through the voice of this great "god every day, and the work which they do is to "watch the two comings of the god Khuti."

Concerning the nine serpents it is said:—

"The Majesty of this great god speaketh words to "these male gods who are at the head of this city:— "Hail, O nine forms of the divine spirits, whose faces "are of flames, who are provided with your knives, "burn ye up the enemies of Kheperȧ, hack in pieces "their shades, for ye are the warders of the Hidden "Flesh, which is made of Nu, your habitation, for it is "ye who dwell in the Water of TA-THENEN, and it is "for you that the magical powers of Kheperȧ come "into being. They have their means of living from "the word of Rā every day. The work which they do "in the Ṭuat is to hack asunder the dead, and to cause "the spirits to be destroyed."

CHAPTER VII.

THE SEVENTH DIVISION OF THE ṬUAT, WHICH IS CALLED THEPḤET-ÀSÀR.

THE scene that illustrates the SEVENTH DIVISION of the Ṭuat, which is passed through by the Sun-god during the SEVENTH HOUR of the night, is introduced by three lines of text, which read :—

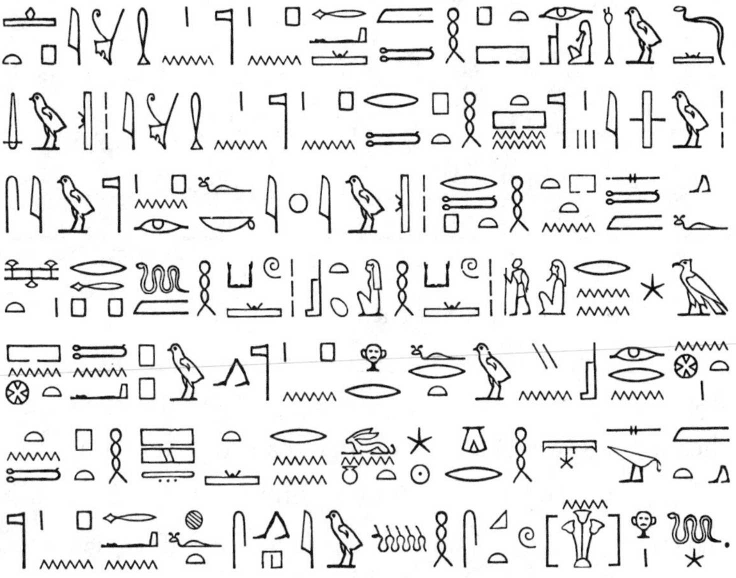

"The Majesty of this great god taketh up his abode "in the Hall of Osiris, and the Majesty of this god "addresseth words to the Hall of the gods who dwell "therein. This god performeth all the rites proper "[for entering] this Hall, and he advanceth on his way "againt Āpep by means of the words of power of Isis, "and by means of the words of power of the Sovereign "God. The name of the gate of this City wherethrough "passeth this god is RUTI-ÀSÀR. The name of this "City is THEPḤET-SHETA. The name of the hour of the "night which guideth this great god into it is KHEFTES-"HÀU-ḤESQET-[NEḤA]-ḤRÀ."

The Boat of Àf, the dead Sun-god, in the Seventh Hour.

In the middle register are:—

1. The boat of Rā, who stands under a canopy formed by the body of the serpent MEḤEN; the god is ram-headed and wears a disk on his head, and his name ÀFU, 𓆑𓆑𓆑, is written twice near him. In front of him stand ḤEKA-SER, 𓎛𓂓𓀙, and SA, and ISIS, who has both arms stretched out before her, and is reciting the words of power which shall make the boat to advance.

Behind the god stand ḤERU-ḤEKEN, KA-SHU, NEHES, ḤU, and the "protector of the boat." Above the boat is written: 

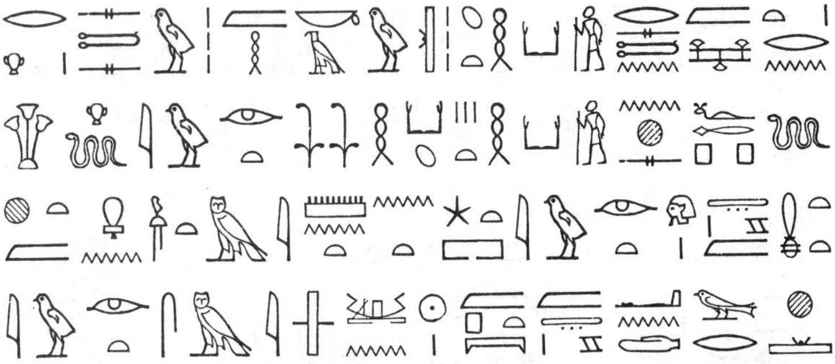

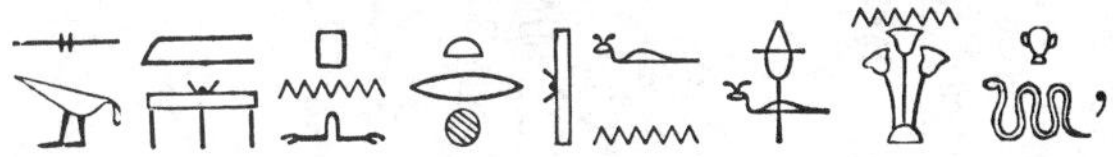, "This great "god journeyeth in this City in the path of the Circle of "SAR (Osiris) by means of the utterances of the words "of power of Isis and of the words of power of SER, so "that he may journey on his way against NEḤA-ḤRÅ. "If these words of power of Isis, and those of SER be "uttered, ĀPEP shall be turned back and shall be shut "up in Åment, in the hidden place of the Ṭuat; if "they be uttered on the earth it shall be so likewise. "Whosoever shall utter them shall become one of those "who are in the boat of Rā, both in heaven and upon "earth; but whosoever knoweth not these figures shall "not know how to repulse NEḤA-ḤRÅ."

2. The serpent NEḤA-ḤRÅ, which is transfixed to the ground by means of six knives. The goddess SERQET, , stands with a band round his neck in the act of

strangling him, and the god Ḥer-ṭesu-f, 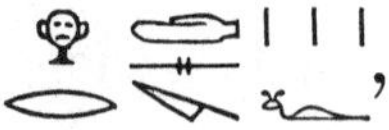, stands by his tail, round which he is tying a fetter. The text which refers to him reads: 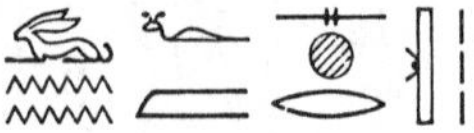

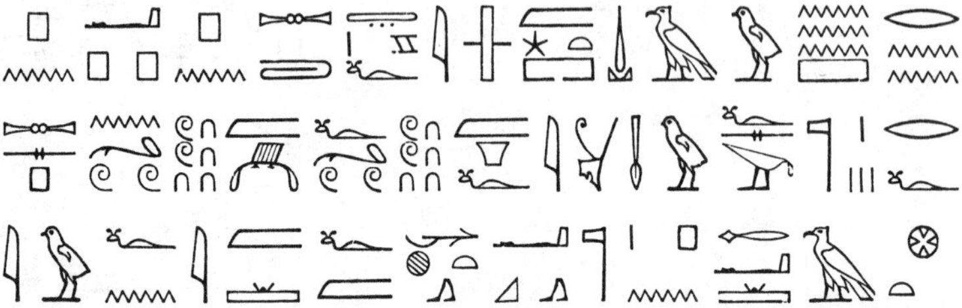

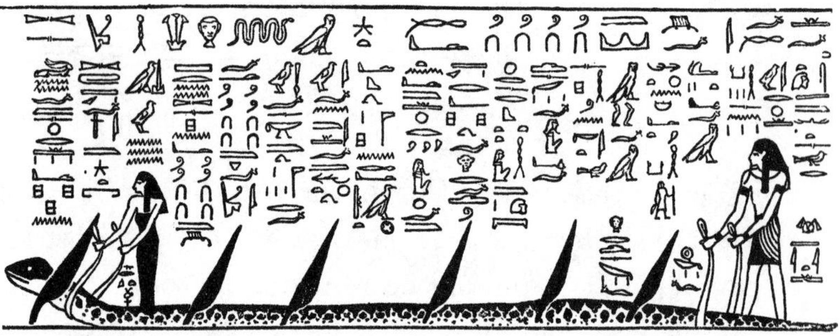

The serpent Nehȧ-ḥrȧ being fettered by Serqet and Ḥer-ṭesu-f.

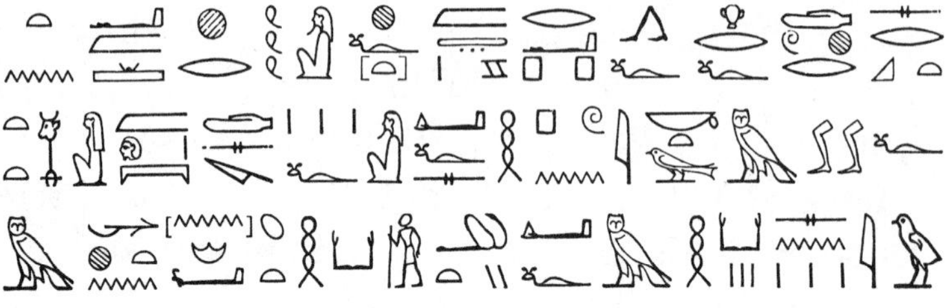

, "He who "is in this picture is Āpep, and he surroundeth his "country, which is in the Ṭuat; Tchau is the name of "this district, which is four hundred and forty cubits

"in length, and four hundred and forty cubits in "breadth, and his voice guideth the gods to him. He "who is with (?) him after this great god hath made "his passage through this City, halteth (?) with ȦFU, "opposite to the country whereover he would make a "way; behold, SERQET is at the head [of Āpep], and "ḤER-ṬESU-F placeth his deadly fetter about his feet "after Isis hath taken possession of the words of power "of SER of two-fold strength, [and Rā] giveth their "words of power. Whosoever knoweth it (i.e., this "picture and the text) upon earth shall not be one of "those of whose water NEḤA-ḤRȦ drinketh."

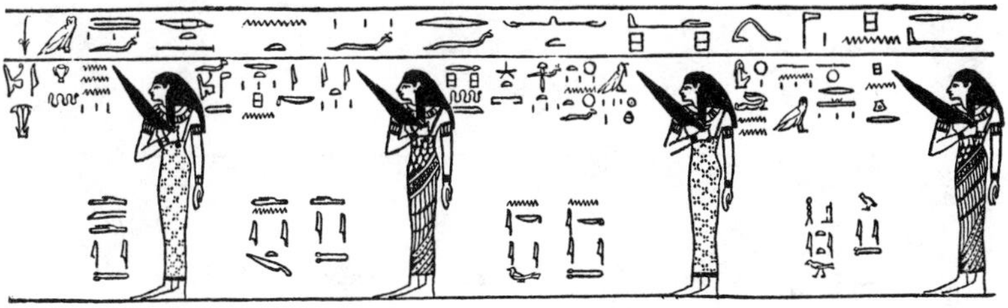

Temṭith. Ṭenith. Nȧkith. Ḥetemtit.

3. The goddess ḤETEMTIT, , armed with a knife.

4. The goddess NȦKITH, , armed with a knife.

5. The goddess ṬENIT,  (var. ), armed with a knife.

6. The goddess ṬEMṬITH, 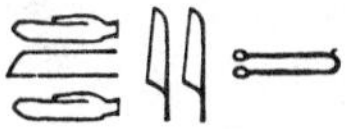 (var. ), armed with a knife. These four goddesses

guard four rectangular coffers, at the end of each of which is a human head; inside each coffer is a mound of sand, beneath which is buried one of the four forms of Osiris. The first coffer "contains the form of TEM," ; the second "contains the form of KHEPERÅ," 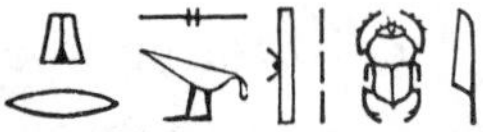; the third "contains the

The coffer of Tem. The coffer of Kheperå.

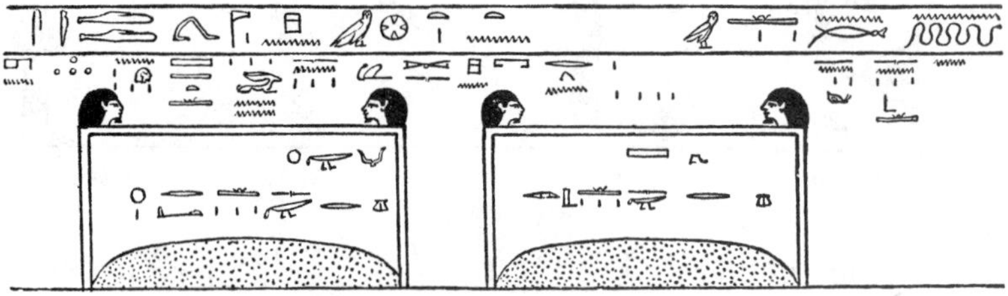

The coffer of Rā. The coffer of Osiris.

form of RĀ," 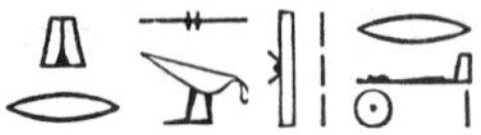; and the fourth "contains the form of OSIRIS," . The goddesses are described as: 

, "The goddesses who hack "at Āpep in the Ṭuat, who repulse (or, bring to nought) "the affairs (or, matters) of the enemies of Rā. Those "who are in this picture, and who hold knives, hack "asunder Āpep in the Ṭuat each day."

7—10. The four coffers of Osiris, concerning which it is said: 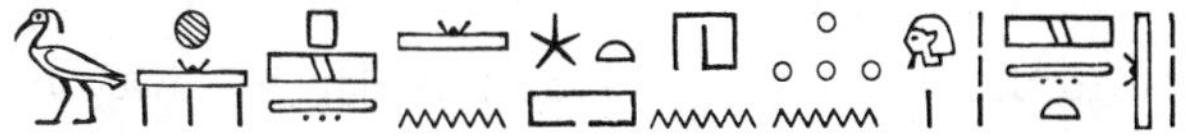

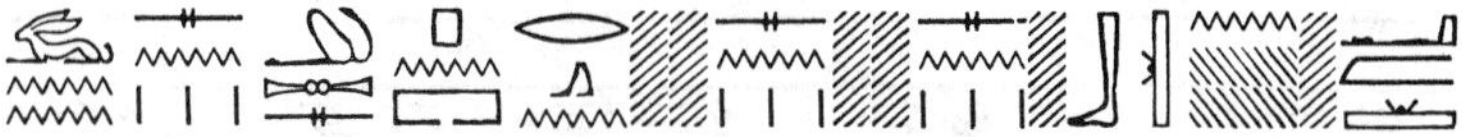

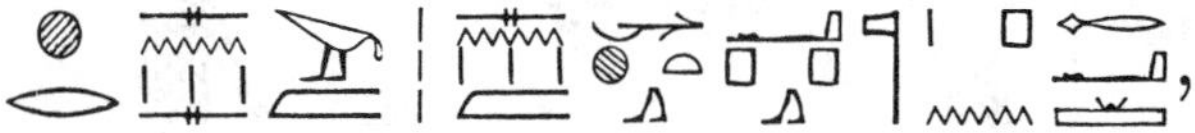, "[These "are the] hidden magical figures of the Ṭuat, the "funeral shrines of the hidden heads. [When] those "who reached this region [come there, the hidden "heads] appear, [and when they have heard the voice of "Rā] they eat their own forms, after this great god hath "passed them by." The line of hieroglyphics above the upper register reads: 

, "The hidden road of Àment. The "great god maketh his way over it in his holy boat, "and he passeth over this road which has no water, "and none to tow. He maketh his way by means of

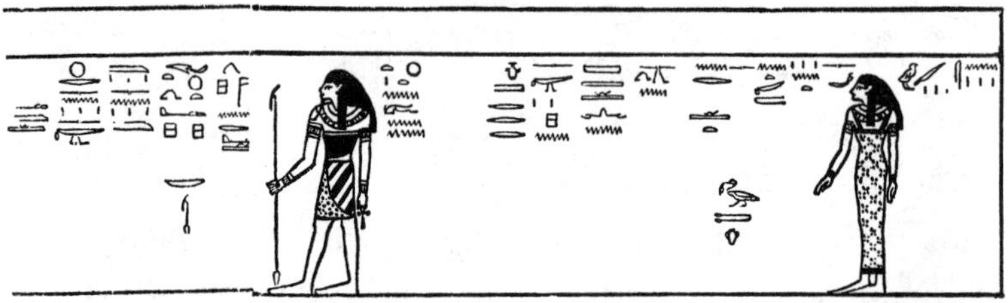

Neb-Uast. Seth-àb (?).

"the words of power of ISIS, and by means of the words "of power of SEMSU (?), and the utterances of this great "god himself [act as] magical protectors, and perform "the slaughters of ĀPEP in the Ṭuat, in this Circle in "his windings in the sky. Whosoever shall make [a "copy of] these [pictures] according to the similitudes "which are in writing at the northern side of the "hidden palace in the Ṭuat they shall act for him that "maketh them as magical protectors in heaven and in "earth. Whosoever knoweth them shall be as the "SPIRITS with Rā."

11. The god NEB-UAST, , standing, and holding a sceptre in his right hand.

12. The goddess SETH-ÅB (?), .

In the upper register are:—

1. The god SHEPES, , in mummied form, seated,

Shepes. Åth. Ankhuithit.

and holding in his right hand some curved object, which resembles a boomerang.

2. The goddess ÅTH, , with the head of a lioness, holding the symbol of "life" in her right hand, and a sceptre in her left.

3. The uraeus ĀNKHUITHIT, , with the head of a woman.

4. A god in human form, seated on a throne, wearing plumes and an uraeus on his head, with "life" in his right hand, and the sceptre  in his left; this god is called ÀFU-ÀSÀR, , and he is seated under a canopy which is formed by the body of a monster serpent called ĀNKH-ÀRU-TCHEFAU-ĀNKH-ÀRU,  . The text which refers to the first three gods reads: 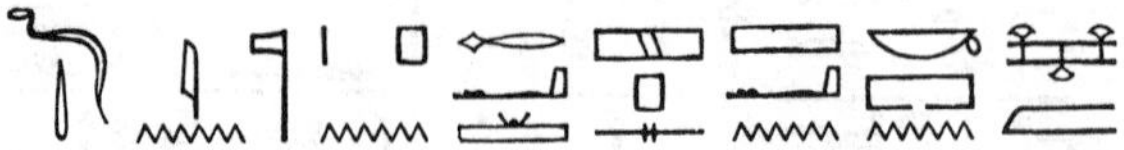

, "The Majesty of this great and holy god saith, "Grant thou me to come forth on the path by thy "spittle (?) and by [thy] throat and let me utter the "word which is *maāt* to Ānkhit, and let me open thy "fold, for I have come to illumine the darkness, and to "embrace him that is in Meḥen." The text which refers to ÀFU-ÀSÀR reads: 

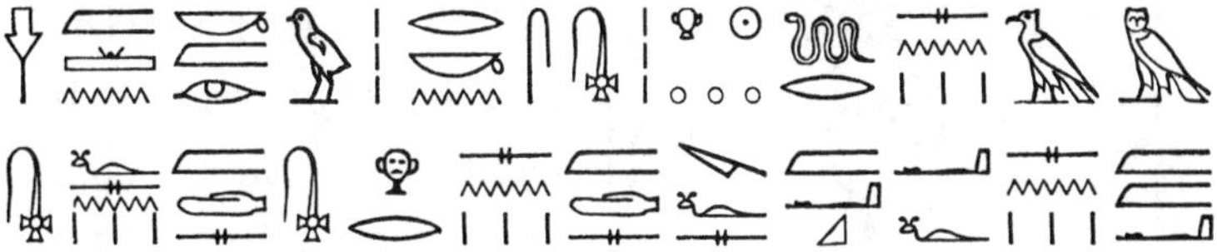

"This god "saith unto Osiris, who dwelleth in the serpent MEḤEN, "Hail, Osiris, Governor of the Ṭuat, thou lord of life, "thou ruler of Åmentet, thou shalt live, live thou life, "thou hast magical power, and shalt prevail by magical

Åfu-Åsår under the serpent Meḥen. The beheading of the enemies of Osiris.

"power in [this] land. Thou dost exalt those who are "in thy following on their arrival before thee. Thine "enemies are beneath thy feet, thou hast gained the "mastery over those who have worked against thee. "The flames [of fire] are against them, he burneth "them up with his blazing knife which is over them, "he hacketh them in pieces and choppeth them up "with his slaughtering knife, and he reckoneth up his "members each day. O let me pass over thee in peace."

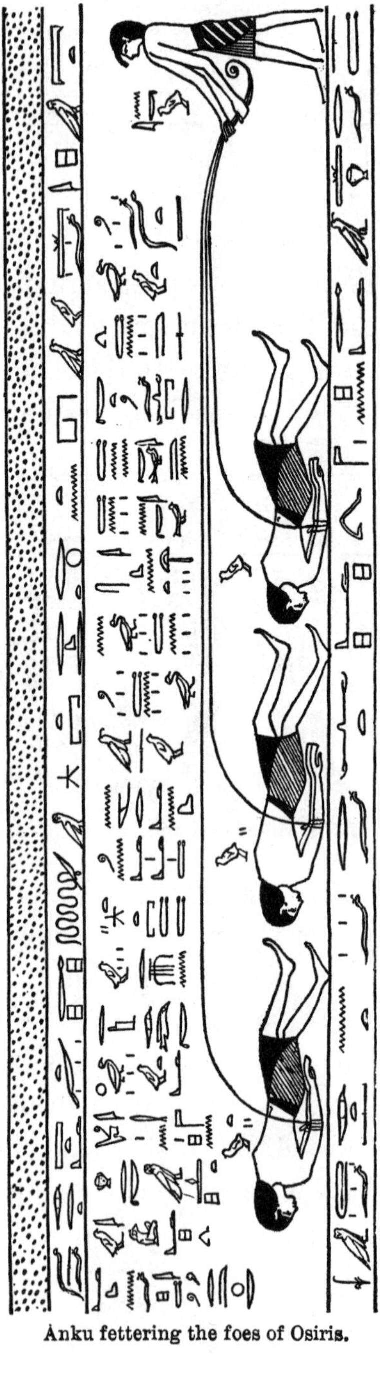

Ȧnku fettering the foes of Osiris.

5. Three headless figures, kneeling, with their arms tied behind their backs; these represent the "enemies of Osiris," , or . Behind these stands a fierce cat-headed (or, lynx-headed) god, who holds a huge pointed stake in one hand, and flourishes a large knife in the other.

6. Three foes, , of Osiris lying on their backs; round the right arm of each a rope is tied, and the other ends of the three ropes are in the hands of a god called ÀNKU, . The passage which refers to these reads:

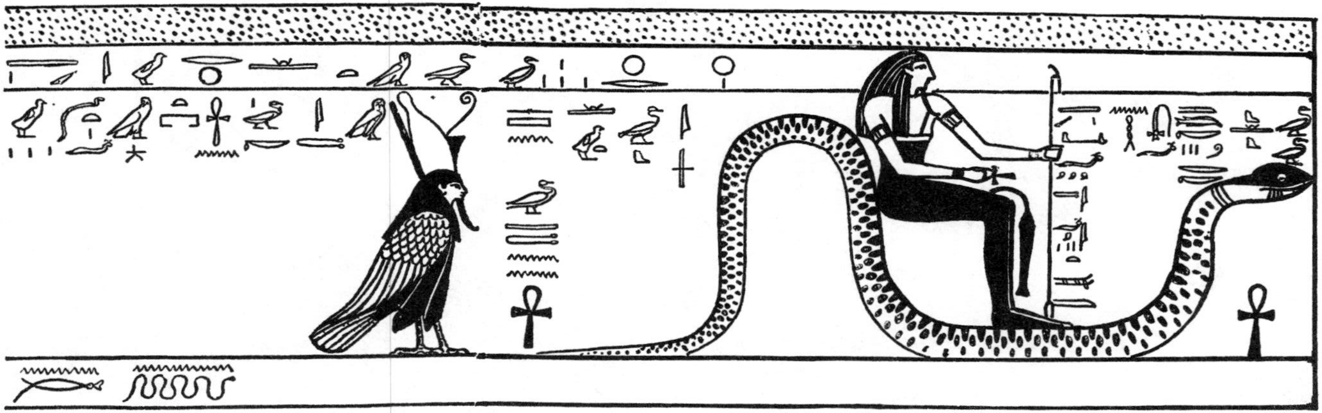

Sa-Tathenen.

The serpent Åfu-Tem.

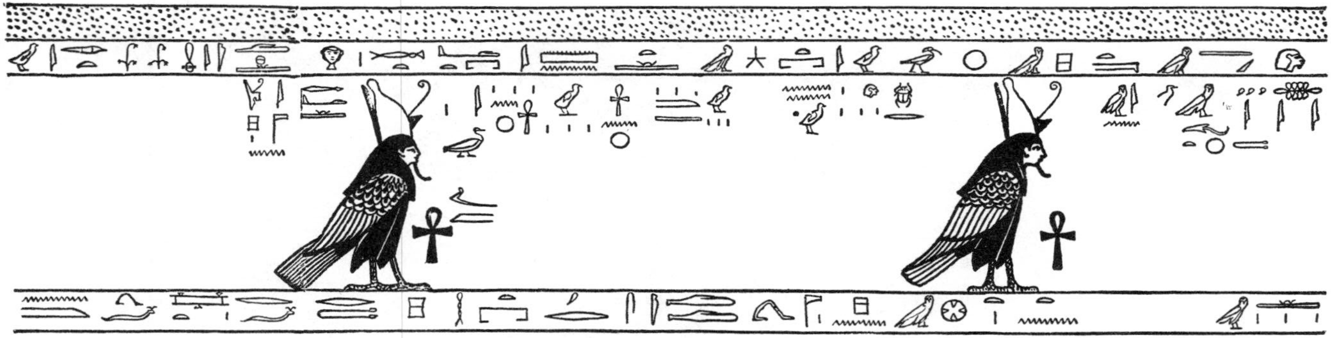

Divine Souls of the Seventh Hour.

, "The Majesty of this god saith:—O ye spirits "who are hostile to Osiris, who have rebelled against "the Governor of the Ṭuat, your hands and arms are "fettered, and [ye] are tied tightly with bonds, and "your souls are kept under ward, and your shades are "hacked in pieces, ÅNKU hath drawn the cords about "you so tightly that ye shall never be able to escape "from his restraint."

7. Three bearded, human-faced hawks, wearing on their heads the double crown of the South and North; the first is called SA-TATHENEN, 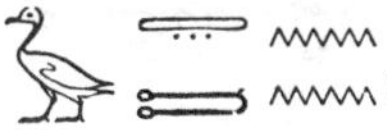, the name of the second is wanting, and the third is called MAM (?), , or MAĀT, .

8. A huge serpent, which bears on its back a god in a sitting posture; the god is called ÅFU-TEM, , and the remains of the text which refers to him say that he shoots forth his flame at those who rebel against Osiris, and that he eats the souls of the enemies of the god.

In the lower register are:—

1. The god ḤERU-ḤER-KHENṬ-F, , seated on a throne, as his name implies. He is hawk-headed, and wears the solar disk encircled by a serpent; in his right hand is the symbol of life, and in his left a sceptre. The other forms of his name are and . Of this god it is said: , "The "work of this figure who is in "this picture is in the Ṭuat, and "it is for him to send the stars "on their way, and to make the "hours to go on their way in the "Ṭuat." The stars are personified by gods, twelve in number, who stand each with a star on his head. Their names are:—

Ḥeru-ḥer-khenṭ-f.

1. UR-ḲERT, .
2. KEKHERT (?), .
3. NEB-KHERT-TA, .
4. ṬUATI, .

5. Ḥiāt,

6. Ḥi-khu-. . . .,

7. Emta-ā,

Ur-ḳert. Kekhert. Neb-khert-ta. Ṭuati. Ḥiāt. Ḥi-khu-. . . .

Emta-ā. Ṭeser-ā. Emma-ā. Sem-nes-f. Ṭesem-em-maat-f. Seqer-ṭepu.

8. Ṭeser-ā,

9. Emma-ā,

10. Sem-nes-f,

11. ṬESEM-EM-MAAT-F, .

12. SEQER-ṬEPU, .

The text relating to these gods reads: 

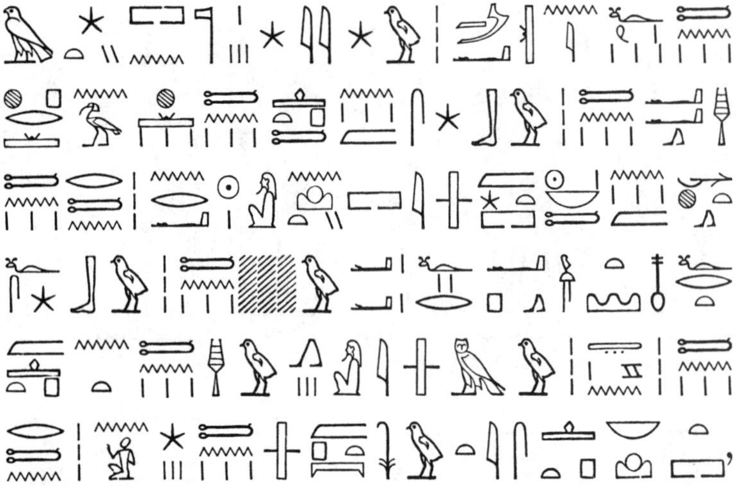,

'The Majesty of Horus of the Ṭuat saith unto the "starry gods:—O ye who are *maāt* in your flesh, whose "magical powers have come into being for you, who "are united unto your stars and who yourselves rise up "for Rā in the horizon which is in the Ṭuat each day, "O be ye in his following, and let your stars guide "his two hands so that he may journey through the "Beautiful Ȧment in peace. And, O ye gods who "stand up, who dwell in our land, light up ye your "stars in the sky so that [I] may unite [myself] with "the master of the horizon."

2. The Twelve Goddesses of the Hours, who face to

the right, having each a star on her head. Their names are:—

1. ḤEKENNUTHETH,
2. NEBT-EN-. . . .,
3. NEBT-NEBT,

Goddesses of the Hours.

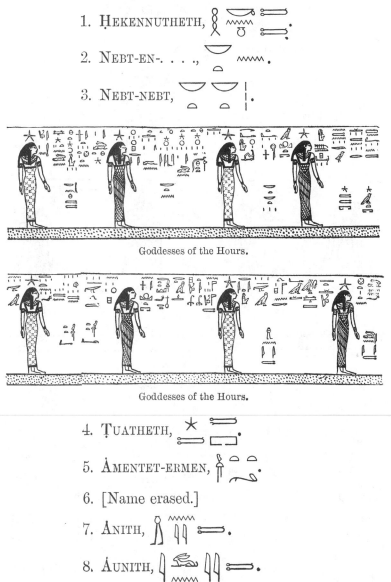

Goddesses of the Hours.

4. ṬUATHETH,
5. ÅMENTET-ERMEN,
6. [Name erased.]
7. ÅNITH,
8. ÅUNITH,

9. TAIT, 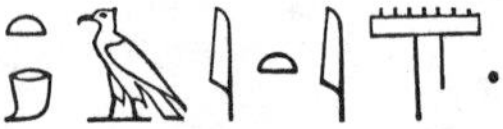.

10. ȦRIT-KHU, .

11. ȦRIT-ȦRU, .

12. UȦAT-TESṬES, 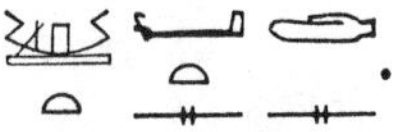.

The text relating to the goddesses of the hours reads:

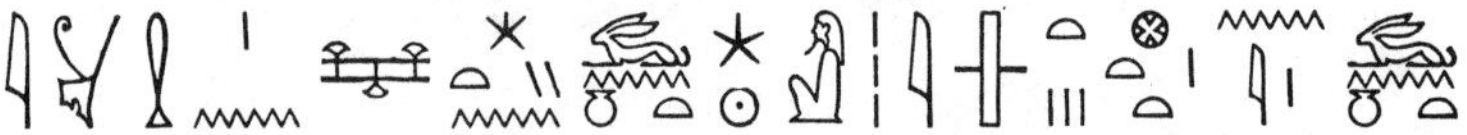

Goddesses of the Hours.

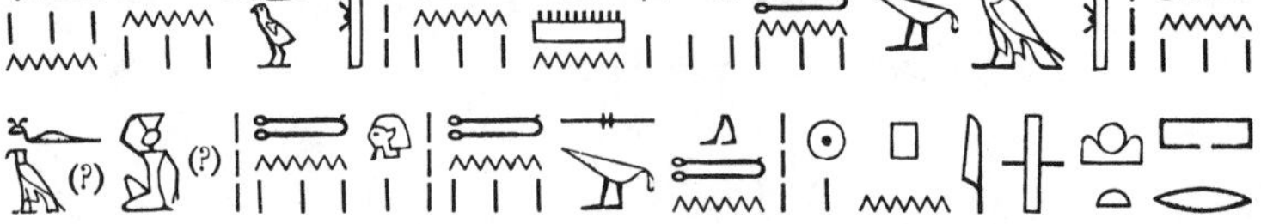

, "The Majesty of Ḥeru-Ṭuati

"saith unto the Hours who are in this City:—O ye "Hours who have the power of coming into being, O "ye Hours who are endowed with stars, O ye Hours "who avenge Rā, fight ye on behalf of Him that is on "the horizon, and take ye your forms (or, attributes), "and carry ye your symbols, and lift ye up your heads "and guide this [god] Rā, who is on the horizon, into "the beautiful Àmentet in peace." The text goes on to say: 

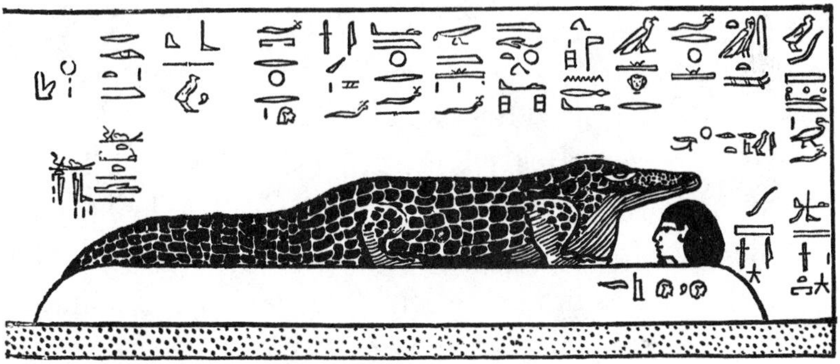

The crocodile Āb-shā-âm-Ṭuat.

, "Behold "the gods and goddesses who guide this great god "along the hidden way of this City."

3. In front of the Hours is an enormous crocodile called ĀB-SHĀ-ÀM-ṬUAT, , which is described as "Osiris, the Eye of Rā,"  . The crocodile stands upon a long funeral

mound, out of the end of which, immediately under the head of the animal, appears a bearded human head, i.e., "the head of Osiris," , or . Of the crocodile the text says: 

,

"He who is in this picture is ĀB-SHĀU, and he is the "warden of the symbols of this city. When he heareth "the voice [of the boat of] Rā which is addressed to the "Eye which is in his cheek (?), the head which is in his "dominion maketh its appearance, and then it eateth "its own form after this great god hath passed it by. "Whosoever knoweth this [picture] ĀB-SHĀU shall not "devour his soul."

CHAPTER VIII.

THE EIGHTH DIVISION OF THE ṬUAT, WHICH IS CALLED ṬEBAT-NETERU-S.

THE scene that illustrates the EIGHTH DIVISION of the Ṭuat, which is passed through by the Sun-god during the EIGHTH HOUR of the night, is introduced by four lines of text which read:—

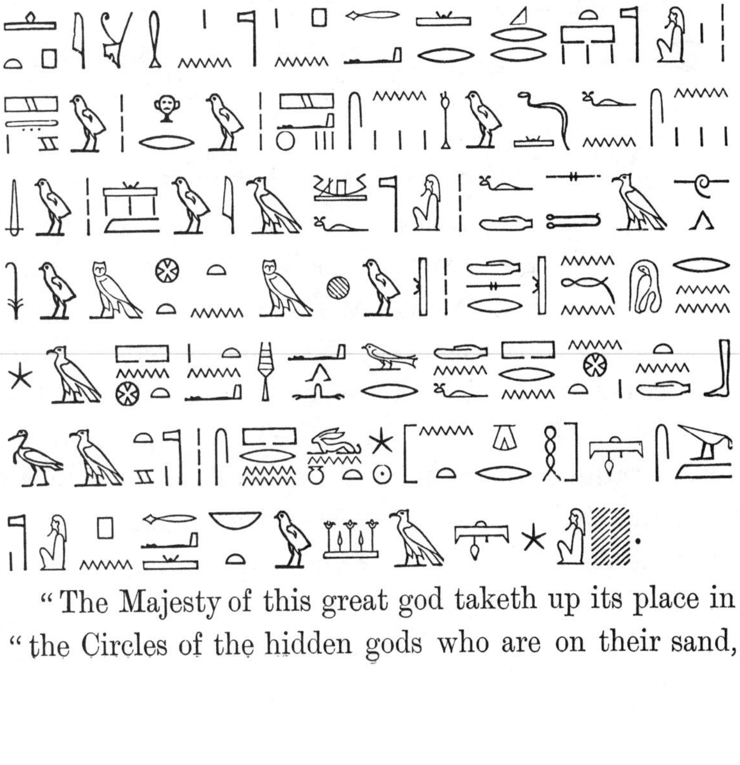

"The Majesty of this great god taketh up its place in "the Circles of the hidden gods who are on their sand,

"and he addresseth to them words in his boat whilst "the gods tow him along through this City by means of "the magical powers of the serpent MEḤEN. The name "of the gate of this City is ĀḤĀ-ȦN-URṬ-NEF. The name "of this City is ṬEBAT-NETERU-S. The name of the "Hour of the night which guideth this great god is "NEBT-USHA."

The Circles of this Division are thus described:—

"The hidden Circles of Ȧment which are passed "through by the great god, his boat being towed along "by the gods who dwell in the Ṭuat; let them be made "according to the figures [which are depicted] on the "north of the hidden palace in the Ṭuat. Whosoever "knoweth them by their names shall be the possessor "of swathings upon earth, and he shall not be repulsed "at the hidden gates, and he shall have offerings in very "great abundance regularly and perpetually."

In the middle register are:—

1. The boat of the sun, in which the god stands

under a canopy formed by the body of the serpent Meḥen, being towed along by nine gods. His passage is thus described: 

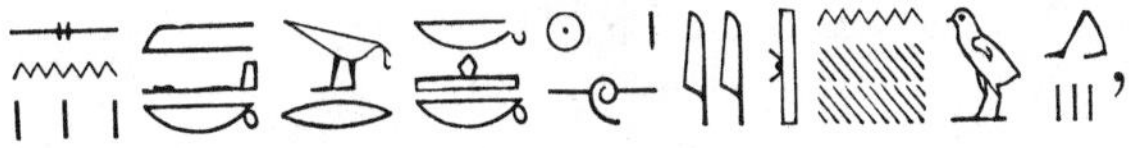, "This god "maketh his way into this City, being towed along "by the gods of the Ṭuat, in his hidden form of "MEḤEN. This god sendeth forth a cry to the regions

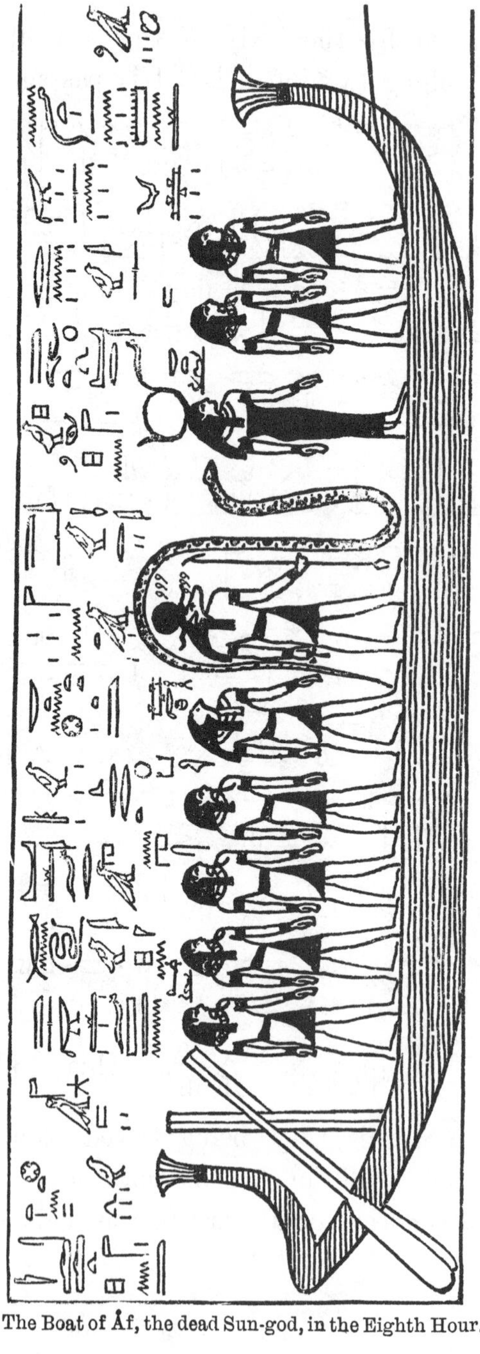
The Boat of Åf, the dead Sun-god, in the Eighth Hour.

"of every Circle "of this City, and "also to the gods "who are there- "in, and it is the "voice of them "which this god "heareth after he "hath sent forth "a cry to them. "The figures of "their bodies "remain always "with their dead "bodies which "are under their "sand, and their "gates open to "the voice of "this god each "day, and then "they hide them- "selves after he "hath passed by "them. Their "work in the "Ṭuat is to tow "Rā along over "the ways of this

"City, and they "rise up after "they have towed "him along into "this Hall, and "they say unto "him:—O thou "god, come thou "to thine hidden "image, O our "god, and to all "the sepulchres "of KHENTI-"ÀMENTI, unite "thyself strong-"ly to it, and "mayest thou "be entreated "to lighten the "darkness of "those who are "on their sands. "We beseech "thee to come "and to unite "thyself, O Rā, "to those who "tow thee along." The eight gods

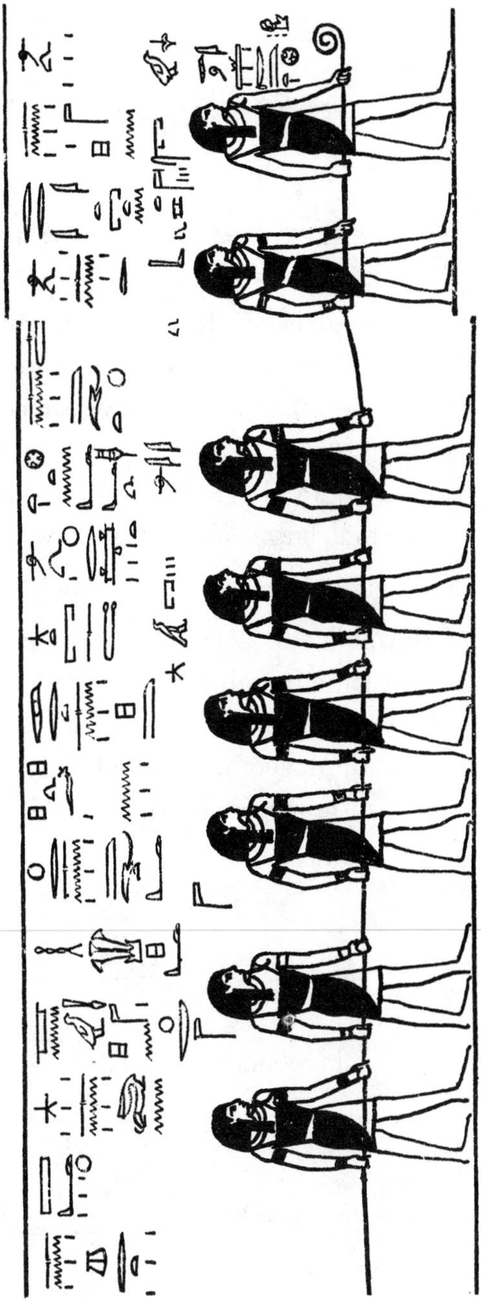

who tow along the boat of Rā are thus described:

, "These "are the gods of the Ṭuat who tow along Rā in the "place where the gods have their sepulchres (ṬEBAT-"NETERU-SET), and he is [acclaimed] by those who are "in this City. The images secret of TATHENEN, of "Horus (?), [and of] the gods are with them."

2. Nine large objects somewhat in the form of the hieroglyphic  *shems,* which has the meaning of "follower" or "servant"; unlike this sign, however, each of the nine objects is provided with a huge knife, and from the curved end of each is suspended a human head. M. Maspero is undoubtedly correct in describing these as the servants of the god. The names of the nine servants are:—

1. ḤETEP-TA, 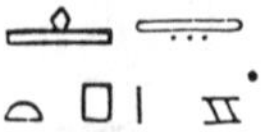.
2. ÀMEN, 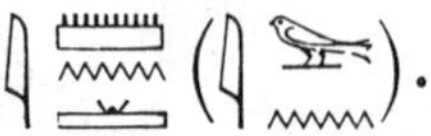.
3. SESHETA-BAIU (?), .
4. SEKHEN-KHAIBIT, 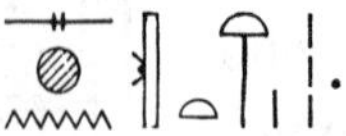.
5. NEB-ER-TCHER, .

6. MENNU, .

7. MĀTHENU, 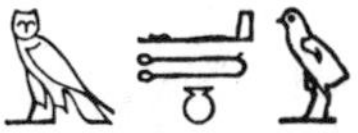.

8. METRUI, .

9. PEREMU (?), .

Of these gods it is said: 

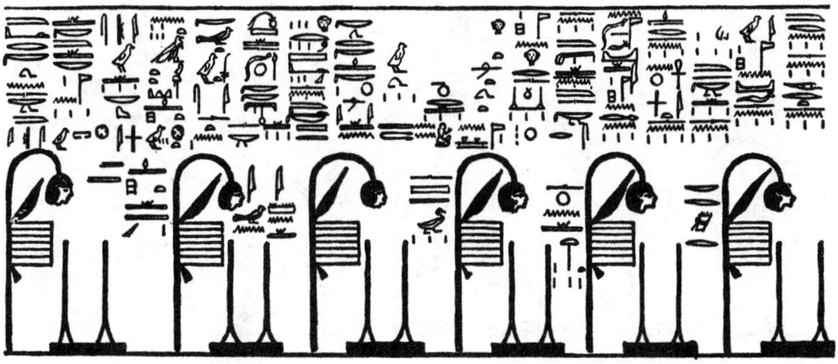

Servants of the god Rā.

, "Those who are in this

"picture are those who are on the path along which this "god is towed, and they have their swathings before "them in the form in which the god himself [had them]. "This our great god crieth out unto those who have "their life in them, in [their] heads in their forms, and "this god crieth out to them by their names. Their work "is [to seize] the enemies of Rā everywhere throughout "this City, and then to make their heads to pass under "their swords after this god hath passed them by."

3. A ram, having the solar disk between his horns,

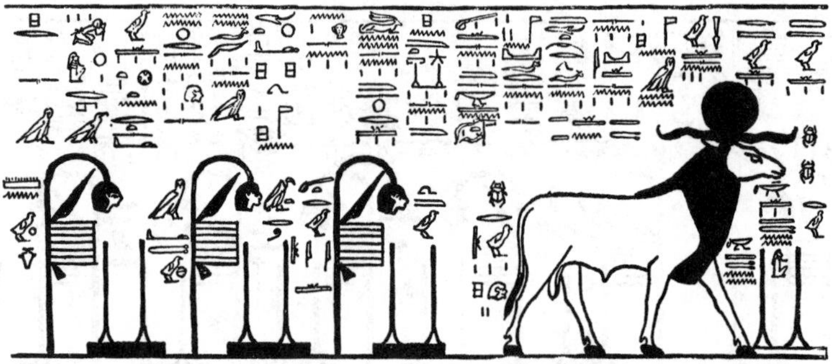

Servants of the god Rā. **First form of Tathenen.**

and the symbol of linen bandages in front of him; he is an image of TATHENEN, 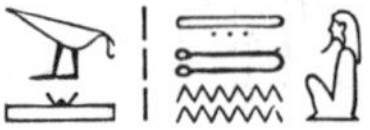, of whom he is the "first form," , or .

4. A ram, having the crown of the South between his horns, and the symbol of linen bandages in front of him; he is an image of TATHENEN, of whom he is the "second form," 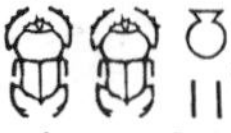, or 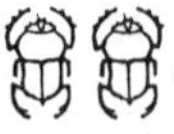.

5. A ram, having the crown of the North between

his horns, and the symbol of linen bandages in front of him; he is an image of TATHENEN, of whom he is the "third form," 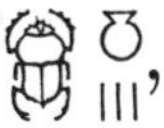, or 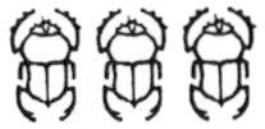.

6. A ram, having the solar disk and a pair of plumes above his horns, and the symbol of linen bandages in front of him; he is an image of TATHENEN, of whom he is the "fourth form," 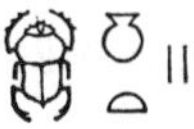, or 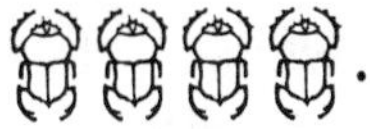.

The text which refers to these reads: 

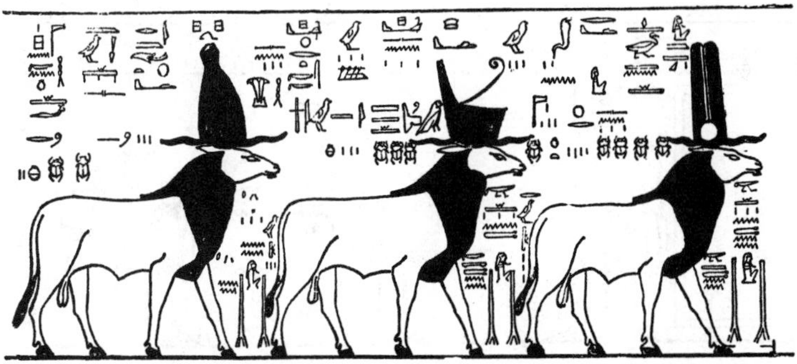

Second form of Tathenen. Third form of Tathenen. Fourth form of Tathenen.

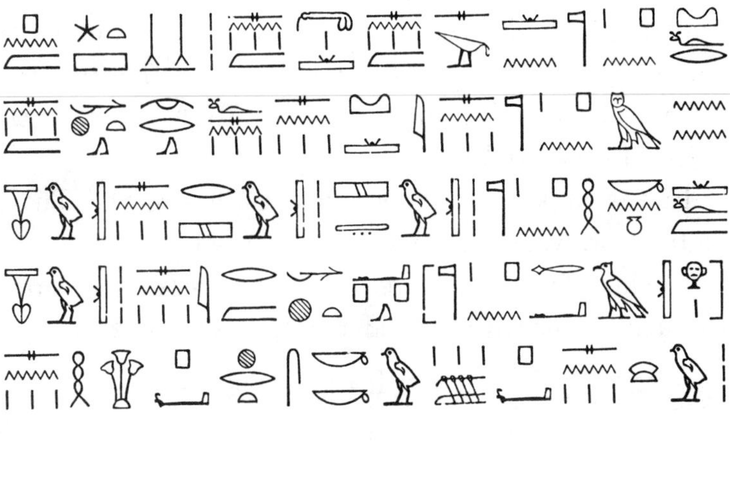

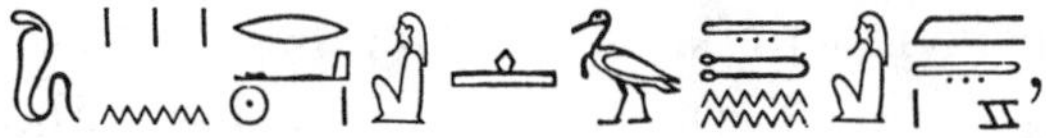, "Those who are "in this picture in the Ṭuat, with their swathings of "linen in front of them, in the form in which the god "himself [had them], are they to whom he crieth out "after he hath come to the place where they are. "And they on their part cry out to this god with their "voices which are joyful but hidden, and this god "singeth a song of joy at their voices. After [this

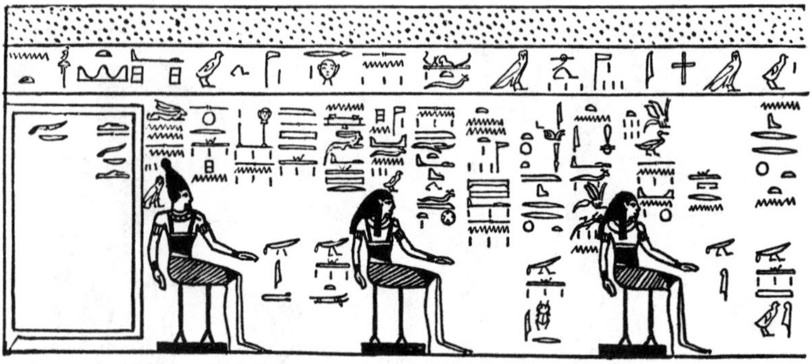

The Circle Sesheta.

"great god] hath passed by them, and when the dark- "ness of night hath covered them over, they receive "the diadems of Rā, and the soul of TATHENEN uniteth "itself to the earth."

In the upper register are five Circles of the Ṭuat, and a door, which may be thus described:—

1. This Circle, which is called SESHETA, is entered through a door with the name of ṬES-NEB-TERER . . . ., , and in it are seated:—

1. The image of TEM, , wearing the White Crown.
2. The image of KHEPERÀ, .
3. The image of SHU, .

Each of these is seated upon an instrument for weaving, . The text reads: 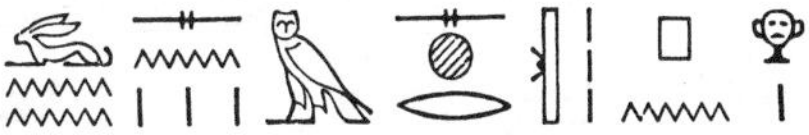

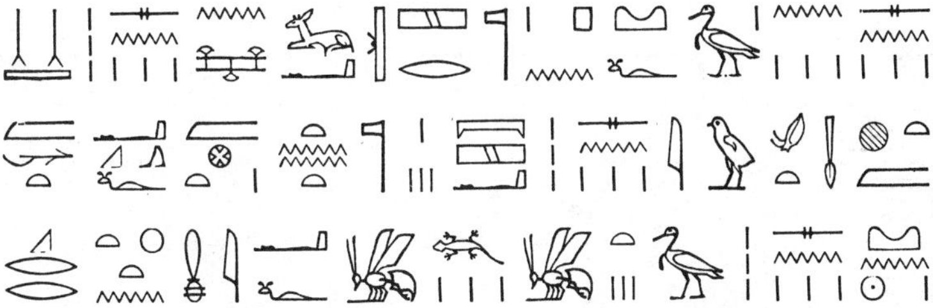

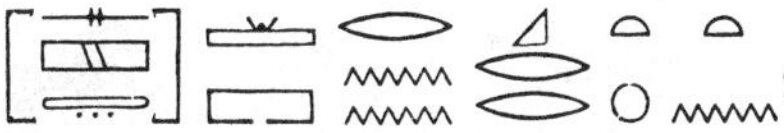, "Those who are in this "picture are [seated] on their instruments for weaving "[after the manner] of Horus, the heir, the youthful "one. This god crieth out to their souls after he hath "entered into this City of the gods who are on their "sand, and there are heard the voices of [those who are] "shut in this Circle which are like [the hum] of many "bees of honey when their souls cry out to Rā. The "name of this Circle is SESHETA."

2. This Circle, which is called ṬUAT, , is entered through a door with the name of ṬES-ĀḤĀ-TATHENEN, 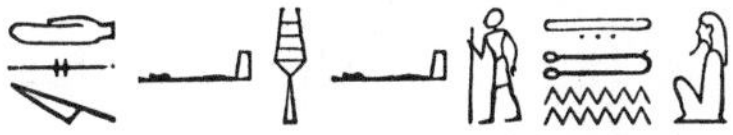, and in it are seated:—

1. The image of TEFNET, .

2. The image of SEB, .

3. The image of NUT, 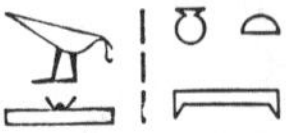.

Each of these is seated upon an instrument for weaving. The text reads: 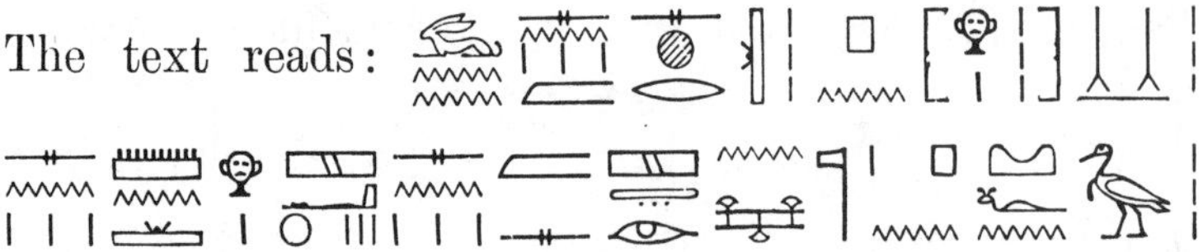

The Circle Ṭuat.

, "Those who are in this picture are "[seated] upon their instruments for weaving, which "are set firmly on their sand, according to the mystery "which Horus made. This god crieth out to their "souls in whatsoever regions they are, and there are

"heard the voices of [those who are] shut in this Circle "which are like the sound of the swathed ones [when] "their souls cry out to Rā. The name of this Circle is "ṬUAT."

3. This Circle, which is called ȦS-NETERU, , is entered through a door with the name of ṬES-ĀKHEM-BAIU, , and in it are seated:—

The Circle Ȧs-neteru.

1. The image of OSIRIS, .

2. The image of ISIS, .

3. The image of HORUS, , hawk-headed.

Each of these is seated as before. The text reads:

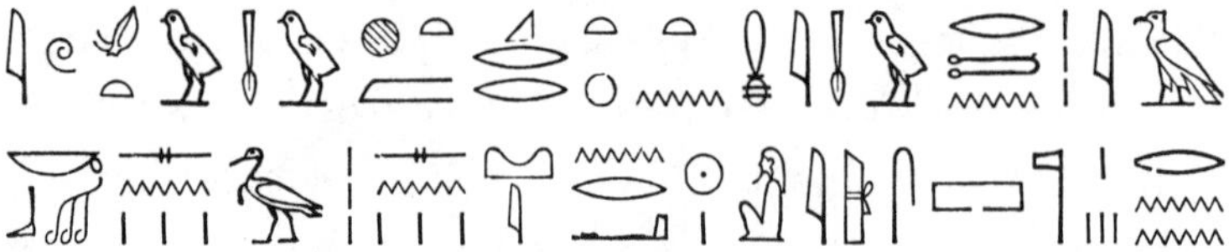

, "Those who are in this picture are [seated] "upon their instruments for weaving, which are set "firmly on their sand, according to the mystery which "Horus made. This god crieth out to their souls in "whatsoever regions they are, and there is heard the

The Circle Åakebi.

"sound of the voices of [those who are] shut in this "Circle, which is like unto the sound of men who "lament when their souls cry out to Rā. The name of "this Circle is ÅS-NETERU."

4. This Circle, which is called ÅAKEBI,  , is entered through a door with the name of ṬES-SHETA-THEḤEN-NETERU, 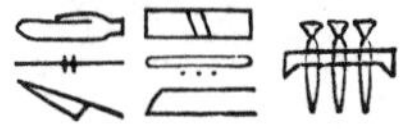 , and in it are seated:—

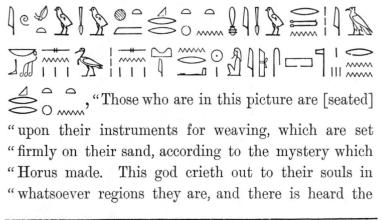

1. The image of KA-ÅMENTET, , bull-headed.

2. The image of BA-NETERU, , ram-headed.

3. The image of REM-NETERU, , ram-headed.

Each of these is seated as before. The text reads:

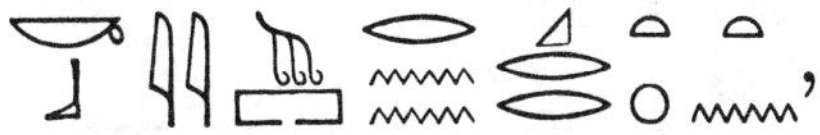, "Those who are in this "picture are [seated] upon their instruments for "weaving, which are set firmly on their sand, according "to the mystery which Horus made. This god crieth "out to their souls in whatsoever regions they are, "and there is heard the sound of the voices of those "who are shut in this Circle, which is like unto the "sounds of bulls and of other male animals when "their souls cry out to Rā. The name of this Circle "is ÅAKEBI."

5. This Circle, which is called NEBT-SEMU-NIFU, 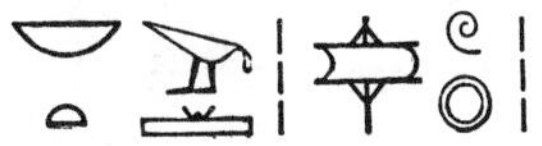, is entered through a door having

the name of ṬENS-SMA-KEKIU, , and in it are seated:—

1. The image of KHATRI, , ichneumon-headed.
2. The image of ȦFFI, , animal-headed.
3. The image of ȦRI-ĀNB-FI, , cynocephalus-headed.

The Circle Nebt-semu-nifu.

Each of these gods is seated as before. The text reads:

, "Those who are in this picture are

"[seated] upon their instruments for weaving, which "are set firmly on their sand, according to the mystery "which Horus made. This god crieth out to their "souls in whatsoever regions they are, and there is "heard the sound of the voices of those who are shut "in this Circle, which is like unto the sound of those "who make supplication through terror when their "souls cry out to Rā. The name of this Circle is "NEBT-SEMU-NIFU."

6. An open door, called ṬES-KHAIBITU-ṬUATIU, , beyond which is a goddess.

The door Ṭes-khaibitu-ṭuatiu.

In the lower register are also five Circles, and an open door, which may be thus described:—

1. This Circle, which is called ḤETEPET-NEB-S, , is entered through a door having the name of ṬET-SEM-ERMEN-TA, ; in it are:—

1. A goddess standing upright, called ÅMEM (?), .

2. The serpent MEḤEN-TA, .

3. Three arrows lying on the top of ; these are the "arrows of Rā."

4. A ram-headed god, seated on ; his name is

NEB-REKHIT, .

The text reads: 

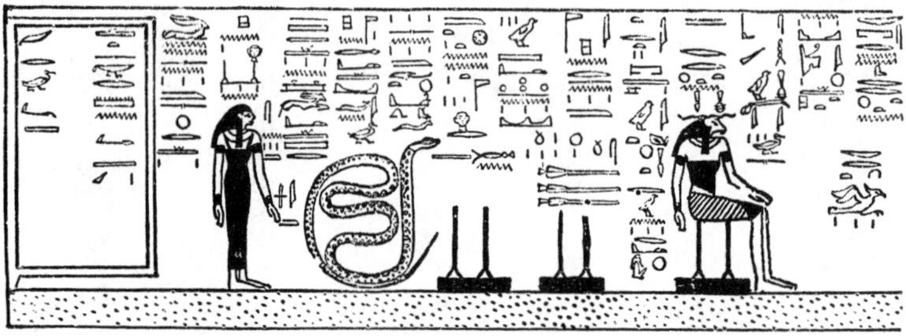

The Circle Ḥetepet-neb-s.

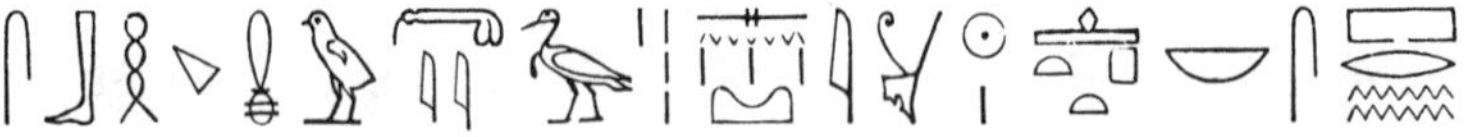

, "Those who are in this picture are [seated] "upon their instruments for weaving, [which are set "firmly on their sand], according to the mystery which "Horus, the heir, the young [god] made. This great "god crieth out to their souls after he hath entered "into this City of the gods who are upon their sand, "and when this god crieth out to them in the two "ȦTERTI there is heard the sound of those who are

"shut in this Circle, which is like unto the voices of "male cats when they cry out and their souls cry out "to Rā. The name of this Circle is ḤETEPET-NEB-S."

2. This Circle, which is called ḤETEMET-KHEMIU, , is entered through a door having the name ṬES-RĀ-KHEFTIU-F, ; in it are:—

1. NUT, , bearded and man-headed.

The Circle Ḥetemet-khemiu.

2. TA, , bearded and man-headed.

3. SEBEQ-ḤRÅ, , crocodile-headed.

The text reads:

"Those who are in this picture are [seated] upon their "instruments for weaving, which are set firmly on their "sand, according to the mystery which Horus made. "This god crieth out to their souls, in whatsoever "regions they are in the two Ȧterti, and there is heard "the sound of the voices of those who are shut in this "Circle which is like unto the sound of the confused "murmur of the living when their souls cry out to Rā. "The name of this Circle is ḤETEMET-KHEMIU."

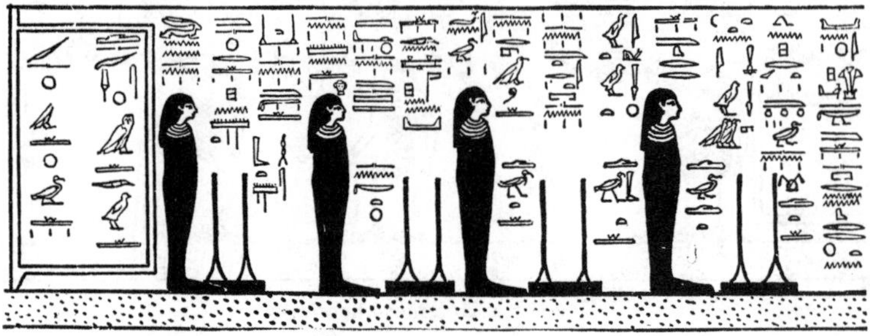

The Circle Ḥap-semu-s.

3. This Circle, which is called ḤAP-SEMU-S, , is entered through a door having the name of ṬES-SEKHEM-ȦRU, ; in it are four mummied gods, each with an instrument for weaving in front of him, and their names are:—

1. ḤEBSET, .

2. SENKET, .

3. ṬEBAT, .

4. ṬEMṬET, .

The text reads: 

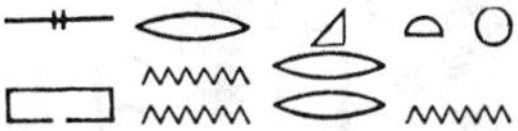, "Those who are in this picture "have their instruments for weaving before them, and "they are set firmly on their sand, according to the "mystery which Horus made. This god crieth out to "their souls, in whatsoever regions they are in the two "ÅTERTI, and there is heard the sound of the voices of "those who are shut in this Circle, which is like unto "the sound of the voices of those who go down to the "battle-field of Nu when their souls cry out to Rā. "The name of this Circle is ḤAP-SEMU-S."

4. This Circle, which is called SEḤERT-BAIU-S, 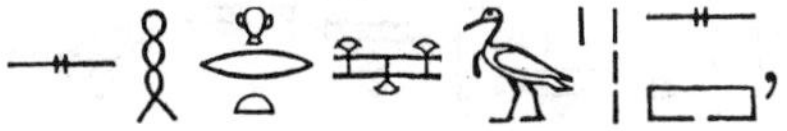, is entered through a door having the name of ṬES-SEPṬ-NESUT,  ; in it are four mummied gods,

each with an instrument for weaving in front of him, and their names are:—

1. KEKU, .
2. MENḤI, 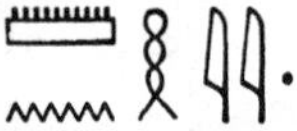.
3. TCHER-KHU, .
4. KHEBS-TA, .

The Circle Seḥert-baiu̦-s.

The text reads: ,
"Those who are in this picture have their instruments

"of weaving before them, and they are set firmly on "their sand, according to the mystery which Horus "made. This god crieth out to their souls in whatsoever regions they are in the two ÅTERTI, and there "is heard the sound of voices of those who are shut in "this Circle, which is like unto the sound of the cry of "the Divine Hawk of Horus when their souls cry out "to Rā. The name of this Circle is SEḤERT-BAIU-S."

5. This Circle, which is called ĀAT-SETEKAU,

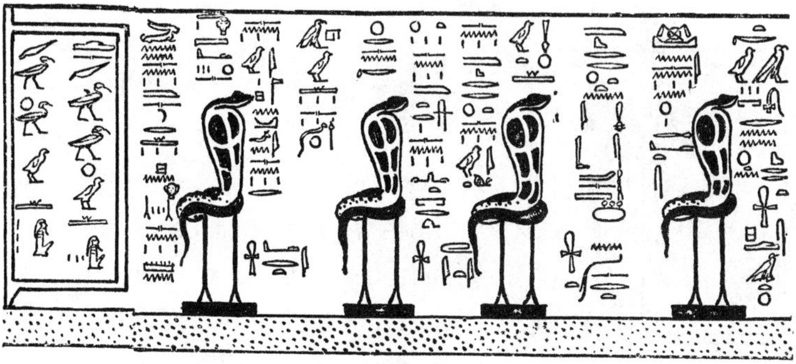

The Circle Āat-setekau.

, is entered through a door having the name of ṬES-KHU, ; in it are four uraei, each of which rests upon its instrument for weaving, and their names are:—

1. ÅĀRET-ĀNKH, .

2. RERIT-ĀNKH, .

3. NESERT-ĀNKHET, .

4. SEPṬAT-ĀNKH, .

The text reads: 

,

The door Ṭes-amem-mit-em-sheta-f.

"Those who are in this picture are "[seated] on their instruments of "weaving, and they are set firmly "on their sand. This god crieth "out to them in whatsoever "regions they are, and they shed "light by means of their radiance [which cometh] "from the depth of their mouths, but they do not "come forth from their Circle; and there is heard "the sound of the voices of those who are shut in "this Circle which is like unto the twittering of the "whole of the birds of a nest of water-fowl when "they cry out to Rā. The name of this Circle is "ĀAT-SETEKAU."

6. A door called ṬES-AMEM-MIT-EM-SHETA-F, 
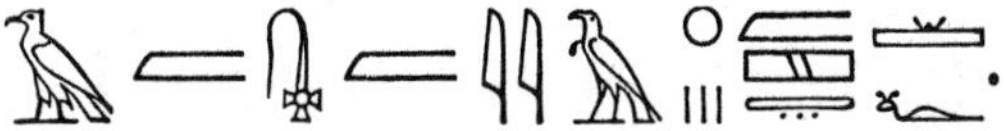. Beyond it is a figure of the god NU, 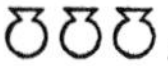, who appears to be over the "chamber of destruction," 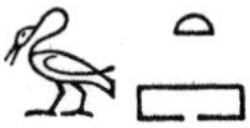.

CHAPTER IX.

THE NINTH DIVISION OF THE ṬUAT, WHICH IS CALLED BEST-ÅRU-ĀNKHET-KHEPERU.

HAVING passed through the EIGHTH DIVISION of the Ṭuat, the boat of the sun arrives at the NINTH DIVISION, which is passed through by the sun during the NINTH HOUR of the night. The opening text reads:—

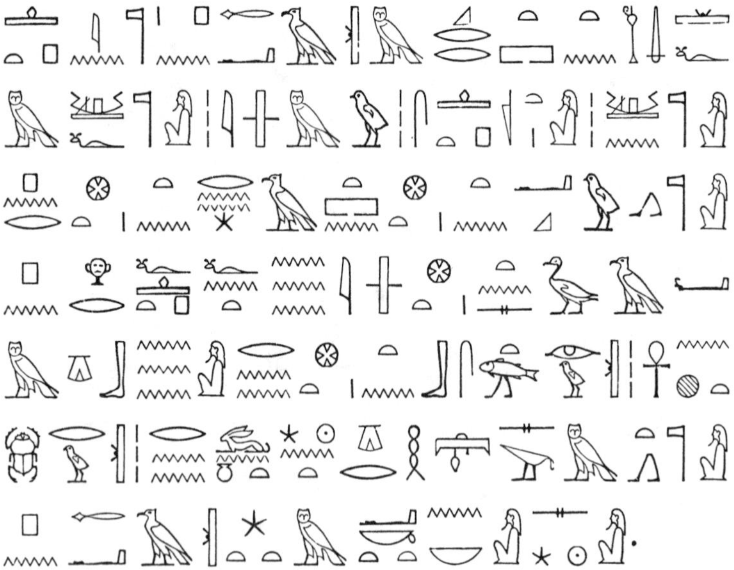

"This great god taketh up his place in this Circle,

"and he addresseth words from his boat to those who "are in it. The divine sailors join the boat of this "great god in this City. The name of the gate of this "City through which this god entereth and taketh up "his place on the stream which is in this City is SAA-"EM-ḲEB; the name of this City is BEST-ȦRU-ĀNKHET-"KHEPERU; the name of the Hour of the night which "guideth this great god is ṬUATET-MĀKETET-EN-NEB-S."

The line of text which runs above the upper register reads:—

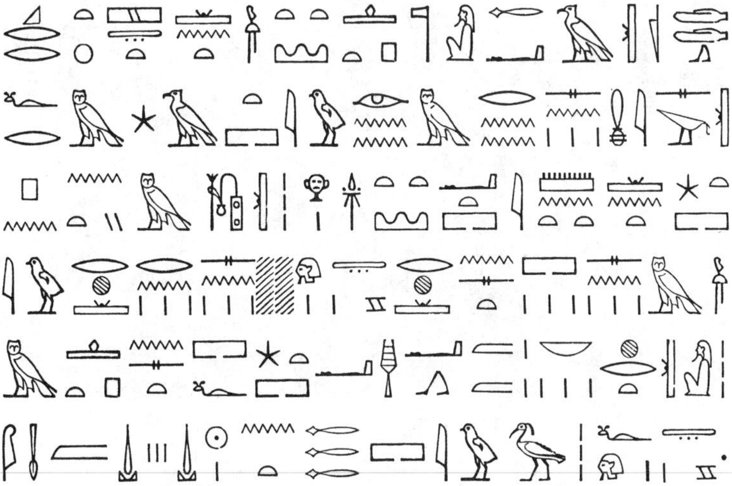

"The hidden Circle of Ȧmentet, through which this "great god travelleth and taketh up his place in the "Ṭuat. If these things be made with their names "after the manner of this figure which is depicted at "the east of the hidden house of the Ṭuat, and if a "man knoweth their names whilst he is upon earth, "and knoweth their places in Ȧmenti, [he shall attain "to] his own place in the Ṭuat, and he shall stand up "in all places which belong to the gods whose voices "(or, words) are *maāt*, even as the divine sovereign "chiefs (*tchatcha*) of Rā, and the mighty ones of the "palace (Pharaohs ?), and [this knowledge] shall be of "benefit to him upon earth."

In the middle register are:—

1. The boat of the sun, with the god ȦFU standing under a canopy formed by the serpent MEḤEN.

The Boat of Ȧfu, the dead Sun-god, in the Ninth Hour.

2. The Twelve Sailors of Rā, each of whom stands upright, and holds a paddle in his hands; their names are:—

1. KHENNU, , i.e., "the sailor" *par excellence*.
2. ȦKHEM-SEK-F, .
3. ȦKHEM-URṬ-F, .

Khennu. Åkhem-sek-f. Åkhem-urṭ-f. Åkhem-ḥemi-f.

Åkhem-ḥep-f. Åhhem-khemes-f. Khen-unnut-f. Ḥepti-ta-f.

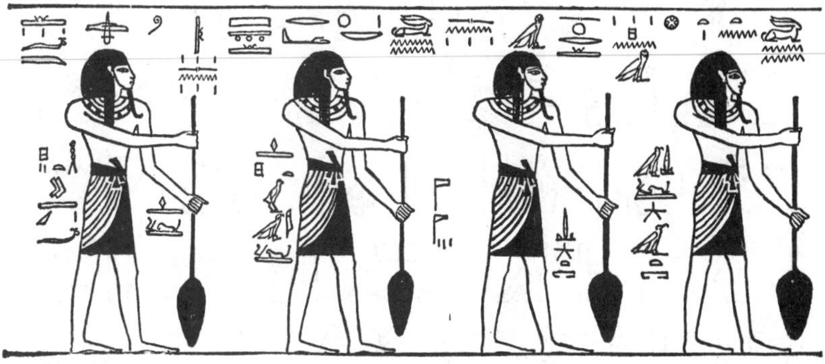

Ḥetep-uāa. Neter-neteru. Tcha-Ṭuat. Ṭepi.

4. ȦKHEM-ḤEMI-F, .

5. ȦKHEM-ḤEP-F, .

6. ȦKHEM-KHEMES-F, .

7. KHEN-UNNUT-F, .

8. ḤEPTI-TA-F, .

9. ḤETEP-UȦA, .

10. NETER-NETERU, .

11. TCHA-ṬUAT, 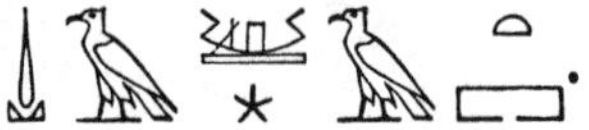.

12. ṬEPI, .

The text which refers to these reads: 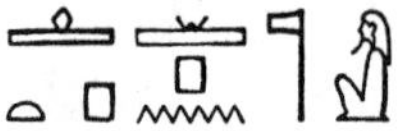

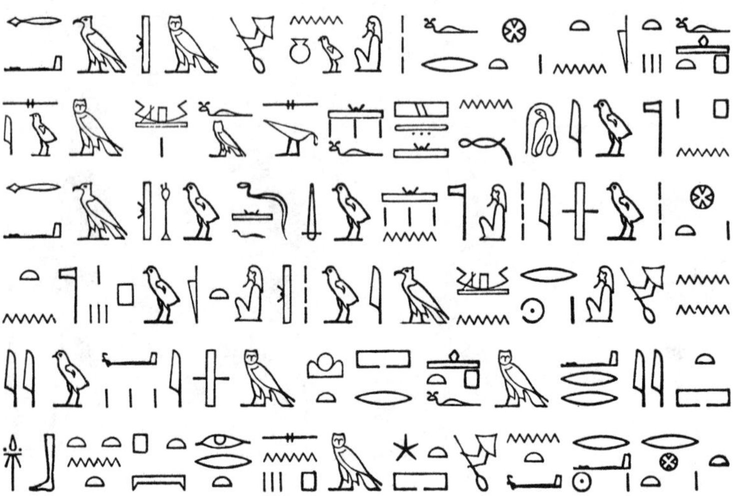

"This "great god joineth those who will transport him "through this City, and his sailors join his boat "wherein he is in his hidden form of MEḤEN. This "great god addresseth words to the gods who dwell "in this City, that is to say, to the gods who are the "sailors of the boat of Rā and to those who will "transport [him] through the horizon so that he may "take up his position in the eastern Hall of heaven. "Their work in the Ṭuat is to transport Rā through "this City every day, and they take their stand by the "stream in this City whereon [saileth] the boat, and "it is they who give water with their paddles to the "spirits who are in this City, and they sing hymns to "the Lord of the Disk, and they make to arise [his] "Soul in his forms by means of their hidden words "every day."

3. A bearded, man-headed hawk, wearing plumes and horns on his head, seated on a basket or bowl; his name is MUTI-KHENTI-ṬUAT, 

4. The ram-god NESTI-KHENTI-ṬUAT, couchant on a basket or bowl.

5. The cow-goddess NEBT-ĀU-KHENTI-ṬUAT, 
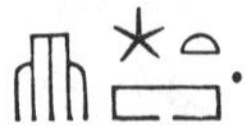.

6. A bearded god, in mummied form, called ḤETEPET-NETER, , or ḤETEPET-NETERU, 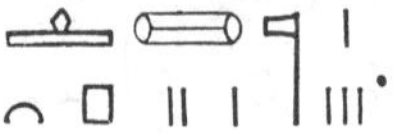.

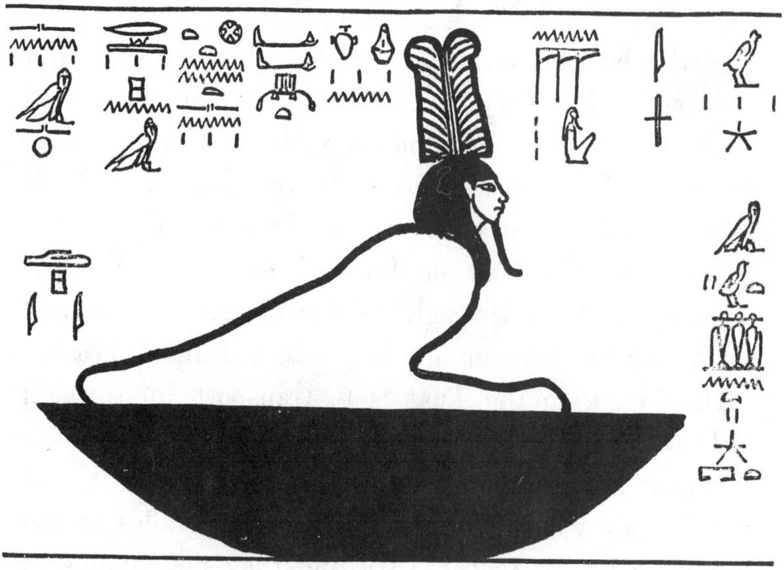

Muti-khenti-Ṭuat.

The text which refers to these reads: 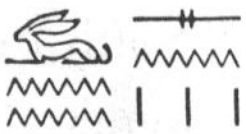

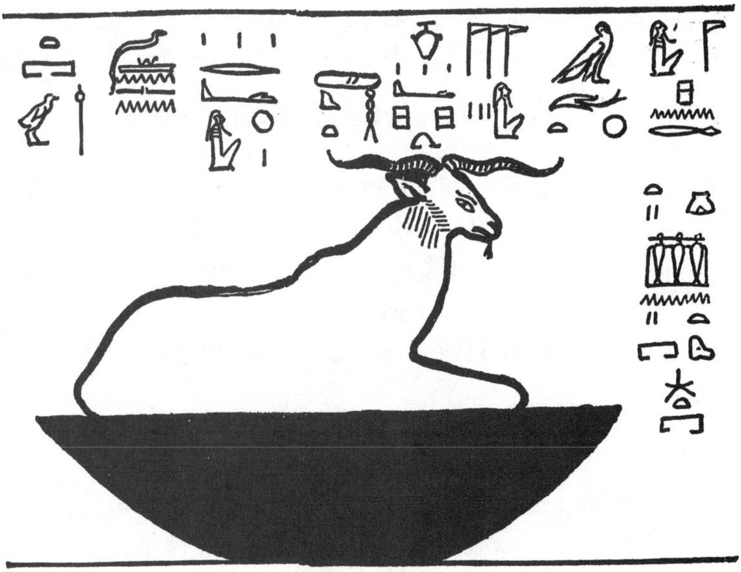

Nesti-khenti-Ṭuat.

Nebt-āu-khenti-Ṭuat. Ḥetepet-neter.

, "Those who are in this picture in this "City are they who give offerings of food to the gods "who are in the Ṭuat; Rā decreeth for them loaves of "bread and vessels of beer, and the gods journey on in "the following of this great god to the Eastern horizon "of the sky, with ḤETEP-NETERU-ṬUAT [also] following "him."

In the upper register are:—

1. Twelve gods, each of whom is seated upon the symbol of linen swathings; their names are:—

1. NEHA-TA, .

2. ṬEBA, .

3. MAATI (or, ȦRITI), .

4. MENKHET, 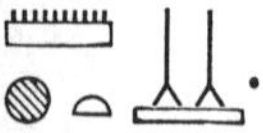.

5. ḤEBS, .

6. NEBTI, .

7. ȦSTI-NETER, 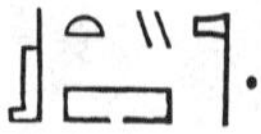.

8. ȦSTI-PAUT, 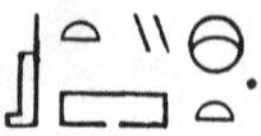.

9. ḤETEMET-KHU, .

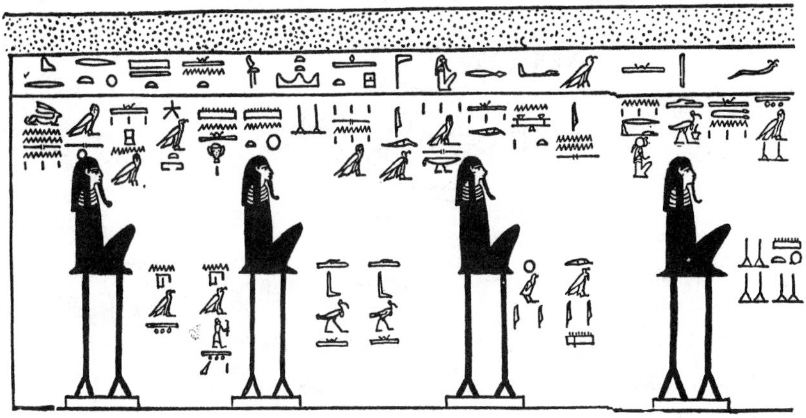

Neha-ta. Ṭeba. Maati. Menkhet.

Ḥebs. Nebti. Ȧsti-neter. Ȧsti-paut.

Ḥetemet-khu. Neb-Pāt. Ṭemṭu. Men-ā.

10. NEB-PĀT, 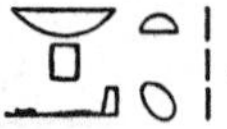.

11. ṬEMṬU, .

12. MEN-Ā, 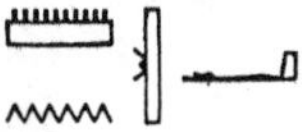.

The text which refers to these reads: 

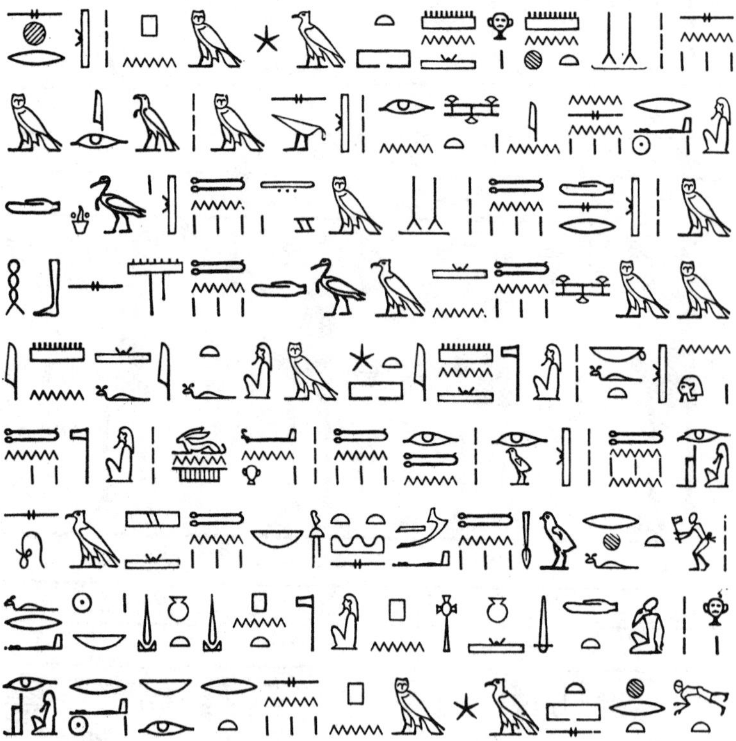

, "Those who are in this picture in "the Ṭuat are seated firmly on their instruments for "weaving, and they are in the form of the figures "which Horus made. Rā saith to them:—O ye who

"are swathed in your holy swathings, who are arrayed "in your garments, whom Horus covered up when he "hid his father in the Ṭuat, which concealeth the gods, "uncover ye your heads, O ye gods, unveil ye your "faces, and perform ye the things which must be done "for Osiris! Ascribe ye praise to the lord of ÅMENTET, "and make ye your word *maāt* against his enemies "every day. These beings are the *tchatcha* (i.e., divine "sovereign chiefs) of this god, and they avenge by their "words Osiris each day; and the work which they do "in the Ṭuat is to overthrow the enemies of Osiris."

2. Twelve goddesses, whose names are:—

1. PERIT, .
2. SHEMAT-KHU, .
3. NEBT-SHĀT, 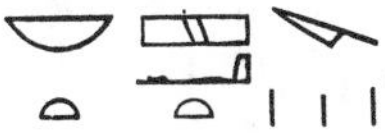.
4. NEBT-SHEFSHEFT, 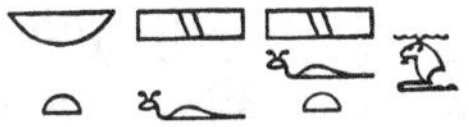.
5. AAT-ÅAṬET, .
6. NEBT-SEṬAU, .
7. ḤENT-NUT-S, .
8. NEBT-MÅT, .
9. ṬESERT-ÅNT, .

10. ĀAT-KHU, .

11. SEKHET-METU, .

12. NETERT-EN-KHENTET-RĀ, 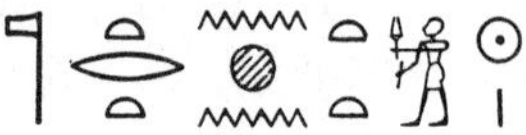.

The text which refers to these reads: 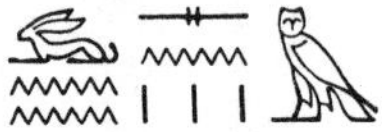

,

"Those who are in this picture with their bodies of the "Ṭuat are they who are in the forms which Horus "made. This great god crieth out to them after he "hath arrived at the place where they are, and they "come to life and they hear [his] voice. Their work "in the Ṭuat is to raise the praises of Osiris, and to "embrace the hidden Soul by means of their words, "and to bring life and strength to the risings of the "god of the Ṭuat [in whatsoever regions they are], and "they utter words on [his behalf] in the chamber each "day."

Perit. Shemat-khu. Nebt-shāt. Nebt-shefsheft.

Āat-âaṭet. Nebt-seṭau. Ḥent-nut-s. Nebt-mȧt.

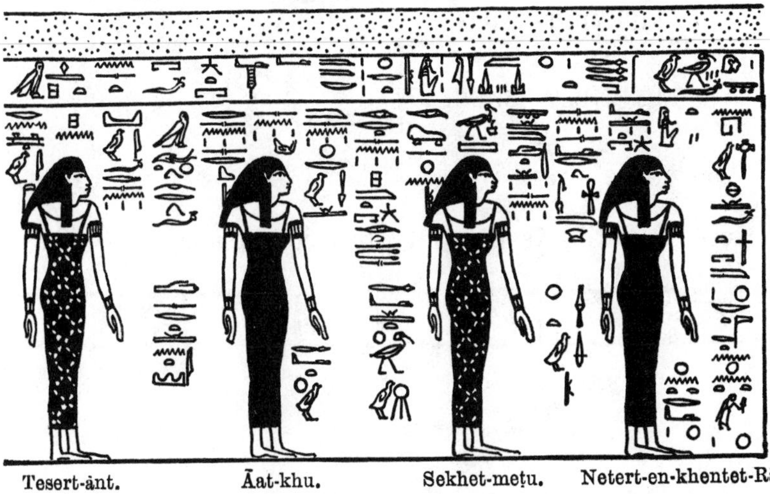

Tesert-ȧnt. Āat-khu. Sekhet-meṭu. Netert-en-khentet-Rā.

In the lower register are:—

1. Twelve uraei, which are mounted each on its instrument for weaving, and each pours forth fire from its mouth; their names are:—

1. . . . .
2. TEKAIT, .
3. . . . .
4. KHUT-ṬUAT, .
5. ṬERTNESHEN, 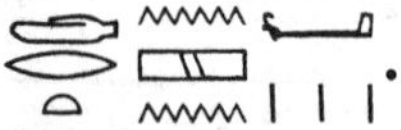.
6. ȦP-SHET, .
7. ĀNKHET, .
8. SHEN-TEN-ȦMM, .
9. . . . .
10. AAT-ȦRU, 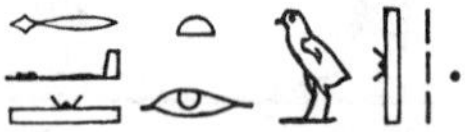.
11. NEBT-UAUAU, .
12. NEBT-REKEḤ, 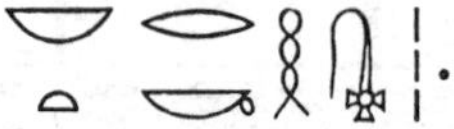.

Above the uraei is a mutilated line of text, which, according to Maspero's restoration, reads: 

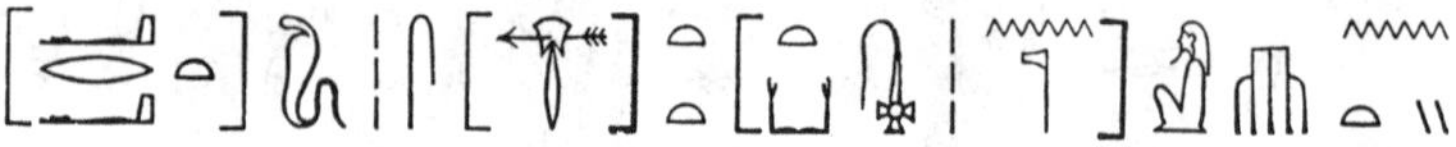

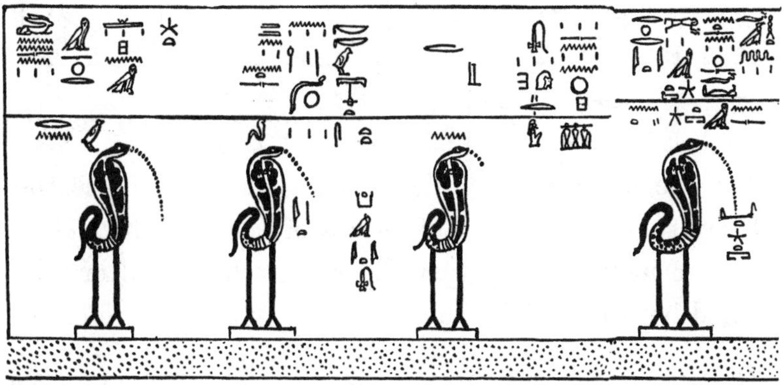

. . . . . Tekait. . . . . . Khut-Ṭuat.

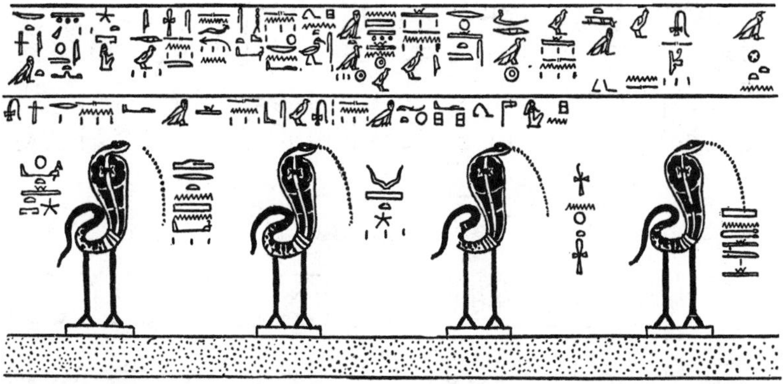

Ṭertneshen. Åp-shet. Ānkhet. Shen-ten-åmm.

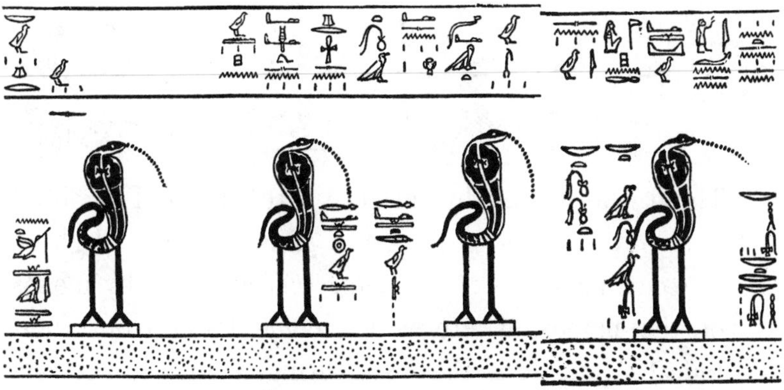

. . . . . Āat-åru. Nebt-uauau. Nebt-Rekeḥ.

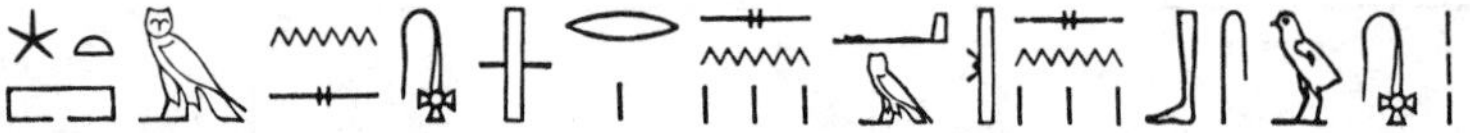
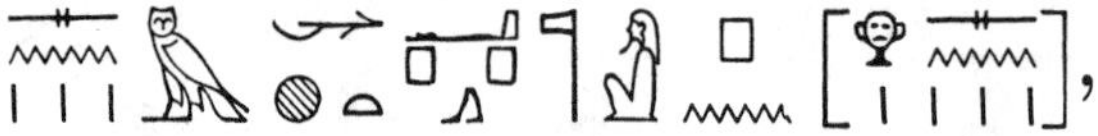, "The names "of the uraei who kindle fires for the god who is the "governor of the Ṭuat by means of the fire which is in "their mouths. They swallow their flames after this "god hath passed by them." The text which refers to them reads: 

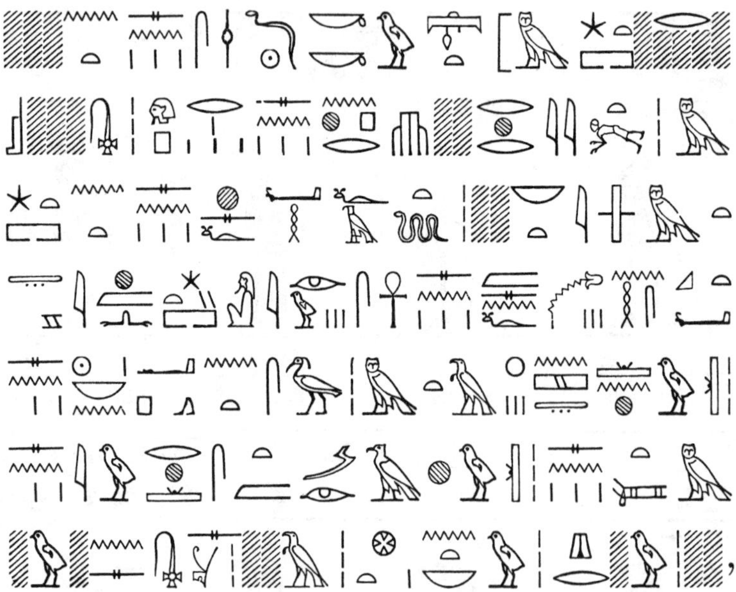,

"Those who are in this picture [are] in the Ṭuat [and "they have bodies of fire], and it is they who lighten "the darkness in the Ṭuat for [Osiris] . . . by means "of the flames of fire which come forth from their "mouths, [and it is they who bring about the destruc-

"tion of] those who are overthrown in the Ṭuat. It is "they who drive back the serpents of every kind which "are on the ground, and which are unknown in their "forms to the god of the Ṭuat. They make themselves "to live by means of the blood of those whom they hack "to pieces each day [when] those advance who endow "with magical power the dead by the mystery of their "formulæ. Those who know this shall see their magical "formulæ, and shall not pass through their flames."

2. Nine bearded gods, who stand upright; each holds the symbol of "life" in his right hand, and a staff, the upper portion of which is in the form of a wriggling snake, in the left hand. These gods are under the direction of a god in mummied form, whose name, or description, is Ḥeru-ḥer-she-Ṭuati,  , i.e., "Horus who is over the lakes in the Ṭuat." The names of the nine gods are:—

1. Sekhti,  (or 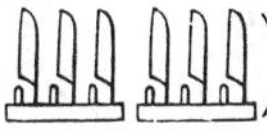).
2. Am-sekhet-f, .
3. Neḥebeti, .
4. Tchāmuti, .
5. Neb-åatti, .
6. Ḥeq-neteru-f, .

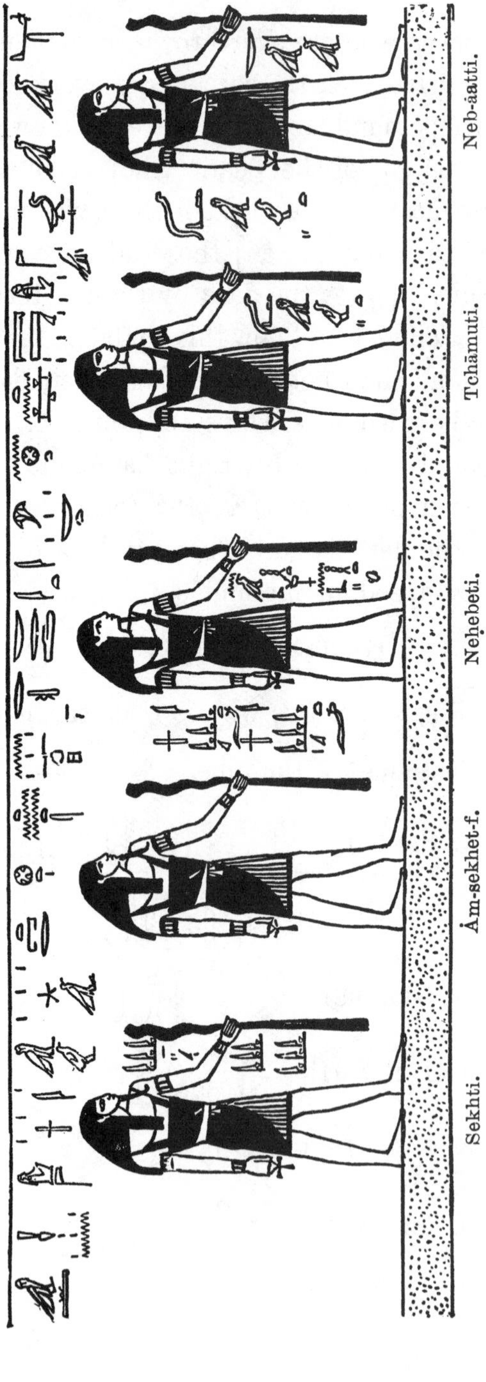
Sekhti.
Ȧm-sekhet-f.
Neḥebeti.
Tchāmuti.
Neb-āatti.

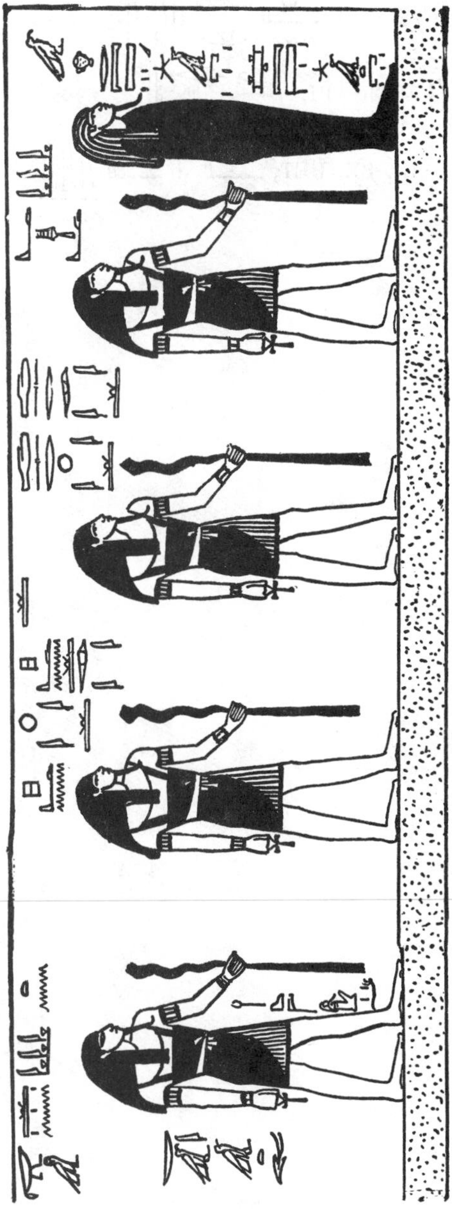

Ḥeq-neteru-f. Pān-ȧri. Ṭeser-ȧri. Āḥā-sekhet. Ḥeru-ḥer-she-ṭuati.

7. PĀN-ȦRI, 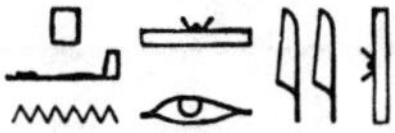.

8. ṬESER-ȦRI, .

9. ĀḤĀ-SEKHET, .

CHAPTER X.

THE TENTH DIVISION OF THE ṬUAT, WHICH IS CALLED MEṬET-QA-UTCHEBU.

HAVING passed through the NINTH DIVISION of the Ṭuat, the boat of the sun arrives at the TENTH DIVISION, which is passed through by the sun during the TENTH HOUR of the night. The opening text reads:—

"This great god taketh up his place in this Circle, "and he uttereth words to the gods who dwell therein.

"The name of the door of this City through which this "great god entereth is ĀA-KHERPU-MES-ȦRU. The name "of this City is MEṬET-QA-UTCHEBU. The name of the "hour of the night which guideth this great god to "the hidden paths of this City is ṬENṬENIT-UḤESET-"KHAK-ȦBU."

In the middle register are:—

1. The boat of the sun, in which the god stands under a canopy formed by the serpent Meḥen; he

The Boat of Ȧf, the dead Sun-god, in the Tenth Hour.

holds the symbol of life in his right hand, and a serpent, which serves as a sceptre, in his left.

2. A large two-headed serpent called THES-ḤRȦU, 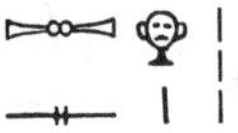, which is depicted in the form of a pair of horns deeply curved towards the ends where they meet. The head which faces to the right has on it a White Crown, and is directly opposite to the face of a goddess, who also wears a White Crown, and is called

ḤERT-ERMENT, [hieroglyphs]; and the head which faces the left has on it a Red Crown, and is directly opposite to the face of a goddess, who also wears a Red Crown and is called SHEMERTI, [hieroglyphs], i.e., "She of the two bows. The serpent is provided with two pairs of legs; one pair is turned to the right and the other to the left

Shemerti. The serpent Thes-ḥrâu. Ḥert-erment.

Within the curve is a large hawk, which bears the name of ḤERU-KHENTI, [hieroglyphs].[1]

3. A boat, wherein lies at full length the serpent ANKH-TA, [hieroglyphs].

[1] Or, KHENT-ḤERU, which became one of the Dekans among the Greeks, i.e., χοντάρ; see Maspero, *op. cit.*, p. 127.

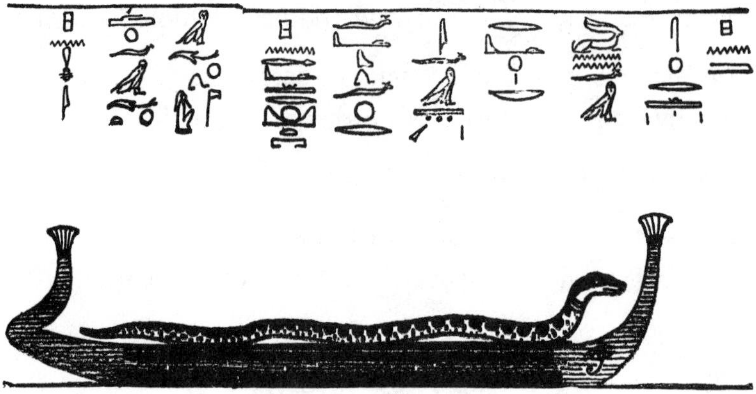

The serpent Ānkh-ta.

4. Four male figures, each of which has a disk, ⊙, in place of a head; each grasps in his right hand an arrow, with a spear-shaped head, which rests on his shoulder, and is pointed downwards; their names are:—

1. ṬEPTHRÀ, . 3. ṬEMAU, .

2. SHESERÀ, 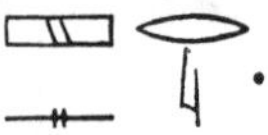. 4. UṬU, .

5. Four bearded, human-headed figures, each of which has in his right hand a short spear, which rests

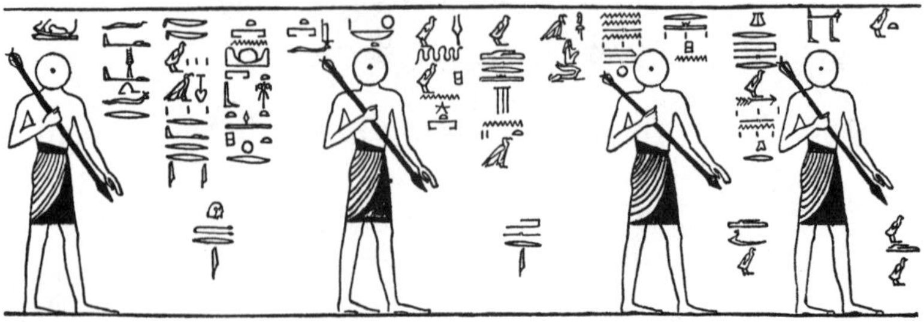

Ṭepthrà. Sheserà. Ṭemau. Uṭu.

on his shoulder, and is pointed upwards; their names are:—

1. SETU,
2. ERṬĀU,
3. KHESEFU,
4. SEKENNU,

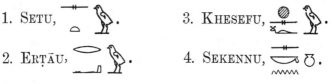

6. Four bearded, human-headed figures, each grasping with both hands a bow, which he holds above his knees; their names are:—

1. PEṬTHI,
2. SHEMERTHI,
3. THESU,
4. KHĀ-Ā,

The texts which refer to the above read:—1. 

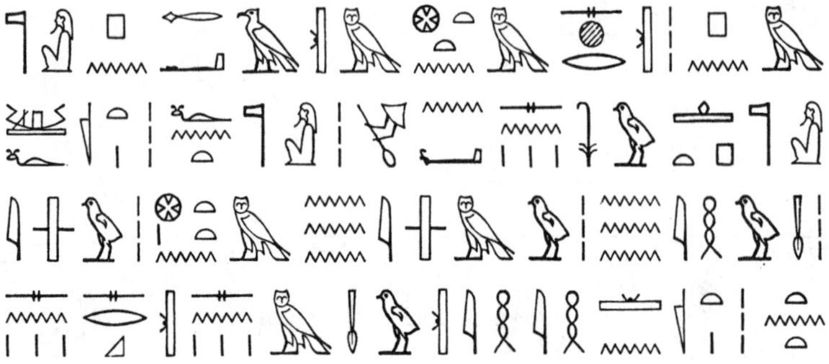

, "This great god maketh his journey through "this City, in this picture, in his boat, and his sailors, "who are the gods, convey him along; this [great] god "taketh up his place in this City in the water, where- "upon those who live in the water make use of their "weapons, and they spring into life at the sound of the "working of the sailors, who are gods, [in the boat of Rā]."

2. 

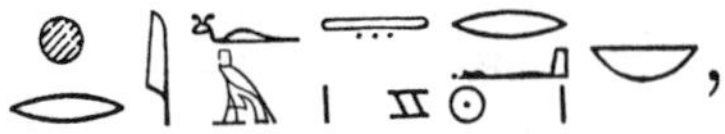, "Those who are in this "picture are they who are on the two sides of THES-ḤRÀU, "who is the son of SEKRI, the governor of the ṬUAT. "This figure (i.e., the serpent) even in the form in which "it is, travelleth after this great god into its horizon,

"and it entereth in with him in the earth every day."

3. 

, "He who is in this picture in his boat "standeth up in the thick darkness in the Hall of the "Eastern Horizon, and he taketh up his position in "his place every day; he formeth the serpent watcher "of the Ṭuat in the holy place of KHENTI-ÅMENTI."

4. 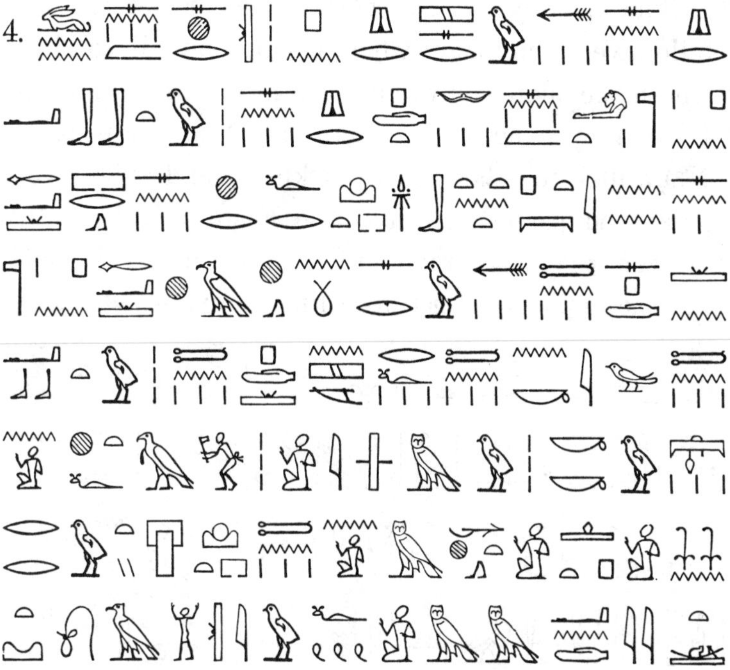

"To those who are in this picture with their arrows, "and to those with javelins, and to those with their "bows, who are in the presence of this great god, and "who make their appearance with him in the Eastern "Horizon of the sky, this great god saith:—Speed ye "your arrows, make ready your javelins, bend your "bows, and destroy ye for me my enemies who are in "darkness; be ye at the portal of your horizon, and "follow ye in my train when I unite myself to those "who make adoration to my flesh in the MĀNṬIT BOAT. "It is they who drive back the SEBI serpent of "NEḤA-ḤRÀ in the thick darkness, and when this "great god passeth on into the Eastern Hall of the "horizon, they also travel on in the train of this god." Over the upper register runs a line of text, which reads:

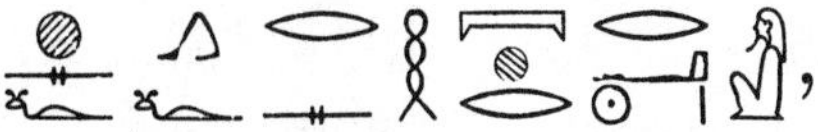, "[This is] the hidden "Circle of Ȧmentet, where KHEPER uniteth himself to "the form of RĀ, and where the gods, and the spirits, "and the dead hasten (?) in the hidden forms of ȦKERT. "If a copy of these things be made according to the "figures which are depicted on the east of the hidden "chamber of the Ṭuat, and if [a man] knoweth it, "together with the names [of the gods], he shall "journey round about and shall pass through the Ṭuat, "and he shall not be turned back from making himself "a companion of Rā."

In the upper register are:—

1. The god PĀNKHI, , who holds in his right hand, and in his left.

2. A beetle, called KHEPER-ĀNKH, , apparently pushing along a zone of sand, , or perhaps entering the horizon. The text which refers to these scenes reads:

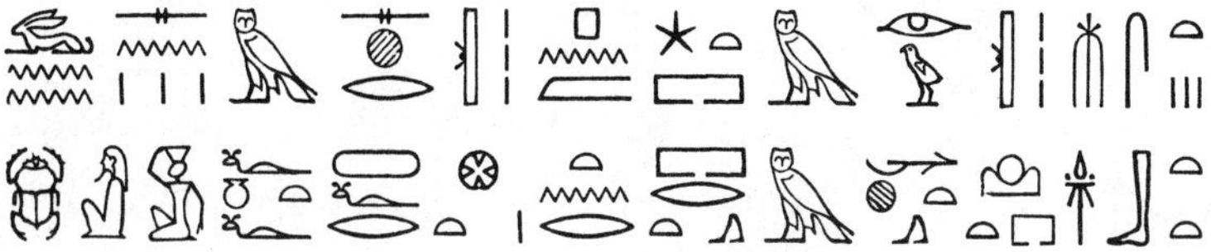

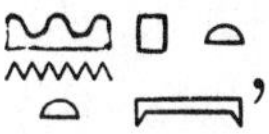, "Those who are in this picture in the Ṭuat "are in the forms of (i.e., they represent) the births of "the god KHEPER, who is carrying his horizon to this

"City, so that he may come forth into the Eastern "Horizon of the sky."

3. Two serpents, standing on their tails, which cross each other near their tips. Their heads and necks are bent at right angles to their bodies, and in the space between them rests a disk; the serpents are called

P-ānkhi. Kheper-ānkh.

MENENUI,  \\. To the right is a youthful goddess wearing a White Crown, and to the left is a similar goddess wearing a Red Crown; each holds the index finger of one hand to her mouth, after the manner of children, and each is depicted in the act of sitting, but lacks a seat or throne.

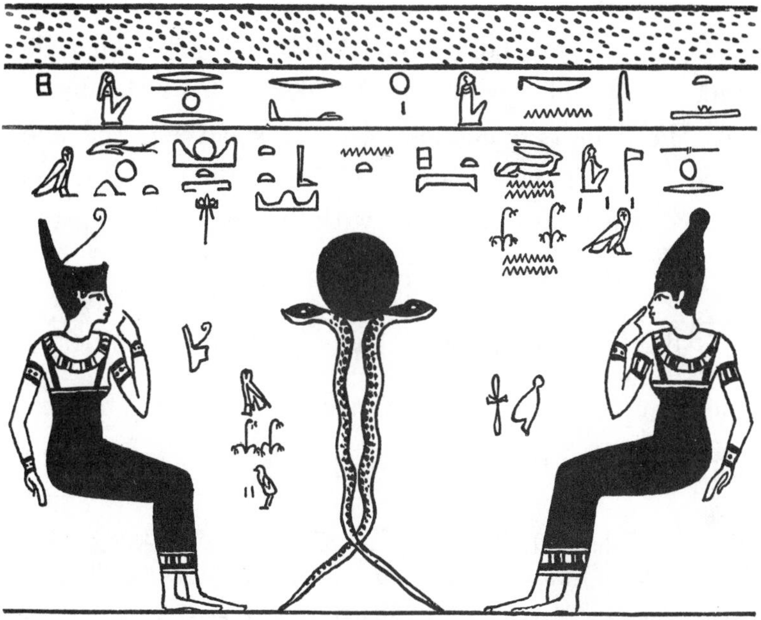

The Menenui serpents and the goddesses of the South and North.

The axe of god and the solar disk

4. An axe, symbol of "god," standing on the handle end, with a disk resting on the side edge of the head. On the left is a goddess who is steadying the axe with her left hand, and on the right is a goddess who is steadying the disk with her right hand; the names of the goddesses are NETHETH, 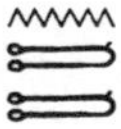, and KENȦT, , respectively. Each goddess is depicted in the act of sitting, but lacks a seat or throne. The text which refers to these scenes reads: 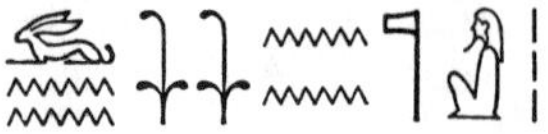

,

"Of those who are in this picture [the two goddesses "on] the left come forth from the double serpent "MĀNENUI, and [the two] on the right come forth from "the axe SEṬFIT. They gather together the souls on "earth, and they make pure the mighty spirits in the "Ṭuat by the hidden figures which are therein, and "[afterwards] they swallow their own spirits (or, souls) "after this great god hath passed them by."

5. Eight goddesses, who stand upright, and hold 

in their right hands, and in their left; they face the ape god, whose tail is stiffened out under him in such a manner as to form a seat for him, and who holds the *utchat*, or eye of the sun, on his two hands. The first four of the goddesses have each the head of a lioness and are called:—

1. SEKHET, .

2. MENKERT, .

Sekhet. Menkert. Ḥuntheth. Usrit.

3. ḤUNTHETH, .

4. USRIT, .

The remaining four have the heads of women, and have the names of:—

1. ABET-NETERU-S, .

2. ÅRIT-TATHETH, .

3. Āḥāt,

4. Themath-ermen (?),

The name of the ape-god is Ȧf (?)-ermen-maat-f, . Concerning the goddesses the text says:

Abet-neteru-s. Ȧrit-Tatheth. Āḥāt. Themath-ermen (?).

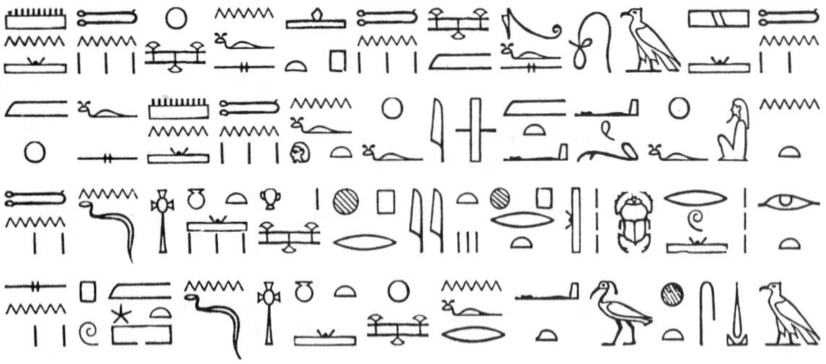

, "To these goddesses who make the

" reckoning of his Eye for Horus in the Ṭuat, Rā saith :— " 'Make ye strong your spirits by means of [your] " strength, and make the reckoning of his Eye for Horus, " stablish ye his Eye for Horus, and make ye Horus to " unite himself to his emanation (or, to that which " floweth from his eyes), praise ye Horus by reason of his " Eye, and stablish ye his first Eye which is in the " hands of the god ÅF-ERMEN-MAAT-F, and utter ye your " words on behalf of Horus, O ye who cause to come

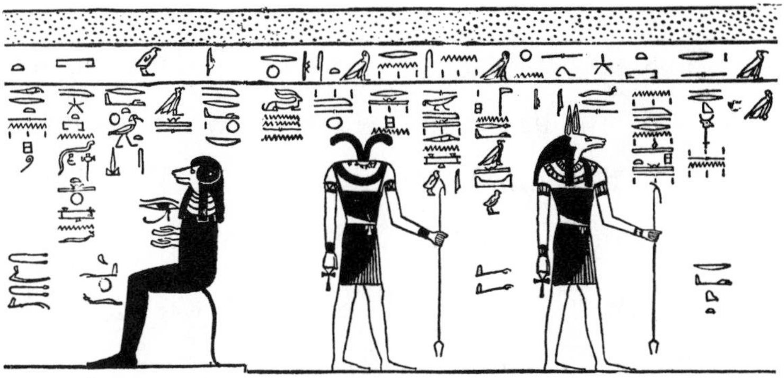

Åf-ermen-maat-f. Ermenui. Neb-āqet.

" into being the becomings of created things.' The work " which they do in the Ṭuat is to utter words on behalf " of his Eye for Horus, and to cause radiant splendour " to proceed from it each day."

6. Eight gods, each of the first seven of whom holds  in his right hand, and  in his left; their names are :—

1. ERMENUI, , who has the double object in the place of a head.

2. NEB-ĀQET, , jackal-headed.

3. ÅMEN-KHU, , hawk-headed.

4. ḤER-SHETA-TAUI, , man-headed.

5. SEM-ḤERU, , man-headed.

6. ÅMEN (?)-ḤERU, , man-headed.

7. KHENT-ÅST-F, , man-headed.

8. KHENT-MENT-F, , a god in mummied form, like Osiris, who wears a White Crown, and grasps a sceptre, , with both hands, which project from his bandages.

The text which refers to these gods reads: 

,

"Those who are in this picture in the forms which "Horus made—when this great god crieth out to them

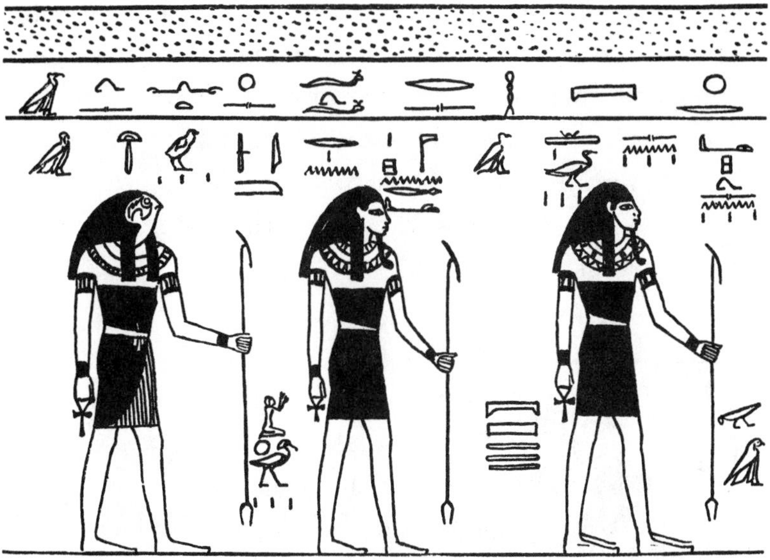

Ȧmen-khu. Ḥer-sheta-taui. Sem-Ḥeru.

Ȧmen Ḥeru. Khent-ȧst f. Khent-ment-f.

"by their names, they unite themselves and come into "life in the shades which are in the mouth of the great "god, and their souls journey onwards in his train to "the horizon. They strip the bodies of the dead of "their swathings and break in pieces the bodies of the "enemies [of Rā], and they give the order for their "destruction in the Ṭuat."

In the lower register are:—

Horus.

1. The god Horus, hawk-headed and wearing a disk, leaning on a staff.

2. Five[1] lakes of water, in each of which is submerged a male form; these figures are called the "submerged," .

3. Three[2] lakes of water, in each of which is a male form swimming, turned over on his breast; these are called the "swimmers," .

4. Four lakes of water, in each of which is a male form floating on his back; these are called the "floaters," . The text reads:

[1] These should be *four* in number.

[2] These should be *four* in number.

The above text is full of *lacunae*, and whole passages, consisting of several lines, are wanting; the following version from Lanzone's edition (*Le Domicile des Esprits*, pl. ii.) will be found useful in obtaining an idea of the contents of the legends which accompanied the lakes of water:

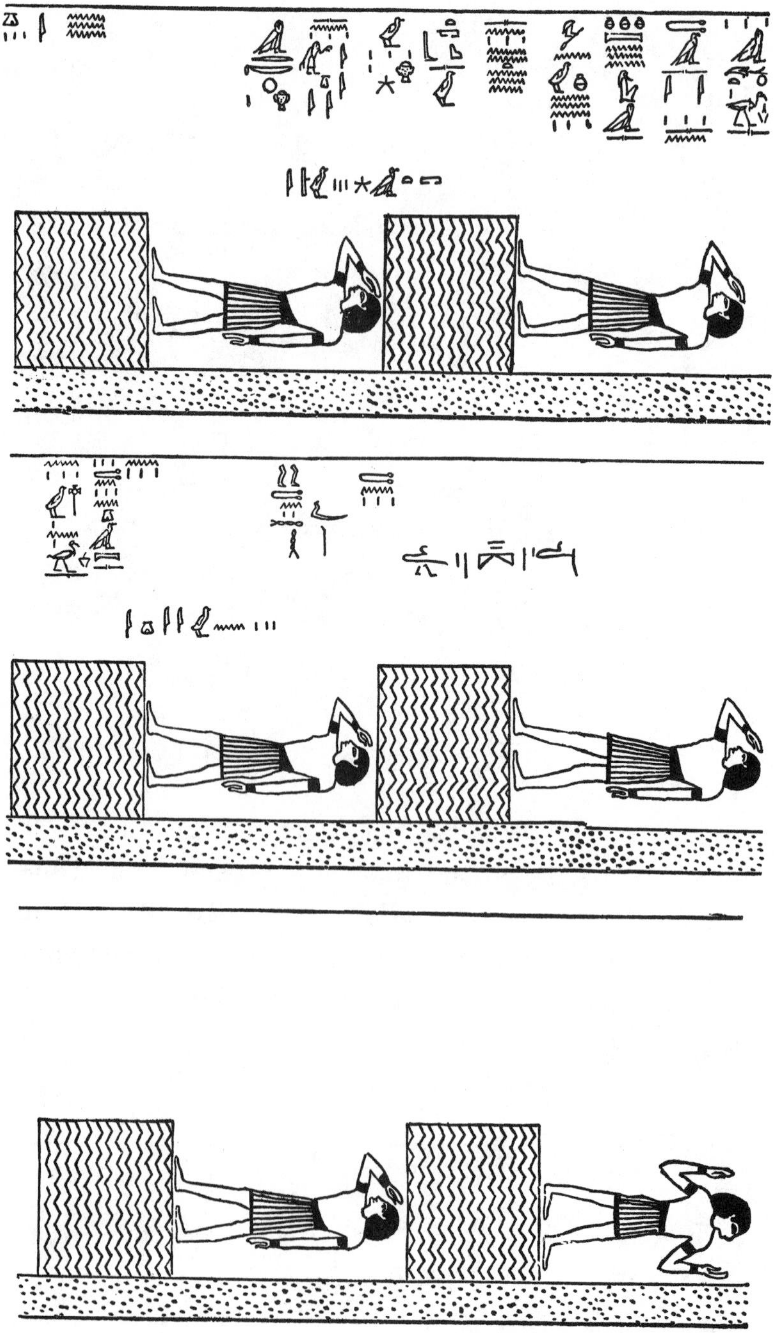

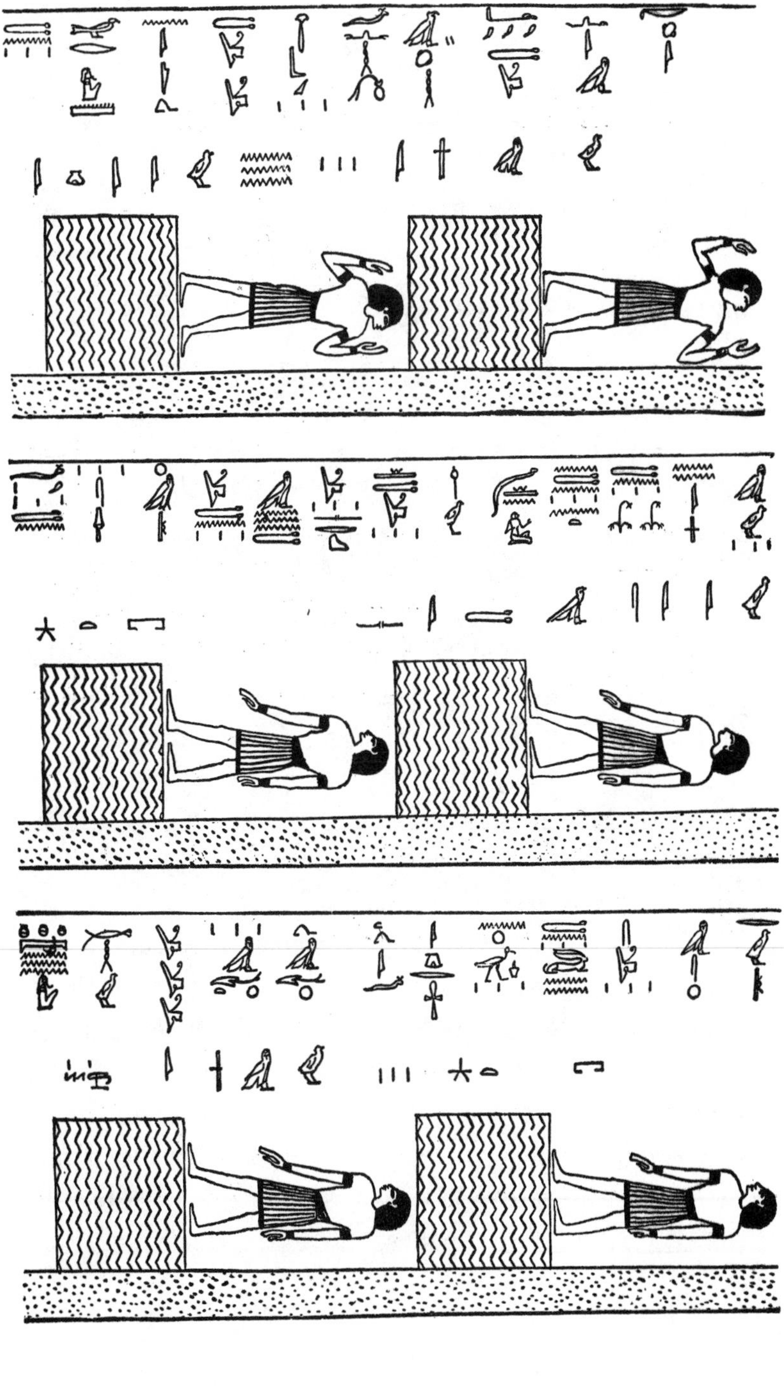

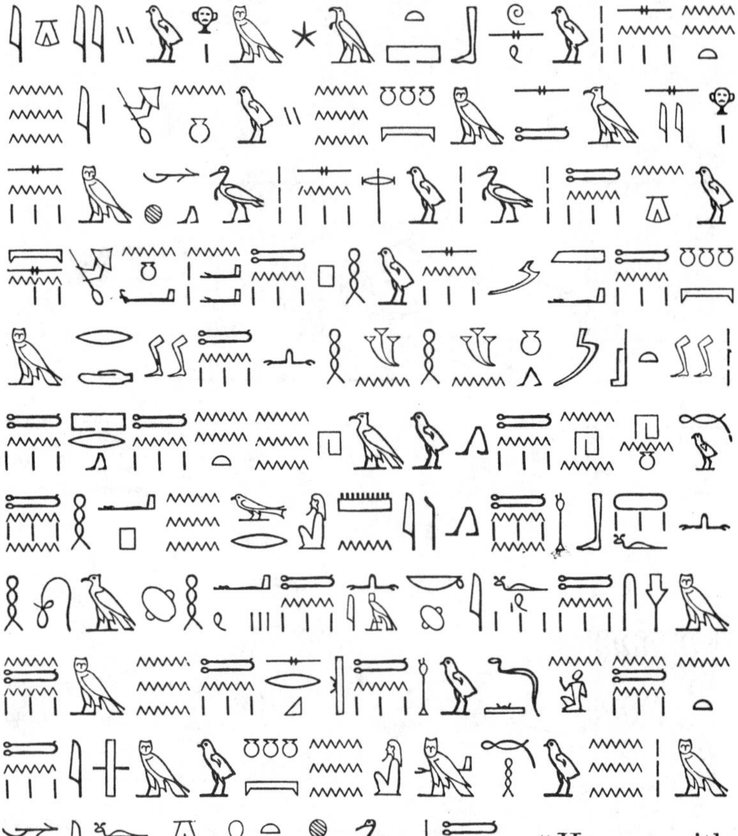

, “Horus saith “unto those who have plunged themselves beneath the “waters, and unto those who swim, and unto those “who float in Nu of the Ṭuat, ‘O ye who have plunged “yourselves beneath the waters, who shine in Nu, O “ye whose hands cover your faces, who swim with “your faces turned towards the water in the Ṭuat, “whose cheeks are filled with water, O ye who paddle “in the waters of Nu, whose faces are turned up into

"the air in the following of your souls, whose souls "have been deprived of their heavenly air, and who "beat the air with your hands in order to obtain it, "O make ye your way in Nu by means of your legs, "and your thighs shall not be in any way impeded. "Come ye forth in this stream, descend ye on these "waves, fill ye ḤĀP-UR, and arrive ye at its furrows,

Ḥetemit. Bekhkhit. Tchetmit. Senthes.

"for your members shall not perish, and your flesh "shall not decay, and ye shall have dominion over your "water, and ye shall have abundance according to my "command, O ye whose duty it is to dwell in NU, "together with those who have plunged themselves "beneath the waters, and are in [his] following, and "whose souls have life."

5. A lake of water.

6. Four female figures, each bearing a serpent on her head and shoulders; the head of each reptile is raised above the head of its bearer, and its tail hangs down her back; their names are:—

1. Ḥetemit, .

2. Bekhkhit, 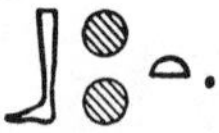.

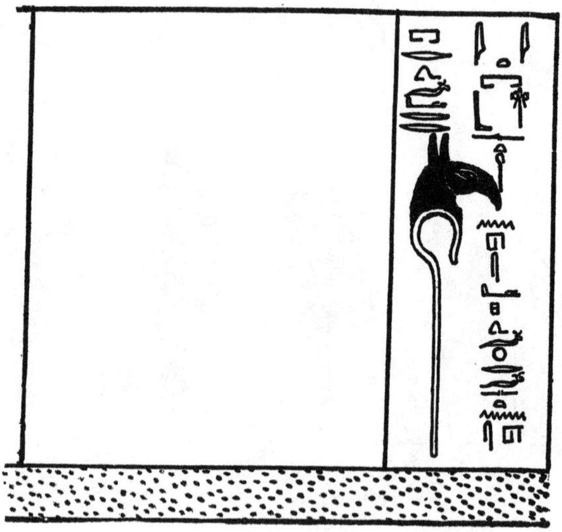

Set-nehes.

3. Tchetmit, 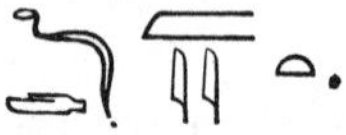.

4. Senthes, 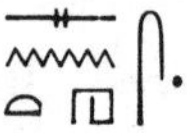.

The text reads: 

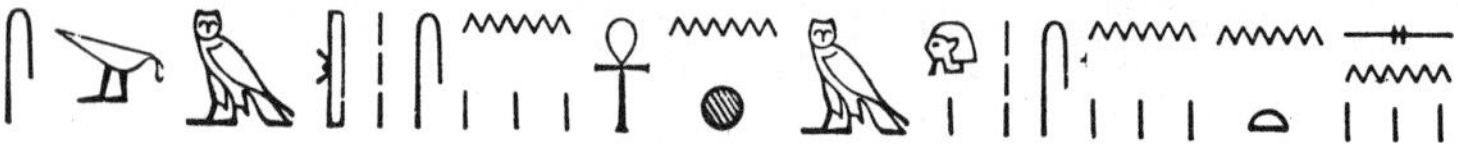

"Those who are in this picture are they whose forms "(or, figures) live by their heads. It is they who shed "light upon the road of Rā in the thick darkness, and "when he cometh forth into the Hall of the East, SET "waketh up and travelleth on with him."

7. A sceptre, , surmounted by the head of Set; its name is SET-NEHES, 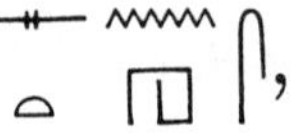, i.e., "Set who wakens."

CHAPTER XI.

THE ELEVENTH DIVISION OF THE ṬUAT, WHICH IS CALLED RE-EN-QERERT-ÅPT-KHATU.

THE ELEVENTH DIVISION of the Ṭuat, which is passed through by the Sun-god during the ELEVENTH HOUR of the night, is introduced by three lines of text, which read:—

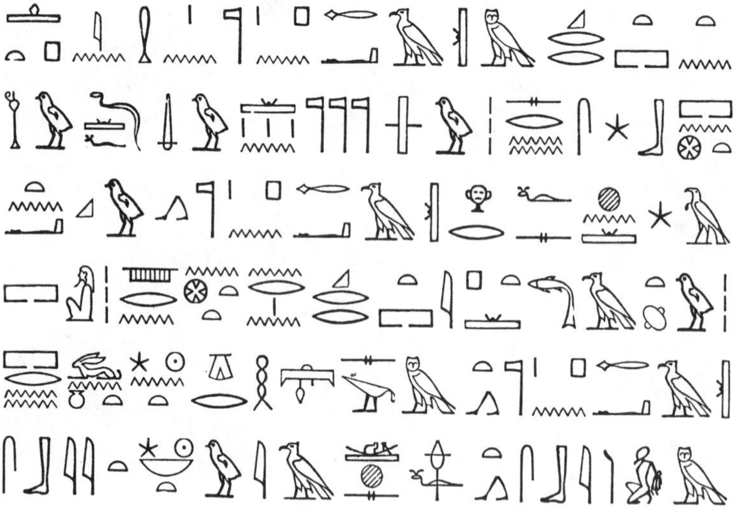

, "The Majesty of this great god taketh "up his position in this Circle, and he addresseth

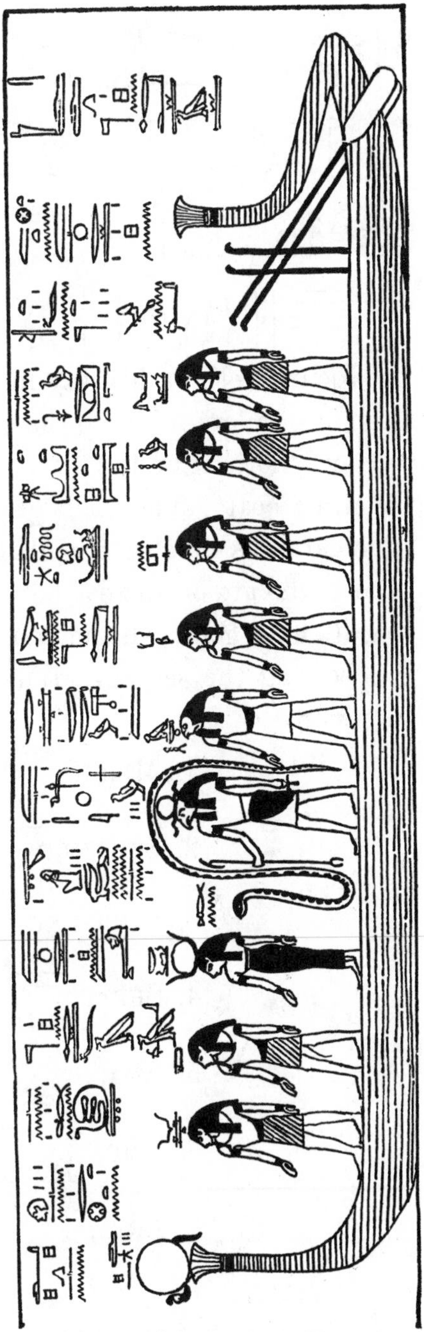

The Boat of the Sun in the Eleventh Division of the Ṭuat.

"words unto the gods "who are in it. The "name of the gate of "this City through "which this great god "hath entered is "SEKEN-ṬUATIU; the "name of this City is "RE-EN-QERERT-ÅPT-"KHATU; the name of "the hour of the night "which guideth this "great god is SEBIT-"NEBT-UÅA-KHESFET-"SEBÅ-EM-PERT-F."

In the middle register are:—

1. The boat of the sun, in which stands the god under a canopy formed by the body of the serpent Meḥen; on his head are horns and a disk. On the high prow of the boat is a disk, encircled by a uraeus, which is called PESṬU, 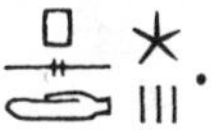. The text reads:

, "This great "god journeyeth on his way in the City in this picture, "and his sailors, who are the gods, guide him into the "eastern horizon of the sky. The star PESṬET which "is on its boat guideth this great god into the ways of "the darkness which gradually lightens, and illumineth "those who are on the earth."

2. Twelve gods, who march before the boat of the god bearing the serpent MEḤEN on their heads; their names are:—

1. MEḤNI, .
2. SEMSEM, .
3. SEKHENNU, 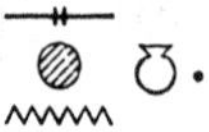.
4. SHEṬU, .
5. ÀMA, .
6. AMU, .
7. ERṬĀ, 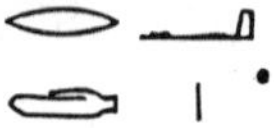.

Meḥni. Semsem. Sekhennu. Sheṭu.

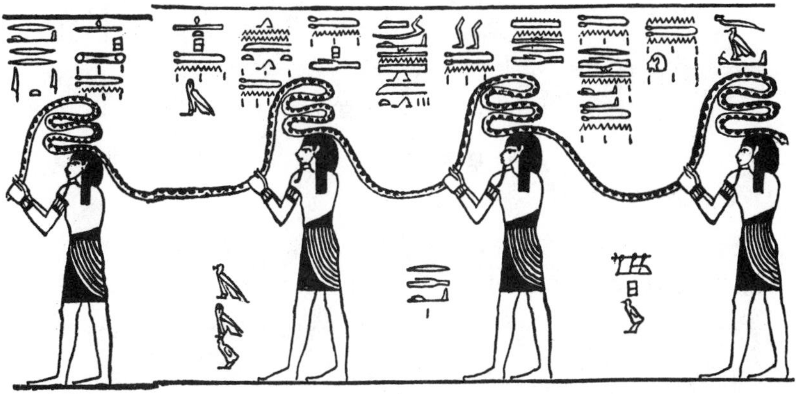

Ȧma. Amu. Erṭā. Shepu.

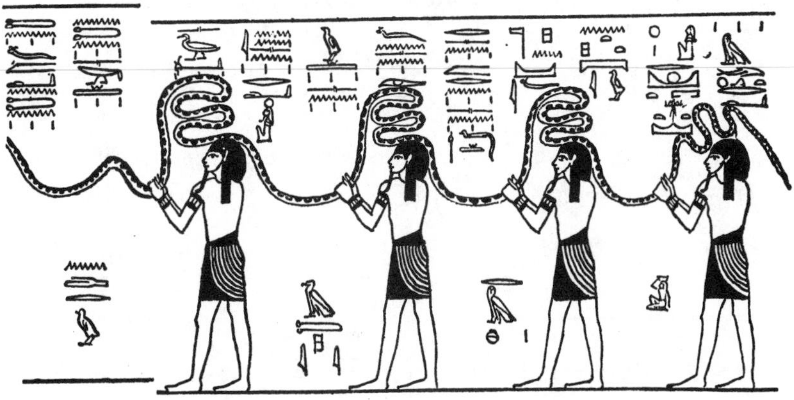

Neṭeru. Athpi. Ermenu. Fa (?).

8. SHEPU, 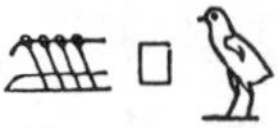.

9. NEṬERU, .

10. ATHPI, 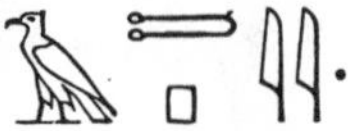.

11. ERMENU, .

12. FA (?), .

The text reads: 

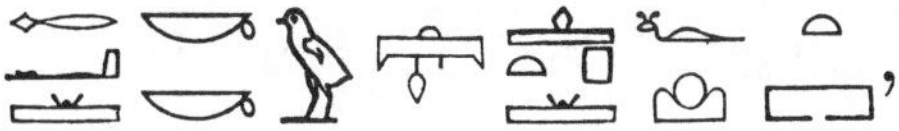, "Those who are in "this picture are in front of this great god, and they carry "the serpent Meḥen-ta on their heads into this City, and "they travel onwards in the following of Rā into the "Eastern Horizon of the sky. This god crieth unto them "by their names, and he decreeth for them what they "have to do. And Rā saith unto them:—'O ye who "keep ward over your serpent-figures with your two

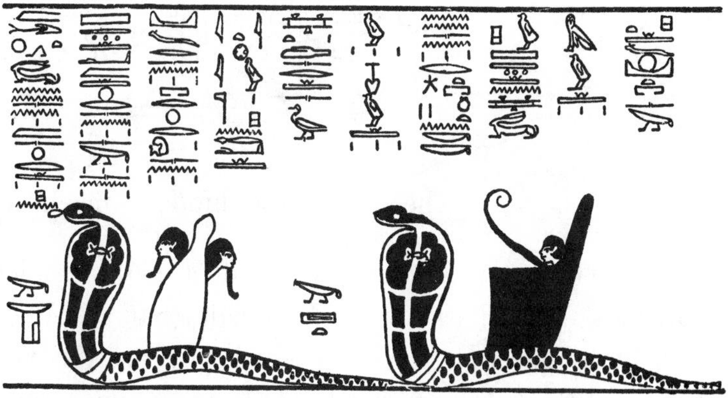

Sem-Nebt-ḥet. Sem-shet.

"hands, lift ye up your heads, whose hands are strong, "whose feet are firm, who perform the journeyings "which ye are bound to make, who make long your "steps as ye go, unite ye yourselves to your offerings in "the Hall of the Eastern Horizon.' Their work is to "make the serpent Meḥen to travel to the Eastern Hall "of the Horizon, and they unite themselves to their habi- "tations after this great god hath passed through the "darkness and hath taken up his place in the horizon."

3. The serpent SEM-SHET, 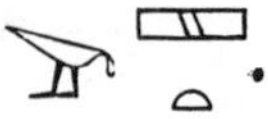. On his back rests the Red Crown, and in an angle of it is a human head.

4. The serpent SEM-NEBTḤET, . On his back rests the White Crown, from each side of which projects a bearded human head. The text reads:

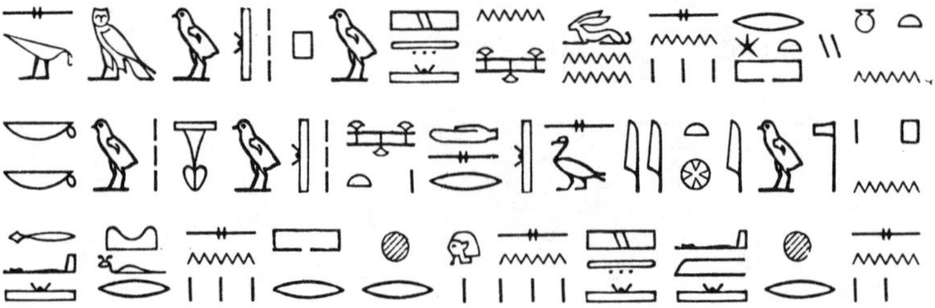

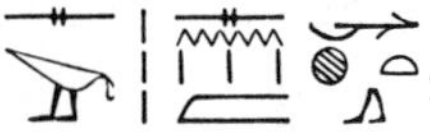, "[These are] the hidden images of "Horus which are at the second door of the thick "darkness, [on] the holy road to Sait (Saïs). When "this great god crieth out to them (i.e., to the two "serpents) these hidden heads make their appearance, "and then they swallow their own forms (i.e., they "disappear)."

5. NEITH of the phallus, , wearing the Red Crown.

6. NEITH of the Red Crown, , wearing the Red Crown.

7. NEITH of the White Crown, , wearing the White Crown.

8. NEITH the Young, , wearing the White Crown. The text reads: 

, "Those who are in

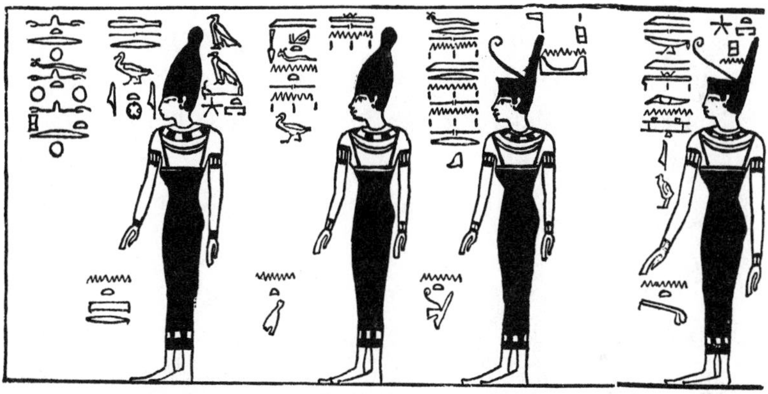

Neith the Young. Neith of the White Crown. Neith of the Red Crown. Neith of the phallus.

"this picture of [this] door [are] in the form which "Horus made; when this god crieth out to them "by their names they spring into life at the sound "of his voice, and it is they who guard the holy "gate of the city of SAIT (Saïs), which is unknown, "and cannot be seen, and cannot be looked at." Above the upper register is a line of text, which reads

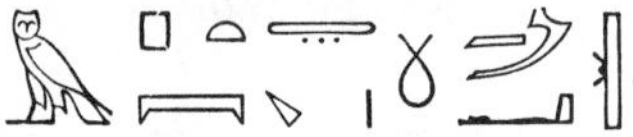, "[This is] the hidden Circle "of the Ṭuat through which this god maketh his "journey so that he may come forth into the Eastern "Horizon of the sky; it swalloweth eternally its images "(or, forms) in the presence of the god REKH (?), who "dwelleth in this City, and then it giveth them to "those who are born and come into being in the earth. "Whosoever shall make an exact copy of these forms "according to the representations of the same at the "eastern [portion] of the hidden Palace of the Ṭuat, "and shall know it, shall be a spirit well equipped "both in heaven and earth, unfailingly, and regularly "and eternally."

In the upper register are:—

1. The god ĀPER-ḤRȦ-NEB-TCHETTA, , above whose body, at the neck, is a disk from which proceed two human heads, the one wearing the White Crown and the other the Red Crown; in his right hand he holds the sceptre , and in the left the

emblem of "life," ☥. The text reads: 

, "He who is in this picture standeth up for Rā, "and he never departeth from his place in the Ṭuat."

2. A huge serpent, with two pairs of human feet and legs, and a pair of large wings. By its side stands a god with a disk upon his head, and on each side of his head is an *utchat*, 𓂀; his hands are stretched out at right angles to his body, and each hand touches the end of one of the serpent's wings. The text reads:

The god Àper-ḥrà-neb-tchetta.

, "When this god crieth out to him that is in "this picture, the form (or, image) of the god Tem pro-"ceedeth from his back; but afterwards it swalloweth "itself (i.e., disappeareth)." The words 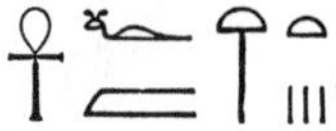, &c., may form the name of the winged serpent.

3. A serpent, with a mummied god seated on his

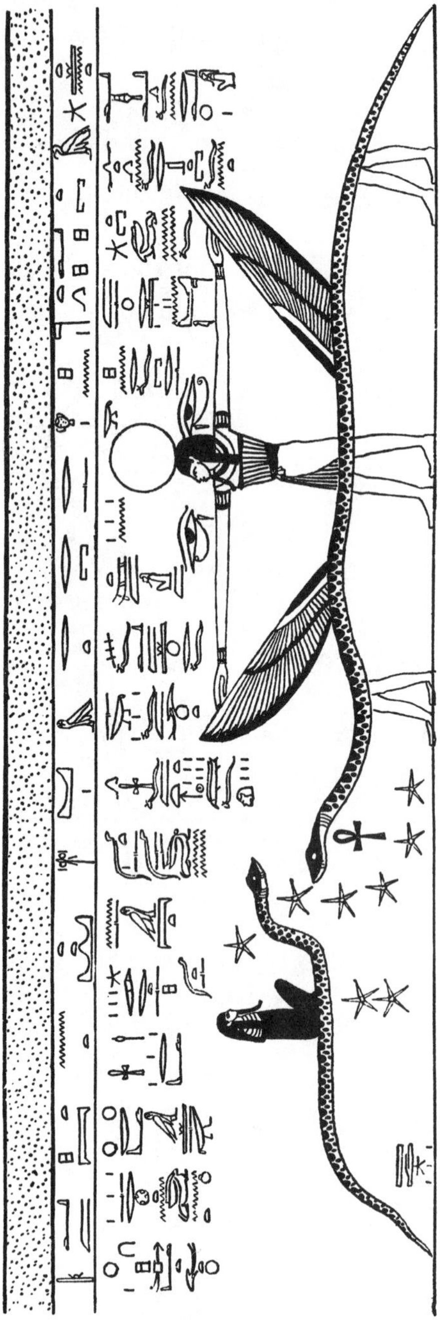

back; above the god is written "TCHET-S," i.e., "its body," and by the tail of the serpent is SHEṬU, 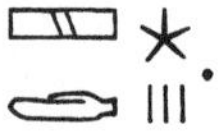. The text reads:

, "TCHET-S "herself is above "the stars (i.e., the "eight stars which "are about the "heads of the two "serpents); her "work is to cast "the living ones to "Rā every day; she "then swalloweth

"her forms in this City of the ELEVENTH HOUR, [and "she is] one of those who follow the god."

4. The god ṬEPUI, , i.e., the "Two-headed"; one head faces to the right and the other to the left.

5. The god KHNEM-RENIT, , ram-headed, holding in his right hand, and in his left.

6. The god NERTA, , with both hands raised in adoration.

7. The god ĀĀUI-F-EM-KHA-NEF, , who has two snakes' heads in the place of a human head; his hands and arms are concealed.

8. The god ÅPT-TAUI, ; his hands and arms are concealed.

The god Ṭepui.

9. The god MER-EN-ĀĀUI-F, , in form similar to the preceding.

10. The god ÅU-EN-ĀĀUI-F, , in similar form.

11. The god RESET-ÅFU (?), , in similar form.

12. The god ṬUA-ḤERU, , in similar form.

13. The god MAĀ, .

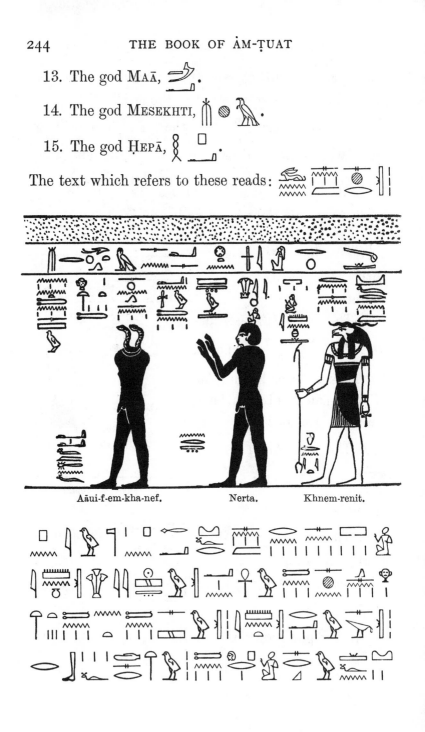

14. The god MESEKHTI, .

15. The god ḤEPĀ, 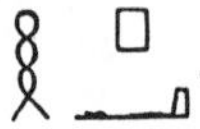.

The text which refers to these reads: 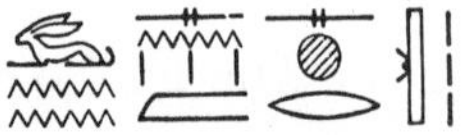

Aāui-f-em-kha-nef. Nerta. Khnem-renit.

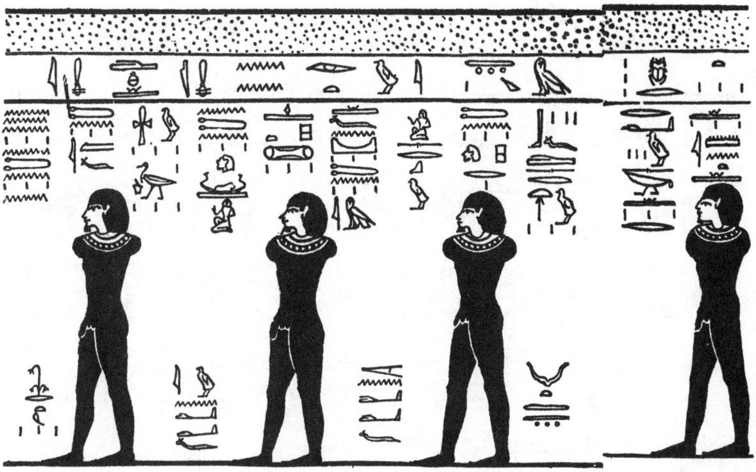

Ṛeset-åfu. Åu-en-åāui-f. Mer-en-åaui-f. Åpt-taui.

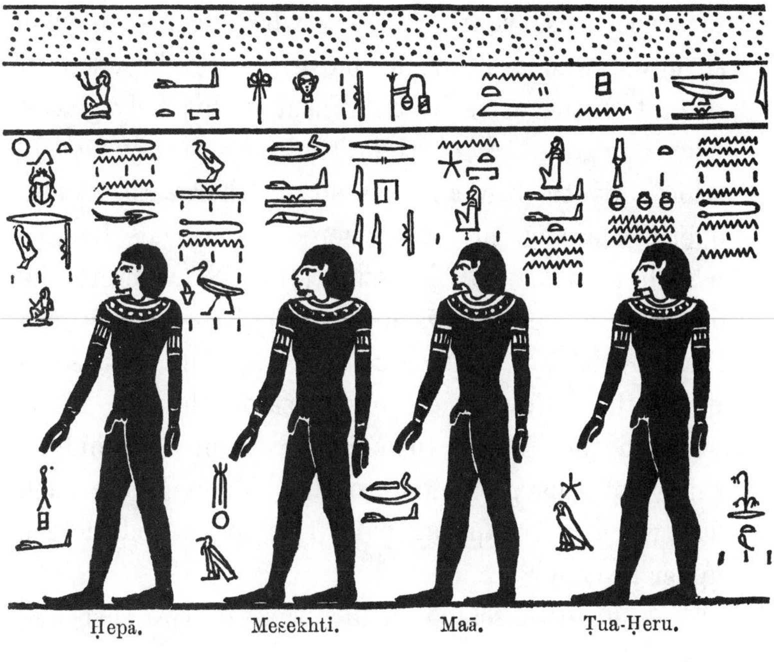

Ḥepā. Mesekhti. Maā. Ṭua-Ḥeru.

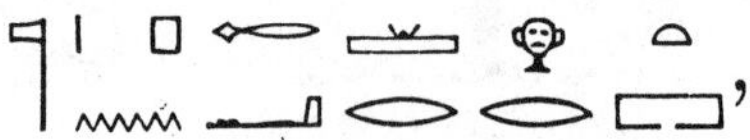, "Those who are in this "picture doth this great god call by their names, "[saying]:—'My hidden appearances and my secret "radiance cause your life, O ye who advance to your "shadows, who are free to move or are shrouded in "respect of the arms by the Form in his holy places, "whose breaths are of the utterances of my mouth, "which giveth life and ye speak therewith, whose "offerings are on my boat whereon your souls live, ye "who have water at the source (?) of NU wherein the "dwellers in the Ṭuat wash with shouts of joy, perform "that which it is your right to do, and let your souls "be in the following of [my] created things.' Their "work in the Ṭuat is to make to advance the hidden "things of this great god to the hidden House each "day when they appear with this great god in the "upper heaven."

16. A goddess, seated on the backs of two serpents,

Nebt-khu. Nebt-ānkhiu.

Mer-ent-neteru. Nert-ābui.

which lie side by side, and appear to issue from her feet; her left hand grasps the body of one serpent, and her right is held up before her face. Her name is NEBT-ĀNKHIU, 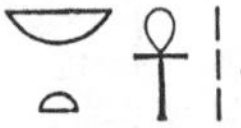. In front of her are three other goddesses, who are similarly seated; their names are NEBT-KHU, , NERT-ĀBUI, , and MER-ENT-NETERU, 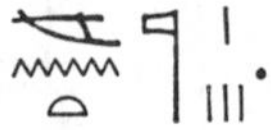. The text reads:

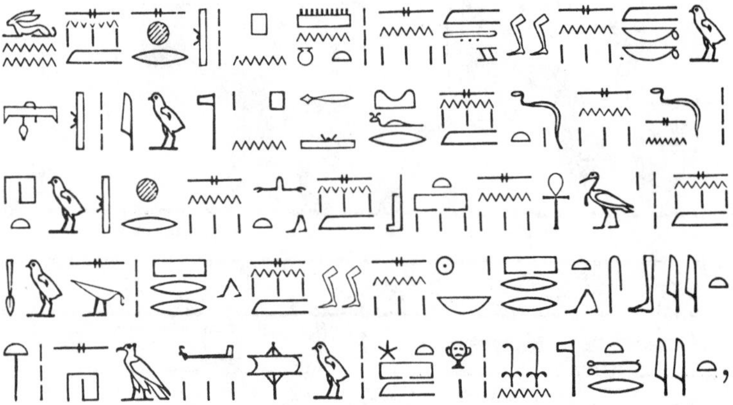,

"Those who are in this picture have their arms on the "earth and their feet and legs in the darkness. When "this great god crieth to them in their own bodies, "they utter cries; they do not depart from their "places, but their souls live in the word of the forms "which come forth from their feet every day. When "the shades appear, the winds which are in the Ṭuat "cease from the faces of these goddesses."

In the lower register are:—

1. Horus, hawk-headed and wearing a disk, leaning

with his right shoulder upon a long staff, and holding in his left hand a boomerang, one end of which is in the form of a serpent's head.

Horus and the serpent Set-ḥeḥ.

2. A huge serpent, called the "Everlasting SET," , standing upon his tail.

3. A large pit, with a vaulted roof, filled with fire, wherein "the enemies," , of Rā are being consumed; the name of the pit is ḤAṬET-KETITS,

The pit of fire, Ḥatet-ketits.

The pit of fire, Ḥaṭet-ḥanṭu-s.

, and is presided over by a goddess with the head of a lioness, who holds in her hands a large knife, and pours fire into it from her mouth.

4. A smaller pit, with a vaulted roof, filled with fire, wherein "the enemies" are being consumed; the name of the pit is ḤAṬET-ḤANṬU-S, 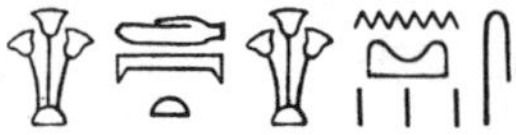(?), and it is presided over by a goddess with a human head, who holds in her hands a large knife, and pours fire into it from her mouth.

5. A pit similar to the above, wherein "the souls," , are being consumed; the name of the pit is ḤAṬ-NEKENIT, , and it is presided over by a goddess as in No. 4.

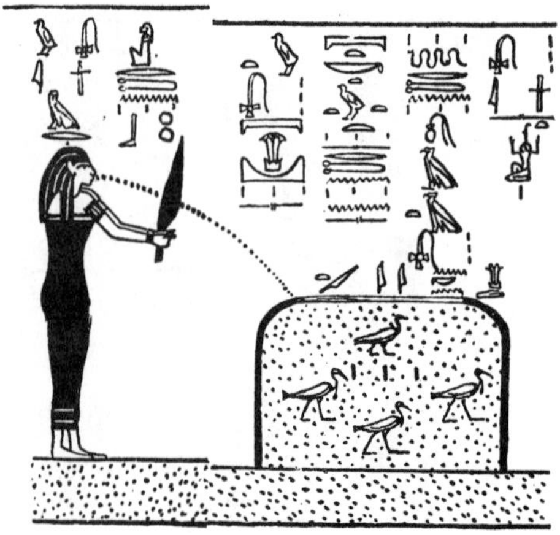

The pit of fire, Ḥaṭ-nekenit.

6. A similar pit, wherein "the shades (or, shadows)" are being consumed; the name of the pit is ḤAṬ-NEMMÀT-SET, , and it is presided over by a goddess as in No. 4.

7. A similar pit, wherein "the heads," , are being consumed; the name of the pit is ḤAṬ-SEFU-S,

The pit of fire, Ḥaṭ-nemmàt-set.

The pit of fire, Ḥaṭ-sefu-s.

, and it is presided over by a goddess as in No. 4.

8. A very large pit, with a vaulted roof, filled with fire, in which are immersed, head downwards, four male figures; the name of this pit is ÀNT-SEKHEṬU, , i.e., "the valley of those who are turned upside down."

9. Four goddesses, each one with the sign for "eastern desert" on her head; their names are:—

1. PESI, .

2. REKḤIT, .

3. ḤER-SHĀU-S, .

4. SAIT, .

10. The god ḤER-UTU-F, , holding a sceptre, , in his left hand, and the sign of "life," , in his right.

The text reads:

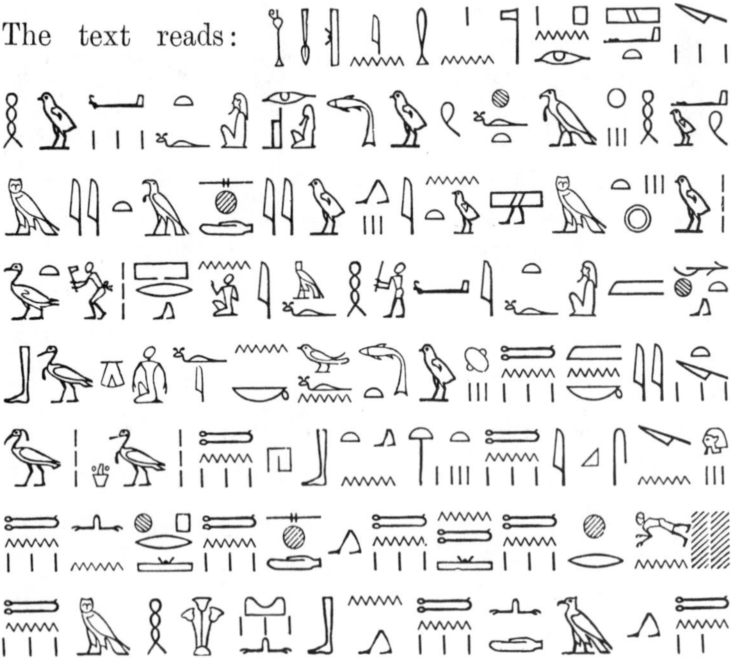

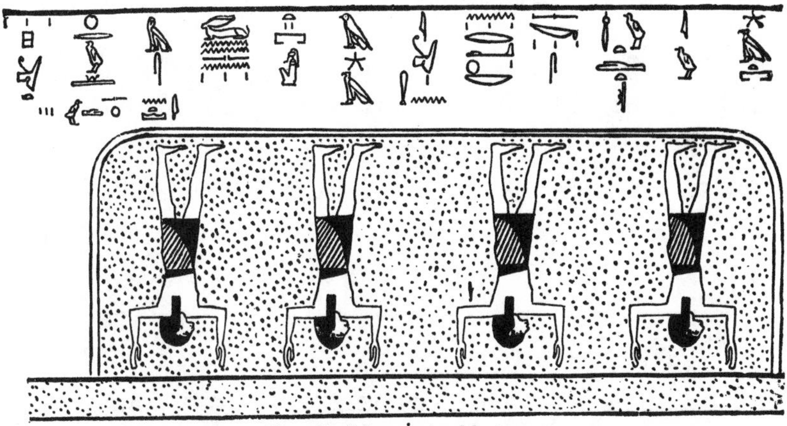

The pit of fire, Ȧnt-sekheṭu.

Ḥer-shāu-s. Rekhit. Pesi.

The god Ḥer-utu-f. Sait.

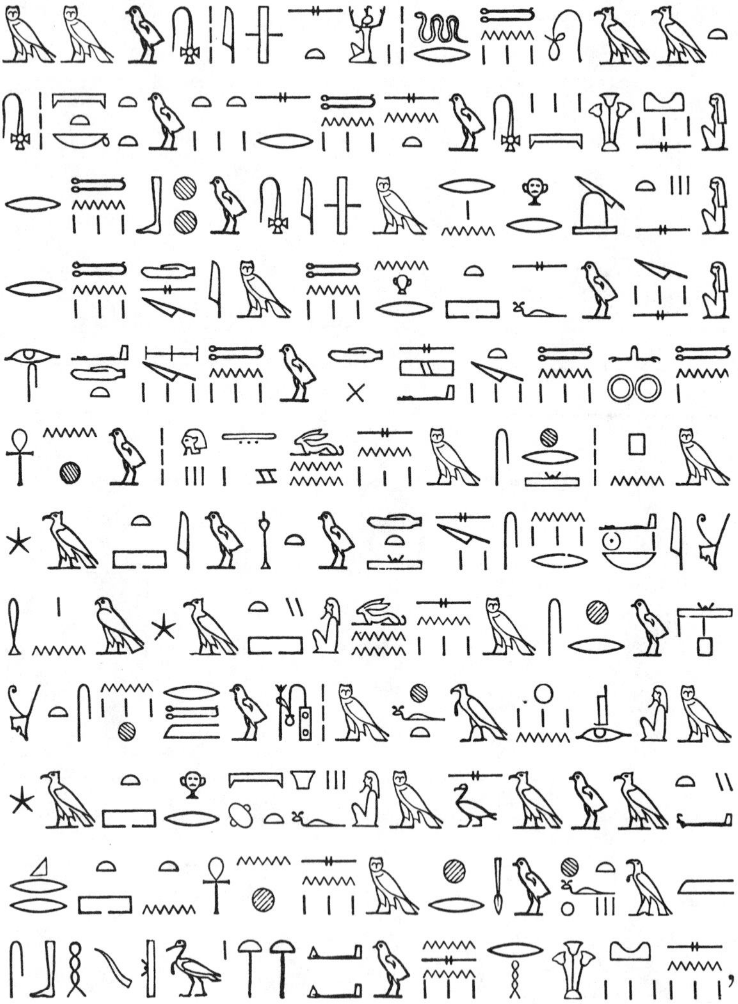

"The Majesty of this god uttereth the decree, [say-
"ing]:—'Hack in pieces and cut asunder the bodies
"of the enemies and the members of the dead who
"have been turned upside down, O my father Osiris
". . . . . and let me come forth from it. My

"father having [once] been helpless hath smitten you, "he hath cut up your bodies, he hath hacked in pieces "your spirits and your souls, and hath scattered in "pieces your shadows, and hath cut in pieces your "heads; ye shall never more exist, ye shall be over-"thrown, and ye shall be cast down headlong into the "pits of fire; and ye shall not escape therefrom, and "ye shall not be able to flee from the flames which are "in the serpent SET-ḤEḤ.

"'The fire of ḤERT-KETTUT-S is against you, the "flames of ḤERT-ḤAṬU-S are against you, the blazing "heat of ḤERT-NEMMȦT-S is against you, ḤERT-SEFU-S "is against you, and she stabs at you, and hacks you "in pieces, and cuts you up in such wise that ye shall "never again see those who are living upon the earth.'

"As for those who are in this picture in the Ṭuat, it "is the Majesty of ḤERU-ṬUATI who giveth the order "for their slaughter each day.

"Those who are in this picture, who are depicted "with the enemies of Osiris of the Ṭuat, and with "ḤER-UTU-F, who is the guardian of this Circle, live by "means of the voice of the enemies, and by the cries of "entreaty of the souls and shadows which have been "placed in their pits of fire."

CHAPTER XII.

THE TWELFTH DIVISION OF THE ṬUAT, WHICH IS CALLED THEN-NETERU.

THE TWELFTH DIVISION[1] of the Ṭuat, which is passed through by the Sun-god during the TWELFTH HOUR of the night, is introduced by three lines of text, which read :—

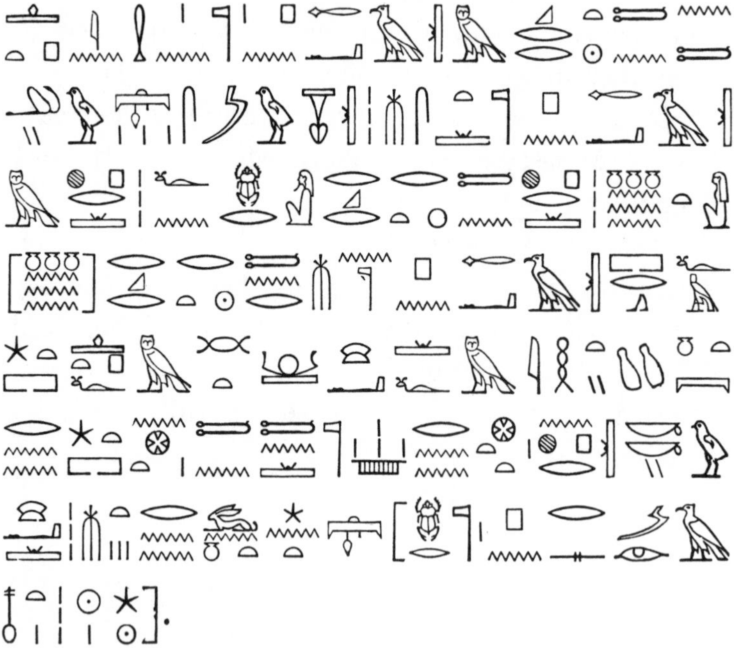

See Lanzone, *Domicile*, pl. v.

"The Majesty of this great god "taketh up his position in this "Circle, which is the uttermost "limit of thick darkness, and this "great god is born in his form of "Kheperá in this Circle, and Nut "and Nu are in this Circle for the "birth of this great god when he "cometh forth from the Ṭuat and "taketh up his position in the "Māṭet Boat, and when he riseth "up from the thighs of Nut. The "name of the Gate of this City is "THEN-NETERU. The name of this "City is KHEPER-KEKIU-KHĀU-"MESTU. The name of the hour of "the night wherein this god cometh "into being is MAA-NEFERT-RĀ."

Above the whole scene is a line of hieroglyphics, which describes it as:—

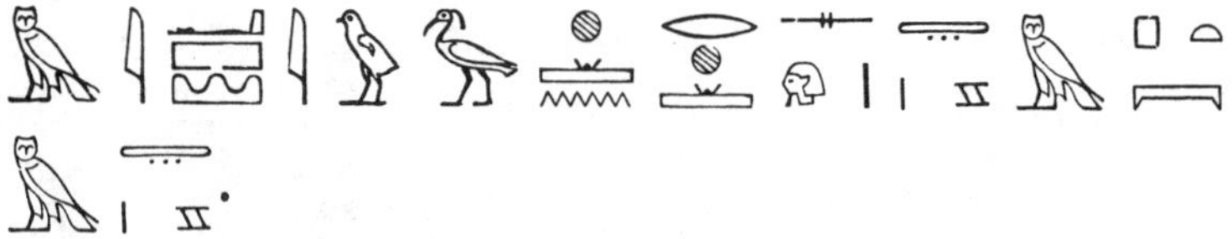

"The hidden Circle in the Ṭuat wherein this great "god is born; he cometh forth into the pool of Nu, "and he taketh up his place in the body of Nut. "Whosoever shall make a copy thereof according to "the copies which exist in writing upon the east [wall

The Boat of the Sun in the last hour of the Night.

"of] the palace, and shall know it upon earth, it shall "act as a magical protector for him both in heaven and "upon earth."

In the middle register are:—

1. The boat of the sun, in which stands the god under a canopy formed by the body of the serpent Meḥen; on his head are horns and a disk. In the fore part of the boat is the beetle of KHEP[R]À, 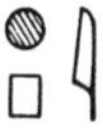,

i.e., Kheperȧ, which takes the place of the solar disk that rested on the prow of the boat in the Eleventh Hour.

The text reads:

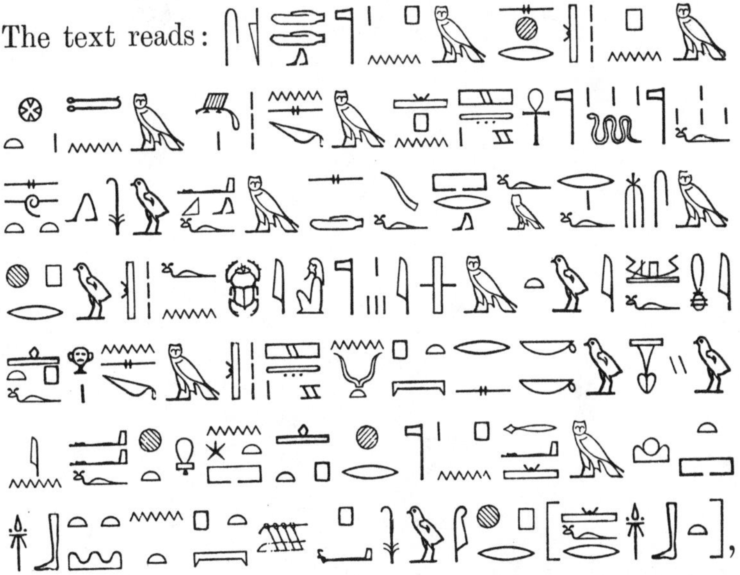

"This great god in this picture journeyeth along "through this City by means of the faithful servants "(*ȧmkhiu*) of this hidden image ĀNKH-NETERU. His "gods draw him along by a cord, and he entereth into "his tail and cometh forth from his mouth, and cometh "to the birth under the form of Kheperȧ, and the gods "who are in his boat [do] likewise. He taketh up his "place on the face of the hidden image of the horn (or, "forehead) of the sky at the end of the thick darkness, "and his hands seal up the Ṭuat. Then this great god "taketh up his position in the Eastern Horizon of "heaven, and Shu receiveth him, and he cometh into "being in the East."

2. Twelve gods, who are occupied in towing along the boat of the Sun, each with his head turned behind him and looking at the boat; their names are :—

1. ḤERU, .
2. SHEMSU, .
3. THENȦ, 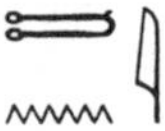.
4. BEQ, .
5. ȦU-ĀNKHIU-F, .
6. SEBEḤU-F, 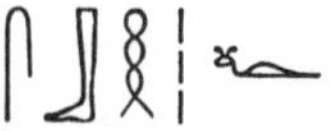.
7. ĀḤĀ-RER, 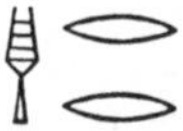.
8. ȦMKHUI, .
9. NEB-ȦMAKH, 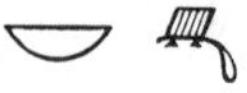.
10. SEKI (?), .
11. ḤEQ-NEK-MU, 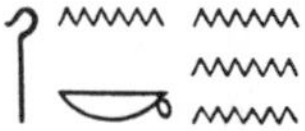.
12. ȦU, .

The text which refers to these reads: 

"Those who are in this picture draw this great god "through the tail (or, bowels) of the serpent Ānkh-"neteru. The loyal servants of Rā who are in his "following are the product of his hands, and they are "born on the earth each day after the birth of this "great god in the eastern portion of the sky. They "enter into this hidden image of Ānkh-neteru in "the form of loyal servants, and they come forth in "the renewed forms of Rā every day. When they "tarry upon the earth it is an abomination to them to "utter the name of the god."

3. The monster serpent KA-EM-ĀNKH-NETERU, .

4. Twelve goddesses, who are occupied in towing the boat of the sun through the body of the serpent KA-EM-ĀNKH-NETERU; each has her head turned behind her, and is looking at the boat. Their names are:—

1. STAT, .

2. KHERU-UTCHAT, .

3. KHET, .

4. SPERT-NETER-S, .

5. NEBTȦMT, 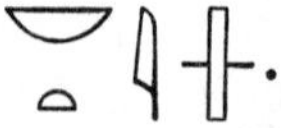.

6. NEB-TCHETTA, .

7. ḤETIT, .

8. ĀNKHET-ERMEN, .

9. KHERUT-ṬEP (?), .

10. ḤETEP-EM-KHUT-S, .

11. BET-NETER-S, .

12. ṬESER-ȦBT, 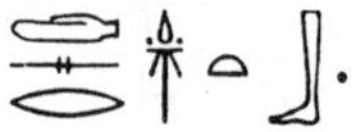.

The text relating to the serpent reads: 

Twelve gods of the last hour of the night.

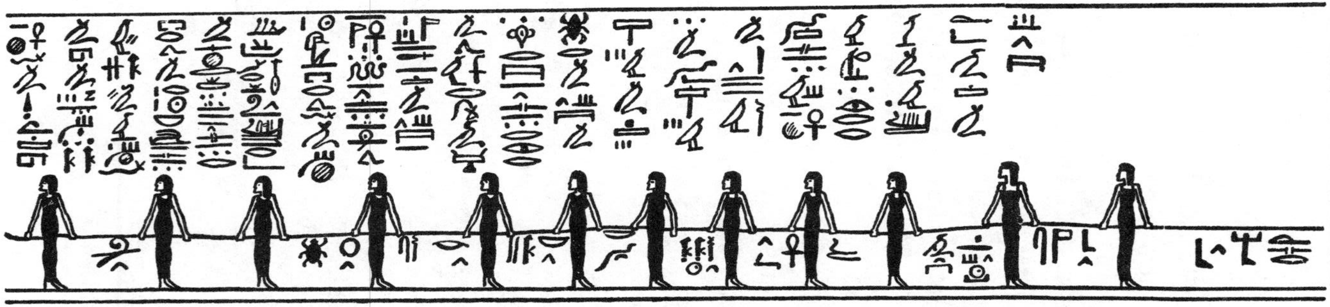

Twelve goddesses of the last hour of the night.

, "Those "who are here are they who have their bodies, and "they come forth in the following of this great god "into heaven. This is the hidden image of the "serpent Ānkh-neteru, which is by his den in the "Ṭuat, and he resteth in [his] place every day. This "great god speaketh to him in [his] name of NĀ, "[and the space covered by] his forepaws and legs is "one thousand three hundred cubits long . . . . ; "he liveth upon the sound of the rumblings "of the earth. The servants who are loyal to his "service come forth from [his] mouth every day." The text relating to the twelve goddesses reads:

, "Those who are in this picture take the "towing rope of the boat of Rā when it cometh forth

"from the serpent ĀNKH-NETERU, and they tow this "great god into the sky, and lead him along the ways "of the upper sky. It is they who make to arise in "the sky gentle winds and humid breezes, and it is "they who order those who live [upon earth] to place "themselves in the great boat in the sky."

In the upper register are:—

1. Twelve goddesses, each of whom stands upright, and bears on her shoulders a serpent which belches forth fire from its mouth; their names are:—

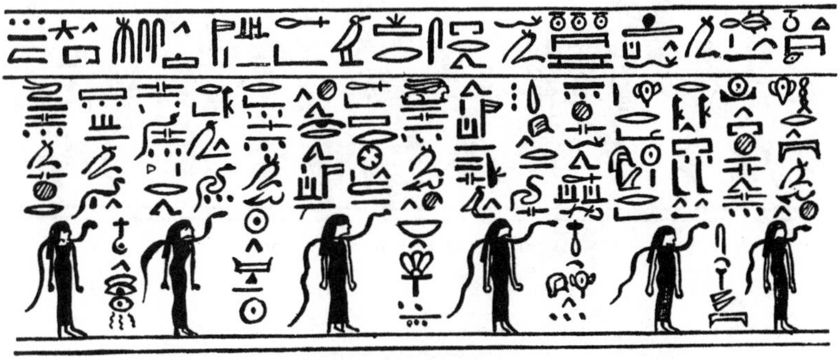

Six goddesses with fiery serpents.

1. NEFERT-KHĀU, 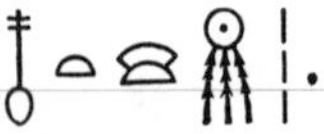.

2. KHET (?)-UAT-EN-RĀ, 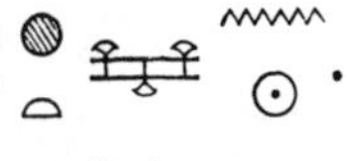.

3. NEBT-SESHESH-TA, .

4. NEFERT-ḤER-ṬEPT, .

5. SEUATCHET-ÅṬEBUI-PET, .

6. Ḥāt-em-taui-s, 

7. Qat-em-sepu-s, 

8. Sekhet-em-khu-s, 

9. Ḥāāt-em-sepu-s, 

10. Khet-ānkh (?)-f, 

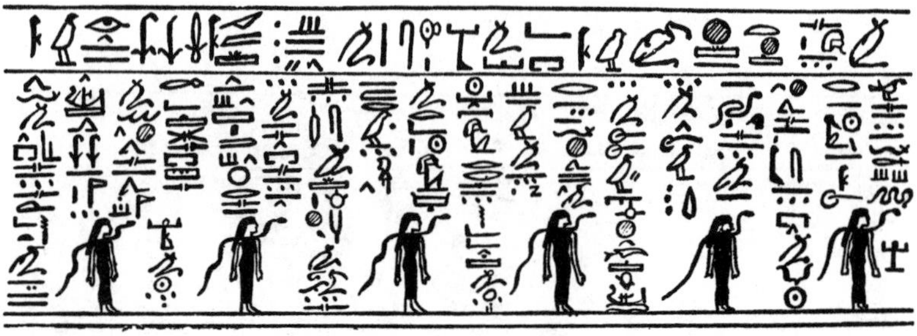

Six goddesses with fiery serpents.

11. Pert-em-Ȧp, 

12. Nebt-ār-em-uȧa-ȧbt, 

The text reads: 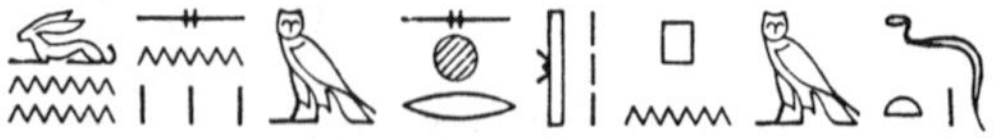

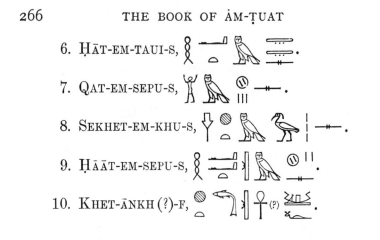

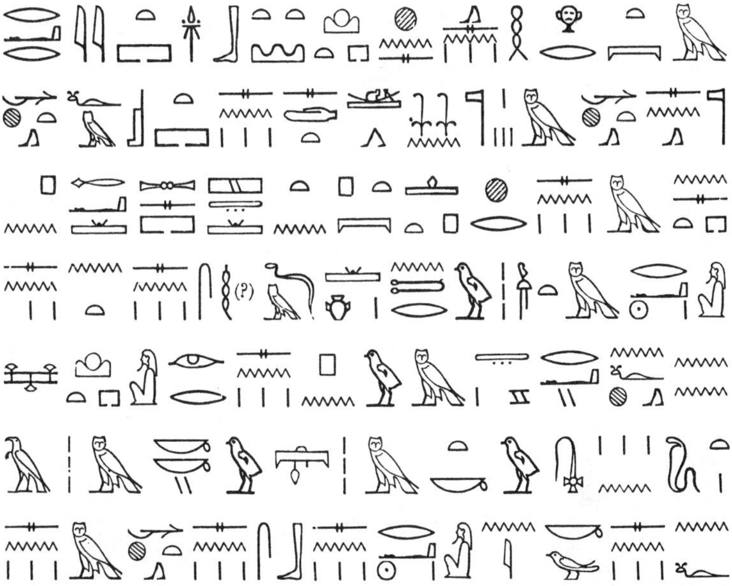

 "Those who are in this picture "with their own bodies, and from whom their uraei "emerge, are in the following of this great god when "he setteth out for this City. They follow after this "god, and the flames which issue from their mouths "drive away Āpep on behalf of Rā into the Hall of "the East of the Horizon. They journey round about "the upper heavens in his following [remaining] in "their places, and they restore these gods after this "great god hath passed by the hidden chamber of the "sky, and then they take up their positions [again] in "their own abodes. They give pleasure to the hearts "of the gods of Åmentet through Rā-Ḥeru-khut, and "their work upon the earth is to drive away those who

"are in the darkness by the flames of their uraei which "are behind them, and they guide Rā along, and they "smite Āpep for him in the sky."

2. Twelve gods, each of whom stands upright, and has both hands raised in adoration before him; their names are:—

1. NEB-ĀNKH, 

2. HI, 

Six gods who praise Rā at dawn.

3. NEB-ȦA, 

4. NEB-ṬUAT, 

5. NETCHEM-ȦB, 

6. ḤĀM, 

7. UA-ȦB, 

8. ḤUNNU, 

9. SENSȦBT, .

10. MA-ṬEPU-NETERU, .

11. THES-ṬEPU-NETERU, .

12. ḤEKENU, 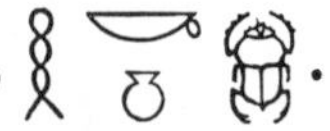.

The text reads: 

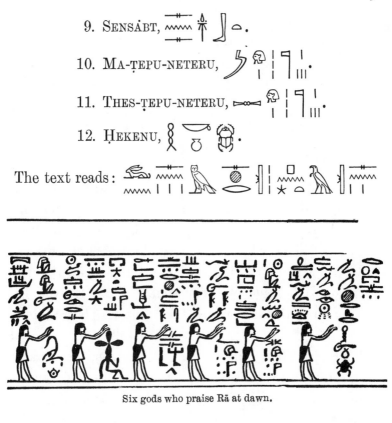

Six gods who praise Rā at dawn.

"Those who are in this picture sing praises unto this "great god from dawn, when he taketh up his position "in the Hall of the east of the sky. They say unto "Rā, 'O thou who art the producer of [thine own] "birth, who dost bring into being [thine own] being, "[lord of] homage of every soul . . . . ., Heaven be- "longeth to thy soul, which taketh up its place therein, "and the earth belongeth to thy body, thou lord of "homage. Thou sailest over the Horizon, thou takest "up thy place in thy shrine, the gods in their bodies "praise thee; descend thou into the sky and take thou "thy two souls through thy magical protectors.' The "work of these gods in the Ṭuat is to praise this great "god, and they stand in this City and they count up "(or, verify) the gods of the country of Māfket (i.e., "Sinai). They descend (?) to earth [before] Rā after "he hath taken up his position in the sky and doth "rise upon the eyes of mankind in their circles."

In the lower register are:—

1. The god Nu, , holding  and  in his left and right hand respectively.

2. The goddess NUT, , holding and .

3. The god ḤEḤU, , holding and .

4. The goddess ḤEḤUT, , holding and .

5. The god ṬEBAI, , man-headed, and holding an oar, or paddle.

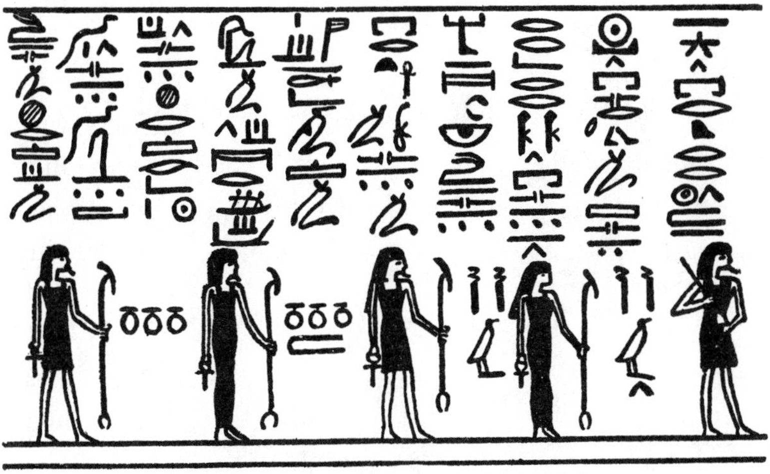

The gods who receive Rā. A god of a paddle.

6. The god QASHEFSHEF, , man-headed and holding a paddle.

7. The god NEHUI, , crocodile-headed, and holding a paddle.

8. The god NI, , with the heads of two birds, and holding a paddle.

9. The deity NESMEKHEF, , in the

form of a serpent, which pours forth fire from its mouth.

10. The god Nebȧ-khu, , man-headed, and holding a paddle.

11. The god Khenti-theth-f, 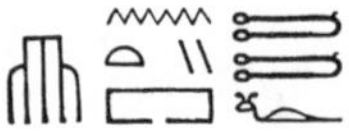, man-headed, and holding a paddle.

12. The god Āḥā-ȧb, , man-headed, and holding a paddle.

13. The god Ṭuati, 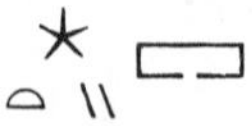, man-headed, and holding a paddle.

14—23. Ten gods, each with his hands raised in adoration; their names are:—

Ṭes-khu, .

Thema-re, .

Ȧākhebu, .

Sekhennu, .

Ermenu, .

Khennu-ermen, .

Bun-ā, .

Khu-re, .

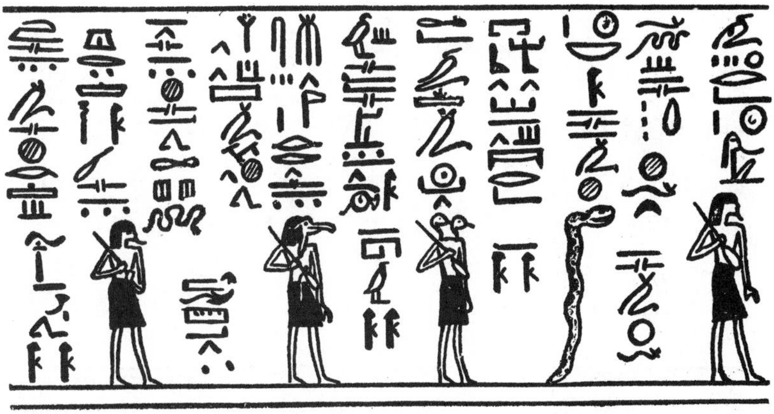

Gods of paddles.

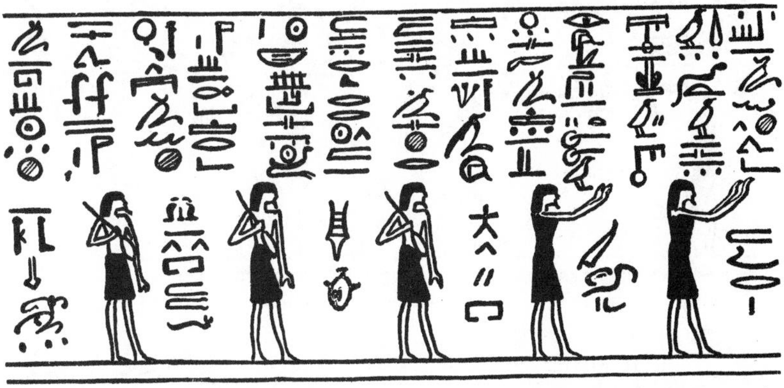

Gods of paddles. Gods who praise Rā at sunrise.

Gods who praise Rā at sunrise.

ȦTHEP, 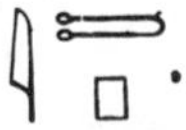.

ȦM-NETER, 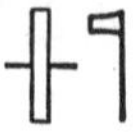.

The texts relating to these gods read:—1. 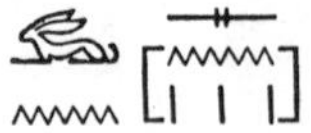

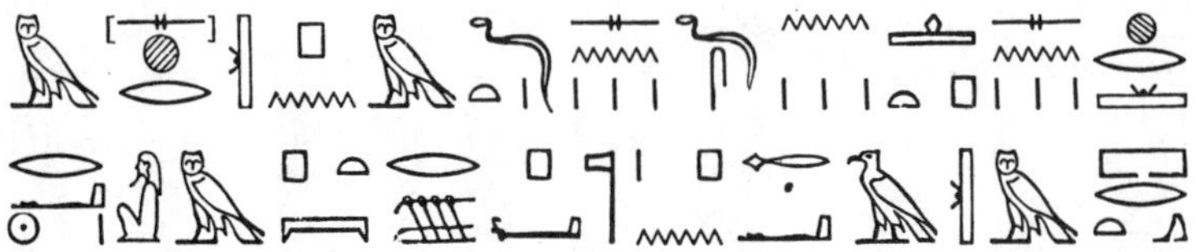

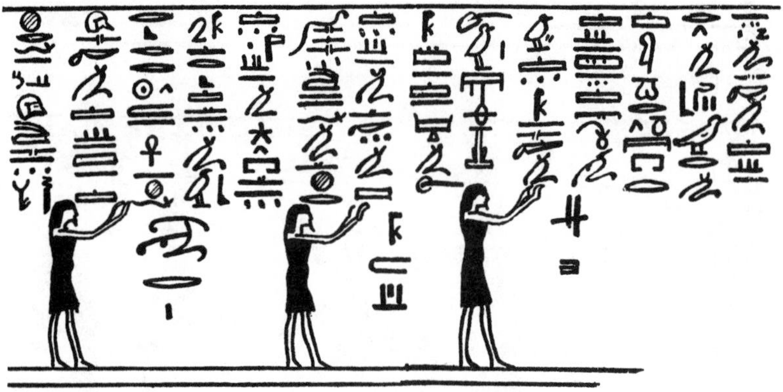

Gods who praise Rā at sunrise.

, "Those "who are in this picture in their own bodies join "themselves unto Rā in the sky to receive this "great god at his coming forth among them in the "east of the sky each day. They themselves belong "to their Halls of the Horizon, but the forms which

they have in the Ṭuat [belong to] this Circle."

2. 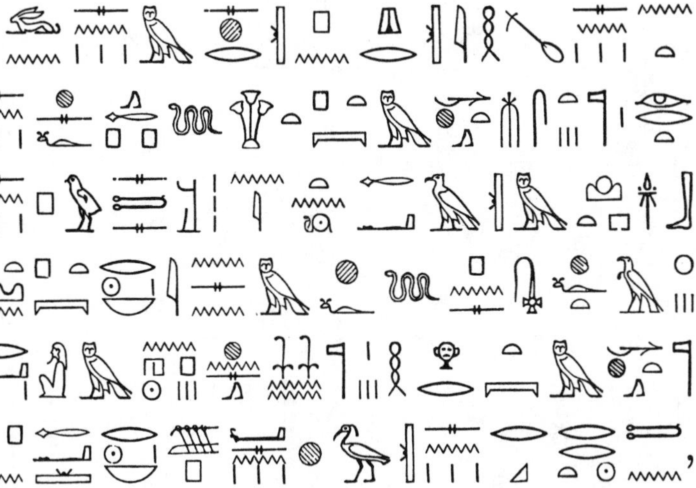

"Those who are in this picture with their paddles drive "Āpep to the back of the sky, after the birth of the god. "Their work is to hold up the Great Disk in the Eastern "Horizon of the sky every day. Behold the serpent "SENMEKHEF which burneth up the enemies of Rā at "the dawn! These gods go round about the heights of "heaven in the following of this great god every day, "and they receive their protection for this Circle."

3. 

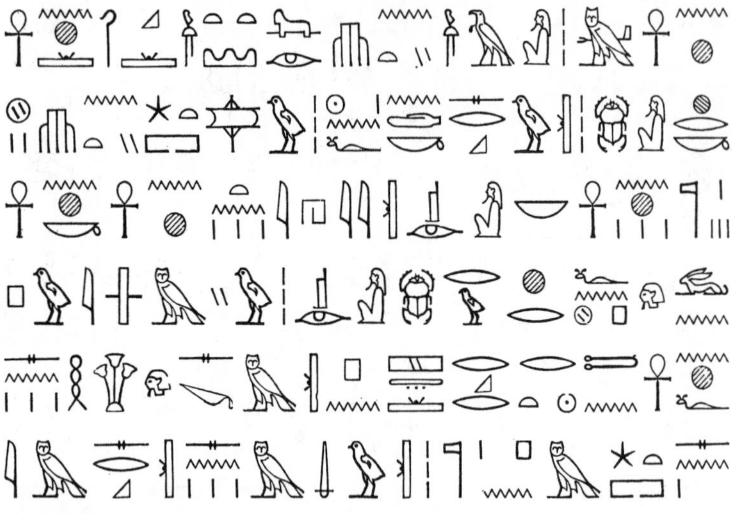

, "Those who are in this picture are behind "the image of Osiris, who is over the thick darkness. "These are the words which this god saith unto them "after this great god hath journeyed by it:—'Life [to "thee], O thou who art over the darkness! Life [to "thee] in all thy majesty! Life [to thee], O governor "of Åmentet, Osiris, who art over the beings of "Åmentet! Life to thee! Life to thee! O thou who "art over the Ṭuat, the winds of Rā are to thy nostrils, "and the nourishment of Kheper is with thee. Thou "livest, and ye live. Hail to Osiris, the lord of the "living, that is to say, of the gods who are with Osiris, "and who came into being with him the first time.' "Those who are behind this hidden Image in this "Circle wherein he liveth have their nourishment "from the words of this god in their own Ṭuat."

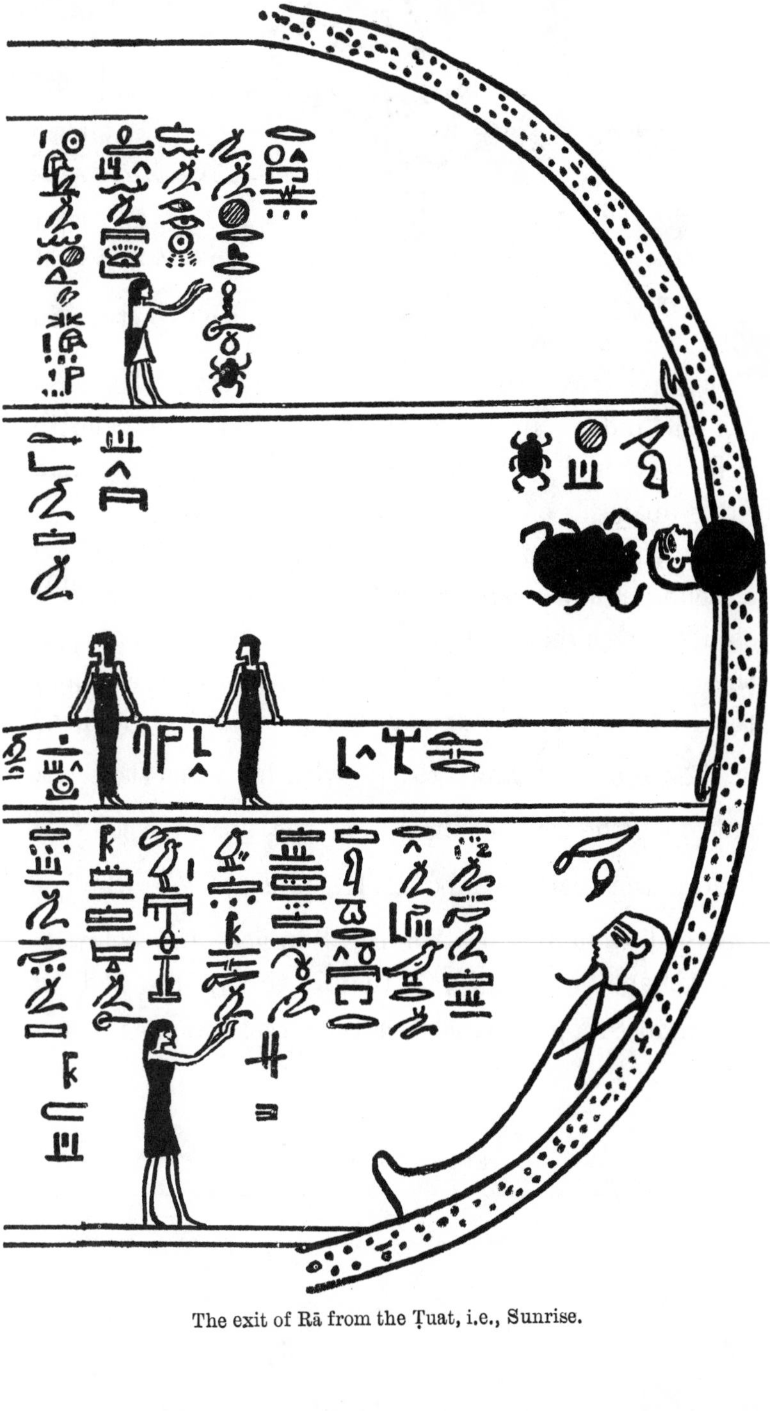

The exit of Rā from the Ṭuat, i.e., Sunrise.

4. 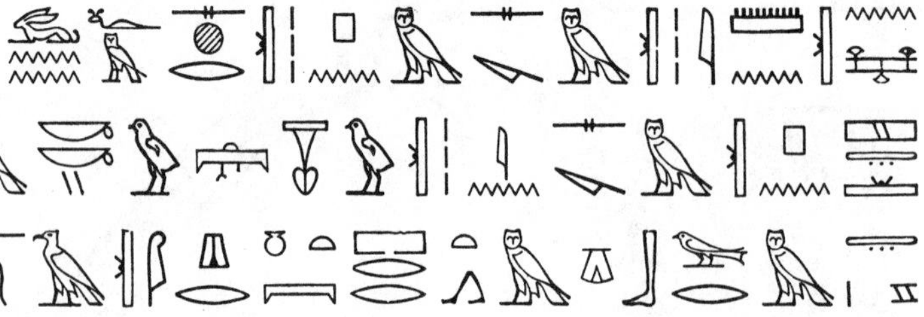

, "He who is in this picture in "the invisible form of Horus in the thick darkness, "is the hidden image which Shu lifteth up beneath "the sky, and ḲEB-UR cometh forth in the earth in "this image."

24. The end of the Ṭuat, which is represented by a semi-circular wall or border formed of earth and stones, or perhaps granite. At the middle point of this border is the disk of the sun which is about to rise on this world, and joined to it is the head of the "image of Shu," , with his arms stretched out along the rounded border of the Ṭuat. Above his head is the beetle, symbol of Khep[er], , who has emerged from the boat of the Sun-god, and below is the "image of Åf," 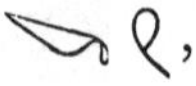, that is to say, the body of the night Sun-god, which has been cast away.

END OF VOL. I.

The Egyptian Heaven and Hell

VOLUME II

THE SHORT FORM OF THE BOOK ÀM-ṬUAT AND THE BOOK OF GATES

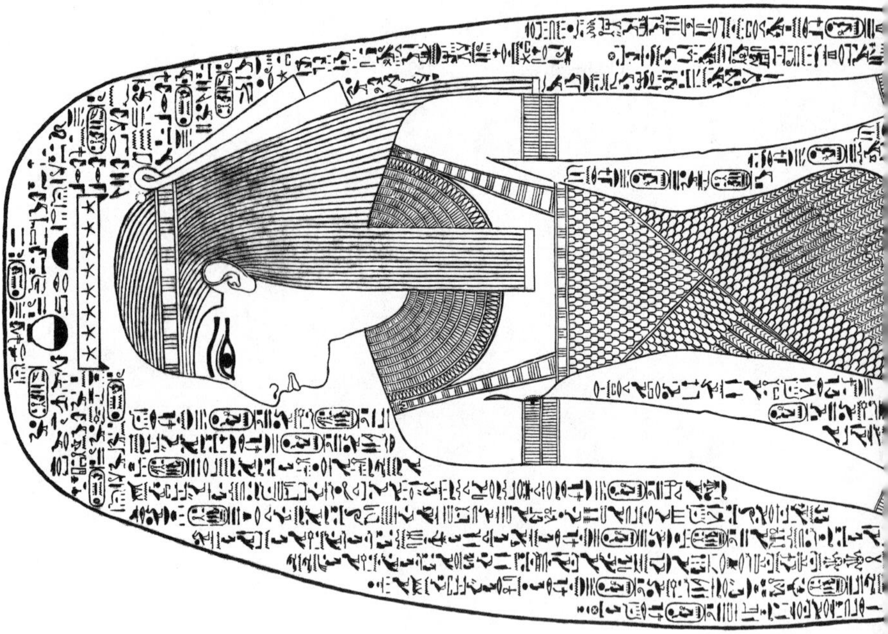

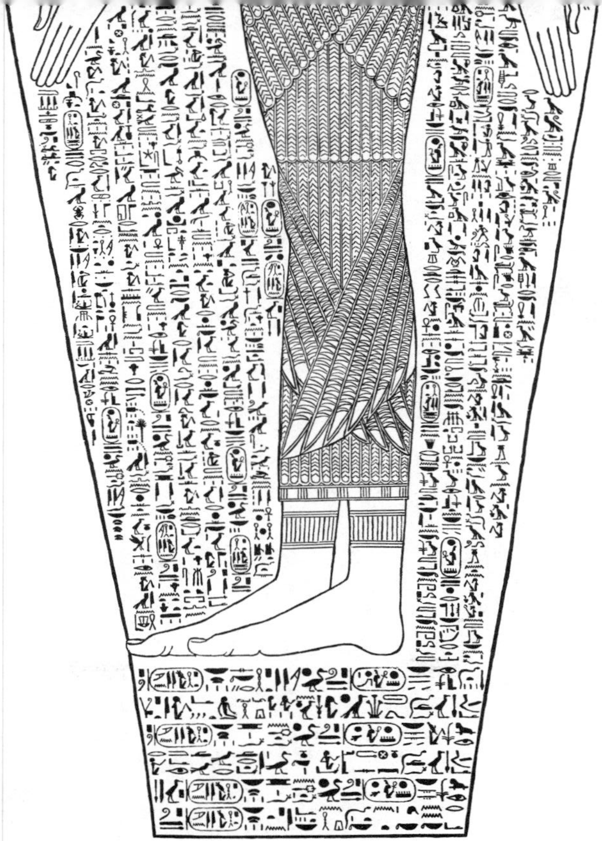

THE GODDESS NUT. (*From the Sarcophagus of Seti I.*)

NOTE

THIS volume is the second of a series of three volumes which treat of the Egyptian Heaven and Hell. It contains the complete hieroglyphic text of the Summary, or short form of the BOOK ÅM-ṬUAT, and the complete hieroglyphic text of the BOOK OF GATES, with translations and reproductions of all the illustrations. A series of Chapters dealing with the origin and contents of Books of the Other World, with prefatory remarks, and a full index to the whole work, will be found in the third volume.

CONTENTS

ERRATA

P. 10, l. 3, for "Then-ṭent-baiu" read "Tent-baiu"; p. 20, l. 10, for "Nebt-mu-ṭuatiu" read "Metchet-mu-nebt-Ṭuatiu"; p. 18, l. 2, for 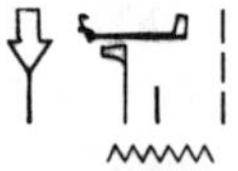 read ; p. 23, l. 3, for  read ; p. 34, l. 1, for  read 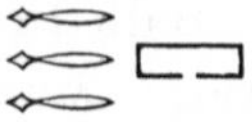; p. 57, l. 3, for "the magical powers" read "her magical powers to those"; p. 113, l. 26, for  read ; p. 115, l. 11, for 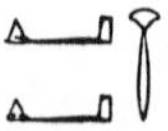 read 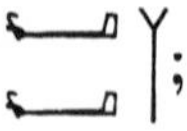; p. 119, l. 3, for "Tchetbi" read "Nebt-tchefau"; p. 147, l. 7. for  read .

THE SHORT FORM

OF THE

BOOK OF ȦM-ṬUAT

THE SUMMARY OF THE BOOK OF WHAT IS IN THE UNDERWORLD.

THE BEGINNING OF THE HORN OF ȦMENTET, [WHICH IS] THE UTTERMOST POINT OF THE DEEPEST DARKNESS.

THE FIRST HOUR.

THIS god entereth into the earth through the Hall of the horizon of Ȧmentet. There are one hundred and twenty ȦTRU to journey over in this Hall before a man arriveth at the gods of the Ṭuat.

The name of the first Field of the Ṭuat is NET-RĀ. He (i.e., Rā) allotteth fields to the gods who are in [his] following, and he beginneth to send forth words to and to work out the plans of the divine beings of the Ṭuat in respect of this Field.

Whosoever shall have these made (i.e., copied)

according to the similitude which is in Àment of the Ṭuat, [and] whosoever shall have knowledge of these similitudes, [which are] the copies of this great god himself, they shall act as magical protectors for him upon earth regularly and unfailingly, and they shall act as magical protectors for him in the Great Ṭuat.

USHEMET-ḤĀTU-KHEFTI-RĀ is the name of the [first] hour of the night which guideth this great god through this Hall.

THE FIRST HOUR.

I.—FROM THE TOMB OF SETI I. (lines 1—22).

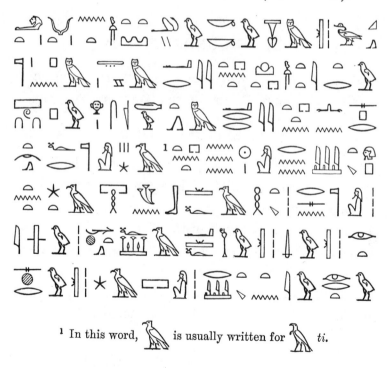

[1] In this word,  is usually written for  *ti.*

THE FIRST HOUR.

II.—From the Leyden Papyrus, T. 71.

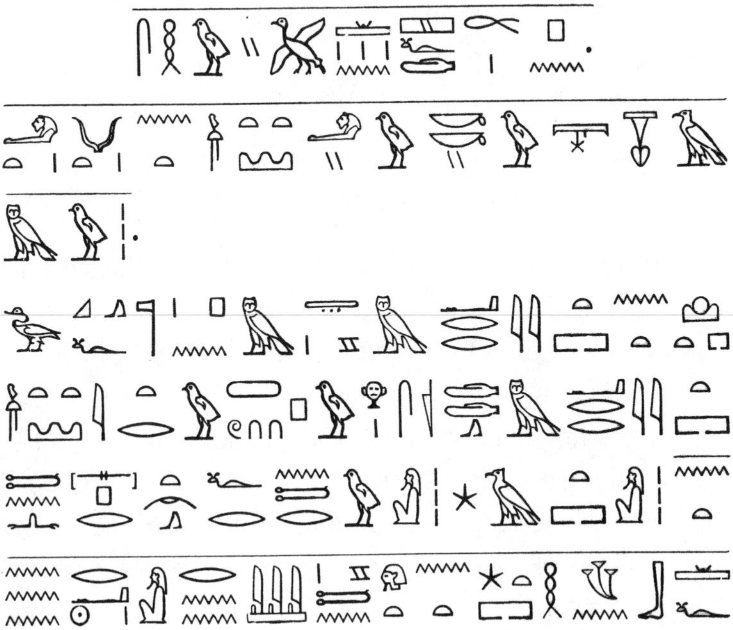

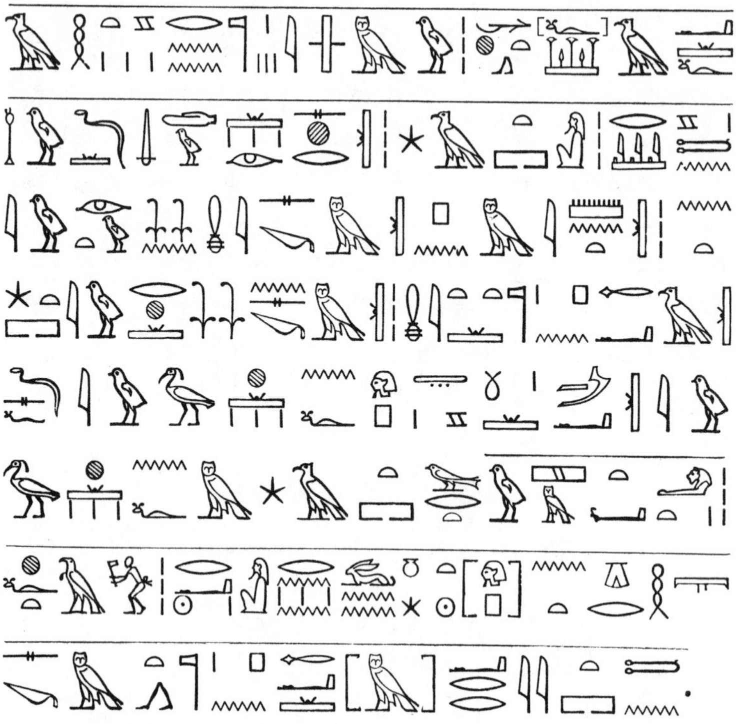

THE SECOND HOUR.

This great god afterwards taketh up his position in UR-NEST, which is three hundred and nine ȦTRU in length, and one hundred and twenty ȦTRU in width.

The name of the gods who are in this Field is BAIU-ṬUATI. Whosoever knoweth their names shall have his existence with them, and unto him shall this great god allot fields in the place wherein they are in the FIELD OF URNES. He shall stand up with the Gods who Stand Up (ĀḤĀU), he shall travel on in the following of this great god, he shall enter into the earth, he shall force a way through the Ṭuat, he shall cleave a passage through the tresses of the gods with flowing hair (Ḥenksu), he shall travel on by the Eater of the Ass (Ām-āa) after the emptying of the lands, he shall eat bread-cakes in the Boat of the Earth, and there shall be given unto him the fore-part of Tatubȧ.

Whosoever shall have made in writing (or, in drawing) similitudes of the Baiu-Ṭuati (i.e., the Souls of the Ṭuat) in the forms in which they are in Ȧment of the Ṭuat—now the beginning of such representations should be from Ȧmentet,—and whosoever shall make offerings unto them upon earth in their names, [these things I say] shall act as magical protectors to that person upon earth, regularly and unfailingly.

And whosoever shall know the words which the gods of the Ṭuat speak to this god, and the words which are said by him to them when he is approaching the gods of the Ṭuat, [these words I say] shall act as magical protectors to him that knoweth them upon earth, regularly and unfailingly.

Shesat-māket-neb-s is the name of the hour of the night which guideth this great god through this Field.

THE SECOND HOUR.

I.—From the Tomb of Seti I. (lines 23—61).

THE SECOND HOUR.

II.—From the Leyden Papyrus, T. 71.

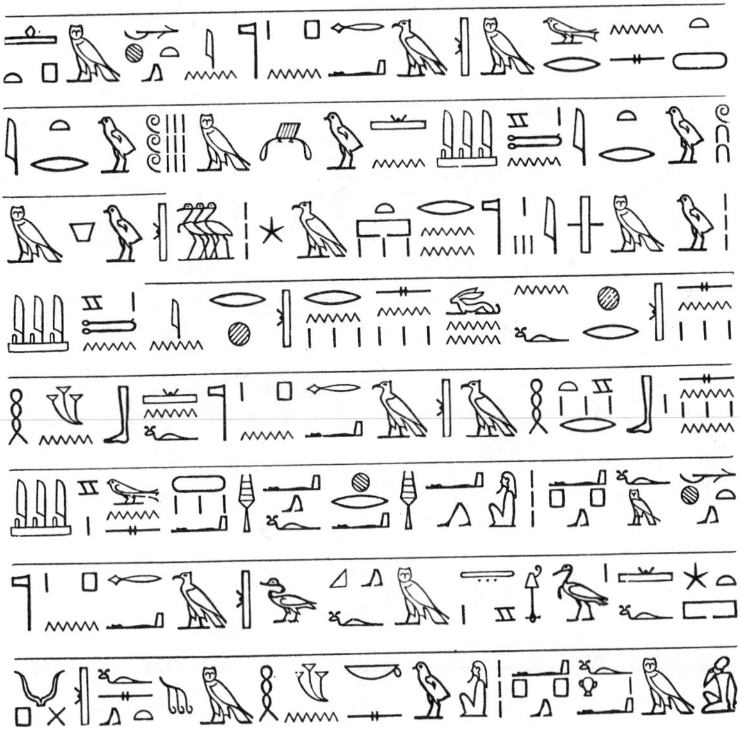

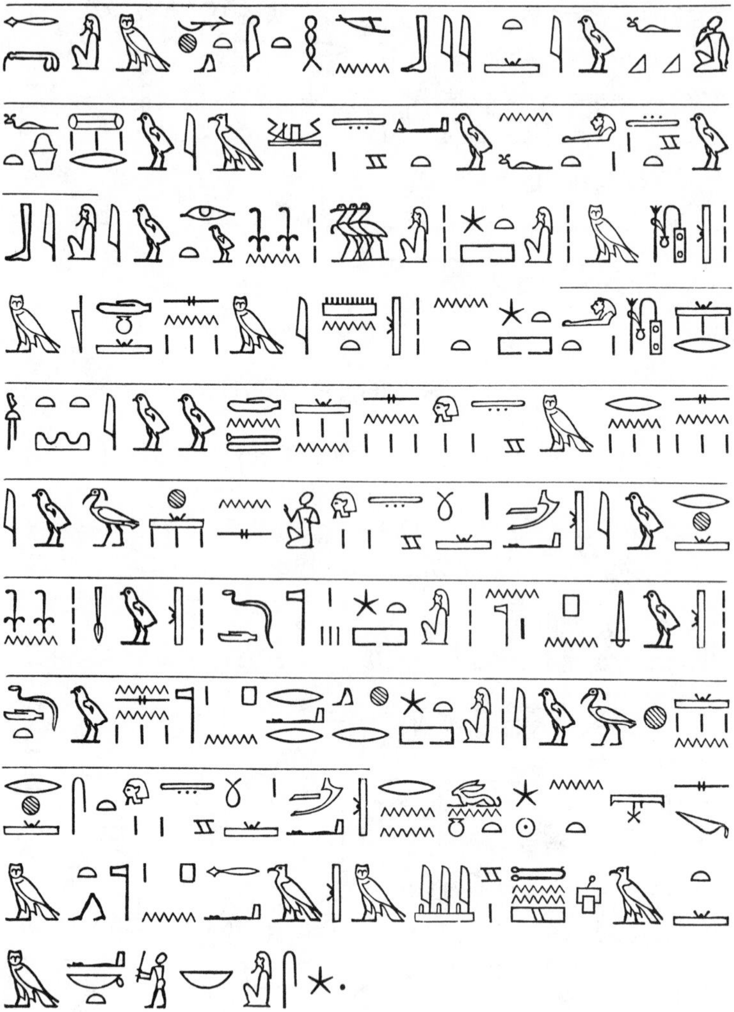

THE THIRD HOUR.

This great god afterwards taketh up his position in the Fields of the PERU-gods (i.e., the Fighters), and this great god paddleth his way over the STREAM OF OSIRIS (NET-ÅSÅR) in sailing up this Field, which is three hundred and nine ÅTRU long, and one hundred and twenty ÅTRU wide. This great god uttereth words to those who are in the following of Osiris to this City, and he allotteth unto them estates which are situated in this Field.

BAIU-SHETAIU (i.e., Hidden Souls) is the name of the gods who are in this Field, and whosoever knoweth their names upon earth shall be able to approach to the place where Osiris is, and there shall be given unto him water for his Field.

NET-NEB-UA-KHEPER-ÅUĀTU is the name of this Field. Whosoever shall know these hidden similitudes of the Hidden Souls in the correct forms wherein they are depicted in Åment of the Ṭuat—now the beginning of such representations should be from Åmentet—[these figures I say] shall act as magical protectors to that man upon earth, [and] in Neter-khert, regularly and unfailingly.

Whosoever knoweth these, when he is making his journey past them shall escape from their roarings, and he shall not fall down into their furnaces (or, pits).

Whosoever knoweth this, when he is keeping ward over [his] seat (or, place), his bread-cake shall be with Rā; and whosoever knoweth this, being soul [and] spirit, shall have the mastery over his legs, and shall never enter into the place of destruction, but he shall come forth with his attributes (or, forms), and shall snuff the air for his hour.

THENṬENT-BAIU is the name of the hour of the night which guideth this great god through this Field.

THE THIRD HOUR.

I.—FROM THE TOMB OF SETI I. (lines 62—105).

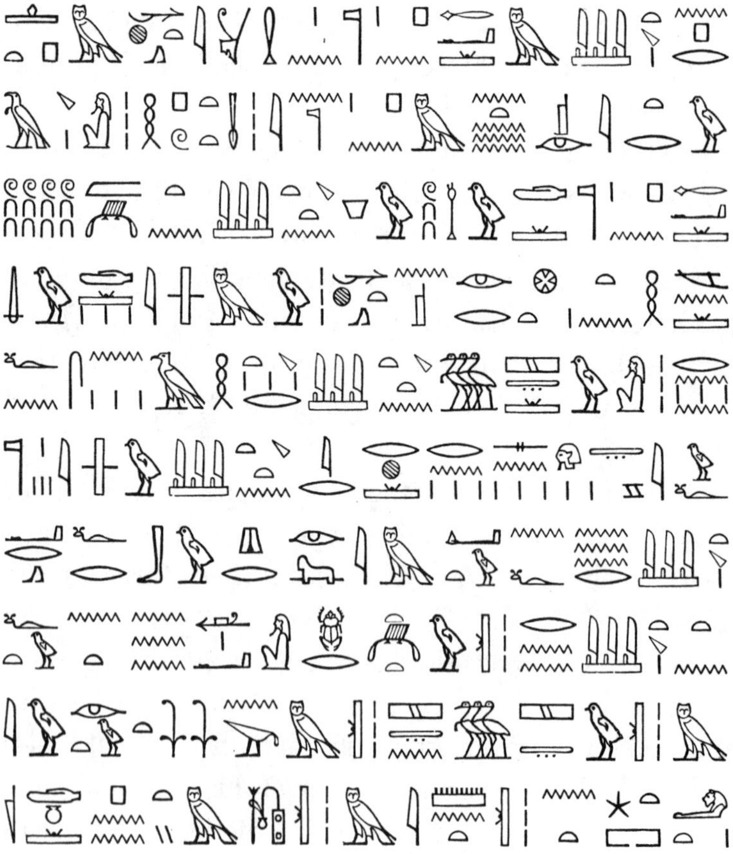

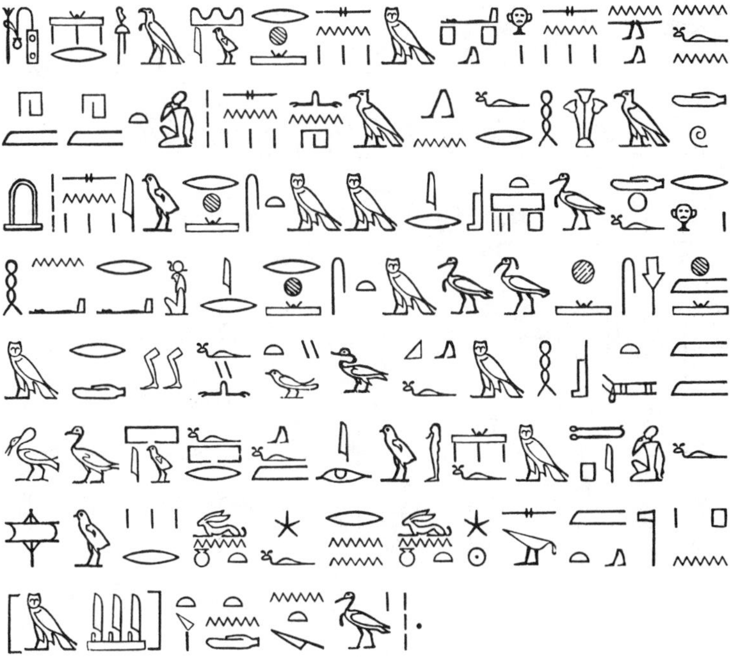

THE THIRD HOUR.

II.—From the Leyden Papyrus, T. 71.

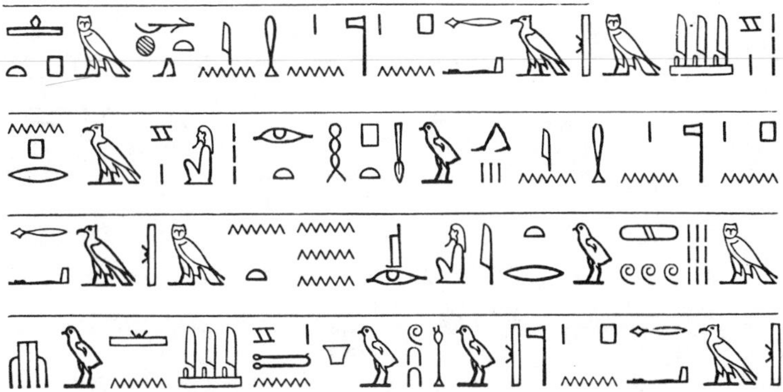

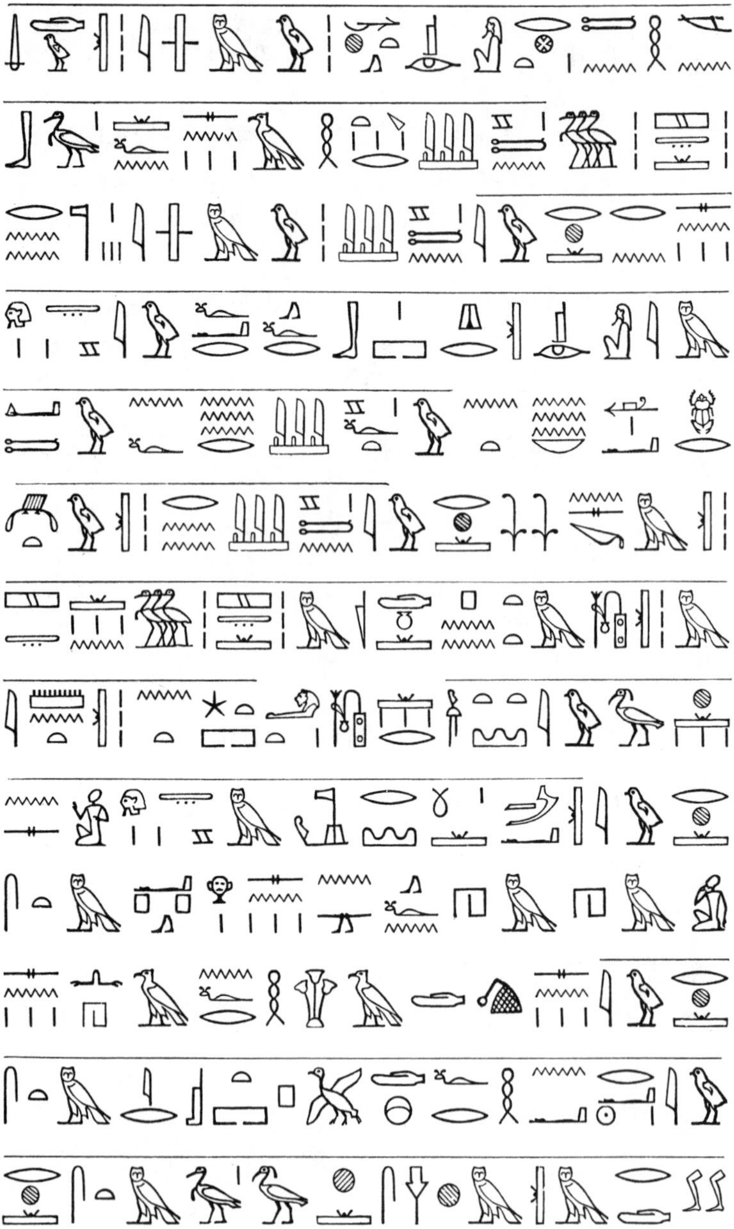

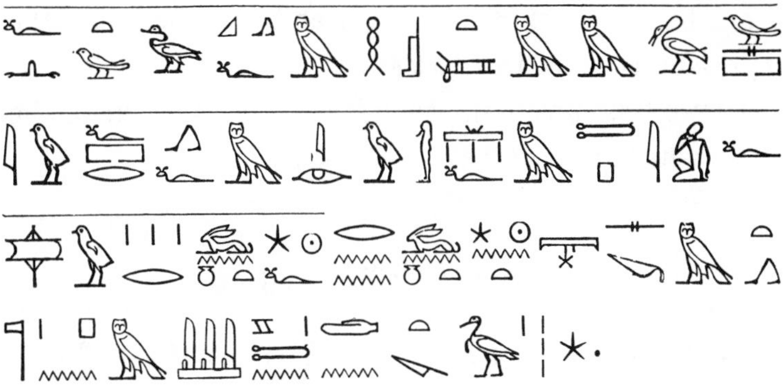

THE FOURTH HOUR.

The majesty of this great god, having been towed along, afterwards taketh up his position in the secret Circle of Ȧmentet, and he performeth the affairs of the gods of the Ṭuat who are therein by means of his voice, but he seeth them not.

Ānkh-kheperu is the name of the gate of this Circle.

Ȧment-sethau is the name of this Circle.

Whosoever knoweth this representation of the hidden roads of Re-statet, and the holy paths of the Ȧmmeḥet, and the secret doors which are in the Land of Seker, the god who is upon his sand, shall be in the condition of him that eateth the bread-cakes which are [made] for the mouth of the Living gods in the Temple of Tem.

Whosoever knoweth this shall be in the condition of him that is *maāt* on the ways, and he shall journey over the roads of RE-SETHAU, and he shall see the representations of the ȦMMEḤET.

URT-EM-SEKHEMU-SET is the name of the hour of the night which guideth this great god.

THE FOURTH HOUR.

I.—FROM THE TOMB OF SETI I. (lines 106—138).

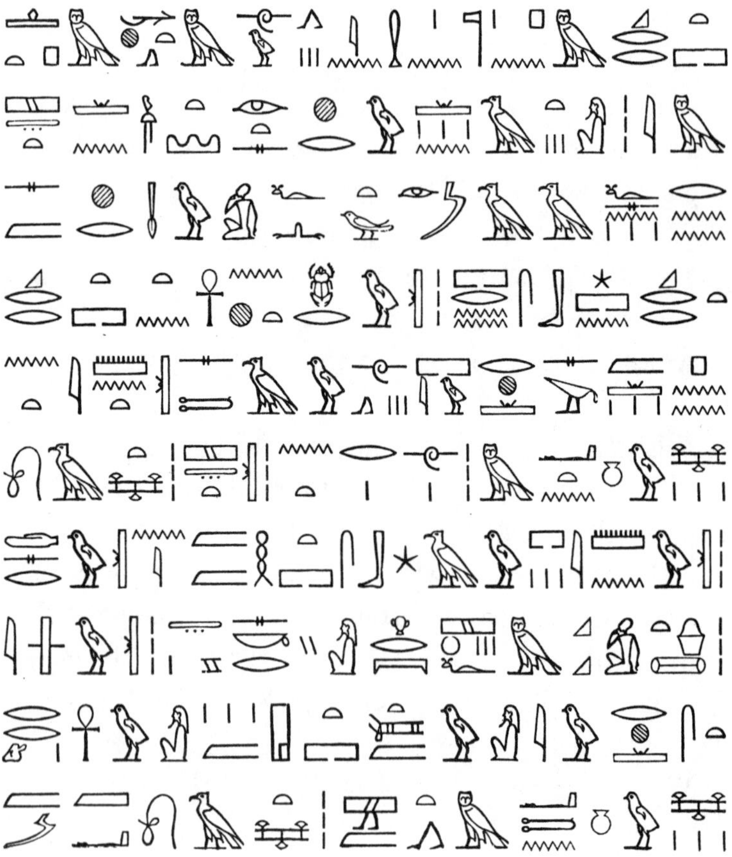

THE FOURTH HOUR.

II.—From the Leyden Papyrus, T. 71.

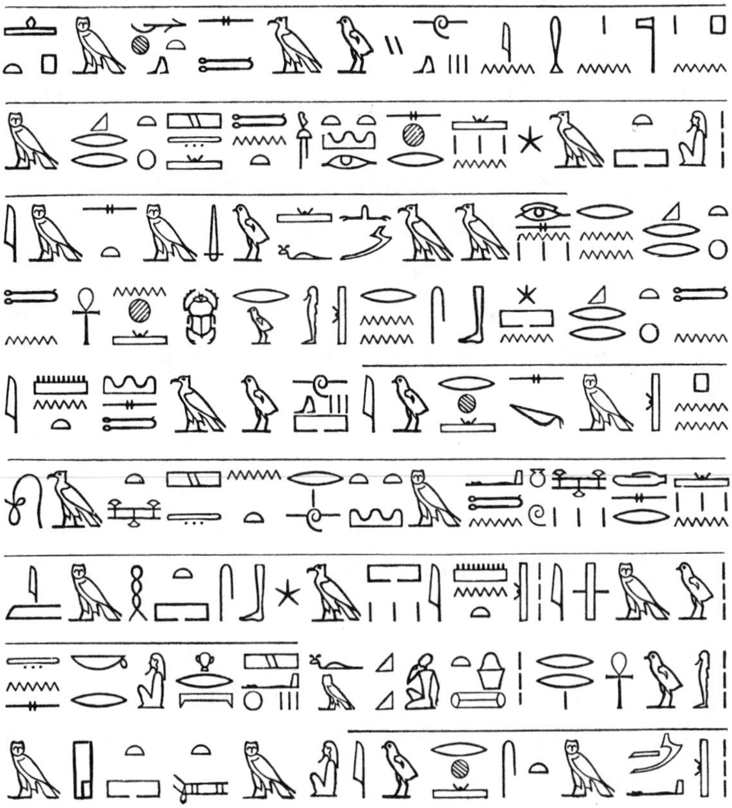

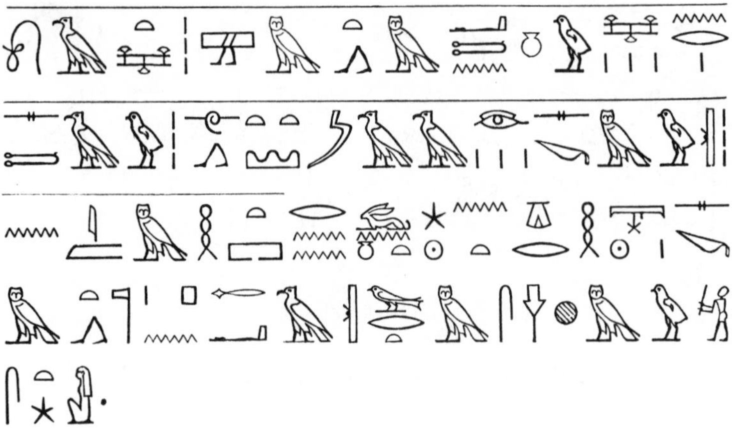

THE FIFTH HOUR.

This great god is towed along over the ways of Maāt of the Ṭuat through the upper half of this secret Circle of the god SEKER, who is upon his sand, and he neither looketh upon nor gazeth at the secret figure of the earth which containeth the flesh of this god. The gods who are in [the train of] this god hear the words of Rā, who crieth unto them from where this god is.

ĀḤĀ-NETERU is the name of the door [of this City].

ȦMENT is the name of the Circle of this god, [and in it are] the secret path of Ȧmentet, and the doors of the hidden palace, and the holy place of the LAND OF SEKER [with his] flesh, and [his] members, [and his] body, in the divine form which they had at first.

BAIU-ȦMU-ṬUAT is the name of the gods who are in [this] Circle. Their forms (*ȧru*) who are in their hour, and their secret shapes (*kheperu*) neither know, nor look upon, nor see this image (or, similitude) of Seker (or, the hawk) himself.

Whosoever shall make these representations according to the image which is in writing in the hidden places of the Ṭuat, at the south of the Hidden Palace, and whosoever shall know them shall be at peace, and his soul shall unite itself to the offerings of Seker, and the goddess Khemit shall not hack his body in pieces, and he shall go on his way towards her in peace. Whosoever shall make offerings to these gods upon earth—[these offerings, I say, shall act as magical protectors to that man upon earth, and in Neter-khert, regularly and unfailingly].

Sem-ḥer-àb-uàa-s is the name of the hour of the night which guideth this great god through this Field.

THE FIFTH HOUR.

I.—From the Tomb of Seti I. (lines 139—173).

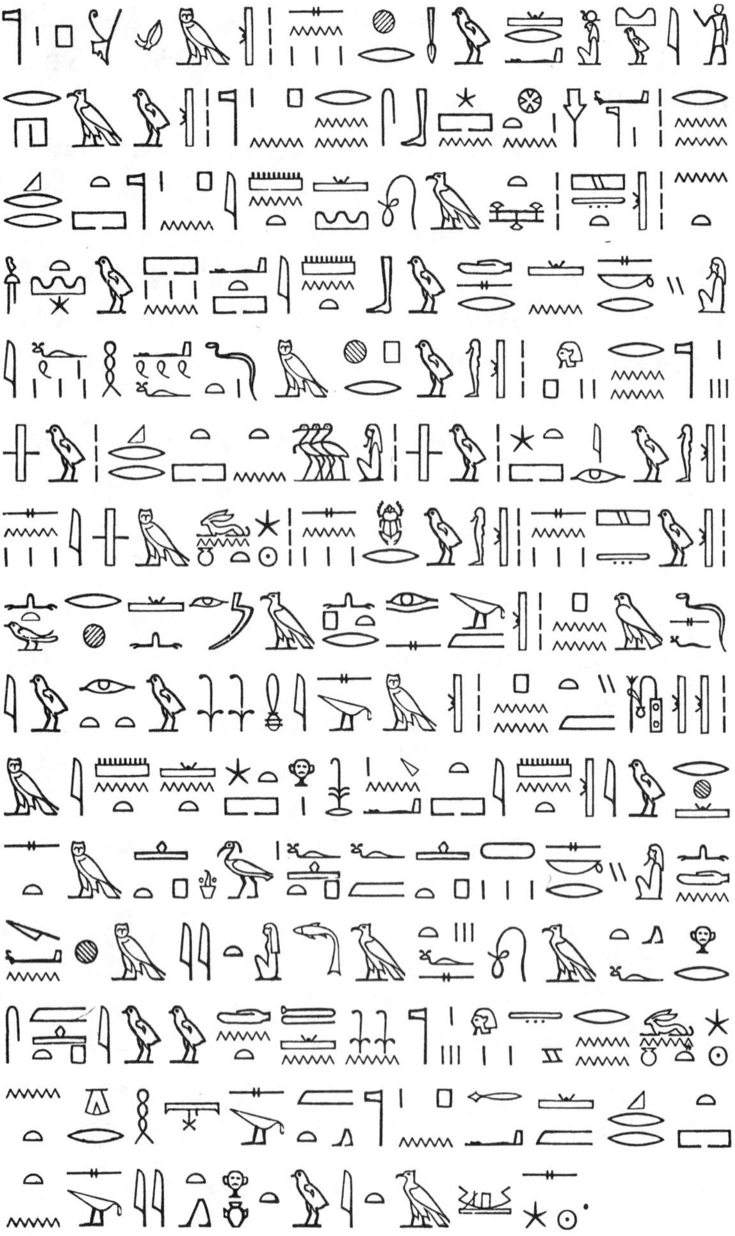

THE FIFTH HOUR.

II.—From the Leyden Papyrus, T. 71.

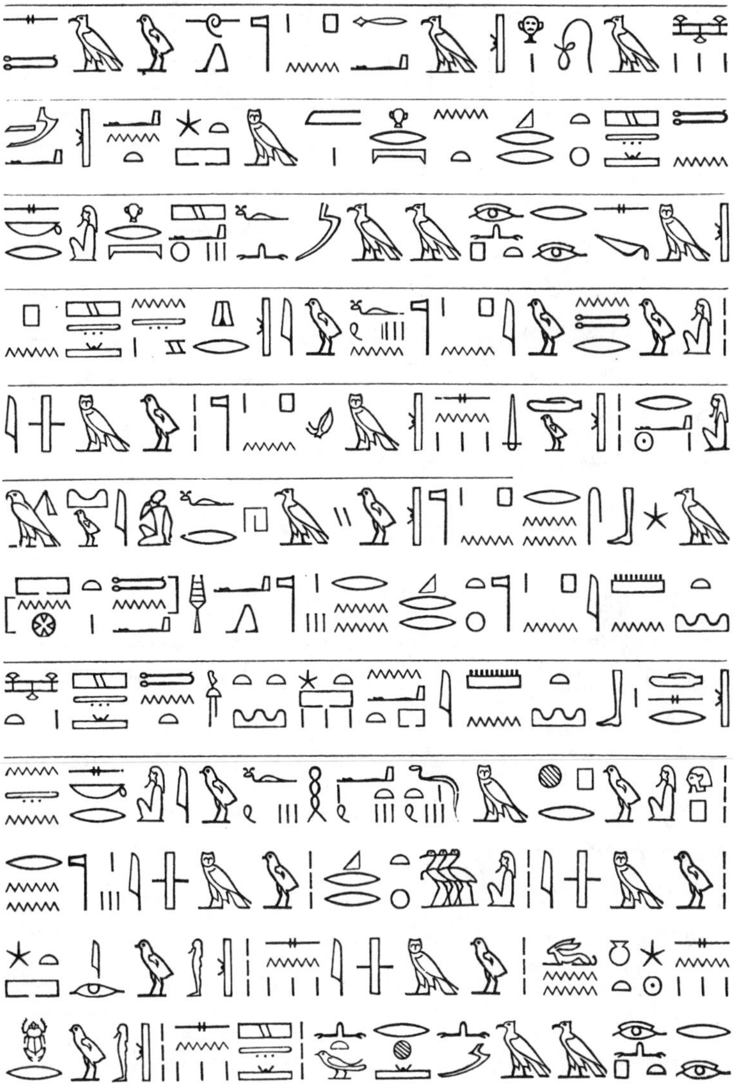

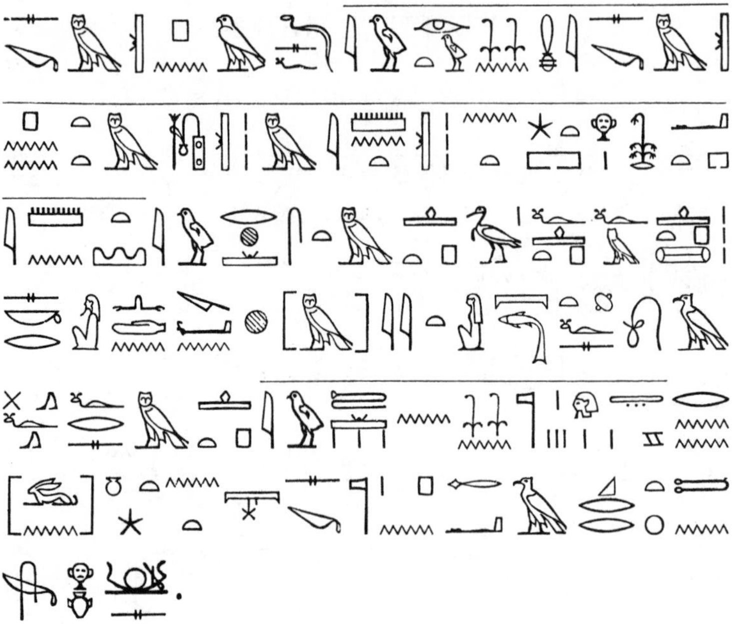

THE SIXTH HOUR.

The majesty of this great god taketh up his position in the stream of NEBT-MU-ṬUATIU (i.e., the Lord of the waters of the gods of the Ṭuat), and he sendeth forth words to the gods who are therein, and he commandeth that they have the mastery over their divine offerings in this City. He maketh his way through this Field, being provided with his Boat, and he setteth apart by his words the estates which are [to produce] their offerings in this City, and he giveth to them water for their lakes, and he travelleth through the Ṭuat every day.

SEPṬ-METU is the name of the door of this City.

The secret roads of Åmentet, and the manner wherein this great god is being rowed along over the water therein in his boat to perform the plans (or, affairs) of the gods of the Ṭuat, the gathering together [of them] by their names, the manifestations of their shapes (or, forms), and [their] secret hours, such are the things of which the secret representation of the Ṭuat is not known to men and women.

Whosoever shall make [a copy of] this image in writing, according to the representation of the same which is in the hidden things of the Ṭuat, at the south of the Hidden Palace, and whosoever shall know them shall be in the condition of one who awardeth offerings in abundance in the Ṭuat, and he shall be united to the offerings of the gods who are in the following of Osiris, and his parents (or, kinsfolk) shall make the offerings which are obligatory on the earth.

The majesty of this great god sendeth forth words, and he giveth divine offerings to [the gods of] the Ṭuat, and he standeth up by them; and they see him, and they have dominion over their Fields and over the gifts made to them, and they effect their transformations by reason of the words which this great god hath spoken unto them.

METCHET-NEBT-ṬUATIU is the name of this Field, which is the road of the Boat of Rā.

MESPERIT-ÅR-MAĀT is the name of the hour of the night which guideth this great god through this country.

THE SIXTH HOUR.

I.—From the Tomb of Seti I. (lines 174—210).

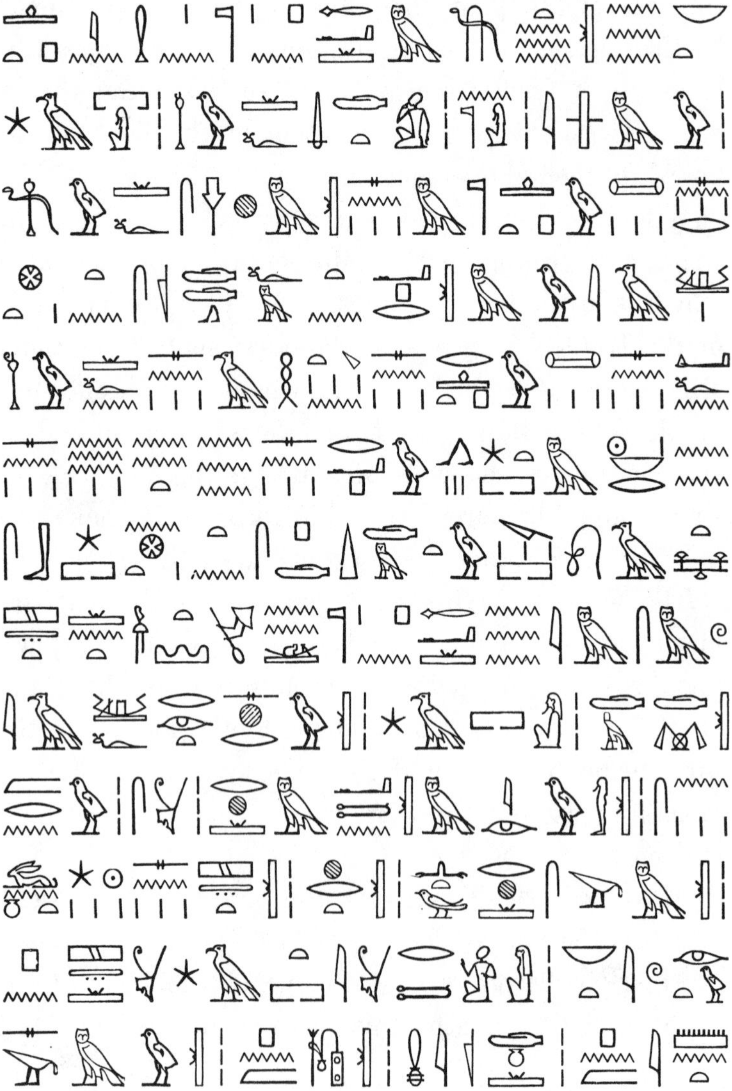

THE SIXTH HOUR.

II.—From the Leyden Papyrus, T. 71.

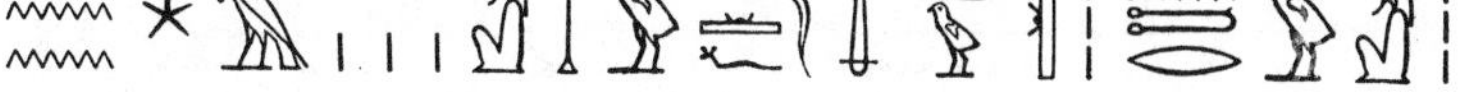

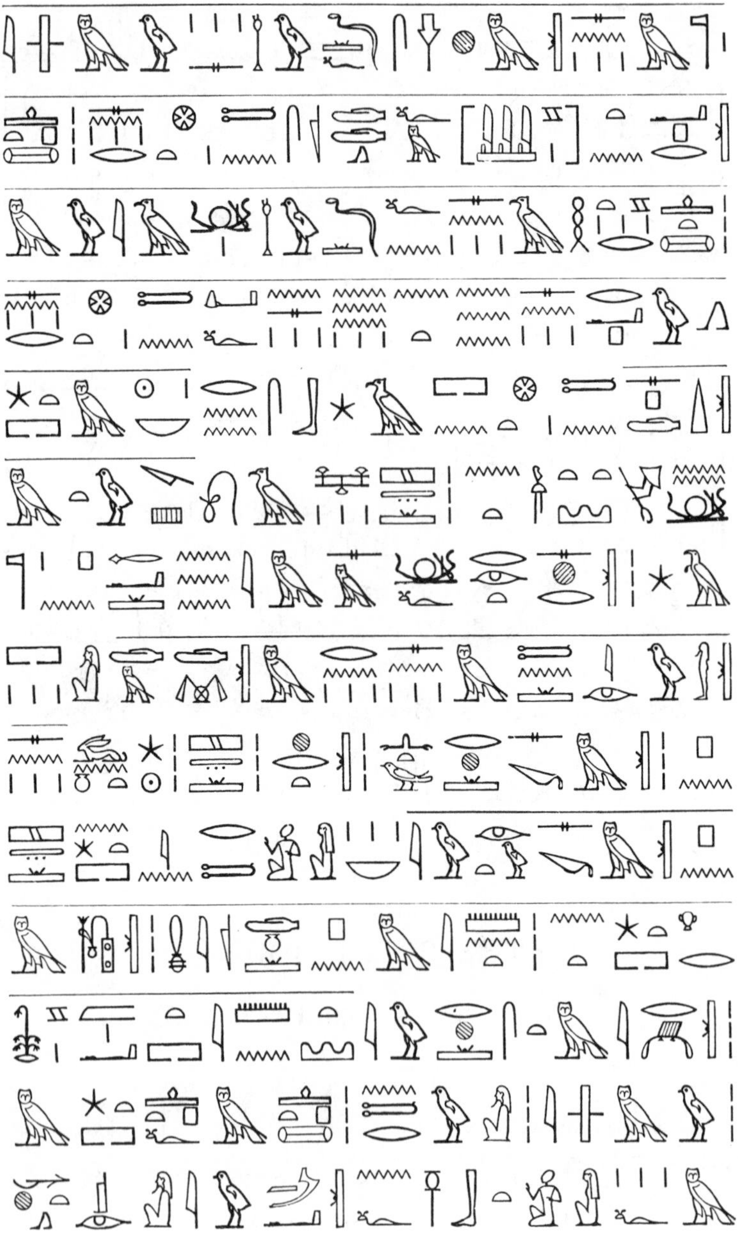

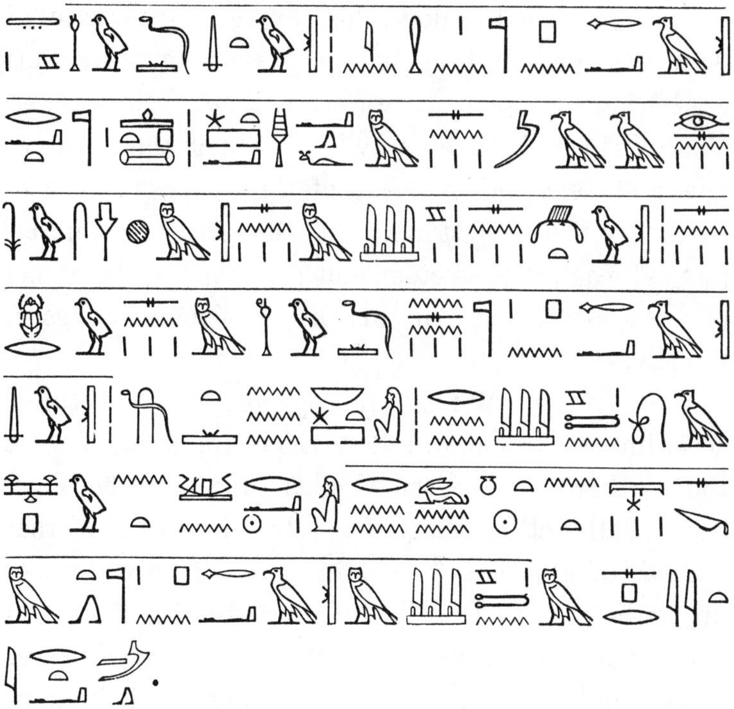

THE SEVENTH HOUR.

The majesty of this great god taketh up his position in the secret place of Osiris, and the majesty of this great god sendeth forth words into this to the gods who dwell therein. This god maketh to himself other forms for this hidden place in order to drive out of his path the serpent fiend ĀPEP by means of the words of power of ISIS, and the words of power of SEMSU (?).

RUTI-ÅSÅR is the name of the gate of this City through which this god passeth.

TEPḤET-SHETA is the name of this City.

This great god maketh his way over the road of Ȧment in the holy boat, and he passeth in it over this road which is without water, without being towed along. He maketh his way by means of the words of power of ISIS, and by means of the words of power of SEMSU (?), and the utterances of this great god himself [act as] magical protectors, and perform the slaughters of Āpep in the Ṭuat, in this Circle, in his windings in the sky.

Whosoever shall make [a copy of] these [pictures] according to the similitudes which are in writing at the northern side of the Hidden Palace in the Ṭuat, they shall act as magical protectors for him that maketh them in heaven and in earth. And whosoever knoweth them shall be a soul of souls with Rā. And whosoever shall make (i.e., recite) the words of power of ISIS and the words of power of SEMSU, shall make to be driven back the Āpep of Rā in Ȧmentet. Whosoever shall do [this] in the Hidden Palace of the Ṭuat, and whosoever shall do [this] upon earth, [the result is] the same. Whosoever knoweth this shall be in the Boat of Rā, both in heaven and upon earth; but he that hath no knowledge of this representation shall not know how to drive back NEḤA-ḤRȦ (i.e., Stinking-Face).

Now the ridge of earth of NEḤA-ḤRȦ in the Ṭuat is four hundred and fifty cubits in length, and he filleth it with the undulations of his body. The regions which belong to him are made (i.e., kept) for him, and the great god doth not make his way over him when he maketh him to turn aside out of the way for him, from the secret place of Osiris, when this god maketh his way through this city in the form of the serpent Meḥen.

Whosoever shall know this upon earth, the serpent Neḥa-ḥrȧ shall not drink his water, and the soul of him that knoweth it shall not be evilly entreated by the gods who are in this Circle; and whosoever knoweth it the crocodile Āb-shau shall not devour his soul.

Khesef-hai-ḥeseq-Neḥa-ḥrȧ is the name of the hour of the night which guideth this great god through this Circle.

THE SEVENTH HOUR.

I.—From the Tomb of Seti I. (lines 210—213).

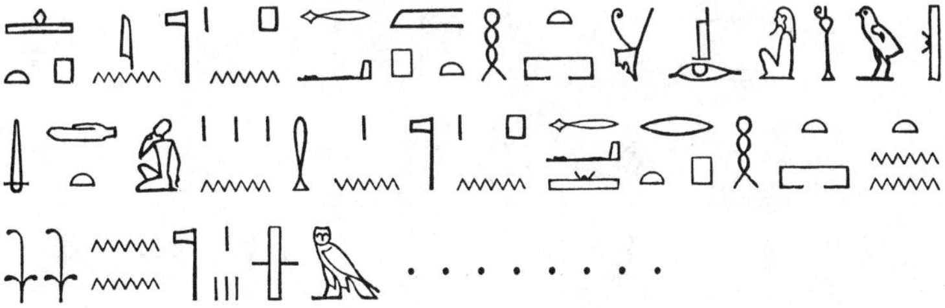

THE SEVENTH HOUR.

II.—From the Leyden Papyrus, T. 71.

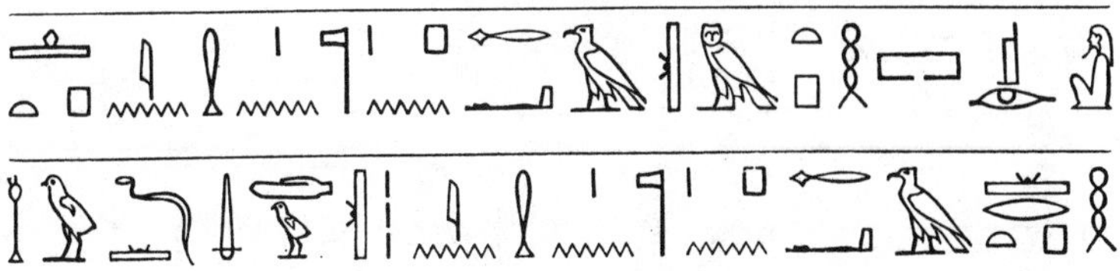

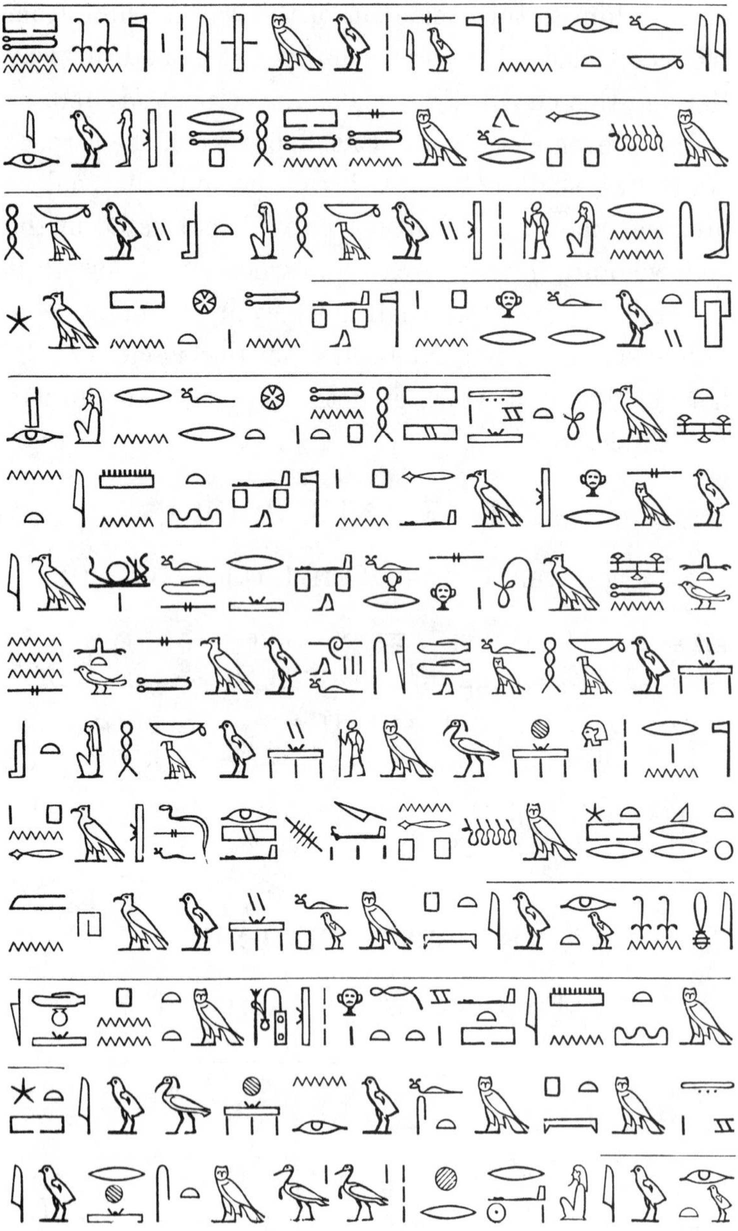

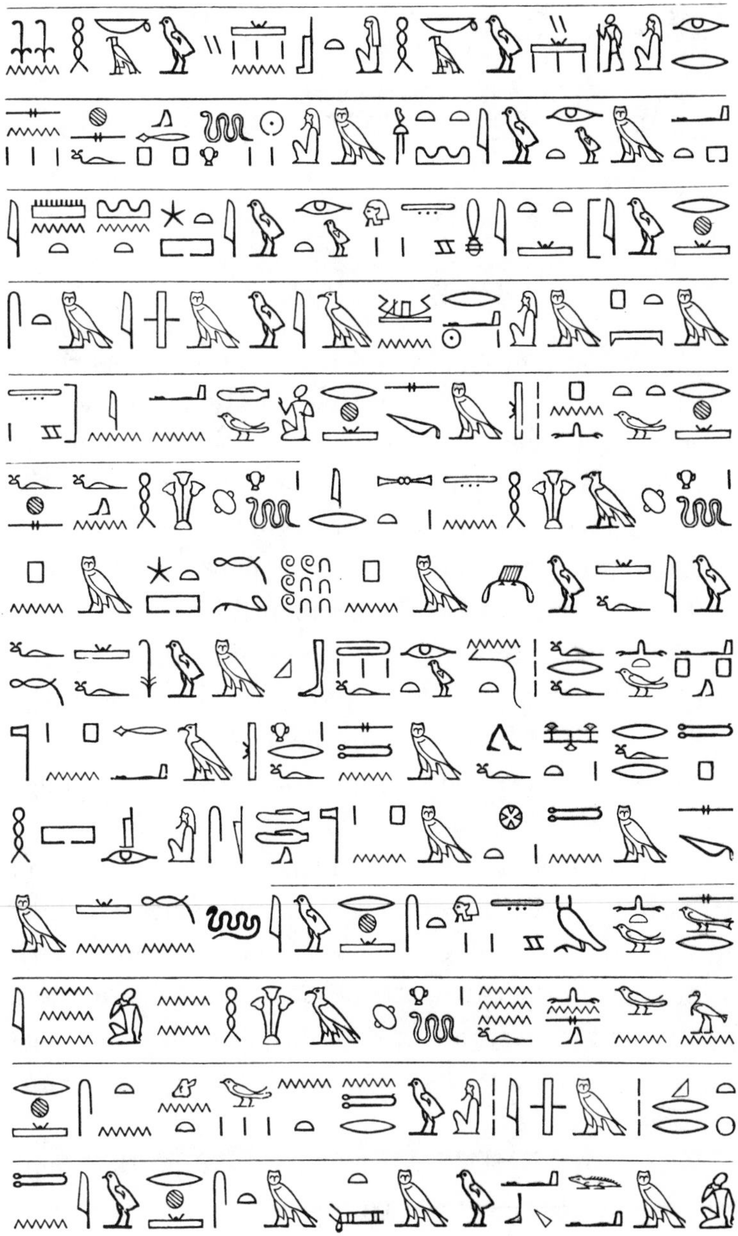

THE EIGHTH HOUR.

When the majesty of this great god hath taken up his position in the secret Circles of those who are in their sand, he sendeth forth words to them from out of his Boat, and the gods tow along him that is in the holy embrace (?) of the serpent MEḤEN.

ĀḤĀ-ȦN-URṬ-F is the name of the gate of this City.

ṬEBAT-NETERU-SET is the name of this City.

As for the secret Circle of ȦMENTET, this great god maketh his way over it in his Boat, by means of the towing of the gods who are in the Ṭuat.

Whosoever shall make [a copy of] these things according to the similitude which is in writing on the north [wall] of the Hidden Palace in the Ṭuat, and whosoever shall know them by their names, shall be in the condition of one who is fully provided with swathings on the earth, and he shall never be repulsed at the secret gates, and he shall have abundant offerings in the great funeral hall regularly and unfailingly for millions of years.

NEBT-USHA is the name of the hour of the night which guideth this great god.

THE EIGHTH HOUR.

From the Leyden Papyrus, T. 71.

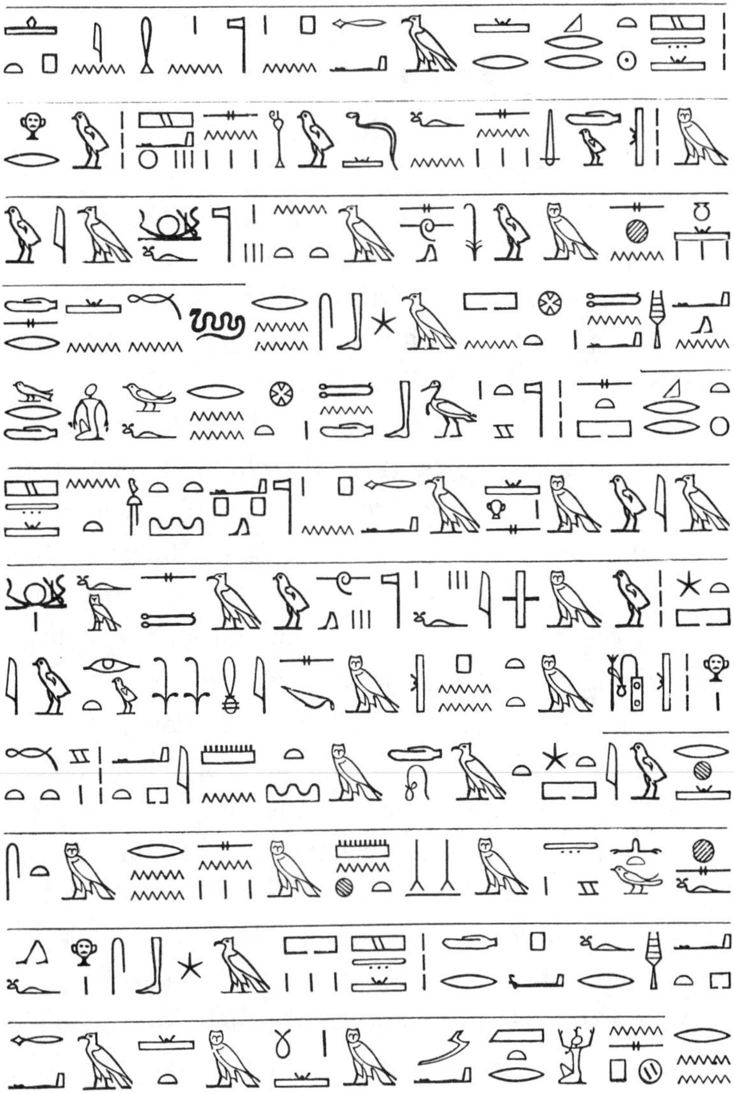

THE NINTH HOUR.

When the majesty of this great god hath taken up his position in this Circle, he sendeth forth words from his Boat to the gods who dwell therein, and the sailors join the Boat of this great god in this City.

SAA-ḲEB is the name of the gate of this City through which this great god passeth to take up his position on the stream which is in this City.

BES-ÀRU is the name of this City, which is the secret Circle of ÀMENTET, wherein take up their positions in the Ṭuat this great god and his sailors.

Whosoever maketh [a copy of] these things in their names according to the similitudes which are in writing on the east [wall] of the Hidden Palace of the Ṭuat, and whosoever knoweth their names upon earth, and knoweth their habitations in Àmentet, shall rest in his habitation in the Ṭuat, and he shall stand up among the lords of the provisions of the gods, and his voice shall be *maāt* before the *tchatcha* beings on the day of the reckoning of Pharaoh (literally, the thrice great house). And these things shall act as magical protectors to him that knoweth them upon earth.

MĀK-NEB-S is the name of the hour of the night which guideth this great god in this Circle.

THE NINTH HOUR.

FROM THE LEYDEN PAPYRUS, T. 71.

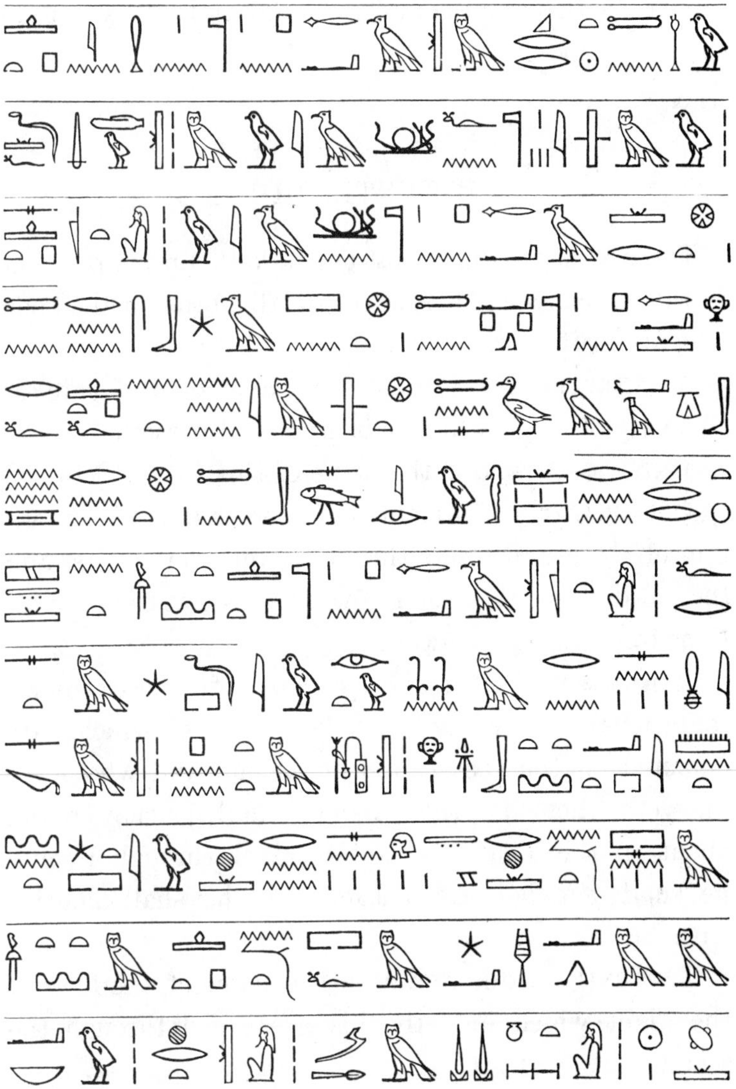

THE TENTH HOUR.

The majesty of this great god taketh up his position in this Circle, and he sendeth forth words to the gods who are in it.

AA-KHEPERU-MES-ȦRU is the name of the gate of this City through which this great god passeth.

METCH-QA-UṬEBU is the name of this City. [This is] the secret Circle of Ȧmentet whereto KHEPERȦ joineth himself before Rā, and the gods, and the spirits, and the dead cry out from it over the secret representations (or, images) of ȦḲERT.

Whosoever shall make [a copy of] these [representations] according to the figures which are depicted on the east [wall] of Ȧment, and whosoever knoweth them by their names shall journey round about in the Ṭuat, and shall travel through it, and he shall not be driven back, and he shall flourish with Rā.

ṬENṬENIT-ḤESQ-KHAKȦBU is the name of the hour of the night which guideth this great god through the secret ways of this City.

THE TENTH HOUR.

FROM THE LEYDEN PAPYRUS, T. 71.

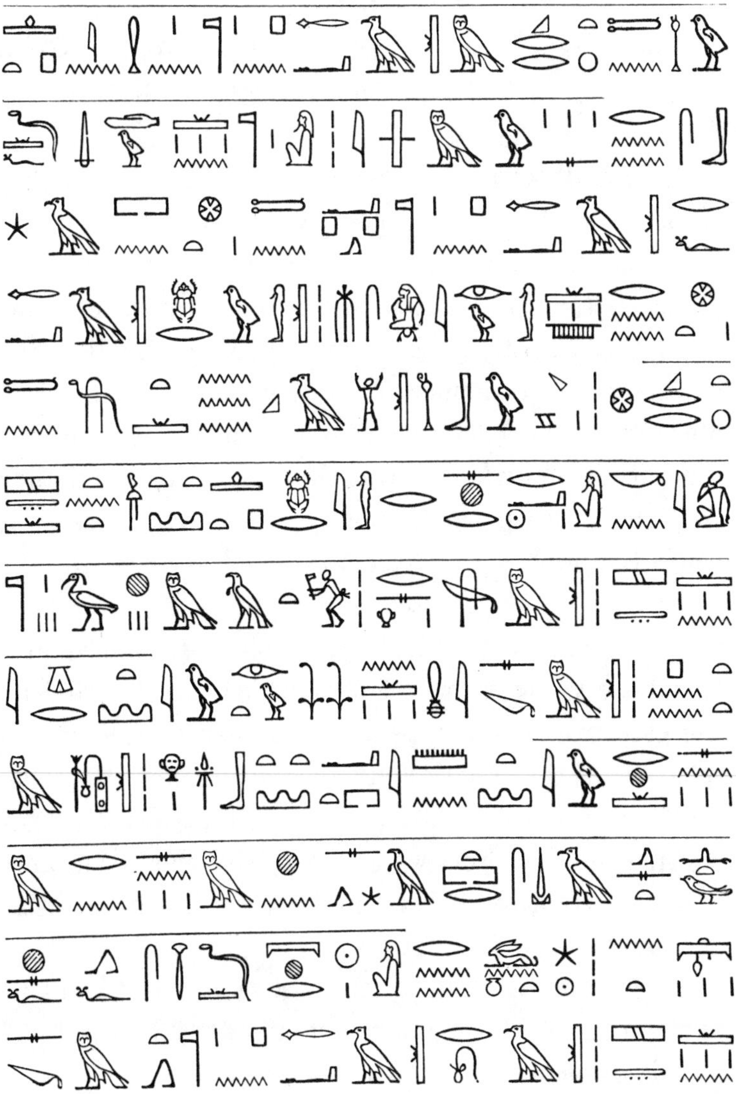

THE ELEVENTH HOUR.

The majesty of this great god taketh up his position in this Circle, and he sendeth forth words unto the gods who are therein.

SEKHEN-ṬUATIU is the name of the gate of this City through which this great god passeth.

RE-EN-QERERT-ȦPT-KHAT is the name of this City. [This is] the secret Circle of the Ṭuat into which this great god passeth on his way, and [he] cometh forth at the eastern mountain of the sky, the eater of eternity. The form thereof is in the presence of the serpent PETRA, which dwelleth in this City, and they (i.e., the gods) place themselves in the train of [Rā] when the birth of KHEPER upon earth is about to take place.

Whosoever shall make [a copy] of these [representations] according to the figures which are depicted on the east [wall] of the palace of Ȧment in the hidden [places] of the Ṭuat, and whosoever knoweth them shall be in the position of him that divideth his offering, and of him who is a spirit who is suitably equipped [to travel] both in heaven and upon earth, regularly and unceasingly.

SEBIT-NEB-UȦA-KHESEF-SEBIU-EM-PERT-F is the name of the hour of the night which guideth this great god in this Circle.

THE ELEVENTH HOUR.

From the Leyden Papyrus, T. 71.

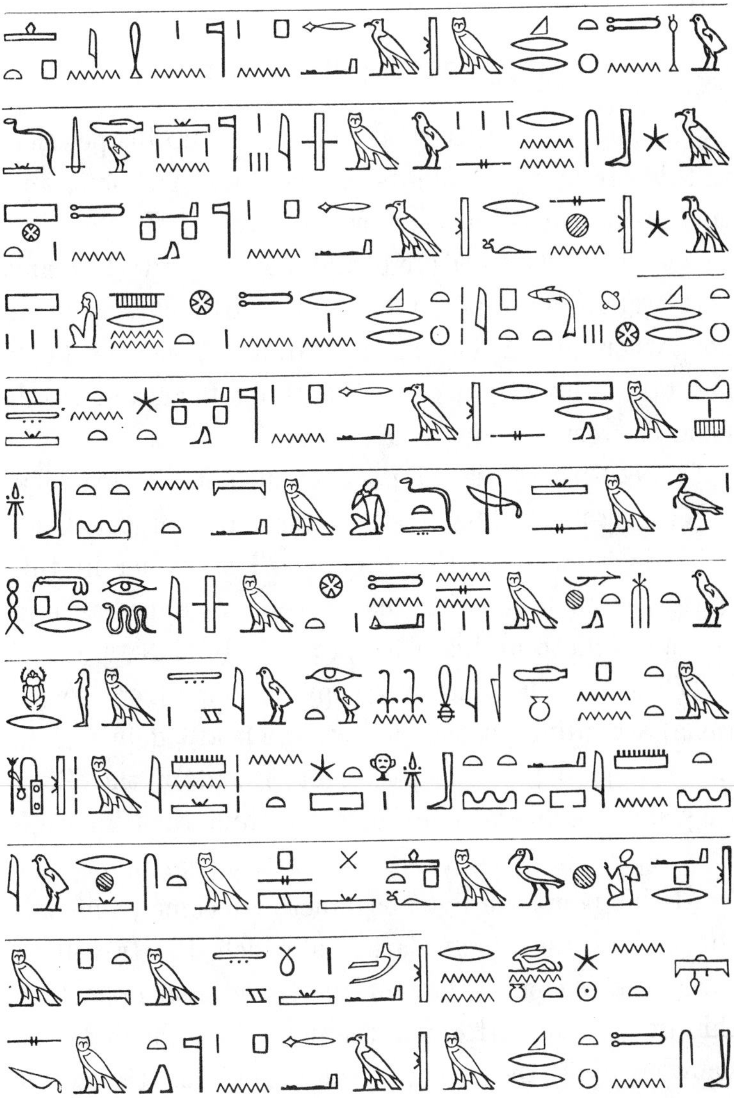

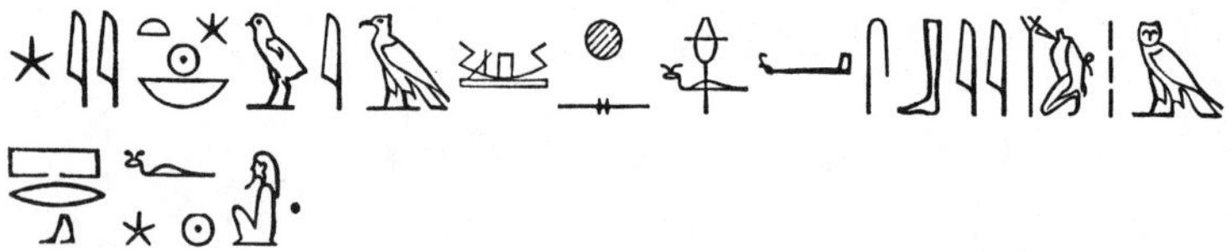

THE TWELFTH HOUR.

The majesty of this great god taketh up his position in this Circle at the limits of the thick darkness, and this great god is born under the form of KHEPERÀ in this Circle. The gods NU and ÀMMUI, and ḤEḤ and ḤEḤ[UT] are in this Circle at the birth of this great god, when he maketh his appearance from the Ṭuat, and taketh up his place in the Māṭeṭ Boat, and riseth from between the thighs of the goddess Nut.

THENEN-NETERU is the name of the gate of this City.

KHEPER-KEKUI-KHĀ-MESTI is the name of this City. [This is] the secret Circle of the Ṭuat, wherein this great god is born, when he maketh his appearance in NU, and taketh up his place in the body of NUT.

Whosoever shall make [a copy] of these [representations] according to the figures which are depicted on the east [wall] of the palace of Àment of the Ṭuat, they shall be magical protectors to him that knoweth them upon earth, both in heaven and on earth.

At this point the light beginneth [to come], and it is the end of the thick darkness which Rā travelleth through in Àmentet, and of the secret matters which this great god performed therein. He who hath no knowledge of the whole(?) or part(?) of the secret representations of the Ṭuat, shall be condemned to destruction.

Whosoever shall make [a copy] of these [representations] according to this copy of what is in the Ȧment of the Ṭuat, [which] cannot be looked at or seen, and whosoever shall know these secret images shall be in the condition of the spirit who is equipped [for journeying], and shall come forth [from] and shall descend into the Ṭuat, and shall hold converse with the men and women who live [there] regularly and unfailingly, millions of times.

THE TWELFTH HOUR.

FROM THE LEYDEN PAPYRUS, T. 71.

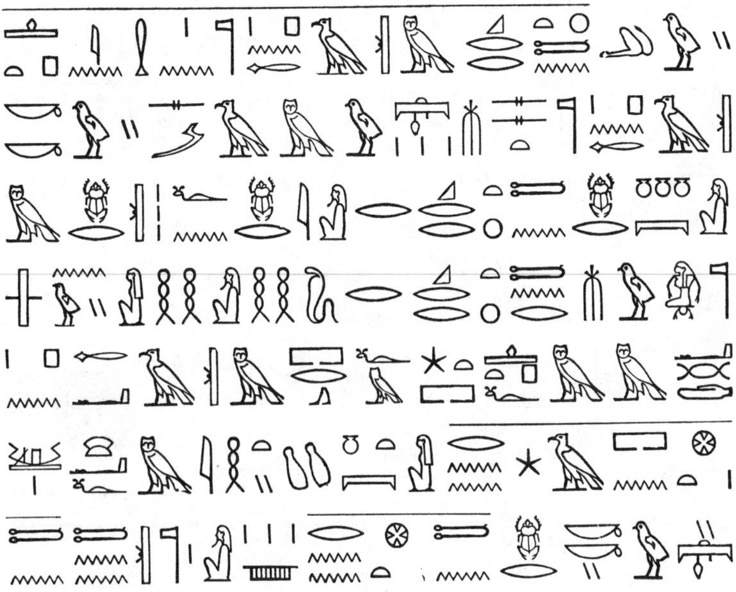

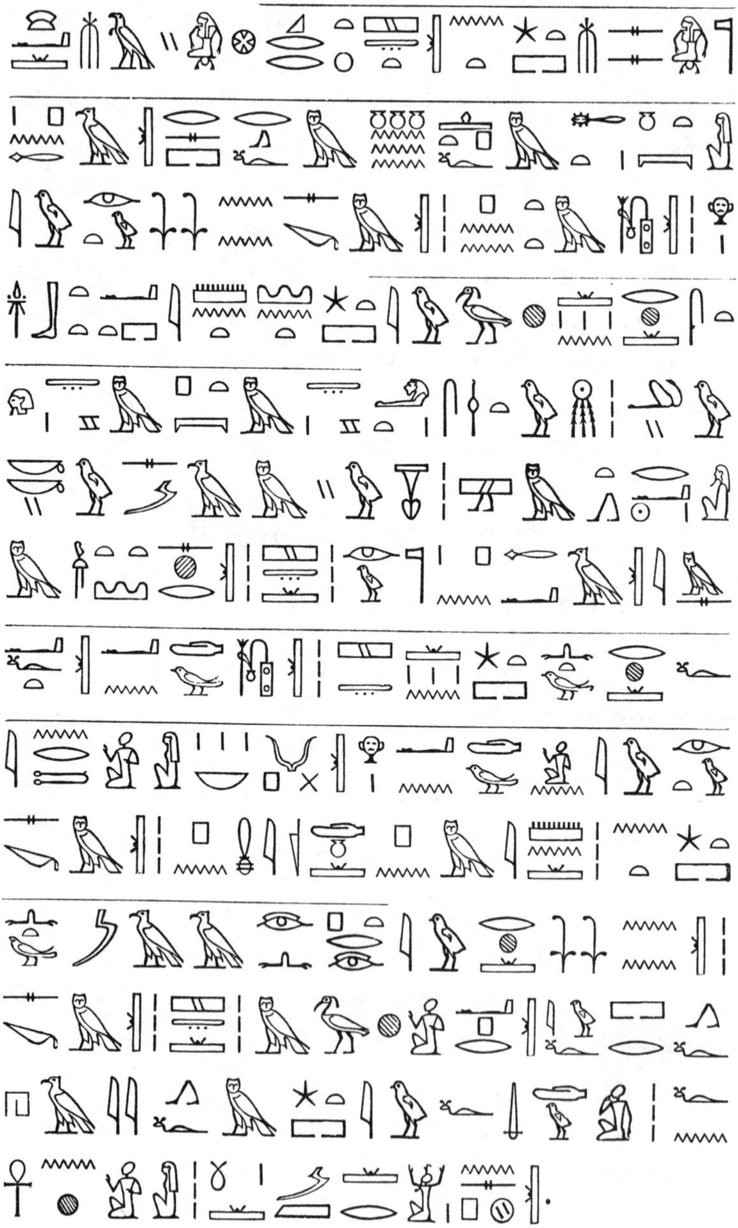

THE BOOK OF GATES

THE BOOK OF GATES

CHAPTER I.

THE ALABASTER SARCOPHAGUS OF SETI I.

THE text of the "Book of Gates," printed in the following pages, is taken from the alabaster sarcophagus of king Seti I., B.C. 1370, which is preserved in the Museum of Sir John Soane, at 13, Lincoln's Inn Fields. This sarcophagus is, undoubtedly, one of the chief authorities for the text of that remarkable book; but before any attempt is made to describe the arrangement of the scenes and the inscriptions which accompany them, it will be well to recall the principal facts connected with its discovery by Giovanni Battista Belzoni, who has fortunately placed them on record in his *Narrative of the Operations and recent discoveries within the pyramids, temples, tombs and Excavations in Egypt and Nubia*, London, 1820, p. 233 ff. In October, 1815, Belzoni began to excavate in the Bibân-al-Mulûk, i.e., the Valley of the Tombs of the Kings, on the western bank of the Nile at Thebes, and in the bed of a watercourse he found a spot where the ground bore traces of having been "moved." On the 19th of the month his workmen made a way through the sand and fragments of stone which had been piled up there, and entered the first corridor or passage of a magnificent tomb, which he soon discovered to have been made for one of the great kings of Egypt. A second corridor led him to a square chamber which, being thirty feet deep, formed a serious obstacle in the way of any unauthorized intruder, and served to catch any rain-water which might make its way down the corridors from the entrance. Beyond this chamber are two halls, and from the first of these Belzoni passed through other corridors and rooms until he entered the vaulted chamber in which stood the sarcophagus.[1] The sarcophagus chamber is situated at a distance of 320 feet from the entrance to the first corridor, and is 180 feet below the level of the ground. Belzoni succeeded in bringing the sarcophagus from its chamber into the light of day without injury, and in due course it arrived in England; the negotiations which he opened with the Trustees of the British Museum, to whom its purchase was first proposed, fell through, and he subsequently sold it to Sir John Soane, it is said for the sum of £2000. An examination of the sarcophagus shows that both it and its cover were hollowed out of monolithic blocks of alabaster,

[1] As Belzoni's narrative is of interest, his account of his discovery of Seti's tomb is given in the Appendix to this Chapter.

and it is probable, as Mr. Sharpe says,[1] that these were quarried in the mountains near Alabastronpolis, i.e., the district which was known to the Egyptians by the name of Ḥet-nub, , and is situated near the ruins known in modern times by the name of Tell al-'Amarna. In the Ḥet-nub quarries large numbers of inscriptions, written chiefly in the hieratic character, have been found, and from the interesting selection from these published by Messrs. Blackden and Fraser, we learn that several kings of the Ancient and Middle Empires carried on works in them, no doubt for the purpose of obtaining alabaster for funeral purposes. The sarcophagus is 9 ft. 4 in. long, 3 ft. 8 in. wide, in the widest part, and 2 ft. 8 in. high at the shoulders, and 2 ft. 3 in. at the feet; the cover is 1 ft. 3 in. high. The thickness of the alabaster varies from 2½ to 4 inches. The skill of the mason who succeeded in hollowing the blocks without breaking, or even cracking them, is marvellous, and the remains of holes nearly one inch in diameter suggest that the drill was as useful to him as the chisel and mallet in hollowing out the blocks. When the sarcophagus and its cover were finally shaped and polished, they were handed over to an artisan who was skilled in cutting hieroglyphics and figures of the gods, &c., in stone, and both the insides and outsides were covered by him

[1] *The Alabaster Sarcophagus of Oimenepthah I., King of Egypt.* London, 1864, p. 14.

with inscriptions and vignettes and mythological scenes which illustrated them. Both inscriptions and scenes were then filled in with a kind of paint made from some preparation of copper, and the vivid bluish green colour of this paint must have formed a striking contrast to the brilliant whiteness of the alabaster when fresh from the quarry. At the present time large numbers of characters and figures are denuded of their colour, and those in which it still remains are much discoloured by London fog and soot.

The first to attempt to describe the contents of the texts and scenes on the sarcophagus of Seti I. was the late Samuel Sharpe, who, with the late Joseph Bonomi, published "The Alabaster Sarcophagus of Oimenepthah I., King of Egypt," London, 1864, 4to; the former was responsible for the letterpress, and the latter for the plates of scenes and texts. For some reason which it is not easy to understand, Mr. Sharpe decided that the hieroglyphic characters which formed the prenomen of the king for whom the sarcophagus was made were to be read "Oimenepthah," a result which he obtained by assigning the phonetic value of O to the hieroglyphic sign for Osiris . The prenomen is sometimes written , or , and , and is to be read either SETI-MER-EN-PTAḤ, or SETI-MEN-EN-PTAḤ. Mr. Sharpe did not, apparently, realize that both the signs  and 

were to be read "Set," and he gave to the first the phonetic value of A and to the second the value of O; he next identified "Aimenepthah" or "Oimenepthah" with the Amenophath of Manetho, and the Chomaepthah of Eratosthenes, saying, "hence arises the support to our reading his name (i.e., the king's) Oimenepthah." Passing over Mr. Sharpe's further remarks, which assert that the sarcophagus was made in the year B.C. 1175 (!), we must consider briefly the arrangement of the texts and scenes upon the insides and outsides of the sarcophagus and its covers. On the upper outside edge of the sarcophagus runs a single line of hieroglyphics which contains speeches supposed to be made to the deceased by the four children of Horus; this line is in two sections, each of which begins at the right hand side of the head, and ends at the left hand side of the foot. Below this line of hieroglyphics are five large scenes, each of which is divided into three registers, and these are enclosed between two dotted bands which are intended to represent the borders of the "Valley of the Other World." On the inside of the sarcophagus are also five scenes, but there is no line of hieroglyphics running along the upper edge. On the bottom of the sarcophagus is a finely cut figure of the goddess Nut, and round and about her are texts selected from the Theban Recension of the *Book of the Dead;* on the inside of the cover is a figure of the goddess Nut, with arms outstretched. On the outside of the cover, in addition to the texts which record the names and titles of the deceased, are inscribed two large scenes, each of which is divided into three registers, like those inside and outside the sarcophagus.

The line of text on the upper outside edge reads :—

I.

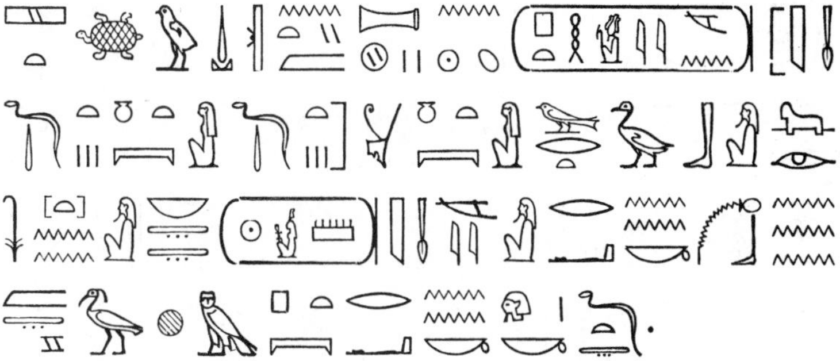

II.

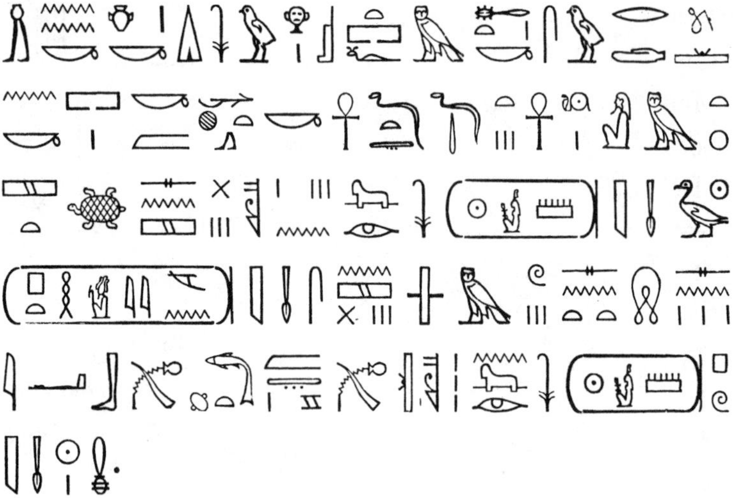

I. Speech of MESTHȦ: "I am Mesthȧ, I am [thy] son, "O Osiris, king, lord of the two lands, Men-Maāt-Rā, "whose word is *maāt*, son of the Sun, Seti Mer-en-Ptaḥ, "whose word is *maāt*, and I have come so that I "may be among those who protect thee. I make to "flourish thy house, which shall be doubly established, "by the command of Ptaḥ, by the command of Rā "himself."

Speech of ȦNPU: "I am Ȧnpu, who dwelleth in (or, "with) the funeral chest." He saith, "Mother Isis "descendeth . . . . bandages for me, Osiris, king "Men-Maāt-Rā, whose word is *maāt*, son of the Sun, "Seti Mer-en-Ptaḥ, whose word is *maāt*, from him "that worketh against me."

Speech of ṬUAMĀTEF: "I am Ṭuamātef, I am thy "son Horus, I love thee, and I have come to avenge "thee, Osiris, upon him that would work his wicked-

"ness upon thee, and I will set him under thy feet "for ever, Osiris, king, lord of the two lands, Men-"Maāt-Rā, son of the Sun, [proceeding] from his "body, loving him, lord of crowns (or, risings) Seti "Mer-en-Ptaḥ, whose word is *maāt,* before the Great "God."

To be said: "Rā liveth, the Tortoise dieth! Strong "are the members of . . . . . Osiris, king Men-Maāt-"Rā, whose word is *maāt,* for Qebḥsennuf guardeth "them. Rā liveth, the Tortoise dieth! In a sound "state is he who is in the sarcophagus, in a sound state "is he who is in the sarcophagus, that is to say, the "son of the Sun, Seti Mer-en-Ptaḥ, whose word is "*maāt.*"

Speech of NUT: Nut, the great one of Seb, saith: "O Osiris, king, lord of the two lands, Men-Maāt-Rā, "whose word is *maāt,* who loveth me, I give unto "thee purity on the earth, and splendour (or, glory) "in the heavens, and I give unto thee thy head for "ever."

II. Speech of NUT, who is over the ḤENNU BOAT: "This is my son, Osiris, king, Men-Maāt-Rā, whose "word is *maāt.* His father Shu loveth him, and his "mother Nut loveth him, Osiris, son of Rā, Seti Mer-"en-Ptaḥ, whose word is *maāt.*"

Speech of ḤĀPI: "I am Ḥāpi. I have come that I "might be among those who protect thee, I bind "together for thee thy head, [and thy members, smiting "down for thee thine enemies beneath thee, and I give "thee][1] thy head, O Osiris, king, Men-Maāt-Rā, whose "word is *maāt*, son of Rā, Seti Mer-en-Ptaḥ, whose "word is *maāt*."

Speech of ÀNPU, the Governor of the divine house: "I am Ànpu, the Governor of the divine house. O "Osiris, king, lord of the two lands, Men-Maāt-Rā, "whose word is *maāt*, son of the Sun, [proceeding] "from his body, the lord of crowns, Seti Mer-en-Ptaḥ, "whose word is *maāt*, the *Shennu* beings go round "about thee, and thy members remain uninjured, O "Osiris, king, Men-Maāt-Rā, whose word is *maāt* for "ever."

Speech of QEBḤSENNUF: "I am thy son, I have "come that I might be among those who protect "thee. I gather together for thee thy bones, and "I piece together for thee thy limbs. I bring unto "thee thy heart, and I set it upon its seat in thy "body. I make to flourish (or, germinate) for thee thy "house after thee, [O thou who] liv[est] for ever."

To be said: "Rā liveth, the Tortoise dieth! Let "enter the bones of Osiris, king Men-Maāt-Rā, whose "word is *maāt*, the son of the Sun, Seti Mer-en-Ptaḥ, "whose word is *maāt*, let them enter into their founda-"tions. Pure is the dead body which is in the earth,

[1] Supplying the words   from the well-known speech on the Canopic jars.

"and pure are the bones of Osiris, king Men-Maāt-Rā, "whose word is *maāt*, like Rā [for ever!]."

On the bottom of the sarcophagus is a large, full-length figure of the goddess NUT, who is depicted in the form of a woman with her arms ready to embrace the body of the king. Her face and the lower parts of the body below the waist are in profile, but she has a front chest, front shoulders, and a front eye. Her feet are represented as if each was a right foot, and each only shows the great toe. One breast is only shown. The hair of the goddess is long and falls over her back and shoulders; it is held in position over her forehead by a bandlet. She wears a deep collar or necklace, and a closely-fitting feather-work tunic which extends from her breast to her ankles; the latter is supported by two shoulder straps, each of which is fastened with a buckle on the shoulder. She has anklets on her legs, and bracelets on her wrists, and armlets on her arms. The inscriptions which are cut above the head, and at both sides, and under the feet of the goddess contain addresses to the king by the great gods of the sky, and extracts from the *Book of the Dead;* they read:—

Inscription on the bottom of the Sarcophagus of Seti I.

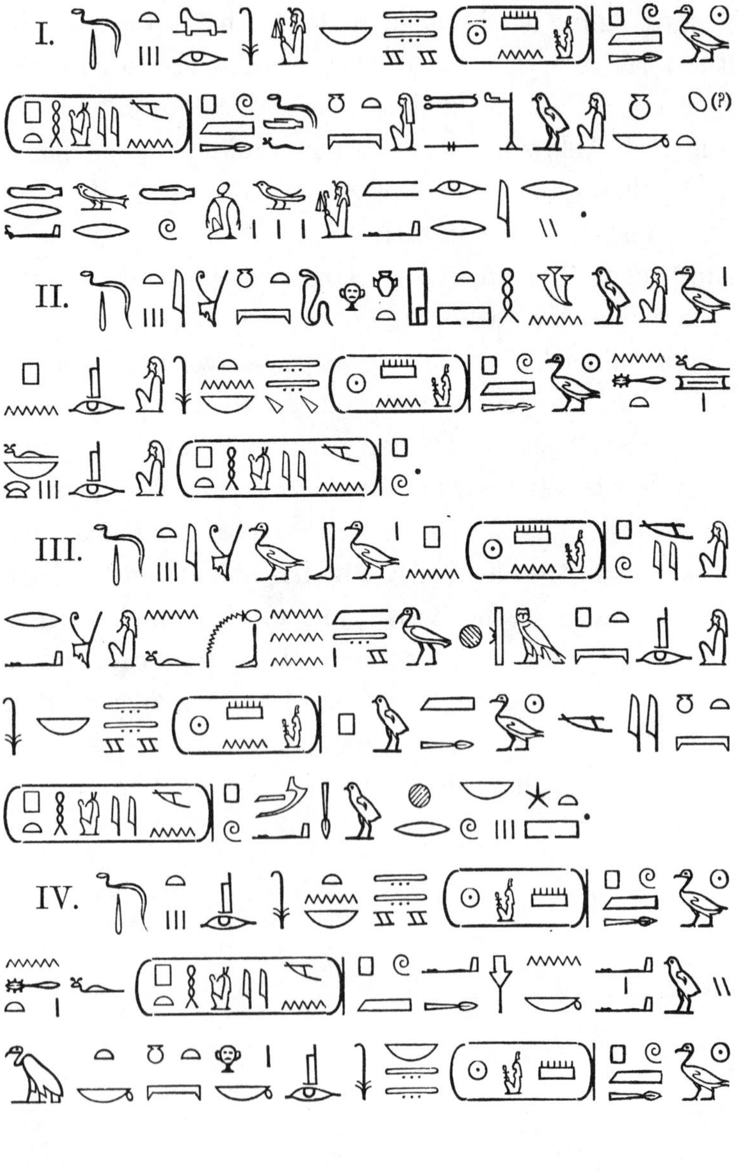

INSCRIPTION ON THE BOTTOM OF THE SARCOPHAGUS OF SETI I.

I. The words of Osiris the king, the lord of the two lands, MEN-MAĀT-RĀ, whose word is *maāt,* the son of Rā (i.e., the Sun), SETI MER-EN-PTAḤ, whose word is *maāt,* who saith, "O thou goddess NUT, support thou "me, for I am thy son. Destroy thou my defects of "immobility, together with those who produce them."

II. The goddess NUT, who dwelleth in ḤET-ḤENNU, saith, "This [is my] son Osiris, the king, the lord "of the two lands, MEN-MAĀT-RĀ, whose word is "*maāt,* the son of Rā, [proceeding] from his body, "who loveth him, the lord of crowns, Osiris, SETI "MER-EN-PTAḤ."

III. The god SEB saith, "This [is my] son MEN-"MAĀT-RĀ, who loveth me. I have given unto him "purity upon earth, and glory in heaven, him the "Osiris, king, the lord of the two lands, MEN-MAĀT-RĀ, "whose word is *maāt,* the son of Rā, the lover of Nut, "that is to say, SETI MER-EN-PTAḤ, whose word is "*maāt,* before the lords of the Ṭuat."

IV. Words which are to be said:—"O Osiris, king, "lord of the two lands, MEN-MAĀT-RĀ, whose word is "*maāt,* the son of Rā, [proceeding] from his body, that "is to say, SETI MER-EN-PTAḤ, whose word is *maāt.* "Thy mother NUT putteth forth [her] two hands and "arms over thee, Osiris, king, lord of the two lands, "MEN-MAĀT-RĀ, whose word is *maāt,* son of Rā,

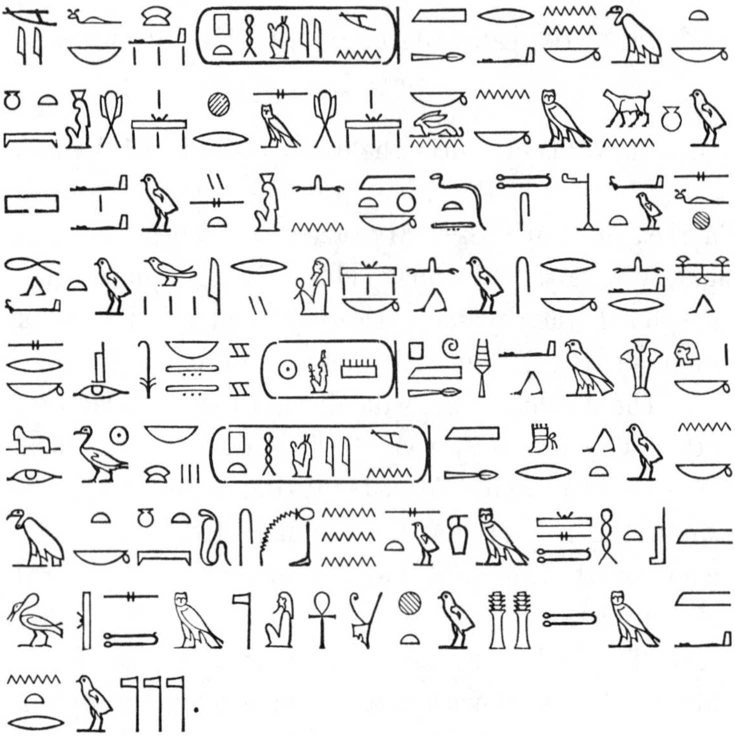

V.

"whom he loveth, lord of diadems, SETI MER-EN-"PTAḤ, whose word is *maāt.* Thy mother NUT "hath added the magical powers which are thine, "and thou art in her arms, and thou shalt never "die. Lifted up and driven away are the calamities "which were to thee, and they shall never [more] "come to thee, and shall never draw nigh unto "thee, Osiris, king, the lord of the two lands, MEN-"MAĀT-RĀ, whose word is *maāt.* Horus hath taken "up his stand behind thee, Osiris, son of Rā, lord "of diadems, SETI MER-EN-PTAḤ, whose word is "*maāt,* for thy mother NUT hath come unto thee; "she hath purified (or, washed) thee, she hath united "herself to thee, she hath supplied thee as a "god, and thou art alive and stablished among the "gods."

V. The great goddess NUT saith, "I have endowed "him with a soul, I have endowed him with a spirit, "and I have given him power in the body of his "mother TEFNUT, I who was never brought forth. I "have come, and I have united myself to OSIRIS, "the king, the lord of the two lands, MEN-MAĀT-RĀ, "whose word is *maāt,* the son of Rā, the lord of "diadems, SETI MER-EN-PTAḤ, whose word is *maāt,* "with life, stability, and power. He shall not "die. I am NUT of the mighty heart, and I took "up my being in the body of my mother TEFNUT "in my name of Nut; over my mother none hath

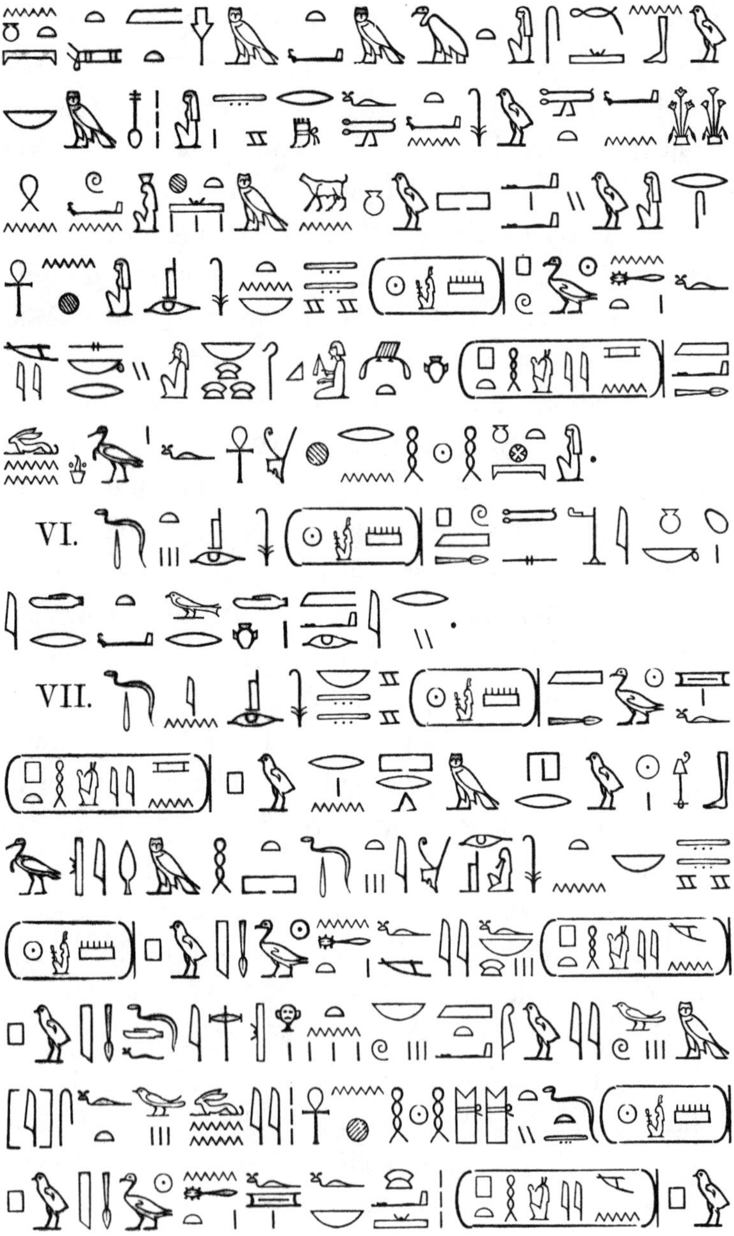
VI.
VII.

"gained the mastery. I have filled every place with my "beneficence, and I have led captive the whole earth; "I have led captive the South and the North, and I "have gathered together the things which are into my "arms to vivify Osiris, the king, the lord of the two "lands, MEN-MAĀT-RĀ, the son of the Sun, [proceeding] "from his body, the lover of SEKER, the lord of diadems, "the governor whose heart is glad, SETI MER-EN-PTAḤ, "whose word is *maāt*. His soul shall live for ever!"

VI. ["Nut,"] saith Osiris, the king MEN-MAĀT-RĀ, whose word is *maāt*, "Raise thou me up! I am [thy] "son, set thou free him whose heart is at rest from "that which maketh [it to be still]."

VII. Osiris, the king, the lord of the two lands, MEN-MAĀT-RĀ, whose word is *maāt*, the son of the Sun, loving him, SETI MER-EN-PTAḤ, saith the

CHAPTER OF COMING FORTH BY DAY AND OF MAKING A WAY THROUGH ĀMMEḤET.[1]

Saith Osiris, the king, the lord of the two lands, MEN-MAĀT-RĀ, whose word is *maāt*, the son of the Sun, [proceeding] from his body, loving him, the lord of crowns, SETI MER-EN-PTAḤ, whose word is *maāt*, "Homage to "you, O ye lords of *maāt*, who are free from iniquity, "who exist and live for ever and to the double *ḥenti* "period of everlastingness, MEN-MAĀT-RĀ, whose word "is *maāt*, the son of the Sun, [proceeding] from his body, "loving him, the lord of diadems, SETI MER-EN-PTAḤ,

[1] This is Chapter LXXII. of the *Book of the Dead*.

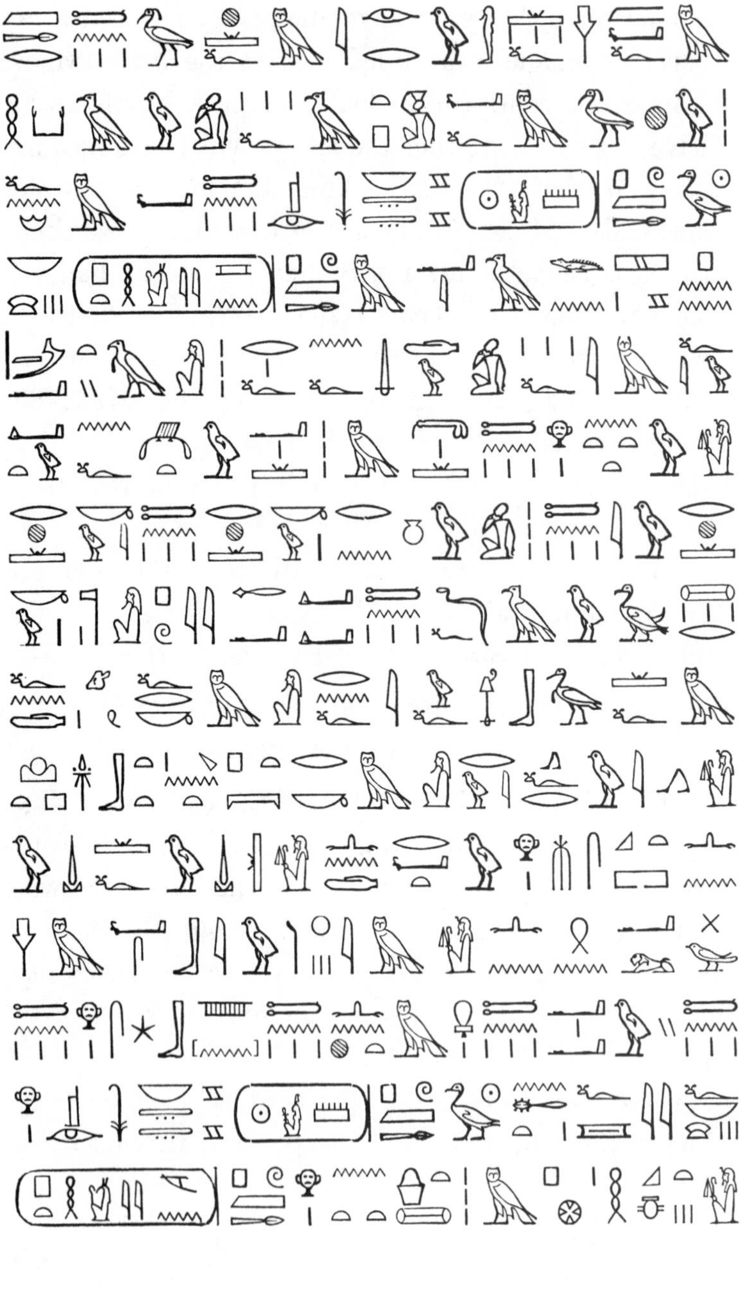

"whose word is *maāt,* before you hath become a "*khu* (i.e., a spirit) in his attributes, he hath gained "the mastery through his words of power, and he "is laden with his splendours. O deliver ye the "Osiris, the king, the lord of the two lands, MEN-"MAĀT-RĀ, whose word is *maāt,* the son of the sun, "the lord of diadems, SETI MER-EN-PTAḤ, whose "word is *maāt,* from the Crocodile of this Pool of "Maāti. He hath his mouth, let him speak there-"with. Let there be granted unto him broad-handed-"ness in your presence, because I know you, and I "know your names. I know this great god unto "whose nostrils ye present offerings of *tchefau.* "REKEM is his name. He maketh a way through "the eastern horizon of heaven. REKEM departeth "and I also depart; he is strong and I am strong. "O let me not be destroyed in the MESQET Chamber. "Let not the Sebàu fiends gain the mastery over "me. Drive not ye me away from your Gates, "and shut not fast your arms against the Osiris, "the king, the lord of the two lands, MEN-MAĀT-"RĀ, whose word is *maāt,* the son of the Sun, [pro-"ceeding] from his body, loving him, the lord of "diadems, SETI MER-EN-PTAḤ, whose word is *maāt,* "because [my] bread is in the city of PE,[1] and my "ale is in the city of ṬEP, and my arms are united

[1] Pe and Ṭep formed a double city in the Delta.

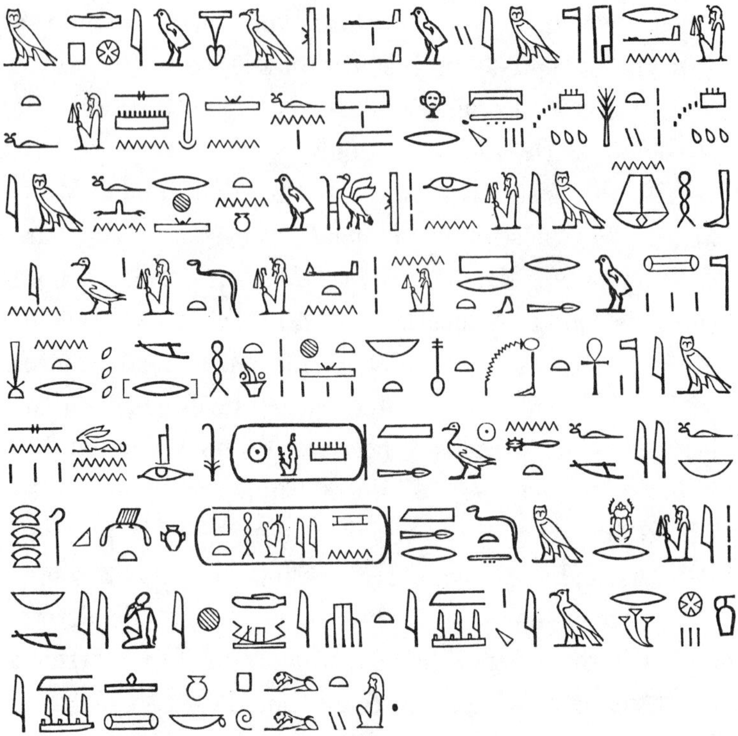

VIII. 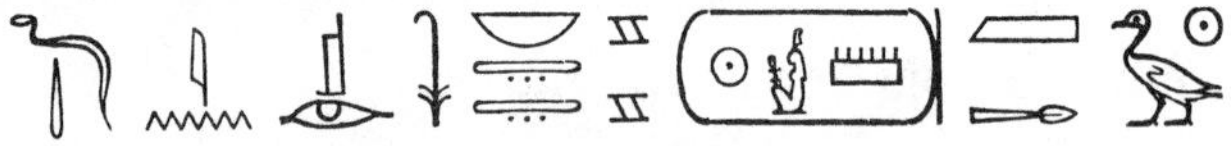

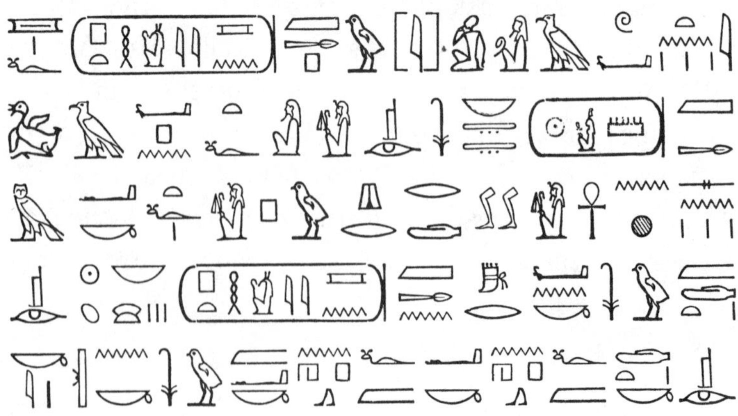

"in the divine house which my father hath given unto "me. He hath stablished for me a house in the high "place of the lands, and there are wheat and barley "therein, the quantity of which is unknown. The son "of my body acteth for me there as *kher-ḥeb.*[1] Grant "ye unto me sepulchral offerings, that is to say, "incense, and *merḥet* unguent, and all beautiful and "pure things of every kind whereon the God liveth. "Osiris, the king, MEN-MAĀT-RĀ, whose word is *maāt,* "the son of the Sun, [proceeding] from his body, loving "him, the lord of diadems, the ruler of joy of heart, "SETI MER-EN-PTAḤ, whose word is *maāt,* existeth for "ever in all the transformations which it pleaseth "[him to make]. He floateth down the river, he saileth "up into SEKHET-ÅARU,[2] he reacheth SEKHET-ḤETEP.[3] "I am the double Lion-god."[4]

VIII. Saith Osiris, the king, the lord of the two lands, MEN-MAĀT-RĀ, whose word is *maāt,* son of the Sun, loving him, SETI MER-EN-PTAḤ, whose word is *maāt* :—"O ward off that destroyer from my father "Osiris, the king, the lord of the two lands, MEN-MAĀT-"RĀ, whose word is *maāt,* and let his divine protection "be under my legs, and let them live. Strengthen "thou Osiris, son of the Sun, lord of diadems, SETI MER-"EN-PTAḤ, whose word is *maāt,* with thy hand. Grasp "thou him with thy hand, let him enter thy hand, let

[1] The *kher-ḥeb* was the priestly official who read the funeral service.

[2] I.e., the Field of Reeds.

[3] I.e., the Field of Peace.

[4] I.e., Shu and Tefnut.

IX.

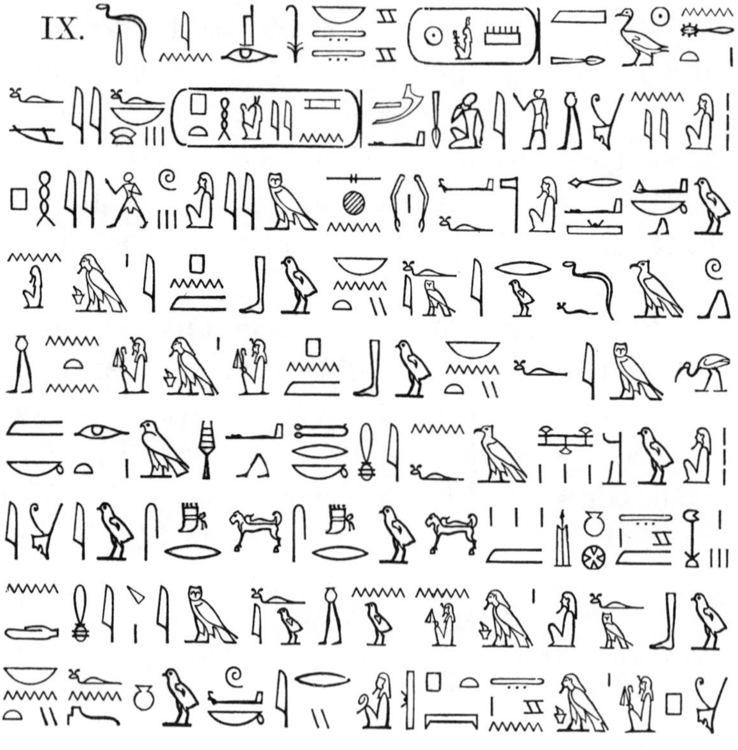

"him enter thy hand, O Osiris, king, lord of the two "lands, MEN-MAĀT-RĀ, whose word is *maāt,* thou shalt "not perish. NUT cometh unto thee, and she fashioneth "thee as the Great Fashioner, and thou shalt never "decay; she fashioneth thee, she turneth thy weak-"ness into strength, she gathereth together thy "members, she bringeth thy heart into thy body, and "she hath placed thee at the head of the living doubles "(*kau*), O Osiris, king, lord of the two lands, MEN-"MAĀT-RĀ, whose word is *maāt,* before the beautiful "god, the lord of TA-TCHESERT."

IX. Saith Osiris, the king, the lord of the two lands, MEN-MAĀT-RĀ, whose word is *maāt,* the son of the Sun, [proceeding] from his body, loving him, the lord of diadems, SETI MER-EN-PTAḤ, whose word is *maāt,*

[THE CHAPTER OF CAUSING THE SOUL TO BE UNITED TO ITS BODY IN THE UNDERWORLD] [1]

"Hail, ye gods who bring (ÅNNIU)! [Hail] ye gods "who run (PEḤIU)! [Hail] thou who dwellest in "his embrace, thou great god, grant thou that may "come unto me my soul from wheresoever it may be. "If it would delay, then let my soul be brought unto "me from wheresoever it may be, for thou shalt find "the Eye of Horus standing by thee like those "watchful gods. If it lie down, let it lie down in "ÅNNU (Heliopolis), the land where [souls are joined "to their bodies] in thousands. Let my soul be brought

[1] This is Chapter LXXXIX. of the *Book of the Dead.*

X.
XI.

"unto me from wheresoever it may be. Make thou "strong, O guardian of sky and earth, this my soul. "If it would tarry, do thou cause the soul to see its "body, and thou shalt find the Eye of Horus standing "by thee even as do those [gods who watch]."

"Hail, ye gods who tow along the boat of the lord of "millions of years, who bring [it] into the upper regions "of the Ṭuat, who make it to pass over Nut, and who "make the soul to enter into its *sāḥu* (i.e., spiritual body), "let your hands be full of weapons, and grasp them "and make them sharp, and hold chains in readiness to "destroy the serpent enemy. Let the Boat rejoice, and "let the great god pass on in peace, and behold, grant "ye that the soul of Osiris, king MEN-MAĀT-RĀ, whose "word is *maāt*, may emerge from the thighs [of Nut] in "the eastern horizon of heaven, for ever and for ever."

X. Osiris, the king, the lord of the two lands, MEN-MAĀT-RĀ SETEP-[EN]-RĀ, whose word is *maāt*, the son of Rā, loving PTAḤ-SEKRI, the lord of diadems, SETI MER-EN-PTAḤ, whose word is *maāt*, saith:—"O ye "*shennu* beings, go ye round behind me, and let not "these my members be without strength."

XI. Osiris, the king, the lord of the two lands, MEN-MAĀT-RĀ AA-RĀ, whose word is *maāt*, the son of the sun, [proceeding] from his body, loving him, lord of diadems, SETI MER-EN-PTAḤ, saith:—"O Nut, lift thou "me up. I am thy son. Do away from me that which "maketh me to be without motion." [Nut saith]:— "O Osiris, the king, the lord of the two lands, MEN-

"MAĀT-RĀ AA-RĀ, whose word is *maāt*, the son of "the sun, [proceeding] from his body, loving him, "the lord of diadems, SETI MER-EN-PTAḤ, whose "word is *maāt*, I have given thee thy head to be "on thy body, and all the members of him that is "SETI MER-EN-PTAḤ, whose word is *maāt*, shall never "lack strength."

On the outside of the cover, beneath the two scenes and texts which occupied the upper part of it, was a horizontal line of hieroglyphics which contained two short speeches, the one by the goddess Nut, and the other by Thoth. The speech of Nut is a duplicate of the opening lines of that found on the bottom of the sarcophagus (see above § v., p. 55); the speech of Thoth is much mutilated, and can have contained little except the promise to be with the king, and a repetition of the royal name and titles. On the inside of the cover were texts, many portions of which are identical, as we see from the fragments which remain, with the Chapters from the *Book of the Dead* which are found on the bottom of the sarcophagus, and which have been transcribed above. At each side of the figure of the winged goddess which was cut on the breast was a figure of the god Thoth, who is seen holding a staff surmounted by the symbol of "night," 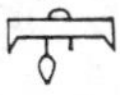. When the cover was complete there were probably four such figures upon it, and the texts which accompanied them were, no doubt, identical with those found in Chapter CLXI. of the *Book of the Dead.*

The scenes and inscriptions which cover the inside and outside of the sarcophagus are described and transcribed in the following chapters.

APPENDIX TO CHAPTER I.

BELZONI'S ACCOUNT OF HIS DISCOVERY OF THE TOMB OF SETI I.

"On the 16th (of October) I recommenced my excava-
"tions in the Valley of Beban el Malook, and pointed
"out the fortunate spot, which has paid me for all the
"trouble I took in my researches. I may call this a
"fortunate day, one of the best perhaps of my life;
"I do not mean to say, that fortune has made me rich,
"for I do not consider all rich men fortunate; but she
"has given me that satisfaction, that extreme pleasure,
"which wealth cannot purchase; the pleasure of
"discovering what has been long sought in vain, and
"of presenting the world with a new and perfect
"monument of Egyptian antiquity, which can be
"recorded as superior to any other in point of
"grandeur, style, and preservation, appearing as if just
"finished on the day we entered it; and what I found
"in it will show its great superiority to all others.
"Not fifteen yards from the last tomb I described, I
"caused the earth to be opened at the foot of a steep
"hill, and under a torrent, which, when it rains, pours
"a great quantity of water over the very spot I have

"caused to be dug. No one could imagine, that the "ancient Egyptians would make the entrance into "such an immense and superb excavation just under a "torrent of water; but I had strong reasons to suppose, "that there was a tomb in that place, from indications "I had observed in my pursuit. The Fellahs who "were accustomed to dig were all of opinion, that "there was nothing in that spot, as the situation of "this tomb differed from that of any other. I con-"tinued the work, however, and the next day, the "17th, in the evening we perceived the part of the "rock that was cut, and formed the entrance. On the "18th, early in the morning, the task was resumed, "and about noon the workmen reached the entrance, "which was eighteen feet below the surface of the "ground. The appearance indicated, that the tomb "was of the first rate; but still I did not expect to "find such a one as it really proved to be. The Fellahs "advanced till they saw that it was probably a large "tomb, when they protested they could go no further, "the tomb was so much choked up with large stones, "which they could not get out of the passage. I "descended, examined the place, pointed out to them "where they might dig, and in an hour there was "room enough for me to enter through a passage that "the earth had left under the ceiling of the first "corridor, which is 36 ft. 2 in. long, and 8 ft. 8 in. wide, "and, when cleared of the ruins, 6 ft. 9 in. high. "I perceived immediately by the painting on the "ceiling, and by the hieroglyphics in *basso relievo*, "which were to be seen where the earth did not reach, "that this was the entrance into a large and magnifi- "cent tomb. At the end of this corridor I came to a "staircase 23 ft. long, and of the same breadth as the "corridor. The door at the bottom is 12 ft. high. "From the foot of the staircase I entered another "corridor, 37 ft. 3 in. long, and of the same width and "height as the other, each side sculptured with "hieroglyphics in *basso relievo*, and painted. The "ceiling also is finely painted, and in pretty good "preservation. The more I saw, the more I was eager "to see, such being the nature of man; but I was "checked in my anxiety at this time, for at the end of "this passage I reached a large pit, which intercepted "my progress. This pit is 30 ft. deep, and 14 ft. by "12 ft. 3 in. wide. The upper part of the pit is "adorned with figures, from the wall of the passage "up to the ceiling. The passages from the entrance "all the way to this pit have an inclination downward "of an angle of eighteen degrees. On the opposite side "of the pit facing the entrance I perceived a small "aperture 2 ft. wide and 2 ft. 6 in. high, and at the "bottom of the wall a quantity of rubbish. A rope "fastened to a piece of wood, that was laid across the "passage against the projections which formed a kind "of door, appears to have been used by the ancients "for descending into the pit; and from the small "aperture on the opposite side hung another, which "reached the bottom, no doubt for the purpose of "ascending. We could clearly perceive, that the water "which entered the passages from the torrents of rain "ran into this pit, and the wood and rope fastened to "it crumbled to dust on touching them. At the "bottom of the pit were several pieces of wood, placed "against the side of it, so as to assist the person who "was to ascend by the rope into the aperture. I saw "the impossibility of proceeding at the moment. Mr. "Beechey, who that day came from Luxor, entered the "tomb, but was also disappointed.

"The next day, the 19th, by means of a long beam "we succeeded in sending a man up into the aperture, "and having contrived to make a bridge of two beams, "we crossed the pit. The little aperture we found to "be an opening forced through a wall, that had "entirely closed the entrance, which was as large as "the corridor. The Egyptians had closely shut it up, "plastered the wall over, and painted it like the rest "of the sides of the pit, so that but for the aperture, "it would have been impossible to suppose, that there "was any further proceeding; and anyone would "conclude, that the tomb ended with the pit. The "rope in the inside of the wall did not fall to dust, but "remained pretty strong, the water not having reached "it at all; and the wood to which it was attached was "in good preservation. It was owing to this method "of keeping the damp out of the inner parts of the "tomb, that they are so well preserved. I observed "some cavities at the bottom of the well, but found "nothing in them, nor any communication from the "bottom to any other place; therefore we could not "doubt their being made to receive the waters from "the rain, which happens occasionally in this moun-"tain. The valley is so much raised by the rubbish, "which the water carries down from the upper parts, "that the entrance into these tombs is become much "lower than the torrents; in consequence, the water "finds its way into the tombs, some of which are "entirely choked up with earth.

"When we had passed through the little aperture "we found ourselves in a beautiful hall, 27 ft. 6 in. by "25 ft. 10 in., in which were four pillars 3 ft. square. "I shall not give any description of the painting, till I "have described the whole of the chambers. At the "end of this room, which I call the entrance-hall, and "opposite the aperture, is a large door, from which "three steps lead down into a chamber with two "pillars. This is 28 ft. 2 in. by 25 ft. 6 in. The pillars "are 3 ft. 10 in. square. I gave it the name of the "drawing-room; for it is covered with figures, which, "though only outlined, are so fine and perfect, that "you would think they had been drawn only the day "before. Returning into the entrance-hall, we saw "on the left of the aperture a large staircase, which "descended into a corridor. It is 13 ft. 4 in. long, "7 ft. 6 in. wide, and has 18 steps. At the bottom we "entered a beautiful corridor, 36 ft. 6 in. by 6 ft. 11 in.

"We perceived that the paintings became more perfect "as we advanced farther into the interior. They "retained their gloss, or a kind of varnish over the "colours, which had a beautiful effect. The figures are "painted on a white ground. At the end of this "corridor we descended ten steps, which I call the "small stairs, into another, 17 ft. 2 in. by 10 ft. 5 in. "From this we entered a small chamber, 20 ft. 4 in. by "13 ft. 8 in., to which I gave the name of the Room of "Beauties; for it is adorned with the most beautiful "figures in *basso relievo*, like all the rest, and painted. "When standing in the centre of this chamber, the "traveller is surrounded by an assembly of Egyptian "gods and goddesses. Proceeding farther, we entered "a large hall, 27 ft. 9 in. by 26 ft. 10 in. In this hall "are two rows of square pillars, three on each side of "the entrance, forming a line with the corridors. At "each side of this hall is a small chamber; that on the "right is 10 ft. 5 in. by 8 ft. 8 in., that on the left "10 ft. 5 in. by 8 ft. 9½ in. This hall I termed the "Hall of Pillars; the little room on the right, Isis' "Room, as in it a large cow is painted, of which I "shall give a description hereafter; that on the left, "the Room of Mysteries, from the mysterious figures "it exhibits. At the end of this hall we entered a "large saloon, with an arched roof or ceiling, which is "separated from the Hall of Pillars only by a step "so that the two may be reckoned one. The saloon "is 31 ft. 10 in. by 27 ft. On the right is a small "chamber without anything in it, roughly cut, as if "unfinished, and without painting; on the left we "entered a chamber with two square pillars, 25 ft. 8 in. "by 22 ft. 10 in. This I called the Sideboard Room, "as it has a projection of 3 ft. in form of a sideboard "all round, which was perhaps intended to contain the "articles necessary for the funeral ceremony. The "pillars are 3 ft. 4 in. square, and the whole beautifully "painted as the rest. At the same end of the room, "and facing the Hall of Pillars, we entered by a large "door into another chamber with four pillars, one of "which is fallen down. This chamber is 43 ft. 4 in. by "17 ft. 6 in.; the pillars 3 ft. 7 in. square. It is covered "with white plaster, where the rock did not cut "smoothly, but there is no painting on it. I named it "the Bull's, or Apis' Room, as we found the carcass "of a bull in it, embalmed with asphaltum; and also, "scattered in various places, an immense quantity of "small wooden figures of mummies 6 or 8 in. long, "and covered with asphaltum to preserve them. "There were some other figures of fine earth baked, "coloured blue, and strongly varnished. On each side "of the two little rooms were wooden statues standing "erect, 4 ft. high, with a circular hollow inside, as if to "contain a roll of papyrus, which I have no doubt "they did. We found likewise fragments of other "statues of wood and of composition.

"But the description of what we found in the centre "of the saloon, and which I have reserved till this place, "merits the most particular attention, not having its "equal in the world, and being such as we had no idea "could exist. It is a sarcophagus of the finest oriental "alabaster, 9 ft. 5 in. long, and 3 ft. 7 in. wide. Its "thickness is only 2 in., and it is transparent, when a "light is placed in the inside of it. It is minutely "sculptured within and without with several hundred "figures, which do not exceed 2 in. in height, and "represent, as I suppose, the whole of the funeral "procession and ceremonies relating to the deceased, "united with several emblems, &c. I cannot give an "adequate idea of this beautiful and invaluable piece "of antiquity, and can only say, that nothing has been "brought into Europe from Egypt that can be com- "pared with it. The cover was not there; it had been "taken out, and broken into several pieces, which we "found in digging before the first entrance. The "sarcophagus was over a staircase in the centre of the "saloon, which communicated with a subterraneous "passage, leading downwards, 300 ft. in length. At the "end of this passage we found a great quantity of bats' "dung, which choked it up, so that we could go no "farther without digging. It was nearly filled up too "by the falling in of the upper part. One hundred feet "from the entrance is a staircase in good preservation; "but the rock below changes its substance, from a beau- "tiful solid calcareous stone, becoming a kind of black "rotten slate, which crumbles into dust only by touching. "This subterraneous passage proceeds in a south-west "direction through the mountain. I measured the "distance from the entrance, and also the rocks above, "and found that the passage reaches nearly halfway "through the mountain to the upper part of the valley. "I have reasons to suppose, that this passage was used "to come into the tomb by another entrance; but this "could not be after the death of the person who was "buried there, for at the bottom of the stairs just "under the sarcophagus a wall was built, which "entirely closed the communication between the tomb "and the subterraneous passage. Some large blocks of "stone were placed under the sarcophagus horizontally, "level with the pavement of the saloon, that no one "might perceive any stairs or subterranean passage "was there. The doorway of the sideboard room had "been walled up, and forced open, as we found the "stones with which it was shut, and the mortar in the "jambs. The staircase of the entrance-hall had been "walled up also at the bottom, and the space filled "with rubbish, and the floor covered with large blocks "of stone, so as to deceive any one who should force "the fallen wall near the pit, and make him suppose, "that the tomb ended with the entrance-hall and the "drawing-room. I am inclined to believe, that who-"ever forced all these passages must have had some "spies with them, who were well acquainted with the "tomb throughout. The tomb faces the north-east, "and the direction of the whole runs straight south-"west."

CHAPTER II.

THE ANTE-CHAMBER OF THE ṬUAT.

In the First Division of the "Book of Gates of the Ṭuat," according to the sarcophagus of Seti I., we see the horizon of the west, or the mountain of the west, , divided into two parts, 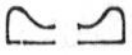, and the boat of the sun is supposed to sail between them, and to enter by this passage into the Ṭuat. On the right hand is fixed a jackal-headed standard, and on each side of it kneels a bearded god; one god is called Ṭat, , and is a personification of the region which is beyond the day, and the other Set, 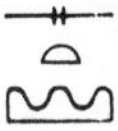, and represents the funeral mountain. On the left hand is a ram-headed standard, and on each side of it also kneels a bearded god; as before, one is called Ṭat and the other Set. The ram's head has the horizontal, wavy horns, which belong to the particular species of ram that was the symbol of the god Khnemu; this animal disappeared from Egypt before the XIIth Dynasty, but the tradition of him remained. In the middle of the scene sails the boat of the sun. The god is symbolized by a beetle within a disk, which is enveloped in the folds of a

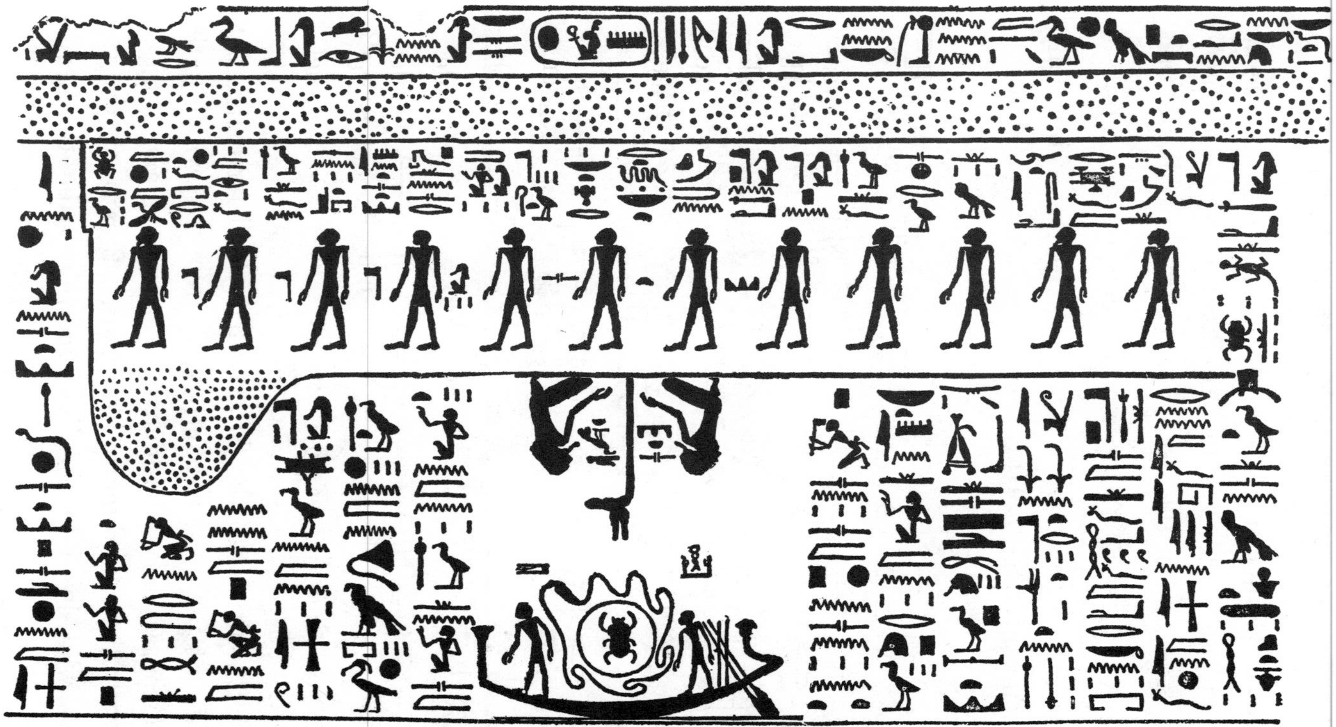

Part of the horizon over which the Boat of the Sun passes to enter the Ṭuat at eventide.
In it are Twelve Gods of the Funeral Mountain.

serpent having its tail in its mouth. In the bows stands the god of divine intelligence, whose name is Sa, , and in the stern, near the two paddles, stands Ḥeka, , i.e., the personification of the word of power, or of magical utterance. The god who usually accompanies Sa is Ḥu. The text which refers to the Sun-god reads:—

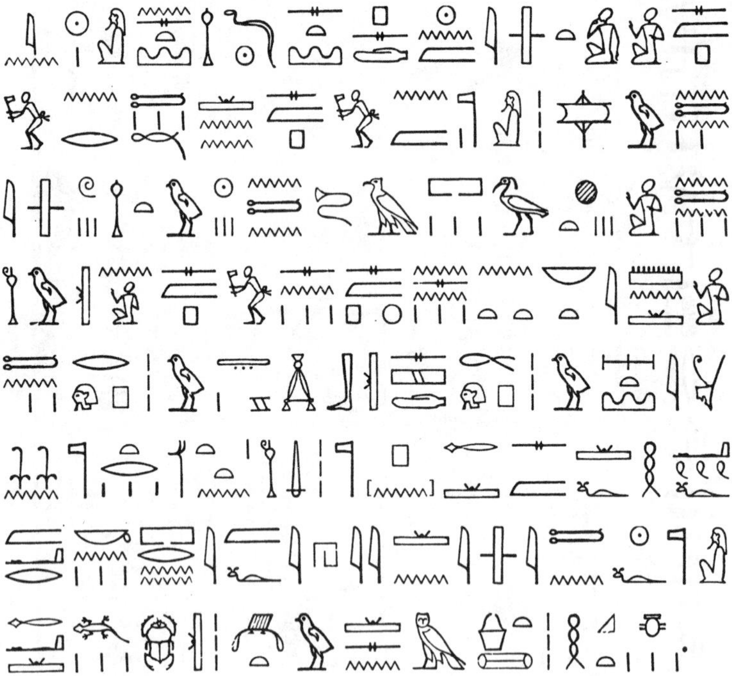

"Rā saith unto the Mountain:—Send forth light, O "Mountain! Let radiance arise from that which hath "devoured me, and which hath slain men and is filled "with the slaughter of the gods. Breath to you, O "ye who dwell in the light in your habitations, my

Part of the horizon over which the Boat of the Sun passes to enter the Ṭuat at eventide.
In it are twelve Gods of Set-Ȧmentet.

"splendours shall be to you. I have decreed their "slaughter, and they have slaughtered everything "which existeth. I have hidden you from those who "are upon the earth, restoring the crown (or, tiara) to "those who are on the Mountain. The gods say:— "'Let this jackal-headed sceptre () emit the words "of this great god who joineth together his members. "Come then unto us, O thou from whom we have come "forth! Cries of joy are to thee, O thou who art in "thy disk, thou great god whose forms (or transforma- "tions) are manifold.' Their provisions [consist] of "bread-cakes and beer."

The paragraph below the above text is practically a duplicate of it, but it contains no mention of either the jackal-headed or the ram-headed sceptre, and it is unnecessary to give it here.

On the right of the boat stand twelve gods, who are called "gods of the mountain," , and the text referring to them reads:—

"[These gods] have come into being from Rā, and "from his substance, and have emerged from his eye. "He hath decreed for them [as] a place (or, abode) the "Hidden Mountain (*Åment Set*), which consumeth men, "and gods, and all cattle, and all reptiles which are "created by this great god. This great god hath decreed "the plans (or, designs) thereof having made [them] to "spring up in the earth which he created."

On the left of the boat stand twelve gods, who are called "gods of Set-Åmentet," 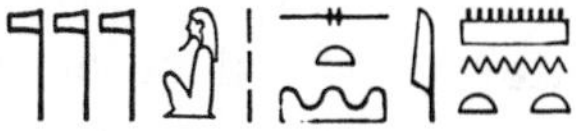, and the text referring to them reads:—

"The hidden place. [These are] those who have "consumed the men, and the gods, and all the cattle, "and all the reptiles which this great god hath created. "This great god hath decreed plans for them after "he made them to spring up in the land which he "created, that is to say, in the Åmentet which he "made."

CHAPTER III.

THE GATE OF SAA-SET.

THE SECOND DIVISION OF THE ṬUAT.

THE boat of Rā, having passed between the two halves of the horizon of the West, now approaches a gateway, the door of which is closed before him; the door of the second division of the Ṭuat is different from the doors of the other divisions, for it consists of a single leaf which turns upon a pivot working in holes in the top and bottom of the framework of the door. This door is guarded by a serpent called SAA-SET, , which stands upon its tail. The text referring to this serpent reads:—

[1] Var. 

"He who is over (i.e., has the "mastery over) this door openeth to "Rā. SA saith unto SAT-SET, 'Open "thy door to Rā, throw wide open thy "door to KHUTI. The hidden abode is "in darkness, so that the transforma-"tions of this god may take place.' "This portal is closed after this god "hath entered in through it, and there "is lamentation on the part of those "who are in their mountain when "they hear this door shut."

In the centre of the scene we see the boat of Rā being towed along by four gods standing, each of whom grasps the tow-line with both hands. The god is now in the form of a ram-headed man, who holds the sceptre  in his right hand, and has the solar disk above his horns. He stands within a shrine which is enveloped in the voluminous folds of the serpent Meḥen, ; a serpent also stands on his tail before him. In front of the shrine stands SA, and behind it ḤEKAU. The gods who tow the boat are called ṬUAIU, .

The sun's boat is met in this section by a company of thirteen gods, who are under the direction of a god who holds a staff in his hand. The names of the first seven gods are :—NEPEMEḤ, ,[1] NENḤĀ, ,[2] BA, , ḤERU, , BEḤĀ-ÅB, , KHNEMU, , and SETCHET, ; the third has the head of a ram, and the fourth that of a hawk. The last six gods

The Boat of the Sun towed by Gods of the Ṭuat.

are described as "gods who are in the entrances," ; the god who bears the staff has no name. The text which refers to the Sun-god reads :—

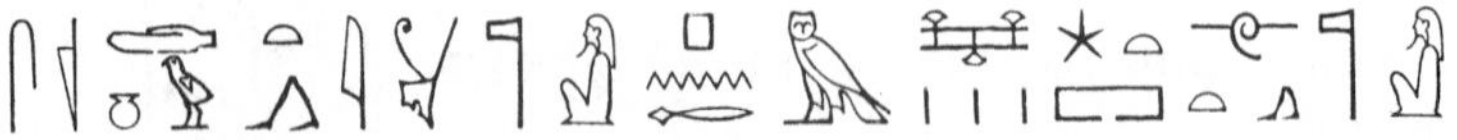

[1] Var., NEPEN, .   [2] Var., NENĀ, .

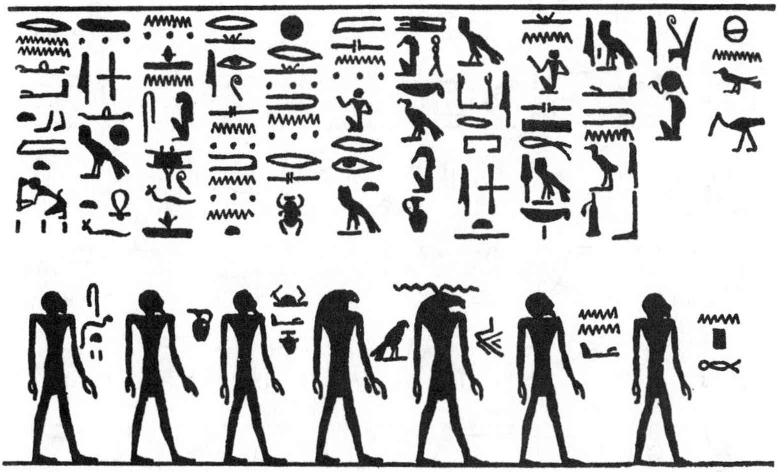

Seven of the Gods of the Entrances who tow the Boat of the Sun through Saa-Set.

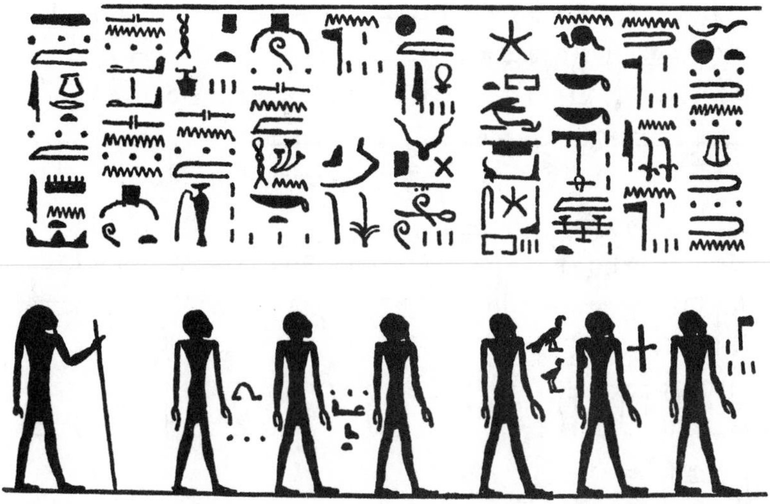

Six of the Gods of the Entrances who tow the Boat of the Sun through Saa-Set, and a god who bears a staff.

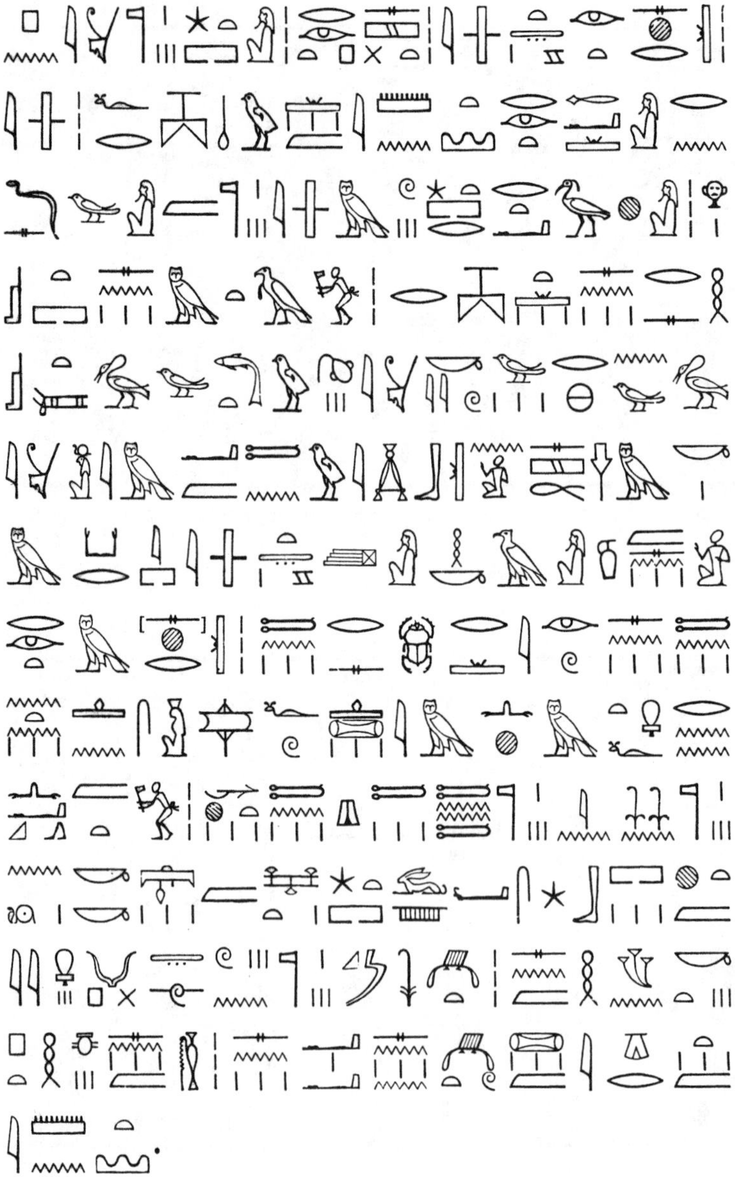

"This great god journeyeth along the roads of the

"Ṭuat. This god is drawn by the gods of the Ṭuat "in order to make divisions (or, distinctions) in the "earth, and to work out [his] designs therein, to weigh "words and deeds in Åment, to magnify the great god "above the little god among the gods who are in the "Ṭuat, to place the KHU (i.e., the blessed dead) upon "their thrones, and the damned [in the place] to which "they have been condemned in the judgment, and to "destroy their bodies by an evil death. Rā saith:—'O "grant ye to me that I may restore the tiara, and that "I may have possession of [my] shrine which is in the "earth. Let SA and ḤEKA unite themselves to me for "the working out of plans for you, and for making to "come into being their attributes (or, forms) ye [have] "what is yours. ISIS hath made to be at peace the "wind, and offerings are there. None shutteth [the "door] against you, and the damned do not enter in "after you. That which belongeth to you is to you, O "gods.' These gods say unto Rā, 'There is darkness "on the road of the Ṭuat, therefore let the doors "which are closed be unfolded, let the earth open, "so that the gods may draw along him that hath "created them.' Their food [i.e., the food of these "gods] is of the funeral offerings, and their drink "is from their cool waters, and their hands are "on meat offerings among the Åḳert regions of "Åment."

On the right of the boat are twenty-four gods, the first twelve of whom are described as "those

who are at peace, the worshippers of Rā," 
, and the second twelve as "the righteous who are in the Ṭuat," ,
These beings are thus described by the accompanying text:—

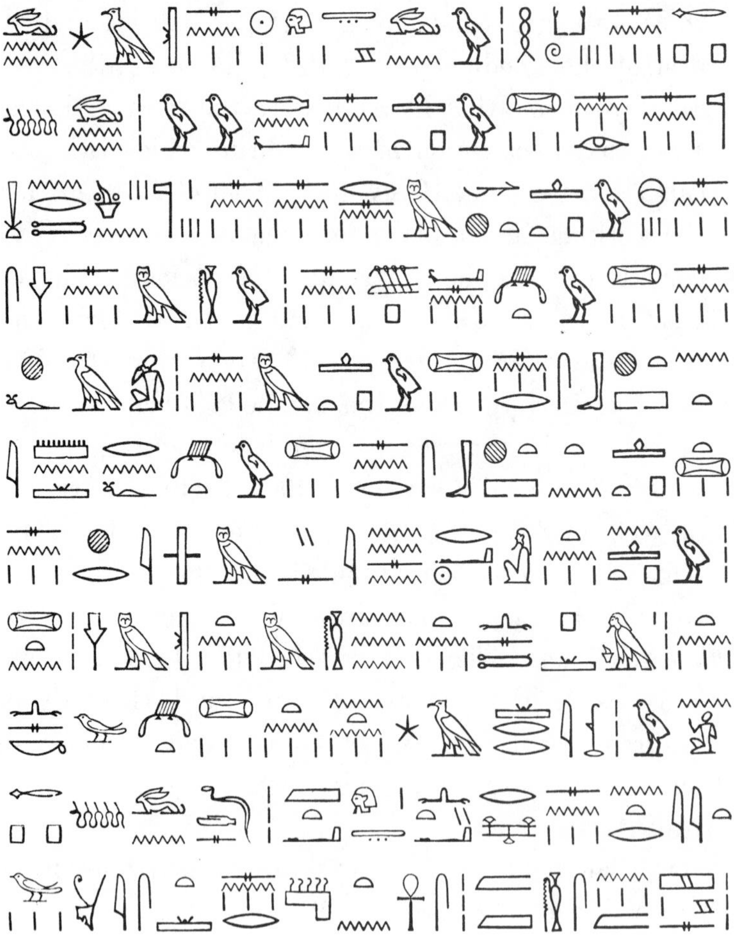

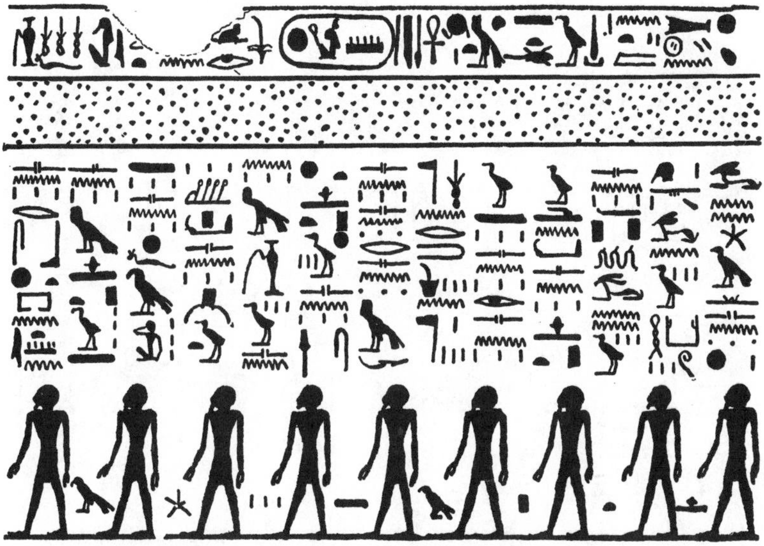

Nine of the gods who adore Rā and are at peace.

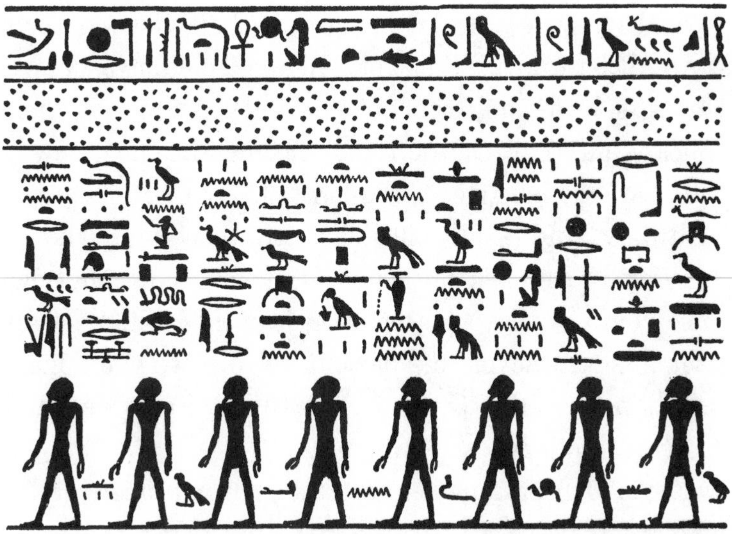

Five of the righteous gods of the Ṭuat.

Three of the gods who adore Rā and are at peace.

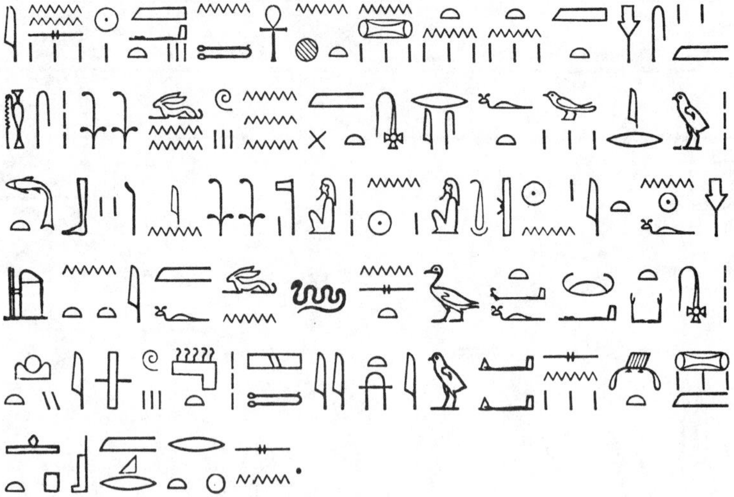

"These [are they who] have worshipped (or, praised) "Rā upon earth, who uttered words of power against "Āpep, who made their offerings unto him, and who "burnt (*literally*, made) incense to their gods on their "own behalf, after their offerings. They have gained "possession of their cool waters, and they receive their "meat, and they eat of their offerings in the gateway "of him whose name is hidden. Their meat is by the "gateway, and their offerings are with him who is "therein. And Rā saith unto them:—'Your offerings "are yours, ye have power over your cool waters, your "souls shall never be hacked to pieces, your meat "shall never fail, [O ye who have] praised [me], and "have vanquished Āpep for me.'"

The above passage refers to the "worshippers of Rā who are at peace."

"[These are] they [who] spake truth upon earth,

"and who were not addicted to evil thought about the "gods. They make their invocations in this gateway, "they live upon maāt (i.e., truth), and their cool "waters are in their cisterns. Rā saith unto them:— "'Truth is yours, live ye on your food. Ye yourselves "are truth;' and they have power over these their cool "waters, which are waters of fire to those who have

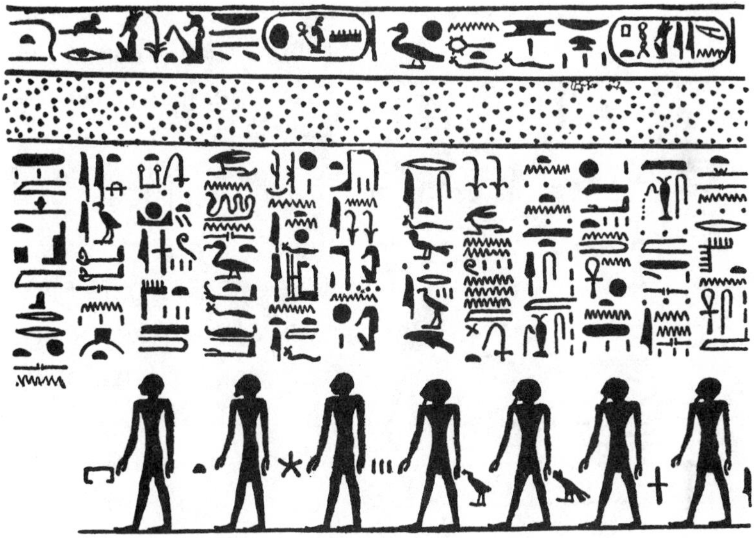

Seven of the righteous gods of the Ṭuat.

"guilt and sin. And these gods say to Rā:—'Let "there be stability to the Disk of Rā. Let him that is "in the shrine have the mastery over it, and let the "serpent [Meḥen] guard him well. May the flames of "Khuti which are in the corners of the hidden shrine "grow stronger.' And there shall be given to them "meat in the place of peace in their circle."

The above passage refers to the "righteous who are in the Ṭuat."

On the left side of the boat of Rā are: 1. The god TEM, , who is depicted in the form of an aged man, leaning heavily on a stick which he grasps in his right hand. 2. Four male beings who are lying prostrate on their backs. 3. Twenty male beings, with their backs bowed, and their arms tied together at their elbows behind their backs. The four beings are described as "the inert," , and the twenty as "the apostates of the Hall of Rā, "who have blasphemed "Rā upon earth, who have "invoked evils upon him "that is in the Egg, who "have thrust aside the "right, and have spoken "words against KHUTI," 

.

The inert Apostates and Blasphemers of Rā.

The text referring to the inert and the apostates reads:—

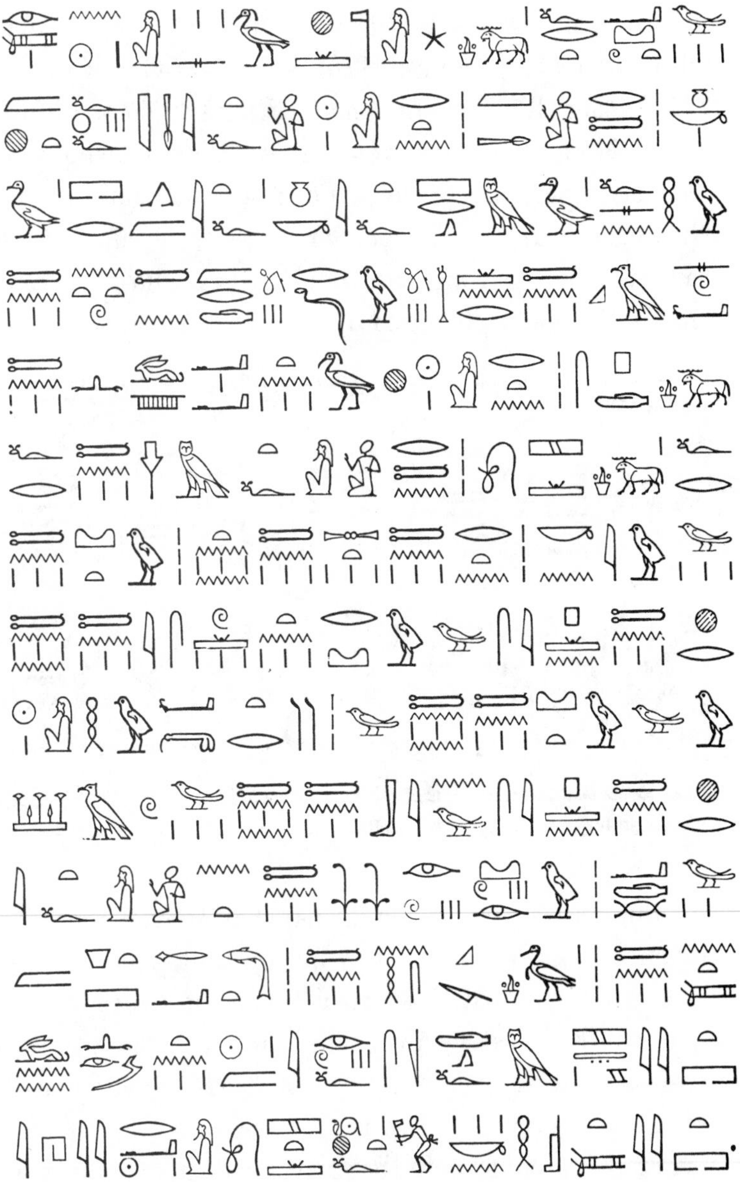

"Tem worketh on behalf of Rā, glorifying the god,

"and singing praises to his soul, and distributing evil "things to his enemies. [He saith]:—'The word of "my father Rā is right (*maāt*) against you, and my "word is right against you. I am the son who pro-"ceedeth from his father, and I am the father who "proceedeth from his son. Ye are fettered, and ye "are tied with strong cord, and it is I who have sent "forth the decree concerning you that ye should be

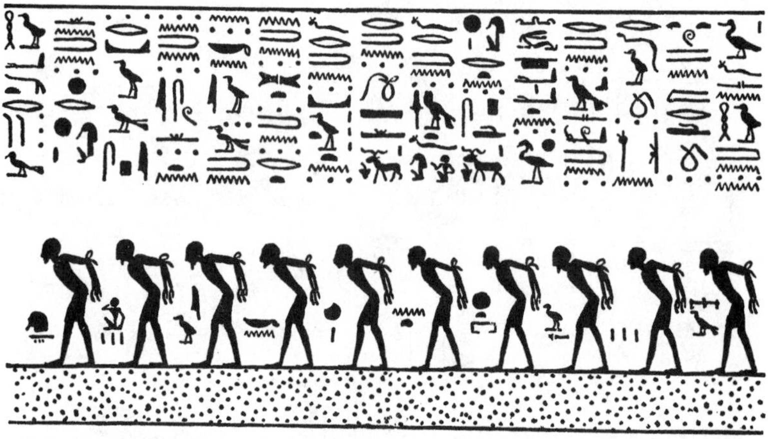

The Apostates and Blasphemers of Rā, who are doomed to destruction, with their arms bound.

"bound in fetters; your arms shall never more be "opened. Rā pronounceth the formula against you, "his soul is prepared to attack you; my father hath "gained the mastery over you, and his soul uttereth "words against you. Your evil deeds [have turned] "against you, your plottings [have come] upon you, "your abominable acts [have recoiled] upon you, your "destinies are for evil, and your doom hath been "decreed before Rā; your unjust and perverted judg-"ments are upon yourselves, and the wickedness of "your words of cursing are upon you. Evil is the doom "which hath been decreed for you before my father. "It is you who have committed sins, and who have "wrought iniquity in the Great Hall; your corruptible

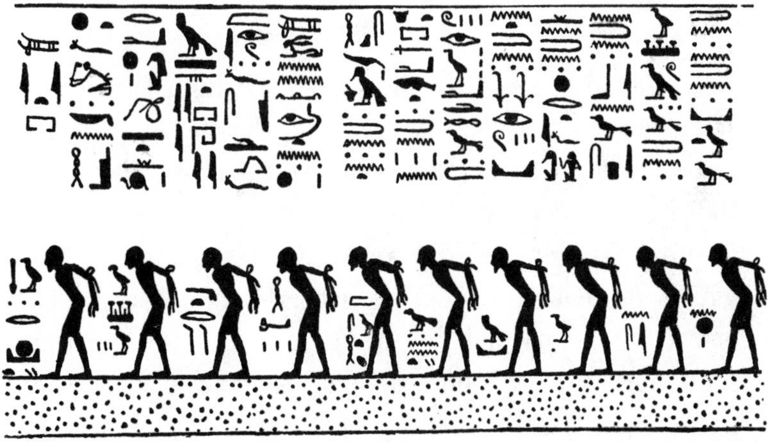

The Apostates and Blasphemers of Rā, who are doomed to destruction, with their arms bound.

"bodies shall be cut in pieces, and your souls shall "have no existence, and ye shall never again see Rā "with his attributes [as] he journeyeth in the hidden "land. Hail, Rā! Adored be Rā! Thine enemies are "in the place of destruction.'"

CHAPTER IV.

THE GATE OF AQEBI.

THE THIRD DIVISION OF THE ṬUAT.

THE boat of the sun having passed through the Second Division of the Ṭuat arrives at the gateway which leads to the THIRD DIVISION. This gateway is unlike the first, which has already been described, for its opening is protected by an outwork, similar to that which protects the door of a fortified building. The outwork is guarded by nine gods, in the form of mummies, who are described as the "second company of the gods," 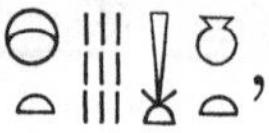, and in this wall, which completely divides the Second Division from the Third, is an opening, which leads to a corridor that runs between two walls, the tops of which are protected by rows of pointed stakes, . At the entrance to the corridor stands a god, in mummied form, called ĀM-ĀUA, , and at the exit is a similar god called SEKHABESNEFUNEN, ; each is said to "extend his arms and hands to Rā," 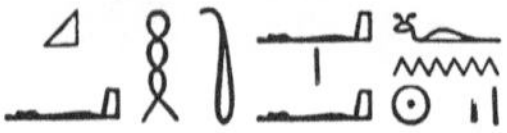. At each side of the angle, near

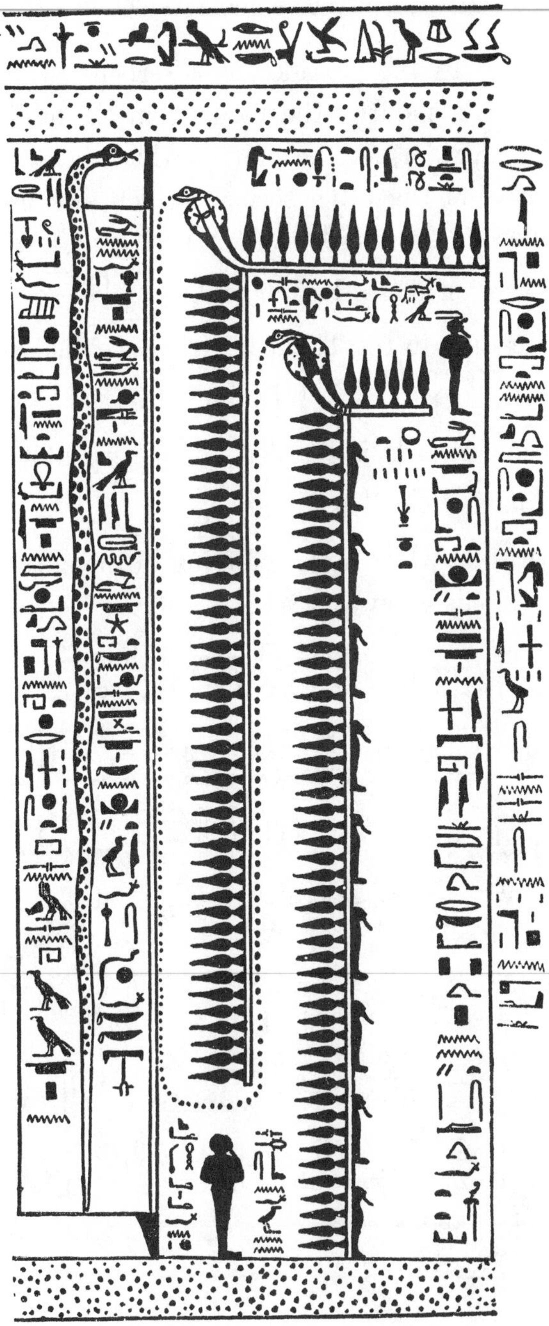

The Gate of the Serpent Aqebi.

the entrance to the corridor, is a serpent, who ejects flames from his mouth; the flame from the one sweeps along the corridor, at the end of which it is met by the flame from the other serpent which sweeps along the inside of the inner wall. The flames of these serpents are said to be for Rā, 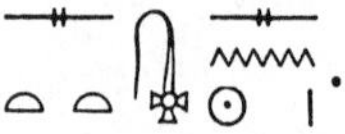. The gateway leading to the Third Division is called SEPṬET-UAUAU, 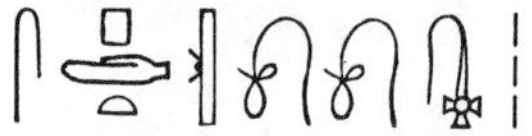, and the door thereof, which opens inwards, is guarded by the serpent standing on his tail, who is called AQEBI, , and faces outwards. The texts referring to the entrance of Rā through this gateway read :—

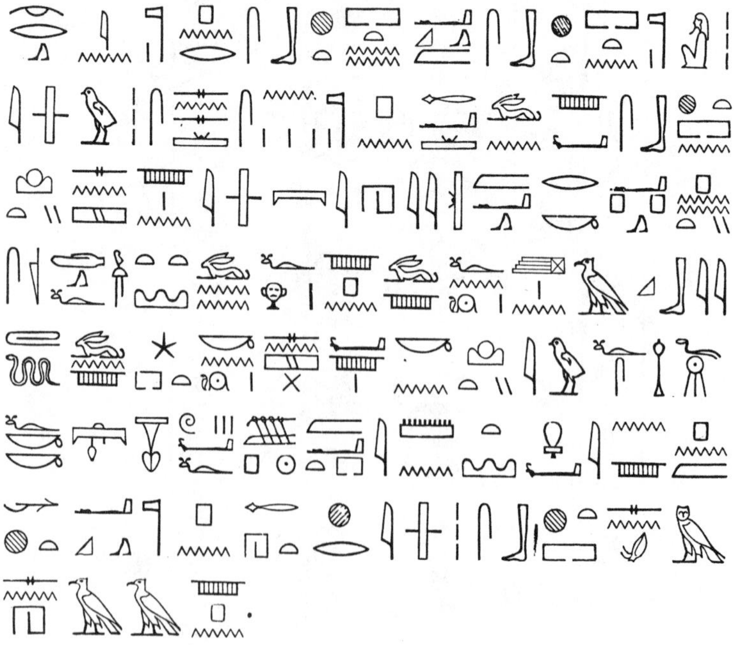

"[When] this god cometh to this gateway, to enter "in through this gateway, the gods who are therein "acclaim this great god, [saying], 'Let this gateway be "unfolded to KHUTI, and let the doors be opened to "him that is in heaven. Come then, O thou traveller, "who dost journey in Ȧmentet.' He who is over this "door openeth [it] to Rā. SA saith unto AQEBI, 'Open "thy gate to Rā, unfold thy door to KHUTI. He shall "illumine the darkness, and he shall force a way for "the light in the habitation which is hidden.' This "door is closed after the great god hath entered "through it, and there is lamentation to those who are "in their gateway when they hear this door close "[upon them]."

Along the middle of the THIRD DIVISION we see the boat of the sun being drawn along by four gods, as before; the god Rā stands in a shrine, similar to that already described, and his companions are SA and ḤEKAU. The rope by which the boat is towed along is fastened to the two ends of a very remarkable object, in the form of a long beam, each end of which terminates in a bull's head. The accompanying text describes it as "his boat," , and from the fact that the four gods who tow the boat are seen again at the other end of the beam-like object, with the towing-rope in their hands, it is clear that the boat of Rā, and the god himself, were believed to pass *through* it, from one end to the other. The object is supported on the shoulders of eight gods, in mummied form, "who are called "Bearers of the gods," ; at each end, immediately behind the bull's head, stands a bull, and at intervals seven gods, who are called "the

The Gods of the Third Division of the Ṭuat towing the Boat of Rā.

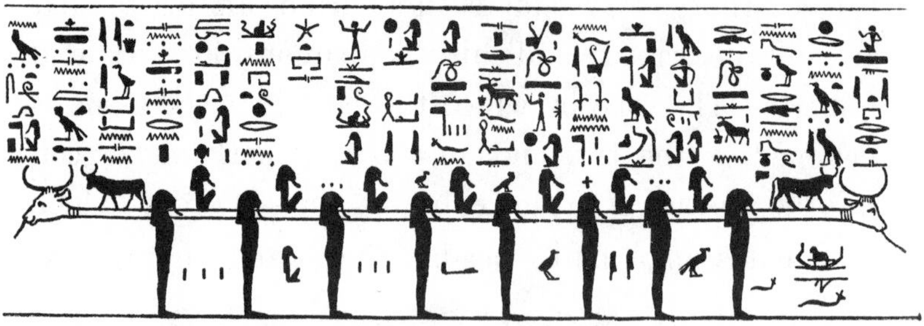

The Eight Bearers of the Boat of the Earth and its Seven Gods.

gods who are within," , are seated upon it. At the end of this Division stand four mummied forms, with their elbows projecting, and their hands crossed on their breasts. The text which refers to the passage of the boat of the sun reads:—

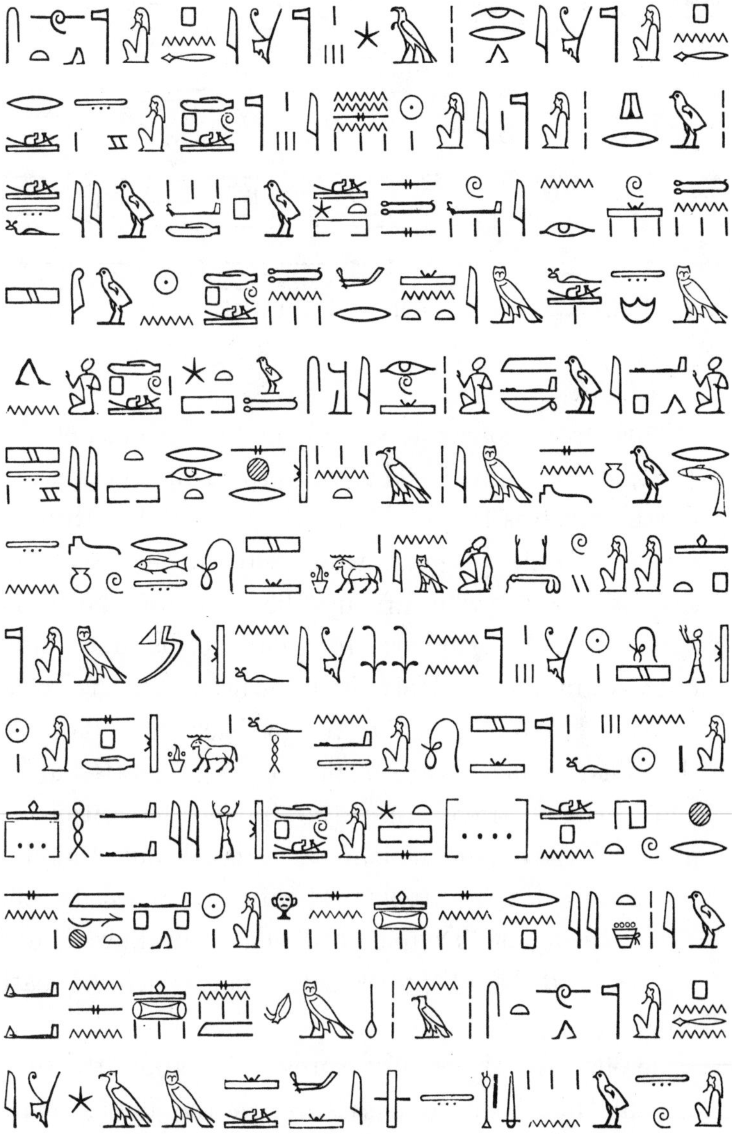

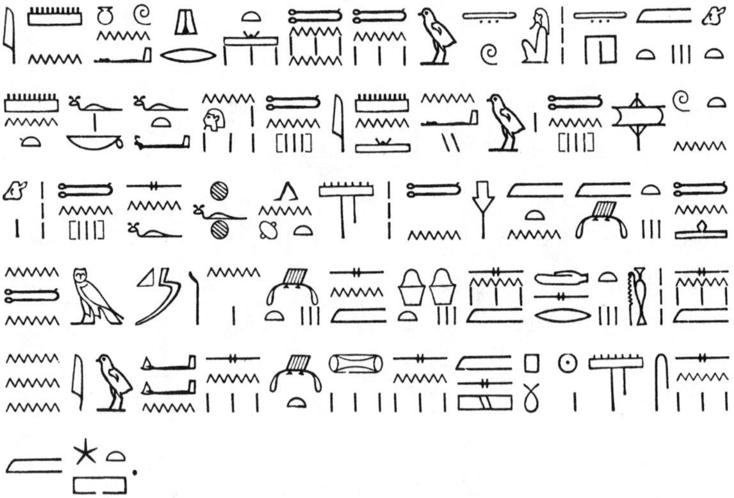

"This great god is towed along by the gods of the "Ṭuat, and this great god advanceth to the Boat of the "Earth, which is the bark of the gods. Rā saith unto "them:—'Hail, ye gods who bear up his Boat of "the Earth, and who lift up the Bark of the Ṭuat, "may there be support to your forms and light "unto your Bark. Holy is he who is in the Boat "of the Earth. I make to go back the Bark of "the Ṭuat which beareth my forms (or, attributes), "and verily I travel into the hidden habitation to "perform the plans which are carried out therein.' "Ennurkhata, Ennurkhata [saith], 'Praised be the "Soul which the Double Bull hath swallowed, and "let the god be at peace with that which he hath "created.'"

The effect of the above words is to allow the Sun-god and his boat to pass through the double bull-headed Boat of the Earth without any let or hindrance, and when he has done this,—

"These gods (i.e., the four gods at the other end of "the Boat of the Earth) say to Rā:—'Praised be Rā, "whose Soul hath been absorbed by the Earth-god! "Praised be the gods of Rā who hath rested [therein].' "This Boat of its Ṭuat rejoiceth, and there are cries "from them after Rā hath passed them as he journeyeth "on his way. Their offerings are the plants of the year,

The Ṭuat-gods address the Utau.

"and their offerings are given to them when they hear "the words of those who draw along this great god. "The gods of the Ṭuat (?) who [draw] the holy Boat "in the earth say unto the UTAU, whose arms are "hidden:—'O ye UTAU of the earth, whose duty it is to "stand (?) near his habitation, whose heads are uncovered, "and whose arms are hidden, may there be air to your "nostrils, O UTAU, and may your funeral swathings "be burst open, and may you have the mastery over

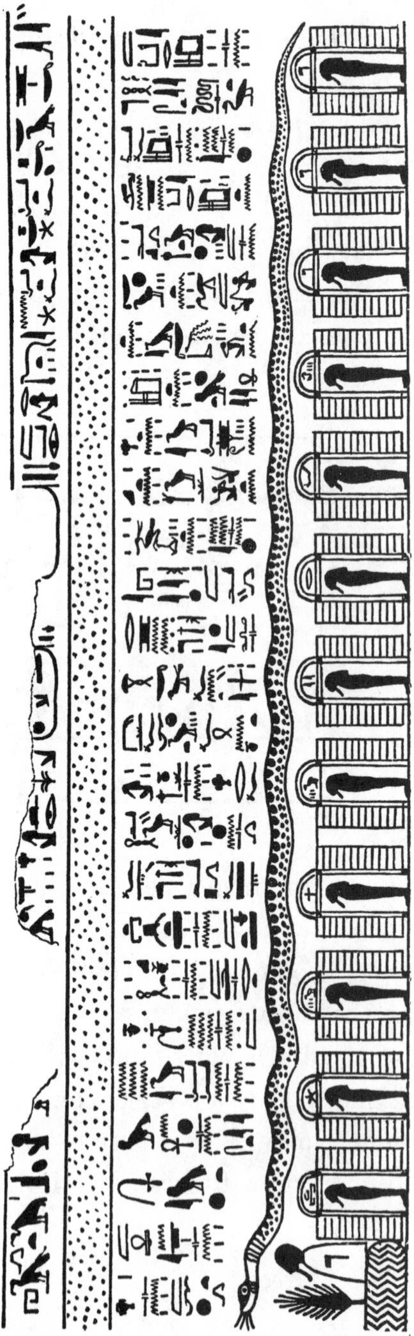
The Twelve holy Gods who are in the Ṭuat.

"your meats, and may "you have peace (or, "rest) in that which I "have created. Their "food is of bread "cakes, and their "bread is made of "the red grain, the "draughts which they "drink are of [cool] "water, and their meat "is given unto them "because of the white- "ness (or, brilliance) "of their apparel in "the Ṭuat."

On the right hand side of this Division of the Ṭuat the boat of the Sun passes twelve shrines, each of which has its doors thrown wide open, and so permits us to see a god in mummied form standing inside it these gods are described as "the holy gods who are in the

Ṭuat," . Along the front of the twelve shrines stretches an enormous serpent, the duty of which is to protect those who stand in them. Beyond the shrines is a long basin or lake of boiling water, with rounded ends, in which stand up to their waists twelve mummied gods, with black heads, who either have white bodies, or are arrayed in white apparel; in front of each god grows a large ear of wheat. These gods are described as "the gods in the boiling lake," 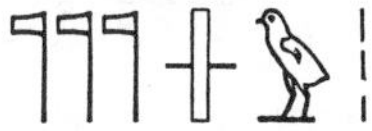 . The texts which relate to both groups of beings are as follows:—

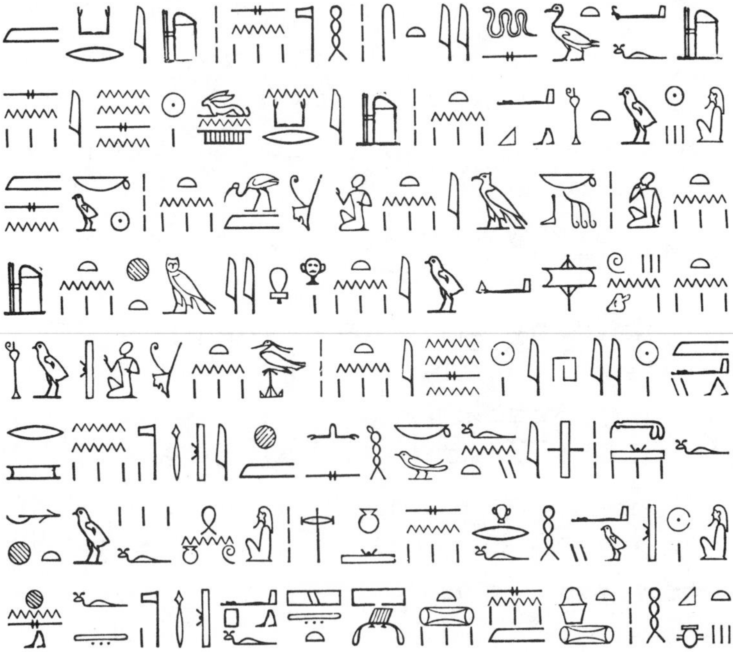

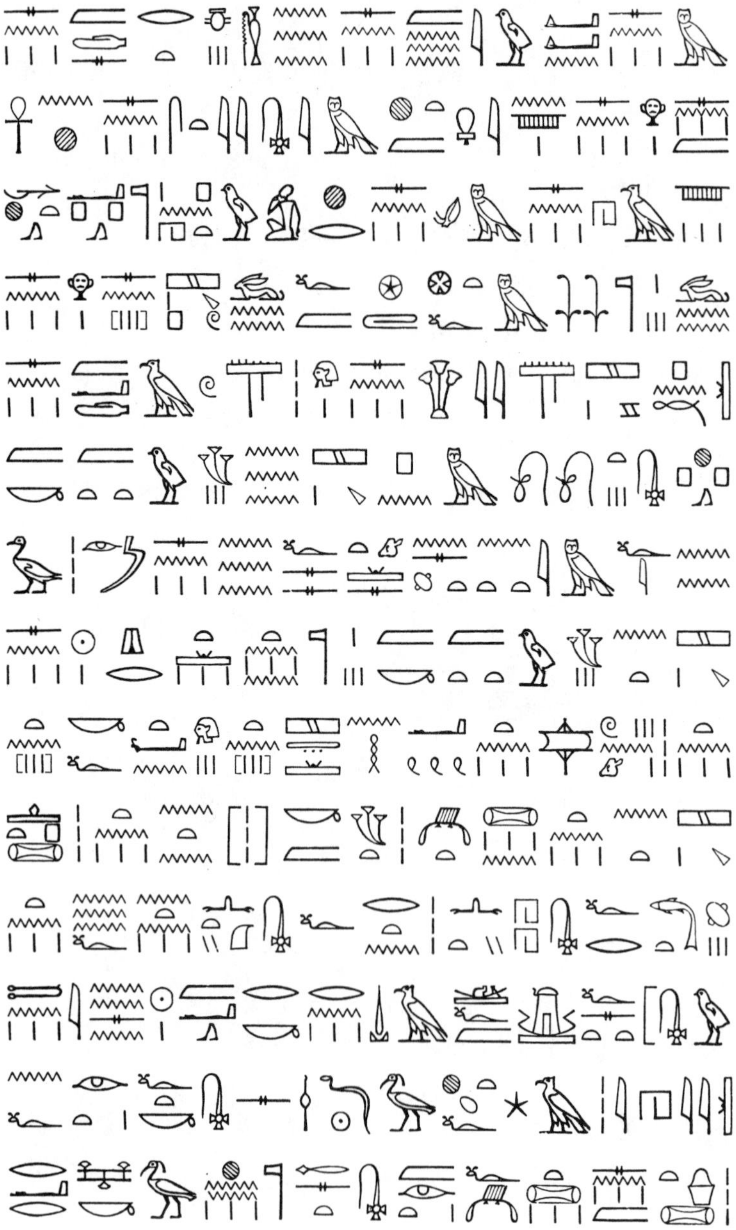

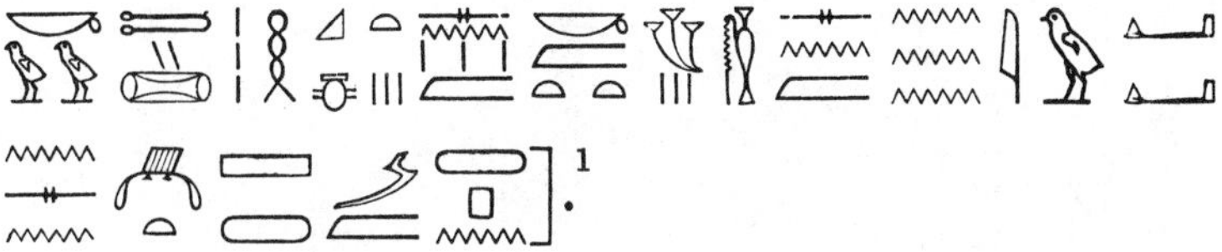
[1]

"[Those who are in] their shrines are the members "of the god whose shrines the serpent SETI guardeth. "Rā saith unto them:—'Open ye [the doors of] your "shrines, so that my radiance may penetrate the "darkness in which ye are! I found you weeping and "lamenting, with your shrines tightly closed, but air "shall be given to your nostrils, and I have decreed "that ye shall have abundance to overflowing [in all "things].' And these gods say unto Rā:—'Hail, Rā, "come thou into our lake, O thou great god who never "failest.' The *Shennu* gods who are before and behind "him pay homage to him, and they rejoice in Rā when "he traverseth [their] region, and when the great god "journeyeth through the secret place. Their food "consisteth of loaves of bread, their drink is made "from the red [barley], and their cool waters come "from [their cisterns of] water, and the serpent of fire, "SETI, giveth unto them the things whereon they live "there. The door which shutteth them in closeth "after this god hath passed through their midst, and "they utter cries of grief when they hear their doors "shut upon them."

[1] The text in brackets is supplied from Lefébure, *Les Hypogées Royaux de Thèbes* (Tombeau de Seti Ier, ive partie, pl. xiv.), Paris, 1886.

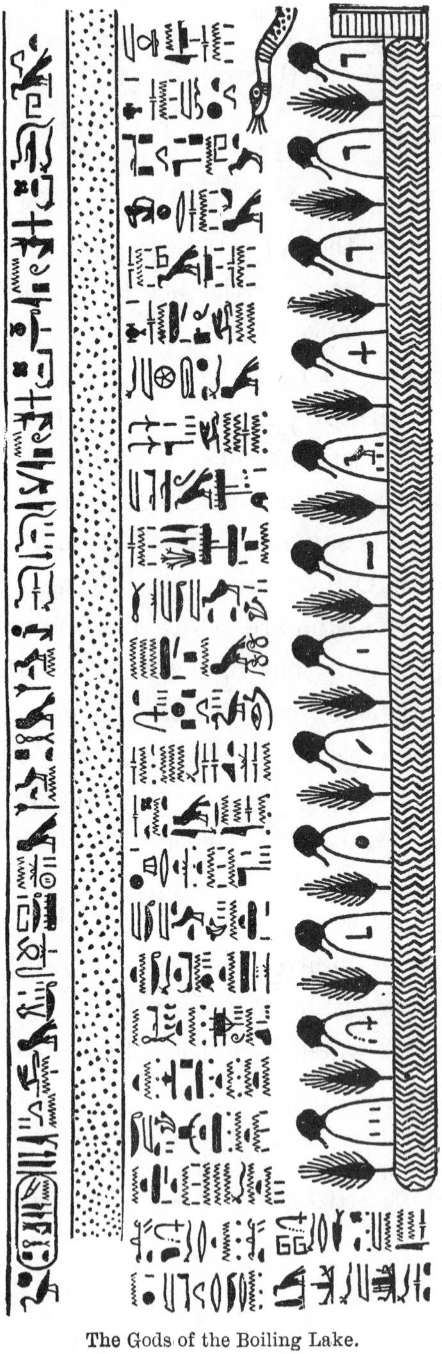
The Gods of the Boiling Lake.

The following refers to the lake of water in this Division:—

"[Here is] the "lake of water "which is in the "Ṭuat, and it is "surrounded by "the gods who are "arrayed in [their] "apparel, and who "have [their] heads "uncovered. This "lake is filled with "green herbs. The "water of this lake "is boiling hot, and "the birds betake "themselves to "flight when they "see the waters "thereof, and when "they smell the "fœtid smell which "is in it. Unto "these gods saith "Rā:—'O ye gods "whose duty it is "[to guard] the green herbs of your lake, whose heads "are uncovered, and whose limbs are covered with "garments, may there be air to your nostrils, and may "offerings be made to you of the green herbs, and may "your meat be from your lake. The water thereof "shall be yours, but to you it shall not be boiling, and "the heat thereof shall not be upon your bodies.' "These [gods] say unto Rā:—'Come thou unto us, O "thou who sailest in thy boat, whose eye is of blazing "fire which consumeth, and hath a pupil which sendeth "forth light! The beings of the Ṭuat shout with joy "when thou approachest; send forth thy light upon us, "O thou great god who hast fire in thine eye.' Their "food consisteth of loaves of bread and green herbs, and "their drink (or, beer) is of the *kemtet* plants, and their "cool water is from [their cisterns of] water. And food "shall be given unto them in abundance from this lake."

On the left of the path along which the boat of Rā passes in this Division of the Ṭuat are two groups of beings. In the first of these we see the god TEM, 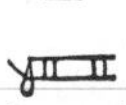, in the form of an aged man, with bent shoulders, leaning upon a staff; coiled up before him in voluminous folds, with its head flat upon the ground, is the monster serpent ĀPEP, . Behind Āpep stand nine men, with their arms hanging by their sides; these are called the "TCHATCHA who repulse ĀPEPI," 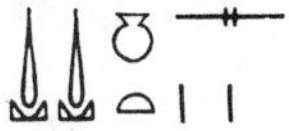 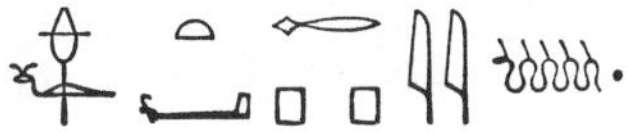. In the second group is TEM,

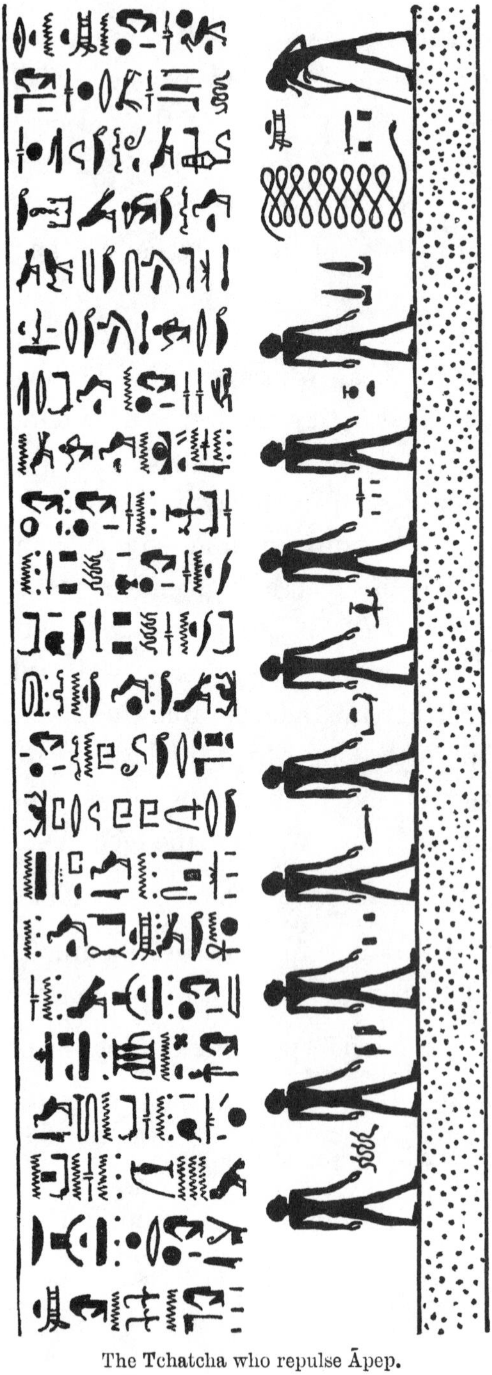

The Tchatcha who repulse Āpep.

in a similar attitude, and before him stand nine gods, each holding the symbol of life in the right hand, and the sceptre  in the left; the nine gods are called "Nebu khert," i.e., "Lords of destinies," 
.

The texts which refer to these groups read:—

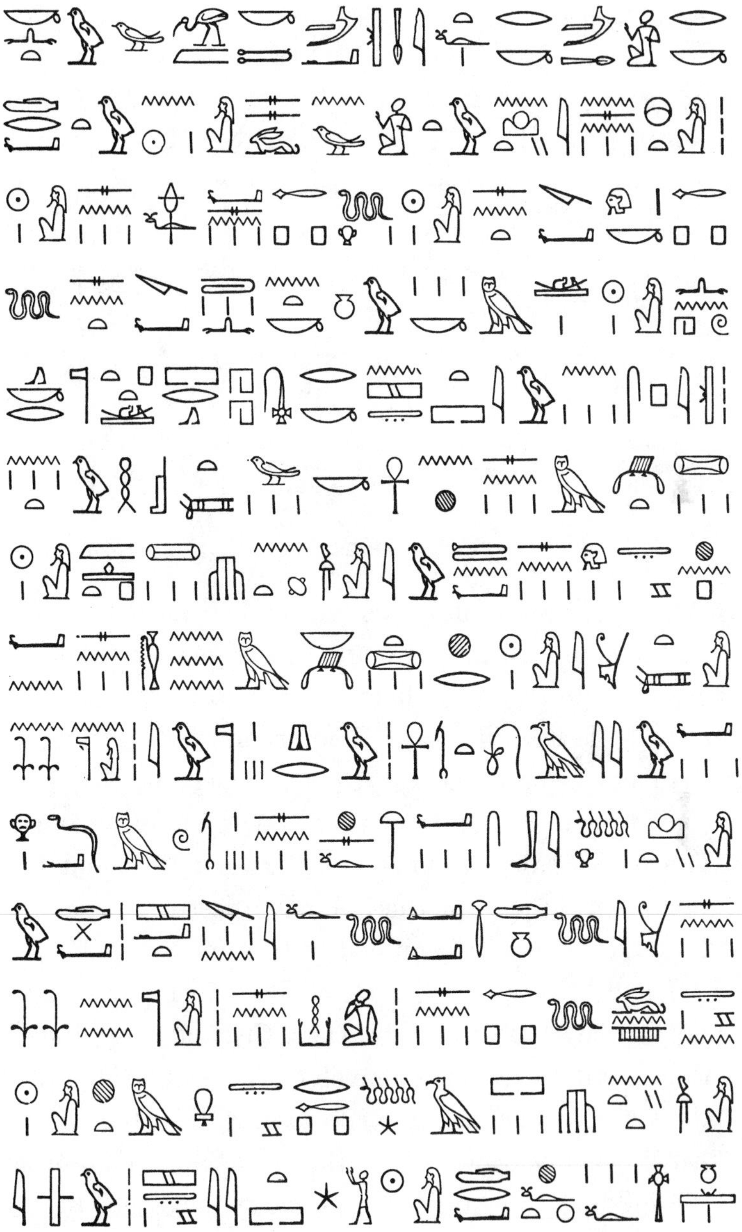

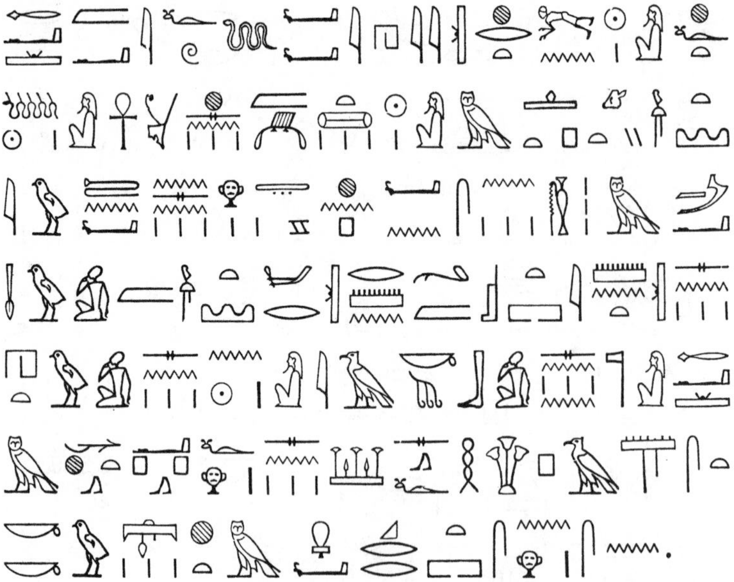

The first group shows us what "TEM hath done for "RĀ, and how he hath protected the god by words of "magical power, and hath overthrown the serpent "SEBȦ. [TEMU saith:—] 'Thou art prostrate, and thou "shalt never more rise up; thou art enchanted by [my "enchantments], and thou shalt never more be found. "The word of my father is *maāt* against thee, and my "word is *maāt* against thee; I have destroyed thee for "RĀ, and I have made an end of thee for KHUTI.'

"The company of the gods of Rā who repulse ĀPEP "say:—'Thy head is slit, O Āpep, thy folds are gashed, "thou shalt never more envelop the boat of Rā, and "thou shalt never again make a way into the divine "bark. A flame of fire goeth out against thee from "the hidden place, and we have condemned thee to thy "dire doom.' They (i.e., 'the nine gods of the "company of Rā) live "upon the food of Rā, "and upon the cakes "of KHENT-ÅMENTI, for "offerings are made on "their behalf upon "earth, and libations of "cool water are made "unto them by the lord "of food (or, as lords of "food) before Rā."

To the second group of nine gods "TEM saith:—'Inasmuch as "ye are the gods who "possess life and sceptre "(i.e., authority), . and "who have mastery over "your sceptres, drive ye "back the serpent SEBÅ "from KHUTI, gash ye "with knives the foul "and evil serpent ÅF.' "These are the gods who "work enchantments on "ĀPEP, who open the "earth to RĀ, and who

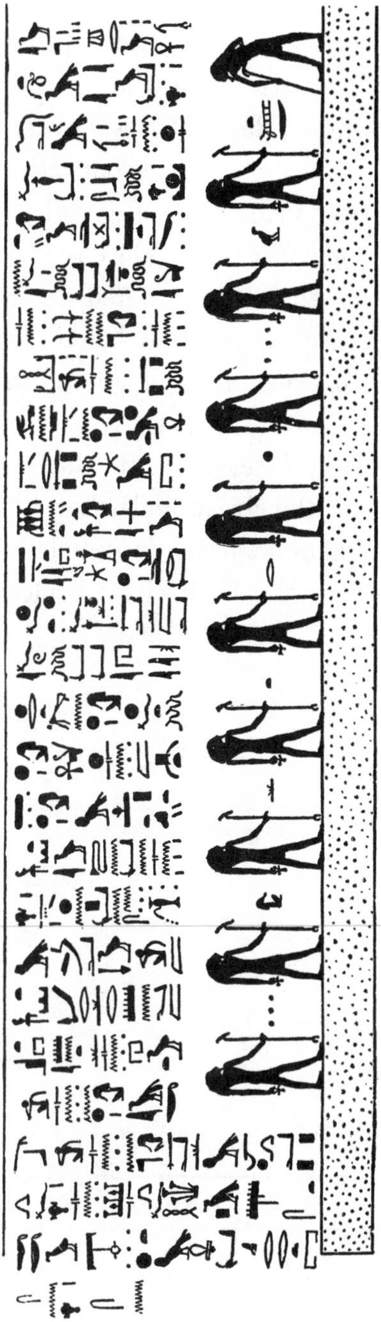

The Lords of Destinies (?).

"shut it against APEP in the gates of KHENTI-ÅMENTI.
"They are those who are in the hidden place, and they "praise Rā, and they destroy his enemies, and they "protect the great one against the serpent ÅFU, and "they utter cries of joy at the overthrow by Rā of the "enemy of Rā. They live upon the meat of Rā, and "on the cakes offered to KHENTI-AMENTI. Offerings "are made on their behalf upon earth, and they receive "libations through [their] word being *maāt* in Åment, "and holy are they of arm in their hidden place. "They utter cries to Rā, and they make lamentation "for the great god after he hath passed by them, for "when he hath departed they are enveloped in dark-"ness, and their circle is closed upon them."

CHAPTER V.

THE GATE OF TCHEṬBI.

THE FOURTH DIVISION OF THE ṬUAT.

THE boat of the sun having passed through the Third Division of the Ṭuat arrives at the gateway which leads to the Fourth Division. This gateway is like that which admitted the god into the Third Division, and its outwork is guarded by nine gods, in the form of mummies, who are described as the "third company of the gods of the great god who are within," . At the entrance to the corridor which runs between the two walls is a god in mummied form called ENUERKHATA, , and at the exit is a similar god called SEṬA-TA, ; each god has a uraeus over his brow, and each is said to "extend his arms and hands to Rā," 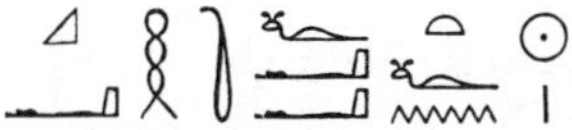. The corridor is swept by flames of fire which proceed from the mouths of two serpents, stationed each at an angle, and their "fire is for Rā." The gateway of the Fourth Division is called NEBT-S-TCHEFAU, 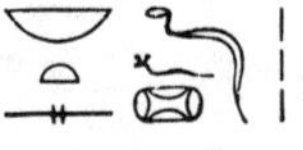, and the text says, "This great god cometh to this "gateway, and entereth in through it, and the gods "who are therein acclaim him,"   . The company of gods say to Rā, "Open thou the earth, force thou a way through "the Ṭuat and the region which is above, and dispel "our darkness; hail, Rā, come thou to us," 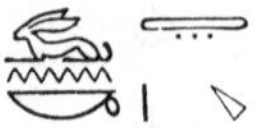  . The monster serpent which stands on his tail and guards the gateway is called TCHEṬBI, , and the two lines of text which refer to his admission of Rā read, "He who is "over this door openeth to Rā. SA saith to TCHEṬBI:— "'Open [thy] gate to Rā, unfold thy doors to KHUTI, "that he may send light into the thick darkness, and "may make his radiance illumine the hidden habitation.' "This door is shut after this great god hath passed "through it, and there is lamentation to those who are "in this gateway when they hear this door close upon "them,"  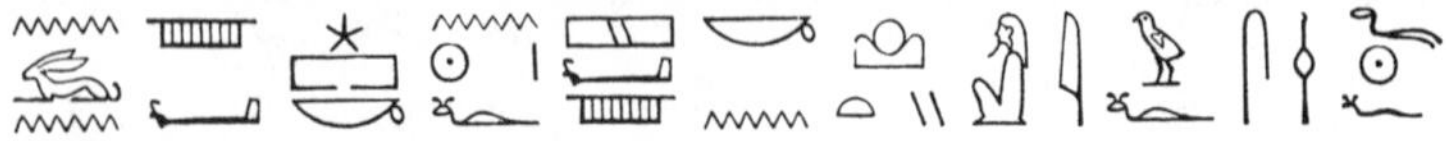

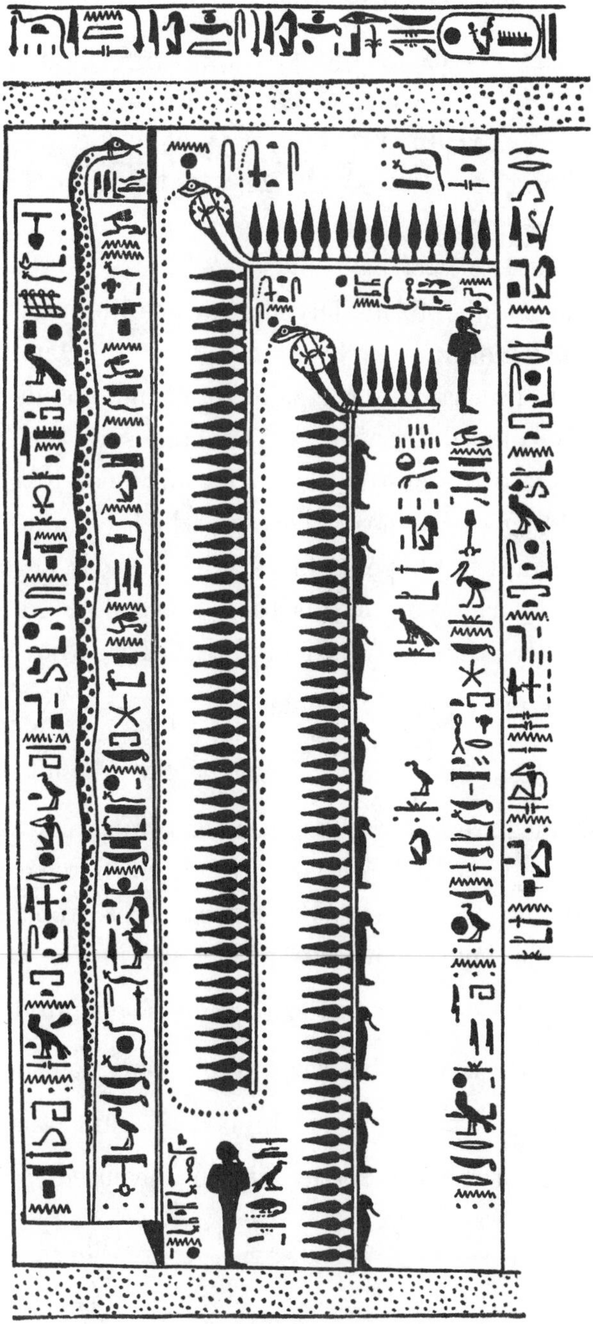

The Gate of the Serpent Tcheṭbi.

In the middle of this Division we see the boat of Rā being towed on its way by four gods of the Ṭuat; the god is in the same form as before, and stands in a shrine enveloped by MEḤEN. SA stands in the bows, and ḤEKA at the stern. The boat advances to a long, low building with a heavy cornice, which contains nine small shrines or chapels; in each of these is a god in mummied form lying on his back. The nine gods are described as the "gods who follow Osiris, who are in their abodes" (literally, "holes"),  . Immediately in front of the nine shrines are two groups, each containing six women, who stand upon a slope, one half of which appears to be land and the other half water; these women are called "the hour goddesses which are in the Ṭuat," . Each group is separated from the other by a monster serpent of many folds called ḤERERET, , and of him it is said that he "spawneth twelve serpents to be devoured by the hours," .

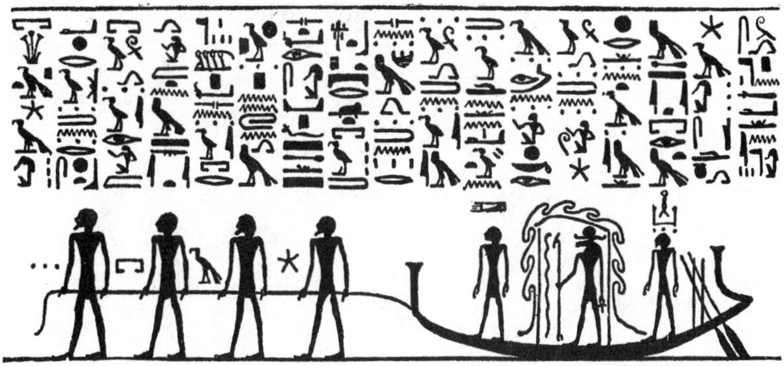

The Gods of the Fourth Division of the Ṭuat towing the Boat of Rā.

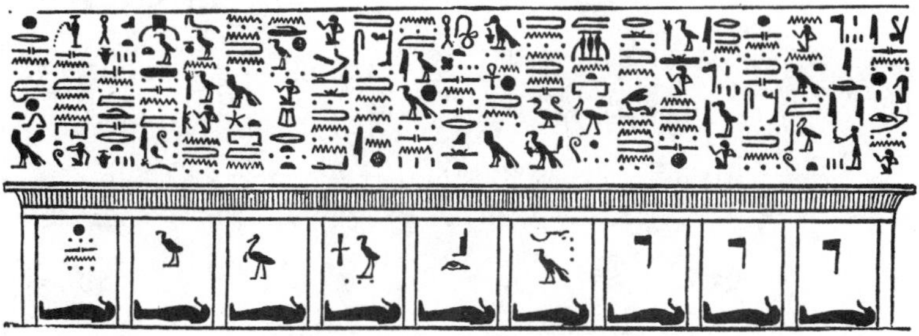

The Nine Gods who follow Osiris.

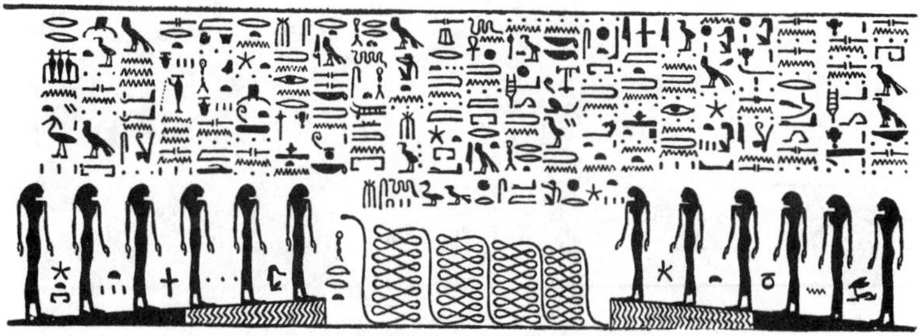

The Serpent Ḥereret and the Goddesses of the Hours.

The text relating to the passage of the boat of the sun reads :—

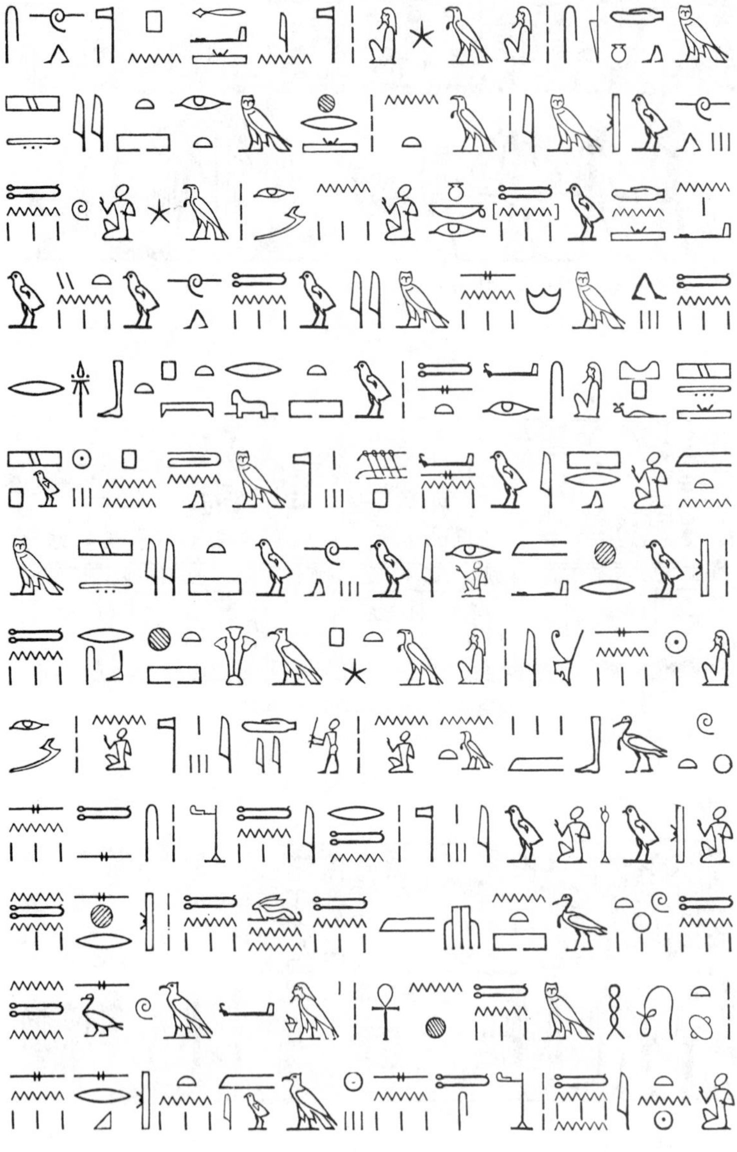

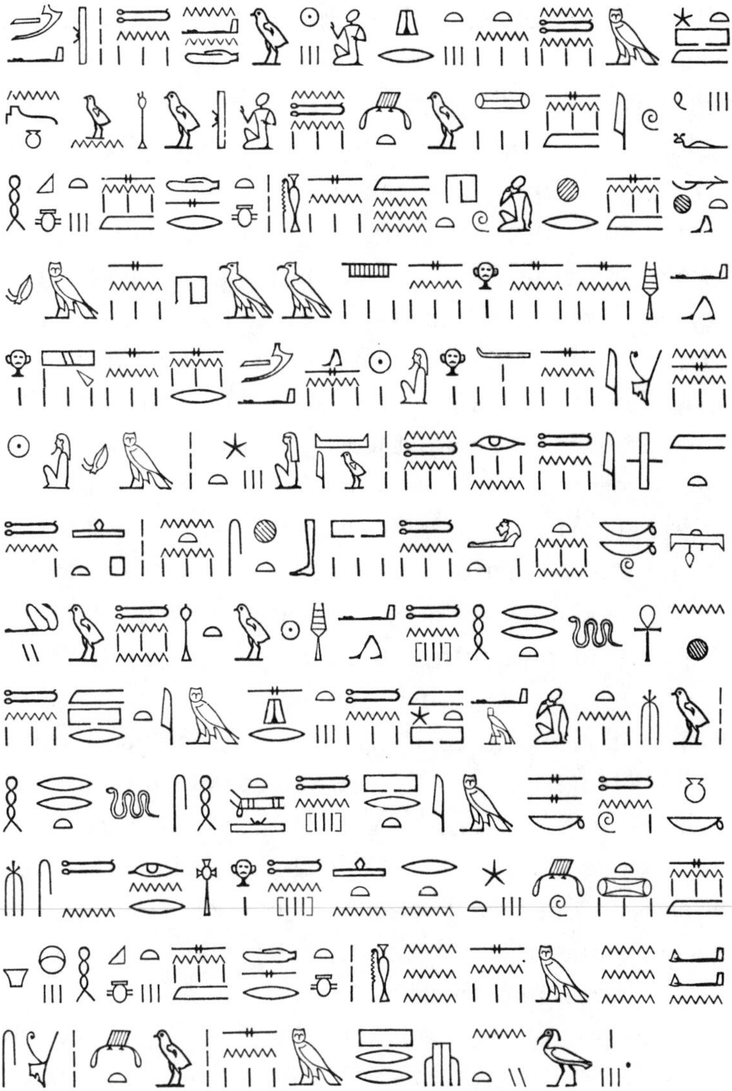

"This great god is drawn along by the gods of the "Ṭuat, and he journeyeth in the hidden place, and "worketh in respect of the things which are there.

"[He saith:—] 'Draw ye me along, O ye beings of the "Ṭuat, look ye upon me, [for] I have created you. "Pull ye with your arms and draw ye me therewith, "and turn ye aside to the eastern part of heaven, to "the habitations which surround ÅRES (or, SÅR) [and "to] that hidden mountain, the light (or, radiance) of "which goeth round about among the gods who receive "me as I come forth among you into the hidden place. "Draw ye me along, [for] I work on your behalf in the "gateway which covereth over the gods of the Ṭuat.'"

"And Rā saith unto them:—'Look ye upon me, O "gods, for I strike those who are in their sepulchres, "[saying], Arise, O ye gods! I have ordered for you the "plan and manner of your existence, O ye who are in 'your sepulchres, whose souls are broken, who live "upon your own filth and feed upon your own offal, "rise up before my Disk, and put ye yourselves in a "right state by means of my beams. The duties which "ye shall have in the Ṭuat are in conformity with the "things which I have decreed for you.' Their food "consisteth of flesh, and their ale is [made] of the red "[barley], and their libations are of cool water. There "is lamentation to them after they have heard their "doors close upon them."

In respect of the twelve goddesses of the hours it is said:—"[These are] they who stand upon their lake, "and it is they who guide Rā in a straight line by "means of their instruments. To them Rā saith:— "'Hearken, O ye goddesses of the hours of the night "sky. Work ye, and eat ye, and rest ye in your "gateways, with your breasts towards the darkness, "and your hind-parts towards the light. Make to "stand up the serpent Ḥereret, and live ye upon that "which cometh forth from it. It is your duty in the "Ṭuat to eat up the spawn of Ḥereret, and ye shall "destroy that which cometh forth from it. Draw ye "me, for I have begotten you in order that ye may pay "homage [to me]. Take ye your rest (or, be at peace), "O ye Hours!' Their food consisteth of cakes of "bread, and their ale is [made] of the red [barley], and "their draughts are of cool water, and there is given "unto them as their food that which cometh forth with "the *khu* (i.e., the beatified dead)."

On the right hand of the path of the boat of the Sun in the Fourth Division we see:—1. Twelve gods, bearded and standing upright, who are called "the gods who carry along their doubles," 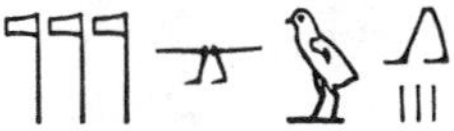 . 2. Twelve jackal-headed gods, who stand round the "Lake of Life," , who are called the "jackals in the lake of life,"  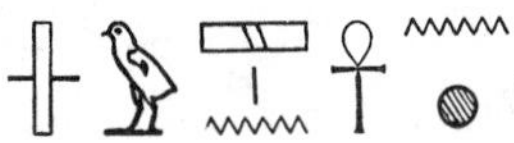. 3. Ten uraei, which stand round the "Lake of the Uraei," , and are called the "Living Uraei," . The texts which refer to these three groups of beings read:—

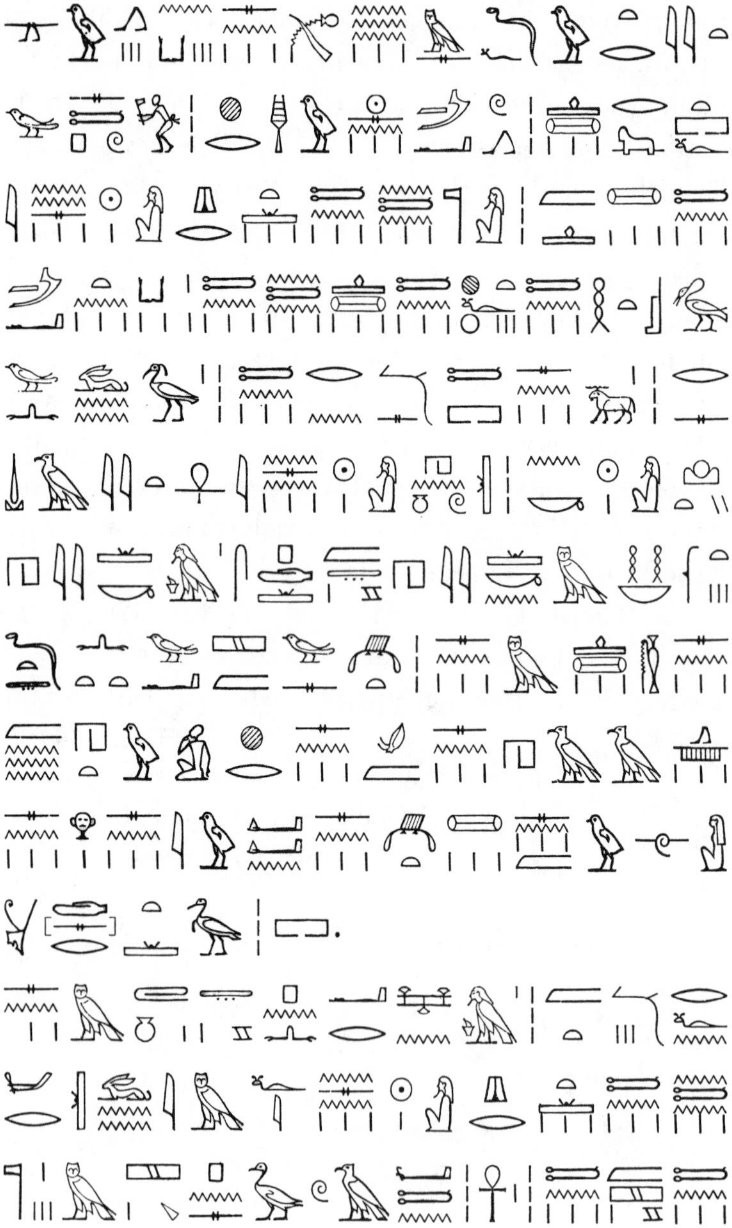

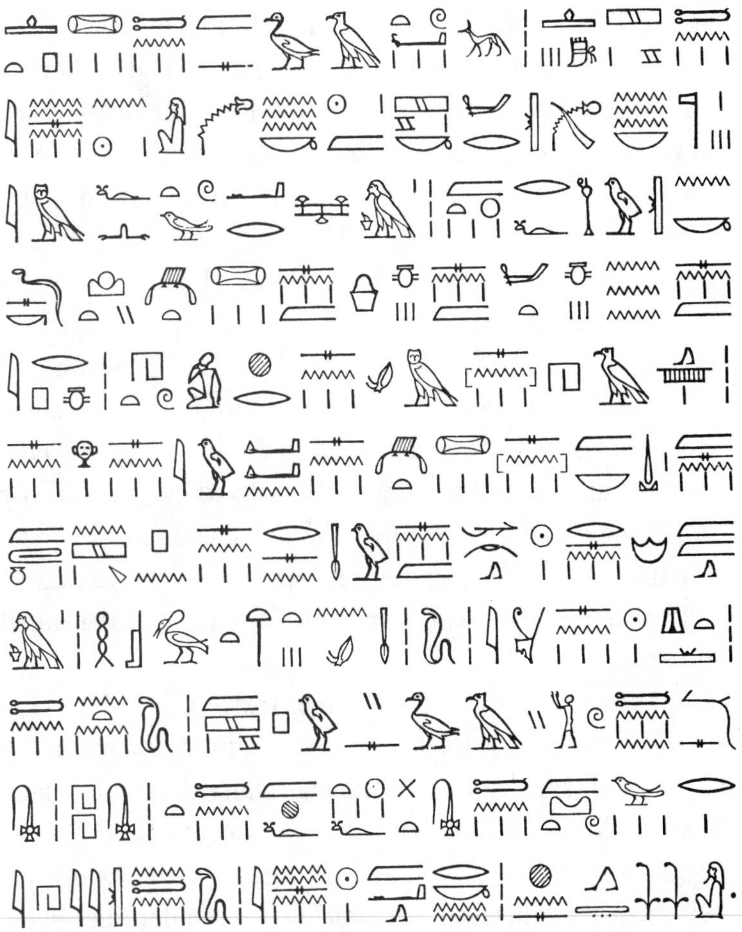

The paragraph which refers to the first twelve gods reads:—

"[These are] they who bear along their doubles, "who immerse themselves in that which floweth in "abundance from the slaughtered ones during the time "of their existence, and who carry the offerings which "are rightly due [to the god] to his abode. Unto them "saith Rā:—'That which belongeth to you [to do], O "ye gods who are among your offerings, is to offer as "an obligatory offering your doubles. Ye have your "own offerings, your enemies are destroyed, and they "are not. Your spirits are on their thrones, [and your] "souls are on their places.' They say unto Rā, 'Adora- "tions be unto thee, O RĀ-KHUTI! Hail to thee, O "thou Soul who art protected in the earth! Hail to "thee, as being eternity, the lord of the years and of "the everlastingness which hath no diminution.' Their "food consisteth of offerings, their drink is of cool "water, and there is lamentation to them when they "hear their doors close upon them. Their food is given "to them from the goddess Mu-sta (?) by ṬESERT-BAIU."

The paragraph which refers to the jackal-headed gods reads:—

"[These are] they who come forth from this lake "whereunto the souls of the dead cannot approach by "reason of the sanctity which is therein. Unto them "saith Rā:—'That which belongeth to you [to do], O ye "gods who are in this lake, is to keep guard upon your "lives in your lake; your offerings are under the guard "of the jackals which have set themselves on the edge "of your lake.' They say unto Rā:—'Immerse thyself, "O Rā, in thy holy lake, wherein the lord of the gods "immersed himself, whereunto the souls of the dead "approach not; this is what thou thyself hast com- "manded, O KHUTI.' Their food consisteth of bread, "their drink is [made] of the red [barley], and their

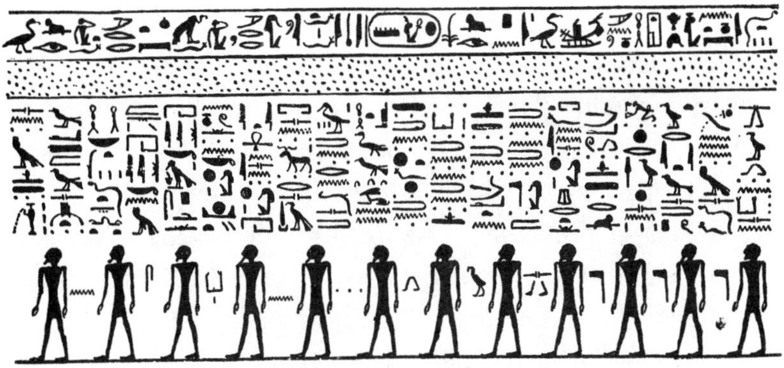

The Twelve Gods who carry their Doubles.

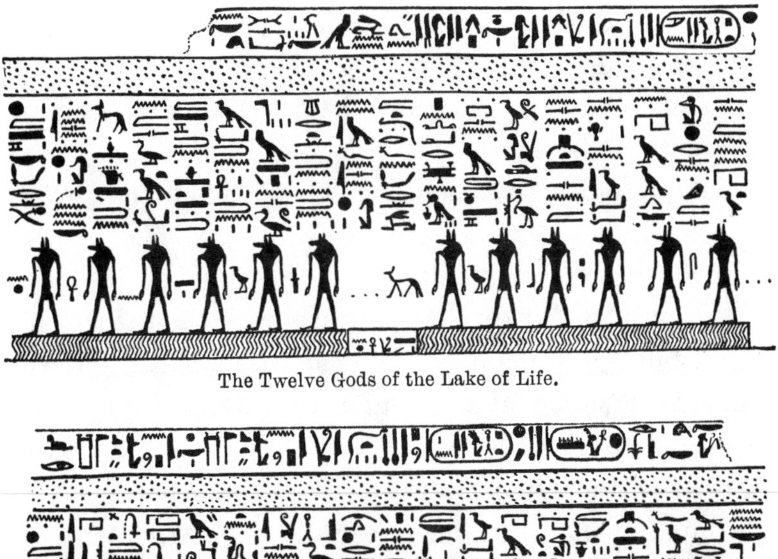

The Twelve Gods of the Lake of Life.

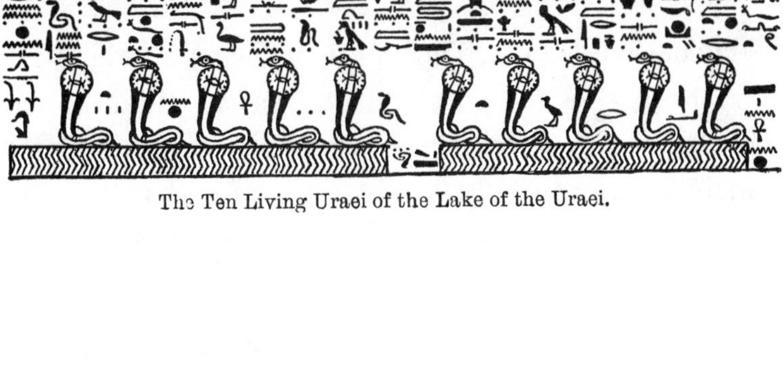

The Ten Living Uraei of the Lake of the Uraei.

"vessels of drink are filled with wine. There is lamentation among them when they hear their doors close "upon them. Their food is given unto them as lord[s] "of their sceptres round about this lake."

The paragraph which refers to the uraei reads:—

"[These are] they who have their speech after Rā "cometh to them, and souls are turned backwards, and "shadows are destroyed at the hearing of the words "(or, voices) of the uraei. Unto them saith Rā:—'That "which belongeth to you [to do], O ye URAEI who are "in this lake, is to guard your flames and your fires [so "that ye may hurl them] against my (literally, his) "enemies, and your burning heat against those whose "mouths are evil. Hail to you, O URAEI.' They "say unto Rā:—'Come thou to us, stride thou over "TANEN.'"

On the left of the path of the boat of the sun through the Fourth Division we see the god Osiris, in mummied form, and wearing on his head the crown of the South, standing on a serpent, and partially covered by the earth of a mountain; his head only is above the ground, and he stands in a naos with a vaulted dome. His name or title, KHENT ÅMENTI, , is written by his side. Before the shrine is a Flame-goddess in the form of a uraeus, and behind her are twelve gods, who stand in front of ḤERU-UR (or, Horus the Aged), the Haroeris of the later Greek writers. Ḥeru-ur is in the form of a hawk-headed man, who leans on a staff. Behind the shrine which contains Osiris stand twelve gods, who are described as "the gods who are behind the shrine," . Behind, or by the side of these, are four pits or hollows in the ground, by the side of each of which stands a god, with his body bent forward in adoration before a bearded god, who holds the symbol of life in the right hand and a sceptre in the left. The four gods are called "Masters of their pits," , and their lord is called the "Master of Earths (?)," .

The texts referring to these gods read:—

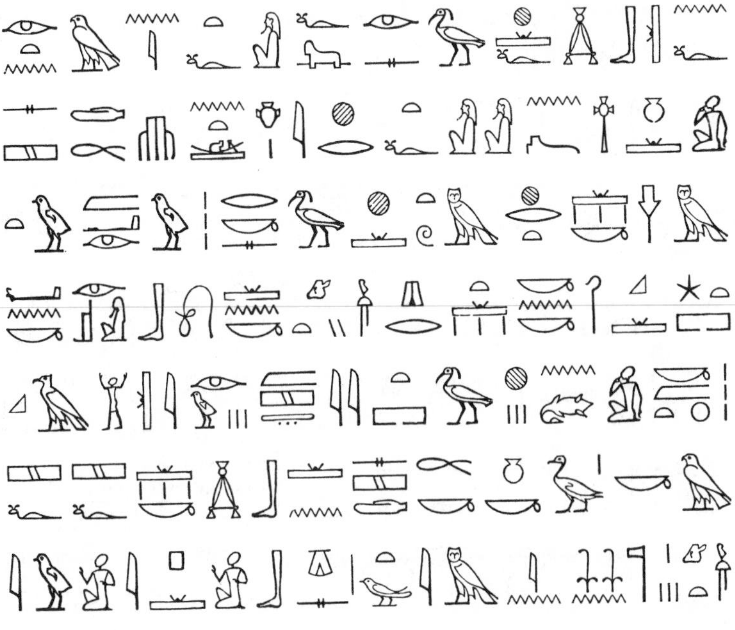

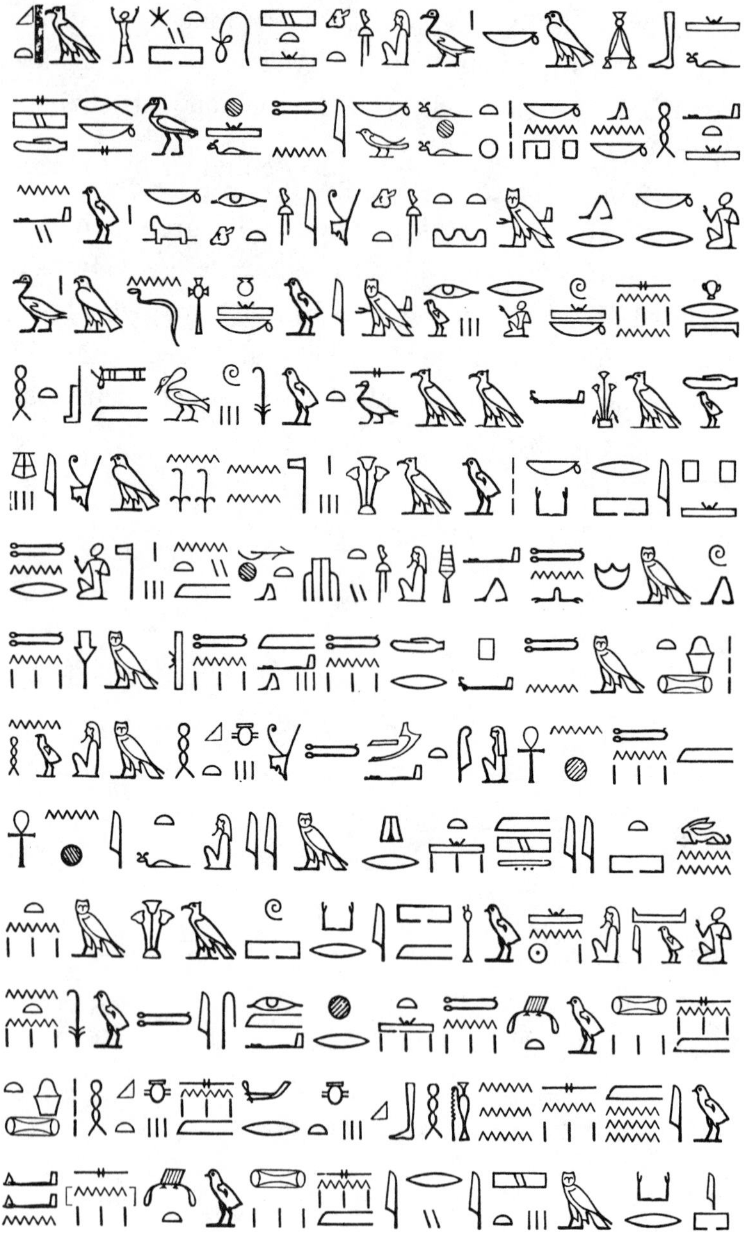

The text referring to Horus reads:—

"Horus worketh on behalf of his father Osiris, he "performeth magical ceremonies for him, and restoreth "to him the crown [, saying], 'My heart goeth out to "thee, O my father, thou who art avenged on those "who would work against thee, and in all the matters "which concern thee thou art guided by magical "ceremonies. Thou hast the mastery, O Osiris, thou "hast the sovereignty, O KHENTI ÅMENTI, thou hast "whatsoever is thine as Governor of the Ṭuat, O thou "whose forms (or, attributes) are exalted in the hidden "place; the beatified spirits hold thee in fear, and "the dead are terrified at thee. Thy crown hath been "restored unto thee, and I, thy son Horus, have "reckoned thy weakness there.'"

The twelve gods who are in front of the shrine of Khenti Åmenti say:—

"Let Him of the Ṭuat be exalted! Let Khenti "Åmenti be adored! Thy son Horus hath restored to "thee thy crown, he hath protected thee by means of "magical ceremonies, he hath crushed for thee thine "enemies, he hath brought to thee vigour for thy arms, "O Osiris, Khenti Ȧmenti."

In reply to this address of the twelve gods Khenti Ȧmenti saith unto his son Horus:—

"Come to me, O my son Horus, and avenge me on "those who work against me, and cast them to him "that is over the things which destroy, [for] it is he "who guardeth the pits [of destruction]."

Then saith Horus unto those gods who are behind the shrine:—

"Make inquisition for me, O gods who are in the "following of Khenti Ȧmenti, stand ye up, and with-"draw ye not yourselves, and be ye masters over "yourselves, and come, and live delicately on the bread "of Ḥu, and drink ye of the ale of Maāt, and live ye "upon that whereon my father liveth there. That "which belongeth to you in the hidden place is to be "behind the shrine, according to the commandment of "Rā. I call unto you, and behold, it is for you to do "what it is your duty [to do].' Their meat consisteth "of cakes of bread, and their ale is of the *tchesert* "drink, and their libations are [made with] cool water. "Their food is given unto them by the guardian of "the things which are in the shrine. And Horus "saith unto these gods:—'Smite ye the enemies of my "father, and hurl ye them down into your pits because "of that deadly evil which they have done against the

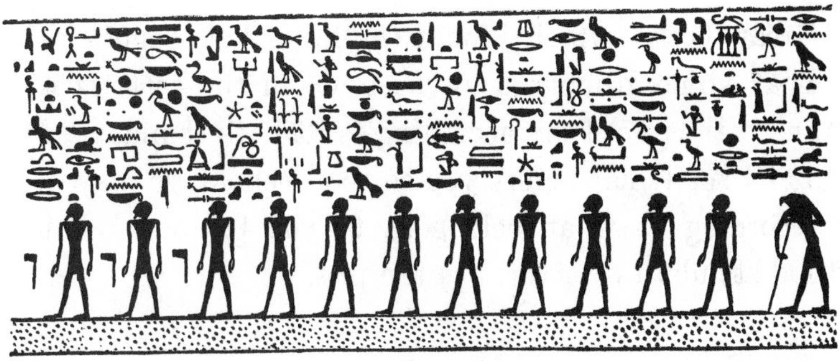

The Twelve Gods before the Shrine. Ḥeru-ur.

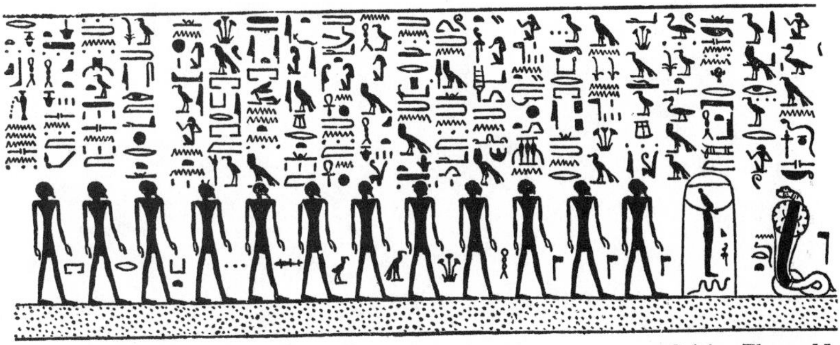

The Twelve Gods behind the Shrine. Osiris Khent-Åmenti. The goddess of Flame (Nesert).

The Master of Earths. The Four Masters of their Pits.

"Great One, [which] found (?) him that begot me. "That which belongeth to you to do in the Ṭuat is to "guard the pits of fire according as Rā hath commanded, "and I set [this] before you so that, behold, ye may do "according to what belongeth to you [to do].' This "god standeth over (or, by) the pits."

CHAPTER VI.

THE GATE OF TEKA-ḤRÀ.

THE FIFTH DIVISION OF THE ṬUAT.

THE boat of the sun having passed through the Fourth Division of the Ṭuat arrives at the gateway which leads to the FIFTH DIVISION. This gateway is similar to that which guards the Fourth Division, and is guarded by nine gods, who are described as the "Fourth Company," ; at the entrance to the corridor and at its exit stands a jackal-headed god, the former being called ĀAU, , and the latter TEKMI, ; each is said to "extend his arms and hands to Rā." The corridor is swept by flames of fire, as before. The gateway is called ÀRIT, 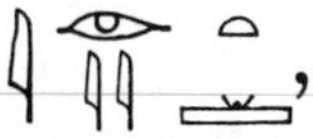, and the text says, "This great god cometh to this "gateway, and entereth in through it, and the gods "who are therein acclaim him," 

. The nine gods say to

Rā, "RĀ-ḤERU-KHUTI unfoldeth our doors, and openeth "our gateways. Hail, Rā, come thou to us, O great "god, lord of hidden nature," 

. The monster serpent which stands on his tail and guards the gateway is called TEKA-ḤRȦ, , and the two lines of text which refer to his admission of Rā read:—"He who is over this door openeth to Rā. "SA saith to TEKA-ḤRȦ:—'Open thy gate to Rā, unfold "thy doors to KHUTI, that he may send light into the "thick darkness, and may make his radiance illumine "the hidden habitation.' This door is shut after the "great god hath passed through it, and there is "lamentation to those who are in this gateway when "they hear this door close upon them." As the hieroglyphic text is identical with that given above on p. 120 it is not repeated here.

In the middle of this Division we see the boat of Rā being towed on its way by four gods of the Ṭuat; the god is in the same form as before, and stands in a shrine enveloped by MEḤEN. SA stands in the bows, and ḤEKA at the stern. In front of those who tow the boat are nine shrouded gods, with projecting elbows; each of these holds in his hands a part of the body of a long, slender serpent, and the group is called "those who hold ENNUTCHI," 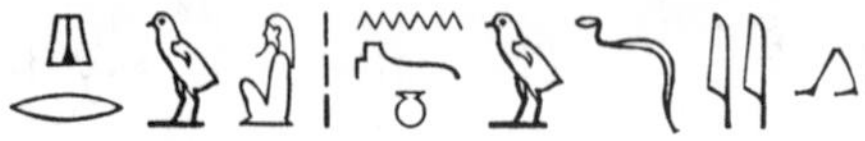. In front of these are

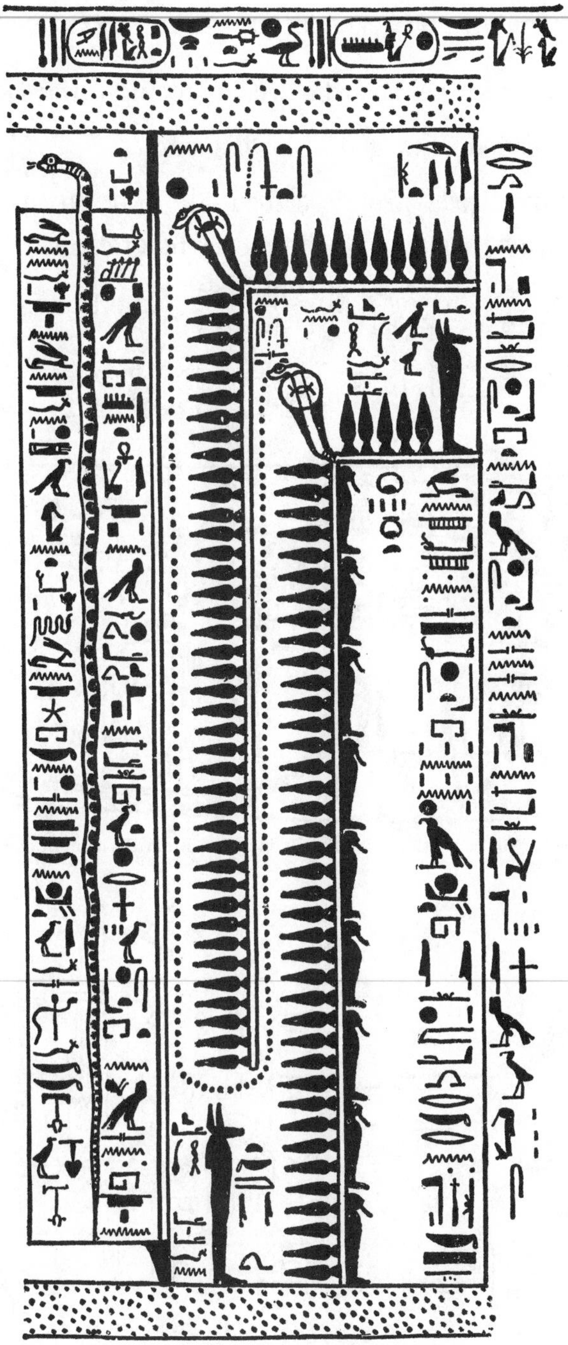

The Gate of the Serpent Teka-ḥrâ.

twelve bearded beings, who are advancing towards a god, who is styled [the god] "of his angle," ; the twelve gods are described as BAIU RETH-ÅMMU-ṬUAT, i.e., "the souls of the men who are in the Ṭuat," 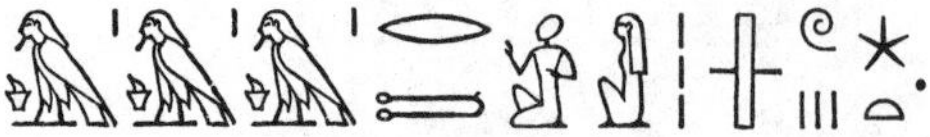. The texts read:—

The Boat of Rā being towed by the Gods of the Fifth Division of the Ṭuat.

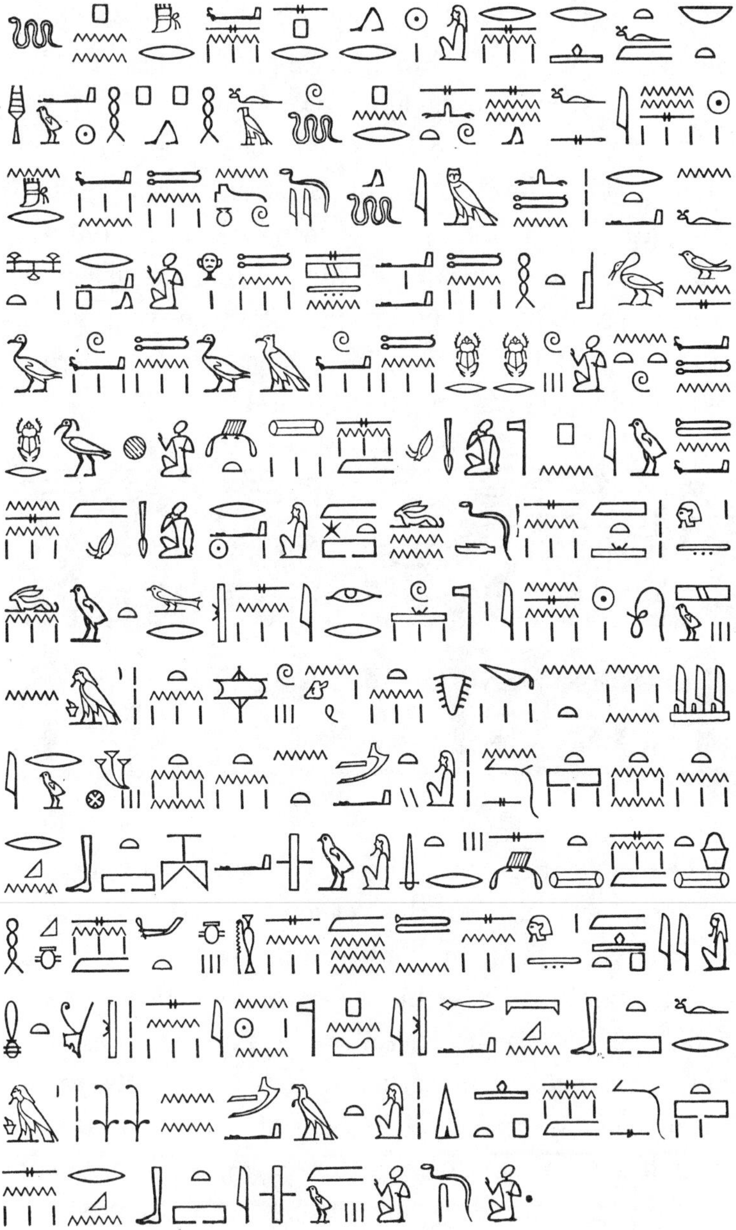

"The gods of the Ṭuat draw along this great god, "and he journeyeth through the hidden place. [Rā "saith:—] 'Draw ye me along, O ye gods of the Ṭuat, "and sing praises unto me, O ye who are at the head "of the stars; let your cords be strong (or, vigorous), "and draw ye me along by means of them, and let "your hands and arms be steady, let there be speed in "your legs, let there be strong intent in your souls, "and let your hearts be glad. Open ye a prosperous "way into the chambers (*qerti*) of hidden things.'"

The Nine Gods who hold Ennutchi.

The text relating to the bearers of the serpent reads:—

"Those who are in this scene carry this serpent. "Rā striketh them and advanceth towards them to "make himself to rest in [the gateway called] NEBT-"ĀḤĀU. This serpent travelleth as far as it (i.e., this "gateway), but he passeth not beyond it. Rā saith "unto them:—'Strike ye the serpent ENNUTCHI there, "give him no way [whereby to escape], so that I may "pass by you. Hide your arms, destroy that which "you guard, protect that which cometh into being "from my forms, and tie ye up (or, fetter) that which "cometh into being from my strength.' Their food "consisteth of the hearing of the word of this god, and "offerings are made to them from the hearing of the "word of Rā in the Ṭuat."

"Unto those who have spoken what is right and "true upon earth, and who have magnified the forms "of the god, Rā saith:—'Praises shall be [sung] to

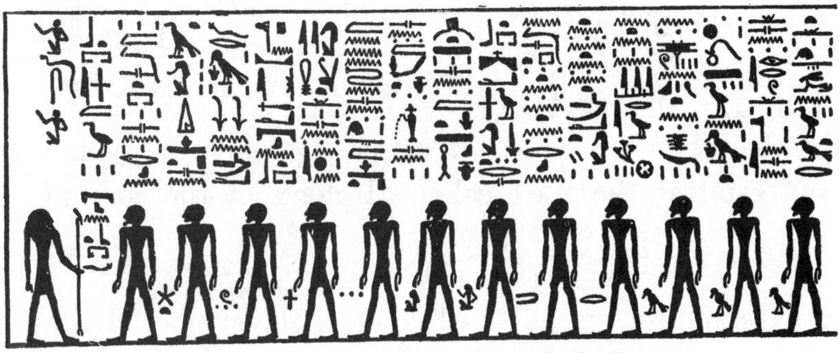

Ḥeri-qenbet-f. The souls of men who are in the Ṭuat.

"your souls, and there shall be breath to your nostrils, "and there shall be to you joints in SEKHET-ÅRU. "That which shall be indeed yours is what belongeth "to the MAĀTI GODS. The habitations which shall be "yours shall be (or, are) at the corner where [live] "those who are with me who weigh words for them.' "Their food is of bread-cakes, and their drink of "*tchesert* drink, and their libations are of cool water. "Offerings are made unto them upon earth as to the "god Ḥetepi, according to what should be offered unto "them."

Rā saith unto this god:—"Let him that is over his "Corner (Ḥeri-qenbet-f) cry out to those souls who "are right, and true, and divine, and make them to sit "at peace in their habitations at the Corner of those "who are with myself."

On the right hand of the path of Rā in the Fifth Division of the Ṭuat are:—1. Twelve male beings bowing in adoration; they are described as "those who make adorations in the Ṭuat,"  . 2. Twelve male beings who bear in their hands a cord for measuring plots of ground and estates; these are called "Holders of the cord in the Ṭuat," . 3. Four gods, standing upright, each holding the symbol of life in his right hand, and a sceptre in the left. The hieroglyphic texts which relate to these groups read:—

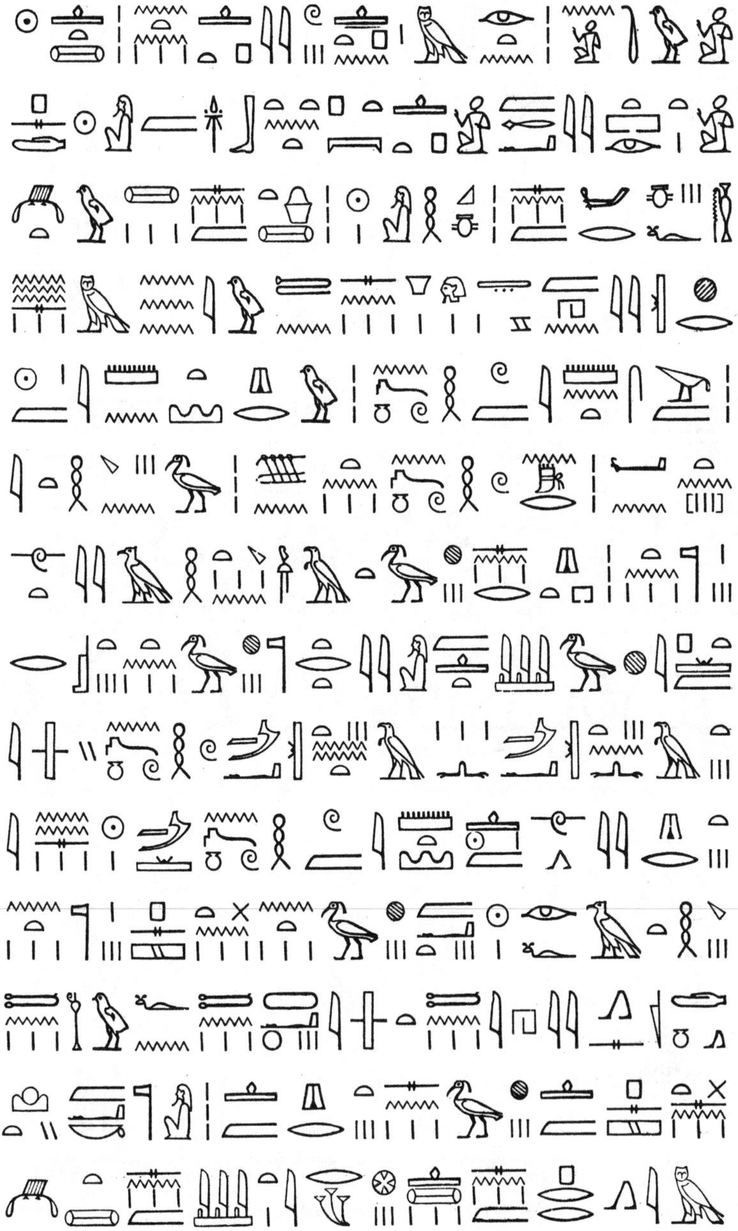

The Twelve Gods who make adoration in the Ṭuat.

The passage in the text which refers to the adorers reads:—

"[These are] they who make songs to Rā in Ȧmentet "and exalt Ḥeru-khuti. [These are they who] knew "Rā upon earth, and who made offerings unto him. "Their offerings are in their place, and their glory "is in the holy place of Ȧment. They say unto "Rā:—'Come thou, O Rā, progress through the Ṭuat. "Praise be to thee! Enter thou among the holy "[places] with the serpent Meḥen.' Rā saith unto "them:—'There are offerings for you, O ye who made "offerings. I am content with what ye did for me, "both when I used to shine in the eastern part of "heaven, and when I was sinking to rest in the "chamber of my Eye.' Their food is of the bread-

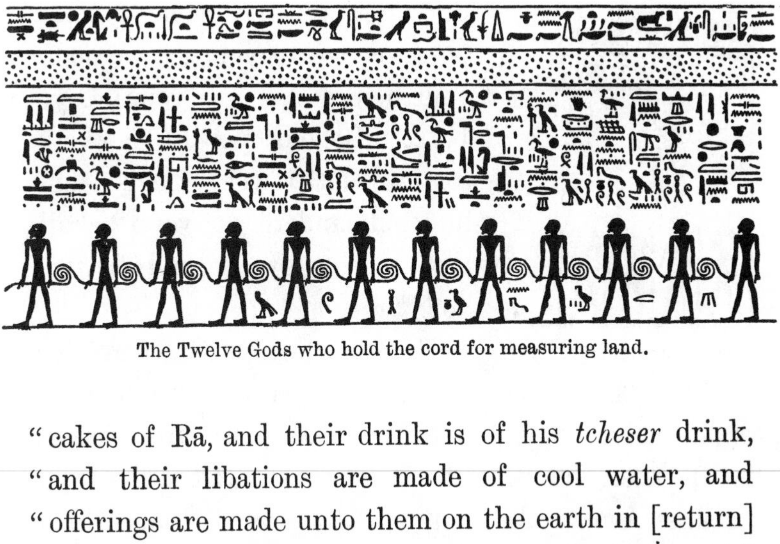

The Twelve Gods who hold the cord for measuring land.

"cakes of Rā, and their drink is of his *tcheser* drink, "and their libations are made of cool water, and "offerings are made unto them on the earth in [return] "for the praisings which they make unto Rā in Ȧment."

The passage in the text which refers to the holders of the measuring cord reads:—

"[These are they who] hold the measuring cord in "Ȧment, and they go over therewith the fields of "the KHU (i.e., the beatified spirits). [Rā saith to "them]:—'Take ye the cord, draw it tight, and mark "out the limit (or, passage) of the fields of Ȧmentet, "the KHU whereof are in your abodes, and the gods "whereof are on your thrones.' The KHU of NETERTI "are in the Field of Peace, [and] each KHU hath been "judged by him that is in the cord. Righteousness "is to those who are (i.e., who exist), and unrighteous-"ness to those who are not. Rā saith unto them:— "'What is right is the cord in Ȧment, and Rā is "content with the stretching (or, "drawing) of the same. Your "possessions are yours, O ye gods, "your homesteads are yours, O ye "KHU. Behold ye, Rā maketh "(or, worketh) your fields, and "he commandeth on your behalf "that there may be sand(?) with "you.'"

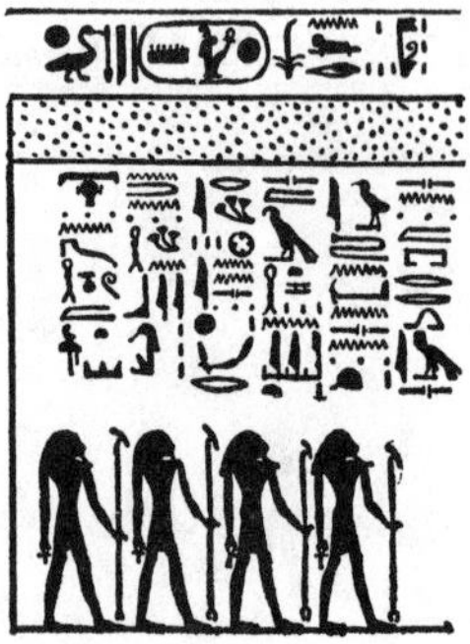

The Four Ḥenbi Gods.

"Hail, journey on, O KHUTI, for "verily the gods are content with "that which they possess, and the KHU are content "with their homesteads. Their food [cometh] from "Sekhet-Ȧru, and their offerings from that which "springeth up therein. Offerings are made unto them "upon earth from the estate of Sekhet-Ȧru."

To the four bearded gods Rā saith:—"Holy are ye, "O ḤENBI gods, ye overseers of the cords in Ȧmentet. "[O stablish ye fields and give [them] to the gods and "to the KHU (i.e., spirits) [after] they have been "measured in Sekhet-Åaru. Let them give fields and "sand to the gods and to the souls who are in the Ṭuat. "Their food shall be from Sekhet-Åaru, and their "offerings from the things which spring forth therein]."

On the left of the path of the boat of Rā are:—1. A hawk-headed god, leaning upon a staff; he is called Horus, . 2. Four groups, each group containing four men. The first are RETH, , the second are ĀAMU, , the third are NEḤESU, , and the fourth are THEMEḤU, . The RETH are Egyptians, the ĀAMU are dwellers in the deserts to the east and north-east of Egypt, the NEḤESU are the black races and NEGROES, and the THEMEḤU are the fair-skinned Libyans. 3. Twelve bearded beings, each of whom grasps with both hands the body of a long serpent; these are called the "Holders of the period of time in Åment," , . 4. Eight bearded gods, who are called the "Sovereign chiefs of the Ṭuat," 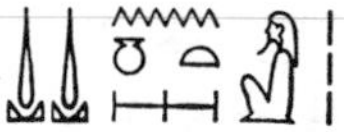 . The hieroglyphic text which relates to these groups reads:—

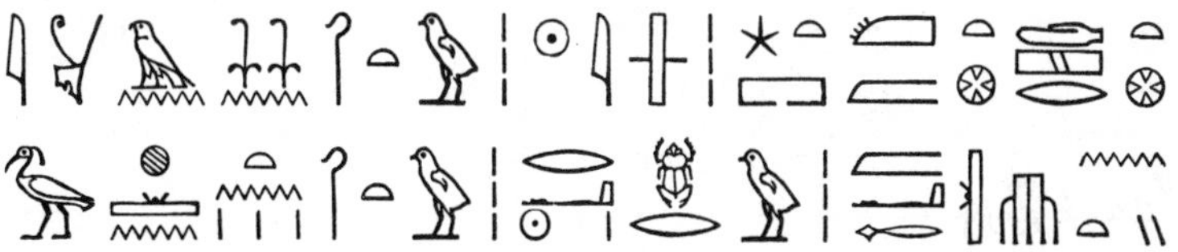

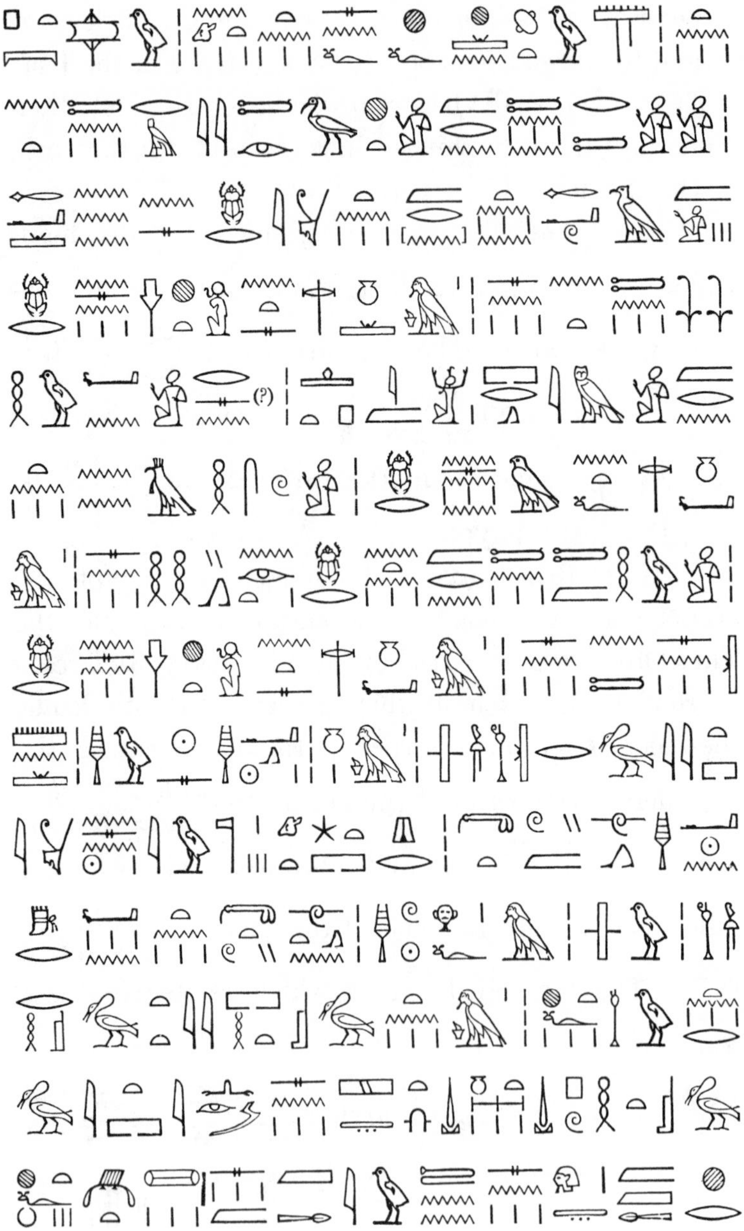

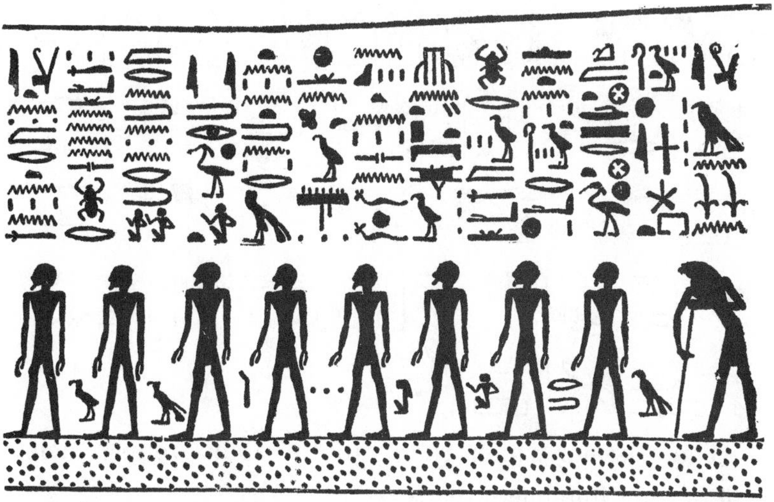

The Āamu, i.e., Asiatics. The Reth, i.e., Egyptians. Horus.

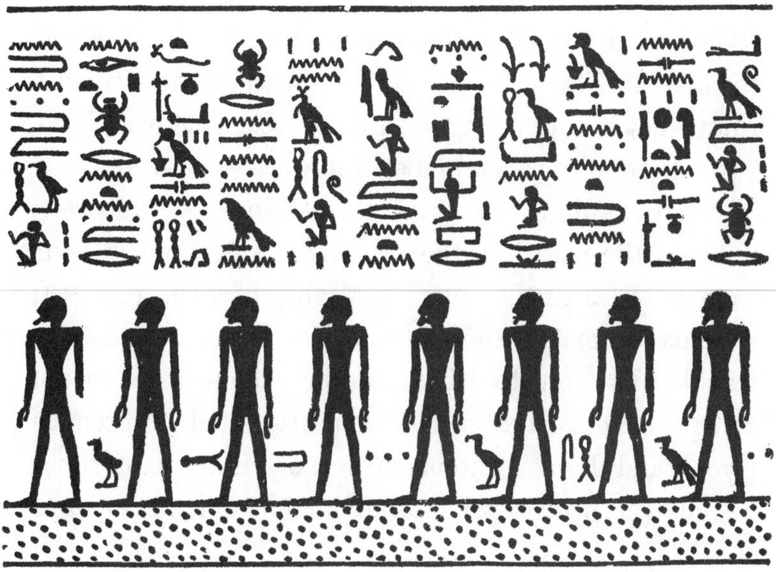

The Themeḥu, i.e., Libyans. The Neḥesu, i.e., Negroes.

The passage which refers to the four groups, each containing four men, reads:—

Horus saith unto the creatures of Rā who dwell in the Black Land (Qemt, i.e., Egypt) and in the Red Land (i.e., the deserts which lie on each side of the Black Land formed of the mud of the Nile):—"Magical "protection be unto you, O ye creatures of Rā, who "have come into being from the Great One who is at "the head of heaven! Let there be breath to your "nostrils, and let your linen swathings be unloosed! "Ye are the tears[1] of the eye of my splendour in your "name of RETH (i.e., men). Mighty of issue (ĀA-MU) "ye have come into being in your name of ĀAMU; "Sekhet hath created them, and it is she who delivereth "(or, avengeth) their souls. I masturbated [to produce "you], and I was content with the hundreds of thou-"sands [of beings] who came forth from me in your

[1] Or, the weeping.

"name of NEḤESU (i.e., Negroes); Horus made them to "come into being, and it is he who avengeth their "souls. I sought out mine Eye, and ye came into being in your name of THEMEḤU; Sekhet hath created "them, and she avengeth their souls."

The passage which refers to the gods who make stable the period of life (KHERU-ĀḤĀU-EM-ÅMENT) reads:—

Those who make firm (or, permanent) the duration

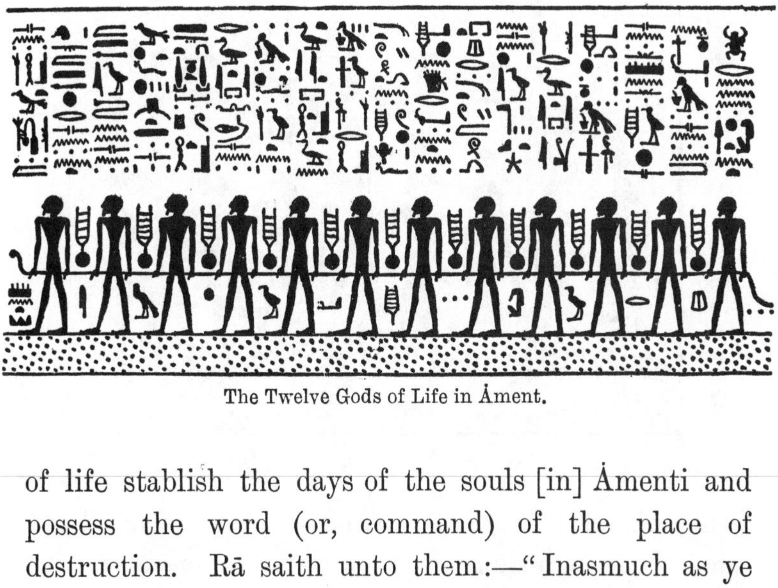

The Twelve Gods of Life in Åment.

of life stablish the days of the souls [in] Åmenti and possess the word (or, command) of the place of destruction. Rā saith unto them:—"Inasmuch as ye "are the gods who dwell in the Ṭuat, and who have "possession of [the serpent] METERUI, by means of "whom ye mete out the duration of life of the souls "who are in Åmenti who are condemned to destruc- "tion, destroy ye the souls of the enemies according "to the place of destruction which ye are commanded "to appoint, and let them not see the hidden "place."

The passage in the text which refers to the divine sovereign chiefs reads:—

"[Here are] the divine sovereign chiefs who shall "destroy the enemies. They shall have their offerings

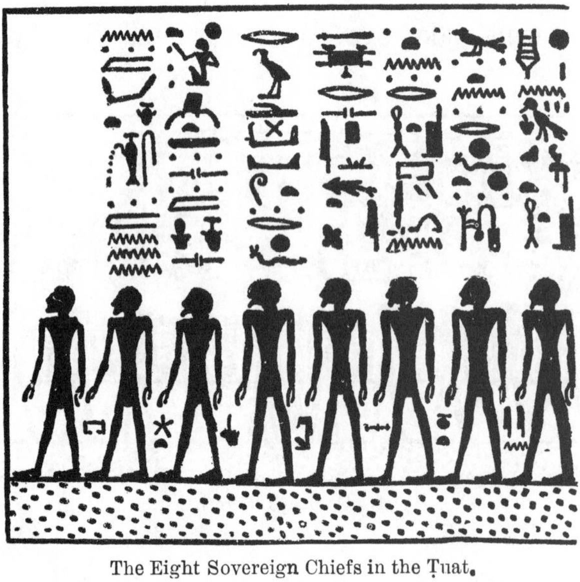

The Eight Sovereign Chiefs in the Ṭuat.

"by means of the word [which becometh] Maāt; they "shall have their oblations upon earth by means of the "word [which becometh] Maāt, and it is they who "destroy and who pass the edict concerning (literally, "write) the duration of the life of the souls who dwell "in Åmenti. The destruction which is yours shall be "[directed] against the enemies, and the power to write "which ye possess shall be for the place of destruction. "I have come, even I the great one Horus, that I may "make a reckoning with my body, and that I may "shoot forth evils against my enemies. Their food is "bread, and their drink is the *tchesert* wine, and they "have cool water wherewith to refresh (or, bathe) "themselves. [Offerings are made to them upon earth. "One doth not enter into the place of destruction.][1]

[1] Supplied from Champollion, *Notices*, p. 772.

CHAPTER VII.

THE JUDGMENT HALL OF OSIRIS.

The Sixth Division of the Ṭuat.

The boat of Rā having passed through the Fifth Division of the Ṭuat arrives at the gateway which leads to the Sixth Division, or, as the text says:  , "This god "cometh forth to this pylon, and he passeth in through "it, and those gods who are in the secret place acclaim "him." The gateway is guarded by twelve bearded mummy forms, who are described as the "gods and goddesses who are in this pylon,"  , and it is called Nebt-āḥā, . The gate which admits to the Sixth Division resembles those already described; at the entrance to the corridor and at its exit stands a bearded mummied form, the former being called Maā-àb, 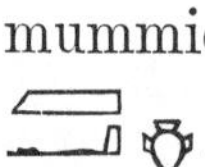, and the latter Sheta-àb, 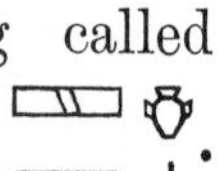. These names mean "Right (or, true) of heart" and

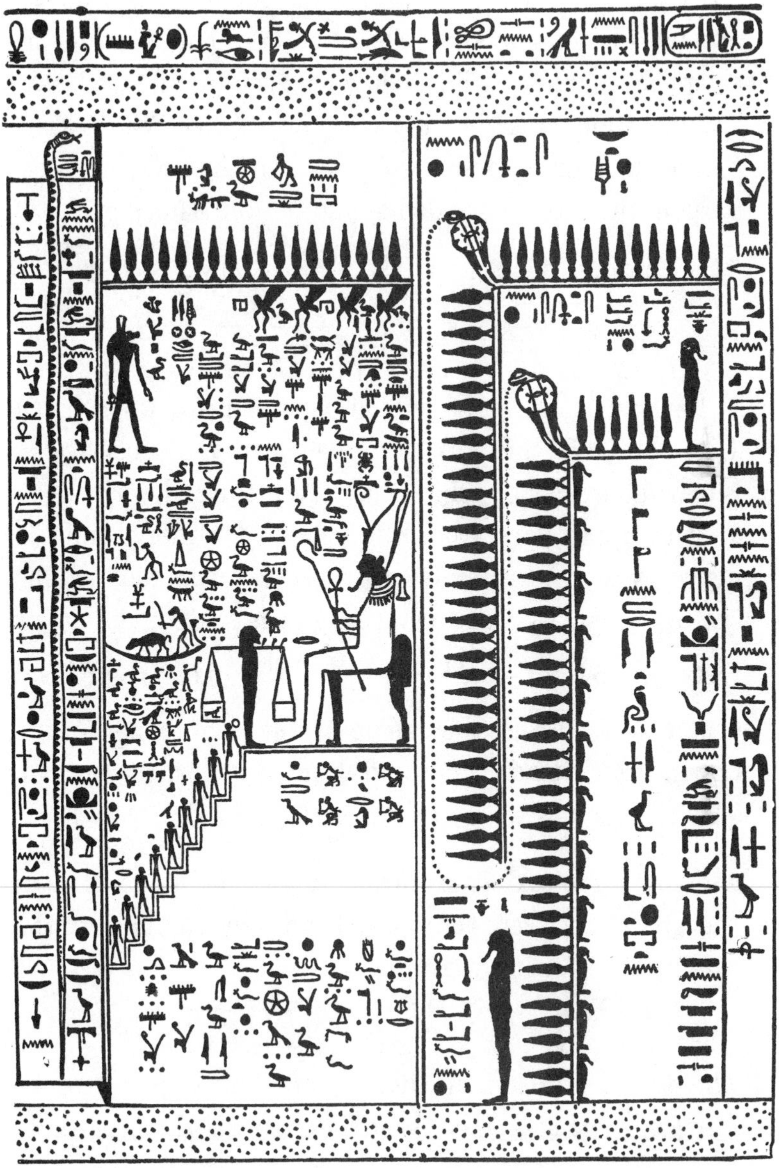

The Judgment Hall of Osiris. The Gate of the Serpent Set-em-maa-f.

"Hidden of heart" respectively, and each is said to extend his hands and arms to Rā. The corridor is swept by flames. The gods who acclaim the god say, "Come thou to us, O thou who art at the head of the "horizon, O great god, who dost open the hidden place. "Open thou the holy doors, and unfold the portals of "the hidden place," 
.

Between the gate which leads into the SIXTH DIVISION and the Division itself we find inserted a remarkable scene, which may be thus described:—In the upper part, from one side to another, a line is drawn, which is intended to represent the roof of the shrine or canopy in which the god is seated, and on it rests a row of *kakheru* , i.e., spear-head ornaments. From the inside of the roof hang, upside down, four heads of some kind of horned animal. These are called *Hahaiu* , and are supposed to be heads of gazelle[1] or oxen. In the space between the spear-head ornaments and the side of the Ṭuat is written

.

The transliteration of these characters appears to be *Ser ḥer Ṭuat sath then;* the meaning of the first three

[1] "Têtes de gazelles" (Champollion, *Monuments*, tom. ii., p. 495).

words is tolerably clear, i.e., "Osiris, governor of the Ṭuat," but the signification of the last signs is doubtful. M. Lefébure translates the inscription, "Osiris, master of Hades, Earth, and Tanen." Osiris, who wears the double crown of the South and North, and holds in his right hand the symbol of "life," and in his left a sceptre, , is seated on a chair of state, which is set on the top of a platform with nine steps. On each step stands a god, and the nine gods are described as the "company which is with SAR, i.e., Osiris," 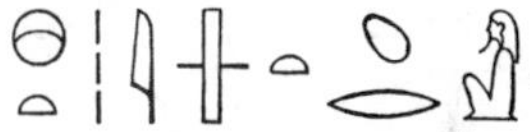. On the topmost step is a Balance, in which the actions of the deceased are weighed; the beam of the Balance is supported either by the deceased, or by a stand which is made in the form of a bearded mummy. One pan of the Balance contains some rectangular object, and the other a figure of the bird which is symbolic of evil and wickedness. Behind the Balance is a boat, which is sailing away from the presence of Osiris; in it is a pig being driven along by a dog-headed ape which flourishes a stick. In the top left-hand corner is a figure of Anubis, jackal-headed, and under the floor of the platform on which Osiris is seated are figures of the enemy of SAR, or Osiris. From the variant of this scene which is found on the sarcophagus of Tcheḥrȧ at Paris,[1] as well as from the sarcophagus of Seti I., we may see that the pig in the

[1] Sharp, *Inscriptions*, part ii., pl. 9.

boat is called ĀM-Ā, , i.e., "Eater of the Arm," and the boat is piloted by a second ape which stands in the bows. On the Paris monument we see a man wielding a hatchet in a threatening manner and standing near the Scales, probably with the view of destroying the deceased if the judgment of Osiris prove adverse to him.

The nine short lines of text at the foot of the scene read:—

This inscription is in the so-called "enigmatic" writing,[1] a fact which was first noticed by Champollion, but a transcript of it exists on the sarcophagus of Tcheḥrȧ in characters which have the ordinary values,[2] and this reads as follows:—

[1] See Goodwin, *Aeg. Zeit.*, 1873, p. 138; Renouf, *ibid.*, 1874, p. 101; and Champollion, *Monuments*, pl. 272.

[2] Lefébure renders, "O ye who bring the word just or false to me, he, Thoth, examines the words" (*Records of the Past*, vol. x., p. 114).

, i.e., "His enemies are under his "feet, the gods and the spirits are before him; he is "the enemy of the dead (i.e., the damned) among the "beings of the Ṭuat, Osiris putteth under restraint "[his] enemies, he destroyeth them, and he performeth "the slaughter of them."

The text which refers to Anubis reads:—

and this Mr. Goodwin transcribed:—

, i.e., "Hail, O ye who make to be *maāt* "the word of your little one, may Thoth weigh the "words, may he make to eat his father."

Immediately over the boat is the short inscription:—

This Goodwin renders by, "[When] this god entereth, "he (i.e., the Ape) riseth and putteth under restraint "Ām-ā (i.e., the Eater of the Arm)."[1]

[1] "The diver [when] this god rises, he gives up [the pig] to the plagues" (Lefébure, *op. cit.*, p. 114).

Behind the pair of scales is the following legend[1]:—

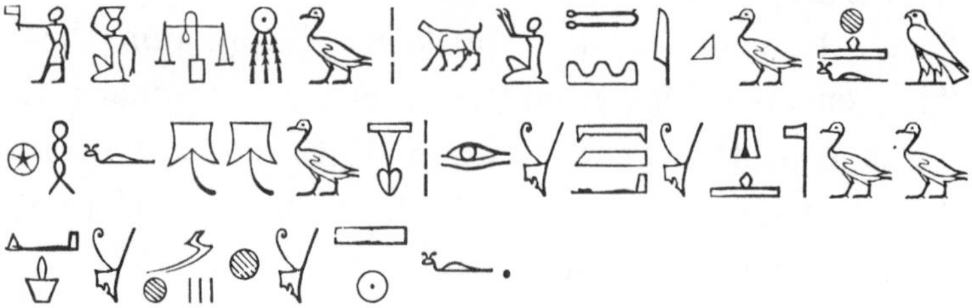

This Mr. Goodwin transcribes by:—

, and renders, "The balance-bearer does homage; the blessed spirits "in Ȧmenti follow after him; the morning star "disperses the thick darkness; there is good will "above, justice below. The god reposes himself, he "gives bread to the blessed, who throng towards him." The translation by M. Lefébure reads, "The bearer of "the hatchet and the bearer of the scales protect the "inhabitant of Ȧmenti, [who] takes his repose in "Hades, and traverses the darkness and the shadows. "Happiness is above, and justice below. The god "reposes and sheds light produced by truth which he "has produced."

[1] See also Champollion, *Monuments*, tom. ii., p. 490.

The upper part of the space between the roof and the platform on which Osiris sits is occupied by two short inscriptions, which are full of difficulty; they read:—

I.

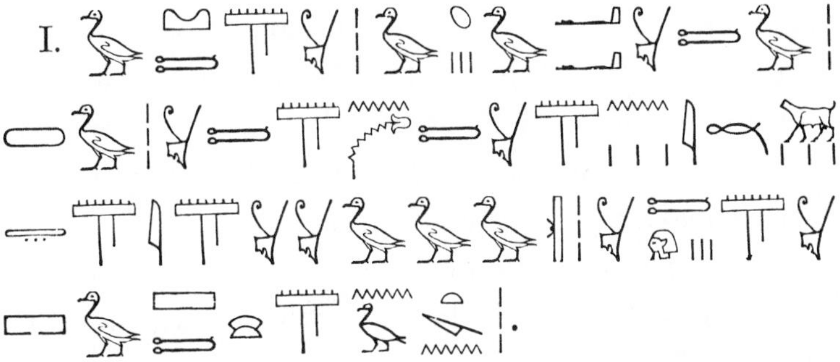

II.

The meaning of these texts has puzzled several workers, and even the order in which the characters are to be read has given rise to differences of opinion. One of the chief difficulties in the matter is caused by the way in which the two legends are written on the sarcophagus of Seti I. Looking at the hieroglyphics as they stand, they seem to form one continuous inscription, but, if we examine the scene as it appears in the tomb of Rameses II., we see that we must divide them as above. Mr. Goodwin made an attempt to transcribe and translate a part of the texts, but as he considered them to form only one inscription we cannot accept his rendering. M. Lefébure has made translations of both texts, and they read [1] :—

I. "They, they hide those which are in the state of "the elect. They the country [belonging] to them, is "Ameh in the land. Behold, these are they whose "heads issue. What a mystery is their appearance, "[the appearance] of your images!"

II. "The examination of the words takes place, and "he strikes down wickedness, he who has a just heart, "he who bears the words in the scales, in the divine "place of the examination of the mystery of mysteries "of the spirits. The god who rises has made his "infernal [companions] all."

For purposes of comparison, the versions of the texts from the tomb of Rameses VI., as given by Champollion (*Monuments*, pl. 252) are given. It will be noted that a part of the line immediately over the head of Osiris, , is given in different places in the latter scene, for 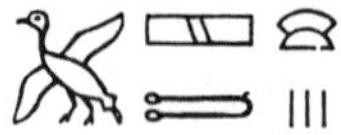 is immediately in front of the double crown of Osiris, and  is immediately in front of the sceptre of the god. The other lines read:—

I. 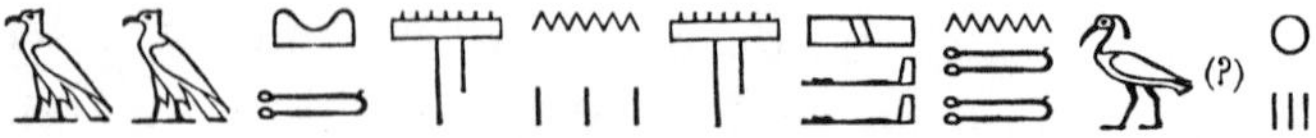

[1] *Records of the Past*, vol. x., p. 114.

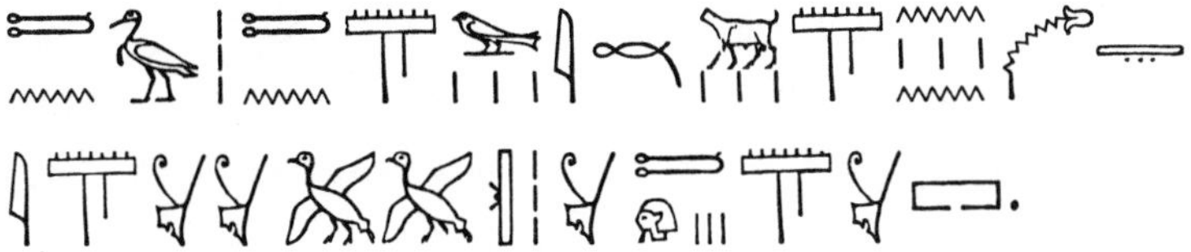

II. 

CHAPTER VIII.

THE GATE OF SET-EM-MAAT-F.

THE SIXTH DIVISION OF THE ṬUAT—*continued.*

THE pylon which gives access to the SIXTH DIVISION of the Ṭuat has already been described. The monster serpent which stands on his tail and guards the gateway is called SET-EM-MAAT-F, 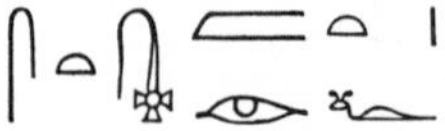, and the two lines of text which refer to his admission of Rā read:—

"He who is over this door openeth to Rā. SA "saith to SET-EM-MAAT-F:—'Open thy gate to Rā, "unfold thy doors to KHUTI, that he may send light "into the thick darkness, and may make his radiance "illumine the hidden habitation.' This door is shut "after this great god hath passed through it, and there "is lamentation to those who are in this gateway when "they hear this door close upon them" (see p. 169).

The scenes and texts which illustrate the Sixth Division of the Ṭuat cannot be obtained in a complete state from the sarcophagus of Seti I., and recourse must therefore be had to other documents. In the following pages, however, the fragments of the texts and scenes from the sarcophagus are first given, and these are followed by the complete texts as they are found in the tomb of Rameses VI., as published by Monsieur E. Lefébure in the third volume of the *Mémoires* of the French Archæological Mission at Cairo.

The fragmentary texts and scenes from the sarcophagus of Seti I. may be thus described:—

In the middle register are:—

1. Two of the four gods of the Ṭuat whose duty it is to tow along the boat of the Sun through this Division.

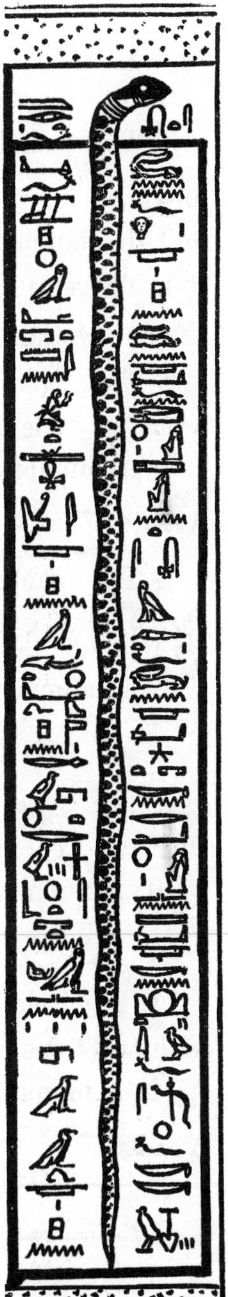

The Serpent Set-em-maat-f.

2. The god TEM, , in the form of an aged man, with bent shoulders, and leaning on a staff.

3. The jackal-headed standard called RĀ, , to which are tied two "enemies," who probably represent the damned.

4. The two UTCHATS, , which appear to be keeping watch on the "enemies."

5. The jackal-headed standard called TEM, , with two "enemies" tied to it.

6. A mummied form, with projecting elbows, called AFAT, .

7. The jackal-headed standard called KHEPER, (?), with two "enemies" tied to it.

8. A mummied form, with projecting elbows, called Ṭ . . . . Ȧ, , or MEṬ, .[1]

9. The jackal-headed standard called SHU, , with two "enemies" tied to it.

10. A mummied form, with projecting elbows, called SENṬ, .

11. The jackal-headed standard called SEB, , with two "enemies" tied to it.

12. A mummied form, with projecting elbows, called AQA-SA, .

[1] The names are supplied from Champollion, *Notices*, p. 502.

13. The jackal-headed standard called Sar,  (Osiris).[1]

14. A mummied form, with projecting elbows, called Āā-kher (?), .[1]

15. The jackal-headed standard called Ḥeru, .[1]

16. A god holding a sceptre called Shef-ḥrȧ, .[1]

The text which refers to the above-mentioned gods reads:—

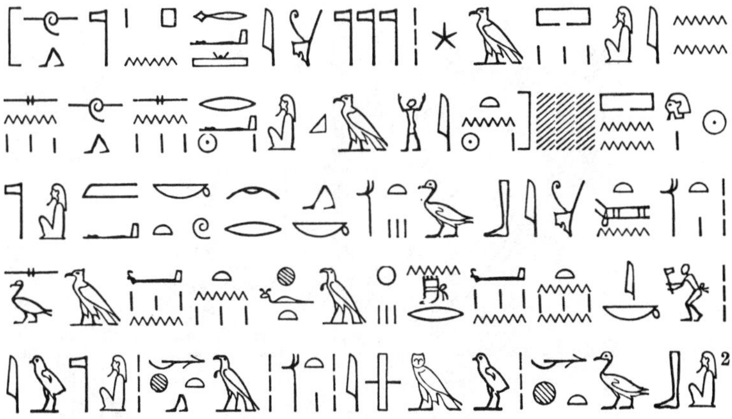[2]

---

[1] The names are supplied from Champollion, *Notices*, p. 502.

[2] Champollion's text reads: 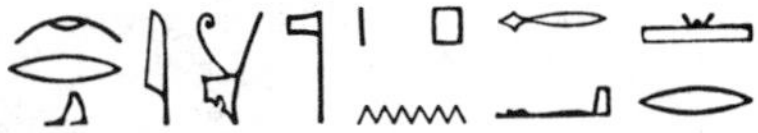

 (*Notices*, tom. ii., p. 503).

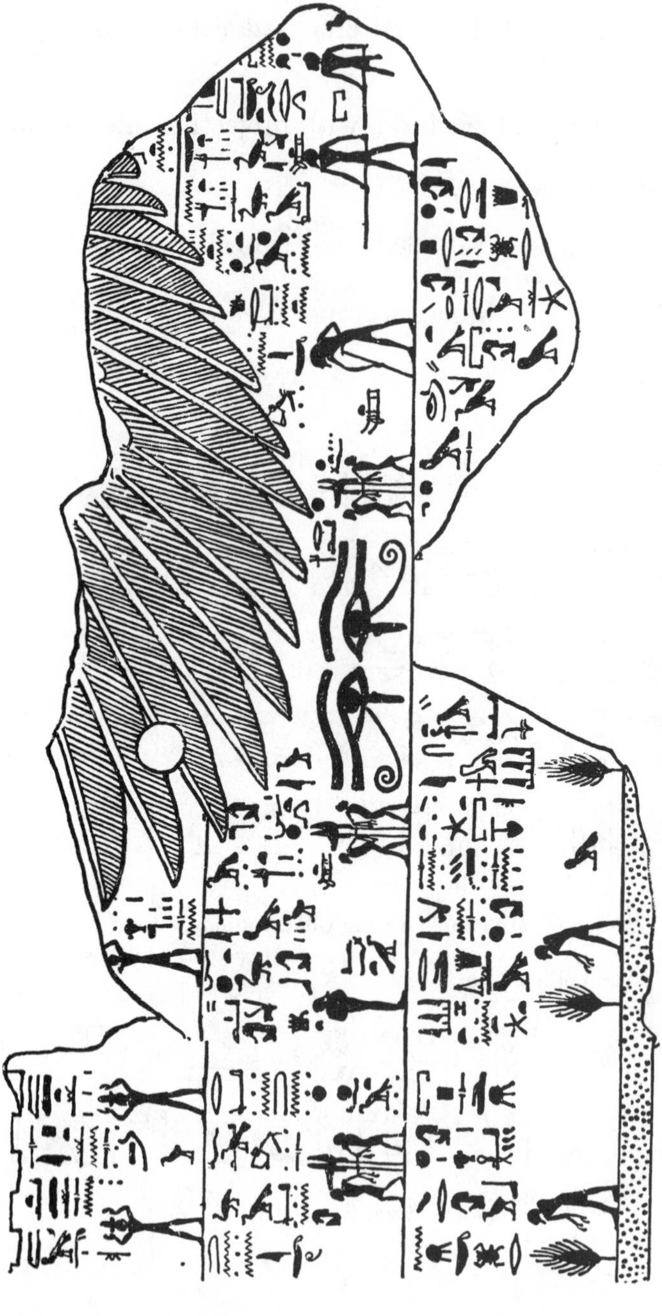

Fragment of the Sixth Division of the Ṭuat, from the Cover of the Sarcophagus of Seti I.

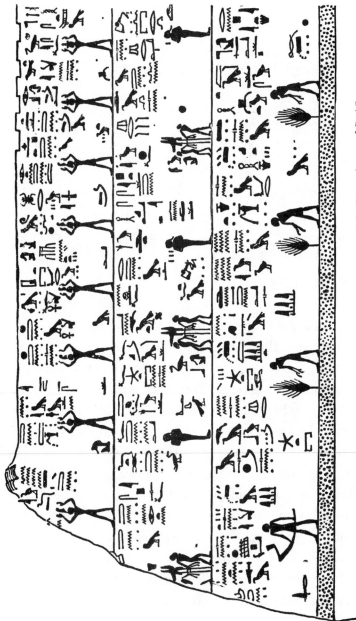

Fragment of the Sixth Division of the Ṭuat, from the Cover of the Sarcophagus of Seti I.

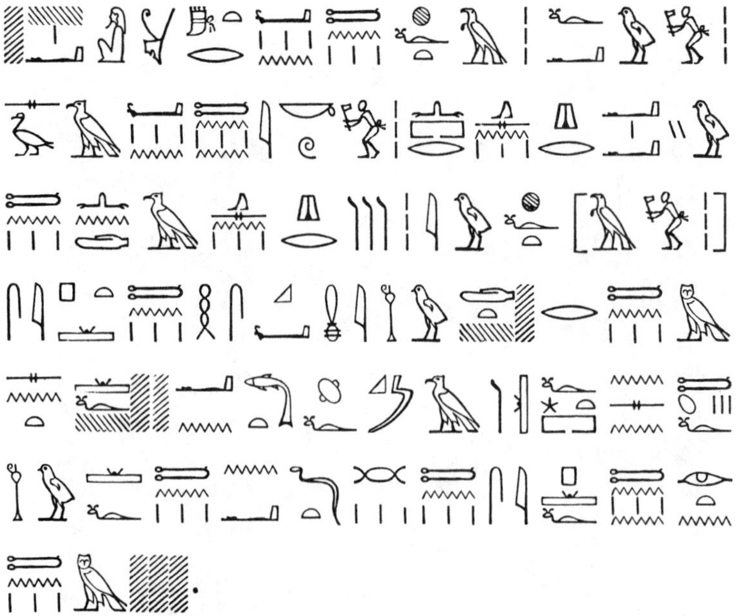

"[This great god is towed along by the gods in the "Ṭuat, and those who tow Rā along say, 'Rise up, O "disk,] . . . . god, verily get thee forth to "the standards of Seb.' Tem saith unto the standards:— "'Keep ward over the enemies, and bind ye fast those "who shall be smitten. O ye gods who are behind the "standards, and who are in the following of Seb, I give "ye the power to bind fast the enemies and to keep "ward over the wicked. Let them not go forth from "under your hands, let them not slip through your "fingers. O enemies, ye are reckoned for slaughter "according to the decree which [was given] to you by "him that . . . . . . with his body, and created the Ṭuat "by his members (?). He hath passed the decree for "you to be punished, and he taketh count of you and "what ye do . . . .'"

The upper register is much mutilated on the cover of the sarcophagus of Seti I.; on it we see:—

1. Five upright male figures, each of whom holds a large loaf of bread, , with both hands on his head; when the scene was complete these figures were twelve in number, as we learn from the variants published by Champollion,[1] and they are called ḤETEPTI-KHEPERU,

2. Six upright male figures, each of whom holds the feather of Maāt with both hands on his head; when the scene was complete these figures were twelve in number, and they are called ĀUTU-MAĀMU-KHERU-MAĀT, [2]

The text which remains reads:—

[1] *Notices*, ii., p. 501.

[2] Supplied from Champollion, *Notices*, ii., p. 502.

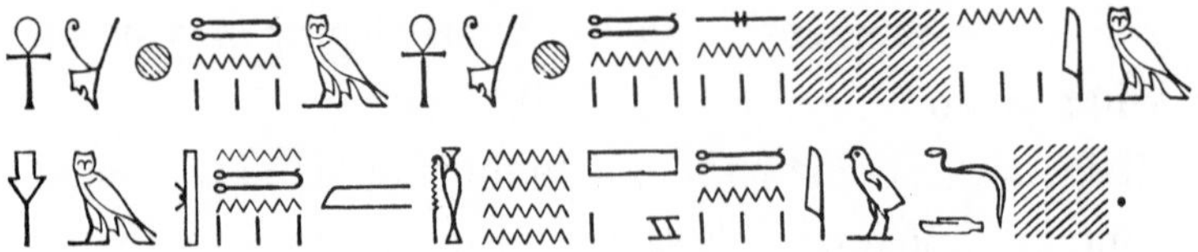

"[These are they who have offered up incense to the

Fragment of the Cover of the Sarcophagus of Seti I. in the British Museum.

"gods, and whose doubles have been washed, 

"maāt, they have been reckoned up and they are maāt

"in the presence of the great god, who destroyeth "iniquities. Osiris saith unto them:—'Ye are *maāt* of "*maāt*. Be ye at peace [because of what] ye have "done, O ye who are in the forms of those who are "in my following, and who dwell in the house of him "whose souls are holy. Live ye on what ye live ...... "there, and have the mastery "over the cool waters which "are in your Lake .....'"

A few years ago I purchased from a native at Luxor a fragment of the cover of the sarcophagus of Seti I. (see p. 176); this is now in the British Museum (No. 29,948), and it gives the following:—

1. Three male figures, each of which bears a loaf on his head.

2. The following fragmentary text: 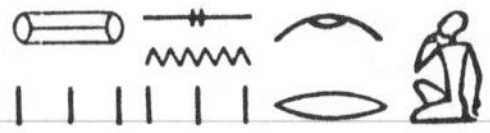

, "Their bread cakes are ordered for

"them by their gods; their *kau* are in their hands, "and they enter into their abodes at the pylon which "destroyeth its gods. The god SAR (Osiris) saith unto "them:—'Your bread shall be to you from that which "cometh forth from your mouths, O ye ḤETEPTI-"KHEPERU . . . . . .'"

In the lower register are:—

1. Five male figures, who are occupied in tending very large ears of corn; when the scene was complete these figures were twelve in number, and they were called, "Those who work about the plants of grain in "the fields of the Ṭuat," 

2. A man holding a sickle; he is one of the seven "reapers," , of which this section of the scene originally consisted.

The text which relates to those who tend the grain reads:—

[1]

[1] The passage in brackets is from Champollion, *Notices*, ii., p. 503.

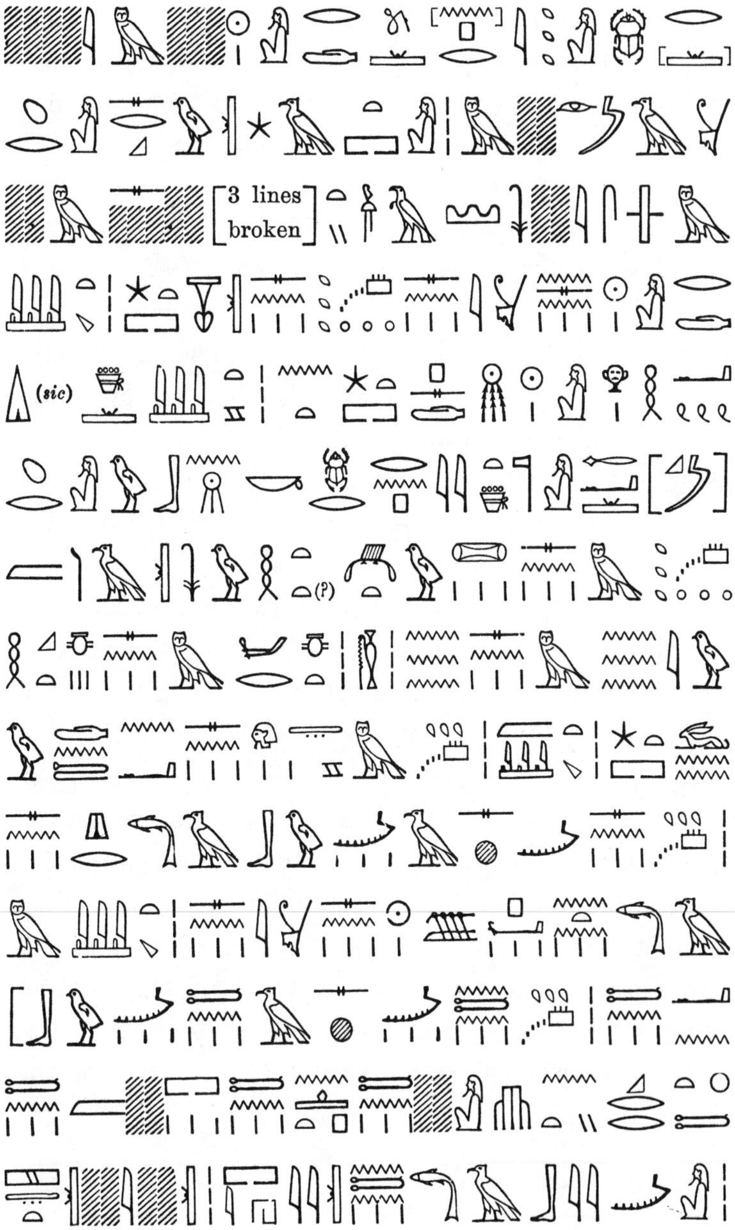
3 lines broken
(sic)
(?)

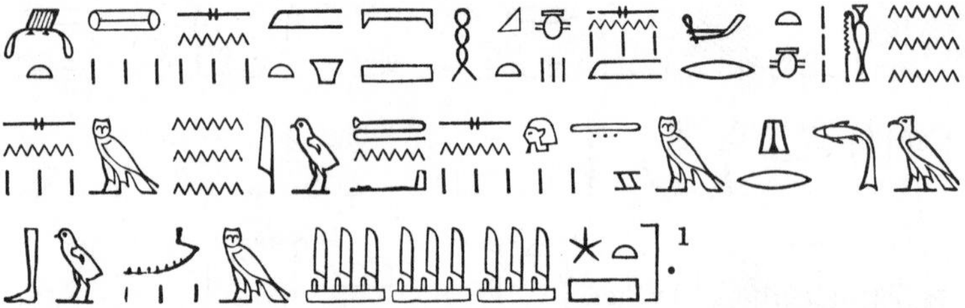 [1]

"[They perform the works in connection with the "grain, and they embrace the god of wheat (NEPRȦ) "which is eaten (?). Their grain becometh glorious in "the land through the light of Rā, when he appeareth, "and sendeth forth heat, and maketh his way by them. "The lord of joy of heart saith unto them:—'Let your "grain be glorious, and let the young shoots of your "grain germinate, and let your offerings be for Rā] ". . . . there . . . . Rā. Let NEPER germinate, and "let SAR (Osiris) be the source of food of the gods in "the Ṭuat . . . . ȦMENTI . . . . behold, in the "fields of the Ṭuat.' They gather together their grain, "and they say unto Rā:—'Let the fields of the Ṭuat be "green with young plants. May Rā shine upon the "members of SAR (Osiris). When thou dost shine the "young plants come into being, O great god, thou "creator of the grain.' Their offerings of food are of "grain, and their drink offerings are of *tcheser*, and "their libations are made with cool water. Offerings "are made unto them on the earth of the grain of the "fields of the Ṭuat."

[1] The words in brackets are supplied from Champollion, *Notices*, ii., p. 503.

Of the reapers it is said:—

"These are they who have their scythes, and who "reap the grain in their fields. Rā saith to them:— "'Take ye your scythes, and reap ye your grain, for it "is granted to you . . . . . . your habitations, and to "join yourselves [to] me in the Circle of the Hidden "Forms. Hail to you, O ye reapers!' Their food is of "bread, and their drink is of *tcheser*, and their libations "are made with cool water. Offerings are made unto "them upon earth as being those who hold scythes in "the fields of the Ṭuat."

The text which describes the middle register of the Sixth Division as it appears in the tomb of Rameses VI. reads:—

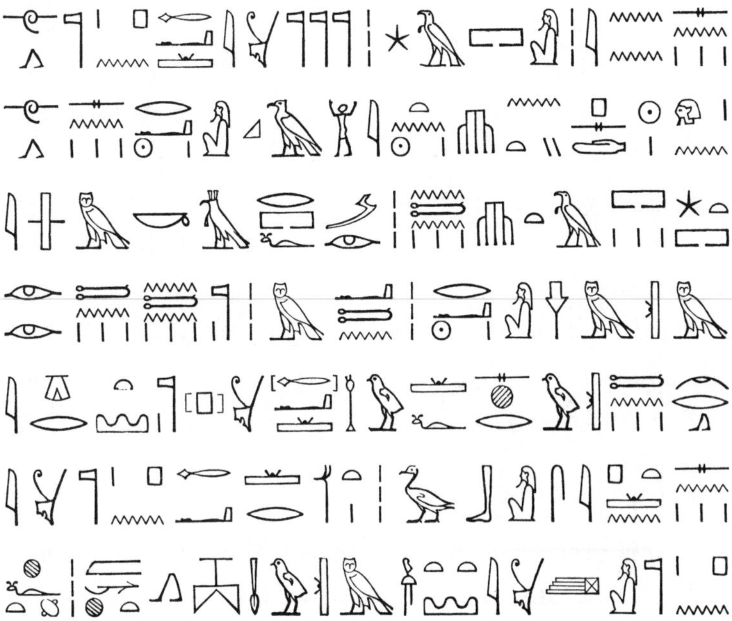

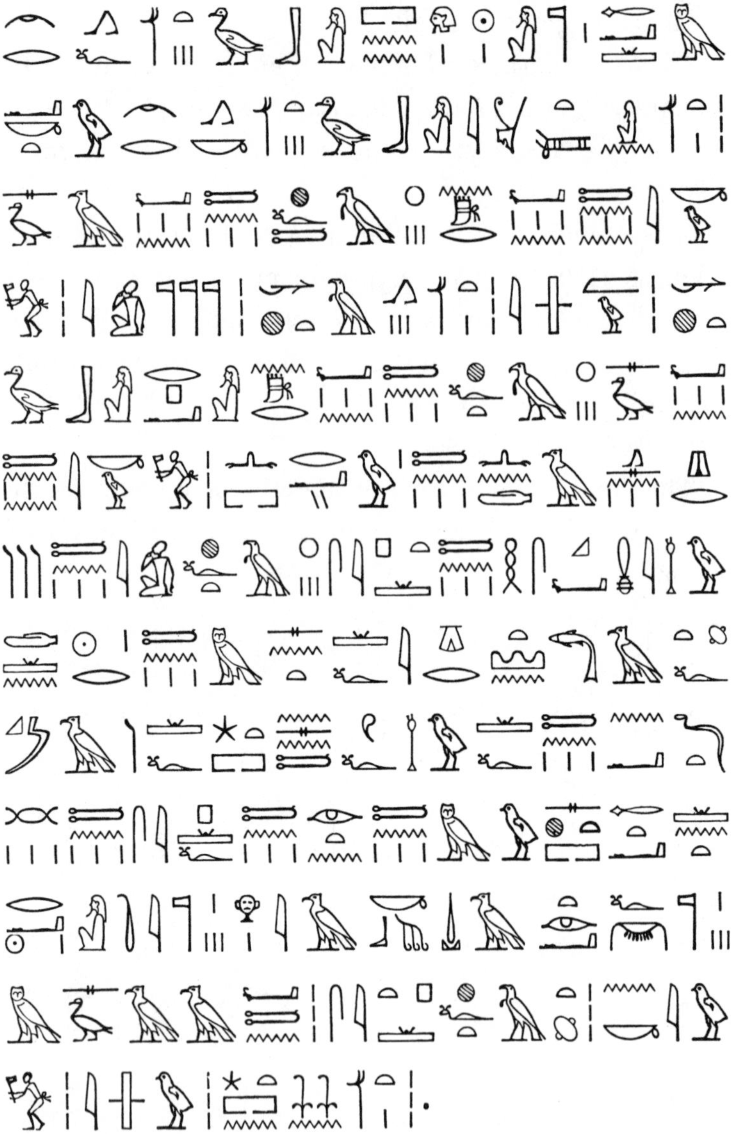

"This great god is being towed along by the gods of "the Ṭuat, and those who tow Rā along say:—'Be "exalted, O Åten (i.e., Disk), who art at the head of "..... the Light, the head .... Look ye at the "abodes of the Ṭuat. Your eyes are to you, O gods, "observe ye Rā, the Power in Åkert. This great god "decreeth your destinies. This great god cometh forth "to the standards of Seb, which reckon up the enemies "after the weighing of words in Åmentet. Behold, Sa "saith unto this god [when] he cometh forth to the "standards of Seb ...... the head of Rā, the great "god .... verily, get thee forth to the standards of "Seb. Tem saith unto the standards:—'Keep ward "over the enemies, and bind ye fast those who are to "be smitten. O ye gods who are in the following of "the standards, and who are in the following of Seb, I "give ye power to bind fast the enemies, and to keep "ward over the wicked (or, those who are to be "smitten). Let them not come forth from under your "hands, let them not slip through your fingers. O ye "enemies, ye are doomed to slaughter, according to the "decree of Rā concerning you. His person is the body "of Åkert, and he hath created the Ṭuat of his frame-"work. He hath issued the decree for you to be put "into restraint, he hath ordered your doom which shall "be wrought upon you in the great hall of Rā .... "the gods weep [and] lament, he setteth the gods "to ward you, and the enemies and those who are to "be smitten in the Ṭuat are condemned to these "standards.'"

In the upper register are twelve gods, each of whom

stands upright, and has the feather of Maāt on his head, and twelve gods, each of whom stands upright, and has a large loaf on his head. These gods are described as "MAĀTI gods bearing Maāt,"  , and the "ḤETEPTIU gods bearing provisions," 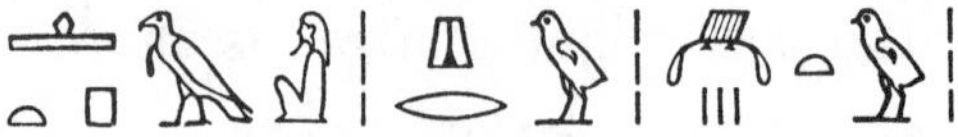. The text reads:—

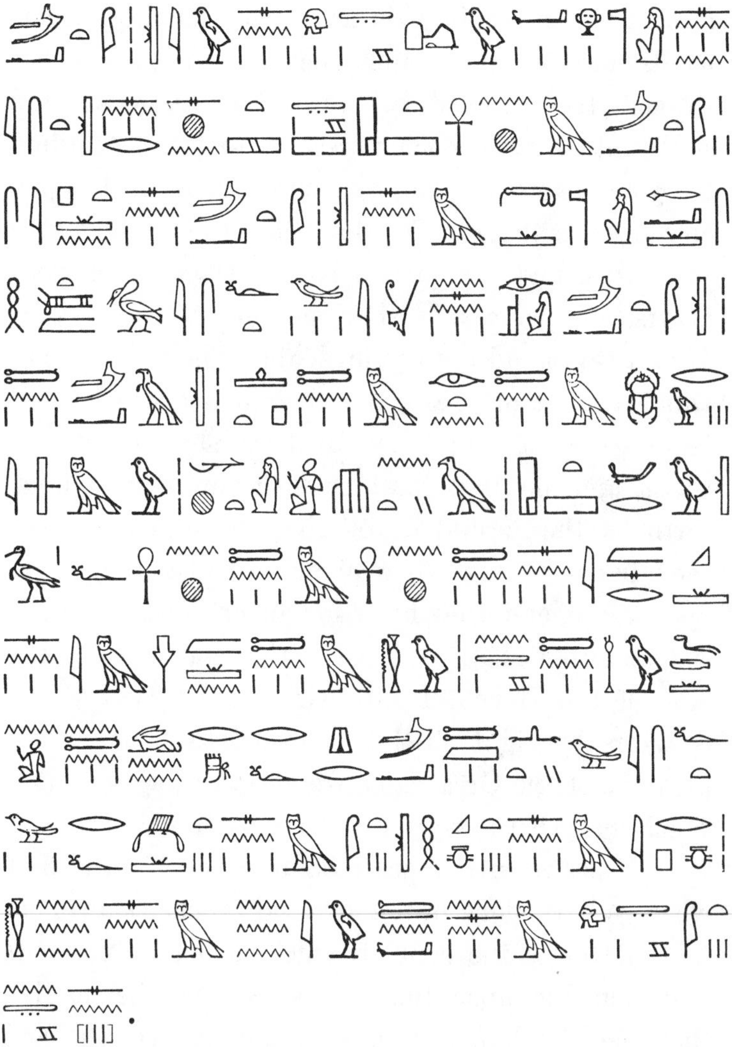

"Offerings of incense to their gods, libations of cool "water to their doubles, and fillings of the mouth ". . . . . . by his sustenance afterwards by their offer- "ings of drink and their offerings of bread. Come "forth to them their gods and their doubles. Their "hands are to them, and they go to their cakes "through the pylon of . . . . . and to its gods. SAR "saith unto them:—'Your bread is to you, [according "to] your utterances, and the peace cakes of Kheper, "and loaves of bread. Ye shall have the mastery over "your legs, and ye shall have satisfaction in your "hearts, and your gods shall present unto you your "*khenfu* cakes and unto your doubles their provisions, "which consist of bread, and their drink, which shall "be of *tcheser* ale, and their libations shall be of cool "water, and offerings shall be made unto them upon "earth as the lord[s] of offerings in Åmentet. For "they have done what was right whilst they were "upon earth, and they have fought on behalf of their "god, and they shall be called to the enjoyment of the "land of the House of Life with *maāt*. That which "is theirs by right shall be allotted to them in the "presence of the Great God, who doeth away iniquity.' "Then shall Osiris say unto them:—'*Maāt* be to you, "O ye MAĀT gods, and peace be unto you by reason of "what ye have done in following after me, O dwellers "in the House, the soul of which is holy. Ye shall "live your life upon that whereupon those who live "there feed, and ye shall have dominion over the cool "waters of your land. I have decreed for you that ye "shall have your being in all of it with *maāt*, and "without sin (or, defects).' Their bread shall be *maāt* "cakes, their drink shall be of wine, and their libations

"shall be of cool water. And there shall be offered
"unto them upon earth the offerings which must be
"made from their land."

In the lower register are the figures of twelve men, each of whom tends a monster ear of corn (?), or a tree, under the superintendence of a god who leans on a staff, and a group of reapers, each holding a sickle. The text, which is mutilated in places, reads:—

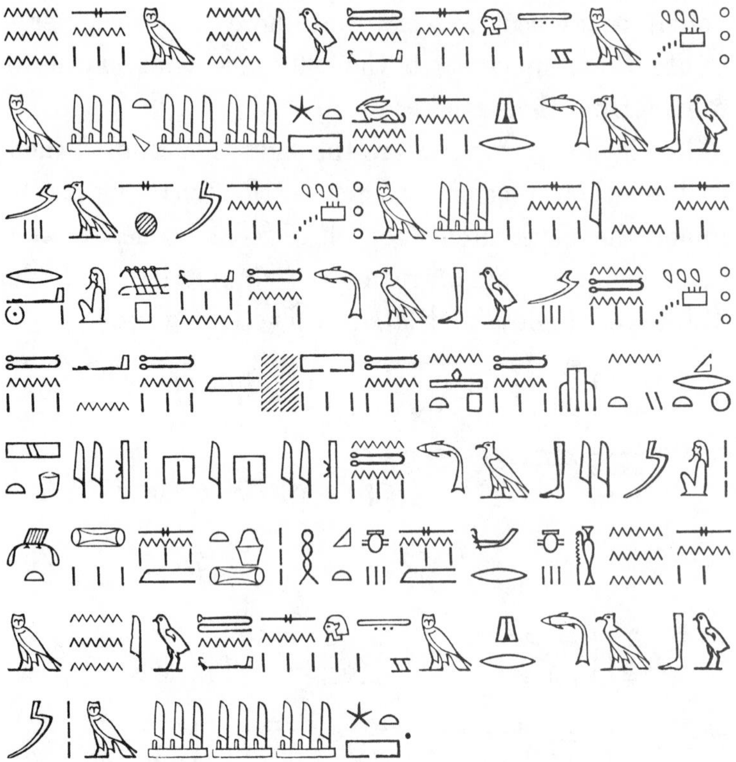

"They perform their work in connection with the "grain, and they embrace (i.e., cultivate) the divine "grain (or, NEPRÀ), and the spirits feed upon their "grain in the land of the god of light (KHU), who "cometh forth and passeth by them, and [NEB-ĀUT-ÀB, " , i.e., the Lord of joy of heart, saith unto "them:—'Let your grain be glorious], and let your ears "of wheat germinate, and let your offerings be for Rā. "Your *khenfu* cakes are in the Ṭuat, your offerings are "to you, the offerings which are yours by *maāt* are "decreed (?) for you. Herbs . . . . . . among you. "SAR . . . . . germinate . . . . . .' and they say unto "Rā :—'Let plants spring up in the Fields of the Ṭuat, "and let Rā shine upon the members of SAR. When "thou dost shine the young plants come into being, "O great god, thou creator of the Egg.' Their food "offerings are of grain, their drink is of *tcheser* ale, and "their libations are made with cool water. Offerings "are made unto them upon earth of the grain from the "Fields of the Ṭuat."

Of the reapers it is said:—

"These are they who have their sickles and who "reap the grain in their Field. Rā saith unto them:— "'Take ye your sickles, and reap ye your grain, for it is "granted unto you . . . . . . your habitations, and to "join yourselves to the Circle of the Hidden of Forms. "Hail to you, O ye reapers!' Their food is of bread-"cakes, and their drink is of *tcheser* ale, and their "libations are made with cool water. Offerings are "made unto them upon earth as being those who reap "the grain in the Fields of the Ṭuat."

CHAPTER IX.

THE GATE OF ĀKHA-EN-MAAT.

THE SEVENTH DIVISION OF THE ṬUAT.

THE boat of the Sun having passed through the Sixth Division of the Ṭuat arrives at the gateway which leads to the SEVENTH DIVISION. This gateway is similar to that which guards the Sixth Division, and is guarded by nine gods, who are described as the "Seventh Company," 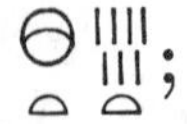; at the entrance to the corridor, and at its exit, stands a bearded god, with arms hidden, the former being called SHEPI, , and the latter HEQES (?), , and each is said to extend his arms and hands to Rā. The corridor is swept by flames of fire as before. The gateway is called PESṬIT, , and the text says, "This "great god cometh to this gateway, and entereth in "through it, and the gods who are therein acclaim him,"

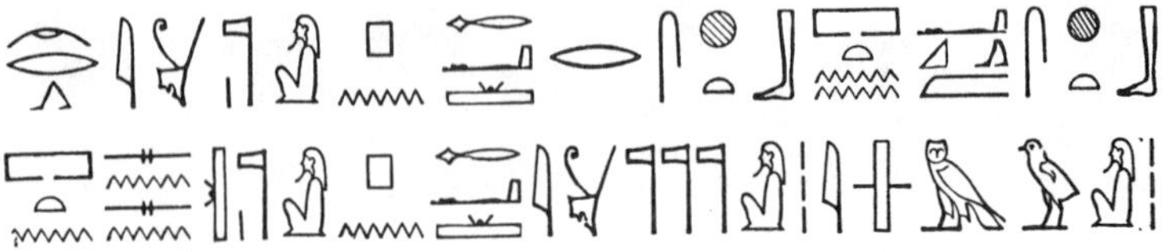

. Part of the text of the speech which the nine gods make to Rā is broken away, but what remains reads, "Open the secret places, open the holy pylons, "and unfold the hidden portals,"  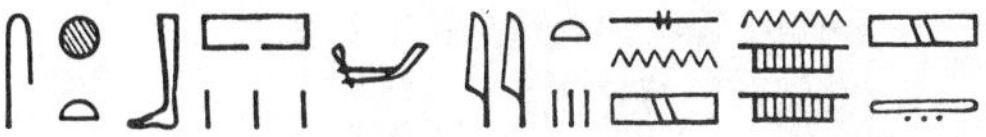. The monster serpent which stands on his tail and guards the gateway is called ĀKHA-EN-MAAT, 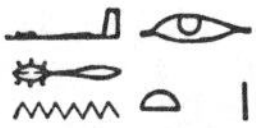, and the two lines of text which refer to his admission of Rā read, "He who is over this door openeth to Rā. SA saith to "ĀKHA-EN-MAAT[1]:—'Open thy gate to Rā, unfold thy "doors to KHUTI, that he may send light into the "thick darkness and may make his radiance illumine "the hidden habitation.' This door is shut after the great "god hath passed through it, and there is lamentation "to those who are in this gateway when they hear this "door close upon them." A portion of the text is mutilated, but it can be restored with certainty.[2]

In the middle of this Division we see the boat of Rā being towed on its way by four gods of the Ṭuat; the god is in the same form as before, and stands in a shrine enveloped by MEḤEN. SA stands in the bows and ḤEKA at the stern. The text relating to the god reads:—

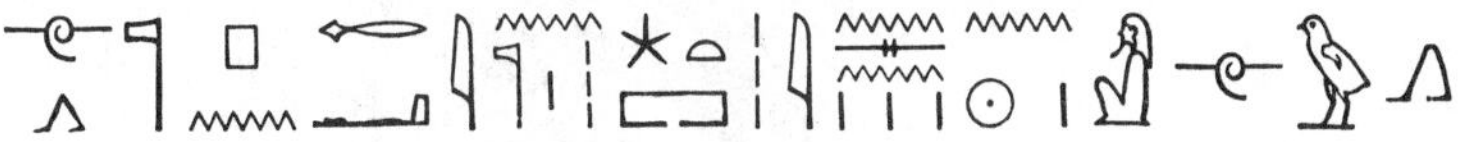

[1] Var., , ĀKHA-ḤRÅ.

[2] See Lefébure, *Mémoires*, tom. ii., part ii., pl. 11 ff.

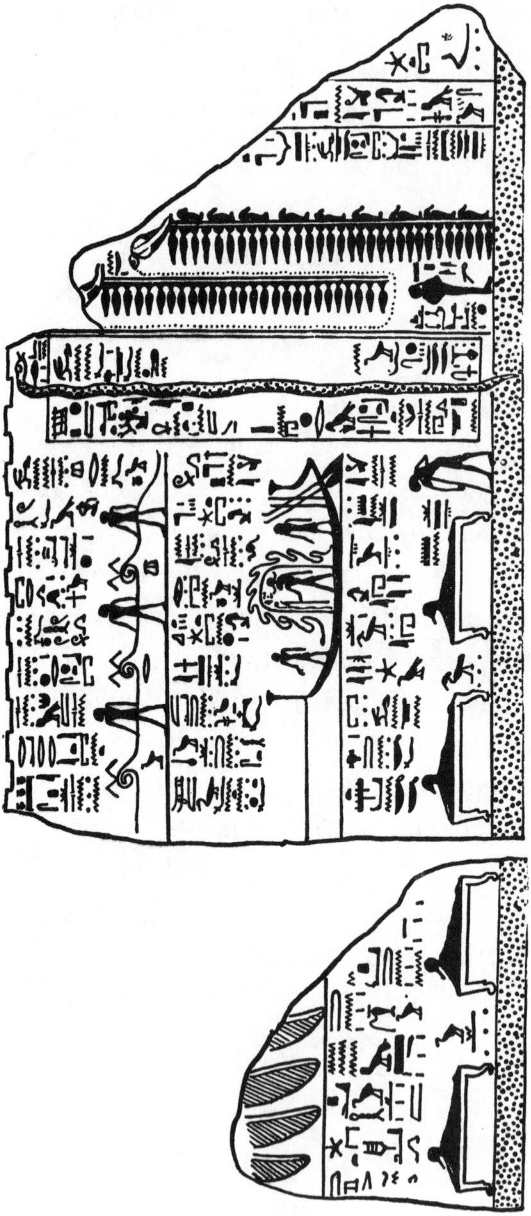

Fragment of the Seventh Division of the Ṭuat, from the Cover of the Sarcophagus of Seti I.

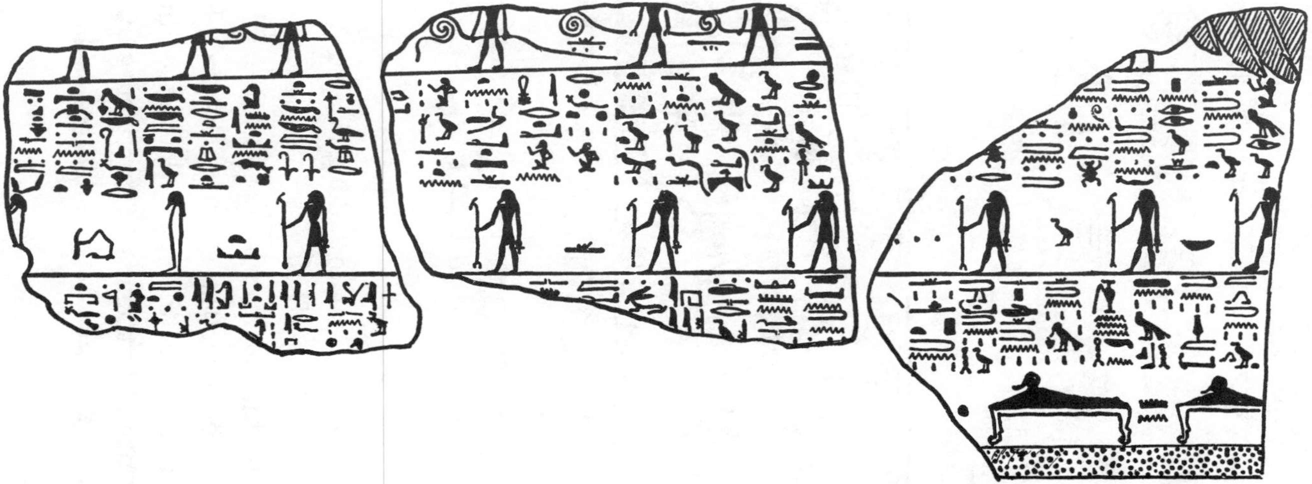

Fragments of the Scenes and Texts of the Seventh Division of the Ṭuat, from the Sarcophagus of Seti I.

The Boat of Rā being towed through the Seventh Division of the Ṭuat by the gods thereof.

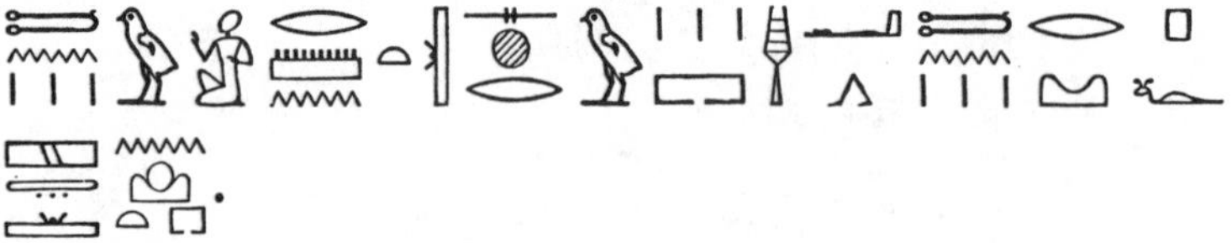

"The gods of the Ṭuat tow along this great god, and "they say unto Rā:—'Thou art towed along, O great "god, lord of the hours, who dost work on behalf of "those who are under the earth.' The gods have life "in his attributes, and the spirits look upon his forms. "And Rā saith unto them:—'There is magical protec-"tion to you, O ye who tow, and there is holiness to "you, O ye who tow and bring me into the nethermost "parts of the Ṭuat, tow ye me along until [ye arrive] "at the chambers (?), and take ye your stand upon the "hidden mountain of the horizon."

In front of the divine towers of the boat march:—

1. Twelve bearded gods, the ÅMENNU-ĀĀIU-KHERU-SHETAU, whose hands and arms are hidden; they are described as "hidden of hands and arms and possessing hiddenness," 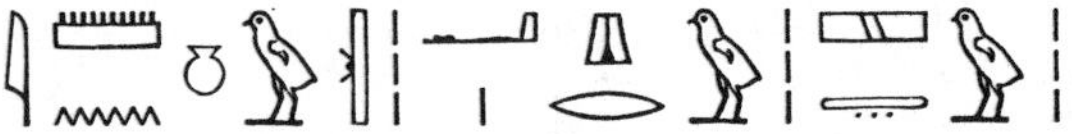.

The text relating to them reads:—

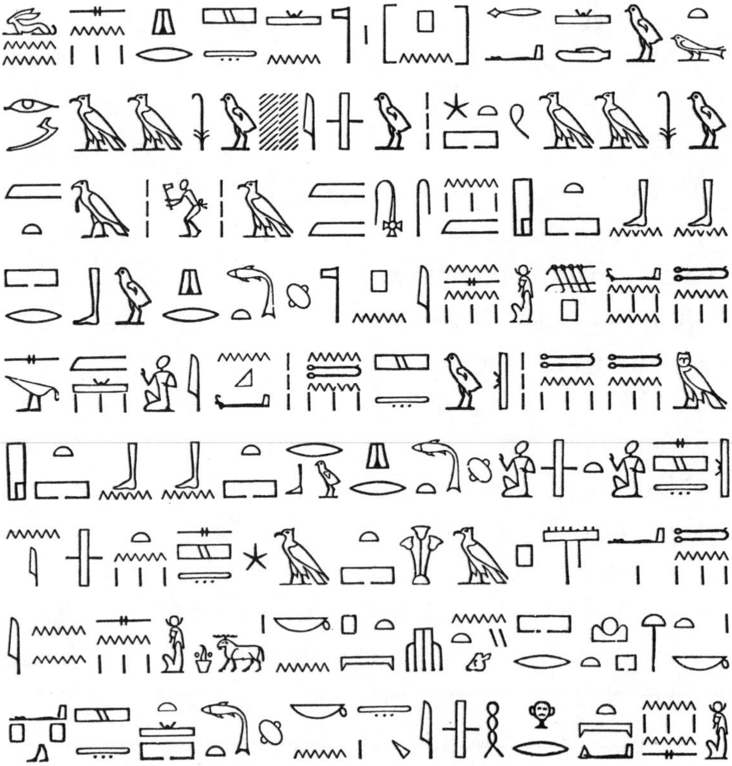

"These are they who possess the hiddenness (or, who "hold the mystery) of this great god. Verily those "who are in the Ṭuat see him, and the dead see him, "who burn in Ḥet-Benben (or, the temple of Rā), and "they come forth to the place where is the body of this "god. Rā saith unto them:—'Receive ye my forms, "and embrace ye your hidden forms (or, mysteries). "Ye shall be in Ḥet-Benben, the place where my body "is. The hiddenness which is in you is the hiddenness "of the Ṭuat, and cover ye your arms therewith.' And "they say unto Rā:—'Let thy soul be in heaven, at "the head of the horizon, let thy shadow penetrate "the hidden place, and let thy body be to the earth; "as for the upper regions of the sky we ascribe Rā "thereto . . . . . Fulfil thou thyself, and take thou "thy place [with] thy body in the Ṭuat.' Their food "consisteth of offerings of every kind whereby souls "become content, and offerings are made unto them "upon earth by reason of the sight of the light in the "Ṭuat."

2. Eight bearded gods, the NETERU-ḤETI, who stand

The Twelve Gods whose hands and arms are hidden.

upright, with their hands hanging by their sides, and are described as "the gods of the temples,"  ; and eight gods, the SENNU, who stand upright, with their arms held straight together in front of them, at a little distance from their bodies. The text which refers to them reads:—

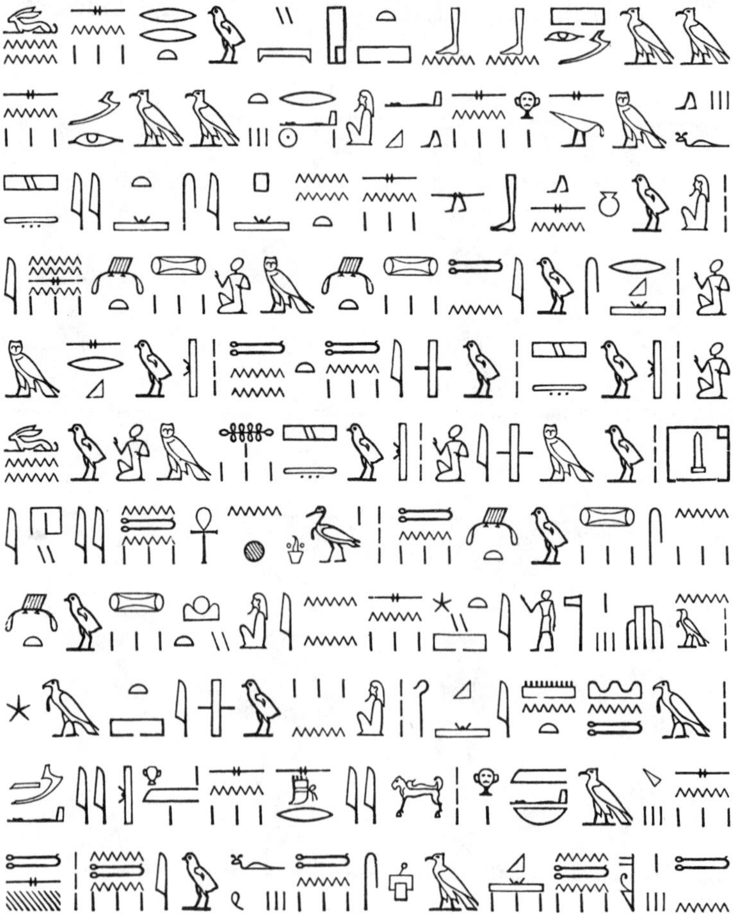

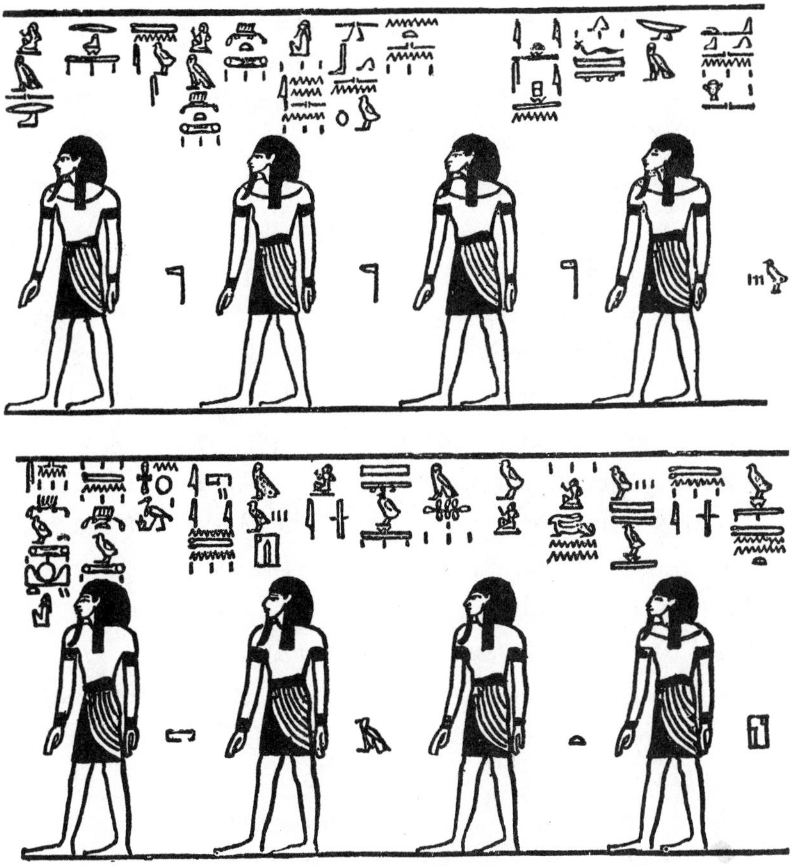

The Eight Neteru-ḥeti.

Four of the Sennu Gods.

"These are they who are outside Ḥet-Benben, and "they see Rā with their eyes, and they enter into his "secret (or, hidden) images; that which is theirs is "apportioned, and the SENNU gods bring it. [And Rā] "saith unto them:—'My offerings (or, provisions) are "from your offerings, and my nourishment is from "your nourishment which is to you, O ye who are in "my secret places. I protect my secret things which "are in Ḥet-Benben. Hail to you! Your souls live, "and their offerings are the offerings of KHUTI.' ṬUATI "saith unto them:—'O ye gods who dwell in the Ṭuat, "who are in the divine [places] of the governor of "Åment, to whom what is their due is given upon "their ground, who lie down upon their own lands, "your own flesh is to you, ye have gathered together "your bones, ye have knit together your members, and "ye have collected your flesh. There are, moreover, "sweet winds to your nostrils, ye have girded on your "apparel, and ye have put on your wigs.'"

In the upper register are:—

1. Twelve gods, the KHERU-METAU[Ḥ], each of whom holds a stake or weapon, forked at one end; they are described as "those who hold the *metau* weapons,"

 The text relating to these reads:—

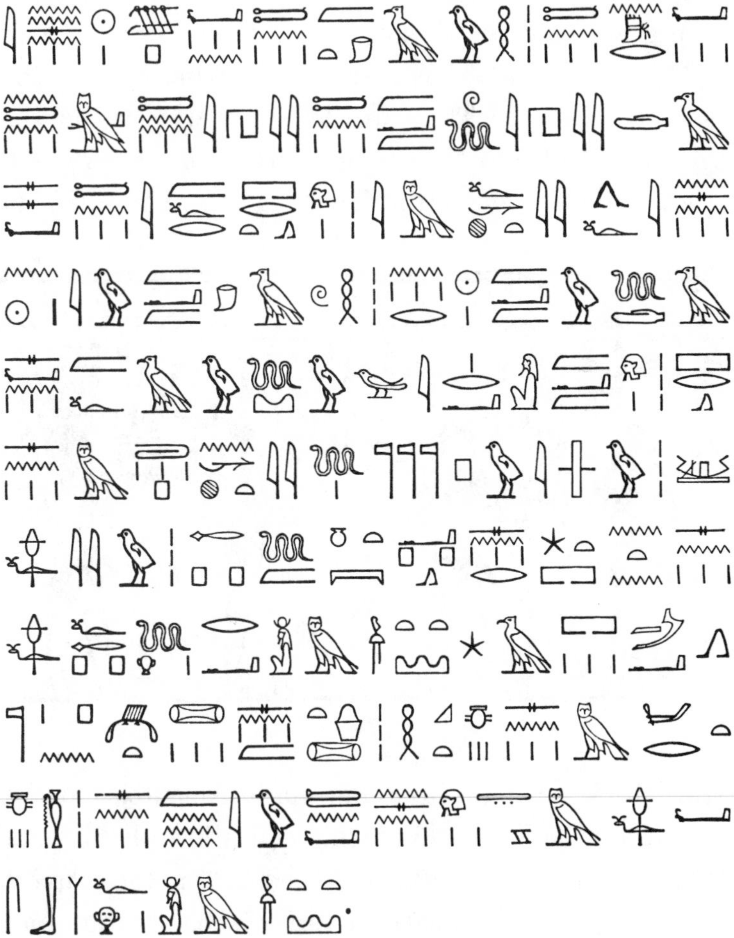

"Rā saith unto them:—'Receive ye your *metauḥ* "weapons, and take ye them with you. Hail to you, "[go against] the serpent fiend MĀMU; hail to you, "make ye gashes in him when the heads appear from "out of him, and turn ye him backwards.' They say "unto Rā:—'Our *metauḥ* weapons in our hands are for "Rā [and against] MĀMU, and we will make gashes in "the great and evil WORM. O Rā, do away the heads "when they come forth from the windings of the "serpent KHETI.' These are the gods who are in the "[Boat of Rā], and they repulse Āpep in the sky, and "they travel through the Ṭuat. It is their duty to

The Kheru-Metauḥ Gods.

"turn back Āpep on behalf of Rā in Åmentet and the "places of the Ṭuat. And this god allotteth to them "their provisions of bread, and their beer is the *tchesert* "drink, and their libations are of cool water, and "offerings are made to them upon earth because they "repulse the Enemy of Rā in Åmentet."

2. The gods KHERU-ĀMU-PERERU-ṬEPU-EM-QEBU-F, and the monster serpent SEBÅ-ĀPEP, the body of which is held

The Kheru-Metauḥ Gods.

up above the ground by twelve bearded gods, who are described as "those who have food when the heads appear from his folds,"  . Twelve human heads grow out from his body,

The Kheru-Metauḥ Gods.

the first appearing from his head, and the other eleven from his back. The text which relates to them reads :—

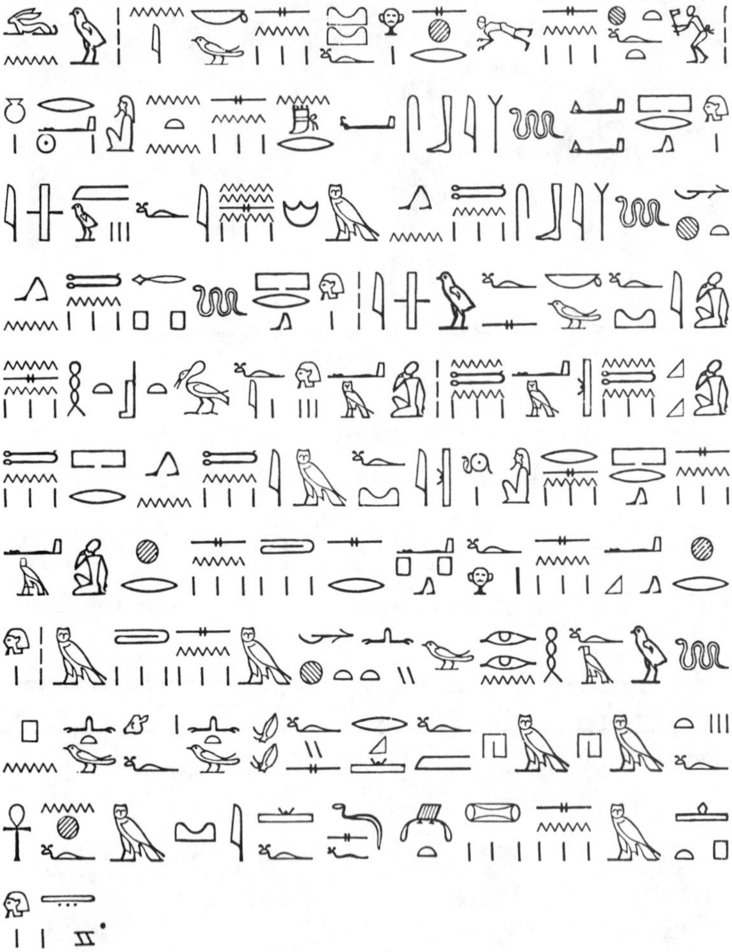

"These are they who are the adversaries of his "two-fold evil, and who overthrow the enemies of Rā, "and it is their duty to seize the SEBȦ-Fiend when he "maketh heads to come forth from him. [Rā] saith to "them:—'Turn ye back SEBȦ, make ye to go back-"wards ĀPEP when the heads appear from out of him, "and let him perish.' [Rā] ordereth for him his "destruction. 'O heads, ye shall be eaten, ye shall be "eaten, ye shall be consumed, when ye come forth from "him.' Rā ordereth for them when they come forth "that they shall be consumed (or, swallowed up) [in] "their folds when he journeyeth to them, and that the "heads shall retreat within their folds. The WORM "ḤEFAU shall be without eyes, and he shall be without "his nose, and he shall be without his ears, and he "shall exist upon his roarings, and he shall live upon "that which he himself uttereth. The food [of these "gods] consisteth of the offerings [which are made to "them] upon earth."

3. An upright, bearded mummied form called QĀN, . To the neck of this figure are attached two ropes, which are twisted together symmetrically, and are grasped by twelve bearded men with both hands. Each god stands within a loop formed by the two ropes, and has a star before him. The gods are described as "those who hold the rope which cometh forth . . . . ." 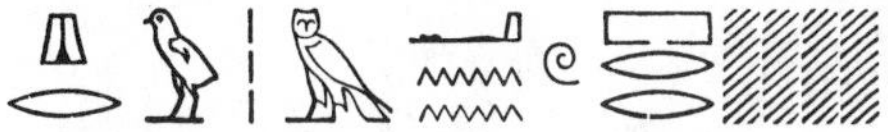. Before the figure are the words 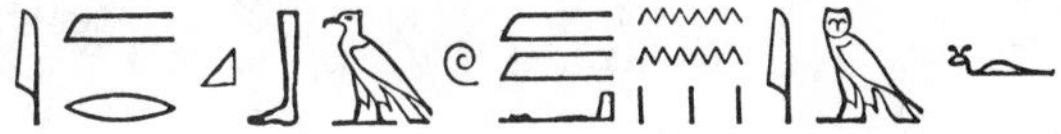. The text reads:—

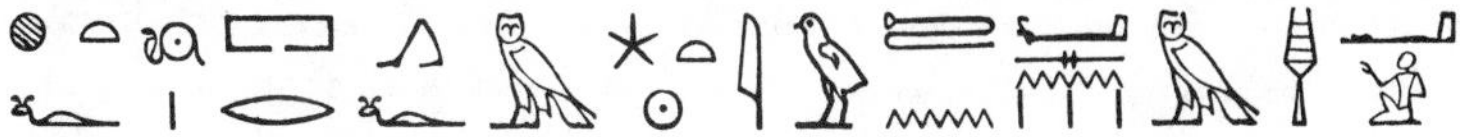

The Serpent Sebȧ-Āpep, with the twelve human heads which grow out of his body and his twelve attendant gods.

The Serpent Sebå-Āpep, with the twelve human heads which grow out of his body and his twelve attendant gods.

The god Qenā, and the gods who hold the rope.

"The Enemy of Rā cometh forth from the Ṭuat.
"Offerings shall be made unto the gods of that whereby
"I exist under the trees. Seize ye the rope, and tie ye

The gods who hold the rope.

"therewith the mouth of ĀQEN. Your hours come "forth, and there is benefit to you therein. Rest ye "upon your throne[s], and let the rope enter into the "mouth of the god ĀQEN when he cometh to the place

The gods who hold the rope.

"where the hours are born; Rā crieth out, and it "resteth in its place, and it maketh an end of ĀNEQ. "They say unto Rā:—'The god NĀQ is tied up with "the rope, the hours of the gods (?) are to thee, O Rā, "with light. Rest thou and thy hidden body . . . . .' "Their provisions of loaves of bread are to them, their "beer is *tchesert*, and their libations are of cool water, "and offerings are made to them upon earth."

The god Ṭuati.

In the lower register are:—

1. A god, standing, and leaning upon a long staff; his name is ṬUATI, .

2. The serpent NEHEP, , the long body of which is made to serve as biers for twelve gods in mummied form; the serpent's body is provided with twenty-four legs of lions, and a mummied god rests over each pair of them. These gods are described as "those who are in the body of Osiris asleep," , and "those who are in inactivity," .

3. Four gods, each with his arms stretched straight together before him at an acute angle with his body. The legend reads, *khast-ta-ruṭ* .

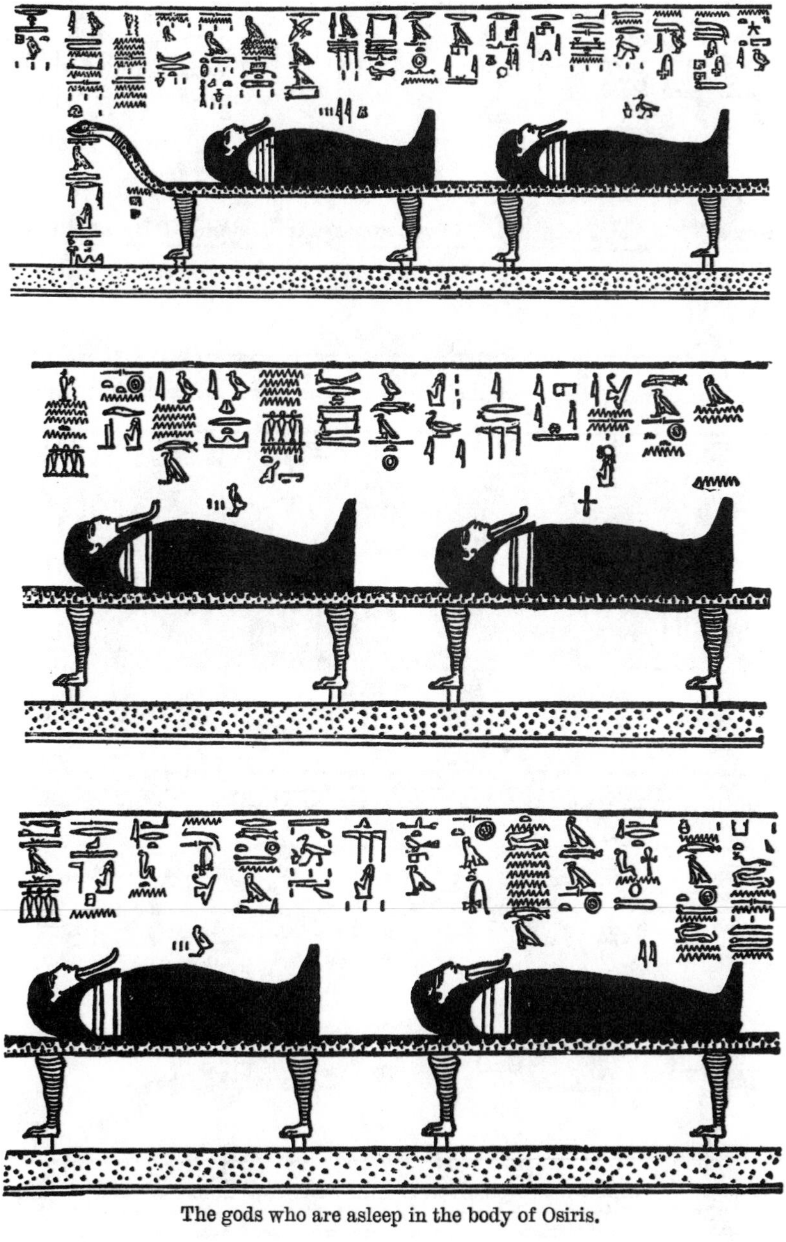

The gods who are asleep in the body of Osiris.

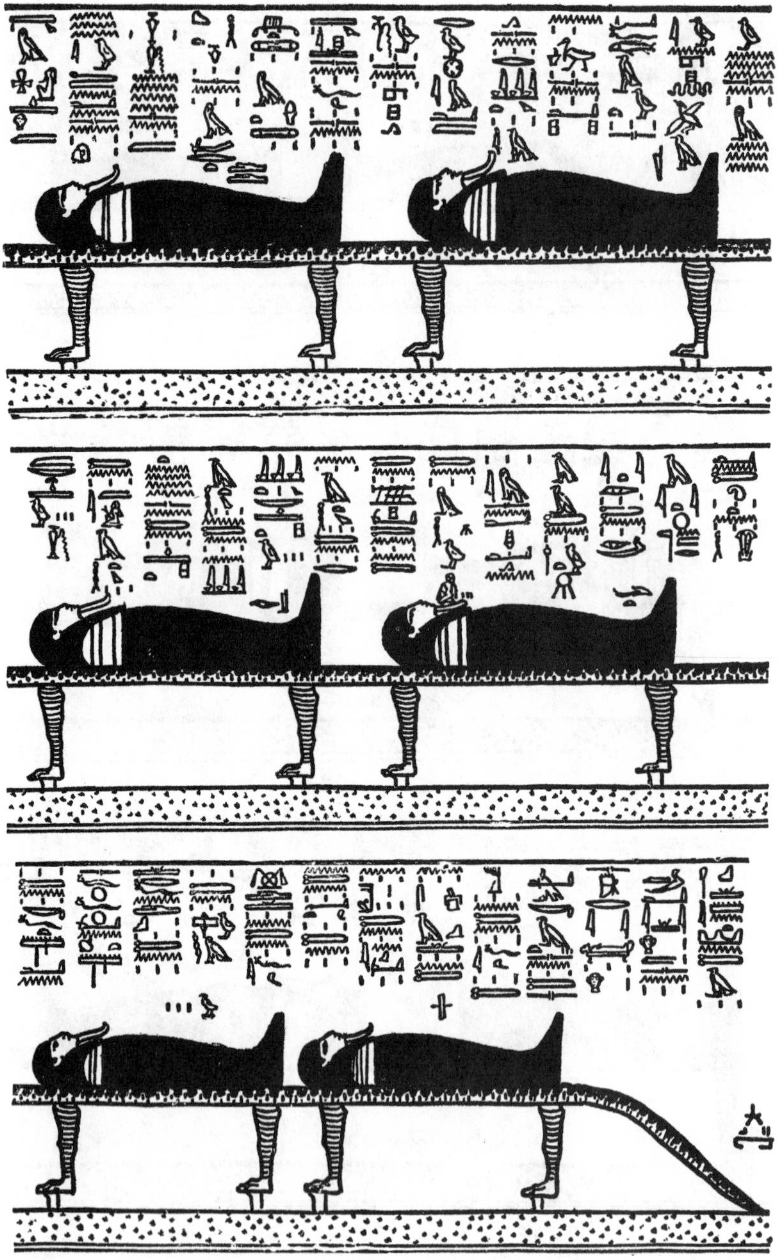

The gods who are asleep in the body of Osiris.

Four Khast-ta-ruṭ Gods.

A god in mummied form.

The serpent in the round pool of fire.

Four Khast-ta-ruṭ Gods.

4. Four gods.
5. A serpent within a circle filled with water.
6. A god in mummied form.

The text relating to these reads:—

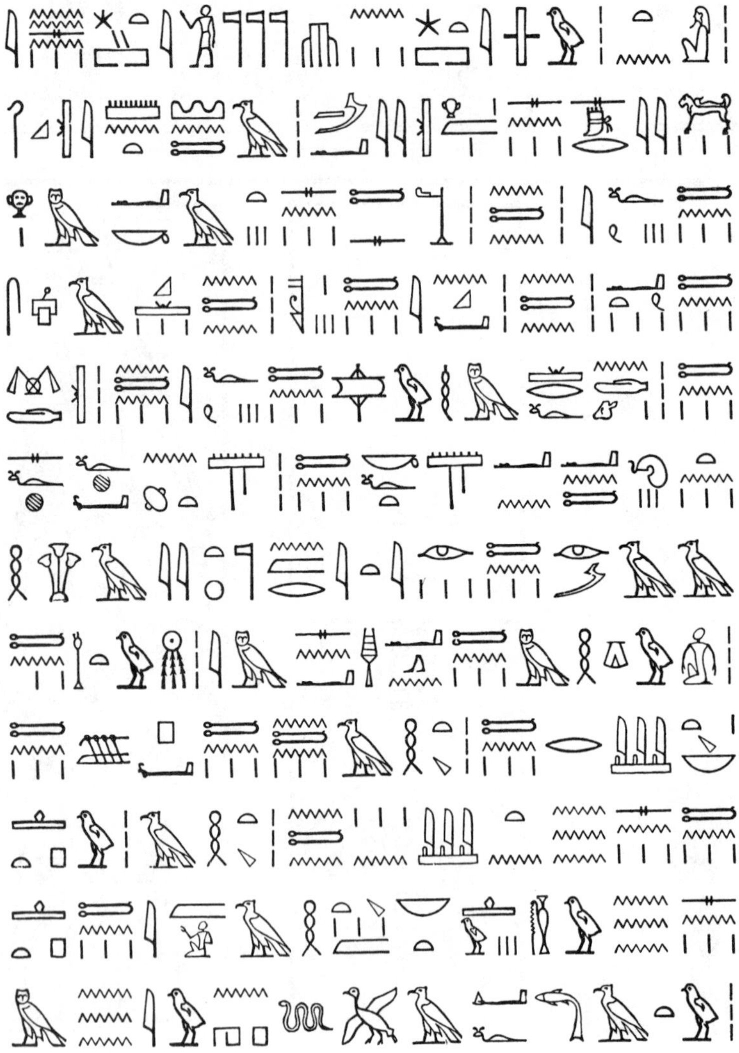

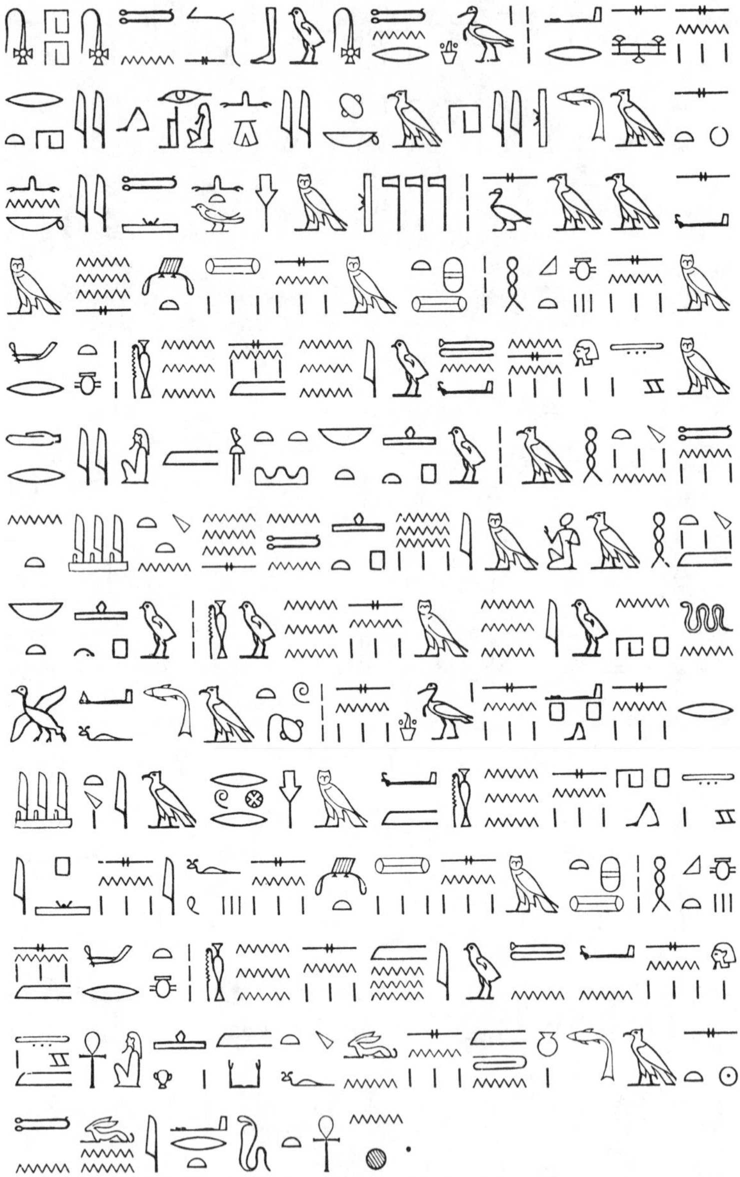

"The god Ṭuati saith unto them:—'Hail, O ye gods

"who are over the Ṭuat, ye gods who dwell in this "[place] of the governor of Åment, who abide per-"manently on your places, and who lie down upon "your couches, lift up the flesh of your bodies, and "gather together your bones, and gird up your "members, and bring ye into one place your flesh! "There is sweet (or, fresh) air for your nostrils. Loose "and take off your funeral swathings, untie and remove "your wigs, unclose your eyes and look ye at the light "therewith, rise ye up from out of your inert and "helpless state, and take possession yourselves of your "fields in Sekhet-nebt-ḥetepu (i.e., Field, lord of offer-"ings). There are fields for you in this Field, and the "waters thereof are for you. Let your offering be "there, [and] fields from Nebt-ḥetepu.' Their libations "shall be of water. It is the serpent NEHEP who "giveth their bodies [and] their souls, and they journey "on to SEKHET-ÅARU to have dominion over their "libations, and to walk over the earth. They count "up their flesh, their food is of bread-cakes, and "their drink is of *tchesert* ale, and their libations "are of water. Offerings are made unto them upon "earth as [unto] the god SĀḤ, who resteth upon his "ground."

"These are they who are in the circuit of this pool. "There is a serpent living in this pool, and the water "of the pool is of fire, and the gods of the earth and "the souls of the earth cannot descend thereto by "reason of the flames of fire of this serpent. This "great god who is the governor of the Ṭuat liveth "in the water of this pool."

And Rā saith unto them:—"Hail to you, O ye gods "who guard this holy pool, give ye yourselves to him "that is the Governor of Åuḳert. The water of this "pool is Osiris, and this water is KHENTI-ṬUAT. This "flame consumeth and destroyeth the souls which dare "to approach Osiris, and the awe of this pool cannot "be done away, or made an end of, or overcome. As "for the gods who keep ward over its waters, their "food is bread, and their drink is *tchesert* ale, and "their libations are of water. Offerings are made unto "them upon earth as unto ṬERI in Åmentet, lord of "offerings. There are fields for you in this Field, "and the waters thereof are for you. Let your offer-"ings be there [and] fields from Nebt-ḥetepu. Their "libations shall be of water. It is the serpent NEHEP "who giveth their bodies [and] their souls, and they "journey into SEKHET-ÅARU to have dominion over "their libations, and to walk on the earth. They "count up their limbs, their food is of bread-cakes, and "their drink is of *tchesert* ale, and their libations are "of water. Offerings are made unto them upon earth "as unto SĀḤ, who resteth upon his ground.

"These are they who are in the circuit of this pool. "There is a serpent living . . . . ."

CHAPTER X.

THE GATE OF SET-ḤRÅ.

THE EIGHTH DIVISION OF THE ṬUAT.

HAVING passed through the Seventh Division of the Ṭuat, the boat of the Sun arrives at the gateway called BEKHKHI, , which leads to the EIGHTH DIVISION, or, as the opening text reads: 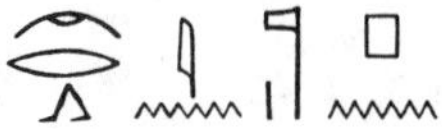  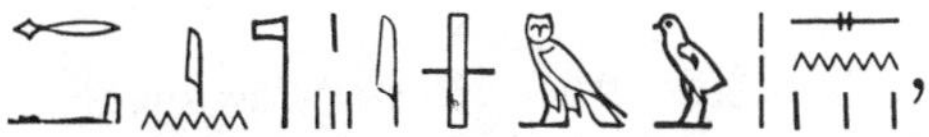, "This great god "cometh forth to this gate, and entereth through it, "and the gods who are therein acclaim this great god." The gateway is like that through which the god passed into the previous Division, and its outwork is guarded by nine gods in the form of mummies, who are described as the PAUT, i.e., the company of the nine gods, 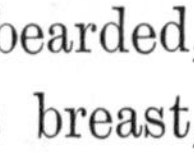. At the entrance to the gate proper stands a bearded, mummied form, with his hands folded on his breast, called BENEN, 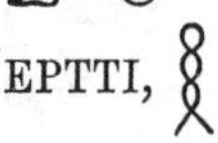, and at its exit stands a similar form called ḤEPTTI, ; each of these is said

to "extend his arms and hands to Rā," 
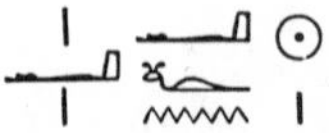. The corridor is swept by flames of fire, which proceed from the mouths of two uraei, as before. The company of the gods who guard the outwork address Rā, and say, "Come thou to us, O thou who "art at the head of the horizon, O thou great god "who openest hidden places, open for thyself the holy "pylons, and unfold the doors thereof," 

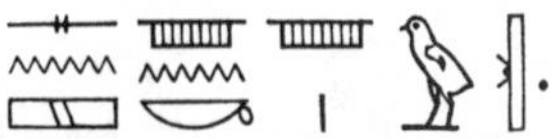. The monster serpent, which stands on his tail and guards the door, is called SET-ḤRÀ, , and the two lines of text which refer to his admission of Rā read, "He who is over this door "openeth to Rā. SA saith unto SET-ḤRÀ:—Open thy "gate to Rā, unfold thy portal to KHUTI, so that he "may illumine the thick darkness, and may send light "into the hidden abode. This gate closeth after the "great god hath passed through it, and the souls who "are on the other side of it wail when they hear the "door closing upon them," 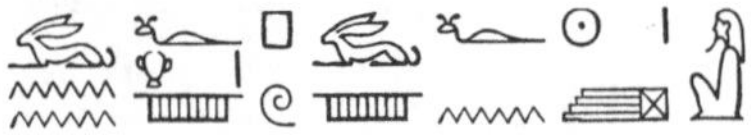

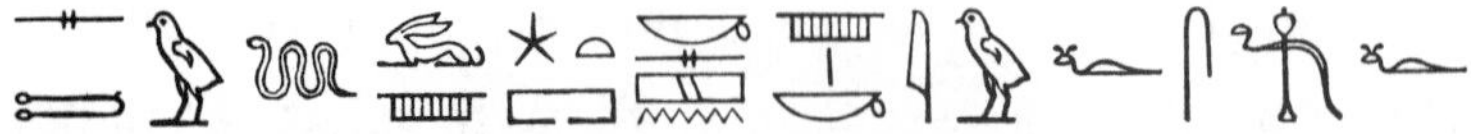

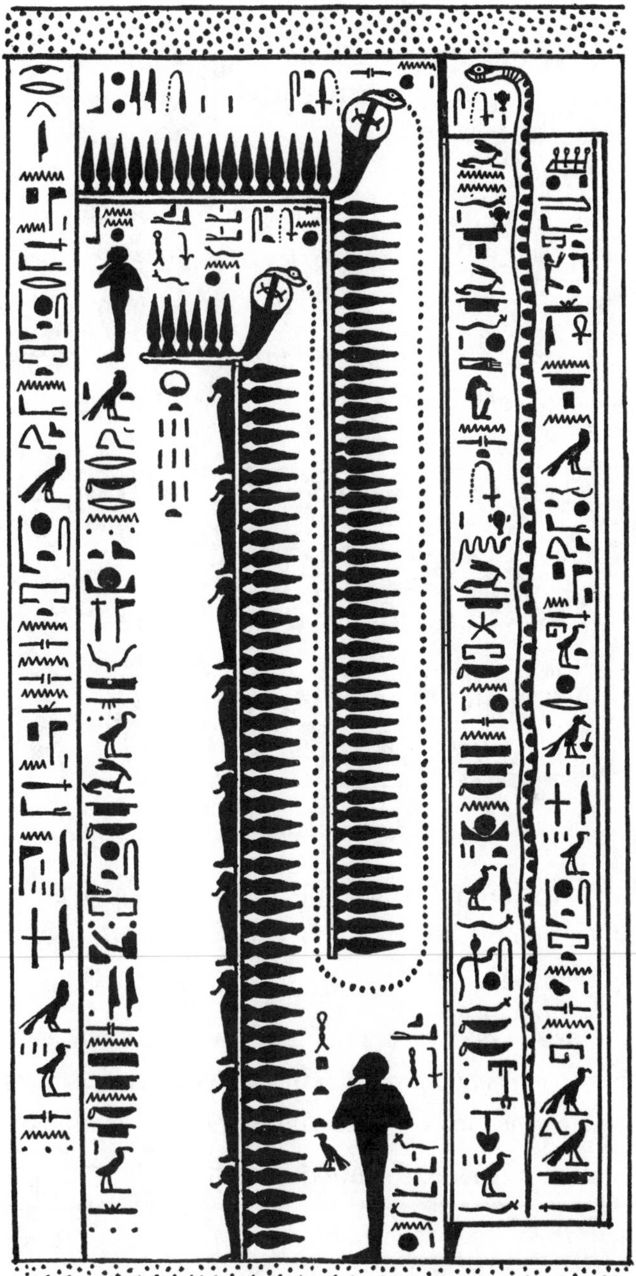

The gate of the Serpent Set-ḥrȧ.

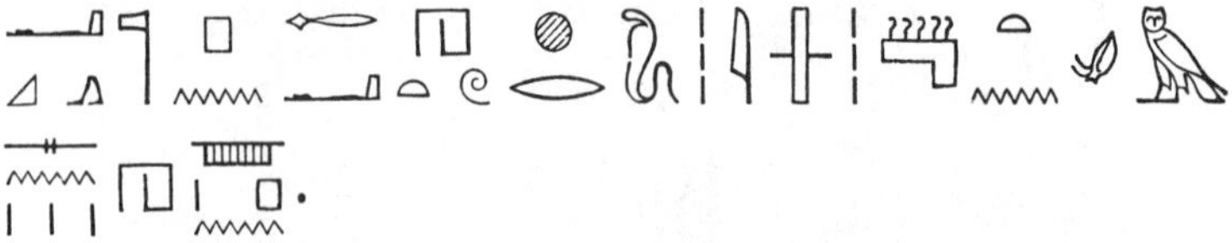

In the middle of the Division we see the boat of Rā being towed on its way by four gods of the Ṭuat, ; the god is in the same form as before, and SA stands on the look-out, and Ḥeka obeys his instructions as to the steering. At the head of the

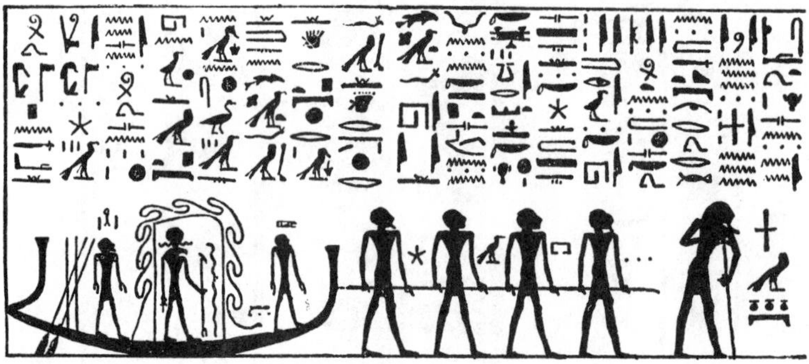

The Boat of Rā being towed through the Eighth Division of the Ṭuat by the gods thereof.

four gods who tow the boat stands an aged god, who leans on a long staff, and is called "He who dwelleth in Nu," . Immediately in front of the divine procession is a long tank, wherein we see four groups, each containing four beings, who are represented in the act of performing various evolutions in the water. These are called HERPIU, , ÅḲIU, , NUBIU, , and KHEPAU,

, which names may be translated "Bathers, Floaters, Swimmers, and Divers." The text which refers to this section reads:—

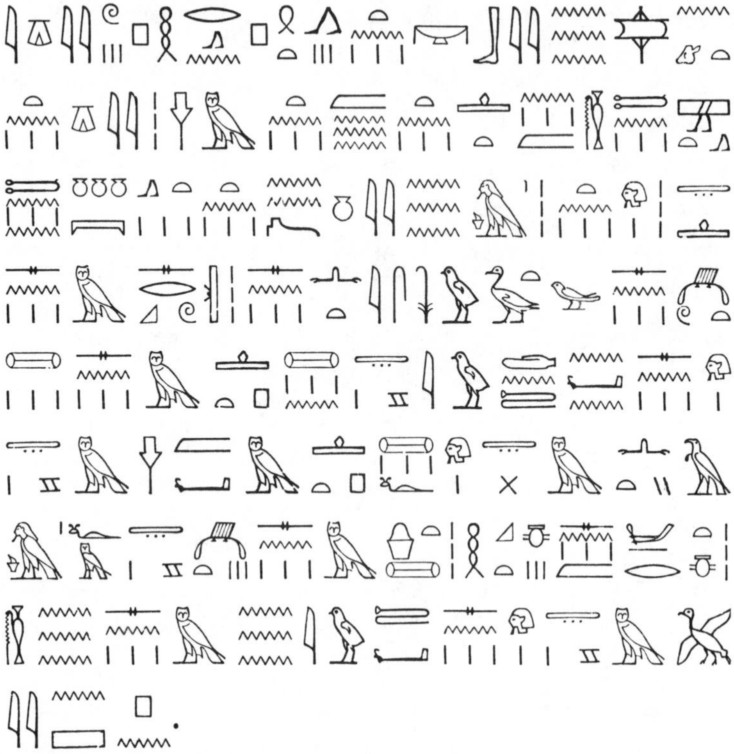

The first section of this text reads:—

This great god is towed along by gods of the Ṭuat, and behold, those who tow Rā along say, "Let there be "praise in heaven to the soul of Rā, and let there be "praise on earth to his body, for heaven is made young "by means of his soul, and earth is made young by "means of his body. Hail! We open for thee the "hidden place, and we make straight for thee the roads "of Åḳert. Be thou at peace, O Rā, with thy hidden "things, O thou who art praised [by] thy secret things "in thy forms (or, attributes). Hail! We tow thee "along, O Rā, we guide thee, O thou who art at the "head of heaven, and thou comest forth to those who "are immersed in the waters, and thou shalt make thy "way over them."

The passage which refers to the aged god reads :—

"He (literally, those) who is in Nu saith to those "who are immersed in the water, and to those who are "swimming in the pools of water, 'Look ye at Rā, who "journeyeth in his boat, [for he is] Great of Mystery.

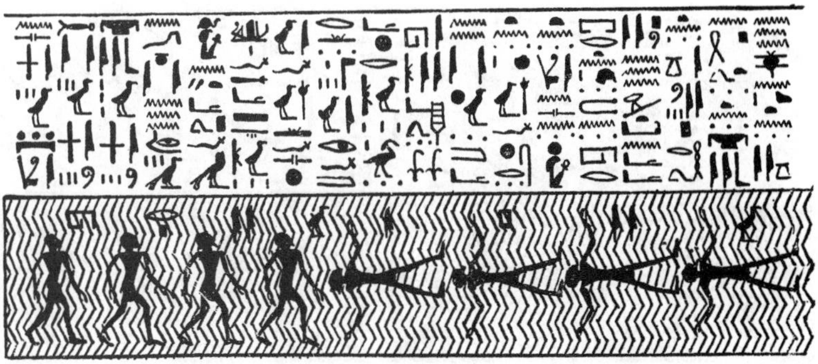

The Four Herpiu Gods, and the Four Åḳiu Gods.

"It is he who ordereth the destinies (or, affairs) of the "gods, it is he who performeth (or, maketh) the plans "of the Khu (i.e., the spirits). Hail! Rise up, O ye "beings of time, pay ye heed to Rā, for it is he who "ordereth your destinies.'"

The speech of Rā reads :—

"Put forth your heads, O ye who are immersed in "the water, thrust out your arms, O ye who are under "the waters, stretch out your legs, O ye who swim, let "there be breath to your nostrils, O ye who are deep "in the waters. Ye shall have dominion over your "waters, ye shall be at peace in your tanks of cool "waters, ye shall pass through the waters of Nu, and ye "shall make a way through your cisterns. Your souls "are upon earth, and they shall be satisfied with their "means of subsistence, and they shall not suffer destruc-"tion. Their food shall consist of the offerings of the "earth, and meat and drink shall be given unto them "upon earth, even as to him that hath obtained dominion

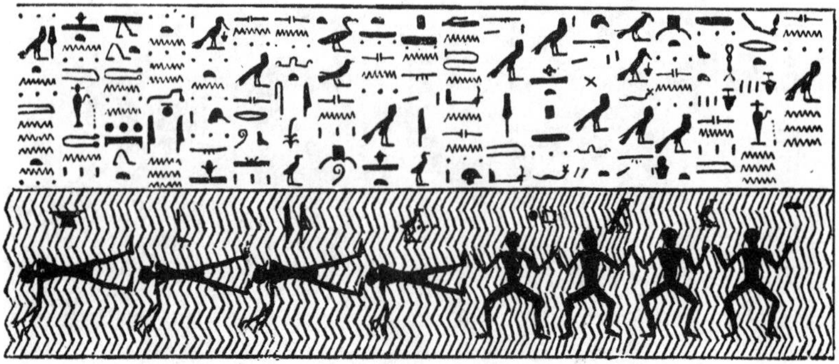

The Four Nubiu Gods, and the Four Khepau Gods.

"over his offerings upon earth, and whose soul is not "upon the earth. Their food shall consist of bread, "and their drink shall be *tchesert* wine, and their "cisterns shall be full of cool water, and there shall be "offered unto them upon earth of that which this lake "produceth."

In the upper register are the following:—

1. Twelve bearded gods, who stand with their arms hanging by their sides, and are described as the "divine "sovereign chiefs who give the bread which hath been

"allotted and green herbs to the souls who are in the "Lake of SERSER (i.e., blazing fire)," 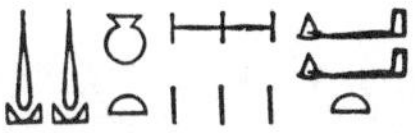

.

The Tchatchau who give the bread of Maāt.

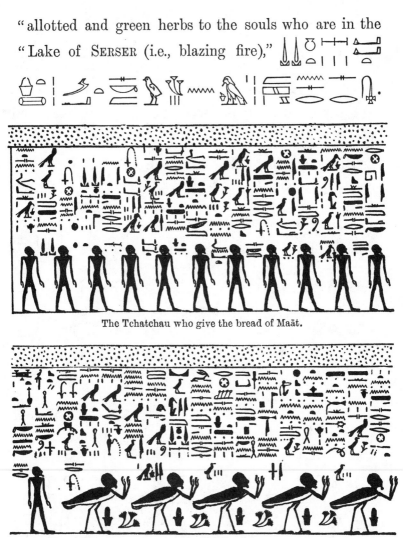

Souls who are in the Lake of Serser.

2. Nine bearded, human-headed and human-handed hawks, which stand with their hands raised in adoration; before each is a loaf of bread, , and a few

green herbs, . These are described as the "souls "who are in the Lake of Serser," .

3. A god, who holds a sceptre in his right hand, and in his left.

The texts which relate to these read:—

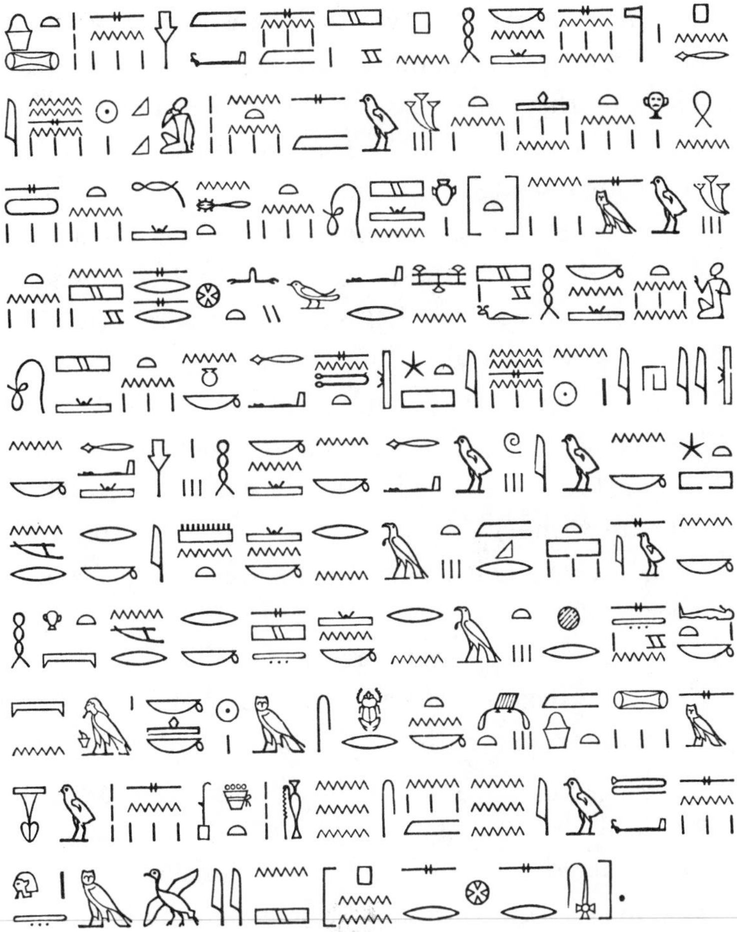

The portion of the text which refers to the twelve sovereign chiefs reads:—

"These are they who make souls to have a right to "the green herbs in the Lake of Serser. Rā saith "unto them:—'[Hail, ye] divine sovereign princes of "the gods, and ye chiefs of the Lake of Serser, who "place souls over their green herbs, let them have "dominion themselves over their bread; give ye your "bread which is appointed, and bring ye your green "herbs to the souls who have been ordered to exist "in the Lake of Serser.' They say unto Rā:—'The "bread appointed hath been and the green herbs have "been brought to the divine souls whom thou hast "ordered to exist in the Lake of Serser. Hail! Verily, "the way is fair; for KHENTI-ÅMENTI praiseth thee, "and those who dwell in TA-THENEN praise thee.' Their "food is of bread-cakes, and their beer is the *tchesert* "beer, and their libations are of cool water; and "offerings are made unto them upon earth by those "who are with (?) ṬUI by the divine sovereign princes."

The passage which refers to the souls in the Lake of Serser reads:—

"These are they who are in the Land of Serser; "they have received their bread, and they have gained "the mastery over this Lake, and they praise this "great god. Rā saith unto them:—'Eat ye your "green herbs, and satisfy ye yourselves with your "cakes; let there be fulness to your bellies, and satis-"faction to your hearts. Your green herbs are of "the Lake of Serser, the Lake which may not be "approached. Praise ye me, glorify ye me, for I am "the Great One of terror of the Ṭuat.' They say "unto Rā:—'Hail to thee, O thou Great One of the "SEKHEMU (i.e., Powers)! Praise is thine, and majesty "is thine. The Ṭuat is thine, and [is subservient] to "thy will; it is a hidden place [made] by thee for "those who are in its Circles. The height of Heaven "is thine, and [is subservient] to thy will; it is a "secret place [made] by thee for those who belong "thereto. The Earth is for thy dead Body, and the "Sky is for thy Soul. O Rā, be thou at peace (or, be "content) with that which thou hast made to come "into being.' Their food consisteth of bread-cakes, "their green herbs are the plants of the spring, and "the waters wherein they refresh themselves are cool·

Souls who are in the Lake of Serser. A god with a sceptre.

"Offerings are made unto them upon the earth as "[being] the product of this Lake of Serser."

In the lower register are:—

1. Horus [the Aged], in the form of a bearded man, leaning upon a staff.

2. Twelve bearded beings, who are described as the "burnt enemies of Osiris," 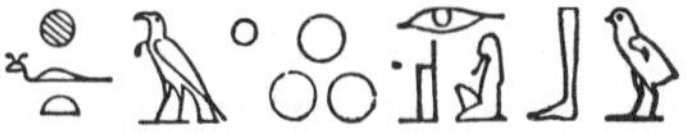 . The first four have their arms tied

behind their back in such a way that the right hand projects at the left side, and the left hand at the right side. The second four have their hands tied together at the elbows, and the upper parts of the arms are at right angles to their shoulders. The third four have their arms tied together at the elbows, and their elbows are on a lower level than their shoulders.

3. A monster speckled serpent, which lies in undulations immediately in front of the enemies of Osiris,

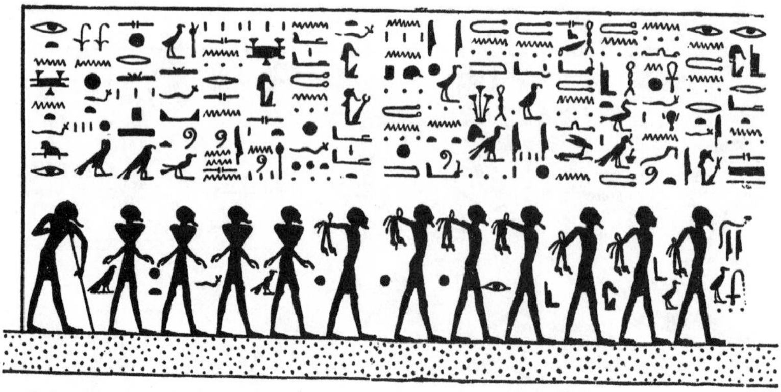

Horus the Aged. The Burnt Enemies of Osiris.

and belches fire into the face of their leader; the name of this serpent is KHETI, . In each undulation stands a bearded god in mummied form, and the hieroglyphics written above describe them as "the gods who are above KHETI," . The text reads:—

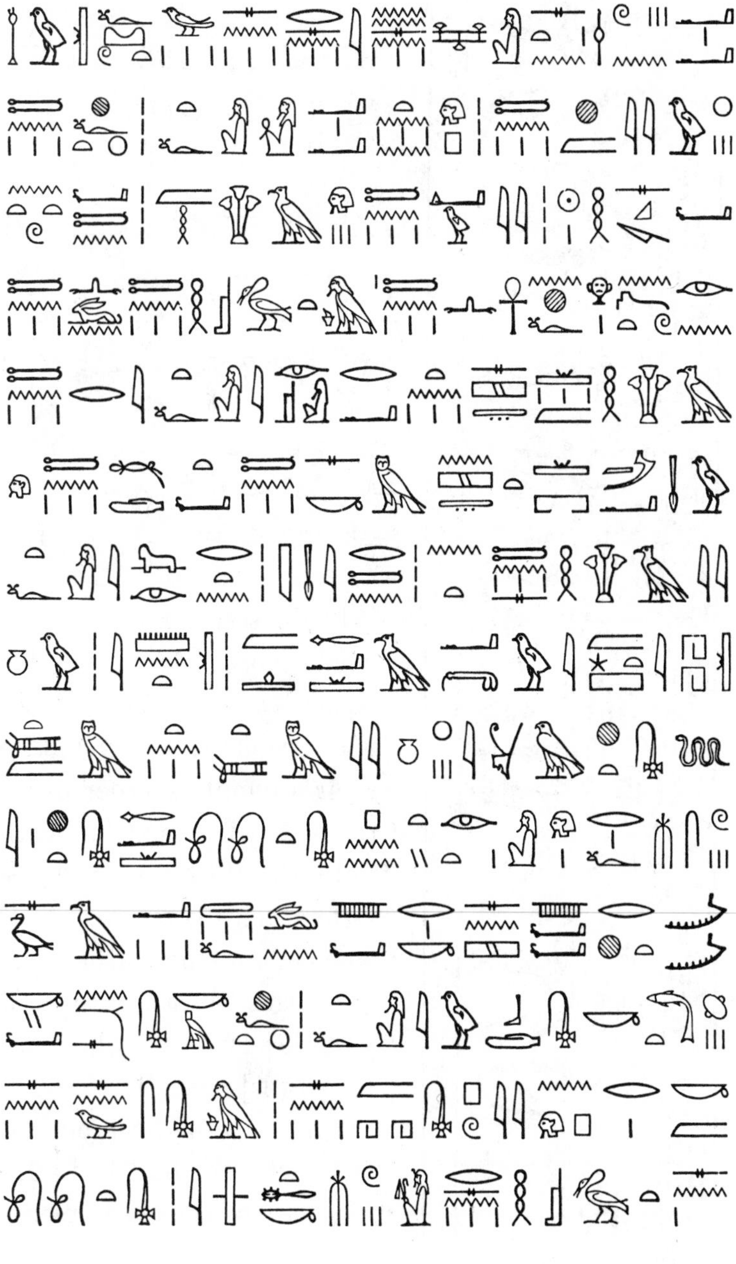

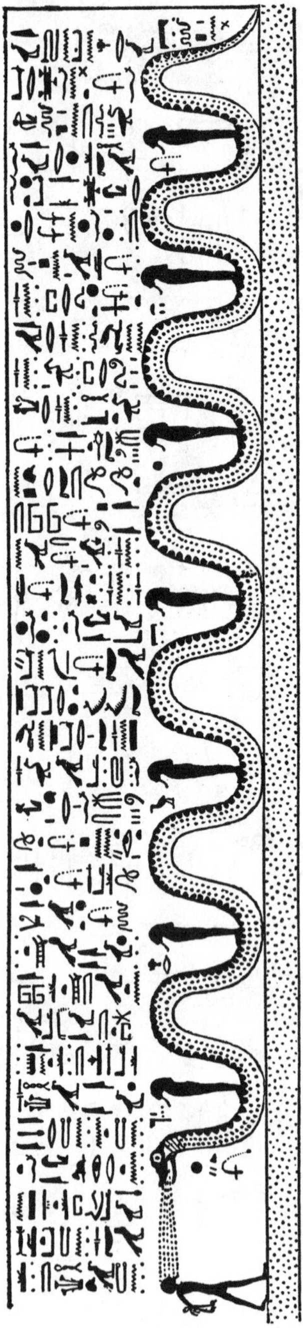

"[This scene representeth] "what Horus doeth for his "father Osiris. The enemies "who are in this scene have "their calamities ordered for "them by Horus, who saith "unto them:—'Let there be "fetters on your arms, O "enemies of my father, let "your arms be tied up towards "your heads, O ye who have "no [power], ye shall be fettered "[with your arms] behind you, "O ye who are hostile to Rā. "Ye shall be hacked in pieces, "ye shall nevermore have your being, your souls shall "be destroyed, and none [of you] shall live because of "what ye have done to my father Osiris; ye have "put [his] mysteries behind your backs, and ye have "dragged out the statue [of the god] from the secret "place. The word of my father Osiris is *maāt* against "you, and my word is *maāt* against you, O ye who "have desecrated (literally, laid bare) the hidden things "which concern the rest (or, resting-place) of the Great "One who begot me in the Ṭuat. O ye shall cease to "exist, ye shall come to an end.'"

"Horus saith:—'[O] my serpent KHET, thou Mighty "Fire, from whose mouth cometh forth this flame "which is in my Eye, whose undulations are guarded "by [my] children, open thy mouth, distend thy jaws, "and belch forth thy fires against the enemies of my "father, burn thou up their bodies, consume their "souls by the fire which issueth from thy mouth, "and by the flames which are in thy body. My "divine children are against them, they destroy "[their] spirits, and those who have come forth from "me are against them, and they shall never more "exist. The fire which is in this serpent shall come "forth, and shall blaze against these enemies whenso- "ever Horus decreeth that it shall do so.' Whosoever "knoweth how to use words of power [against] this "serpent shall be as one who doth not enter upon his "fiery path."

The end of this text on the sarcophagus of Seti I. is

defective, but from the tomb of Rameses VI. we see that it should end thus:—"Offerings shall be made "to these gods who are upon this great serpent. Their "food is of bread, their drink is of *ṭesher* beer, and the "waters of their libations are cool."

CHAPTER XI.

THE GATE OF ĀB-TA.

THE NINTH DIVISION OF THE ṬUAT.

HAVING passed through the Eighth Division of the Ṭuat, the boat of the sun arrives at the gateway called ĀAT-SHEFSHEFT, 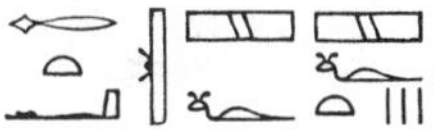, which leads to the NINTH DIVISION, or, as the opening text reads: 

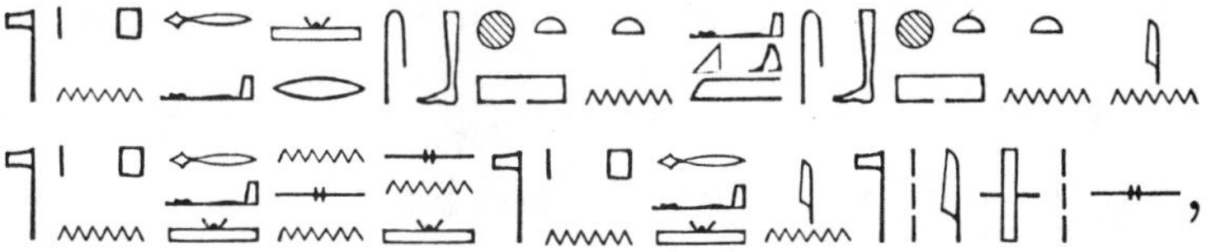,

"This great god cometh to this gate, and entereth "through it, and the gods who are therein acclaim this "great god." The gateway is like that through which the god passed into the previous Division, and its outwork is guarded by nine gods in the form of mummies, who are described as the PAUT, i.e., the company of the nine gods, 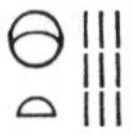. At the entrance to the gate proper stands a bearded, mummied form, with his hands folded on his breast, called ÅNḤEFTA, 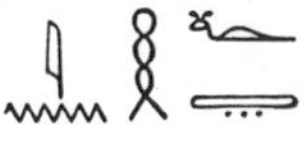, and at its exit stands a similar form called ERMEN-TA, 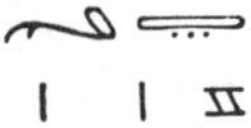; each of these is said to "extend his arms and hands to Rā," , or 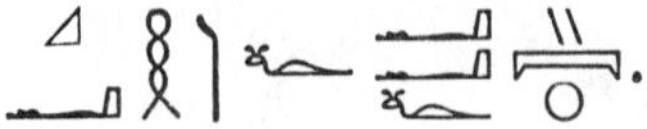. The corridor is swept by flames of fire, which proceed from the mouths of two uraei, as before. The company of the gods who guard the outwork address Rā, and say, "Come thou to us, O "thou who art the head of the horizon, O thou great "god who openest the secret places, open for thyself "the holy pylons, and unfold for thyself the holy doors "thereof," 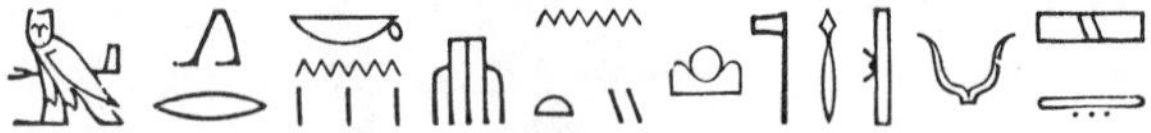

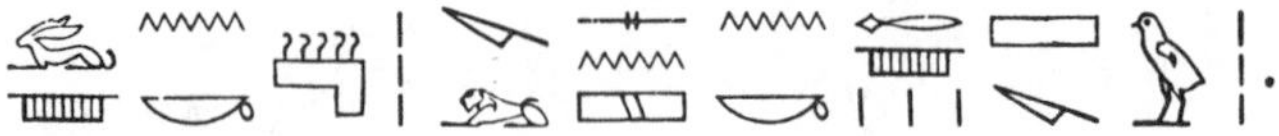. The monster serpent which stands on his tail and guards the door is called ĀB-TA, , and the two lines of text which refer to his admission of Rā read, "He "who is over this door openeth to Rā. SA saith unto "ĀB-TA, 'Open thy gate to Rā, unfold thy portal to "KHUTI, so that he may illumine the thick darkness, "and may send light into the hidden abode.' This gate "closeth after this god hath passed through it, and the "souls who are on the other side of it wail when they "hear this door closing upon them," 

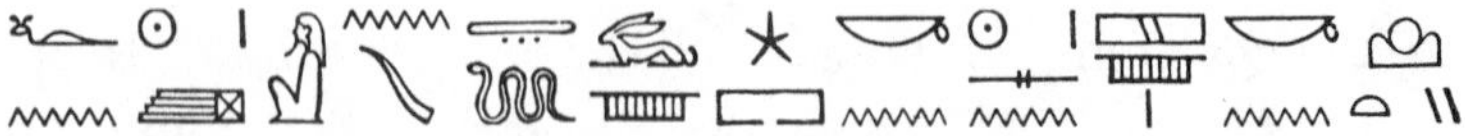

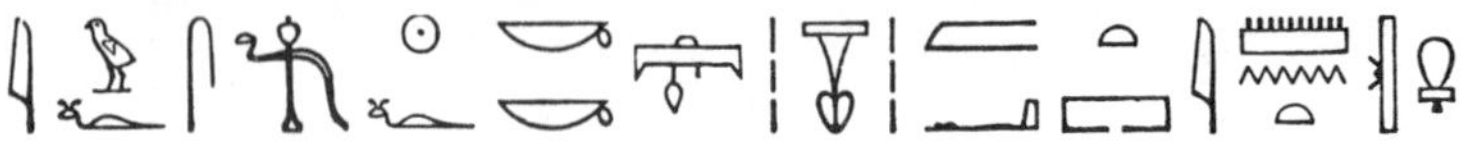

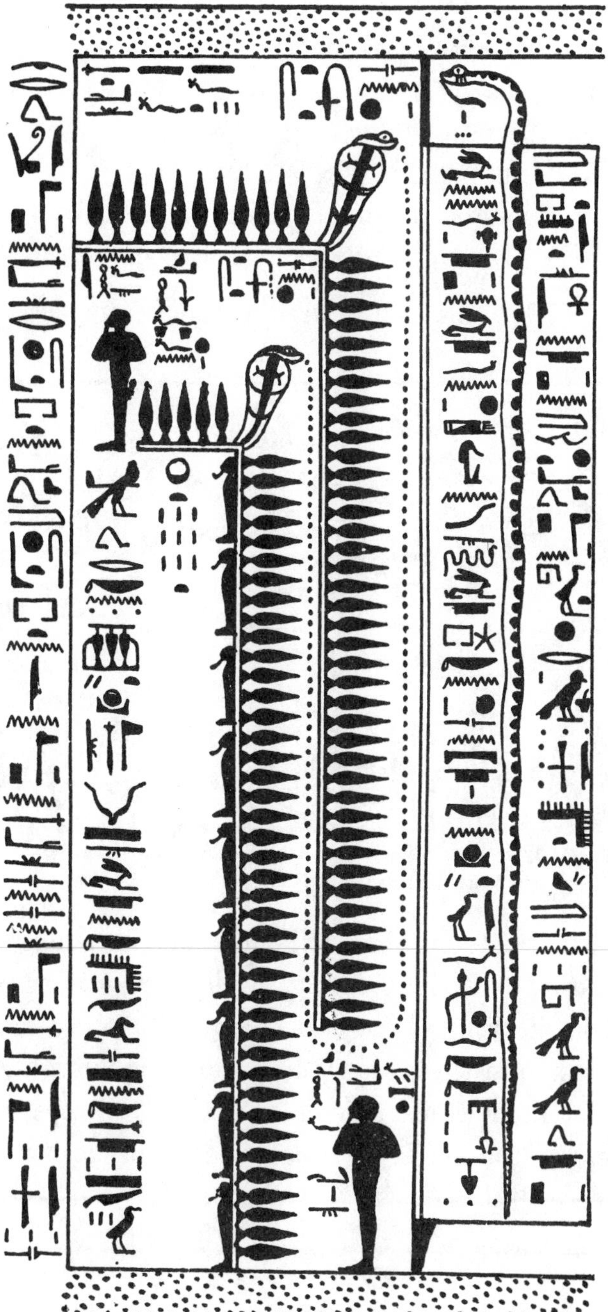

The Gate of Āb-ta.

In the middle of the Division we see the boat of Rā being towed on its way by four gods of the Ṭuat, ; the god is in the same form as before,

The Boat of Åf-Rā in the Ninth Division of the Ṭuat.

and SA stands on the look-out, and ḤEKA obeys his instructions as to steering. The procession which marches in front of the boat consists of :—

1. Six bearded male figures, standing upright, who hold in their hands the ends of a rod, or rope, which is bent in the shape of a bow over their heads; these are described as "those who are over the words of magical power," .

2. Four dog-headed apes, which hold a rod bent as already described; these are described as "those who work magic by means of knots for Rā," .

3. Four women, who stand upright, and hold a bent

Gods, goddesses, and apes casting spells on Āpep.

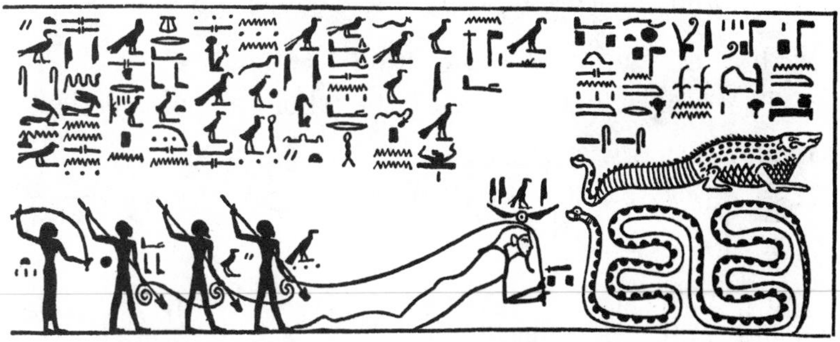

The spearmen. Åai. Shesshes and Āpep.

rod, or rope, over their heads like the four apes and the six male figures; they are described as "those who work magic by means of knots for Rā," 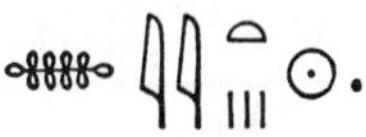.

4. Three male figures, each holding a harpoon in

his right hand, and a cord in his left; they are called "spearmen," . Immediately in front of these is a bearded male figure, who has been lying prostrate on his face; he has upon his head a small solar disk and a pair of ass's ears, and his name is ÅAI, , i.e., the ASS. In his hands he grasps a rope, which passes over his head and along his back, and is held by each of the three spearmen in his left hand; from the knees upwards his body is raised in a diagonal position, and this attitude suggests that he has either raised himself by means of the rope, or has been pulled into this position by the spearmen. Facing the Ass are:—1. The monster serpent ĀPEP, , and 2. The crocodile SHESSHES, , with a tail ending in the head of a serpent.

The text, which refers to the whole of this section, reads:—

"This great god is towed along by the gods of the "Ṭuat, and those who tow Rā along say:—'The god "cometh to his body, and the god is towed along to his "shadow. O be thou at peace with thy body, and we "will tow thee along in thy integrity into thy (literally, "his) secret place. Come thou, O Rā, and be thou at "peace with thy body, for thou shalt be protected by "those who are over the curved ropes (?).'"

The text which refers to the six men, four apes, and four women, with nets over their heads, reads:—

"Those who are in this picture march before Rā, and "they utter words of power against Āpep, and [then] "return to the Ārit (or, Hall) of the horizon. They "journey onwards with him into the height of heaven, "and they come into being for him in the Ȧterti "(i.e., the two portions of the sky in which Rā rises "and sets), and they cause him to rise in Nut. And "they say their words of power which are these:—'Out "upon thee, O thou Rebel Serpent! Out upon thee, "thou monster that destroyest, thou Āpep that sendest "forth thy evil emanations (or, deeds)! Thy face shall "be destroyed, O Āpep. Thou shalt advance to the "block of execution. The Nemu are against thee, and "they shall hack thee in pieces. The Ȧaiu are against "thee, and they shall destroy thee. The Ābebuiti "(i.e., the three spearmen) shall drive [their harpoons] "into thee, and they shall enchant thee by means of "their Hail! Thou art destroyed, dashed in pieces, "and stabbed to death, O serpent Sessi.'"

"Those who are in this scene, and who have their

"spears, keep ward over the rope of Ai, and they do "not permit this Worm to approach the boat of the "great god. They pass behind this god upwards. "These gods who do battle on behalf of this god in "heaven say":—(The speech is wanting).

Gods of the South raising the Standard of the South.

In the upper register are the following:—

1. Four gods, who in the place of heads have each a crown of the South, to which is affixed a uraeus, upon his body, and who, aided by a bearded male figure, are engaged in raising up from the ground, by means of a rope, a pole or staff, which is surmounted by a bearded

human head wearing a crown of the South; the gods are called "gods of the South," , and the bearded male figure "he who is over the front end," 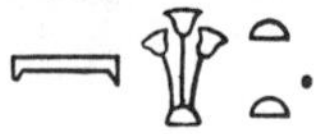.

2. Four gods, who in the place of heads have each a

Gods of the North raising the Standard of the North.

crown of the North, to which is affixed a uraeus, upon his body, and who, aided by a bearded male figure, are engaged in raising up from the ground, by means of a rope, a pole or staff, which is surmounted by a bearded human head wearing a crown of the North; the gods are called "gods of the North," , and the bearded male figure is "he who is over the hind part," .

3. Between the two groups described above is the hawk-headed sphinx which typifies "Horus in the Boat," . Above its hind-quarters spring the head and shoulders of a bearded human figure called ĀNĀ, , and on the head of the hawk and that of Ānā is a crown of the South. Standing on the back of the sphinx is the figure of HORUS-SET with characteristic heads, with his arms outstretched, and with each hand laid upon the upper part of the crowns of the South. The hawk head of this figure faces the back of the hawk head of the sphinx, and the animal's head, which is characteristic of Set, faces the back of the human head of Ānā. It is thus quite clear that

Heru-âm-uàa with Set-Horus on his back.

Horus was regarded as a form of the Sun-god of the South, and Set as a form of the Sun-god of the North.

4. The serpent SHEMTI, , which has four heads and necks at each end of its body, and each head and neck are supported on a pair of legs. A male figure called ÅPU, , stands and grasps the middle of the body of the serpent with both hands.

5. The serpent BÅTA, , with a bearded head at each end of his body; each head wears a crown of the South. Above the back of this serpent is another serpent, from each end of the body of which spring the upper portions of the bodies and heads of four bearded male figures; the first figure of each group has a pair of hands and arms which are raised in adoration, and each figure of the two groups has a pair of legs, which rest on the back of the serpent BÅTA. A male figure called ÅBETH stands and grasps the middle of the body of the serpent ṬEPI, , with both hands.

6. Two male beings, swinging over their heads a net, wherewith they are going to attack the serpent, or to resist him.

The text which refers to the above reads:—

The Shemti Serpent and his warder Ȧpu.

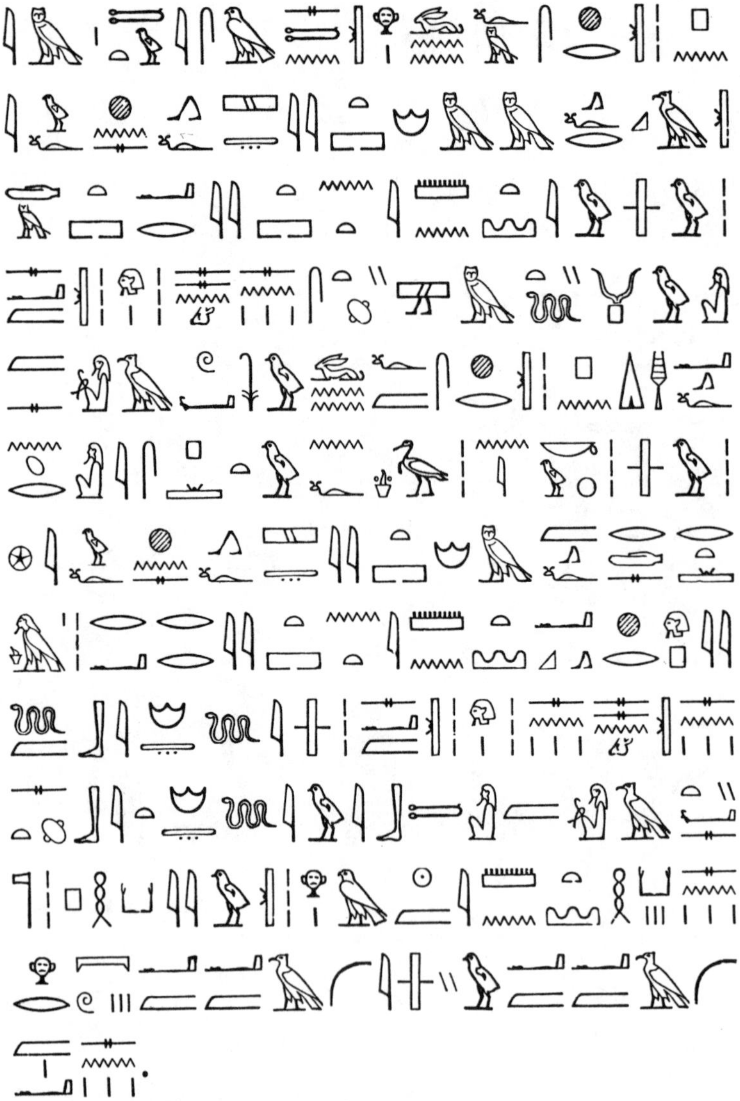

The passage which refers to the gods of the South reads:—

"Those who are in this scene rise up for Rā, who

"saith unto them:—'Receive ye your heads, O ye gods, "and draw tightly the front end of your rope. Hail, "O ye gods, come into being! Hail, possess ye the "power of light, O ye gods, and come ye into being, O "ye gods. Possess ye the power of light, O ye gods, by

The Serpents Båta and Ṭepi and the warder Åbeth.

"my coming into being in the secret place, and by my "power of light in the hidden place (Åment), in the "chambers of things.'"

The passage which refers to Horus-Set reads:—

"Rā maketh to arise this god. This god with his "two faces goeth in after Rā hath passed by him."

The passage which refers to the gods of the North reads:—

"Rā saith unto them:—'Let your heads be to "you, O ye gods! Receive ye your crowns of "the North, and pull ye tightly at the hinder "end of the boat of him that cometh into being "from me. Behold now Horus of the handsome "Face!'"

The passage which refers to the serpent SHEMTI reads:—

"He who is in this picture strideth through the secret "place, and he withdraweth to QA-ṬEMT, the Hall (or, "Court) of Ȧment. Those who are in it are the heads "which have been devoured, and they breathe the "odour of SHEMTI, of which ȦPU is the warder."

The passage which refers to the serpent BȦTA reads:—

"He who is in this picture maketh his rising up for "SAR, and he keepeth count of the souls which are "doomed in the Ṭuat. He strideth through the secret "place, and he withdraweth to ṬESERT-BAIU, to the "Hall (or, Court) of Ȧment; then ṬEPI entereth into "BȦTA. Those who are in it are they whose heads "have been devoured. They breathe the odour of "BȦTA, of which ȦBETH is the guardian."

The passage which refers to the two gods with nets reads:—

"These are the gods who make use of words of "power for Horus-Rā in Ȧment. [They have power] "over the net, and they make use of words of power on "those who are in the net[s] which are in their hands."

In the lower register are:—

1. Sixteen gods, who stand at one end of the scene, and grasp a rope with both hands. The first four are bearded, man-headed beings, and are said to be "the souls of Ament," 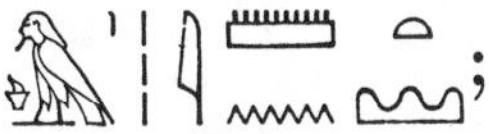; the second four are ibis-headed, and are "the followers of Thoth," ; the third four are hawk-headed, and are "the followers of Horus," 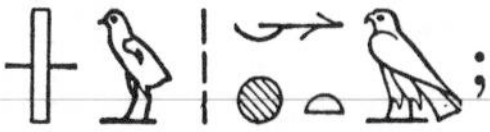; and the last four are ram-headed, and are "the followers of Rā," .

Two gods with nets.

2. Eight bearded, man-headed beings, who stand at the other end of the scene in two groups of four, and who are described as "Powers," ;

each grasps a rope with both hands. The rope which is held by these groups of beings is attached to the legs of the enormous serpent Khepri, . This serpent has a head at each end of its body, the foremost part of which is supported on a pair of human legs; from each end of that portion of its body which lies flat on the ground springs a uraeus. On the centre fold of the body is seated a hawk, which wears on its head the double crown, . This hawk is the symbol of "Horus of the Ṭuat," *Ḥeru ṭuati* .

The text which refers to this section of the scene reads:—

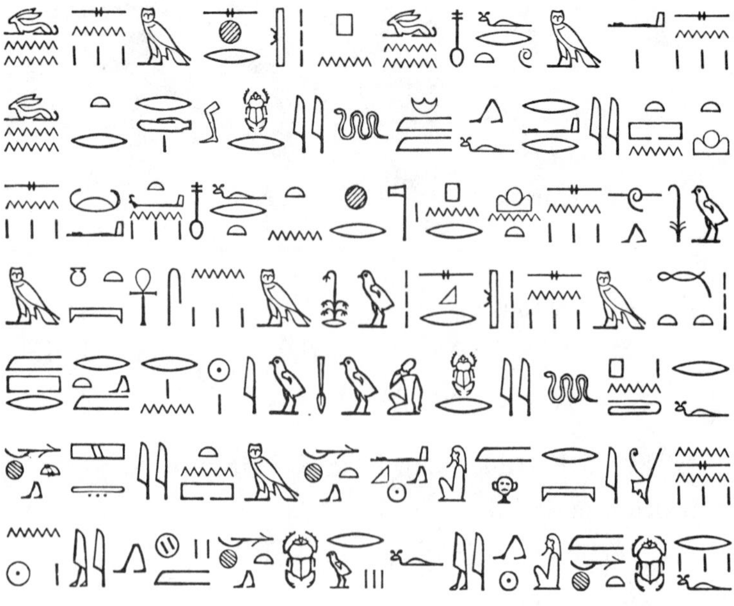

The Souls of Ȧment, and the Followers of Thoth who tow Khepri.

The Followers of Horus and the Followers of Rā who tow Khepri.

"Those who are in this scene have the rope in their "hands, and it is fastened to the leg[s] of KHEPRI, who "moveth backwards to the Hall of their horizon. They "draw this rope with the god into their horizon, and "they tow him along in the sky (NUT). They live upon "the things of the South, and their sustenance is from "the things of the North, [and they exist] on that which "cometh forth from the mouth of Rā. The voice of "this serpent KHEPRI goeth round about and travelleth "into the secret place after Rā hath entered into the "height of heaven."

The four groups, each containing four beings, "say "unto Rā:—'Come, O come, after thy transformations! "Come, O Rā, after thy transformations! Appear,

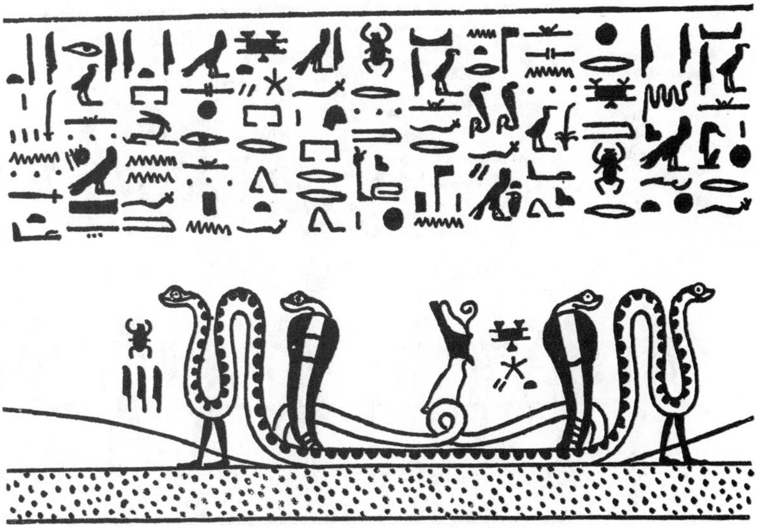

The Serpent Khepri and Horus of the Ṭuat.

"appear, after thy transformations! Appear, O Rā, "after thy transformations in heaven, in the great "heaven! Hail! We decree for thee thy habitations "by the excellence which is in the words of the Mighty "One of Forms in the secret (or, hidden) place.'"

The passage which refers to Horus reads:—

"He who is in this scene is ḤERU ṬUATI (i.e., Horus

"of the Ṭuat). The head cometh forth from him, "and the forms [in which he appeareth] from the "coiled [serpent]. Rā crieth unto this god to whom "the two divine URAEI unite themselves; he entereth "in upon the way into KHEPRI, who listeneth when Rā "crieth to him."

The two groups, each containing four beings, "have

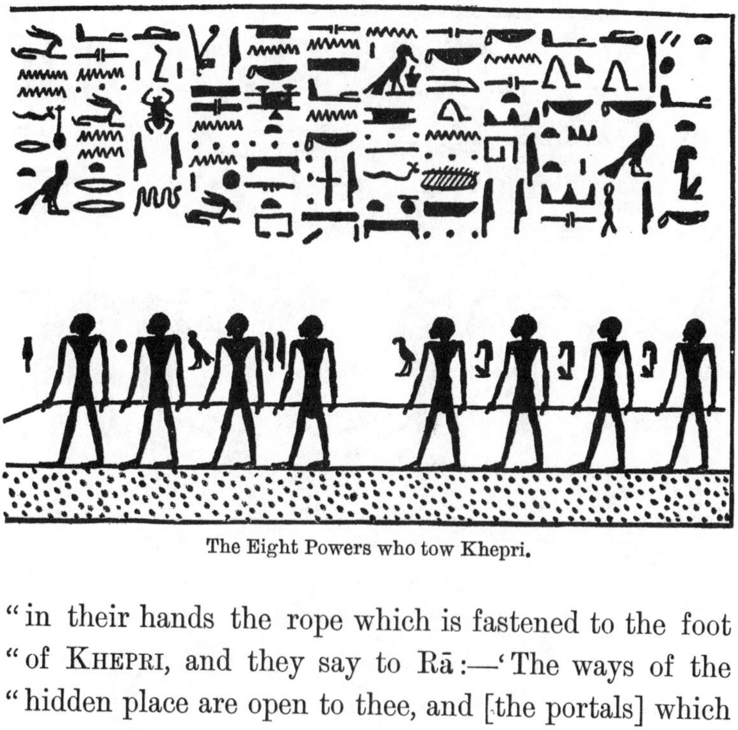

The Eight Powers who tow Khepri.

"in their hands the rope which is fastened to the foot "of KHEPRI, and they say to Rā:—'The ways of the "hidden place are open to thee, and [the portals] which "are in the earth are unfolded for thee, the SOUL which "Nut loveth, and we will guide thy wings to the moun-"tain. Hail! Enter thou into the East, and make thou "ṭhy passage from between the thighs of thy mother.'"

CHAPTER XII.

THE GATE OF SETHU.

THE TENTH DIVISION OF THE ṬUAT.

HAVING passed through the Ninth Division of the Ṭuat, the boat of the sun arrives at the gateway TCHESERIT, , which leads to the Tenth Division, or, as the opening text reads:   , "This great god cometh "forth to this gate, and entereth through it, and the "gods who are therein acclaim the great god." The gateway is like that through which the god passed into the previous Division, and its outwork is guarded by sixteen uraei. At the entrance to the gate proper stands a bearded, mummied form called NEMI, 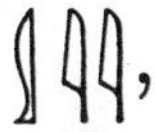, who holds a knife in his hands, and at its exit stands a similar mummied form called KEFI, 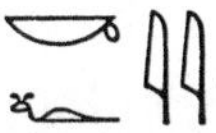. The corridor is swept by flames of fire, which proceed from the mouths of two uraei, as before. The uraei which guard the outwork address Rā, and say, "Come thou to "us, O thou who art at the head of the horizon, O thou "great god who openest the secret place, open thou "the holy pylons and unfold the portals of the earth,"

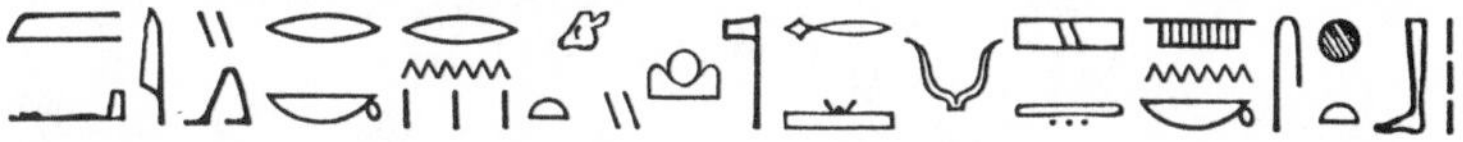

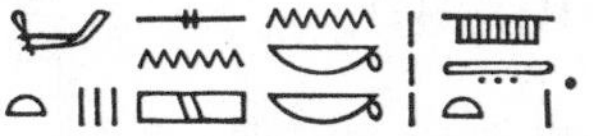 The monster serpent which

The Boat of Åf-Rā in the Tenth Division of the Ṭuat.

stands on his tail and guards the door is called SETHU, , and the two lines of text which refer to his admission of Rā read:—"He who is over this gate "openeth to Rā. SA saith unto SETHU, 'Open thy "gate, unfold thy portal, so that he may illumine the "thick darkness, and may send light into the hidden "abode.' This gate closeth after the great god hath

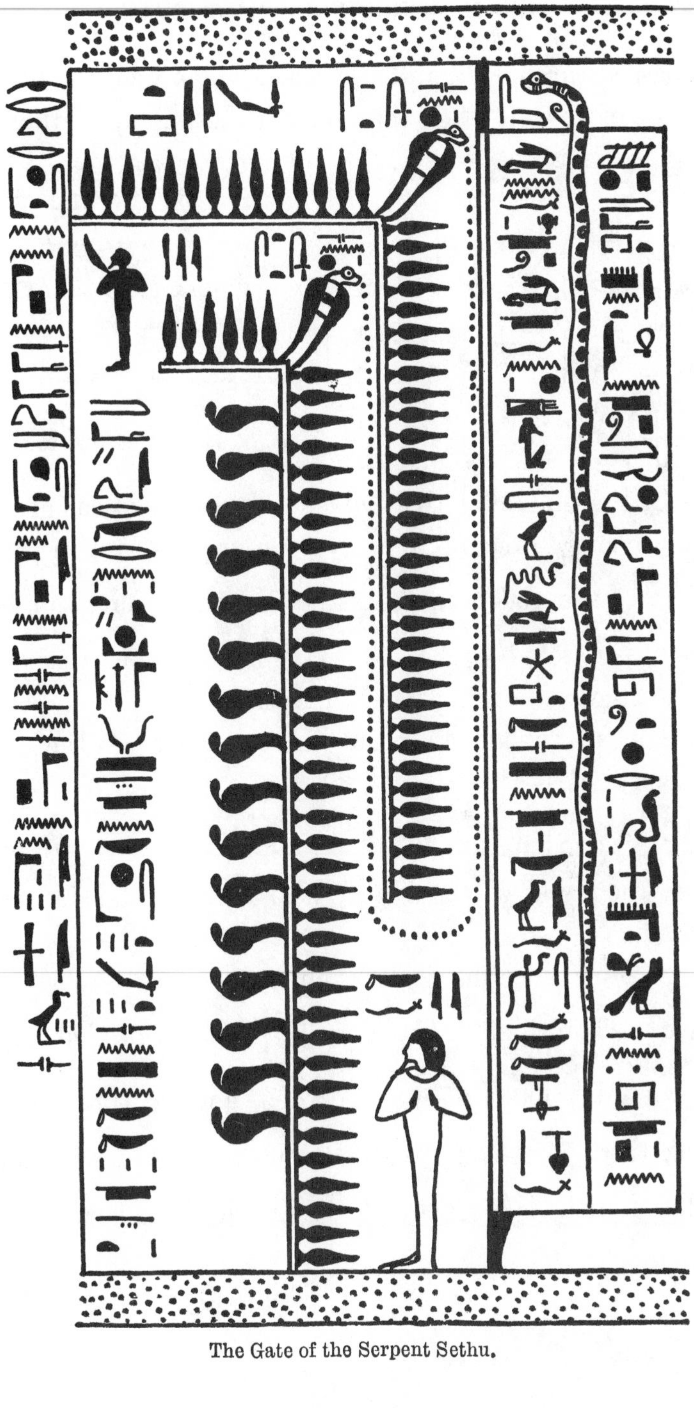

The Gate of the Serpent Sethu.

"passed through it, and the uraei who are on the other "side of it wail when they hear it closing upon them,"

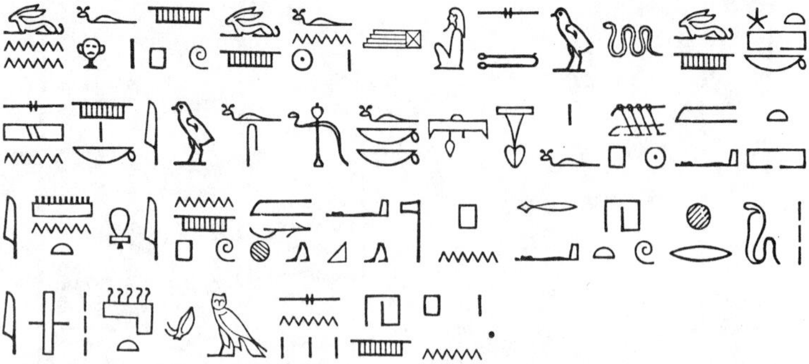

In the middle of this Division we see the boat of the sun being towed on its way by four gods of the Ṭuat, 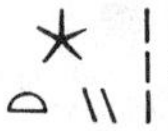; the god is in the same form as before, and his boat is piloted by SA, who commands, and by ḤEKA, who steers according to his directions.

The procession in front of the boat of the sun consists of:—

1. A bearded male figure called UNTI, , i.e., the "god of the hour," who holds a star in each hand.

2. Four kneeling gods, each with a uraeus over his head. The first is HORUS, , hawk-headed; the second is SEREQ, 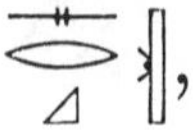, bearded, and wearing a wig; the third is ĀBESH, bearded and without a wig; and the fourth is SEKHET, , with the head of a lioness.

3. Three bearded beings, the "Star-gods," , each holding a star in his right hand, which is stretched aloft, and with his left towing a small boat containing the "Face of the Disk."

4. A small boat holding a uraeus, which has the latter part of its body bent upwards; within the curve is the "Face of the Disk," .

5. The winged serpent SEMI, standing on its tail, with its body in folds.

6. The bearded figure BESI, , receiving in his hand the flame which spouts up from the head of a horned animal, which forms the top of a staff, and is transfixed by a knife.

7. The serpent ĀNKHI, , from each side of the neck of which grows a bearded, mummy figure.

8. Four women, each with both hands raised in adoration; they are described as "Criers," .

9. Two bows, set end to end, , on each of which three uraei rear their heads. Standing over the place where the two ends of the bows meet, with a foot on the end of each, is the two-headed figure HORUS-SET, with two pairs of hands, one pair on each side of his body, raised in adoration. HORUS-SET is called "he of the two heads," , and the two bows are "the Crown of the Uraei," .

The text which refers to the above groups reads:—

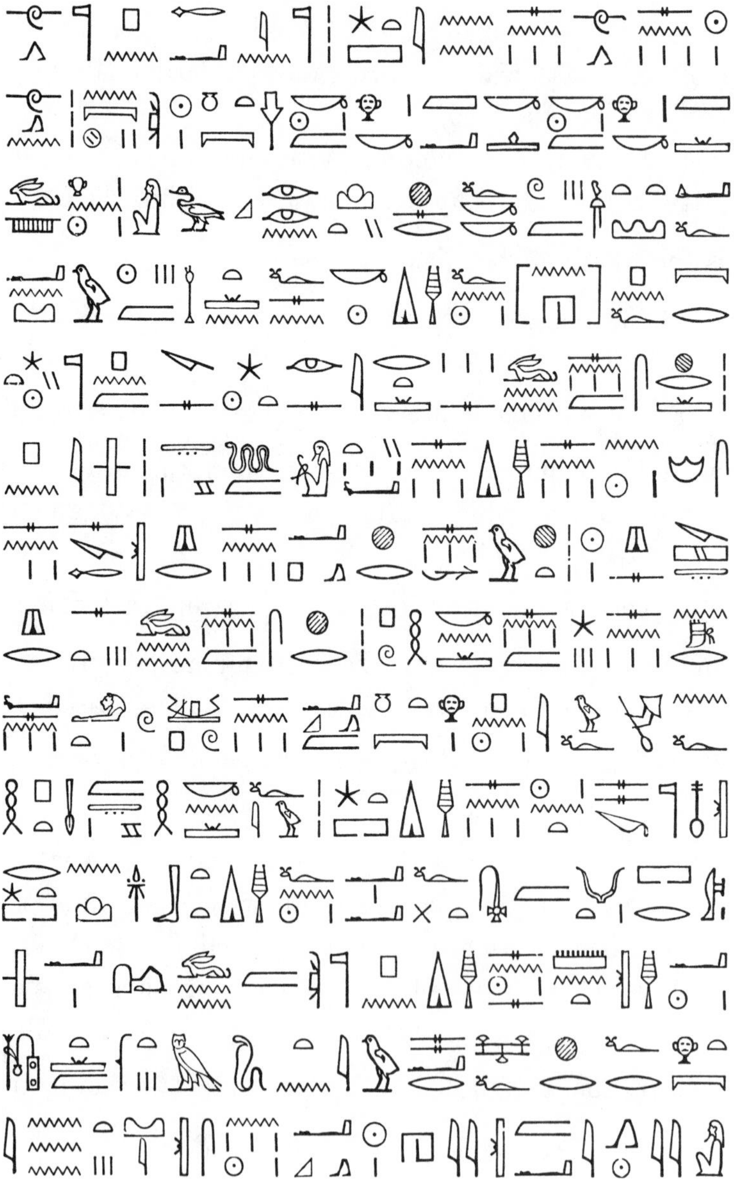

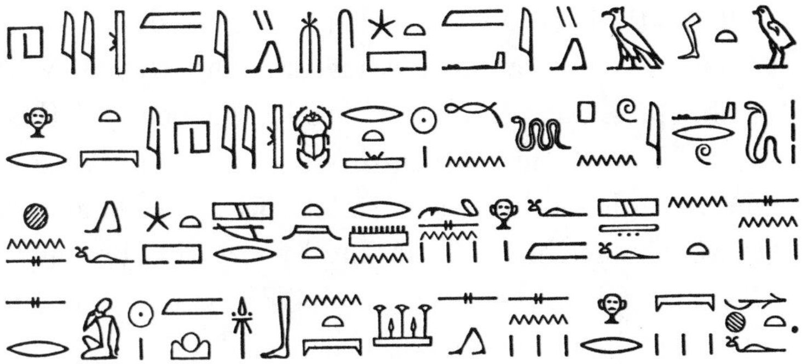

"This great god is towed along by the gods of the "Ṭuat, and those who tow Rā along say:—'We are "towing Rā along, we are towing Rā along, and Rā "followeth [us] into Nut. O have the mastery over "thy Face, indeed thou shalt unite thyself to thy Face, "O Rā, [by] Maāt. Open, O thou Face of Rā, and let "the two Eyes of Khuti enter into thee; drive away "thou the darkness from Åmentet. Let him give light "by what he hath sent forth, the light.'"

Of the god with stars it is said:—

"He maketh a rising up for Rā (or, he stablisheth "Rā), UNTI maketh to be light the upper heaven; this "god leadeth the hour, which performeth that which "belongeth to it to do."

Of the four seated gods it is said:—

"The [four] serpents who are in the earth keep ward "over those who are in this picture. They måke a "rising up for Rā, and they sit upon the great image[s "which are] under them, and they pass onwards with "them in the following of Rā, together with the hidden "images which belong to them."

Of the three gods who hold stars it is said:—

"Those who are in this picture sing hymns with "their stars, and they grasp firmly the bows of their "boat, [and it] entereth into Nut. And this Face of "Rā moveth onwards, and saileth over the land, and "those who are in the Ṭuat sing hymns to it, and make "Rā to stand up (i.e., establish Rā)."

Of the winged serpent SEMI it is said:—

"[It maketh a rising up for Rā], and it guideth the

Gods of Light and Fire. Star-gods. Face of the Disk. Semi.

"Well-doing god into the Ṭuat of the horizon of the "East."

Of the god BESI it is said:—

"He maketh a rising up for Rā, and he placeth fire "on the head and horns (or, [in] his hands is the fire "from the head and horns), and the weapon which is in "the hand of the Fighter is in the follower of this god."

Of the uraeus with the double male figure it is said:—

"It maketh a rising up for Rā. The stablishing of

"Time which is reckoned in writing by years is with "this uraeus, and it maketh it to go with him into the "heights of heaven."

Of the "Criers" it is said:—

"Those who cry unto Rā say, 'Enter in, O Rā! "Hail, come, O Rā! Hail, come, O thou who art born "of the Ṭuat! Come, O offspring of the heights of "heaven! Hail, come thou into being, O Rā!'"

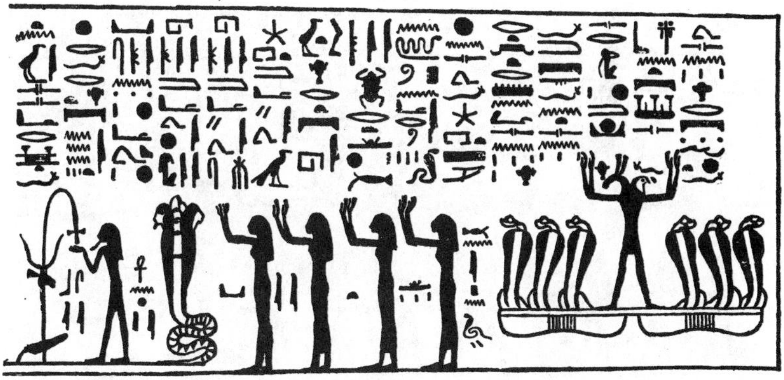

Besi. Ānkhi. The goddesses who hail the god. Meḥen and Horus-Set.

Of the double bow it is said:—

"This is the MEḤEN serpent of the uraei, which "strideth through the Ṭuat. The two bows are "stretched out, and they bear up on themselves him of "the Two-Faces (or, Two-Heads, i.e., Horus-Set) in his "mystery which [appertaineth] to them. They lead "the way for Rā in the horizon of the east of heaven, "and they pass on into the heights of heaven in his "train."

In the upper register are:—

1. The four Ȧntiu gods, , each of whom holds a knife in his right hand, and a short staff with one end curved and curled in his left.

2. The four Ḥenātiu gods, , each having four uraei in the place of a head; they are armed with weapons similar to those of the Ȧntiu gods.

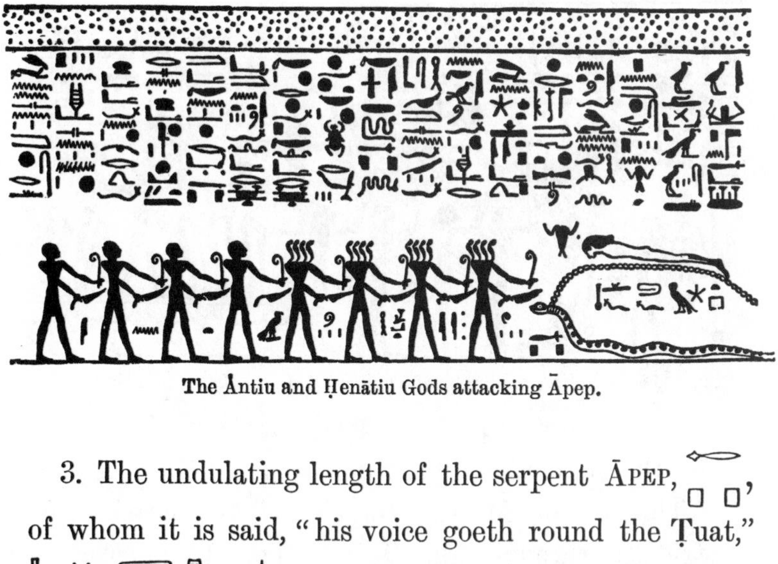

The Ȧntiu and Ḥenātiu Gods attacking Āpep.

3. The undulating length of the serpent Āpep, , of whom it is said, "his voice goeth round the Ṭuat," . Attached to the neck of the monster is a very long chain, which rises in an oval curve, and, passing along through the hands of sixteen male figures, is then grasped and held down by a large hand, from which it again rises in an oval curve, and passing on for some distance descends into the earth

immediately in front of Khenti-Åmenti. On the first curve of the chain, lying flat on her face, is the goddess Serq. Of the sixteen bearded figures who grasp the chain with both hands, four are called SEṬEFIU, , and face to the left; the twelve are described as the "TCHAṬIU gods, strong of arm," . The right hand which grasps and pulls down the chain is called "HIDDEN BODY," . Lengthwise on the second curve of the great chain lean the upper portions of the figures of five gods, each of whom grasps the chain with his right hand, and holds in his left a sceptre and the end of a chain which fetters a serpent in coils. The name of the first serpent is UAMEMTI, , but of the remaining four no names are given. The five gods appear to grow out of the great chain, and are called SEB, , MEST, , ḤĀPI, , ṬUAMUTEF, , and QEBḤSENNUF, . At the end of this section of the scene stands the bearded mummied figure of KHENTI-ÅMENTI, wearing the White Crown and the *menåt*, and holding the sceptre in his two hands.

The text which refers to these groups reads:—

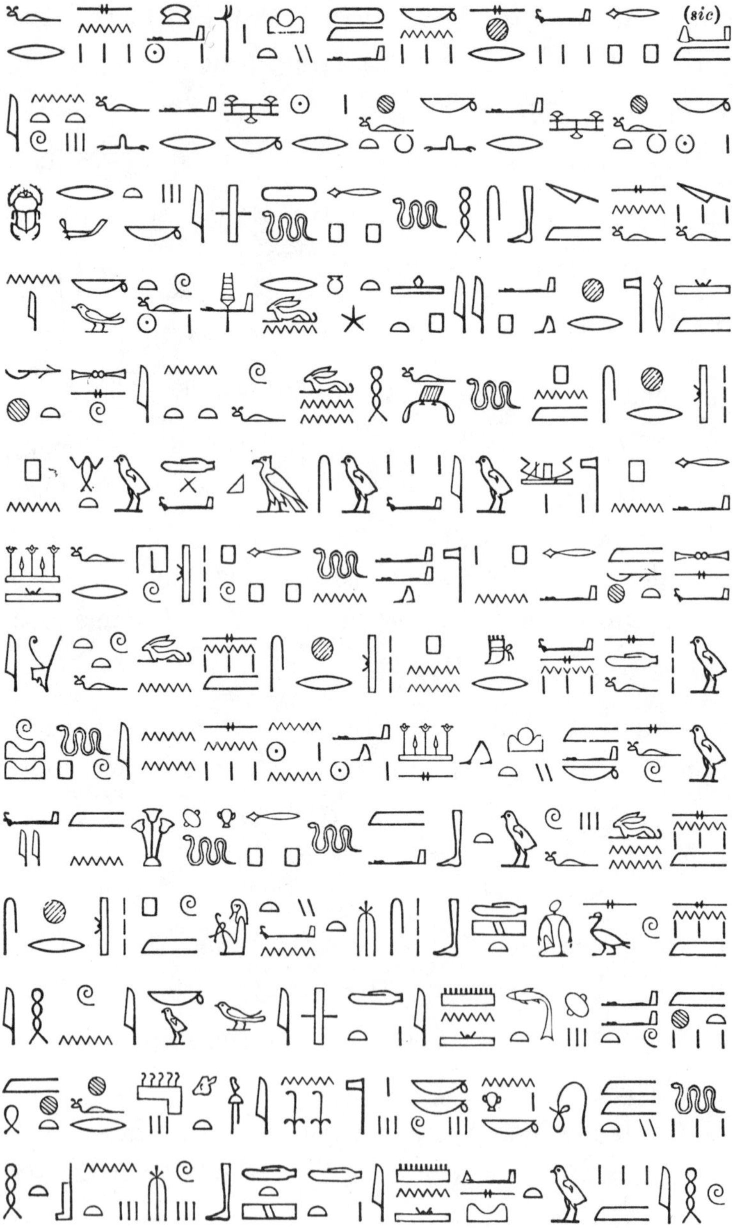
(sic)

The Seṭefiu and other gods holding Āpep in restraint.

Of the eight gods (i.e., the ÅNTIU and ḤENĀTIU) it is said:—

"Those who are in this picture rise up (or, stand) for "Rā, and Rā riseth and cometh forth for them, [and "they say], 'Rise, Rā, be strong, Khuti; verily we will "overthrow Āpep in his fetters. Approach not thou, "O Rā, towards thine enemy, and thine enemy shall "not approach thee; may thy holy attributes come "into being within the serpent. The serpent Āpep is "stabbed with his knives, and gashes are inflicted on "him. Rā shall stand up in the hour wherein he is "content (or, the hour of peace), and the great god "shall pass on in strength when his chain (i.e., Āpep's) "is fixed.'"

"The reptile (literally, worm) who is in this picture "breaketh asunder the fetters, and the boat of this "great god beginneth [to move] towards the region

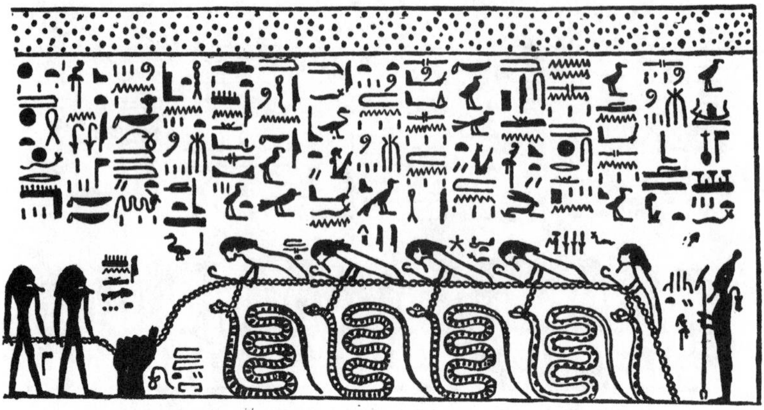

Seb and the Children of Horus holding Apep and his sons in restraint.

"of Āpep; this great god travelleth on after he (i.e., "Āpep) hath been put in restraint by means of his "fetters."

Of the four SEṬEFIU gods it is said:—

"Those who are in this picture grasp the fetters of "the being of two-fold evil, and they say to Rā, 'Come "forward, Rā, pass onwards, Khuti. Verily fetters "have been laid upon NEḤA-ḤRÀ, and Āpep is in his "bonds.'"

Of the twelve other gods who grasp the chain it is said :—

"Those who are in this picture [act] as warders of "the sons of the helpless one, and they keep guard "over the deadly chain which is in the HIDDEN HAND, "for the dead bodies are placed with the things [which "belong to them] in the circuit of the battlements of "KHENTI-ÅMENTI. And these gods say, 'Let darkness "be upon thy face, O UAMEMTI, and ye shall be "destroyed, O ye sons of the helpless one, by the "HIDDEN HAND, which shall cause evils [to come upon "you] by the deadly chain which is in it. SEB keepeth "ward over your fetters, and the sons of the fetters "(i.e., Mest, Ḥāpi, Ṭuamutef, and Qebḥsennuf) put "upon you the deadly chain. Keep ye [your] ward "under the reckoning of KHENTI-ÅMENTI.'"

Of the children of Horus it is said :—

"Those who are in this picture make heavy the "fetters of the sons of the helpless one, and the boat of "the Well-doing God travelleth on its way."

In the lower register are :—

1. Twelve male beings, each of whom carries a paddle; they are called "gods who never diminish,"

2. Twelve female beings, each of whom grasps a rope with both hands; above the head of each is a star. They are called the "hours who tow along [the boat of Rā],"

3. The god BĀNTI, , with the head of a cynocephalus ape, holding a sceptre, .

4. The god SESHSHȦ, , man-headed, with a star above him, holding a sceptre, .

5. The god KA-ȦMENTI, , bull-headed, and holding a sceptre, .

The Twelve Ȧkhemu-Seku Gods with their Paddles.

6. The god RENEN-SBAU, , man-headed, with a star above him, holding a sceptre, .

7. A monkey, with a star over his head, standing on a bracket, ; he is called the "god of Rethenu" (Syria), .

8. A bracket, whereon rests the Utchat, .

9. A god called ḤER-NEST-F, 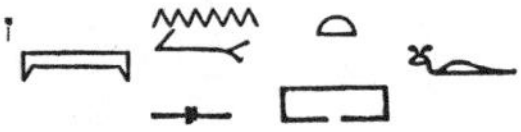, holding a sceptre.

The text which refers to the above reads:—

Of the twelve gods (the ÅKHEMU SEKU) it is said:—

"Those who are in this picture make a rising up for "Rā, and they take their paddles in this Circle of "UNTI. They come into being of their own accord at "the seasons when Rā is born in Nut; they come into "being for the births of Rā, and they make their "appearance in Nu along with him. It is they who "transport this great god after he hath taken his place "in the horizon of the East of heaven. Rā saith unto "them:—'Take ye your paddles and unite ye your-"selves to your stars. Your coming into being taketh "place when [I] come into being, and your births take "place when my births take place. O ye beings who "transport me, ye shall not suffer diminution, O ye "gods ÅKHEMU SEKU.'"

Of the twelve goddesses of the hours it is said:—

"Those who are in this scene take hold of the rope "of the boat of Rā to tow him along into the sky. It "is they who tow Rā along, and guide him along the "roads into the sky, and behold, they are the goddesses "who draw along the great god in the Ṭuat. Rā saith "unto them:—'Take ye the rope, set ye yourselves in "position, and pull ye me, O my followers, into the "height of heaven, and lead ye me along the ways. "My births make you to be born, and behold, my "coming into being maketh you to come into being. "O stablish ye the periods of time and years for him "who is among you.'"

1. "The god who is in this picture adjureth the

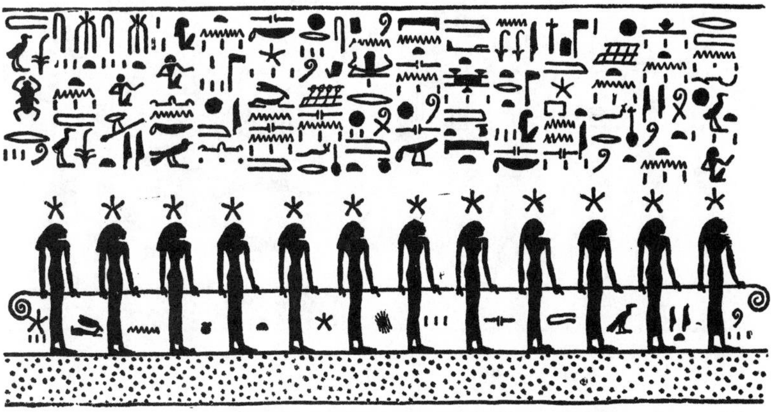

The Twelve Goddesses of the Hours.

"pylons to open to Rā, and he goeth on his way by his "side."

2. "The god who is in this picture crieth out to the "stars concerning the births of this great god, and he "goeth on his way with them."

3. "The god who is in this picture crieth to the gods "of the Boat of Rā, and he goeth on his way with "him."

4. "The god who is in this picture setteth the stars

"in their places (literally, towns), and he goeth on his "way with the great god."

The above four paragraphs must refer to the four gods Bānti, Seshshȧ, Ka-Ȧment, and Renen-sbau, and therefore the god of Rethenu, the Utchat, and the god Ḥer-nest-f remain without descriptions. From the tomb of Rameses VI. M. Lefébure adds the two

Bānti. Seshshȧ. Ka-Ȧmenti. Renen-sbau. Neter-Rethen. Eye of Rā. Ḥer-nest-f.

following paragraphs which concern the Utchat and Ḥer-nest-f, 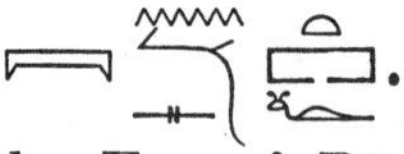.

"This is the Eye of Rā, which the god uniteth to "himself, and it rejoiceth in its place in the boat."

"This is he who openeth the door of this Circle; he "remaineth in his position, and doth not go on his way "with Rā."

CHAPTER XIII.

THE GATE OF ȦM-NETU-F.

THE ELEVENTH DIVISION OF THE ṬUAT.

HAVING passed through the Tenth Division of the Ṭuat, the boat of the sun arrives at the gateway SHETAT-BESU, , which leads to the Eleventh Division, or, as the opening text reads:  , "This "[great] god cometh forth to this gate, this great god "entereth through it, and the gods who are therein "acclaim the great god." The gateway is like that through which the god passed into the previous Division; at the entrance to the gate proper stands a bearded, mummied form called METES, 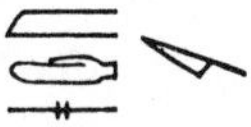, and at its exit stands a similar form called SHEṬĀU, . The corridor is swept by flames of fire, which proceed from the mouths of two uraei, as before. In the space which is usually guarded by a number of gods stand two sceptres, , each of which is surmounted by a White Crown; the one on the right is the symbol of OSIRIS,  (SAR), and the other of HORUS, . Between the sceptres is a line of text, which reads:—"They say to Rā, '[Come] in peace! "[Come] in peace! [Come] in peace! [Come] in peace! "O thou whose transformations are manifold, thy soul "is in heaven, thy body is in the earth. It is thine "own command, O great one," 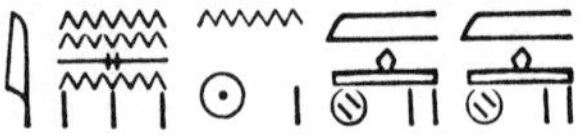

The monster serpent which stands on his tail and guards the door is called ÅM-NETU-F, 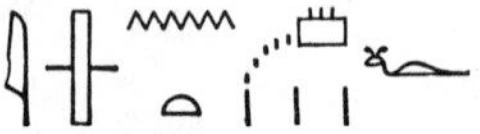, and the two lines of text which refer to his admission of Rā read:—"He who is over this door openeth to Rā. "SAU saith to ÅM-NETU-F, 'Open thy gate to Rā, unfold "thy portal to KHUTI, so that he may illumine the "thick darkness, and may send light into the hidden "abode.' This gate closeth after the great god hath "passed through it, and the gods who are on the battle-"ments wail when they hear it closing upon them,"

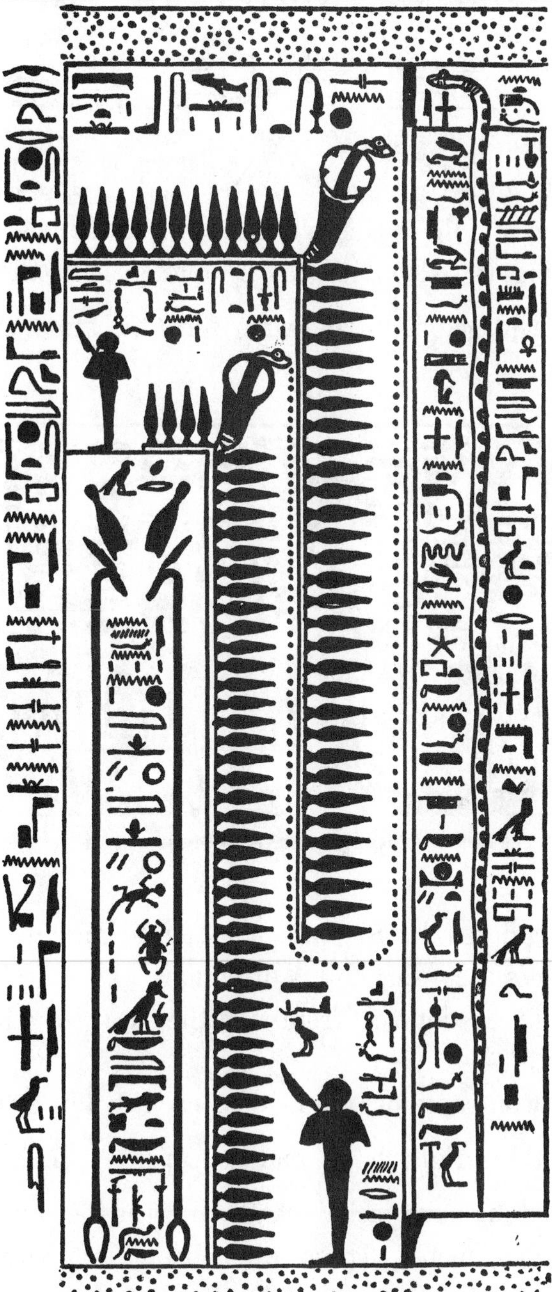

The Gate of the Serpent Àm-netu-f.

In the middle of this Division we see the boat of the sun being towed on its way by four gods of the Ṭuat, 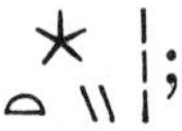; the god is in the same form as before, and his

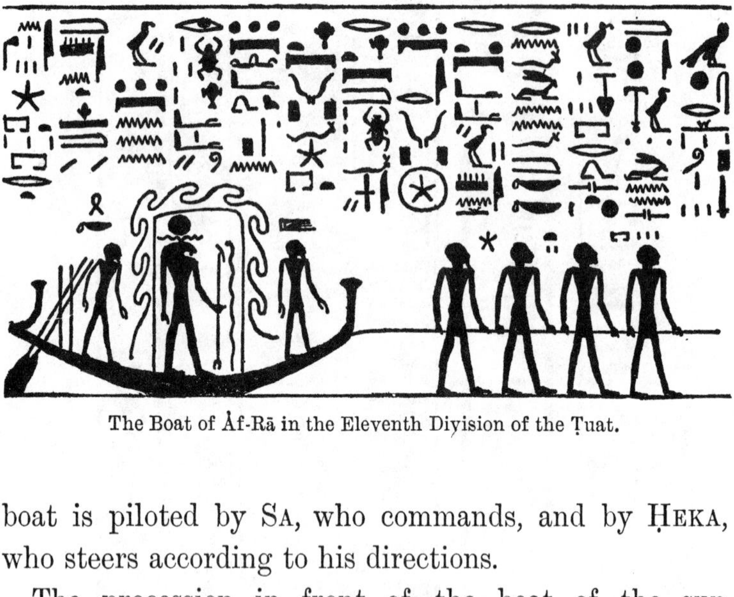

The Boat of Åf-Rā in the Eleventh Division of the Ṭuat.

boat is piloted by SA, who commands, and by ḤEKA, who steers according to his directions.

The procession in front of the boat of the sun consists of:—

1. A company of nine gods, each holding a huge knife in his right hand, and a sceptre, , in his left; the first four have jackal heads, and the last five heads of bearded men. These nine beings represent the

"company of the gods who slay ĀPEP,"

2. The serpent ĀPEP, fettered by five chains which enter the ground; the fetters are further strengthened by small chains, which are linked to the larger ones, and are fastened to the ground by means of pegs with a hook at the top. In an earlier picture we have

The Slaughterers of Āpep.

seen ĀPEP fettered by Seb, Mest, Ḥāpi, Ṭuamutef, and Qebḥsennuf, who were represented by five gods, but here the figures of the gods are wanting, and it is only the legend "Children of Horus," , that tells us the chains represent the gods.

3. Four Apes, , each holding up a huge hand and wrist.

4. The goddess of Upper Egypt, wearing the White Crown, and styled ÅMENTI, .

5. The goddess of Lower Egypt, wearing the Red Crown, and called ḤERIT, .

6. The bearded god SEBEKHTI, 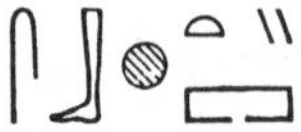, who holds the emblem of "life" in his right hand, and a sceptre in his left.

The text which refers to the above gods reads:—

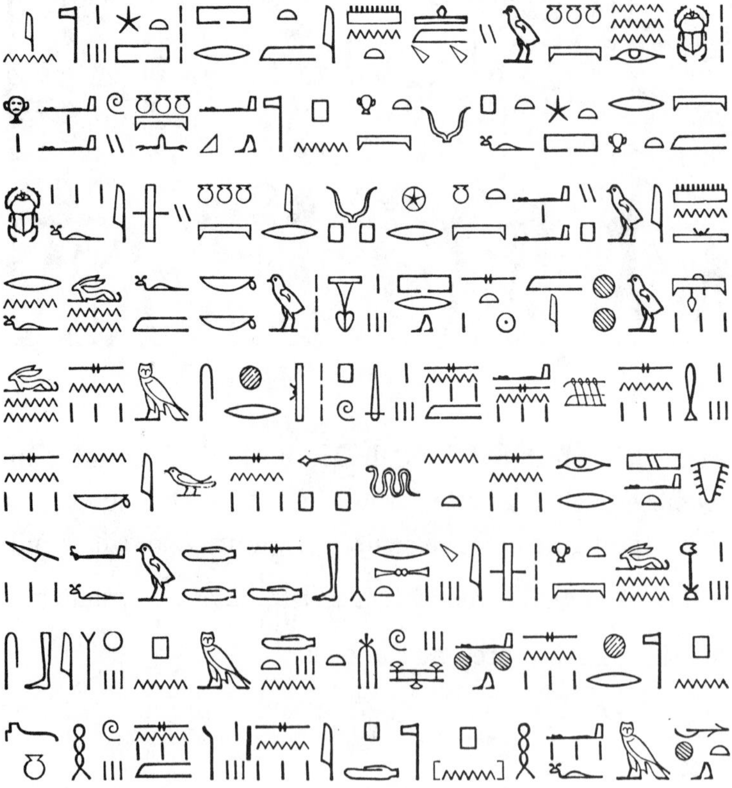

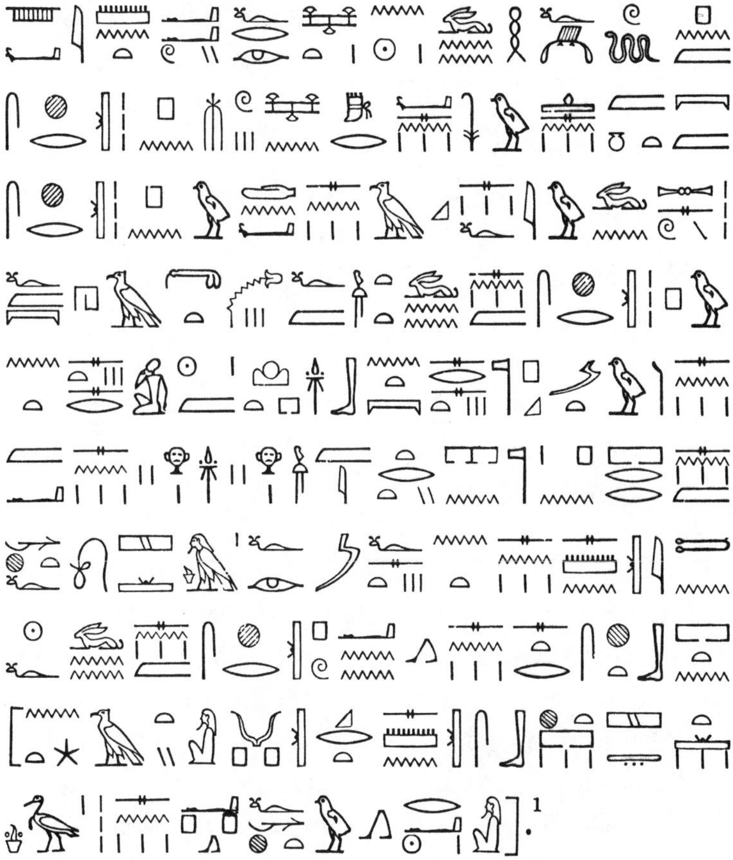[1]

Of the gods of the Ṭuat who tow the boat of Rā it is said:—

"The gods of the Ṭuat say, 'Behold the coming "forth [of Rā] from Åment, and [his] taking up [his] "place in the two divisions of Nu, and [his] perform-"ance of [his] transformations on the two hands of Nu. "This god doth not enter into the height of heaven,

[1] Supplied from Champollion, *Monuments*, tom. ii., p. 537.

"[but] he openeth [a way through] the Ṭuat into the "height of heaven by his transformations which are in "Nu. Now, what openeth the Ṭuat into Nut (i.e., the "sky) are the two hands of ÅMEN-REN-F (i.e., he whose "name is hidden). He existeth in the thick darkness, "and light appeareth [there] from the starry night.'"

Of the nine gods with knives and sceptres it is said:—

"Those who are in this scene [with] their weapons "in their hand take their knives and hack [with them] "at Āpep; they make gashes in him and slaughter "him, and they drive stakes whereby to fetter him in "the regions which are in the upper height. The "fetters of the REBEL are in the hands of the Children "of Horus, who stand threateningly by this god "with their chains between their fingers. This god "reckoneth up his members after he whose arms are "hidden hath opened [the door] to make a way for Rā."

Of the serpent Āpep it is said:—

"The Children of Horus grasp firmly this serpent "which is in this picture, and in this picture they rest "in Nut (i.e., the sky). They heap their fetters upon "him, and whilst his folds (?) are in the sky his poison "drops down from him into Åmentet."

Of the four apes holding hands it is said:—

"It is those who are in this picture who make ready "for Rā a way into the eastern horizon of heaven, and "they lead the way for the god who hath created them "with their hands, [standing] two on the right hand

"and two on the left in the double *ātert* of this god; "then they come forth after him, and sing praises to "his soul when it looketh upon them, and they stablish "his Disk."

Of the three remaining deities it is said:—

"Those who are in this picture turn away SET from "this Gate [of the god ṬUATI. They open its cavern,

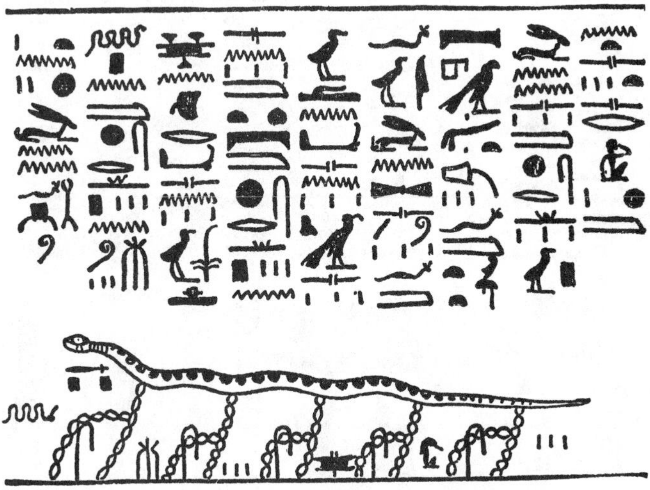

Āpep fettered by the chains of Seb and the Children of Horus.

"and stablish the hidden pylons, and their souls remain "in the following of Rā]."

In the upper register of this Division are:—

1. Four gods, each holding a disk in his right hand; these are "they who hold light-giving disks," 

.

2. Four gods, each holding a star in his right hand; these are "they who hold stars," .

3. Four gods, each holding a sceptre, , in his left hand; these are "they who come forth," .

4. Four ram-headed gods, each holding a sceptre in

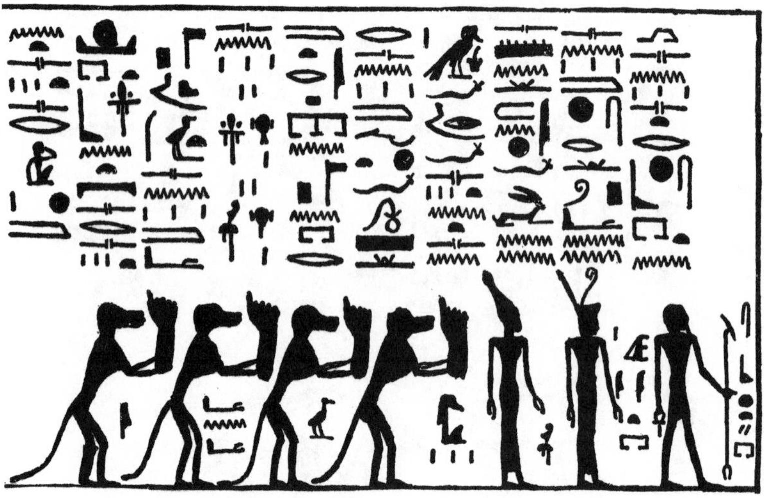

The Apes who praise Rā. Ȧmenti. Ḥerit. Sebekhti.

his left hand; their names are BA, , KHNEMU, , PENṬER, , and ṬENṬ, .

5. Four hawk-headed gods, each holding a sceptre in his left hand; these are called HORUS, , ĀSHEMTH, , SEPṬ, , and ȦMMI-UȦA-F, .

6. Eight female figures, each seated on a seat formed by a uraeus with its body coiled up, and holding a star in her left hand; these are called "the protecting hours," .

7. A crocodile-headed god called SEBEK-RĀ, who grasps a fold of a serpent that stands on its tail in his right hand, and a sceptre in his left.

The text which refers to these reads:—

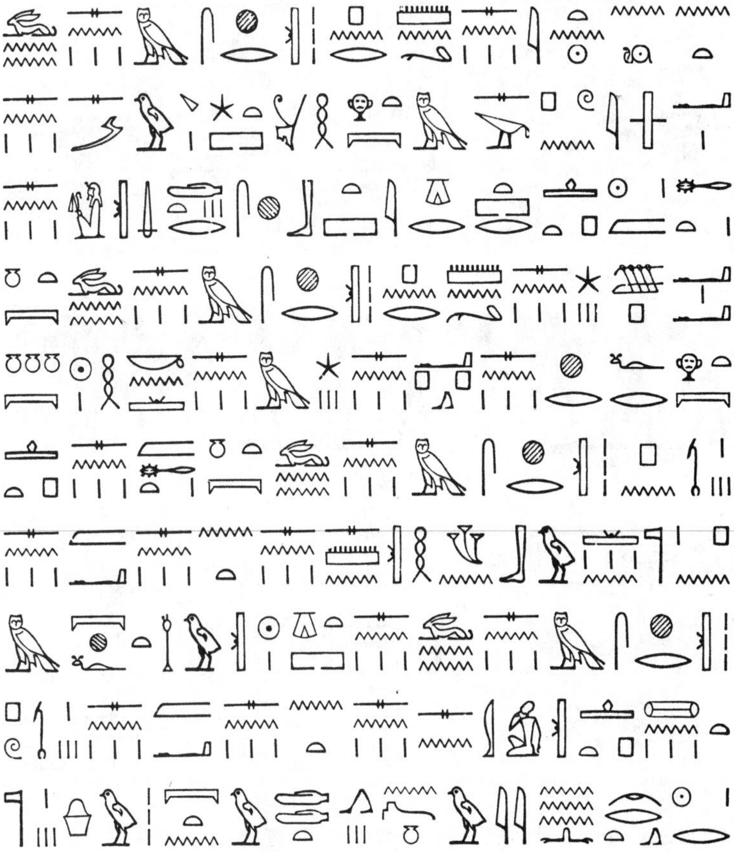

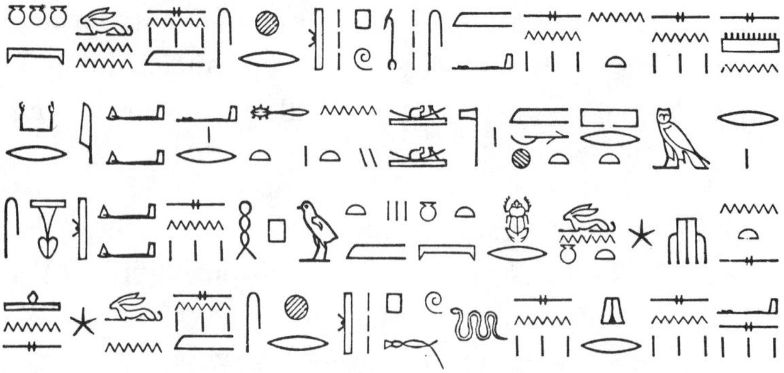

The gods who bring Disks and Stars for Rā.

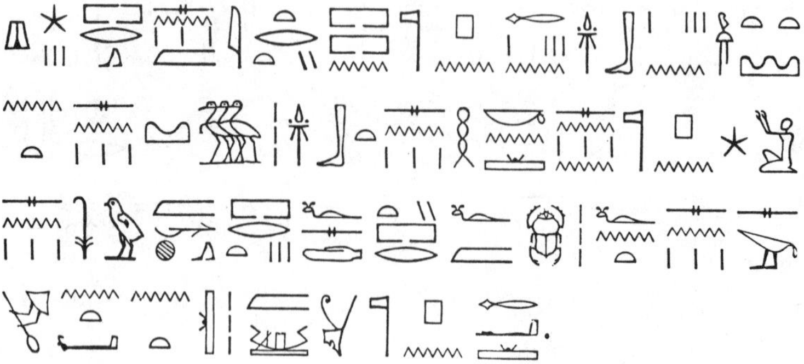

Of the four gods bearing disks it is said:—

"Those who are in this picture carry the disk of Rā, "and it is they who make a way through the Ṭuat and "the height of heaven by means of this image which is "in their hands. They utter words to the Pylon of "Åkert so that Rā may set himself in the body of Nut "(i.e., the sky)."

Of the four gods bearing stars it is said:—

The gods who prepare the Offerings and Shrine of Rā.

"Those who are in this picture carry stars, and "when the two arms of Nu embrace Rā they and their "stars shout hymns of praise, and they journey on "with him to the height of heaven, and they take up "their places in the body of Nut."

Of the four gods bearing sceptres it is said:—

"Those who are in this picture [having] their "sceptres in their hands, are they who stablish the "domains of this god in the sky, and they have "their thrones in accordance with the command of "Rā."

Of the four ram-headed gods it is said:—

"Those who are in this picture [having] their "sceptres in their hands, are they who decree [the "making ready] of the offerings of the gods [from] the "bread of heaven, and it is they who make to come "forth celestial water when as yet Rā hath not emerged "in Nu."

Of the four hawk-headed gods it is said:—

"Those who are in this picture [having] their "sceptres in their hands, are they who stablish the "shrine [in the boat of Rā], and they lay their hands "on the body of the double boat of the god after it "hath appeared from out of the gate of Sma, and they "place the paddles [of the boat] in Nut, when the "Hour which presideth over it (i.e., the boat) cometh "into being, and the Hour [which hath guided it] goeth "to rest."

Of the goddesses who are seated on uraei it is said:—

"Those who are in this picture with their serpents "under them, and their hands holding stars, come "forth from the two ÅTERT of this great god, four to "the East and four to the West; it is they who call "the Spirits of the East, and they sing hymns to this "god, and they praise him after his appearance, and "SEṬTI cometh forth in his forms. It is they who "guide and transport those who are in the boat of this "great god."

There is no description of the crocodile-headed god Sebek-Rā in the text.

In the lower register are:—

1. Four gods, each wearing the Crown of the South; these are the "Kings of the South in chief," .

The goddesses of the Återti.

2. Four bearded gods, "the WEEPERS," .

3. Four gods, each wearing a Crown of the North; these are the KHNEMIU, .

4. Four bearded gods, the RENENIU, , i.e., "those who give names."

5. Four females, each wearing the Crown of the South; these are the "Queens of the South," 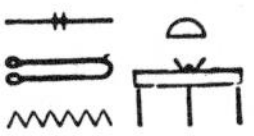.

6. Four females, each wearing the Crown of the North; these are, presumably, the "Queens of the North;" these are the KHNEMUT, 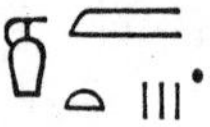.

7. Four females, without crowns.

8. Four bearded gods, with their backs slightly bowed; these are the gods who praise Rā.

9. A cat-headed god called MÀTI, .

The text which refers to these gods reads:—

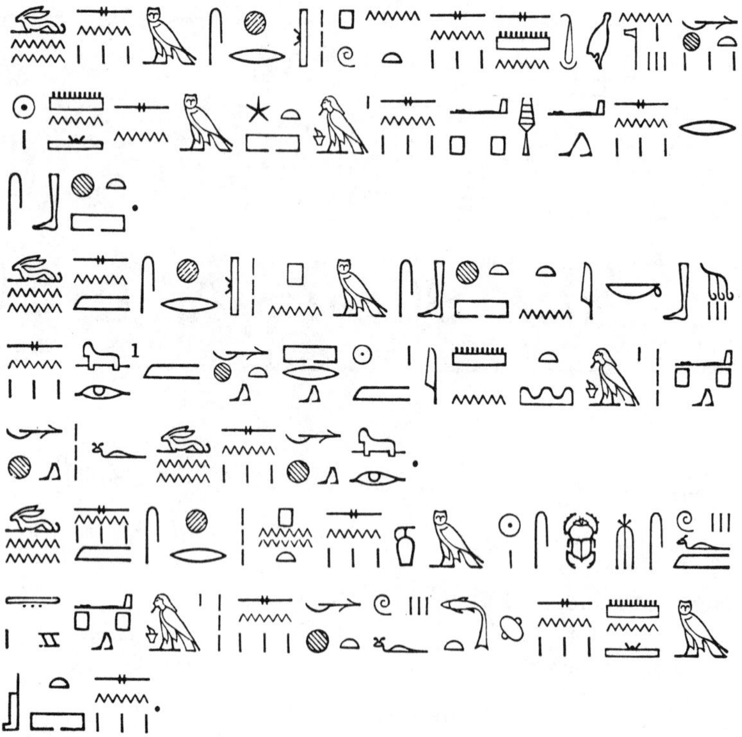

[1] Var., , SAR, Champollion, *Monuments*, tom. ii., p. 539.

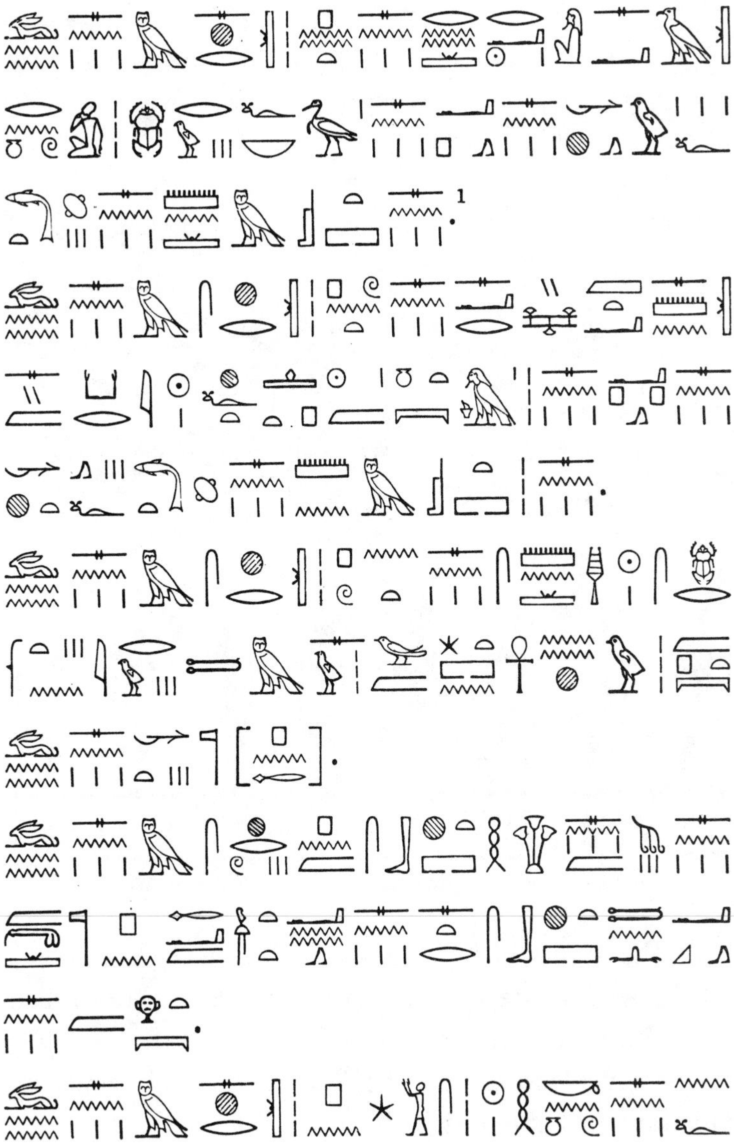

[1] Champollion, *Monuments*, tom. ii., p. 539.

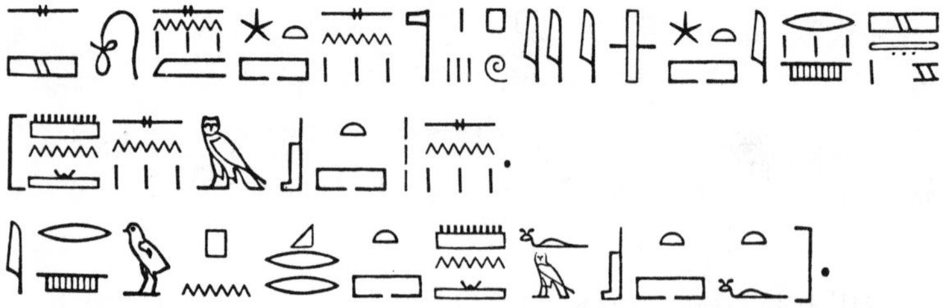

The Stablishers of the White Crown. The Four Weepers.

Of the gods wearing the White Crown it is said:—

"Those who are in this picture are they who stablish "the White Crown on the gods who follow Rā; they "themselves remain in the Ṭuat, but their souls go "forward and stand at [this] gate."

Of the four Weepers it is said:—

"Those who are in this picture in this gate make

"lamentation for Osiris after Rā hath made his appear-"ance from Ȧment; their souls go forward in his train, "but they themselves follow after Osiris."

Of the four gods wearing the Red Crown it is said:—

"Those who are in this picture are those who unite "themselves to Rā, and they make his births to come

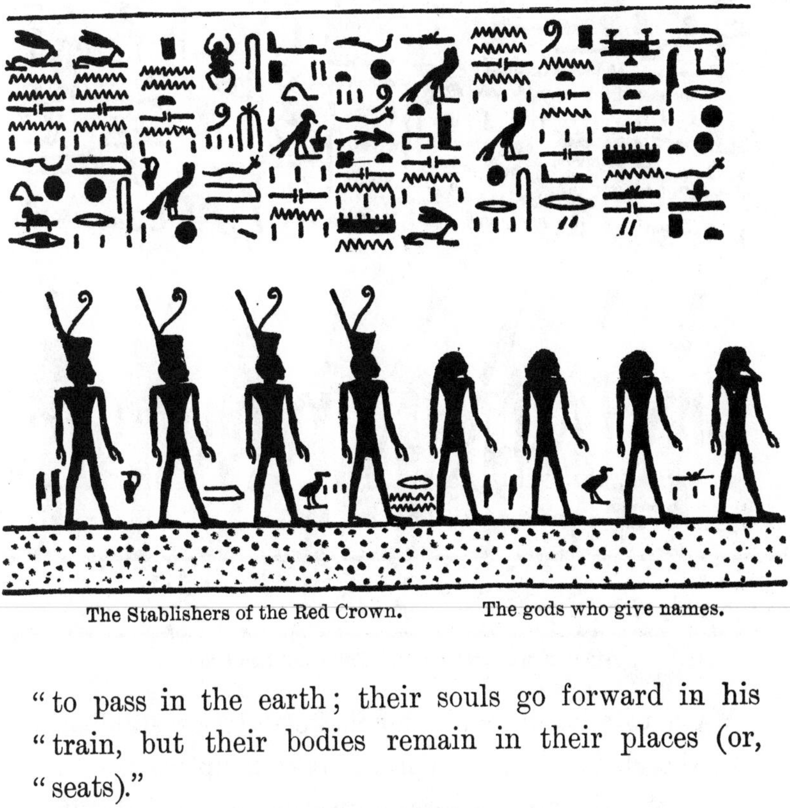

The Stablishers of the Red Crown. The gods who give names.

"to pass in the earth; their souls go forward in his "train, but their bodies remain in their places (or, "seats)."

Of the four Reneniu it is said:—

"[Those who are in this picture are they who give "the name to Rā, and they magnify the names of all "his forms; their souls go forward in his following, "but their bodies remain in their places (or, seats)."][1]

Of the four goddesses wearing the White Crown it is said:—

"Those who are in this picture are they who make

Goddesses who stablish the White and Red Crowns.

"MAĀT to advance, and who make it to be stablished "in the shrine of Rā when Rā taketh up his position "in Nut; their souls pass onwards in his following, "but their bodies remain in their places."

[1] Supplied from the tomb of Rameses VI.

Of the four goddesses wearing the Red Crown it is said:—

"Those who are in this picture are they who stablish "time, and they make to come into being the years for "those who keep ward over the condemned ones in the "Ṭuat and over those who have their life in heaven; "they follow in the train of this great god."

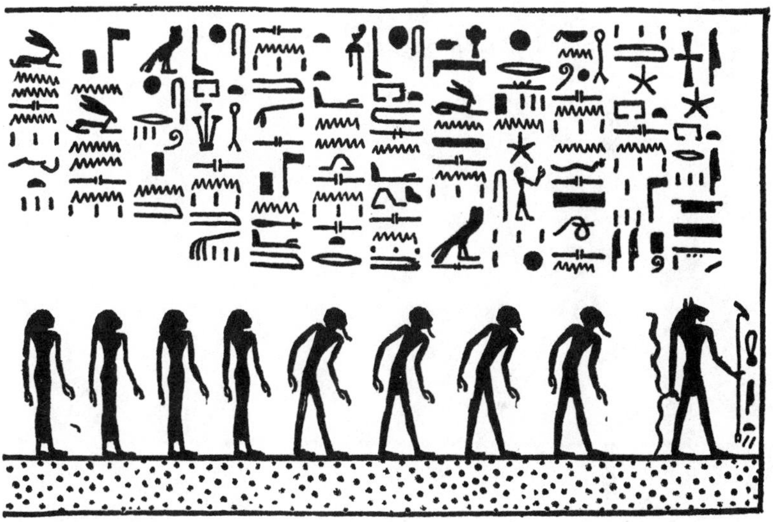

Goddesses who drive away Set. Gods who adore and praise Rā. Māti.

Of the four females who are without crowns it is said:—

"Those who are in this picture in [this] gate make "lamentation and tear their hair in the presence of "this great god in Åmentet; they make SET to with-"draw from this pylon, and they do not enter into the "height of heaven."

Of the four gods with their backs bowed it is said:—

"Those who are in this picture make adoration to "Rā and sing praises unto him, and in their place in "the Ṭuat they hymn those gods who are in the Ṭuat, "and who keep guard over the Hidden Door. [They "remain in their places."] [1]

["The warder of the door of this Circle remaineth "in his place."] [1]

[1] Supplied from the tomb of Rameses VI.

CHAPTER XIV.

THE GATE OF SEBI AND RERI.

THE TWELFTH DIVISION OF THE ṬUAT.

HAVING passed through the Eleventh Division of the Ṭuat, the boat of the sun arrives at the gateway ṬESERT-BAIU, , which is the last that he will have to pass through before emerging in heaven in the light of a new day. "This great god cometh "forth to this gate, this great god entereth through it, "and the gods who are therein acclaim the great god." The gateway is like that through which the god passed into the previous Division; at the entrance to the gate proper stands a bearded mummied form called PAI, , and at its exit stands a similar form called ÅKHEKHI, 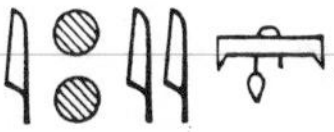. The corridor is swept by flames of fire, which proceed from the mouths of uraei, as before. In the space which is usually guarded by a number of gods stand two staves, each of which is surmounted by a bearded head; on one head is the disk of TEM, , and on the other a beetle, the symbol of Kheperå. The text which refers to these reads:

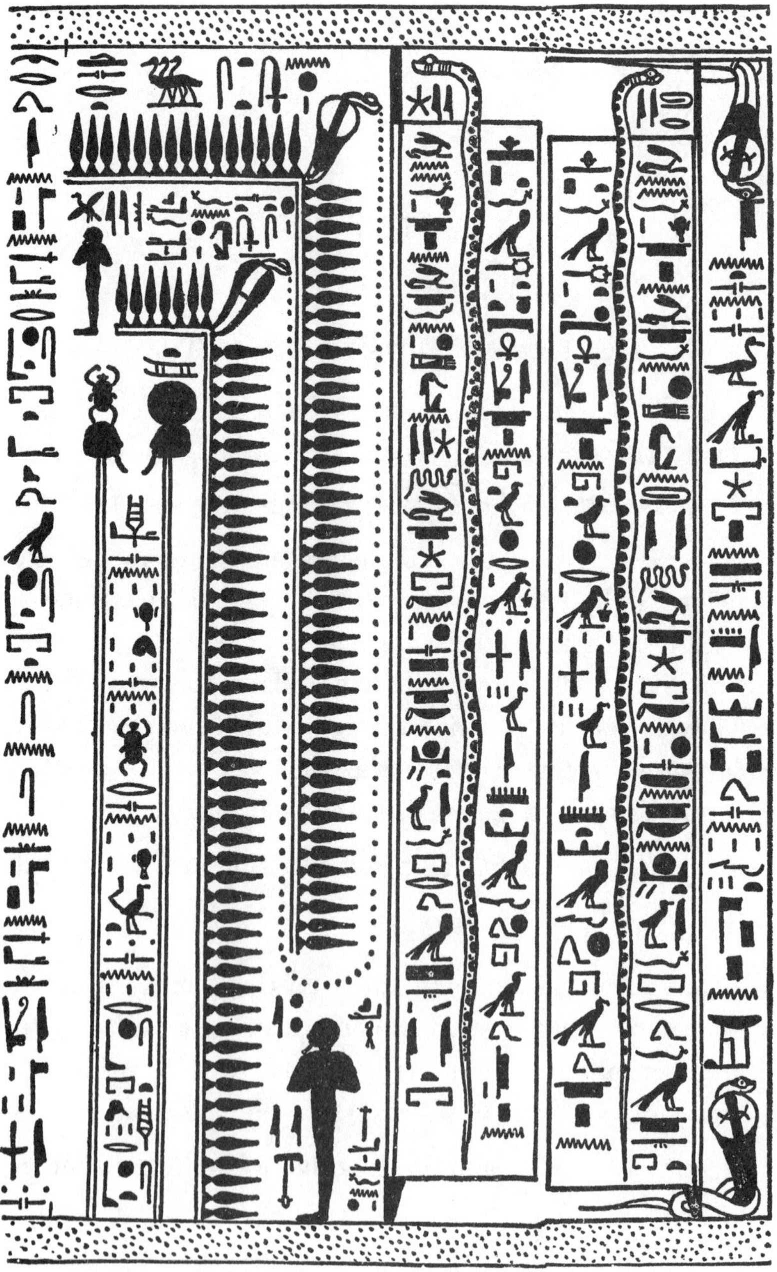

The Gate Ṭesert-Baiu. The doors of Sebi and Reri.

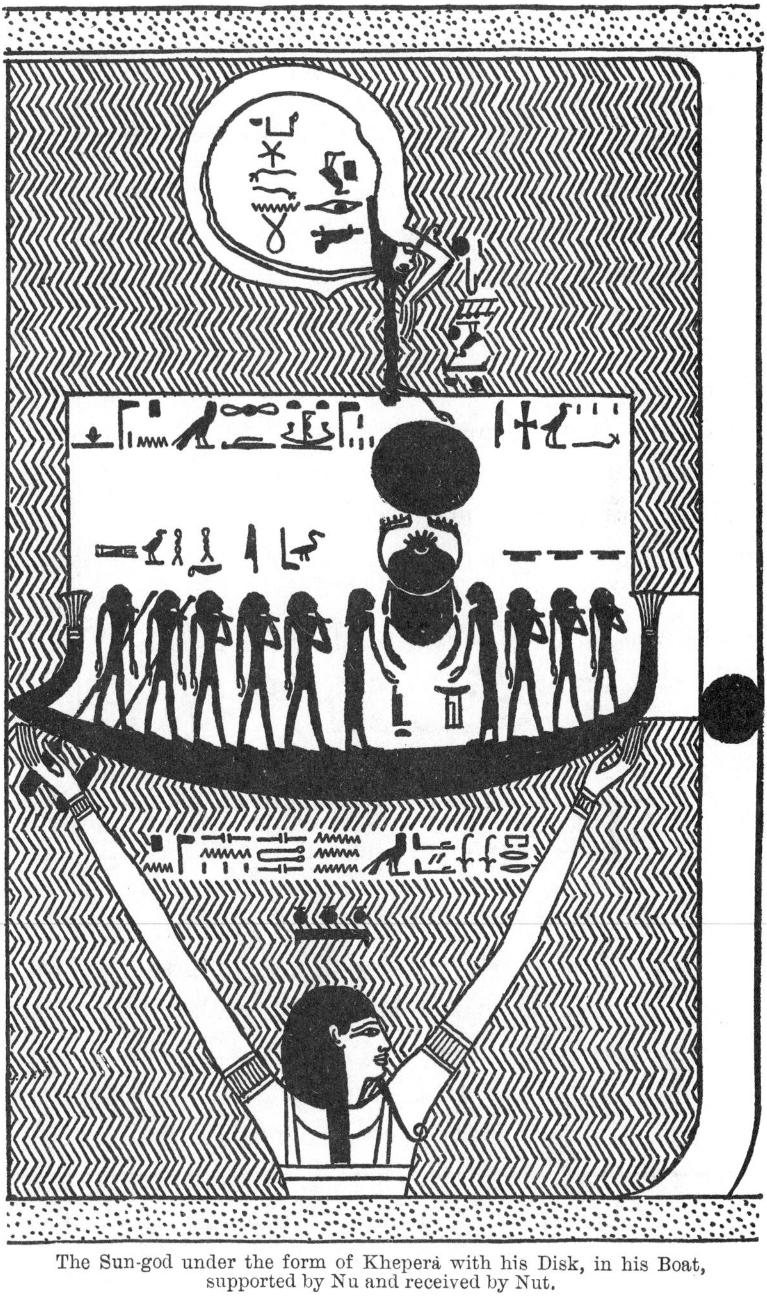

The Sun-god under the form of Kheperȧ with his Disk, in his Boat, supported by Nu and received by Nut.

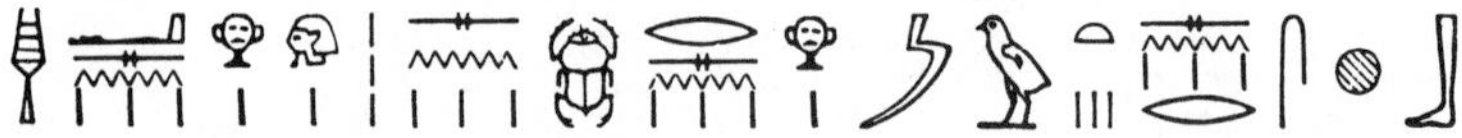

, "They stand up on their heads, "and they come into being on their staves by the "gate; the heads stand up by the gate."

The monster serpent which stands on its tail and guards the one door is called SEBI, , and the two lines of text which refer to his admission of Rā read, "He who is over this door openeth to Rā. SA saith "unto Sebi, 'Open thy gate to Rā, unfold thy portal to "Khuti, so that he may come forth from the hidden "place, and may take up his position in the body of "NUT.' Behold, there is wailing among the souls "who dwell in Åment after this door hath closed,"

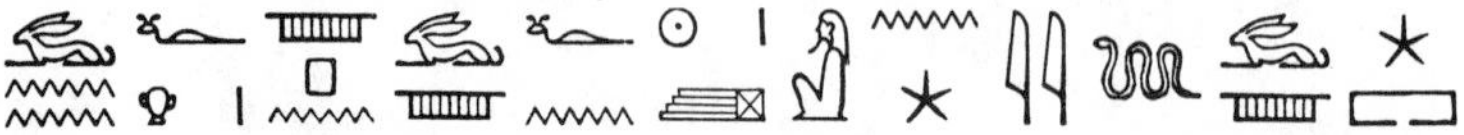

, &c.

The monster serpent which stands on its tail and guards the other door is called RERI, , and the two lines of text which refer to his admission of Rā read, "He who is over this door openeth to Rā. SA "saith unto RERI, 'Open thy gate to Rā, unfold thy "portal to KHUTI, so that he may come forth from the "hidden place, and may take up his position in the "body of Nut.' Behold, there is wailing among the "souls who dwell in Åment after this door hath closed."

The text, being similar to that which refers to SEBI, is not repeated here.

On each side of the door is a uraeus, the one representing ISIS and the other NEPHTHYS, and of them it is said, "They it is who guard this hidden gate of Ȧment, "and they pass onwards in the following of this god,"

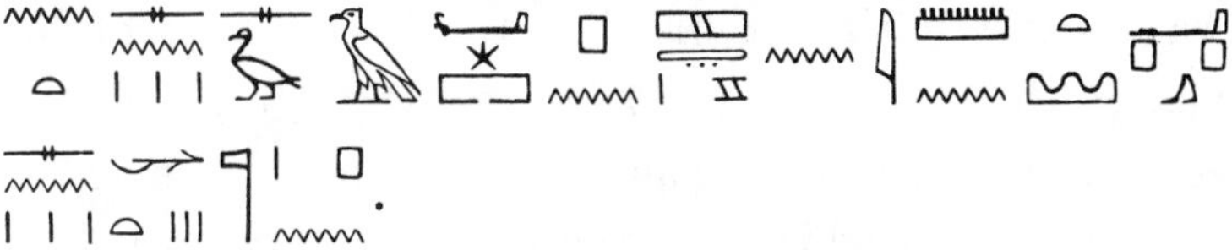

Here we see that the end of the Ṭuat is reached, and the boat of the sun has reached that portion of it through which he is about to emerge in the waters of Nu, and thence in the form of a disk in the sky of this world. Having passed on to the water the boat is supported by the two arms of NU himself, or, as the text says, "These two arms come forth from the "waters, and they bear up this god,"  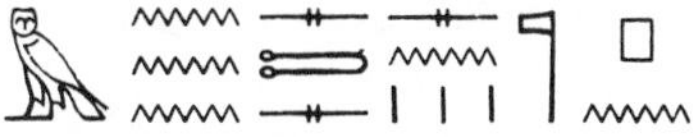. The god appears in the boat in the form of a beetle, which is rolling along a disk; on the left of the beetle is Isis, and on the right Nephthys. The three beings in the front of the boat are probably the personifications of doors, , and the gods to the left are SEB, , SHU, , ḤEK, , ḤU, , and SA, . In the hieroglyphics at the top of the open space above the boat is

written, "This god taketh up his place in the MĀṬETET "Boat [with] the gods who are in it," 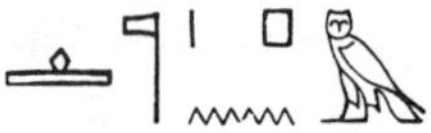
. Away in the waters above, or beyond the boat, is a kind of island, formed by the body of a god, which is bent round in such a way that the tips of his toes touch the back of his head. On his head stands the goddess Nut, with her arms and hands raised and stretched out to receive the disk of the sun, which the Beetle is rolling towards her; the text says, "Nut receiveth Rā," . The island formed by the body of the god is said to be "Osiris, whose circuit is the Ṭuat," 
.

END OF VOL. II.

The Egyptian Heaven and Hell

The Egyptian Heaven and Hell

VOLUME III

THE CONTENTS OF THE BOOKS OF THE OTHER WORLD DESCRIBED AND COMPARED

Scene from the Papyrus of Nekht, showing the deceased and his wife worshipping Osiris in the Other World, and the manner of the house in which they expected to live, and their vineyard and garden with its lake of water. (British Museum, No. 10,471, sheet 21.)

PREFACE

THE present work is the outcome of two lectures on the Books of the Ṭuat, i.e., the Egyptian Underworld, or "Other World," which I had the honour to deliver at the Royal Institution in the spring of 1904, and it has been prepared at the suggestion of many who wished to continue their inquiries into the beliefs of the Egyptians concerning the abode of the departed, and the state of the blessed and the damned.

The object of all the Books of the Other World was to provide the dead with a "Guide" or "Handbook," which contained a description of the regions through which their souls would have to pass on their way to the kingdom of Osiris, or to that portion of the sky where the sun rose, and which would supply them with the words of power and magical names necessary for making an unimpeded journey from this world to the abode of the blessed. For a period of two thousand years in the history of Egypt, the Books of the Other World consisted of texts only, but about B.C. 2500 funeral artists began to represent pictorially the chief features of the "Field of Peace," or "Islands of the Blessed," and before the close of the XIXth Dynasty, about 1300 years later, all the principal books relating to the Ṭuat were profusely illustrated. In the copies of them which were painted on the walls of royal tombs, each division of the Ṭuat was clearly drawn and described, and each gate, with all its guardians, was carefully depicted. Both the living and the dead could learn from them, not only the names, but also the forms, of every god, spirit, soul, shade, demon, and monster which they were likely to meet on their way, and the copious texts which were given side by side with the pictures enabled the traveller through the Ṭuat—always, of course, provided that he had learned them—to participate in the benefits which were decreed by the Sun-god for the beings of each section of it.

In primitive times each great city of Egypt possessed its own Other World, and, no doubt, the priests of each city provided the worshippers of their gods with suitable "guides" to the abode of its dead. In the beginning of the Dynastic Period, however, we find that the cult of Osiris was extremely popular, and therefore it was only natural that great numbers of people in all parts of Egypt should hope and believe that their souls after death would go to the kingdom in the Other World over which he reigned. The beliefs connected with the cult of Osiris developed naturally out of the beliefs of the Predynastic Egyptians, who, we have every reason to think, dealt largely in magic both "Black" and "White." Many of the superstitions, and most of the fantastic and half-savage ideas about the gods and supernatural powers enshrined in the great collection of religious texts called PER-EM-HRU, were inherited by the Dynastic Egyptians from some of the oldest dwellers in the Nile Valley. Those who died in the faith of Osiris believed in the efficacy of the Book PER-EM-HRU, and were content to employ it as a "Guide" to a heaven which was full of material delights; the number of those who were "followers" of Osiris was very large under every dynasty in Egypt. On the other hand, from the IVth Dynasty onwards there was a very large class who had no belief in a purely material heaven, and this being so, it is not surprising that Books of the Other World containing the expression of their views should be composed.

The principal Books of the Underworld in vogue under the XVIIIth and XIXth Dynasties were:—1. PER-EM-HRU, or, "[The Book] of the Coming Forth by Day." 2. SHĀT ENT ȦM ṬUAT, or, "The Book of that which is in the Ṭuat." 3. The composition to which the name "Book of Gates" has been given. Now the first of these, which is commonly known as the "Theban Recension of the Book of the Dead," has supplied us with much valuable information about the beliefs which flourished in connection with an early form of the ancient cult of Osiris in the Delta, and with the later form of his worship, after he had absorbed the position and attributes of Khenti-Ȧmenti, an old local deity of Abydos. The two other Books, however, are as important, each in its own way, as the "Book of the Dead," for they throw considerable light on the development of the material and spiritual elements in the religion of Egypt, and commemorate the belief in the existence of numbers of primitive gods, who are unknown outside these Books. The "Book Ȧm-Ṭuat," in the form in which we know it, was drawn up by the priests of the confraternity of Ȧmen-Rā at Thebes, with the express object of demonstrating that their god was the overlord of all the gods, and the supreme power in "Pet Ta Ṭuat," or, as we should say, "Heaven, Earth, and Hell." The Ṭuat, or Other World, which they imagined included the Ṭuat of every great district of Egypt, viz., the Ṭuat of Khenti-Ȧmenti at Abydos, the Ṭuat of Seker of Memphis, the Ṭuat of Osiris of Mendes, and the Ṭuat of Temu-Kheper-Rā of Heliopolis.

In the Book Ȧm-Ṭuat the god Ȧmen-Rā was made to pass through all these Ṭuats as their overlord and god, and his priests taught that all the gods of the dead, including Osiris, lived through his words, and that such refreshing as the beings of the Ṭuat enjoyed each day was due to his grace and light during his passage through their regions and Circles. Moreover, according to the dogmas of the priests of Ȧmen-Rā, only those who were fortunate enough to secure a place in the divine bark of the god could hope to traverse the Ṭuat unharmed, and only those who were his elect had the certainty of being re-born daily, with a new supply of strength and life, and of becoming of like nature and substance with him.

In the Book of Gates the dogmas and doctrines of Osiris are far more prominent, and the state of the beatified closely resembles that described in the "Book of the Dead." In primitive times in Egypt men thought that they would obtain admission into the kingdom of Ḥetep by learning and remembering the secret name of this god and certain magical formulae, and by pronouncing them in the correct way at the proper time. The need for a consciousness of sin, and repentance, and a life of good works, were not then held to be indispensable for admission into the abode of the beatified. From the "Book of Gates," however, we learn that in the later Dynastic Period a belief was prevalent that those who worshipped the "great god" on earth, and made all the duly-appointed offerings, and turned not aside to "miserable little gods," and lived according to *maāt*, i.e., uprightness and integrity, would receive a good reward *because* they had done these things. The texts in these Books state that the beatified live for ever in the kingdom of Osiris, and feed daily upon the heavenly wheat of righteousness that springs from the body of Osiris, which is eternal; he is righteousness itself, and they are righteous, and they live by eating the body of their god daily. On the other hand, the wicked, i.e., those who did not believe in the great god or make offerings, are hacked to pieces by the divine messengers of wrath, and their bodies, souls, and spirits are consumed by fire once and for all.

The Egyptians had no belief in a purgatory. The fires of the Other World were, it is true, occupied daily in burning up the damned and the opponents of the Sun-god, but each day brought its own supply of bodies, souls, spirits, demons, etc., for annihilation. In all the Books of the Other World we find pits of fire, abysses of darkness, murderous knives, streams of boiling water, foul stenches, fiery serpents, hideous animal-headed monsters and creatures, and cruel, death-dealing beings of various shapes, etc., similar to those with which we are familiar in early Christian and mediæval literature, and it is tolerably certain that modern nations are indebted to Egypt for many of their conceptions of hell.

In the present work the object has been to give the reader the complete hieroglyphic texts of the BOOK ÅM-ṬUAT and the BOOK OF GATES, with reproductions of all their illustrations in black and white, and English translations and descriptions. The illustrations of the former work have been specially traced from the plates of the excellent edition of the tomb of Seti I. published by MM. G. Lefébure, U. Bouriant, V. Loret, and E. Naville, in the second volume of the *Mémoires de la Mission Archéologique Française au Caire*, Paris, 1886. The illustrations of the BOOK OF GATES have been traced from Bonomi's *Sarcophagus of Oimenepthah I.*, London, 1864, but for certain scenes I was permitted by the late Mr. G. Birch, Keeper of Sir John Soane's Museum, to compare the tracings with the scenes on the sarcophagus itself. A copy of the scene on the portion of the cover, which I acquired for the Trustees of the British Museum a few years ago, has also been included.

The plan followed has been to devote a chapter to each Division of the Ṭuat, and to give the hieroglyphic texts, with short descriptions of the various gods, &c., and translations, as near to the scenes to which they refer as possible. With a view of making the edition as complete as possible, I have added a transcript of the "Summary" of the BOOK ÅM-ṬUAT from Dr. Pleyte's facsimile of the Leyden Papyrus, and a translation for the convenience of the reader who may wish to compare the Divisions of Åm-Ṭuat with those of the BOOK OF GATES. The former have been printed in one volume, and the latter in another; the full index given at the end of the introductory volume will, it is hoped, make reference and comparison easy. All general descriptions, and such explanations of the scenes as are possible in the present state of our knowledge, have been given in a series of chapters in this volume, together with an account of the origin and development of "guides" to the Other World, and a rendering of a recently published and very important text from a coffin at Cairo. This text proves that the

Egyptians believed in the reconstitution of family life in the Other World, and thought that every man, and woman, and child would possess such a measure of individuality that they would know their relatives and friends in the Other World, and would be known by them (see within, Chapter III.).

The first translation of the BOOK ȦM-ṬUAT was published by Prof. G. Maspero in the *Revue des Religions*, 1888, tom. xvii., pp. 251—310; tom. xviii., pp. 1—67. This has been reprinted, with certain modifications and additions, in his *Bibliothèque Égyptologique*, tom. ii., pp. 1—181, Paris, 1893. The text chosen by him for elucidation was that published by M. G. Lefébure in his edition of the tomb of Seti I., and this he supplemented with extracts from other versions of the work given on sarcophagi, papyri, etc. The "Summary," or Short Form of ȦM-ṬUAT, was first published in a complete form, with variant readings, by M. G. Jéquier (see his *Le Livre de ce qu'il y a dans l'Hades*, Paris, 1894). In Prof. Maspero's work mentioned above he also discussed and analysed the earlier sections of the BOOK OF GATES, of which M. E. Lefébure published a translation of the texts, as found on the sarcophagus of Seti I., in the *Records of the Past*, vol. x., pp. 79—134, London, 1878, and vol. xii., pp. 1—35, London, 1881. In preparing the present edition of the two great Books of the Other World I have availed myself of these works, and also of the valuable editions of the texts from the royal tombs at Thebes, which M. E. Lefébure has published in the first and second fasciculi of the third volume of the *Mémoires de la Mission Archéologique Française au Caire*, Paris, 1889.

E. A. Wallis Budge.

London,
October, 1905.

CONTENTS

LIST OF ILLUSTRATIONS.

THE

EGYPTIAN HEAVEN AND HELL

CHAPTER I.

ORIGIN OF ILLUSTRATED GUIDES TO THE OTHER WORLD.

THE inhabitants of Egypt during the Dynastic Period of their history possessed, in common with other peoples of similar antiquity, very definite ideas about the abode of departed spirits, but few, if any, ancient nations caused their beliefs about the situation and form, and divisions, and inhabitants of their Heaven and Hell, or "Other World," to be described so fully in writing, and none have illustrated the written descriptions of their beliefs so copiously with pictorial representations of the gods and devils, and the good and evil spirits and other beings, who were supposed to exist in the kingdom of the dead. It is now generally admitted that Egyptian Dynastic History covers a period of nearly five thousand years, but it must not be assumed for one moment that it is at present possible to describe in a connected or complete form all the views and opinions about their Other World which were held by the theologians and the uneducated classes of Egypt during this long space of time, and it must be said at once that the materials for such a work are not forthcoming. All that can be done is to collect from the copies that have come down to us of the books which relate to the state and condition of the dead, and to the abode of departed spirits, the beliefs which are enunciated or referred to therein, and, taking them so far as possible in chronological order, to piece them together and then make deductions and draw general conclusions from them. We must always remember that the texts of the various Books of the Dead are far older than the illustrations found in the later recensions of them which are now in our hands, and that such illustrations, in matters of detail at least, reflect the opinions of the priestly class that held religious supremacy at the time when they were drawn or painted. In cases where archetypes were available the artist was careful to follow in all general matters the ancient copies to which he had access, but when new beliefs and new religious conceptions had to be illustrated, he was free to treat them pictorially according to his own knowledge, and according to the wishes of those who employed him.

The oldest Books of the Dead known to us, that is to say, the religious compositions which are inscribed on the walls of the chambers and corridors of the pyramids of kings Unȧs, Tetȧ, Pepi I., Mer-en-Rā, and Pepi II., are without illustrations of any sort or kind, and it is not easy to account for this fact. That the Egyptians possessed artistic skill sufficient to illustrate the religious and general works which their theologians wrote or revised, under their earliest dynasties of kings of all Egypt, is evident from the plain and coloured bas-reliefs which adorn the walls of their *maṣṭabas*, or bench-shaped tombs, and we can only point out and wonder at the fact that the royal pyramids contain neither painted nor sculptured vignettes, especially as pictures are much needed to break the monotony of the hundreds of lines of large hieroglyphics, painted in a bluish-green colour, which must have dazzled the eyes even of an Egyptian. The reason, however, why such early texts are not illustrated is probably not far to seek. Professor Maspero has proved that the "pyramid texts" contain formulae and paragraphs which, judging from the grammatical forms that occur in them, it is easy to see must have been composed, if not actually written down, in the earliest times of Egyptian civilization. These formulae, &c., are interspersed with others of later periods, and it seems as if, at the time when the "pyramid texts" were cut into stone, these religious compositions were intended to contain expressions of pious thought about the hereafter which would satisfy both those who accepted the ancient indigenous beliefs, and those who were prepared to believe the doctrines which had been promulgated by the priests of the famous brotherhood of Rā, the Sun-god, who had made their head-quarters in Egypt at Ȧnnu, i.e., On, or Heliopolis. The old native beliefs of the country were of a more material character than the doctrines which the priests of Heliopolis taught, but it was found impossible to eradicate them from the minds of the people, and the priests therefore framed religious works in such a manner that they might be acceptable both to those who believed in the old animal-gods, tree-gods, plant-gods, &c., of Egypt, and those who preferred a purely solar cult, such as that of the worship of the Sun-god Rā. The oldest Books of the Dead, in fact, represent the compromise arrived at under the IVth, Vth, and VIth Dynasties, between the priests of the old and the new religions. This being so, the religious texts of the period represent too much a patch-work belief for purposes of systematic illustration, and in the result, and perhaps also through the funeral customs of the day, the growth in men's minds of the wish for illustrated guides to the Underworld was retarded.

When the glory of sovereignty departed from the kings who held court at Memphis after the end of the rule of the VIth Dynasty, the system of solar theology, which had been promulgated in Lower Egypt by the priests of Heliopolis, began to make its way into Upper Egypt, and wherever it came it assumed a leading position among the religious systems of the day. The kings of the VIIth and VIIIth Dynasties, like those of the IIIrd, IVth, and VIth, came from Memphis, but they had comparatively little power in the land, and, so far as we know, they did not build for themselves pyramids for tombs, and there is no evidence forthcoming to show that they filled the walls of their sepulchres with religious texts. They carried on neither wars nor building operations of any importance, and it seems that their tombs were neither large nor magnificent. Owing to their feeble rule the governors of Suten-ḥenen, or Herakleopolis, and those who ruled in the provinces near that city, succeeded in gaining their independence, and the kings of the IXth and Xth Dynasties were Herakleopolitans; their rule gradually extended to the south, and the religious influence of their priests was so great that they succeeded in forcing many of their mythological legends and beliefs into the accepted religion of the country, and these subsequently became part and parcel of the great Recension of the Theban Book of the Dead. The dominion of the Herakleopolitans, however, was of comparatively short duration, and it collapsed under the attacks of the bold and vigorous governors of the Thebaïd, whose capital was at Thebes. Judging from the historical evidence concerning the period which lies between the VIth and the XIth Dynasties, neither the two last Memphitic nor the two Herakleopolitan Dynasties of kings did anything to improve the general condition of the country, and it seems as if they found it necessary to employ all their energies to maintain their position and the little real power in the country which they possessed.

As this was the case, we need not wonder that all magnificence disappeared from funeral rites and ceremonies, and that the tombs of the period were small and unimportant. The gods were worshipped and the dead were buried as matters of course, but it goes without saying that kings, whose authority was not consolidated, and whose power was ineffective except in the immediate neighbourhood of the towns in which they lived, who were unable to wage wars in Syria and Sinai and to bring back much spoil, could neither establish Colleges of priests nor endow new temples; for in ancient Egypt, as elsewhere, the fortunes of the gods and the wealth of their sanctuaries increased or declined according as the inhabitants of the land were prosperous or otherwise. Similarly also, when the community was suffering from the evil effects of a long period of civil wars, and business was at a standstill, and farmers were unable to carry on the usual agricultural operations on which both the government and the priesthood ultimately depended for support, it was impossible for men to bury their dead with all the pomp and ceremony which were the characteristics of funerals in times of peace and prosperity. The innate conservatism of the Egyptians made them cling to their ancient beliefs during this period of stress, but no important pyramids were built, and very few private funeral chapels were maintained at expensive rates, and the souls of the dead were committed to such protection as could be obtained by the prayers of their relatives and friends, and by the utterance of religious formulae, and by inexpensive amulets.

With the rise to power of the Princes of Thebes, things took a turn for the better so far as worship in the temples and the care for the dead were concerned. So soon as they had overcome their enemies the Princes of Herakleopolis, and their confederates the Princes of Asyût, and had firmly established themselves on the throne of Egypt, they sent men to reopen the quarries in the First Cataract and in the Wâdî Ḥammâmât near Coptos. This is a sure proof that the new line of kings, most of whom bear the name of Menthu-ḥetep, had need of large quantities of granite, and of sandstone of various kinds, and such materials can only have been required for the building of temples and palaces, and funeral altars and stelae, sarcophagi, &c. The fact that the work was begun again in the quarries also proves that the authority of the Menthu-ḥeteps was well established. Menthu-ḥetep II., we are told by an inscription set up in the Wadî Ḥammâmât by his officer Åmen-em-ḥāt, caused to be quarried a block of stone which measured eight cubits, by four cubits, by two cubits, i.e., about thirteen feet six inches long, six feet six inches wide, and three feet six inches thick, and it is probable that he required this for a sarcophagus. This king is also famous as the maker of a well in the desert, the mouth of which was about sixteen feet six inches square; and at one time he employed several thousands of men, including three thousand carriers or boatmen, in his stone-works. His successor, Menthu-ḥetep III., continued the work in the quarries, and built himself a pyramid, called Khu-ȧst, 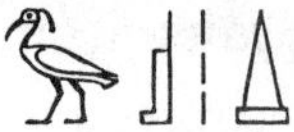, in the mountain of Tchesert at Thebes, which may now be identified with that portion of the great Theban cemetery to which the name Dêr al-Baḥarî was given by the Arabic-speaking Egyptians.

This building is mentioned in the great Abbott Papyrus preserved in the British Museum (No. 10,221), where it is declared to have been found unviolated by the members of the Commission which was appointed to inquire into the condition of the royal tombs, after the robberies which had taken place in them about the period of the rule of the priest-kings of Thebes, B.C. 1,000. The remains of the tomb of Menthu-ḥetep III. have been recently discovered,[1] and though at the time of writing it has not been completely excavated, sufficient has been done to show that it is a very remarkable building. It is clear that the lower part of it is rectangular, and that it was surrounded by a colonnade; the outside is cased with limestone slabs, behind which is a "wall of rough and heavy nodules

[1] See a letter in the *Times* of June 22nd, 1905 (p. 4), on the "Most Ancient Temple at Thebes," by Prof. E. Naville and Mr. H. R. Hall.

of flint, and the middle is filled with rubbish and loose stones." On this rectangular building, or base, a small pyramid probably stood, at least, this is what we should expect. The remains already excavated prove that this base was surrounded by a triple row of columns, which supported a ceiling and formed a hypostyle passage or colonnade, which "must have been quite "dark, or nearly so (like the ambulatories surrounding "the shrines in later temples), for the outside was "closed by a thick wall." Between this wall and the edge of the platform on which the building stood was an outer colonnade of square pillars, but the pillars no longer exist. In the rock below the pavement of this colonnade a number of tombs were hewn; each consisted of a pit from twelve to fifteen feet deep, which led to a small rectangular chamber, wherein originally stood a limestone sarcophagus. In these tombs women who were both priestesses of Hathor and members of the royal *harîm* were buried, and further excavations will no doubt reveal the fact that Menthu-ḥetep's high officers of state were buried in somewhat similar tombs in the immediate neighbourhood of the remarkable monument which the Egypt Exploration Fund has brought to light through the exertions of Prof. E. Naville and Mr. H. R. Hall.

The facts given above indicate that Menthu-ḥetep III. built a splendid tomb at Thebes, and it seems that in certain particulars he copied the royal pyramid tombs of the IVth, Vth, and VIth Dynasties. It is unlikely that the superstructure which he set upon the rectangular base, to which reference has been made above, and which is assumed to have been in the form of a pyramid, was as large as any of the important pyramids of Gîza, and the base on which it rested is "a "new and interesting fact in Egyptian architecture"; but when he set his funeral monument on the rocky platform in the mountain of Tchesert it is more than probable that either he or his architect had in mind the rocky platform on which the great Pyramids of Gîza stand, and it seems as if he built it on a massive rectangular base, so that it might appear conspicuous and imposing from a distance. Like the earlier royal builders of pyramids, Menthu-ḥetep built a funeral temple in connexion with his pyramid, and established an order of priests, who were to perform the services and ceremonies connected with his worship, and he allowed the ladies of his court to be buried round about it, just as did the kings of old who reigned at Memphis. The great feature of Menthu-ḥetep's monument, which has no parallel in the older pyramids in the north of Egypt, is the ramp, with a double row of square columns on each side of it, which he built on the front or eastern face of the temple platform.

Now whilst Menthu-ḥetep III. was employed in building his pyramid and funeral temple, the hereditary governors and nobles of important provinces in Upper Egypt were not slow to avail themselves of the opportunity which peace and the renewed prosperity of the country gave them, and they began to make rock-hewn tombs for themselves and the members of their families in the hills, and to cause their bodies to be buried in elaborately inscribed or painted wooden coffins. Of coffins of this period, one of the oldest examples is that of ȦMAMU , which was purchased by the Trustees of the British Museum so long ago as 1834.[1] On the inside of this coffin is inscribed in black ink in the hieratic character a series of texts which are extracts from the Heliopolitan Recension of the Book of the Dead; these are enclosed within a coloured border, formed of rectangles, painted in blue, green, yellow, and red. Above the texts are carefully drawn, and painted as nearly as possible in their natural colours, representations of most of the objects which the deceased hoped he would use in the Underworld, and these pictures prove that the knowledge of the elaborate funeral rites and ceremonies, which were observed at Memphis under the IVth Dynasty, had descended in a complete state to the period when Ȧmamu's coffin was made and ornamented.

In connection with Ȧmamu's coffin reference must be made to a large group of coffins which was excavated a few years ago at Al-Barsha, a place situated on the north side of a rocky valley, just behind the modern Coptic village of Dêr An-Nakhla, near Shêkh Abâda

[1] See Birch, *Ancient Egyptian Texts from the Coffin of Amamu in the British Museum*, London, 1886.

(the ancient Antinoë), in Upper Egypt. All the coffins found here are rectangular in shape, and have so much in common with the coffin of Åmamu, in respect of shape, and in the arrangement of their texts and pictures, including the representations of *maṣṭaba* doors, that it seems impossible to assign to them a date much earlier or later than the period of the XIth Dynasty. For our present purpose, however, whatever be their exact date, they are of the greatest importance, for on the insides of the panels of some of them are painted the oldest known illustrations of certain sections of Books of the Dead. The texts inscribed on them contain extracts from the Heliopolitan Recension of the Book of the Dead, of which we know so much from the selections given in the Pyramids of Unås, Tetå, and other kings, but side by side with these are copies of chapters belonging to Books of the Dead, which seem to have been originally composed at some anterior period, and which were intended to reflect the more popular and more materialistic religious views and beliefs. Among such books must be mentioned the "Book of Two Ways," or the "Two Ways of the Blessed Dead," of which a version inscribed on a coffin in the Berlin Museum has been recently published.[1] The rubrical directions of this work show that it was compiled when implicit belief existed in the minds of the Egyptians as to the efficacy of

[1] Schack-Schackenburg, *Das Buch von den Zwei Wegen des Seligen Toten*, Leipzig, 1903.

certain "words of power" (*ḥekau*, ) and of pictures of the gods, and it is clear that many portions of it are purely magical, and were intended to produce very material results. Thus concerning one passage a rubric says, "Whosoever knoweth this "Chapter may have union with women by night or "by day, and the heart (or, desire) of the woman shall "come to him whensoever he would enjoy her." This rubric follows a text[1] in which the deceased is made to pray for power of generation similar to that possessed by the god Beba, and for the will and opportunity of overcoming women, and it was to be written on a bandlet which was to be attached to the right arm. Moreover, the soul which had knowledge of certain sections of the work would "live among the living ones," and would "see Osiris every day," and would have "air in his nostrils, and death would never draw nigh unto him."[2] The illustrations which accompany the texts on the coffins from Al-Barsha make it evident that under the XIth Dynasty the Egyptian theologian had not only divided the Underworld in his mind into sections, with doors, &c., but that he was prepared to describe that portion of it which belonged to the blessed dead, and to supply a plan of it! Besides the sections from the "Pyramid Texts," to which reference has already been made, and the "Book of the Two Ways," the coffins of Al-Barsha

[1] See page 49, l. 9—p. 51, l. 11. [2] See page 49, ll. 4—9.

contain a number of texts of various lengths, many of which have titles, and resemble in form the Chapters of the great Theban Recension of the Book of the Dead. Examples of these have been published in Prof. Maspero's *Recueil de Travaux*, tom. xxvi., p. 64 ff., by M. P. Lacau, e.g., "Chapter of the Seven Addresses of homage to the goddess Meḥ-urt"; [Chapter of] "the reassembling of the kinsfolk of a man in Neter-khert"; "Chapter of driving back Ḳebḳa"; "Chapter of setting out for Orion," &c.

From the considerations set forth above it is quite clear that the practice of illustrating certain sections of Books of the Dead existed under the XIth Dynasty, and there is no good reason for doubting that it continued to be observed during the prosperous rule of the kings of the XIIth Dynasty. Under the IVth, Vth, and VIth Dynasties the selections of extracts from Books of the Dead which were intended to benefit royal souls in the Underworld were cut upon the walls of the chambers and corridors of their pyramids, and in the case of private individuals texts intended to produce the same effect were usually cut into the walls of the chambers wherein their stone sarcophagi were placed. The pyramids of the kings of the XIth and XIIth Dynasties, whether in the north or south of Egypt, are not, so far as the information at present available goes, characterized by lengthy extracts from Books of the Dead, and officials and men of rank in general were content to dispense with the cutting of religious inscriptions into the sides of stone sarcophagi, and into the walls of the passages and chambers of their tombs in the mountains, and to transfer them to the sides of their brightly painted, rectangular wooden coffins. The practical advantages of this change are obvious. Wooden coffins were easier to obtain and cheaper than stone sarcophagi, longer and fuller selections from religious texts could be easily and quickly traced upon them in the hieratic character, which an expert scribe could, no doubt, write at a rapid rate, the expense of adding coloured drawings was small, and, above all, the deceased would have close to his mummy the sacred writings on which he so greatly relied for assistance in the Other World. The coffin which was fully inscribed could easily be made to hold copies of all the texts deemed to be of vital importance to the dead, and such a coffin when, as was frequently the case, it was placed in a massive, outer, wooden coffin, served the purpose of the large rolls of papyri inscribed with religious and funeral texts, and illustrated with elaborately painted vignettes, which were buried with the dead from the XVIIIth to the XXVIth Dynasty.

After the death of Ȧmen-em-ḥāt III., who was perhaps the greatest king of the XIIth Dynasty, the whole country fell into a state of confusion, and the kings of Thebes ceased to be masters of all Egypt. The kings of the XIIIth Dynasty were Theban and reigned at Thebes, and appear to have maintained their hold in a considerable degree upon Upper Egypt; but the kings of the XIVth Dynasty reigned at Xoïs, in the Delta, and many of them were contemporaries of the kings in Upper Egypt. The kings of the XVth and XVIth Dynasties were Hyksos, or "Shepherd Kings," and their rule was overthrown by Seqenen-Rā III., a king of the XVIIth Dynasty, and a Theban, probably about B.C. 1800. In the interval between the XIIth and the XVIIIth Dynasties the ceremonies connected with the worship of the gods in their temples, and the funerals of kings and officials, lost the magnificence which had characterized them under the XIIth Dynasty, and the building of pyramids and the making of rock-hewn tombs ceased for a period of some hundreds of years. With the rise to power of the Theban kings, who formed the XVIIIth Dynasty, a marvellous development of temple and funeral ceremonies took place, and, thanks chiefly to the vast quantities of spoil which were poured into Thebes by the victorious armies of Egypt on their return from Western Asia, the cult of the gods and of the dead assumed proportions which it had never reached before in Egypt.

The chief deity of Thebes was Ȧmen, the "Hidden," or perhaps "unknown," god, in whose honour a shrine was built to the north of the city, in a place called "Ap," or "Apt," by the Egyptians, and "Karnak" by the modern inhabitants of Luxor. It is impossible to say at present exactly when the first sanctuary of this god was built at Thebes, but the discovery of the large collection of 457 votive statues of kings and officials and other objects, made by M. Legrain[1] in 1901-2, indicates that the foundation of the sanctuary of Ȧmen dates from a very early period of Dynastic History.[2] Be this as it may, the god Ȧmen seems to have enjoyed no special importance or popularity in Egypt until the XIIth Dynasty, when his sanctuary appears to have been rebuilt and enlarged; but so long as his priests were dependent for maintenance upon the revenues of Upper Egypt alone neither they nor their god can have enjoyed any very great wealth. When Seqenen-Rā III. defeated the Hyksos, and made himself master of all Egypt, and when Ȧāhmes I. (Amasis) drove the Hyksos out from their stronghold Avaris, in the Delta, thus completing the work of the deliverance of the country from a foreign yoke, which Seqenen-Rā III. had begun, they attributed the success of their arms to their god Ȧmen, who was from this time forward regarded not only as the principal god of the Egyptians, but as the "king of the gods." Soon after Ȧmen-ḥetep I., the successor of Ȧāhmes I., came to the throne, he made war against the Nubians, and became master of the gold-producing districts of the Eastern Sûdân. His next care was to rebuild, or perhaps to repair and add to, the sanctuary

[1] See Maspero's *Recueil de Travaux*, tom. xxvii., p. 67.

[2] According to M. Legrain, the IIIrd Dynasty (*Recueil*, tom. xxvii., p. 67).

of Åmen, and he founded the famous College of priests of Åmen, whose counsels guided, both for good and for evil, the destinies of Egypt for several hundreds of years. He richly endowed these priests and their god and his temple, and on many of the coffins of this brotherhood are representations of members of the order in the act of worshipping his names, and of pouring out libations before his cartouches. The priests of Åmen had, no doubt, good reason for worshipping Åmen-ḥetep with such devotion.

It is unnecessary to describe in detail the growth of the cult of Åmen under the XVIIIth Dynasty, and it will suffice to say that the history of his cult is, practically, the history of Egypt for nearly one thousand years. His priests made him possessor of the principal attributes and titles of all the ancient gods of Egypt, and their absolute power enabled them to modify the old systems of belief of the country. They introduced the primitive gods of the land into their own system of theology, but assigned to them subordinate positions and powers inferior to those of Åmen, or Åmen-Rā, as he was called, and the new editions of most of the old religious works which appeared at Thebes bore the traces of having been edited in accordance with their views and opinions. In many of its aspects the cult of Åmen was less material than that of many of the old gods, and the religion of the priests themselves ruthlessly rejected many of the primitive beliefs which survived among the populace in general. They were obliged to tolerate and respect the universal belief in Osiris as the judge, king, and god of the dead, for they, of course, found it impossible to eliminate from the minds of the people the effect which the traditions of a material heaven, handed down for untold generations, had made upon them. Among the servants of Åmen and his temple, however, there were some who preferred to put their faith in the religious writings which had satisfied their ancestors many centuries before, and to these we owe the great collection of religious and funeral texts called PER EM HRU, "[The Book of] Coming forth by Day," which is now commonly known as the Theban Recension of the Book of the Dead.

It is true that the subject matter of many of the texts is older than the IVth Dynasty, and that the phraseology of some dates from the period of the Vth and VIth Dynasties, and that the forms in which most of them are cast are not more recent than the XIth or XIIth Dynasty, but it is equally true that the editing and arrangement of them by the Theban priests, to say nothing of the addition of supplementary hymns, Chapters, and coloured illustrations, produced a very decided change in the general teachings of the collection.

"The Book of Coming Forth by Day," in its Theban form, was an illustrated guide to the kingdom of Osiris, but its teachings did not satisfy the strict followers of Åmen-Rā, and they brought into use a Recension of a work in which they were able to promulgate the particular ideas of their order as to the future state of the dead. The followers of Osiris believed that the righteous dead would find their everlasting abode in the kingdom of that god, and would enjoy in a fertile land, with running streams, a life very like that which the well-to-do Egyptian lived upon earth. The followers of Ȧmen-Rā aimed at securing a place in the boat of the Sun-god, i.e., the "Boat of Millions of Years," so that they might sail over the sky with him each day, and enjoy the sight of the earth on which they had lived, and might, under his all-powerful protection, pass through the regions of darkness by night, and emerge in heaven, being reborn each day. In the kingdom of Osiris the beatified dead ate bread-cakes made from one wonderful kind of grain, and drank beer made from another kind, and enjoyed conjugal intercourse, and the company of their relations and friends; all their material comforts were supplied by the use of words of power, &c., by which they even obtained entrance into that kingdom.

Entrance to the Boat of Millions of Years was likewise obtained by the knowledge of magical words and formulae, and of the secret names of the great gods, but the food on which lived the beatified souls who succeeded in securing a place in the Boat consisted of the emanations of the god Rā, or, according to the priests of Ȧmen, Ȧmen-Rā. In other words, the beatified souls in the Boat became beings formed of the light of Rā, on which they subsisted. The belief that the souls of the righteous flew into the Boat of Rā is a very old one, but the doctrine in the form in which it was developed by the priests of Ȧmen can never have been universally accepted in Egypt, for it was not sufficiently material to satisfy any but the educated classes. The great kings of the XVIIIth and XIXth Dynasties, being convinced that their military successes were due to the influence and operation of Ȧmen-Rā, dutifully accepted the instructions of the priests of the god in all matters relating to his worship, and they permitted them to prepare tombs for them in the Valley of Bîbân al-Mulûk at Thebes, which were built and ornamented according to the views held by the followers of Ȧmen-Rā concerning the Other World. The oldest tombs here, i.e., those of the XVIIIth Dynasty, are usually entered by means of long, sloping corridors that lead down into the the chambers which held the sarcophagi, and into smaller halls which adjoin the large chambers; in the later tombs the corridors are often very long, and it is this characteristic which caused certain Greek writers to call them Σύριγγες, i.e., "shepherd's pipes." Of the forty-five tombs in this valley (Strabo mentions forty only), the oldest royal tomb appears to be that of Thothmes I., and the most recent that of Rameses XII., of the XXth Dynasty. These tombs vary greatly in details, just as they do in size and in the arrangement and number of their chambers, but it seems that each tomb was intended to represent the Underworld, and that the ceremonies, which were performed in it as the mummy was taken from the entrance to the last chamber in which it was to rest, were highly symbolical, and that the progress of the body through the tomb was, so far as it was possible, made to resemble that of the Sun-god through the hours of the night in the Other World.

The religious texts with which the walls of the royal tombs are decorated do not consist of extracts from the funeral works of the Ancient and Middle Empires, but of sections from a work entitled ÀM-ṬUAT, i.e., [The Book of] "what is in the Ṭuat," or Underworld, and many of these are illustrated more or less fully with coloured pictures of the gods, mythological scenes, &c. The rubrics show that portions of this work belong to remote antiquity, and many of the beliefs which appear in it are the products of the period when the Egyptians were partly, if not wholly, savages. In the book itself numbers of gods and mythological beings are mentioned whose names are not found elsewhere in Egyptian literature. As we find it in the tombs of the royal followers of Àmen, the Book "Àm-Ṭuat" contains all the dogmas and doctrines which the priests of Àmen held concerning the future life and the state and condition of the dead, and it is quite easy to see that the great object of those who compiled it was to prove that Àmen-Rā was not only the head of the gods in heaven, and the ruler of the world which he had created, but also the king of all the gods of the dead, and the master of all the beings who were in the

Underworld. In other words, the priests of Àmen asserted the absolute sovereignty of their god, and their own religious supremacy. It is, however, interesting to note that certain kings did not entirely shake off their belief in Osiris, and in the efficacy of the Chapters of the Book of Coming Forth by Day, for Thothmes III. was swathed in a linen sheet on which was written a copy of the CLIVth Chapter, and Àmenḥetep III. was rolled up in sheets whereon extracts from several Chapters of that work were inscribed. Seti I. went a good deal further, for although fully illustrated copies of Divisions I.—XI. of the Book "Àm-Tuat" were painted on the walls of his tomb, he took care to have a complete copy of the Book of Gates,[1] with full illustrations, and copies of the LXXIInd and LXXXIXth Chapters of the Book of Coming Forth by Day cut on his alabaster sarcophagus.

The Chapter which Thothmes III. believed to be all-powerful is entitled "Chapter of not letting the body perish," and if its words really express his convictions, he must have been terrified at the idea of his material body falling into dust and decay, and must have hoped for its resurrection through Osiris. The Chapters which Seti I. had cut on his sarcophagus are entitled the "Chapter of Coming Forth by Day, and of making a way through Àmmeḥet," and the "Chapter of causing the soul to be united to its body in the Underworld." In the former he declares that

[1] See within, Chapter IV., p. 85.

he knows the names of the gods who preside over the Other World, and also the proper words of power, and because he has this knowledge he demands admission into Sekhet-Ȧaru, a portion of Osiris's kingdom of Sekhet-ḥetepet, and a constant and abundant supply of wheat (for bread), barley (for beer), incense, unguents, &c., and the power to assume any form he pleases at will. In the latter he calls upon certain gods to make his soul rejoin its body, and, addressing the gods who tow the Boat of Millions of Years, he asks them to cause him to be born from the womb of the Sky-goddess Nut in the eastern horizon of heaven, [daily,] for ever.

It has already been said that a complete illustrated copy of the Book of Gates was also inscribed on the sarcophagus of Seti I., and it is not easy to explain this fact until we remember the important position which it makes Osiris to hold in the Other World. That the book is formed of very ancient materials is evident from the last sections, which certainly contain magical texts and pictures specially prepared with the object of making the sun to rise, and there is little doubt that the latter are representations of the ceremonies which the primitive Egyptians actually performed to produce that most desirable effect. The earlier sections of the Book are full of magical ideas, but scattered among them are expressions of beliefs which, it seems, must belong to a later period of civilization, and passages which impress the reader with the idea that they were composed by men who believed that the righteous would be rewarded and the wicked punished in the world to come. Special prominence is given to the conception of the Judgment, wherein Osiris is the Judge of the dead. As the result of this Judgment the righteous have allotments of land meted out to them, which vary in size according to their deserts, and the wicked are slain, and their bodies cut in pieces, and their souls destroyed. In many particualrs the views of the Book of Gates concerning the future state agree closely with those of the Book of Coming Forth by Day.

The net result of the facts stated in the last two paragraphs proves that Seti I. relied for salvation upon the protection, part magical and part religious, afforded by the sacred writings of two great schools of religious thought, the leaders of which in his day preached opposing and contradictory doctrines. It may be argued that by filling the walls of his tomb and sarcophagus with the texts of such books he was merely acting from the point of view of religious expediency, wishing to indicate his impartiality in respect of the followers of Åmen and the followers of Osiris, and his respect for the ancient traditional beliefs, however material, crude, and impossible they may have appeared to him personally. This, however, is unlikely to have been the case, and it is far more probable that he believed every religious or funeral text to have its own special value as a means of salvation, and that he selected for inscribing on the walls of his tomb and sarcophagus those which he thought would be the most likely to secure for him in the next world an existence which would be at once happy and everlasting. Therefore Seti I. provided himself with amulets, *ushabtiu* figures, magical formulae, pictures of gods and fiends to be used in working sympathetic magic, religious formulae and copies of hymns and funeral works, an inscribed tomb and sarcophagus, &c.; in fact, he was painfully anxious to omit nothing from the inscriptions in his tomb which would propitiate any god, or appease the wrath and turn aside the opposition of any of the fiends wherewith he had filled his Underworld.

CHAPTER II.

THE EARLIEST EGYPTIAN CONCEPTION OF THE OTHER WORLD.

HAVING briefly referred to the origin and development of the magical, religious, and purely funeral texts which, sometimes with and sometimes without illustrations, formed the "Guides" to the Ancient Egyptian Underworld, the form of the conceptions concerning the place of departed spirits as it appears in the Recensions of the XVIIIth and XIXth Dynasties must now be considered. To reconstruct the form which they took in the Predynastic Period is impossible, for no materials exist, and the documents of the Early Empire are concerned chiefly with providing the deceased with an abundance of meat, drink, and other material comforts, and numbers of wives and concubines, and a place in Sekhet-Ȧaru, a division of Sekhet-ḥetepet, to which the name "Elysian Fields" has not inaptly been given. In later times Sekhet-Ȧaru, or Sekhet-Ȧanru, comprised all Sekhet-ḥetepet. Of Sekhet-ḥetepet as a whole the earliest known pictures are those which are painted on the coffins of

Al-Barsha, and of no portion of this region have we any detailed illustrations of the occupations of its inhabitants older than the XVIIIth Dynasty. To the consideration of Sekhet-Åaru, which was the true heaven of every faithful worshipper of Osiris, from the time when he became the judge and benevolent god and friend of the dead down to the Ptolemaïc Period, that is to say, for a period of four thousand years at least, the scribes and artists of the XVIIIth Dynasty devoted much attention, and the results of their views are set forth in the copies of PER-EM-HRU, or the Theban Book of the Dead, which have come down to us.

In one of the oldest copies of PER-EM-HRU, i.e., in the Papyrus of Nu,[1] is a vignette of the Seven *Ārits*, or divisions of Sekhet-Åaru; the portion shown of each *Ārit* is the door, or gate, which is guarded by a gatekeeper, by a watcher, who reports the arrival of every comer, and by a herald, who receives and announces his name. All these beings save two have the head of an animal, or bird, on a human body, a fact which indicates the great antiquity of the ideas that underlie this vignette. Their names are:—

Ārit	I.	*Gatekeeper.*	SEKHET-ḤRÅ-ĀSHT-ÅRU.
		Watcher.	SEMETU.
		Herald.	HU-KHERU.

[1] British Museum, No. 10,477, sheet 26 (Chapter cxliv.).

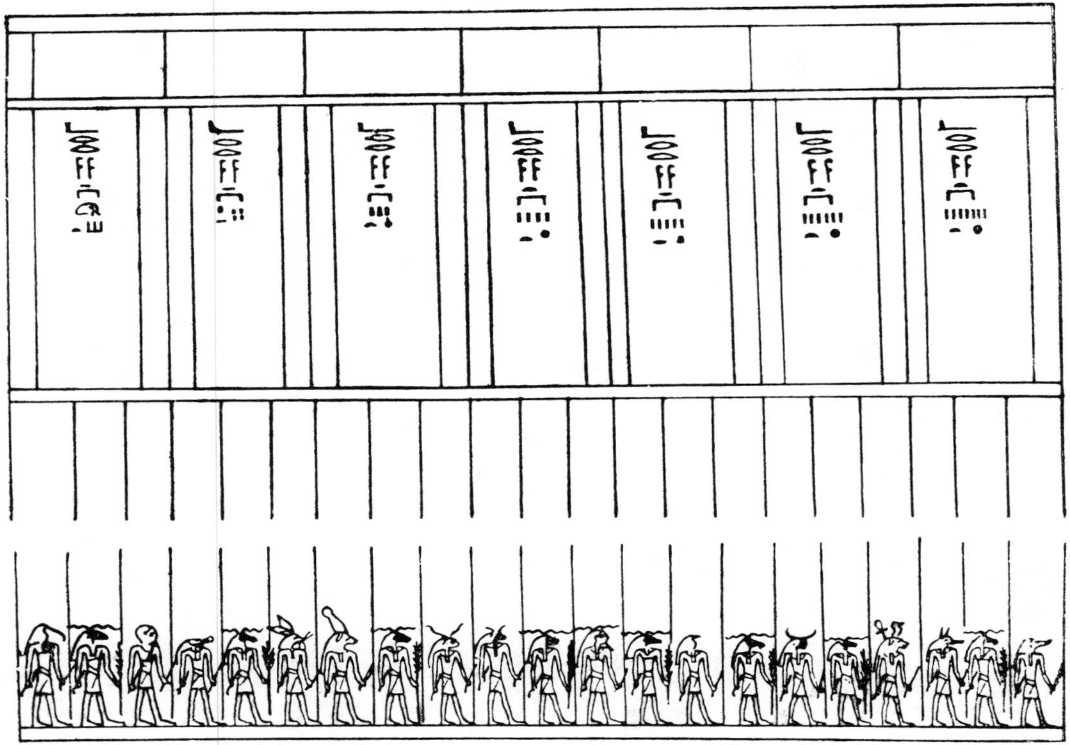

The Seven Ārits, each with its Gatekeeper, its Watcher, and its Herald.

Arit II.	*Gatekeeper.*	ṬUN-ḤĀT.
	Watcher.	SEQEṬ-ḤRȦ.
	Herald.	SABES.
Arit III.	*Gatekeeper.*	ȦM-ḤUAT-ENT-PEḤUI-FI.
	Watcher.	RES-ḤRȦ.
	Herald.	UĀAU.
Arit IV.	*Gatekeeper.*	KHESEF-ḤRȦ-ĀSHT-KHERU.
	Watcher.	RES-ȦB.
	Herald.	NETEḲA-ḤRȦ-KHESEF-AṬU.
Ārit V.	*Gatekeeper.*	ĀNKH-EM-FENṬU.
	Watcher.	ASHEBU.
	Herald.	ṬEB-ḤER-KEHAAT.
Arit VI.	*Gatekeeper.*	ȦKEN-TAU-K-HA-KHERU.
	Watcher.	ȦN-ḤRȦ.
	Herald.	METES-ḤRȦ-ȦRI-SHE.
Ārit VII.	*Gatekeeper.*	MEṬES-SEN.
	Watcher.	ȦĀA-KHERU.
	Herald.	KHESEF-ḤRȦ-KHEMIU.

From another place in the same papyrus,[1] and from other papyri, we learn that the "Secret Gates of the House of Osiris in Sekhet-Ȧaru" were twenty-one in number; the Chapter (CXLVI.) gives the name of each Gate, and also that of each Gatekeeper up to No. X., thus:—

I. *Gate.* NEBT - SEṬAU - QAT - SEBT - ḤERT - NEBT - KHEBKHEBT - SERT - MEṬU-

[1] Sheet 25.

KHESEFET-NESHENIU-NEḤEMET-UAI-EN-I-UAU.

Gatekeeper. NERI.

II. *Gate.* NEBT-PET-ḤENT-TAUI-NESBIT-NEBT-TEMEMU-TENT-BU-NEBU.

Gatekeeper. MES-PEḤ (or, MES-PTAḤ).

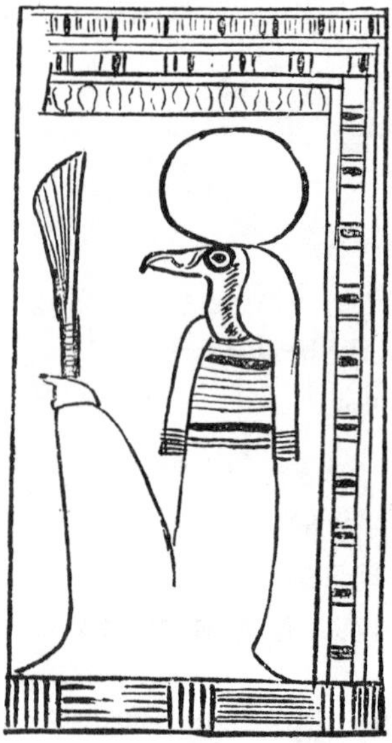

Gate I.

Gate II.

III. *Gate.* NEBT-KHAUT-ĀAT-ĀABET-SENETCHEMET-NETER-NEB-ÅM-S-HRU-KHENT-ER-ÅBṬU.

Gatekeeper. ERTĀT-SEBANQA.

IV. *Gate.* SEKHEMET-ṬESU-ḤENT-TAUI-ḤETCHET-KHEFTI-NU-URṬ-ÅB-ÅRIT-SARU-SHUT-EM-ĀU.

Gatekeeper. NEḲAU.

Gate III.

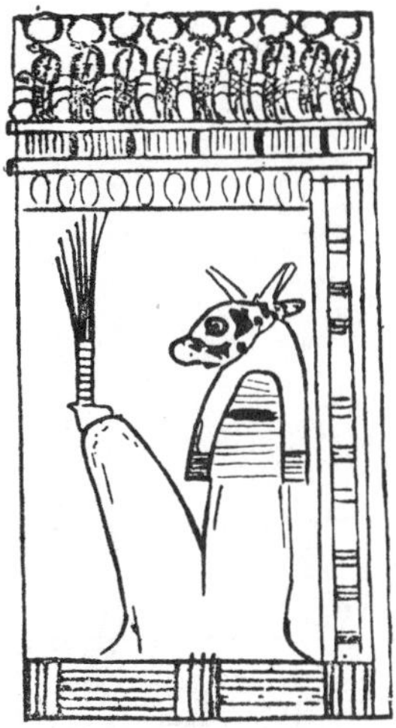

Gate IV.

V. *Gate.* NEBT - REKḤU - RESHT - TEBḤET - ṬĀTU - NES - ÅN - ĀQ - ERES - UN - ṬEP-F.

Gatekeeper. ḤENTI-REQU.

Gate V.

Gate VI.

VI. *Gate.* Nebt-senket-āat-hemhemet-ȧn-rekh-tu-qa-s-er-usekh-s-ȧn-qemtu-qeṭ-s-em-shaā-ȧu-ḥefu-ḥer-s-ȧn-rekh-tennu-mes-en-thu-kher-ḥāt-urṭu-ȧb.

Gatekeeper. Smamti.

Gate VII.

Gate VIII.

VII. *Gate.* Ȧkkit-ḥebset-baḳ-aakebit-mert-seḥap-khat.

Gatekeeper. Ȧkenti.

VIII. *Gate.* Rekḥet-besu-ākhmet-tchafu-sepṭ-pāu-khat-ṭet-smam-ȧn-netchnetch-ȧtet-sesh-ḥer-s-en-senṭ-nȧh-s.

Gatekeeper. Khu-tchet-f.

IX. *Gate.* ÅMT-ḤĀT-NEBT-USER-HERT-ÅB-MESTET-NEB-S-KHEMT-SHAĀ-....-EM-SHEN-S-SATU-EM-UATCHET-QEMĀ-THESET-BES-ḤEBSET-BAḲ-FEQAT-NEB-S-RĀ-NEB.

Gatekeeper. TCHESEF.

Gate IX.

Gate X.

X. *Gate.* QAT-KHERU-NEHESET-ṬENÅTU-SEBḤET-ER-QA-EN-KHERU-S-NERT-NEBT-SHEFSHEFT-ÅN-ṬER-S-NETET-EM-KHENNU-S.

Gatekeeper. SEKHEN-UR.

XI. *Gate.* NEMT-ṬESU-UBṬET-SEBÅU-ḤENT-ENT-SEBKHET-NEBT-ÅRU-NES-ÅHEHI-HRU-EN-ÅNKHEKH.[1]

[1] The names of the gatekeepers of Gates XI.—XXI. are not given in the papyri.

XII. *Gate.* NAST-TAUI-SI-SEKSEKET-NEMMȦTU-EM-NEHEPU-QAḤIT-NEBT-KHU-SETEMTH-KHERU-NEB-S.

XIII. *Gate.* STA-EN-ȦSȦR-ĀĀUI-F-ḤER-S-SEḤETCHET-ḤĀP-EM-ȦMENT-F.

XIV. *Gate.* NEBT-ṬENṬEN-KHEBT-ḤER-ṬESHERU-ȦRU-NES-HAKER-HRU-EN-SETEMET-ĀU.

XV. *Gate.* BAṬI-ṬESHERU-QEMḤUT-ȦARERT-PERT-EM-ḲERḤ-SENTCHERT-SEBȦ-ḤER-QABI-F-ERṬĀT-ĀĀUI-S-EN-URṬU-ȦB-EM-ȦT-F-ȦRT-ITET-SHEM-S.

XVI. *Gate.* NERUTET-NEBT-ȦAṬET-KHAĀ-KHAU-EM-BA-EN-RETH-KHEBSU-MIT-EN-RETH-SERT-PER-QEMAMET-SHĀṬ.

XVII. *Gate.* KHEBT-ḤER-SENF-ȦḤIBIT-NEBT-UAUIUAIT.

XVIII. *Gate.* MER-SETAU-ĀB-ȦBTU-MERER-S-SHĀṬ-ṬEPU-AMKHIT-NEBT-AḤĀ-UḤSET-SEBȦU-EM-MĀSHERU.

XIX. *Gate.* SERT-NEHEPU-EM-ĀḤĀ-S-URSH-SHEMMET-NEBT-USERU-ANU-EN-TEḤUTI-TCHESEF.

XX. *Gate.* AMT-KHEN-TEPEḤ-NEB-S-ḤEBS-REN-S-ȦMENT-QEMAMU-S-THETET-ḤĀTI-EN-ȦM-S.

XXI. *Gate.* ṬEM-SIA-ER-MEṬUU-ȦRI-ḤEMEN-HAI-NEBȦU-S.

From the above lists, and from copies of them which are found in the Papyrus of Ani, and other finely illustrated Books of the Dead, it is quite clear that, according to one view, Sekhet-Ȧaru, the land of the blessed, was divided into seven sections, each of which was entered through a Gate having three attendants, and that, according to other traditions, it had sections varying in number from ten to twenty-one, for each of the Gates mentioned above must have been intended to protect a division. It will be noted that the names of the Ten Gates are in reality long sentences, which make sense and can be translated, but there is little doubt that under the XVIIIth Dynasty these sentences were used as purely magical formulae, or words of power, which, provided the deceased knew how to pronounce them, there was no great need to understand. In other words, it was not any goodness or virtue of his own which would enable him to pass through the Gates of Sekhet-Ȧaru, and disarm the opposition of their warders, but the knowledge of certain formulæ, or words of power, and magical names. We are thus taken back to a very remote period by these ideas, and to a time when the conceptions as to the abode of the blessed were of a purely magical character; the addition of pictures to the formulae, or names, belongs to a later period, when it was thought right to strengthen them by illustrations. The deceased, who not only possessed the secret name of a god or demon, but also a picture of him whereby he could easily recognize him when he met him, was doubly armed against danger.

In addition to the Seven Ārits, and the Ten, Fourteen, or Twenty-one Gates (according to the manuscript authority followed), the Sekhet-Ḥetepet possessed Fourteen or Fifteen Ȧats, or Regions, each of which was presided over by a god. Their names, as given in the Papyrus of Nu,[1] are as follows:—

Ȧat I. AMENTET, wherein a man lived on cakes and ale; its god was ȦMSU-QEṬ, or MENU-QEṬ.

Ȧat II. SEKHET-ȦARU. Its walls are of iron. The wheat here is five cubits high, the barley

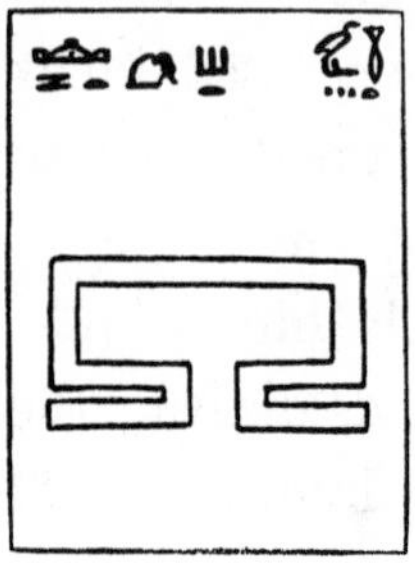

Ȧat I.

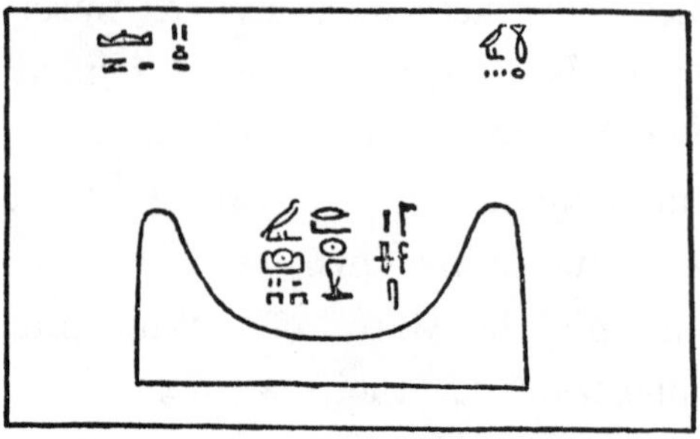

Ȧat II.

is seven cubits high, and the Spirits who reap them are nine cubits high. The god of this Ȧat is RĀ-ḤERUKHUTI.

Ȧat III. ȦATENKHU. Its god was OSIRIS or RĀ.

Ȧat IV. ṬUI-QAUI-ĀȦUI. Its god was SATI-ṬEMUI.

Ȧat V. ȦATENKHU. The Spirits here live upon the inert and feeble. Its god was probably OSIRIS.

[1] Sheets 28, 29, and 30.

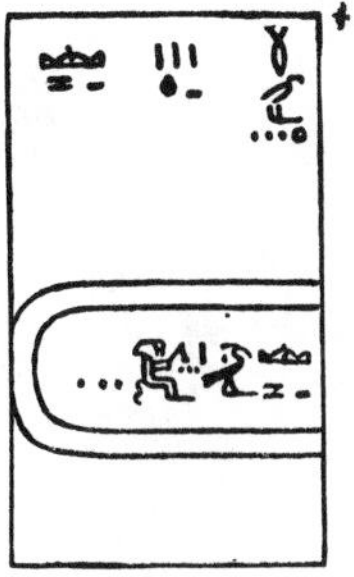

Ȧat III.

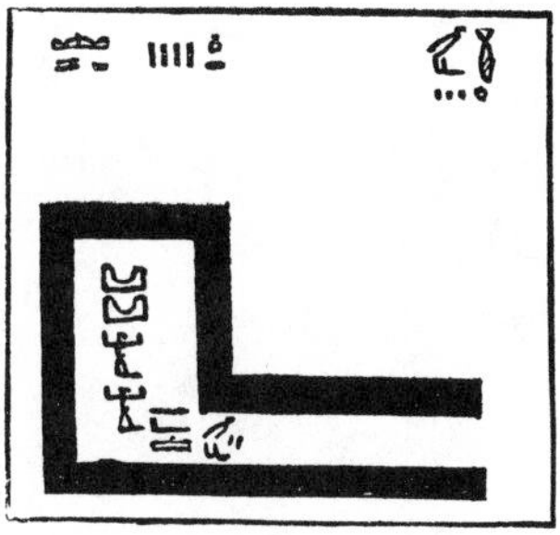

Ȧat IV.

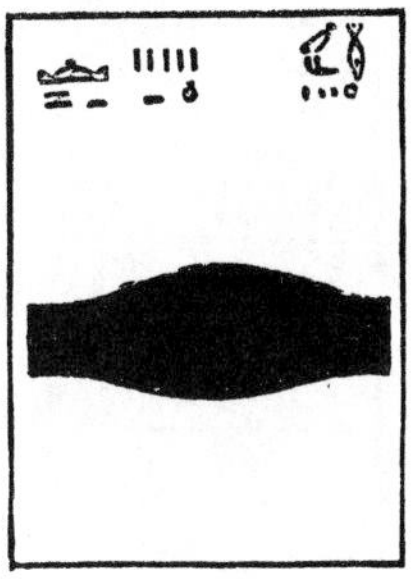

Ȧat V.

Ȧat VI. Ȧmmeḥet, which is presided over either by Sekher-Āṭ or Sekher-remus. This Ȧat was sacred to the gods, the Spirits could not find it out, and it was accursed for the dead.

Ȧat VII. Ȧses, a region of burning, fiery flame, wherein the serpent Rerek lives.

Ȧat VIII. Ha-ḥetep, a region containing roaring torrents of water, and ruled over by a god called Qa-ha-ḥetep. A variant gives the name of this Ȧat as Ha-sert, and that of its god as Fa-pet.

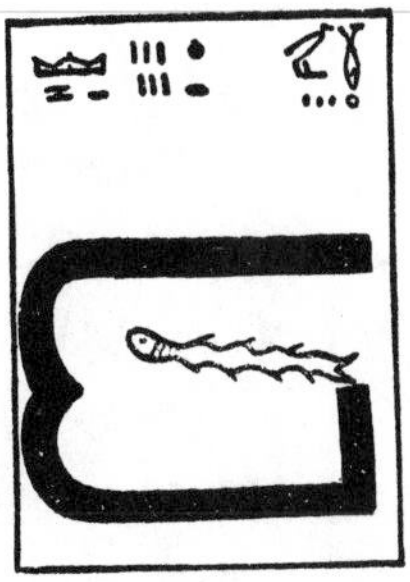

Ȧat VI.

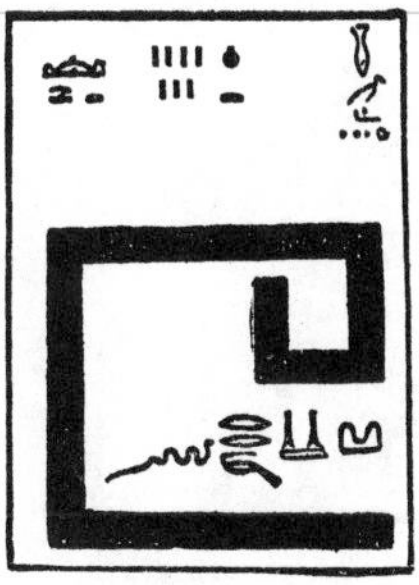

Ȧat VII.

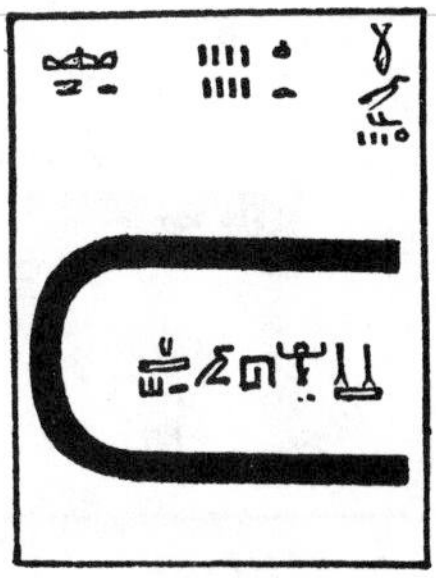

Ȧat VIII.

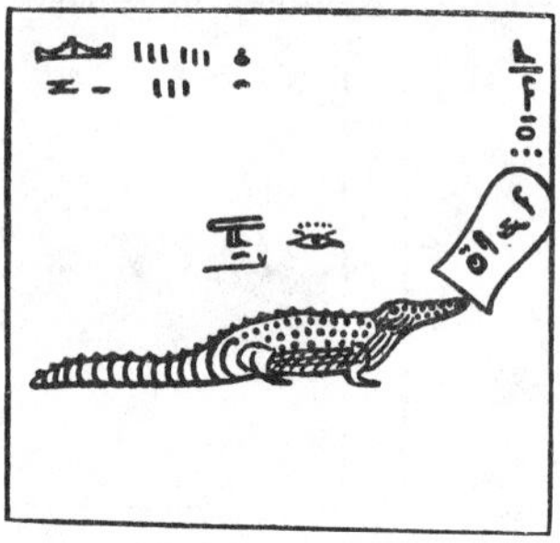

Åat IX.

Aat X.

Åat IX. ÅKESI, a region which is unknown even to the gods; its god was MAA-THETEF, and its only inhabitant is the "god who dwelleth in his egg."

Åat X. NUT-ENT-QAḤU, i.e., the city of Qaḥu. It was also known by the name ÅPT-ENT-QAḤU. The gods of this region appear to have been NĀU, KAPET, and NEḤEB-KAU.

Åat XI. ÅṬU, the god of which was SEPṬ (Sothis).

Åat XII. UNT, the god of which was ḤETEMET-BAIU; also called ÅSTCHEṬET-EM-ÅMENT.

Åat XI.

Åat XII.

Aat XIII. UĀRT-ENT-MU: its deity was the hippopotamus-god called HEBṬ-RE-F.

Åat XIV. The mountainous region of KHER-ĀḤA, the god of which was ḤĀP, the Nile.

A brief examination of this list of Åats, or Regions, suggests that the divisions of Sekhet-ḥetepet given in it are arranged in order from south to north, for it is well known that Åmentet, the first Åat, was entered from the neighbourhood of Thebes, and that the last-mentioned Åat, i.e., Kher-āḥa, represents a region quite

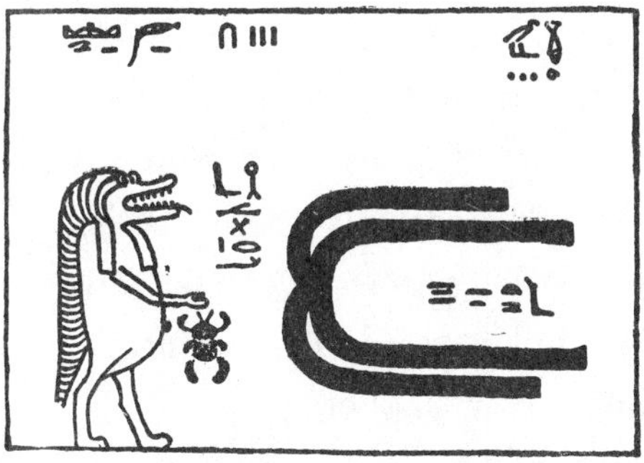

Aat XIII.

Åat XIV.

close to Heliopolis; if this be so, Sekhet-Åaru was probably situated at no great distance from Abydos, near which was the famous "Gap" in the mountains, whereby the spirits of the dead entered the abode set apart for them. We see from this list also that the heaven provided for the blessed was one such as an agricultural population would expect to have, and a nation of farmers would revel in the idea of living among fields of wheat and barley, the former being between seven and eight feet, and the latter between nine and ten feet high. The spirits who reaped this grain are said to have been nine cubits, i.e., over thirteen feet, in height, a statement which seems to indicate that a belief in the existence of men of exceptional height in very ancient days was extant in Egypt traditionally.

Other facts to be gleaned from the list of Ȧats concerning Sekhet-Ȧaru are that:—1. One section at least was filled with fire. 2. Another was filled with rushing, roaring waters, which swept everything away before them. 3. In another the serpent Rerek lived. 4. In another the Spirits lived upon the inert and the feeble. 5. In another lived the "Destroyer of Souls." 6. The great antiquity of the ideas about the Ȧats is proved by the appearance of the names of Ḥāp, the Nile-god, Sepṭ, or Sothis, and the Hippopotamus-goddess, Hebṭ-re-f, in connection with them.

The qualification for entering the Ȧats was not so much the living of a good life upon earth as a knowledge of the magical figures which represented them, and their names; these are given twice in the Papyrus of Nu, and as they are of great importance for the study of magical pictures they have been reproduced above.

Of the general form and the divisions of Sekhet-Ȧaru, or the "Field of Reeds," and Sekhet-ḥetepet, or the "Field of Peace," thanks to the funeral papyri of the XVIIIth Dynasty, much is known, and they may now be briefly described. From the Papyrus of Nebseni[1] we learn that Sekhet-ḥetep was rectangular in shape, and that it was intersected by canals, supplied from the stream by which the whole region was enclosed. In one division were three pools of water,

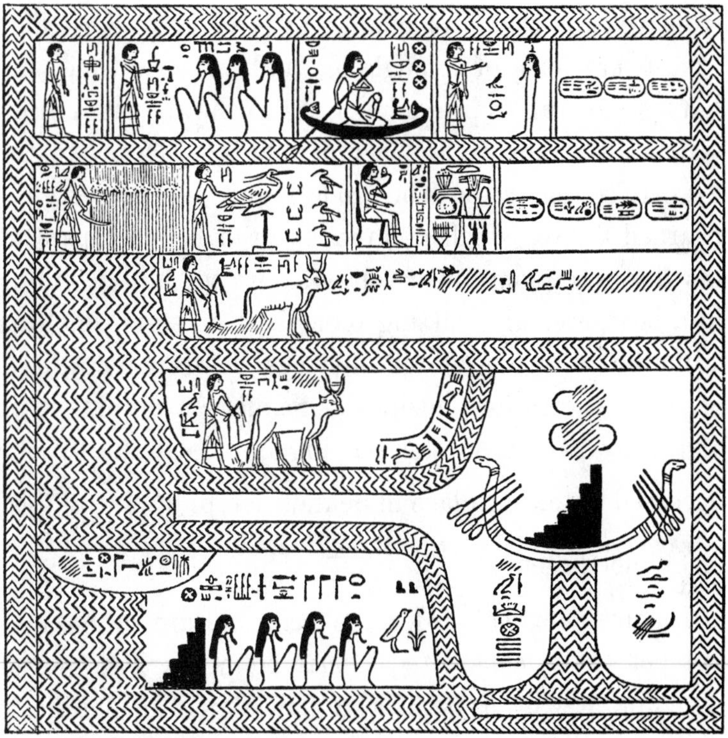

Sekhet-Ḥetepet (Papyrus of Nebseni, British Museum, No. 9900, sheet 17).

in another four pools, and in a third two pools; a place specially set apart was known as the "birthplace of the god of the region," and the "great company of the

[1] British Museum, No. 9,900, sheet 17.

gods in Sekhet-ḥetep" occupied another section of it. At the end of a short canal was moored a boat, provided with eight oars or paddles, and each end of it terminated in a serpent's head; in it was a flight of steps. The deceased, as we see, also possessed a boat wherein he sailed about at will, but its form is different from that of the boat moored at the end of the canal. The operations of ploughing, and of seed-time and harvest, are all represented. As to the deceased himself, we see him in the act of offering incense to the "great company of the gods," and he addresses a bearded figure, which is intended probably to represent his father, or some near relation; we see him paddling in a boat, and also sitting on a chair of state smelling a flower, with a table of offerings before him. None of the inscriptions mentions Sekhet-Åaru, but it is distinctly said that the reaping of the grain by the deceased is taking place in Sekhet-ḥetep, , or Sekhet-ḥetepet, 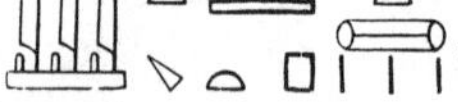.

In chronological order the next picture of Sekhet-ḥetepet to be considered is that from the Papyrus of Ani, and it will be seen at a glance that in details it differs from that already described. Ani adores the gods in the first division, but he burns no incense; the boat in which he paddles is loaded with offerings, and he is seen dedicating an offering to the bearded figure. The legend reads, "Living in peace in Sekhet—winds for the nostrils." The second division contains scenes

Sekhet-Ḥetepet (Papyrus of Ani, British Museum, No. 10,470, sheet 32).

of reaping and treading out of corn, but only three pools of water instead of four. In the third division we see Ani ploughing the land by the side of a stream of untold length and breadth, which is said to contain neither fish nor worms. It is important to note that this division is described as SEKHET-ȦANRU, . The eyot which represents the birthplace of the god of the city has no title, and the larger island, which is separated from it by a very narrow strip of ground, contains a flight of steps, but no gods. In the left-hand corner is a place which is described as "the seat of the Spirits, who are seven cubits in height"; the "grain is three cubits high, and it is the perfect Spirits who reap it." In the other portion of this section are two boats instead of one as in the Papyrus of Nebseni.

In connection with the two pictures of Sekhet-ḥetepet described above, it is important to consider the text which accompanies the older of them, i.e., that of the Papyrus of Nebseni. The deceased is made to say that he sails over the Lake of Ḥetep (i.e., Peace) in a boat which he brought from the house of Shu, and that he has come to the city of Ḥetep under the favour of the god of the region, who is also called Ḥetep. He says, "My mouth is strong, I am equipped [with words "of power to use as weapons] against the Spirits "let them not have dominion over me. Let me be "rewarded with thy fields, O thou god Ḥetep. That "which is thy wish do, O lord of the winds. May I "become a spirit therein, may I eat therein, may I "drink therein, may I plough therein, may I reap "therein, may I fight therein, may I make love therein, "may my words be powerful therein, may I never be "in a state of servitude therein, and may I be iṇ "authority therein. . . . . . [Let me] live with the "god Ḥetep, clothed, and not despoiled by the 'lords "of the north,'[1] and may the lords of divine things "bring food unto me. May he make me to go forward "and may I come forth; may he bring my power to "me there, may I receive it, and may my equipment "be from the god Ḥetep. May I gain dominion over "the great and mighty word which is in my body in "this my place, and by it I shall have memory and "not forget." The pools and places in Sekhet-ḥetepet which the deceased mentions as having a desire to visit are UNEN-EM-ḤETEP, the first large division of the region; NEBT-TAUI, a pool in the second division; NUT-URT, a pool in the first division; UAKH, a pool in the second division, where the *kau*, or "doubles," dwell; TCHEFET, a portion of the third division, wherein the deceased arrays himself in the apparel of Rā; UNEN-EM-ḤETEP, the birthplace of the Great God; QENQENTET, a pool in the first division, where he sees his father, and

[1] Probably the marauding seamen who traded on the coasts of the Mediterranean, and who sometimes landed and pillaged the region near which the primitive Elysian Fields were supposed to have been situated.

looks upon his mother, and has intercourse with his wife, and where he catches worms and serpents and frees himself from them; the Lake of TCHESERT, wherein he plunges, and so cleanses himself from all impurities; ḤAST, where the god ÅRI-EN-ÅB-F binds on his head for him; USERT, a pool in the first division, and SMAM, a pool in the third division of Sekhet-ḥetepet. Having visited all these places, and recited all the words of power with which he was provided, and ascribed praises to the gods, the deceased brings his boat to anchor, and, presumably, takes up his abode in the Field of Peace for ever.

From the extract from the Chapter of Sekhet-Åaru and Sekhet-ḥetepet given above, it is quite clear that the followers of Osiris hoped and expected to do in the next world exactly what they had done in this, and that they believed they would obtain and continue to live their life in the world to come by means of a word of power; and that they prayed to the god Ḥetep for dominion over it, so that they might keep it firmly in their memories, and not forget it. This is another proof that in the earliest times men relied in their hope of a future life more on the learning and remembering of a potent name or formula than on the merits of their moral and religious excellences. From first to last throughout the chapter there is no mention of the god Osiris, unless he be the "Great God" whose birthplace is said to be in the region Unen-em-ḥetep, and nowhere in it is there any suggestion that the permission or favour of Osiris is necessary for those who would enter either Sekhet-Åaru or Sekhet-ḥetep. This seems to indicate that the conceptions about the Other World, at least so far as the "realms of the blest" were concerned, were evolved in the minds of Egyptian theologians before Osiris attained to the high position which he occupied in the Dynastic Period. On the other hand, the evidence on this point which is to be deduced from the Papyrus of Ani must be taken into account.

At the beginning of this Papyrus we have first of all Hymns to Rā and Osiris, and the famous Judgment Scene which is familiar to all. We see the heart of Ani being weighed in the Balance against the symbol of righteousness in the presence of the Great Company of the Gods, and the weighing takes place at one end of the house of Osiris, whilst Osiris sits in his shrine at the other. The "guardian of the Balance" is Anubis, and the registrar is Thoth, the scribe of the gods, who is seen noting the result of the weighing. In the picture the beam of the Balance is quite level, which shows that the heart of Ani exactly counter-balances the symbol of righteousness. This result Thoth announces to the gods in the following words, "In very truth the heart of Osiris hath been weighed, "and his soul hath stood as a witness for him; its case "is right (i.e., it hath been found true by trial) in the "Great Balance. No wickedness hath been found in "him, he hath not purloined the offerings in the "temples,[1] and he hath done no evil by deed or word "whilst he was upon earth." The gods in their reply accept Thoth's report, and declare that, so far as they are concerned, Ani has committed neither sin nor evil. Further, they go on to say that he shall not be delivered over to the monster Āmemet, and they order that he shall have offerings, that he shall have the power to go into the presence of Osiris, and that he shall have a homestead, or allotment, in Sekhet-ḥetepet for ever. We next see Ani being led into the presence of Osiris by Horus, the son of Isis, who reports that the heart of Ani hath sinned against no god or goddess; as it hath also been found just and righteous according to the written laws of the gods, he asks that Ani may have cakes and ale given to him, and the power to appear before Osiris, and that he may take his place among the "Followers of Horus," and be like them for ever.

Now from this evidence it is clear that Ani was considered to have merited his reward in Sekhet-ḥetepet by the righteousness and integrity of his life upon earth as regards his fellow-man, and by the reverence and worship which he paid to every god and every goddess; in other words, it is made to appear that he had earned his reward, or had justified himself by his works. Because his heart had emerged

[1] Ani was the receiver of the ecclesiastical revenues of the gods of Thebes and Abydos, and the meaning here is that he did not divert to his own use any portion of the goods he received.

triumphantly from its trial the gods decreed for him the right to appear in the presence of the god Osiris, and ordered him to be provided with a homestead in Sekhet-ḥetep. There is no mention of any repentance on Ani's part for wrong done; indeed, he says definitely, "There is no sin in my body. I have not "uttered wittingly that which is untrue, and I have "committed no act having a double motive [in my "mind]." As he was troubled by no remembrance of sin, his conscience was clear, and he expected to receive his reward, not as an act of mercy on the part of the gods, but as an act of justice. Thus it would seem that repentance played no part in the religion of the primitive inhabitants of Egypt, and that a man atoned for his misdeeds by the giving of offerings, by sacrifice, and by worship. On the other hand, Nebseni is made to say to the god of Sekhet-ḥetep, "Let me be rewarded "with thy fields, O Ḥetep; but do thou according to "thy will, O lord of the winds." This petition reveals a frame of mind which recognizes submissively the omnipotence of the god's will, and the words "do thou according to thy will" are no doubt the equivalent of those which men of all nations and in every age have prayed—"Thy will be done."

The descriptions of the pictures of Sekhet-ḥetep given above make it evident that the views expressed in the Papyrus of Nebseni differ in some important details from those which we find in the Papyrus of Ani, but whether this difference is due to some general

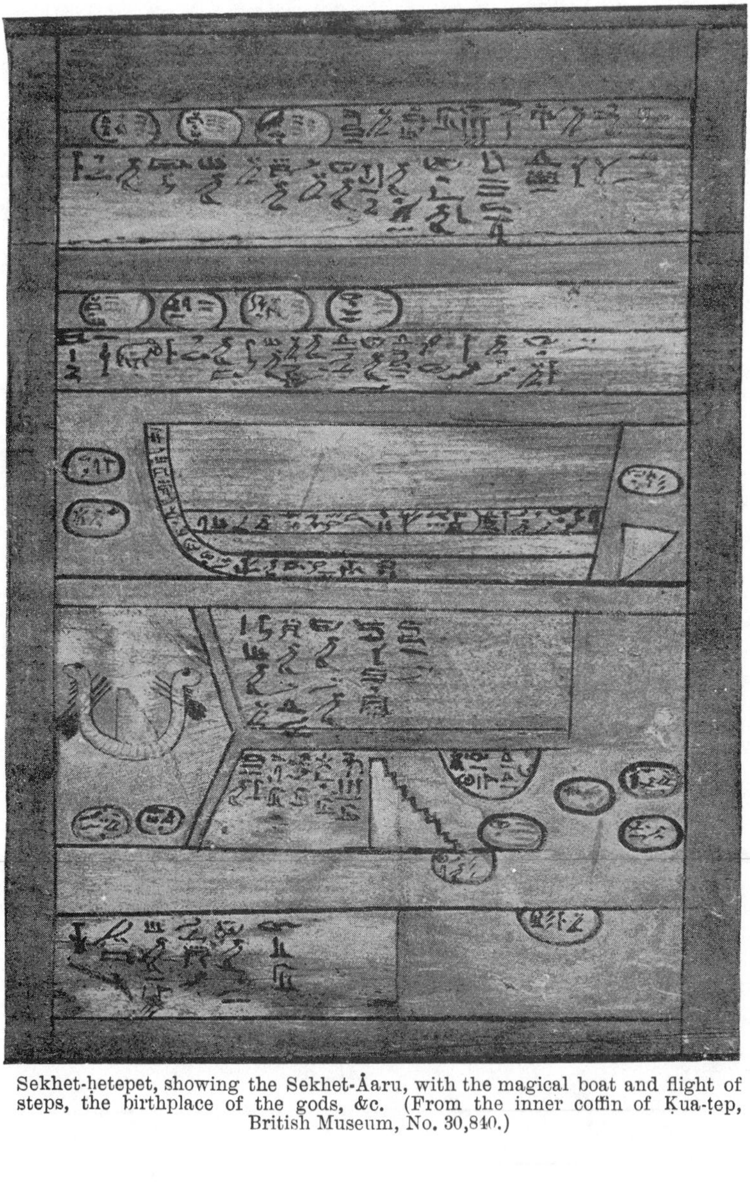

Sekhet-ḥetepet, showing the Sekhet-Åaru, with the magical boat and flight of steps, the birthplace of the gods, &c. (From the inner coffin of Ḳua-ṭep, British Museum, No. 30,840.)

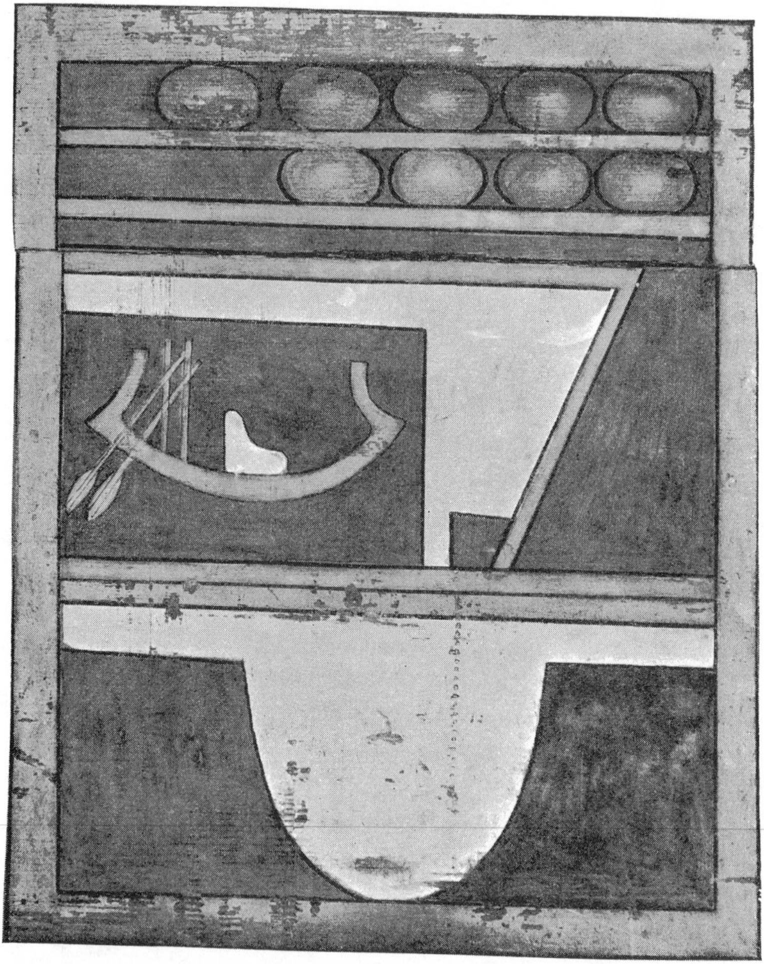

Sekhet-ḥetepet, showing the Sekhet-Aaru, with the magical boat, the nine lakes, the birthplace of the gods, &c. (From the outer coffin of Sen, British Museum, No. 30,841.)

development in religious thought, which took place in the interval between the periods when the papyri were written, cannot be said. There is abundant evidence in the Papyrus of Ani that Ani himself was a very religious man, and we are not assuming too much when we say that he was the type of a devout worshipper of Osiris, whose beliefs, though in some respects of a highly spiritual character, were influenced by the magic and gross material views which seem to have been inseparable from the religion of every Egyptian. Though intensely logical in some of their views about the Other World, the Egyptians were very illogical in others, and they appear to have seen neither difficulty nor absurdity in holding at the same time beliefs which were inconsistent and contradictory. It must, however, in fairness be said that this characteristic was due partly to their innate conservatism in religious matters, and their respect for the written word, and partly to their fear that they might prejudice their interests in the future life if they rejected any scripture or picture which antiquity, or religious custom, or tradition had sanctioned.

Certain examples, however, prove that the Egyptians of one period were not afraid to modify or develop ideas which had come down to them from another, as may be seen from the accompanying illustration. The picture which is reproduced on p. 53 is intended to represent Sekhet-ḥetepet, and is taken from the inner coffin of Ḳua-Ṭep, which was found at Al-Barsha, and is now in the British Museum (No. 30,840); it dates from the period of the XIth Dynasty. From this we see that the country of the blessed was rectangular in shape, and surrounded by water, and intersected by streams, and that, in addition to large tracts of land, there were numbers of eyots belonging to it. In many pictures these eyots are confounded with lakes, but it is pretty clear that the "Islands of the Blessed" were either fertile eyots, or oases which appeared to be green islands in a sea of sand. Near the first section were three, near the second four, near the third four, three being oval, and one triangular; the fourth section was divided into three parts by means of a canal with two arms, and contained the birthplace of the god, and near it were seven eyots; the fifth is the smallest division of all, and has only one eyot near it. Each eyot has a name which accorded with its chief characteristic; the dimensions of three of the streams or divisions are given, the region where ploughing takes place is indicated, and the positions of the staircase and the mystic boat are clearly shown. The name of the god Ḥetep occurs twice, and that of Osiris once.

If now we compare this picture with that from the Papyrus of Nebseni we shall find that the actual operations of ploughing, reaping, and treading out of the corn are depicted on the Papyrus, and that several figures of gods and the deceased have been added. The text speaks of offerings made by the deceased, and of his sailing in a boat, &c., therefore the artist

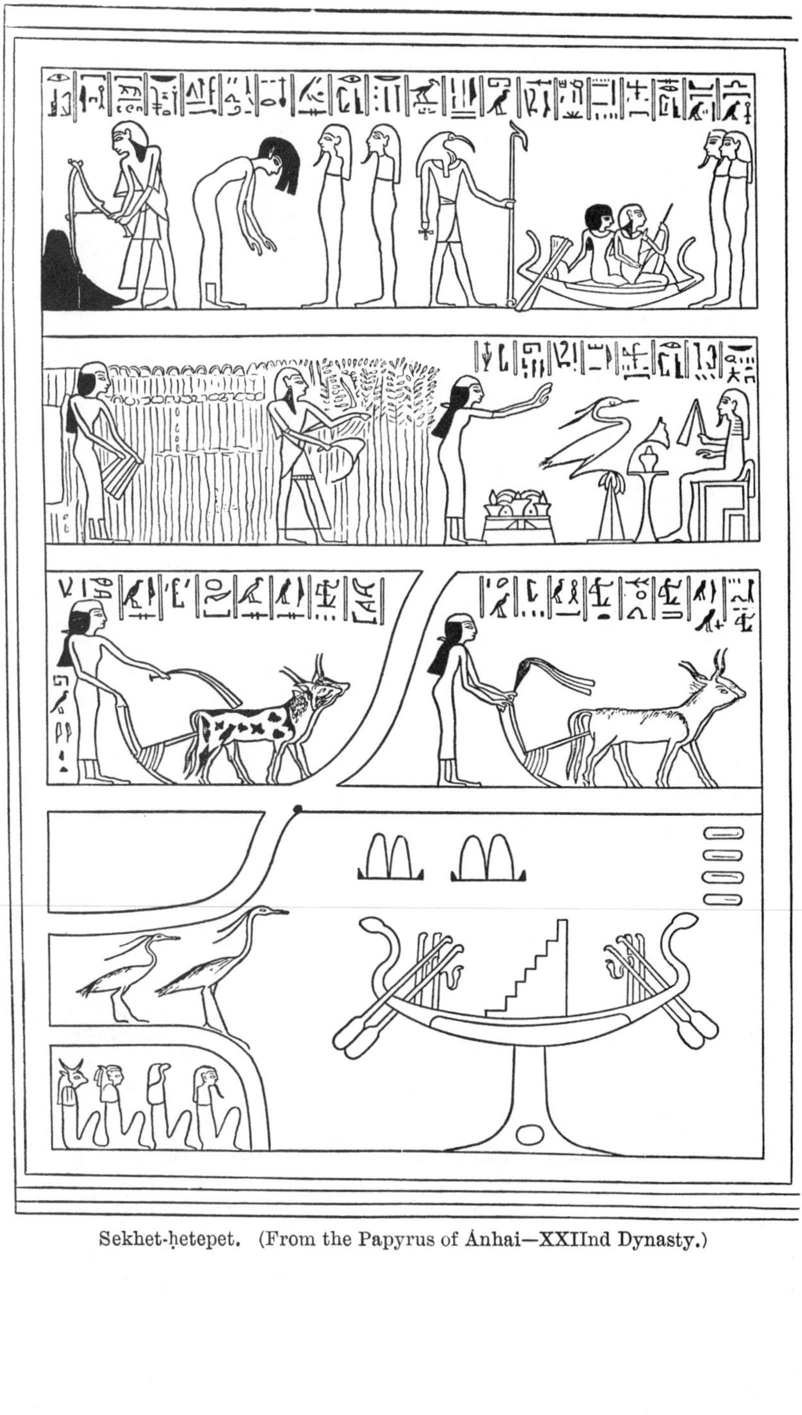

Sekhet-ḥetepet. (From the Papyrus of Ȧnhai—XXIInd Dynasty.)

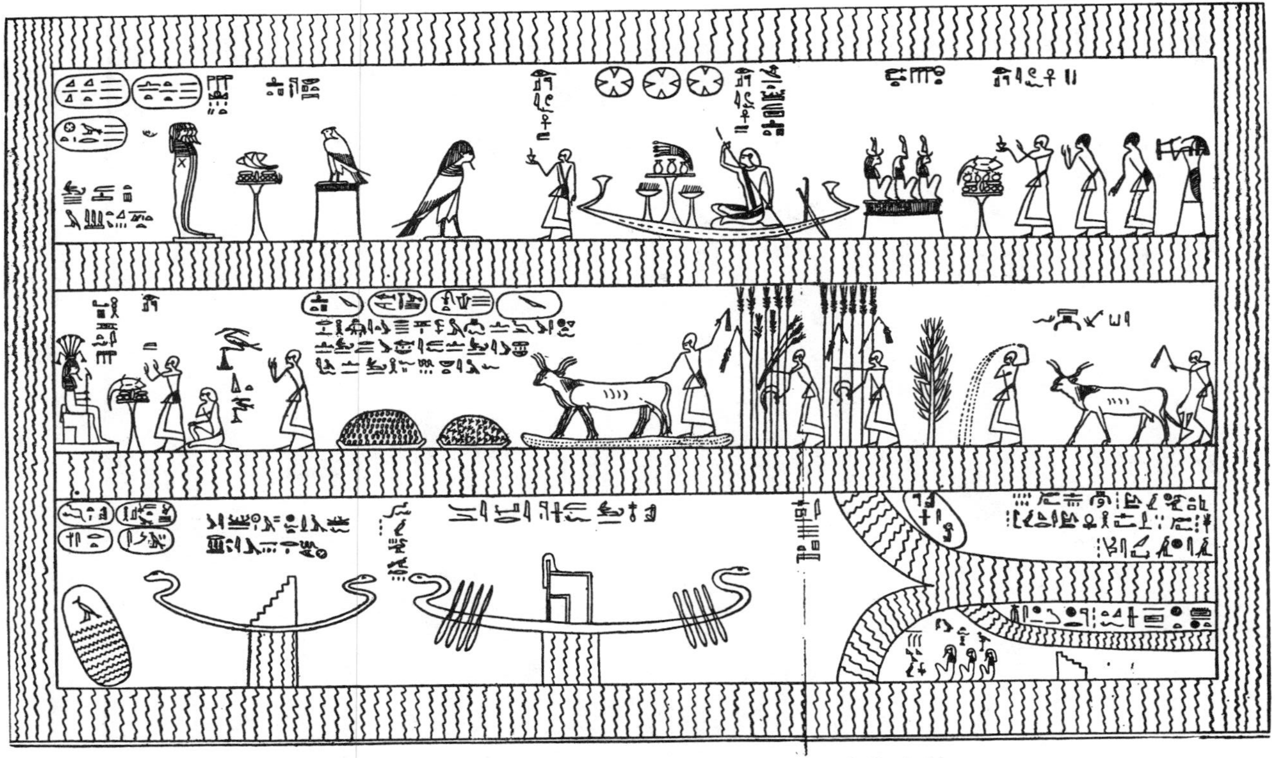

Sekhet-ḥetepet. (From the Turin Papyrus—Ptolemaïc Period.)

added scenes in which he is depicted doing these things; and the lower part of the picture in the Papyrus has been modified considerably. In the second division it may be noted that Nebseni is seen laying both hands on the back of the Bennu bird; there is no authority for this in the older copy of the picture. In the illustration on p. 55, which is reproduced from the coffin of Sen, in the British Museum (No. 30,841), a still simpler form of Sekhet-ḥetepet is seen; here we have only nine eyots, which are grouped together, and no inscription of any kind.

Still further modifications were introduced into the pictures of Sekhet-ḥetepet drawn in later times, and, in order that the reader may be enabled to trace some of the most striking of these, copies of Sekhet-ḥetepet from the Papyrus of Ȧnhai (about B.C. 1040), and from that of Ȧuf-ānkh (Ptolemaïc Period), are reproduced on pp. 59 and 61.

CHAPTER III.

THE REUNION OF THE BEATIFIED AND THEIR RECOGNITION OF EACH OTHER IN THE OTHER WORLD.

HAVING now described Sekhet-ḥetep and the Halls and Gates of the Other World according to the Book of Coming Forth by Day (PER-EM-HRU), we may pass on to consider how far souls in Sekhet-ḥetep had the power to know and recognize each other, and to enjoy intercourse with relatives and friends. From many scenes and passages in texts it has for some time past been clear that husband met wife, and wife met husband again beyond the grave, for in the Papyrus of Ani we see Ani accompanied by his wife in the House of Osiris and in many other places, and in the Papyrus of Ȧnhai [1] we see Ȧnhai bowing before two mummied forms, which represent her father and mother, and seated in a boat side by side with her husband. From the Papyrus of Nebseni [2] we know that the meeting of the deceased with his mother, father, and wife was believed to take place on the island in the first division of Sekhet-ḥetep called Qenqentet, for he says,

[1] See page 59.

[2] *Book of the Dead*, Chapter CX., line 39.

"O Qenqentet, I have entered into thee, and I have "seen the Osiris (*i.e.*, his father) and I have gazed "upon my mother, and had union [with my wife]."[1] Other passages in the PER-EM-HRU indicate that the Egyptian hoped to meet again other people besides his father, mother, and wife, in Sekhet-ḥetep. Thus in the LIInd Chapter the deceased is made to say, "Let me "have the power to manage my own fields in Ṭaṭṭu "(Mendes), and my own growing crops in Ȧnnu (Helio- "polis). Let me live upon bread made from white grain, "and let my beer be made from red grain, and may my "ancestors, and my father and my mother be given unto "me as guardians of my door and for the ordering of "my territory." This petition is repeated in Chapter CLXXXIX., lines 7-9, which was written with the object of preventing a man from being hungry, and so being obliged to eat filth or offal.

From another passage (Chapter LXVIII., lines 13, 14) it is clear that the deceased expected to find in the Other World slaves, or domestic servants, who would help him to cultivate the land which he believed would be allotted to him, and there is reason for supposing that such beings would have been known to him upon earth. He says, "I have gained the mastery over the

[1] 
From this passage it seems that a man who died before his wife expected to find another woman in Sekhet-ḥetep whom he might marry.

"waters, I have gained the mastery over the canal, I "have gained the mastery over the river, I have gained "the mastery over the furrows, I have gained the "mastery over the men who work for me, I have "gained the mastery over the women who work for "me in Neter-khert, I have gained the mastery over "the things which were decreed to me on earth in "Neter-khert." Thus we see that every pious Egyptian hoped to live again with the members of his household after death in Sekhet-ḥetepet.

Now the word which I have rendered "ancestors" in the extract given above is *abtu*, , or *abut*, and its form and evident meaning suggest a comparison with the common Semitic word for "fathers"; the determinatives  prove that the word describes people of both sexes. It occurs twice in the PER-EM-HRU, viz., in Chapter LII., line 6, and Chapter CLXXXIX., line 7,[1] and was translated "persons" by me in 1896; the oldest example of the use of the word was published by M. P. Lacau in *Recueil*, 1904, p. 67.

The very short form of the prayer of the deceased that he may enjoy the companionship of his father and mother in Sekhet-ḥetep is the outcome of a belief which is very ancient; and it finds its fullest expression in an

[1] See my edition of the *Chapters of Coming Forth by Day*, text, pp. 124, 493.

important Chapter, which M. Lacau has published[1] according to the texts on two coffins of the XIth Dynasty, which were found at Al-Barsha, and are now in the Egyptian Museum at Cairo.[2] This Chapter supplies us with some valuable information concerning the reunion and recognition of relatives and friends in Sekhet-ḥetep, and M. Lacau's excellent edition of the text is a useful contribution to the literature which specially concerns Sekhet-ḥetep. The words which stand at the head of the Chapter read, "THE GATHERING TOGETHER OF THE ANCESTORS OF A MAN TO HIM IN NETER KHER,"[3] and the text begins:

"Hail, Rā! Hail, Tem! Hail, Seb! Hail, Nut! Grant "ye unto Sepȧ that he may traverse the heavens (or "sky), that he may traverse the earth, that he may "traverse the waters, that he may meet his ancestors, "may meet his father, may meet his mother, may meet "his grown up sons and daughters, and his brethren, "and his sisters, may meet his friends, both male and "female, may meet those who have been as parents to "him,[4] and his kinsfolk (cousins ?),[5] and those who have "worked for him upon earth, both male and female, and "may meet the concubine whom he loved and knew."

[1] See RECUEIL, 1904, pp. 67-72, and *La Réunion de la Famille*, by M. J. Baillet, in *Journal Asiatique*, Xème Série, tom. iv., p. 307, where a rendering of the Chapter into French will be found.

[2] They bear the numbers 28083 and 28087.

[3] A name of the Underworld.

[4] Perhaps "his uncles and aunts," or "foster-parents."

[5] Or "connexions."

"Behold, O Qema-ur (i.e., Great Creator), make Sepȧ "to rejoin his grown up sons and daughters, and his "concubines whom it is his heart's desire [to meet], and "make thou Sepȧ to rejoin his friends, both male and "female, and those who have worked for him upon earth."

"And if it happen that his father should be turned "aside, or opposed or removed, when he would appear "to him, or his mother when she would reveal herself to "him, when Sepȧ wisheth to rejoin his ancestors, and "his father and his mother, and his men and his women, "and if it happen that there should be turned aside, "or opposed, or done away the reunion of Sepȧ with "his little children, or his reunion with his brethren "and sisters, and with his friends, and with his foster-"parents, and with his kinsfolk, and with those who "have worked for him upon earth: then verily the "heart which is provided [with words of power] shall "be removed from Rā, and the choice oxen for sacrifice "shall be driven away from the altars of the gods, "and the bread-cakes shall not be shattered, and the "white bread-cakes shall not be broken in pieces, the "meat-offering shall not be cut up in the divine "chamber of sacrifice, and for you ropes shall not "be coiled, and for you boats shall not be manned.

"But if he shall be with his father when he "appeareth, and if he shall receive his mother when "she maketh herself visible, and if he shall be "rejoined to his ancestors and to his fathers and his "mothers, and his men and his women, and his little "children, and his beloved ones, and his foster-parents, "and his kinsfolk, and his [grown-up] sons and "daughters, and his concubines, whom it is his heart's "desire [to meet], and his friends, and those who have "worked for him upon earth; and if he shall rejoin all "his ancestors in heaven, and on earth, and in Neter-"kher, and in the sky, and in Ȧakeb (i.e., a region of the "sky), and in Ḥāp (the Nile), and in Aḳeb (i.e. the "watery abyss of the sky), and in Ḥet-ur-kau, and in "Ṭeṭu, and in Ṭeṭet (?), and in Pa-ur, and in Āḥakher, "and in Ābṭu: then verily the bread-cakes shall be "shattered, and the white bread-cakes shall be broken "in pieces, and verily the meat offerings shall be cut up "in the divine chamber of sacrifice, and verily ropes "shall be coiled, and verily boats shall be manned, and "verily the Boat of Rā shall journey on its way, being "rowed by the mariners of the ȦKHEMU-SEKU and the "ȦKHEMU-URTCHU; now his name is unknown, his "name is unknown.

"The goddess Hathor surroundeth Sepȧ with the "magical protection of life, but it is Seb who equippeth "him.[1] The sister of Sepȧ [and] wife [is] the guardian "of the wood of the Great Field.[2] And, moreover,

[1] Or, It is Seb who is the funeral chest, or sarcophagus, the allusion being to the fact that it was in the body of Seb, i.e., the earth, that the deceased was laid.

[2] The meaning of this line is not clear to me. The word *khet* , is often applied to wheat or barley, as the "wood," or "plant" of life. By "Great Field" I understand Sekhet-ḥetep.

"the sister of Sepȧ, the guardian of the wood of the "Great Field, saith, 'Verily thou shalt come with "rejoicing, and thy heart shall be glad, and there shall "be food to Sepȧ, and winds shall be given unto thee, "yea, thy ancestors have commanded this [to be done]'; "therefore shall Sepȧ come with gladness, and his heart "shall be glad, and his ancestors shall be given unto "him. And the great ones of the ancestors of Sepȧ "shall come [to meet him] with joy, and their hearts "shall be glad when they meet him; and they shall "bear in their hands their staves, and their mattocks, "and their tools for ploughing, and their metal (?) "weapons of the earth, and shall deliver him from the "things which the goddess . . . . . . doeth, and from "the actions (?) of Nut, and from the mighty things "which the Two-Lion[1] God doeth to every soul, and "to every god. The ancestors of Sepȧ shall make him "to be delivered . . . . . [Rubric]. May be rejoined "ancestors, and father, and mother, and foster-parents, "and kinsfolk, and young children, and wives, and "concubines, and beloved ones (i.e., friends) male and "female, and servants (i.e., slaves), and the property "of every kind which belongeth to a man, to him in "Neter-kher (the Underworld)."

The Rubric ends with the words, "rope of Maāt, millions of times," which indicate that the whole Chapter, probably including the Rubric, was to be said by the person who wished to rejoin his friends in the

[1] I.e., Shu and Tefnut.

Underworld regularly and unceasingly for millions of times. The phrases *shes maāt ḥeḥ en sep* occur very often in the Theban Recension of the Book of the Dead, and a full list of the passages will be found in the *Vocabulary* to my edition of that work, page 328.

A perusal of the above Chapter shows that it is the expression of beliefs and ideas concerning the future life which belong to a very early period of civilization, and to a time when the Egyptians held most primitive views about their gods. The first paragraph calls upon two forms of the Sun-god, and the god of the earth, and the god of the sky, to allow the deceased to pass through the sky, and the earth, and the waters, to meet his ancestors, mother, father, wives, women of pleasure, sons and daughters of all ages, brothers and sisters, foster-parents (or perhaps uncles and aunts), cousins, connexions, friends of both sexes, "the doers of things," both men and women, etc. Portions of the second paragraph are difficult to render exactly, but it seems that in it the deceased is made to say that in the event of his being prevented from meeting or rejoining his father, mother, and other near and dear relatives and friends, the customary funeral offerings shall be promptly discontinued, and the heart of Rā, which is equipped with its word (of power), shall be removed from him; if, on the other hand, he is made to rejoin all his near and dear relatives and connexions, and is allowed and enabled to travel about and visit them in the various holy cities in heaven, bread and meat offerings shall be duly made on earth for the gods, and the Boat of Rā shall travel on its way. In other words, the deceased undertakes to provide offerings to the gods whom he mentions so long as he is allowed to rejoin his relatives at will, but if he is hindered in any way, he threatens that the progress of Rā himself shall be hindered, and that the god shall suffer the loss of his heart with its word of power.

The Cow-goddess Hathŏr is said to endue him with the protection of her magical power, and the earth-god Seb to supply him with all he needs, and the guardian of the staff [of life] promises that he shall be supplied with food and air in the Great Field, because the ancestors of the deceased who are already living there have given orders to this effect. These same ancestors, it is declared, shall come out to meet him, and as it is possible that some attempt may be made to stop or injure him by Seb (?), Nut, Shu and Tefnut, they shall bring their sticks, and staves, and clubs, and other weapons in their hands, so that they may be ready to defend their relative, and lead him to their abode. Here we have a good description of the manner in which Egyptian peasants have always turned out to defend a friend, and how they have always armed themselves with clubs, and sticks, and handles of ploughs, or flails, whenever a fellow villager had to be rescued from the clutches of foes or from the authorities, and have gone forth to his assistance. Not only would their spirits defend their spirit relative in the Other-

World, but they would also defend him by exactly the same means which their bodies would have employed to defend his body upon earth.

From one end of the chapter to the other there is no mention of Osiris, who in later times became the god of the Resurrection, and it is quite clear that the deceased believed that his reunion with his ancestors and family could be brought about without the help of any god, simply by the recital of the Chapter "Millions of times with never-ending regularity." The repetition of the whole chapter was unnecessary, for if a man recited the words of the Rubric an infinite number of times he would not only be able to rejoin his relatives, but also to regain in the Other World possession of all the property of every kind which he had enjoyed on this earth. The Rubric had, in fact, so far back as B.C. 2600, become a traditional magical formula of a most powerful character, and it must have been composed at the time when the abode of the blessed was supposed to resemble the "great field" in which the men of a village assembled to celebrate a festival, and before the ideas concerning Sekhet-Åaru and Sekhet-ḥetep, with which we are familiar from the "Book of Coming Forth by Day," were evolved. The texts of the Chapter and Rubric are of such interest that copies of them are printed as an Appendix to the present section.

We have now before us all the principal facts which are necessary for forming an opinion as to the kind of heaven which the primitive Egyptian hoped and expected to enjoy, and of the means which he took to obtain admission therein. He either bought, or persuaded, or forced, the "servant of the god," or priest, to give him words of power, i.e., names of gods, and magical formulae, which he learned, or had written down for him, and he relied for admission into the next world upon his knowledge of these, or copies of them which were buried with him, and upon the recitals of them at proper times and seasons by his relatives and friends, and upon offerings made upon earth to the gods on his behalf. Once in the abode of the blessed he was free to go wherever he pleased, to travel from one sacred place to another, to visit his friends, to eat, to drink, to enjoy the society of his wives and women of pleasure, and to rejoice in a family life which was only a glorified duplicate of that which he had known on earth. The gods he knew there were much like himself, and the extent and fervour of the worship which he devoted to them was exactly in proportion to the assistance which they rendered to him; his chief anxiety was not to forget the words of power which he had learned. His occupation consisted in watching the growth of crops, for all the necessary work was performed by beings who carried out his every behest. We now pass on to describe the abode of the blessed according to the "Book Ȧm-Ṭuat" and the "Book of Gates."

APPENDIX TO CHAPTER III.

THE CHAPTER OF THE GATHERING TOGETHER OF A MAN'S ANCESTORS TO HIM IN NETERKHER.

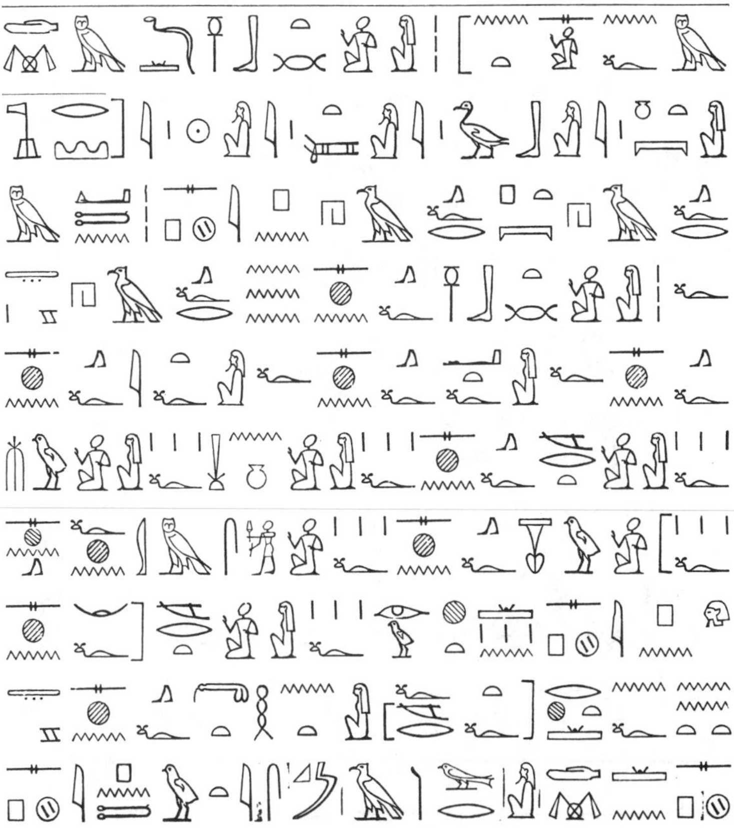

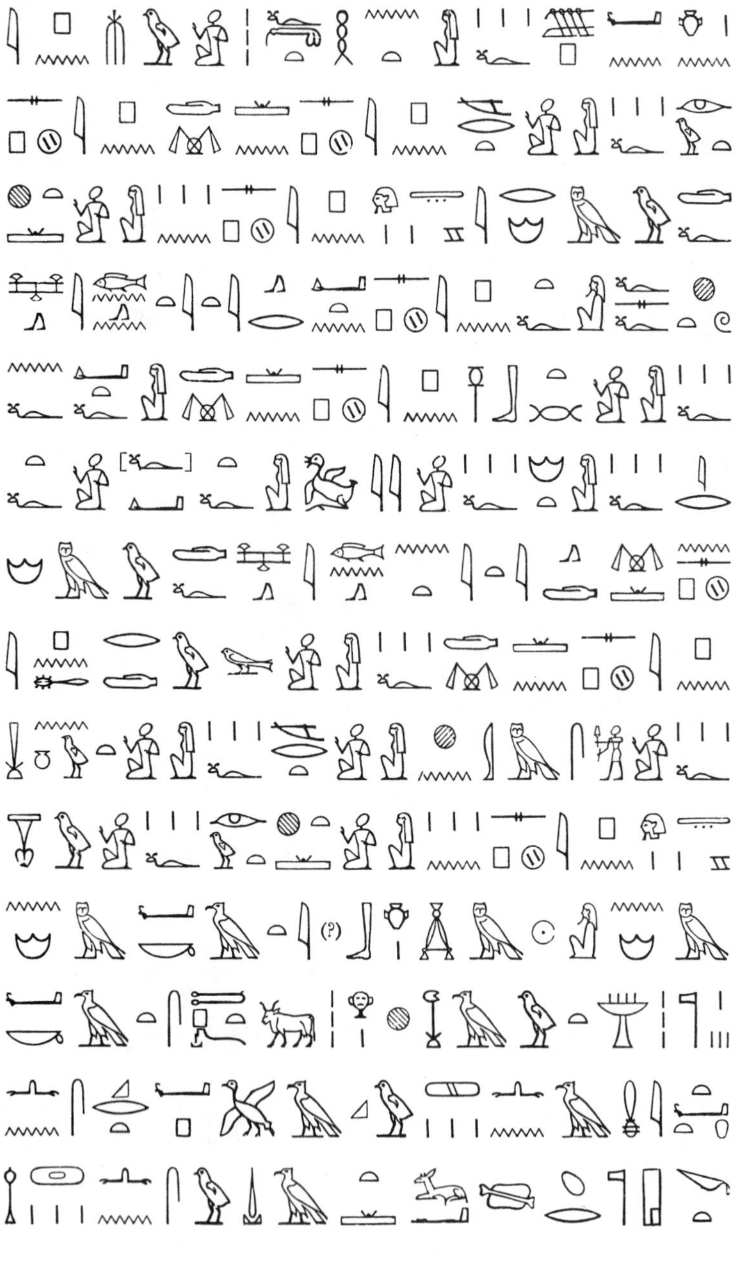

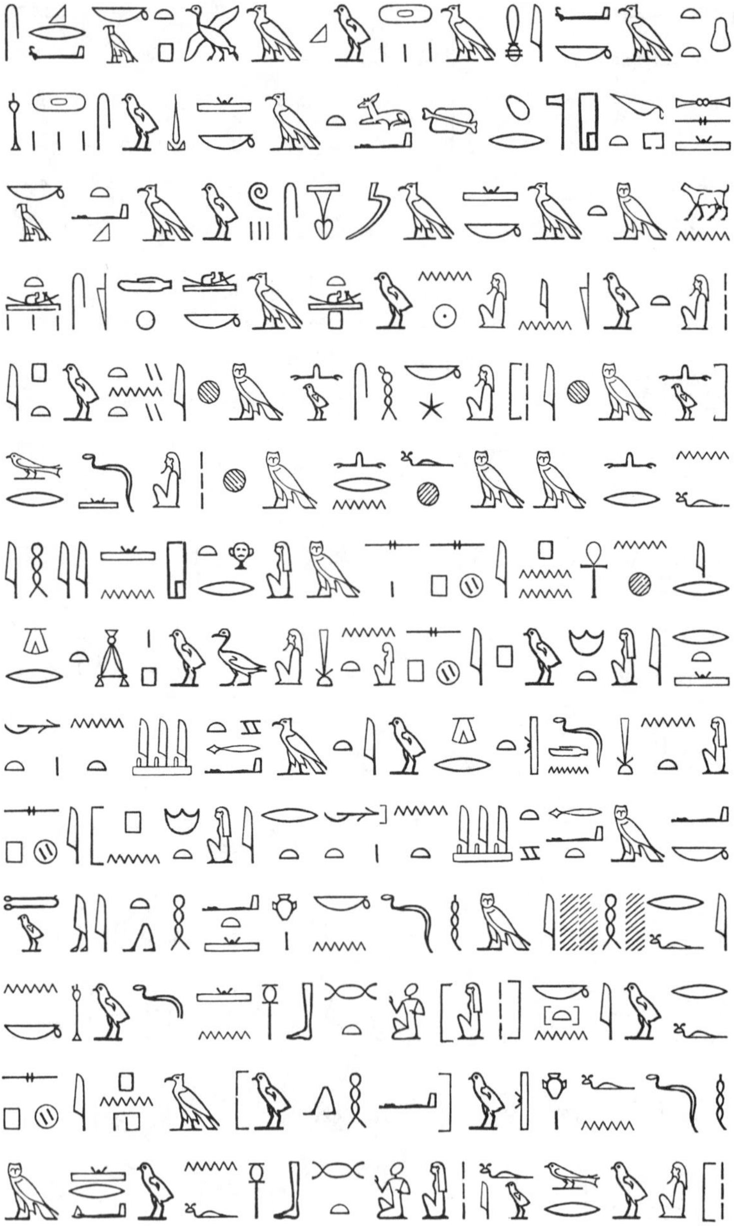

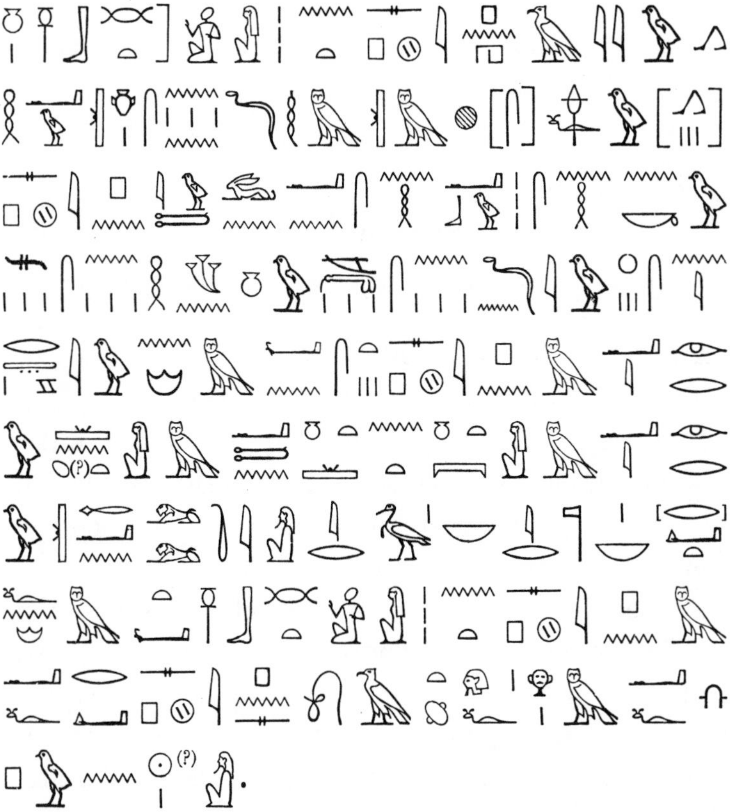

RUBRIC: 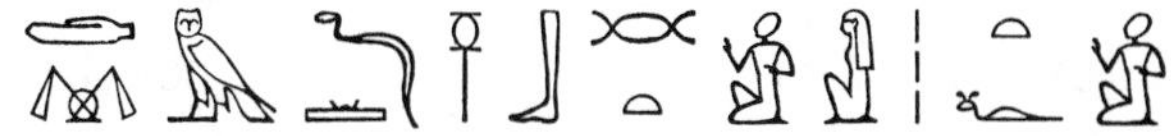

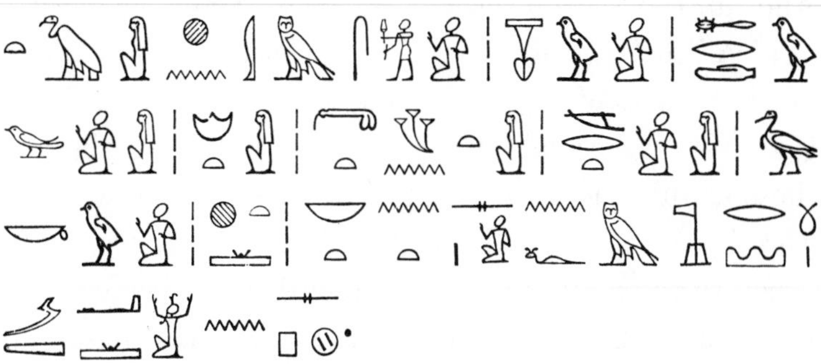

CHAPTER IV.

THE BOOK ȦM-ṬUAT AND THE BOOK OF GATES.

"ȦM-ṬUAT," or SHĀT ȦM-ṬUAT, i.e., the "Book of what is in the Ṭuat," is the name given by the Egyptians to the large funeral book in which the priests of Ȧmen describe the Other World according to the views of their order, and the passage of their god Ȧmen-Rā through the mysterious country which he traversed during the hours of the night. Its object, in the first place, was to impress the followers of Ȧmen and others with the idea of the absolute supremacy of that god in the realms of the dead, and to show that all the gods of the dead in every place of departed spirits throughout Egypt rendered to him homage in one form or another, and in return received benefits from him. And in the second place, the book, being an actual "guide" to the Underworld, with pictures of its various divisions and of the gods and demons of every kind that were to be met with in them, was invaluable for the faithful, who were able to learn from it, whilst they were living upon earth, how to find their way from this world to the next, and how to identify the beings who would attempt to bar their way, and what to say to them. The BOOK ÀM-ṬUAT was a very lengthy work, and a complete copy of it occupied much space whether on walls or on papyrus, and, as poor folk could not afford tombs with chambers and corridors sufficiently large to hold all its texts and pictures, they were obliged to be content with sections, and smaller extracts from it. The need of a shortened form of the work was felt at a comparatively early period after it came into general use, and it is therefore not suprising to find that the priests collected all the facts, which were absolutely essential for the soul that had to travel by itself through the Other World, into a small book that may for convenience be called the "SUMMARY OF ÀM-ṬUAT." In this "Summary" all the lengthy speeches of Àmen-Rā, and the answers of the gods, and, of course, all pictures are omitted.

The oldest copies of the BOOK ÀM-ṬUAT are found in the tombs of Thothmes III., Àmen-ḥetep II., and Àmen-ḥetep III., at Thebes.[1] The most complete and best illustrated copy is that which is found on the walls of

[1] The tombs of Àmen-ḥetep II. and Thothmes III. were discovered by M. Loret in 1898, and, according to the description of them published in the French journals, the copies of Àm-Ṭuat on their walls were in a good state of preservation. The copy of the work in the tomb of Àmen-ḥetep III., written in hieratic, was well preserved in Champollion's time, but is now illegible; see Champollion, *Lettres*, 13e Lettre; and Champollion, *Monuments*, iii. 232-234. The text of the Third Hour was published by Lepsius, *Denkmäler*, iii. 78 and 79. See also *Description de l'Égypte*, Antiq. tom. iii. 193, tom. x., 218, and plates, tom. ii., 80, 81; and Lefébure in *Mémoires Mission Arch. Française*, tom. iii., p. 172.

the tomb of Seti I. at Thebes; here we have eleven out of the twelve sections of the BOOK ȦM-ṬUAT, and the first six divisions of the SUMMARY of the work. The texts and pictures of this fine copy have been completely published by M. Lefébure, assisted by MM. Bouriant, Loret,[1] and Naville, and M. Maspero has translated and discussed the work at length in one of the most important of his luminous dissertations on Egyptian mythology.[2] The next fullest copy is found in the tomb of Rameses VI.,[3] and provides us with eleven divisions, but the drawings are less careful, and the texts are less accurate, and contain numerous additions which appear to represent beliefs of a later period. The history of the BOOK ȦM-ṬUAT shows us that the Egyptians treated it as they treated their older Books of the Dead; they first copied it on the walls of tombs, then on the sides of stone sarcophagi and wooden coffins, and next on rolls of papyrus. We have seen how the kings of the XVIIIth and XIXth Dynasties had it copied on the walls of their tombs, and it must now be noted that Rameses III. decorated his red granite sarcophagus with scenes relating to the course of the sun in the Other World.[4] This sarcophagus is preserved in the Museum

[1] See *Mémoires publiés par les membres de la Miss. Arch. Française*, tom. ii., Paris, 1886.

[2] See *Études de Mythologie et d'Archéologie Egyptiennes*, in *Bibliothèque Égyptologique*, tom. ii., p. 1 ff., Paris, 1893.

[3] See Lefébure, *op. cit.*, tom. iii., fasc. 1, p. 48 ff.

[4] See E. de Rougé, *Notice Sommaire des Monuments Égyptiens exposés dans les Galeries du Musée du Louvre*, Paris, 1876, p. 51.

of the Louvre in Paris, and its cover is in the Fitzwilliam Museum, Cambridge. Among other sarcophagi inscribed with text and pictures from the BOOK ȦM-ṬUAT may be mentioned those of: 1. Horus, son of Tarut-en-Sekhet;[1] 2. Tcheṭ-ḥrȧ, a priest of Ptaḥ;[2] 3. Qem-Ḥāp,[3] the son of Takhāau; and Nekht-neb-f. Now, whilst on the walls of tombs, and on the side of sarcophagi, divisions Nos. I.-XI. are found, the only divisions which are met with on papyrus are Nos. IX.-XII. Thus the Louvre Papyrus, No. 3071, which formed the subject of a special study by Devéria[4] and Pierret,[5] and the Turin Papyrus, published by Lanzone,[6] and the Leyden Papyrus T. 71,[7] contain each the last four divisions only. The Leyden Papyrus T. 72[8] contains divisions X., XI., and XII., the Berlin Papyrus No. 3001 contains divisions IX., X. and XII., and the Berlin Papyrus No. 3005 contains divisions X. and XI. only. There are several papyri in the British Museum inscribed with similar selections.

[1] See E. de Rougé, *Notice Sommaire*, p. 52. It contains the figures of the eleven divisions, with very few inscriptions; see Jéquier, *Le Livre de ce qu'il y a dans l'Hades*, p. 25.

[2] See E. de Rougé, *Notice Sommaire*, p. 52. This sarcophagus is made of basalt, is beautifully cut, and was brought to France by Champollion. See also Sharpe, *Egyptian Inscriptions*, vol. ii., plates 1-24.

[3] See Schäfer in Jéquier, *op. cit.*, p. 26, notes 3 and 4.

[4] See *Catalogue des Manuscrits Égyptiens*, Paris, 1881, p. 15.

[5] See Pierret, *Études Égyptologiques*, tom. ii., p. 103-148.

[6] See Lanzone, *Le Domicile des Esprits*, Paris, 1879, folio.

[7] See *Catalogue du Musée Égyptien de Leyde*, pp. 253-255.

[8] See Jéquier, *op. cit.*, p. 27.

The principal authorities for the text of the SUMMARY of ȦM-ṬUAT are those which M. Jéquier consulted when preparing his edition, viz., the Berlin Papyrus No. 3001, the Leyden Papyrus T. 71, the Louvre Papyrus No. 3071, the Papyrus of Turin, published by Lanzone, and, of course, the tomb of Seti I., which gives the text of the first six divisions. The most valuable of all these is the Leyden Papyrus T. 71, of which an excellent fac-simile, with a complete translation, was published by Drs. Pleyte and Boeser in 1894;[1] in this papyrus the text of the SUMMARY only fills 119 short columns, and the great popularity of the work is attested by the fact that the priests of Ȧmen were induced to compress all the most important portions of Ȧm-Ṭuat into so small a compass.

Similar in many details, but widely different from the BOOK ȦM-ṬUAT in point of fundamental doctrine, is the great funeral work to which the names "Book of the Lower Hemisphere,"[2] "Book of Hades," "Livre de l'Enfer," have been given. A glance at the pictures which accompany the texts of this Book is sufficient to show that it deals with the passage of the Sun-god through the Other World during the hours of the night, but, as M. Maspero pointed out long ago, it is wrong to

[1] *Papyrus Funéraire Hiéroglyphique, Shā-ȧm-Ṭûa* (T. 71). Publié dans la 32ième Livraison des *Monuments Égyptiens du Musée*, Leyden, 1894.

[2] See Devéria, *Catalogue*, Sect. ii., *Le Livre de L'Hémisphère Inférieur*. .

call the region through which the god passes by the name of "Lower Hemisphere," for it suggests that it is below the surface of our earth, which is not the case. There is much to be said also against the titles "Book of Hades," and "Book of Hell," and as among the prominent characteristics which distinguish it from the BOOK ÅM-ṬUAT is a series of gates, it will be convenient and more correct to call it the "BOOK OF GATES." The form in which we first know this work is, clearly, not older than the XVIIIth or XIXth Dynasty, but many parts of it are very much more ancient. As the BOOK ÅM-ṬUAT was composed with the view of asserting the absolute supremacy of Åmen-Rā in the Other World, so the BOOK OF GATES was compiled to prove that, in spite of the pretensions of the priests of Åmen-Rā, Osiris, the ancient god of the dead, was still the over-lord of the Underworld, and that his kingdom was everlasting. The BOOK ÅM-ṬUAT practically ignores Osiris, and is silent even concerning the doctrines of the Judgment and Sekhet-Ḥetepet, and in fact about all the fundamental principles of the religion of Osiris as regards the dead, which had been universally believed throughout Egypt for thousands of years.

The most complete copy of the BOOK OF GATES known to us is found inscribed on the alabaster sarcophagus of Seti I,[1] king of Egypt about B.C. 1375,

[1] See *The Alabaster Sarcophagus of Oimenephtah I., King of Egypt, now in Sir John Soane's Museum, Lincoln's Inn Fields, drawn*

and it consists of two parts:—1. A series of texts and pictures which describe the progress of the Boat of the Sun-god to the kingdom of Osiris, the Judgment of the Dead, the life of the beatified in Sekhet-Ḥetepet, the punishment of the wicked, and the foes of the Sun-god. 2. A series of texts and pictures which represent the magical ceremonies that were performed in very ancient times with the view of reconstructing the body of the Sun, and of making him rise each day. That the BOOK OF GATES embodied many of the most ancient Egyptian religious beliefs and traditions is evident, but it is quite certain that it never became as popular as the BOOK ȦM-ṬUAT; it must always be a matter for wonder that Seti I., having covered several walls in his tomb with the texts of this Book, should fill several more with sections of the BOOK OF GATES, and then have a complete copy of it cut and inlaid on the sides of his alabaster sarcophagus and its cover!

We may now consider the region through which the Sun-god passed during the hours of the night, and the descriptions of its divisions and their inhabitants which are furnished by the BOOK ȦM-ṬUAT

y *Joseph Bonomi, and described by Samuel Sharpe*, London, 1864. description of the pictures and texts was given by M. Pierret in e *Revue Archéologique* for 1870; small portions of the text were scussed by Goodwin and Renouf in *Aeg. Zeit.*, 1873, p. 138, and 74, p. 101; and an English rendering of the whole text was given E. Lefébure, in the *Records of the Past*, vol. x., p. 79 ff., vol. xii., 1 ff.

and the BOOK OF GATES. This region was called by the Egyptians "Ṭat," or "Ṭuat," or "Ṭuaut";[1] the oldest form of the name, and that which is met with in the earliest of the Pyramid Texts is "Ṭat," ; the chief god of the Ṭuat was called "Ṭuat," or "Ṭuaut," , and the beings who lived therein were called "Ṭuatiu," , or . The meaning of the name Ṭat, or Ṭuat, is unknown, and it is useless to speculate upon it or to invent etymologies for it; it was applied to the home of the beatified spirits and the damned, no doubt in predynastic times, and the exact meaning which it conveyed to the minds of those who first used it has been lost. To describe its general situation is less difficult, but not many details as to its exact extent are forthcoming.

To find a word which shall at once describe the situation and character of the Ṭuat is impossible, for the reason that the Egyptian conception of the place of departed spirits is unique. The Ṭuat is not the "Lower Hemisphere," because it is not under the ground, and though for want of a better word I have frequently used "Underworld," when speaking of

[1] The common forms of the names are: 
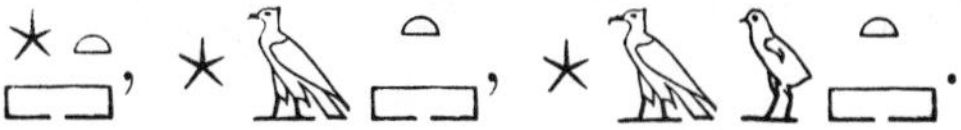.

the Ṭuat, it is unsatisfactory, for unless it is specially defined to mean the place of departed spirits in general, it produces a wrong impression in the mind. Again, the word Ṭuat must not be rendered by "Hades," or "Hell," or "Sheol," or "Jehannum," for each of these words has a limited and special meaning. On the other hand, the Ṭuat possessed the characteristics of all these names, for it was an "unseen" place, and it contained abysmal depths of darkness, and there were pits of fire in it wherein the damned, i.e., the enemies of Osiris and Rā, were consumed, and certain parts of it were the homes of monsters in various shapes and forms which lived upon the unfortunate creatures whom they were able to destroy. On the whole, the word Ṭuat may be best rendered by "The Other World,"[1] or "Underworld," always provided that it be clearly understood that the Egyptians never believed it to be under the earth.

In inventing a situation for the Ṭuat the Egyptians appear to have believed that the whole of the habitable world, that is to say, Egypt, was surrounded by a chain of mountains lofty and impassable, just like the Jebel Ḳâf[2] of Muhammadan writers; from one hole in this mountain the sun rose, and in another he set. Outside this chain of mountains, but presumably quite close to them, was the region of the Ṭuat; it ran parallel with

[1] See Maspero, *Études de Mythologie*, tom. ii. p. 27.

[2] See Yâḳûṭ's Geographical Dictionary, ed. Wüstenfeld, tom. iv., page 18.

the mountains, and was on the plane either of the land of Egypt or of the sky above it. On the outside of the Ṭuat was a chain of mountains also, similar to that which encompassed the earth, and so we may say that the Ṭuat had the shape of a valley; and from the fact that it began near the place where the sun set, and ended near the place where he rose, it is permissible to say that the Ṭuat was nearly circular in form. That this is the view taken by the Egyptians themselves is proved by the scene which is reproduced in the Book of Gates (page 303). Here we have the body of Osiris bent round in a circle, and the hieroglyphics enclosed within it declare that it is the Ṭuat. With the identification of Osiris with the Ṭuat we need not deal here, but it is important for our purpose to note that in the time of Seti I. the Egyptians assigned a circular form to the Ṭuat. The view put forward by Signor Lanzone to the effect that the Ṭuat was the place comprised between the arms of the god Shu and the body of the sky-goddess Nut, whom, according to the old legend, he raised up from the embrace of her husband the Earth-god Seb, so forming the earth and the sky, thus appears to be untenable.[1]

Now as the Ṭuat was situated on the other side of the mountains which separated it from Egypt, and from the sun, moon, and stars which lighted the skies of that country, it follows that it must have been a region which was shrouded in the gloom and darkness of night,

[1] See Lanzone, *Le domicile des Esprits*, p. 1.

and a place of fear and horror. At each end of the Ṭuat was a space which was neither wholly darkness nor wholly light, the western end being partially lighted by the setting sun, and the eastern end by the rising sun. From the pictures in the BOOK ÅM-ṬUAT and the BOOK OF GATES we learn that a river flowed through the Ṭuat, much as the Nile flowed through Egypt, and we see that there were inhabitants on each of its banks, just as there were human beings on each side of the Nile. At one place the river of the Ṭuat joined the great celestial waters which were supposed to form the source of the earthly Nile.

How, or when, or where the belief arose it is impossible to say, but it seems that at a very early period the inhabitants of Egypt thought that the souls of the dead when they departed from this world made their way into the Ṭuat, and took up their abode there, and long before the Dynastic Period the Ṭuat was regarded throughout Egypt as the kingdom of the dead. Certain sections of it were considered to belong by traditional right to certain cities, e.g., Heliopolis, Memphis, Herakleopolis, Abydos, etc., each possessing its own "Other World" and gods of the dead, and all these had to be considered by the theologians who formulated general plans of the Ṭuat. How the Egyptians imagined the dead to live in the Ṭuat, or upon what, is not clear, but they seem to have thought that all their wants could be provided for by the use of words of power, amulets, talismans, etc. In the earliest times of all the souls of the dead remained in the "Other World" which belonged to their town or city, but when Osiris attained to the supreme power over the dead, it was only natural that departed spirits should flock from all parts of Egypt to his kingdom, wherein the beatified enjoyed a life very much like that which they had lived upon earth. The celestial kingdom of Osiris, that is to say, Sekhet-Ḥetepet or Sekhet-Ȧaru, was originally a copy of some very fertile region in the Delta, and, to the very end of the period of native Egyptian rule, the Egyptian Paradise consisted of green fields intersected by streams of living, i.e., running water, with abundant crops of wheat and barley, and its appearance represented a typical middle-Delta landscape. So long as Osiris had his kingdom in the Delta, probably near the ancient city of Mendes, the souls of the dead travelled from south to north, but at a later period, when Osiris had absorbed the position and attributes of KHENT-ȦMENTI, perhaps the oldest god of the dead of Abydos, departed spirits made their way from north to south, so that they might enter the Ṭuat by the "Gap" in the mountains there. Still later, the Egyptians reverted to their old belief as to the situation of the domain of Osiris, and the books which deal with the Ṭuat always assume that it lies far away to the north, and were intended to guide souls on their way to it.

The ultimate fate of the souls of human beings who had departed to the Ṭuat must always have been a matter of speculation to the Egyptians, and at the best they could only *hope* that they had traversed the long, dark, and dangerous valley in safety. The same may be said of numbers of the gods, who in very early times were believed to possess a nature which closely resembled that of men and women, and to be in danger of extermination in the Ṭuat. Of the gods the only one about whose successful passage of the Ṭuat there was no doubt was Rā, or according to the priests of Ȧmen, Ȧmen-Rā, for he rose each morning in the East, and it was manifest to all that he had overcome whatsoever dangers had threatened him in the Ṭuat during the past night. This being so, it became the object of every man to obtain permission to travel in the boat of Rā through the Ṭuat, for those who were followers of Osiris could disembark when it arrived at his kingdom, and those who wished to remain with Rā for ever could remain in it with him. To each class of believer a guide to the Ṭuat was necessary, for up to a certain place in that region both the followers of Osiris and the followers of Rā required information about the divisions of the Ṭuat, and knowledge of the names of the Halls and Gates, and of the beings who guarded them and who were all-powerful in the land of darkness. For the worshippers of Ȧmen, or Ȧmen-Rā, the Book Ȧm-Ṭuat was prepared, whilst the followers of Osiris pinned their faith to the Book of Gates. From each of these Books we find that the Sun-god was not able to pass through the Ṭuat by virtue of the powers which he possessed as the great god of the world, but only through his knowledge of the proper words of power, and of magical names and formulae, before the utterance of which every denizen of the Ṭuat was powerless. Osiris had, of course, passed through the Ṭuat, and seated himself on his throne in the "House of Osiris," but even he would have been unable to perform his journey in safety through the Ṭuat without the help of the words of power which "Horus, the son of Isis, the son of Osiris," had uttered, and the magical ceremonies which he had performed. Words and ceremonies alike he learned from Isis, who, according to a later tradition, obtained the knowledge of them from Thoth, the Divine Intelligence. Now if Osiris and Rā had need of such magical assistance in their passage through the Ṭuat, how much greater must have been the need of man!

The Ṭuat was, according to the authors of the funeral works of the XVIIIth and XIXth Dynasties, divided into twelve portions, some of which are called "SEKHET" 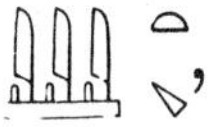, i.e., "Field," others "NUT" , i.e., "City," others "ĀRRIT" 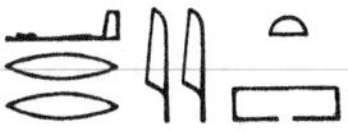, i.e., "Hall," and others "QERRET" , i.e., "Circle." The first indicates that the region to which it was applied was believed to consist of cultivated lands, the second suggests a place where there were many buildings and houses, the third a territory which was vast and spacious, and which, in some respects, represented an empty courtyard, or hall, or compound of a house, and the fourth probably describes the circular form of some divisions. Now since the Ṭuat was traversed by the sun-god during the hours of the night, the Egyptians regarded each of these divisions as the equivalent of an hour, and hence it came that the sections of the Books of the Ṭuat were often called "Hours," the First Hour corresponding to the First Division, and so on up to the Twelfth Hour. It will, however, be urged that during the summer in Egypt the night is not twelve hours long, but the answer to this objection is that the first division is in reality only the ante-chamber of the Ṭuat, and the twelfth the ante-chamber of the sky of this world, into which the Sun-god enters to begin the new day. The divisions II. to XI. of the Ṭuat have an entirely different character from the ante-chamber of the Ṭuat and that of the sky.

It has already been said that a river flows from one end of the Ṭuat to the other, and its existence can only be explained in one way. At a very early period of their history the Egyptians believed that the Sun-god passed over the sky, which they held to be a vast watery mass, in some kind of boat; the belief in the existence of such a boat was absolutely necessary, for unless the fire of the sun was protected from contact with the water of the sky, it would, they argued, be extinguished. So far back as the period when the Pyramids of Gîza were built, the existence of two boats was assumed; in one, called MĀṬET, the Sun-god sailed from the time he rose until noon, and in the other, called SEKTET, he sailed from noon to sunset. When the conception of the existence of the Ṭuat was evolved, and the belief that the Sun-god passed through it each night gained credence, it became necessary to find some means of transport for the god. It was impossible to remove him from his boat, which was, like himself, eternal, hence its name, "Boat of Millions of Years," and even if it had been possible the difficulty remained either of taking his boat back from the place of sunset to the place of sunrise, so that it might be ready for him on the following morning when he emerged from the Ṭuat, or of providing him with a new boat each day. The simplest way was to assume in the Ṭuat the existence of a river which was in direct communication with the watery mass of the sky on which Rā sailed by day, and to make the Sun-god to enter the Ṭuat on it. This was the natural way out of the difficulty, for apart from the fact that no other means of transport for the god could be devised, it was consistent with experience that kings, and nobles, and high officials, always travelled through Egypt by water. No animal and no chariot could convey the god through the Ṭuat, for, even had animals or chariots suitable for the purpose existed, they must have been consumed by the god's fire. We shall see later that there was one division of the Ṭuat through which the Sun-god could not pass even in his boat, and that he was obliged to leave it and travel on the back of a serpent.

From the titles of the Book Ȧm Ṭuat, as it is found in the tomb of Seti I., we may gather that the pictures accompanying the texts were supposed to be exact copies of the divisions of the Ṭuat as they actually existed in Ȧmenti, i.e., the "hidden place," or the "Other World," and the texts were supposed to give the traveller in the Ṭuat all the information he could possibly require concerning the "souls, the gods, the shadows, the spirits, the gods of the Ṭuat, the gates of the Ṭuat, the hours and their gods, and the gods who praise Rā, and those who carry out his edicts of destruction." The divisions of the Ṭuat according to this work are:—

Division I. *Names*—Maāti, , and Net-Rā, 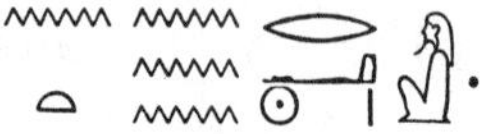.

Warder—Ȧrnebȧui, .

Hour-goddess—Ushem-ḥātiu-kheftiu-nu-Rā, .

Division II. *Name*—Urnes, 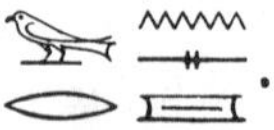.

Warder—Ȧm-nebȧui,  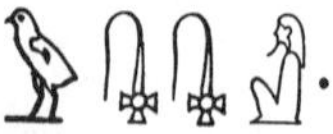.

Hour-goddess—Seshet-māket-neb-s, .

Division III. *Name*—NET-NEB-UĀ-KHEPER-ĀUT,

Warder—KHETRȦ, 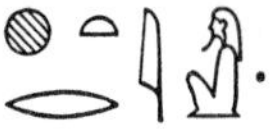

Hour-goddess—ṬENT-BAIU, 

Division IV. *Name*—ĀNKHET-KHEPERU, 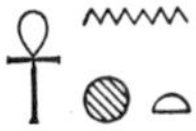

Name of the gate of this Circle—ȦMENT-SETHAU, 

Hour-goddess—URT-EM-SEKHEMU-S,

Division V. *Name*—ȦMENT, 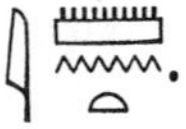

Name of the gate of this Circle—ĀḤĀ-NETERU, 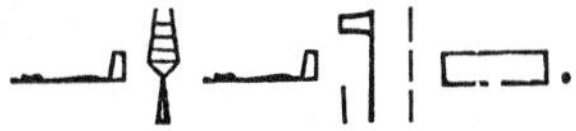

Hour-goddess—SEKMET-ḤER-ȦBT-UȦA-S,

Division VI. *Name*—METCHET-NEBT-ṬUAT,

Name of the gate of this City—SEPṬ-METU, 

Hour-goddess—MESPERIT - ȦR - ĀT - MAĀTU, 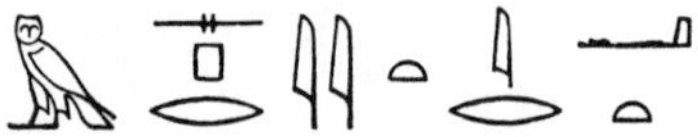

Division VII. *Name*—TEPḤET-SHETAT, 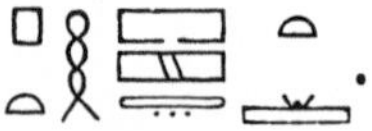

Name of the gate of this City—RUTI-EN-ȦSȦR, 

Hour-goddess--KHESFET-HȦU-ḤESQETU-NEḤA - ḤRȦ, 

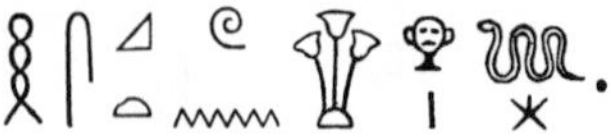

Division VIII. *Name*—ṬEBAT-NETERU-S, 

Name of the Gate—ĀḤĀ-ȦN-URṬ-NEF, 

Hour - goddess — NEBT - USHA, 

Division IX. *Name*—BEST - ȦRU - ĀNKHET - KHEPERU, 

Name of the Gate—SA - EM - ḲEB, [1]

[1] Or, SA-AḲEB, reading  for .

Hour-goddess—ṬUATET - MĀKTET - EN - NEB-S, 

Division X. *Name*—METET-QA-UTCHEBU, 

Name of the Gate—ĀA-KHEPERU-MES-ÀRU, 

Hour - goddess — ṬENṬENIT - UḤETES - KHAK-ÀB, 

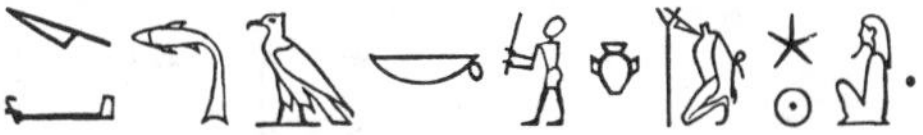

Division XI. *Name*—RE - EN - QERERT - ÀPT - KHATU, 

Name of the Gate—SEKHEN-ṬUATIU, 

Hour - goddess — SEBIT - NEBT - UÀA - KHESFET-SEBÀ-EM-PERT-F, 

Division XII. *Name*—KHEPER - KEKIU - KHĀU - MEST, 

Name of the Gate—THEN-NETERU,

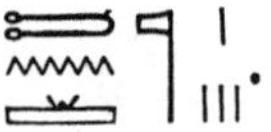

Hour-goddess — MAA-NEFERT-RĀ,

The divisions of the Ṭuat according to the BOOK OF GATES are usually marked by Gates, which are guarded by serpents; they are as follows:—

Division I. *Name of Guardian Gods.*—SET and TAT.

Name of the Region.—SET-ÅMENTET,

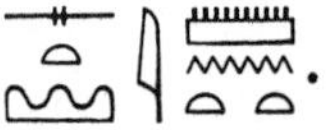 Western Vestibule.

Division II. *Name of the Serpent* — SAA-SET,

Division III. *Name of the Serpent* — AQEBI,

Name of the Gate—SEPṬET-UAUAU,

Division IV. *Name of the Serpent* — TCHEṬBI,

Name of the Gate—NEBT-S-TCHEFAU,

Division V. *Name of the Serpent*—TEKA-ḤRÅ, 

Name of the Gate—ÅRIT, 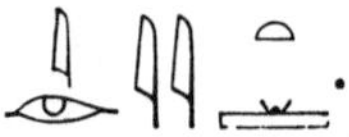

Division VI. At the entrance to this division is the Judgment Hall of Osiris.

Name of the Serpent—SET-EM-MAAT-F,

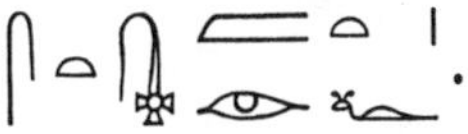

Name of the Gate — NEBT - ĀḤĀ,

Division VII. *Name of the Serpent*—AKHA-EN-MAAT,

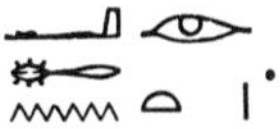

Name of the Gate—PESṬIT, 

Division VIII. *Name of the Serpent* — SET - ḤRÅ,

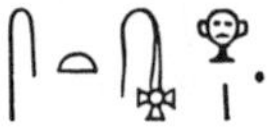

Name of the Gate — BEKHKHI,

Division IX. *Name of the Serpent*—ĀB-TA, 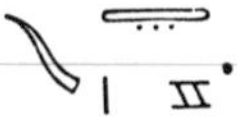

Name of the Gate—ĀAT-SHEFSHEFT,

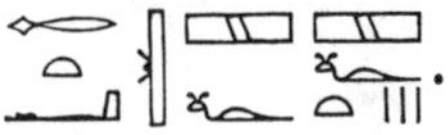

Division X. *Name of the Serpent*—SETHU, 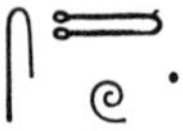

Name of the Gate — TCHESERIT,

Division XI. *Name of the Serpent*—ÅM-NETU-F,

.

Name of the Gate—SHETAT-BESU,

.

Division XII. *Names of the Serpents*—SEBI, ,

and RERI, .

Name of the Gate — ṬESERT-BAIU,

. Eastern Vestibule.

From the above lists it is clear that in the BOOK ÅM-ṬUAT the actual divisions of the Ṭuat are considered without any reference to Gates, even if such existed in the scheme of the priests of Åmen-Rā, and that according to the Book of Gates, the Gates of the divisions in the Ṭuat are the most important and most characteristic features. The absence of Gates in the BOOK ÅM-ṬUAT is not difficult to explain; the compilers of this work, wishing to exalt Åmen-Rā, did away with the Gates, which were the most important features of the kingdom of Osiris, so that the necessity for Åmen-Rā to seek permission of their warders, who were appointed by Osiris, was obviated.

CHAPTER V.

THE CONTENTS OF THE BOOK ÅM-ṬUAT AND THE BOOK OF GATES COMPARED.

THE WESTERN VESTIBULE OR ANTECHAMBER OF THE ṬUAT.

HAVING already briefly described the general character of the BOOK ÅM-ṬUAT and the BOOK OF GATES we may pass at once to the comparison of their contents. For the sake of convenience, in describing the various divisions of the Ṭuat let us assume that we are occupying the position of a disembodied spirit who is about to undertake the journey through the Ṭuat, and that we are standing at the entrance to the First Division awaiting the arrival of the BOAT OF THE SUN-GOD, on which we hope to have permission to travel. Every funeral rite has been duly and adequately performed, the relatives and friends of the deceased have made the legally appointed offerings, and said all the prayers proper for the occasion, amulets inscribed with magical names and formulae have been attached to the body, copies of sacred writings have been laid on it or near it in the tomb, the priests have said the final words which will secure for the soul a passage in the Boat of Rā, and a safe-conduct to the abode of the blessed, whether this abode be in the boat itself or in the kingdom of Osiris. The result of all these things is that we have been enabled to pass through the tomb out into the region which lies immediately to the west of the mountain-chain on the west bank of the Nile, which we may consider as one mountain and call Manu,[1] or the mountain of the Sunset. At this place are gathered together numbers of spirits, all bent on making their way to the abode of the blessed; these are they who have departed from their bodies during the day, and they have made their way to the sacred place in Western Thebes where they can join the Boat of the Sun-god.

Some are adequately equipped with words of power, and amulets, and their ultimate safety is assured, but others are less well provided, and it will be the fate of many of these to remain in the place wherein they now are, and never to enter the House of Osiris or the Boat of Rā. They will not suffer in any way whatsoever, but will simply remain there, protecting themselves as best they can by any words of power they may possess until such time as they are overcome by some hostile being, when they will die and take their places among the other dead spirits, having failed to present themselves in the Judgment Hall of Osiris.

[1] In Egyptian, , or, .

Now the dead who are in the various divisions of the Ṭuat do not, apparently, pass entirely out of existence; for, as we shall see later, they are revivified once each day by light which the Sun-god casts upon them as he passes through the Ṭuat, and for a season they enjoy his rays, and when, as he leaves one division to enter another, the Gate closes upon him, and shuts out his light, they set up dismal cries at his departure, and then sink down into inertness in the darkness which will swallow them up for twenty-four hours. It is possible that the dead here referred to represent the primitive inhabitants of the country, and the gods of the dead whom they worshipped when on earth, but there is no doubt that to these were joined the spirits of those who for some reason or other failed to advance beyond one or other of the divisions of the Ṭuat.

Now, however, the time of evening has come, and the Sun-god in the SEKTET BOAT, wherein he has travelled since noon, draws nigh, flooding the FIRST DIVISION of the Ṭuat with light. This DIVISION, or antechamber, or vestibule, of the Ṭuat is, according to the BOOK ȦM-ṬUAT, called NET-RĀ, and before the Sun-god can come to the dweller in the Ṭuat he must pass over a space which is said to be 120, or 220, *ȧtru*, or leagues, in length. The river URNES, on which the boat moves, is 300 *atru* in extent, and is divided into two portions. On looking into the BOAT OF THE SUN-GOD we see that this deity has transformed himself, and that he no longer appears as a fiery disk, but as a ram-headed man, who stands within a shrine; in other words, Rā has taken the form of Osiris, in order that he may pass successfully through the kingdom of the dead, whose lord and god is Osiris. The name given to this form is ȦF, or ȦFU, , which means literally "flesh," and "a dead body;" it was as a dead body that Osiris first entered the Ṭuat, and those who wished to become what he became subsequently had to enter the Ṭuat as dead bodies and with the attributes wherewith he entered it. The boat then contains the body of the dead Sun-god, or ȦFU-RĀ; he has with him a crew of seven gods and one goddess; one of these acts as guide (ȦP-UAT), another as steersman, another as the "look out," and the goddess, or "lady of the boat," is there as representative of the Division through which they are about to pass. Besides these we have KA-SHU, i.e., the "double of Shu," the god of the atmosphere of this world, who is present in the boat in order to supply the god with air; ḤERU-ḤEKENU, who recites magical formulae; and SA and ḤU, who represent the knowledge and intelligence necessary for the due performance of the journey. We may note that the boat moves by itself, and that the gods who form a procession in front of it do not tow it. As we have already described these in vol. i. (see pp. 4-8), it is needless to say here more than that they are all forms of the Sun-god, or deified aspects of him, and that they accompany their lord, who has transformed himself. Side by side with the boat of

ȦFU-RĀ is a smaller boat, in which the coming into being of Osiris is depicted, and the beetle is there to typify the presence of Osiris, and to lead ȦFU-RĀ on his way through the DIVISION (vol. i., p. 7). As ȦFU-RĀ is preceded by a number of forms of the Sun-god, so the "form of Osiris," KHEPER-EN-ȦSȦR, is preceded by a number of Osirian deities, three snakes and three goddesses, among them being NEITH of the NORTH, NEITH of the SOUTH, and the rare goddess ĀRTET (vol. i., p. 7).

The direction in which ȦFU-RĀ is moving is northwards, and we may glance at the beings who are on the banks of the river of the Ṭuat. On the right hand are nine apes, "which sing to Rā as he entereth the Ṭuat," nine gods and twelve goddesses, who sing praises unto Rā, and twelve serpents, which belch forth the fire that gives light to lighten the god on his way (vol. i., pp. 12-15). On the left hand are nine apes, "which open the gates to the Great Soul" (i.e. ȦFU-RĀ), twelve goddesses, who open the gates in the earth, twelve goddesses, who guide the god, and nine gods, "who praise Rā" (vol. i., pp. 9-11). So soon as ȦFU-RĀ has entered this DIVISION (ĀRRIT) he calls upon the gods to let him proceed, and he asks for light and guiḍance from them; he bids one set of apes to open the doors to him, and the other to welcome him. As he is provided not only with the word of power, but has also the knowledge how to utter it, the gods straightway bid him enter the place where OSIRIS

KHENTI-ÅMENTI dwells. The serpent goddesses sing hymns to him, and they lighten the darkness by pouring out fire from their mouths, the god takes possession of the grain which is in NET-RĀ, his word has its due effect upon every one, and the punishments which he adjudges to the condemned are carried out duly. As for the dead who are in this DIVISION they do not journey on with the god, but they are left behind (vol. i., p. 8), and when they see him pass through the fortified gate which guards the entrance to the SECOND DIVISION "they wail" (vol i., p. 20). The texts say nothing about the actual condition of the dead whom ÅFU-RĀ leaves behind him, and nothing of the place, or places, whence they came; we can only assume that they are those who for some reason or other have failed to obtain a seat in the BOAT of the god. They must not be confounded with the gods and goddesses and apes who are in attendance upon ÅFU-RĀ, for these are, in reality, officers of the Division whose duty it is to escort him to the Gate of the Second Division, and then to return to their places to await his return the following evening. In return for their services they receive food and drink by the command of the god. As the Boat of ÅFU-RĀ was assumed by the priests of Åmen-Rā to begin its journey through the Ṭuat at Thebes, and as we are expressly told that the god was obliged to pass over a space of 120 or 220 *åtru*, or leagues, before he came to the dwellers in the Ṭuat, it is probable that the first group of dead are those who entered the Ṭuat through the opening in the mountains behind Abydos, which was called the "GAP." The oldest god of the dead of Abydos was KHENTI-ȦMENTI, i.e., Governor of Ȧmenti, ȦMENTI, i.e., the "hidden" land, being a name for the Underworld, or "Other World," in general. This being so, it is clear that when ȦFU-RĀ came to the end of the FIRST DIVISION of the Ṭuat he arrived at the beginning of the dominions of KHENTI-ȦMENTI, whose attributes became absorbed subsequently into those of OSIRIS.

In the BOOK OF GATES the FIRST DIVISION is depicted in a different manner. The BOAT OF THE SUN is seen passing through the mountain of the horizon, which is divided into two parts; the god appears in the form of a beetle within a disk, which is surrounded by a serpent with voluminous folds. The only gods with him in the boat are SA and ḤEKA, here the personifications of the intelligence and the word of power. The duty of SA is to make all plans for the god's journey, and ḤEKA will utter the words of power which will enable him to overcome all opposition. On each half of the mountain is a sceptre, one having the head of a jackal, and the other that of a ram; each sceptre is supported by the god TAT and the god SET, the personifications of the Ṭuat and the Mountain respectively. One sceptre is mentioned in the text, which is somewhat obscure in meaning; it seems, however, that the jackal-headed sceptre uttered words on behalf of the god ȦFU-RĀ, and that the other typified him, taking the place of the ram-headed god with a human body which we have in the BOOK ÅM-ṬUAT. On each side of the Boat are twelve gods, who presumably represent the Twelve Hours of the Day, and the Twelve Hours of the Night; one group is called "Neteru Set" (*or* Semt), i.e., "Gods of the Mountain," and the other "Neteru Set-Åmentet," i.e., "Gods of the Mountain of the Hidden Land." The gods of the Mountain are the offspring of Rā himself, and they "emerged from his eye" (vol. ii., p. 85), and to them has Åmentet been given as an abode.

CHAPTER VI.

SECOND DIVISION OF THE ṬUAT.

I. THE KINGDOM OF KHENTI-ÅMENTI-OSIRIS ACCORDING TO THE BOOK ÅM-ṬUAT.

THE god ÅFU-Rā now enters the region URNES 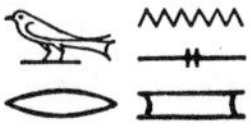, which derives its name from that of the river flowing through it; it is 309, or 480 *åtru* or leagues in length, and 120 wide. URNES is a portion of the dominions of OSIRIS-KHENTI-ÅMENTI, the great god of Abydos, and it, no doubt, formed a section of the SEKHET-ḤETEPET according to the old theology of Egypt. The Boat of ÅFU-Rā is now under the direction of the goddess of the second hour of the night, SHESAT-MĀKET-NEB-S, and the uraei of Isis and Nephthys have been added to its crew. Immediately in front of it are four boats, which move by themselves; the first contains the full moon, of which Osiris was a form, the second the emblem of a deity of harvest, the third the symbols of another agricultural deity, and the fourth the Grain-god personified. All four boats contain either forms or symbols of Osiris, in his different aspects, as the god of ploughing, sowing, and reaping, and of the grain from the time when it germinates to the season of harvest.

When Ȧfu-Rā has come into Urnes, he addresses the gods of the region, who are called "Baiu-Ṭuatiu," and tells them to open their doors so that they may receive air, and fresh food, and fresh water, in return for the deeds of valour which they have done on behalf of Ȧfu-Rā. It seems that at one portion of this Division the followers of Osiris and Rā had to do battle against Āpep and his friends, and that in return for their services the god gave them places here in which to dwell, with an abundance of wheat and barley, etc. The gods in reply welcome Ȧfu-Rā, and beg him to dissipate the darkness in Ȧmenti, and to slay the serpents Ḥau and Neḥa-ḥrȧ (vol. i., p. 40); they promise that those who guide his boat shall destroy Āpep, that Osiris shall come to meet him and shall avenge him, and that he shall rest in Ȧment, and shall appear in the East the following morning under the form of Kheperȧ. After this speech they lead Ȧfu-Rā into a state of peace in Sekhet-en-pertiu, , i.e., the "Field of the Gods of grain," wherein are the boats of the Grain-gods already described. In this fair haven Ȧfu-Rā rests, and every follower of Osiris hoped to follow his example.

If we consider for a moment the group of divine beings which stands on each bank of the river Urnes it becomes evident that each god or goddess belongs to the company of Osiris. To the right of the boat stand six gods, who either hold or wear an ear of corn and are connected with the growth of the grain (vol. i., p. 31), gods armed with knives, and connected with the harvest, gods of the seasons, each holding a notched palm-stick, the god of the year, the gods of Sothis and Orion (vol. i., p. 32) Osiris-Unnefer, Akhabit, Anubis, the "Eater of the Ass,"[1] etc. To the left of the Boat are six deities, each with a phallus in the form of a knife, the double god Horus-set (vol. i., p. 29), various animal- and bird-headed gods, goddesses both with and without uraei on their heads, the "Crook" (*mest* 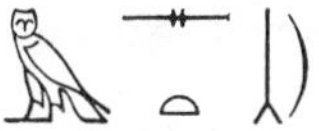) of Osiris, the serpent-protector of Osiris, and so on. The gods on the right of Åfu-Rā are they who give him "the seasons, and the years which are in their hands," and so soon as he speaks to them "they have life through his voice"; he, moreover, tells them what to do, and he orders that the herbs of the field of Urnes shall be given to them in abundance.

Nekht spearing the Eater of the Ass.

The duties of these gods are simple: they supply

[1] This is a name given to the serpent which is seen attacking an ass in the XIth Chapter of the Book of the Dead, and which is a form of the god Set; the Ass is probably a form of the sun-god Rā. The Eater of the Great Phallus, i.e., the Ass, was also a power of evil, yet here he is found seated among beneficent gods.

the followers of ÅFU-RĀ, i.e., those spirits who have succeeded in entering his boat, with green herbs, they give them water, and they light the fires which are to destroy the enemies of Rā. It is not, however, easy to understand their position. All these gods are under the rule of ÅM-NEBÅUI, who is "the lord of this Field," but it seems that they remain in a state of inertness until ÅFU-RĀ enters and shines upon them; and although they have their duties and know how to perform them, it is suggested by the texts that they perform nothing until he speaks to them. In other words, they are merely dead gods, until the word of power spoken by ÅFU-RĀ makes them produce grain on which to feed themselves and the "followers of Rā." In this way is the power of Åmen-Rā shown: his dead body, i.e., the night sun, is able to re-vivify all the gods of the kingdom of Osiris, and to make them work. The gods on the left have, first of all, to praise ÅFU-RĀ after he has entered URNES; they next "guard the day, and bring on the night until the great god cometh out into the East of the sky." Besides this their duty is to bring to the god's notice the words of those who are upon earth, and they make souls to come to their forms (vol. i., p. 34); they are also concerned with the "offerings of the night," and effect the overthrow of enemies.

From this passage it is clear that the Egyptians believed that words uttered on earth were taken to ÅFU-RĀ by his ministers, and it is difficult not to think that such words must have been in the form of petitions, or prayers, if only for sepulchral offerings. So soon as ÅFU-RĀ has passed through the Division, and his light has begun to leave them, all the gods of URNES "cry out in lamentation, and utter wailings because he has left them." From the SUMMARY of the BOOK ÅM-ṬUAT we gather that the pictures and texts referring to this Division of the Ṭuat, or Hour of the night, were believed to possess special efficacy, and the faithful thought that if a man knew the names of its gods he would receive a place of abode in URNES, and would travel about with the god, would have the power of entering the earth and the Ṭuat and of going so far as the pillars which supported the heavens, would travel over the serpent ĀMU-ĀA (i.e., the Eater of the Ass), would eat the bread intended for the Boat of the Earth,[1] and would partake of the perfumed unguent of the god TATUBÅ. Moreover, it is stated that the man who makes offerings to the BAIU-ṬUATIU (i.e., the divine souls of the Ṭuat), mentioning them by their names, shall in very truth receive innumerable benefits upon earth. The texts giving these facts are most important, for they prove that in early times the abode of the blessed was believed to be in URNES, and that the making of offerings to the dead was inculcated as a meritorious act, and that it was believed to bring blessings upon him that made the offering even whilst he was upon earth. It may also be noted in passing

[1] See within, page 126.

that the heaven URNES was somewhat exclusive, for only the followers of Osiris and Rā were admitted.

SECOND DIVISION OF THE ṬUAT.

II. THE KINGDOM OF KHENTI-ȦMENTI-OSIRIS ACCORDING TO THE BOOK OF GATES.

To advance into this Division the Boat of ȦFU-RĀ must first pass through the Gate which is guarded by the huge serpent SAA-SET, and this done the god now takes upon himself the form in which he appears in the BOOK ȦM-ṬUAT, i.e., that of a ram-headed man. The snake-goddess MEḤEN, which surrounded the disk enclosing a beetle, now envelops the shrine in which he stands; it must be noted that SA and ḤEKAU stand, as before, in the Boat, which is now towed along by four gods of the Ṭuat, who represent the four quarters of the earth and the four cardinal points. The Boat is received by a company of thirteen gods, who are apparently under the rule of a god who holds a staff. The object of the visit of ȦFU-RĀ is to "weigh words "and deeds in Ȧment, to make a distinction between "the great and little gods, to assign thrones to the "Spirits [who are pure], to dismiss the damned to the "place set apart for them, and to destroy their bodies." (vol. ii., p. 91). Now this is an important statement, for it distinctly implies that a judgment of the dead takes place in the Second Division, or Hour, of the Ṭuat, which is here called Ȧment, that the positions of the dead are graded, and that reward and punishment are meted out to the dead, according to their deserts. It is said by Ȧfu-Rā to the dwellers in Ȧment, "the dead "(*mitu* ) shall not enter in after you"; which proves that, wherever the place of punishment was, it was not in the Second Division of the Ṭuat. The gods who assist Ȧfu-Rā in his work of judgment are said to live upon the offerings made to them upon earth; here was a direct inducement to the faithful to make offerings regularly to the gods of the Ṭuat, and it was understood that such acts of piety would tell on their behalf when their words and deeds came to be weighed in Ȧment. The reader will note that it is Ȧfu-Rā who is the judge here, and not Osiris.

Examining now the beings who are on both banks of the river we see that they fall naturally into two classes, viz., the good and the bad; the former are on the right hand of the god, and the latter on his left, just as saints and sinners are arraigned before God's throne in mediaeval pictures of the Judgment. The good are divided into two classes, "the Ḥeteptiu who "praise Rā," and the "Maātiu who dwell in the Ṭuat" (vol. ii., p. 93). The Ḥeteptiu are thus called because they made "offerings" (*ḥetepet*) to Rā upon earth, and burned incense to him; they also sang praises to Rā and worshipped him upon earth, and uttered *ḥekau*, or words of power, against Āpep, the arch-foe of Rā (vol. ii., p. 94). From this text we see that it was not enough for the followers of Rā to praise him and give him gifts, but that they must also use magical words and formulae in order that Rā's foe may be destroyed; and, because when they were upon earth they made offerings to the Ṭuat-gods, now that they are themselves in the Ṭuat and have need of food, Rā declares that offerings made to them shall never fail, and their souls shall never be destroyed. The MAĀTIU beings have this name given to them because, as the text says, "they spoke *Maāt*," i.e., what is true, "upon earth"; moreover, "they did not approach the *neterit*," . Now the word *neterit* usually means "goddesses," but here it has an unusual determinative, which, however, suggests that it is used to express some idea of "evil" in connexion with the gods or goddesses, such as blasphemy, or contempt, or apostacy. On the whole it seems most likely that *neterit* means "false gods," that is to say, gods whom Rā would not recognize as such, and that the feminine form of the word, with the unusual determinative, indicates they were weak and miserable beings. As a reward for their veracity and orthodoxy (?) upon earth, the food on which they live is *Maāt*, i.e., truth, and they themselves become *Maāt*, or TRUTH itself, and they are permitted to invoke the god in the Gate. Rā, moreover, gives them the mastery over the waters of the region, which, though cool and refreshing to the MAĀTIU beings themselves, become "waters of fire" (vol. ii., p. 95) to those who are sinners and are involved in wickedness. We have already seen that the wicked were not allowed to enter this Division, therefore it appears that it was held to be possible for the dead round about it to attempt to drink of the cool waters, which straightway turned into fire and consumed them.

Turning now to those beings who stand to the left of the Boat (vol. ii., pp. 96-99), we see that they are twenty-four in number; of these four lie dead, or helpless, and are called ENENIU, i.e., the "Inert," and twenty stand with their backs bowed, and their arms tied at their elbows behind them, in an agonizing position. Here, it is clear, are beings who are fettered and stand awaiting their doom. The charges made against them are to the effect that: 1. They blasphemed Rā upon earth. 2. They invoked evil upon him that was in the Egg. 3. They thrust aside the right. 4. They spoke against KHUTI. The god referred to as being "in the Egg" is, of course, a form of the Sun-god, and we know from the LIVth Chapter of the Book of the Dead, that the EGG was laid by ḲENḲENUR, or the "Great Cackler." The god KHUTI is the form of the Sun-god at sunrise and sunset, and thus we see that all the sins which were committed by the ENENIU and their fettered companions were against Rā, and against forms of him. The name given to these is "STAU," i.e., "Apostates of the Hall of Rā," and sentence of doom is passed upon them by TEMU on behalf of Rā; it is decreed that their arms shall never be untied again, that their bodies shall be cut to pieces, and that their souls shall cease to exist (vol. ii., p. 97). Such are the things which take place in the Second Division of the Ṭuat according to the BOOK OF GATES, and, view them in whatever way we may, it is impossible not to conclude that the Egyptians thought that those who praised and worshipped Rā upon earth were rewarded with good things, whilst those who treated him lightly were punished. It is evident also that the offering up of propitiatory sacrifices and making of peace offerings were encouraged by the religion of Osiris, as being good both for gods and men.

CHAPTER VII.

THIRD DIVISION OF THE ṬUAT.

I. The Kingdom of Khenti-Åmenti-Osiris, according to the Book Åm-Ṭuat.

The Boat of Åfu-Rā, leaving the abode of the Souls of the Ṭuat, now enters that of the Baiu-shetaiu, or the "Secret Souls," and we find that a change has taken place as regards the crew. The goddess of the hour called Ṭent-baiu has taken charge of the Boat, a hawk-headed god acts as steersman, and the number of the other gods is reduced to four. The region now entered by Åfu-Rā is called Net-neb-uā-kheper-āut, and it is 309 (or 480) *åtru* or leagues in length, and 120 in width; it is, in fact, a continuation of the domains of Osiris, and in it is the House of Ṭeṭ wherein the great god of the dead himself dwells. The Boat of Åfu-Ra is preceded by three boats (vol. i., pp. 45-47) of a mystical character, containing hawk-gods, and mummied forms of gods who are akin to Osiris. Facing the boats are four forms of Osiris, with their arms and hands covered. Having arrived in this Division, Åfu-Rā cries out to its god, Osiris, who straightway creates these secret boats and sends them to bring ÅFU-RĀ to the place where he is. The abode of Osiris is situated on the NET-ÅSÅR, 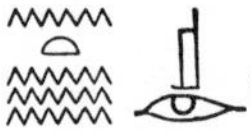, i.e., the "Stream of Osiris," a name given to the river of the Ṭuat in the THIRD DIVISION, and it is at the head of this river that the throne of Osiris rests according to some copies of the Theban Recension of the Book of the Dead. The inhabitants who are seen on both banks of the stream are called PERTIU, , and they live on lands which have beeṇ allotted to them by Åfu-Rā; in return for these they serve Osiris and defend him from the attacks of all his enemies. As the boat in which ÅFU-Rā stands and the three other boats move on, the gods on the banks move with them and guard them, and when they have escorted the great god to the end of their territory, they return to their old places and await his coming on the following night.

On the right of ÅFU-RĀ are twenty-six gods, and of these eight are forms of Osiris, four of Osiris of the North, and four of Osiris of the South; all are under the rule of KHETRÅ, who is the "Warder of this Field" (vol. i., p. 60), but it is only when they hear the words of ÅFU-RĀ that they come to life. The work which they do in this region is to hew and hack souls in pieces, to imprison the shadows of the dead, and to carry out the sentence of death on those who are doomed to destruction in a place of fire; they cause fires to come into being, and flames to burst forth on the wicked.

Now in this case also the beings who are doomed to be burned in a place specially set apart for this purpose cannot be of the number of the gods who protect Osiris, for they were created by Rā to serve this god in this Division of the Ṭuat, and to attend upon himself as he made his journey through it each day! They must, then, be the dead of olden time who have reached this Division, but who through want of friends and relatives upon earth to make proper and sufficient offerings daily, or through some other cause, have failed to find nourishment and have perished in consequence. The realm of Osiris had to be cleared of such beings, and the gods whose duty it was to protect him destroyed them with fire. We may note, too, that in this Division the shadows and souls of the dead were supposed to wander about, and though we do not know how they arrived there, or exactly why they failed to please Osiris, it is quite certain that they were regarded as a danger to the god, and destroyed in consequence.

On the left of ȦFU-RĀ stands a row of deities (vol. i., p. 50 ff.), some wholly in animal forms, who appear to have taken part in the burial ceremonies which were performed for Osiris; the exact functions of many of them are unknown, and the names of certain of them are not found elsewhere. According to the text these gods are clothed with their own bodies of flesh, and their souls speak from them, and their shadows are joined to them. Having been addressed by ȦFU-RĀ they sing praises to the god, and when he has passed from their Division they, as well as the gods on the right of the BOAT, lift up their voices and weep. In return for the lands which were given them by Osiris, in the possession of which they were confirmed by ȦFU-RĀ, these gods have certain duties to perform, viz., to take vengeance upon the fiend SEBȦ, to make NU to come into being, and to cause Ḥāpi to flow. From this it appears that SEBȦ possessed at times power over NU, that is to say, the great celestial watery mass which was the source of the river NILE in Egypt; to destroy this fiend was all-important, for without water the inhabitants of the Ṭuat could not live, and the cessation of the flow of the NILE would cause the ruin and death of the people of Egypt. It is interesting to note the connexion of the NILE with the chief domain of Osiris, and it is, no doubt, a reminiscence of the period in the history of the god when he was a water-god. A knowledge of the beings in these pictures and of the texts of this DIVISION was considered of very great importance for the deceased, for, knowing *their forms* and their names, he would not be terrified by their "roarings," and would not in his haste to escape from them fall headlong into their pits. In this DIVISION of the Ṭuat we see that ȦFU-RĀ was absolute master, and that he is made to create its inhabitants to serve Osiris, and Khenti-Ȧmenti, and himself, and to allot to them places to dwell in, and food to keep them alive. When he withdraws his light from them they weep, and sink into a state of inertness to await his return on the following day.

THIRD DIVISION OF THE ṬUAT.

II. THE KINGDOM OF KHENTI-ÅMENTI-OSIRIS ACCORDING TO THE BOOK OF GATES.

Before ÅFU-RĀ can pass into the THIRD DIVISION it is necessary for him to pass through a Gate which is protected by two strong walls, with a passage running between them. This passage is swept by flames of fire which proceed from two uraei; each end of it is guarded by a warder in mummied form, and on the inner side of the inner wall is a company of gods. The Gate is called SEPṬET-UAUAU, and the name of its monster serpent is AQEBI. So soon as the Boat enters the DIVISION or HOUR four of the gods of the region appear, and take it in tow; the god is in the same form as before, and has in no way suffered by his passage through the Gate, because at the word of SA the Gate opened, the flames which swept between the walls ceased, and the warders of the passage and the guardian gods withdrew their opposition. In this DIVISION a serious obstacle had to be overcome. Immediately in the fair way of the course of ÅFU-RĀ is a group of eight gods, called FAIU-NETERU, who bear on their shoulders a long pole-like object, each end of which terminates in a bull's head. This object is intended to represent the long tunnel in the earth, each end of which was guarded by a bull, through which, according to one tradition, the night-Sun passed on his journey from the place of sunset to the place of sunrise. At intervals on the tunnel are seated seven gods called NETERU-ÅMIU, i.e., the "gods who are within," and they are intended to represent the guardians of the seven portions into which the tunnel was divided; the name given to the tunnel is "UÅA-TA," i.e., "Boat of the Earth," but there is no doubt that it originally re-

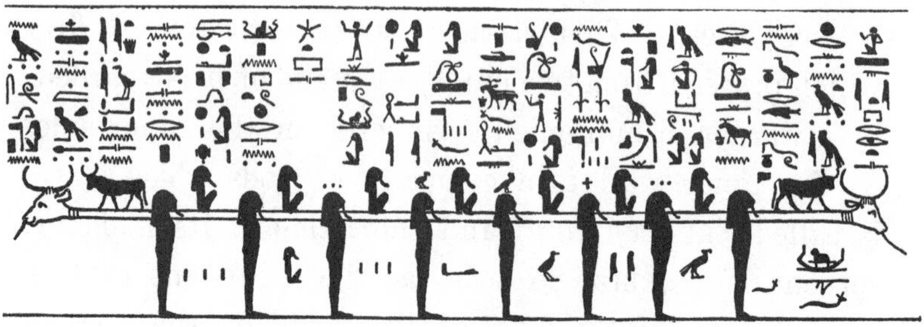

The Boat of the Earth.

presented a kind of Ṭuat which was complete in itself, as the bulls' heads, one at each end of it, prove.

The difficulty of passing through the "Boat of the Earth" is soon overcome, for the gods of the Ṭuat tow ÅFU-RĀ through it, and we see them at the other end of the Division still holding the tow-line in their hands. In front of them are the four gods, whose arms and hands are covered (vol. ii., p. 107), whom we have already seen in the BOOK ÅM-ṬUAT (vol. i., p. 48), where they were in charge of the four boats which filled the picture. It is not difficult to explain why the "Boat of the Earth" was omitted by the Theban priests from their composition; had they kept it in it they would have been obliged to make their god ÅFU-RĀ, the night form of ÅMEN-RĀ, to submit to being towed through an inferior Ṭuat, and to being absorbed by the earth-god. The text which refers to this remarkable scene tells us that ĀFU-RĀ addresses the eight gods who support the "Boat of the Earth," and declares that he who is in it is "holy," and in reply the being or beings ENNURKHATA (?) say, "Praised be the BA," i.e., the ram-headed form of Osiris, which the god has taken, "which the "double bull has swallowed (or, absorbed); let the god "be at peace with that which he hath created." The gods also say, "Praised be RĀ, whose BA hath set him-"self in order with the EARTH-GOD," . Thus it is quite clear that the "Boat of the Earth" is the abode of the "Earth-god."

To the right of ÅFU-RĀ, as he passes through this Division or Hour, are the twelve "holy gods who are in "the Ṭuat," each in his shrine, with its doors thrown wide open; they are guarded by a huge serpent called SETI. These gods are in mummied form, and represent a large class of the beatified dead which exists in the realm of Osiris. According to the text which refers to them ÅFU-RĀ finds the shrines closed when he appears, and the gods within weeping and lamenting; at his word the doors fly open, and the occupants of the shrines obtain air and food and adore him, but when he has passed on the doors of the shrines close again, and the gods betake themselves to lamentations until he reappears on the following night. Thus another class of the dead owes its revivification, light, and food to the beneficence of ȦFU-RĀ rather than to Osiris.

A little beyond the Twelve Shrines is a group of Twelve Gods, who are partially immersed in the "Lake of Boiling Water"; in front of each is a large plant. The waters of this lake have the peculiar property of appearing cool to the taste and touch of the gods who live on it, and who feed upon the plants which grow in it. It is important to notice that the Lake is said to be boiling hot, and that "the birds betake them- "selves to flight when they see the waters thereof, and "when they smell the stench which is in it." Now this description tells us at once that the Lake of Boiling Water is no other than a collection of water which resembles that of the famous "ASPHALTITIS LACUS," or *ἀσφαλτῖτις λίμην*, which is described by Diodorus Siculus (ii. 48; xix. 98). The water of this Lake is said to be very salt, and of an extremely noxious smell, and the fire which burns beneath the ground, and the stench of the bitumen render the inhabitants of the neighbouring country sickly and short-lived. The country round about is nevertheless well fitted for the cultivation of palms, wherever it is traversed by fresh water. It is quite clear that the author of the Egyptian text cannot have borrowed his description of the Lake from later writers, and it is equally clear that his account of it represents the tradition of the existence of some hot sulphur spring or bituminous lake which existed in Egypt, probably in or near one of the Oases. At Khârga, for example, there are several springs the waters of which reach a temperature of 97° Fahrenheit. As we see in the picture (vol. ii., p. 112) a large plant, or small tree, growing before each of its inhabitants, it is evident that some kind of vegetation flourished in the neighbourhood of the Lake, and the quaint costume of the gods, who, of course, typified the inhabitants of the region, suggests that they were not Egyptian. The dwellers in the LAKE OF BOILING WATER entreat ȦFU-RĀ to come to them, saying, "Send forth thy light "upon us, O thou great god who hast fire in thine eye (vol. ii., p. 113). In answer, the god decrees that their food shall consist of loaves of bread and green herbs, and that their beer shall be made from the *kemtet* plant. This plant has not as yet been accurately identified, but it is tolerably certain that it belonged to a species which was characteristic of the neighbourhood of the Lake.

The beings who stand on the left hand of ȦFU-RĀ are divided into two groups: the first consists of nine men, and the second of nine gods, and each group is under the command of TEMU. Between TEMU and the first company, who are called TCHATCHA we see (vol. ii., p. 114) coiled the monster serpent ĀPEP which has collapsed as a result of the utterance of the word of power by TEMU. This serpent tried to envelop the boat of ÅFU-RĀ with its folds, and then to force a way into his boat; but the TCHATCHA, i.e., "Great Chiefs," cut open its head, and slit its body in many places, and its destruction was finished by TEMU. These TCHATCHA live upon the same food as Rā, but they also partake of the offerings made upon earth to KHENTI-ÅMENTI, the ancient god of the dead of Abydos. The nine gods who follow these are called NEBU-KHERT, and their duty is to repulse the serpents SEBÅ and ÅF (vol. ii., p. 115), and to enchant and to render helpless and motionless ĀPEP when he attempts to force the gates of KHENTI-ÅMENTI. Their food is the same as that of the TCHATCHA, but they possess a power of a remarkable character (which is represented by the words "maāt kheru"), for they know how to utter words in such a way, and with such a tone of voice, that the effect which they wish them to have must of necessity take place. Everything which Osiris possessed as god and judge of the dead he owed to the "*maāt* kheru," or "word of *maāt*." As the god ÅFU-RĀ passes out of the THIRD DIVISION both the TCHATCHA and the NEBU-KHERT give themselves up to lamentation, and they return to the entrance, and wait for the re-appearance of his boat on the following night, when they will again attack SEBÅ, and ÅF, and ĀPEP, and overcome them. The exact place which was set apart for the souls of human beings is nowhere described in the texts.

CHAPTER VIII.

FOURTH DIVISION OF THE ṬUAT.

I. The Kingdom of Seker according to the Book Ȧm-Ṭuat.

The Boat of Ȧfu-Rā has now passed out of the dominions of Khenti-Ȧmenti, the ancient god of the dead of the city of Abydos, and has entered the kingdom of Seker, who is probably the oldest of all the gods of the dead in Egypt. The dominions of Seker were situated in the deserts round about Memphis, and were supposed to cover a large extent of territory, and their characteristics were entirely different from those of the regions ruled over by Khenti-Ȧmenti near Abydos, and from those of the kingdom of Osiris, the lord of Busiris and Mendes, in the Delta. The kingdom of Seker was shrouded in thick darkness, and, instead of consisting of fertile plains and fields, intersected by streams of running water, was formed of bare, barren, sandy deserts, wherein lived monster serpents of terrifying aspect, some having two, and some three heads, and some having wings. This region offered so many difficulties to the passage of the Boat of Ȧfu-Rā, that special means had to be found for overcoming them, and for enabling the god and his followers to proceed northwards to the House of Osiris. As there was no river in the land of SEKER a boat was useless to ȦFU-RĀ, and as the god was unable to travel through the FOURTH DIVISION boldly, and to allow himself to be seen by all the inhabitants thereof, it was arranged that he should pass through a series of narrow corridors, which were provided with doors. The pictures which illustrate the passage of the god through this DIVISION, or HOUR, are arranged in three registers, but the actual corridors through which he travelled are drawn across these obliquely.

The main corridor is called RE-STAU. At the end of the first section of it is the door MĀṬES-SMA-TA (vol. i., p. 63), at the end of the second section is the door MĀṬES-MAU-ĀT (vol. i., p. 71), and at the end of the third section is the door MĀṬES-EN-NEḤEḤ (vol. i., p. 75). An inscription in this last tells us that it is the road by which the body of SEKER enters and that his form is neither seen nor perceived; hence it is clear that the road by which ȦFU-RĀ passed through this DIVISION was supposed to be high up above the dominions of SEKER, and that he never saw that god at all. The name given to this DIVISION, or "CIRCLE," as it is called in the Summary, is ĀNKHET-KHEPERU, and that of its Gate is ȦMENT-SETHAU, 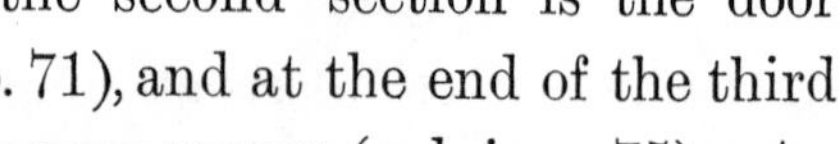; the goddess of the Hour is called URT-EM-SEKHEMU-S. We may now consider the means employed by ȦFU-RĀ for passing through this HOUR. Looking at the middle register (vol. i., p. 63) we see that the god has discarded his ordinary boat, and that he and his crew are standing in a boat which is formed of a two-headed serpent; a serpent was the best means of transport for the god, because it could glide easily along the sandy floor of the rocky corridor. From the "mouth of the boat," which is drawn by four gods, rays of light are emitted; this light is not strong enough to enable ÅFU-RĀ to see the beings who are on each side of him (vol. i., p. 66), but knowing they are there, he cries out to them, and they hear him. The hidden gods who march in front of the boat are few in number, and the names of many of them are unfamiliar; some of them are connected with Osiris, and all of them are under the control of ÅNPU, or ANUBIS, and perform some act which helps the boat along. Among them may be specially noted Thoth and Horus, above whose outstretched hands is the Eye 𓂀, which is here identified with SEKRI (vol. i., p. 75).

As ÅFU-RĀ journeys on his way there are on his right three serpents, a scorpion, a uraeus serpent, a three-headed serpent with wings and human legs, a few of the gods of the HOUR, a serpent with two necks and heads proceeding from one body, and a tail which terminates in another head (vol. i., pp. 67, 71, 75, 79). On his left are a few more gods and goddesses, the serpents ḤETCH-NĀU, ÅMEN, ḤEKENT, and the terrible three-headed serpent MENMENUT, the face of which illumines the chamber in which KHEPERÅ is born daily (vol. i.,

p. 79). Over the back of the last-named serpent are fourteen heads, which, as M. Maspero has well shown, represent the gods of the first fourteen days of the month, and they are being carried by the serpent to fill the EYE which THOTH and HORUS are bringing through RE-STAU. The beings to the right and left of ȦFU-RĀ are ancient gods of the kingdom of SEKER, and each guards some door or corridor in it which leads to the hidden chamber of SEKER himself.

FIFTH DIVISION OF THE ṬUAT.

I. THE KINGDOM OF SEKER ACCORDING TO THE BOOK ȦM-ṬUAT.

This DIVISION, or HOUR, or CIRCLE, as it is described in the text, is called ȦMENT, and it contains the secret ways, and the doors of the hidden chamber of the holy place of the Land of SEKER, and his flesh, and his members, and his body, in the forms which they had in primeval times; the main gate is called ĀḤĀ-NETERU, the gods are called BAIU-ȦMMIU-ṬUAT, and the goddess of the HOUR is SEMIT-ḤER-ȦBT-UȦA-S. The Boat of ȦFU-RĀ is towed by seven gods and seven goddesses, and is preceded by a few gods who are led by Isis (vol. i., pp. 87, 91, 95, 99, 103, 107, 111); the texts make it clear that ȦFU-RĀ continues his journey by the help of KHEPERȦ. The corridor of RE-STAU through which he travels now bends upwards, and passing by the secret abode of SEKER, by which it is hidden, once more descends to its former level. The Land of Seker is in the form of an elongated ellipse, and is enclosed by a wall of sand; it rests upon the backs of two man-headed sphinxes, each of which is called ÅF and lives upon the voice, or word, of the great god. The duty of these is to guard the Image of Seker. The form in which this god is depicted is that of a hawk-headed man, who stands between a pair of wings that project from the back of a huge serpent having two heads and necks, and a tail terminating in a bearded human head. The Land of Seker is covered by a pyramid having its apex in the form of the head of a goddess, and above it is the vault of night, from which emerges the Beetle of KHEPERÅ. When the Boat of ÅFU-RĀ comes to the pyramid, the Beetle ceases to converse with the goddess of the apex, whose duty it is to pass on its words to SEKER, and betakes itself to the Boat, and begins the revivification of ÅFU-RĀ, who is led on without delay to the end of RE-STAU, where he is received by the MORNING STAR and the light of a new day.

The IMAGE of Seker, which has been described above, lives in thick darkness, and any light which is seen there proceeds from the "eyes of the heads of the "great god whose flesh sendeth forth light," and the god himself lives upon the offerings which are made to the god TEMU upon earth. When ÅFU-RĀ has passed by in his boat there is heard in the Land of

Seker a mighty noise which is like unto that heard in the heights of heaven when they are disturbed by a storm. On one side of the Land of Seker is the serpent Tepȧn (vol. i., p. 95), which presents to the god the offerings made to him daily ; on the other is the serpent Ānkhȧapau, which lives upon its own fire, and remains always on guard. Close by are the emblems of the various forms of Seker. Behind the serpent Ṭepȧn is a lake of boiling water, from which project the heads of those who are being boiled therein. This lake or stream is called Netu, , and it is situated in the region of the kingdom of Seker which is called Ȧmmāḥet, ; the unfortunate beings who are in the boiling water weep when the Boat of Ȧfu-Rā has passed them by.

The gods who stand on the other side of the corridor through which Ȧfu-Rā passes are all invoked by him, and they all are assumed to help him on his way, not because they are in duty bound to do so, but because he acknowledged their power by asking their help. Some of them he appealed to because he had created them, but others are manifestly the servants of Seker, and their duty it was to guard his kingdom. A number of them are gods who were set over the waters which lay in the northern part of the Division, and it was all important for Ȧfu-Rā to have their friendly help when he left the back of the serpent and rejoined his own boat. In one portion of the region to the left of Ȧfu-

Rā we see the Ḥetep-neteru, i.e., a company of eight gods, and the goddess Qeṭet-ṭent; the work of these gods is to be present at the destruction of the dead in the Ṭuat, and to consume their bodies by the flames which they emit from their mouths, and the goddess lives partly on the blood of the dead, and partly on what the gods give her. These gods are provided with blocks on which they cut in pieces the dead, and when they are not thus employed they sing hymns to their god, to the accompaniment of the shaking of sistra; they exist by virtue of the word of power which they have received, and their souls have been given to them (vol. i., p. 110). The dead who are here referred to are those who have succeeded in entering the dread realm of Seker, but who, for want of the influence over the gods there, which could only be obtained by sacrifices and offerings made upon earth, and by the knowledge of mighty words of power, were unable to proceed to the abode of Seker.

When they arrived in the Ȧmmāḥet, some of them were cast into a lake of liquid fire, or of boiling water, and others were first cut in pieces, and then consumed by fire. Thus there is no doubt that there was a hell of fire in the kingdom of Seker, and that the tortures of mutilation and destruction by fire were believed to be reserved for the wicked. Of the rewards of the righteous in this kingdom we have no knowledge whatsoever, and it seems as if the scheme of the Other World of Seker made no provision for the beatified dead; at all events, it provided for them no fertile fields like the Sekhet-Ḥetepet of Osiris, and no Boat of Millions of Years wherein as beings of light they could travel in the company of the Sun-god for ever. The religion of Seker proclaimed that the god lived in impenetrable darkness, in a region of sand, closely guarded by terrible monster serpents, and it had little in it to induce the worshippers of the god to wish to be with him after their departure from this world. The cult of SEKER is one of the oldest in Egypt, and in its earliest form it, no doubt, represents the belief as to the future life of some of the most primitive inhabitants of the country; in fact, it must have originated at a period when some influential body of priests taught that death was the end of all things, and when snakes and bulls were the commonest forms under which the gods of the neighbourhood of Memphis were worshipped. The oldest presentment of the Land of Seker which we have is, of course, not older than the XVIIIth or XIXth Dynasty, and it must be remembered that it is the work of the priests of Thebes, who would be certain to remove any texts, figures, or details which they found inconvenient for their views. It is tolerably certain that the form in which they depicted it is much shorter than that in which it existed originally, and that the attributes and duties of many of the gods have been changed to suit the necessities of the cults of Osiris and Ȧmen-Rā. Such changes have resulted in great confusion, and at the present time it is impossible to reduce these most interesting, but at the same time most difficult, scenes and texts to their original forms. The priests of Ȧmen-Rā found it to be impossible to ignore entirely SEKER and his Land, when they were depicting the various Underworlds of Egypt, but it is very suggestive that they make the path of ȦFU-RĀ to be *over* and not *through* his kingdom, and that ȦFU-RĀ had to go on his way without entering the pyramid beneath which reposed the IMAGE of SEKER in the deepest darkness of night, in fact without seeing SEKER at all. On the other hand, they attached the greatest importance to the knowledge of the pictures of the FOURTH and FIFTH DIVISIONS, and they believed that it would enable the body of a man to rejoin his soul, and prevent the goddess KHEMIT, , from hacking it in pieces, and would secure for the believer a share of the offerings made to Seker.

CHAPTER IX.

FOURTH DIVISION OF THE ṬUAT.

II. The Kingdom of Khenti-Åmenti-Osiris according to the Book of Gates.

The pictures and texts of this Division, or Hour, in the Book of Gates vary considerably from those in the Book-Åm-Ṭuat. The god Åfu-Rā appears in his Boat as before with Sa and Ḥekau, and four gods tow him on his way; he has passed through the Gate which is called Nebt-tchefau, and its guardian serpent Tchetbi has in no way resisted his progress. The region now entered by Åfu-Rā has no connexion with the Land of Seker, and it appears to be a continuation of the dominions of Khenti-Åmenti. Immediately in front of the boat are nine sepulchres, each containing a god in mummied form; these are the "gods who are in the following of Osiris, who dwell in their caves" (vol. ii., p. 123). Next come the twelve Hour-goddesses who stand in two groups; between the groups is the monster serpent Ḥereret, which spawns twelve serpents to be consumed by the Twelve Hour-goddesses. As Åfu-Rā goes on his way he adjures the Ṭuat gods to take him to the eastern part of heaven, so that he may visit the habitations of the god ÅRES, (or SÅR) , and when he has come to them, he orders the doors to open, and raises up the beings therein whose "souls are broken," and allots to them meat and drink. The Hour-goddesses are the daughters of Rā, and their work is to guide their father through the night; six of them represent the first six hours of the night, and the other six the last six. These are here (vol. ii., p. 123) depicted together, whilst in the BOOK ÅM-ṬUAT each appears in the boat of ÅFU-RĀ in the Hour to which she belongs.

On the right of ÅFU-RĀ are the Twelve gods who "carry their doubles" (vol. ii., p. 131) and who live upon the offerings which are made to them and upon what is given to them by ṬESERT-BAIU, i.e., the place of holy souls. Their duty is to offer their *kau* or doubles to the god, whom they address as the "lord of years and of everlastingness which hath no diminution" (vol. ii., p. 130). Beyond these gods are two lakes, viz., the LAKE OF LIFE, and the LAKE OF THE LIVING URAEI. Round the LAKE OF LIFE stand twelve jackal-headed gods who invite ÅFU-RĀ to bathe in it, even as the "lord of the gods" did, and who state that the souls of the dead do not come near it because it is holy. When he passes out of this DIVISION they lift up their voices in lamentation (vol. ii., p. 132). The LIVING URAEI turn back the souls from their Lake, and the mere sound of the words which they utter destroys the shadows of the dead who have succeeded in coming near it. They preserve with great care the flames and fire which are in them, so that they may hurl them at the enemies of ÅFU-RĀ.

In the course of his journey through this HOUR ÅFU-RĀ passes the shrine of KHENTI-ÅMENTI, the ancient god of Abydos, which is seen on the left (vol. ii., p. 137); he is in mummied form, wears the white crown, as befits a god of the South, and stands on a serpent. Immediately before the shrine is the Flame-goddess NESERT. Before and behind the shrine are twelve gods, at the head of the first company being ḤERU-UR, or "Horus the Aged." ḤERU-UR addresses the god in the shrine by the names "Osiris" and "Khenti-Åmenti," and declares that he has performed the magical ceremonies which have made KHENTI-ÅMENTI to be the "Governor of the Ṭuat," to such purpose that the spirits of the blessed (*khu*, ) look upon him with awe, and the dead, i.e., the damned, (*mit* ) are in terror of him. Here we have the proof of the existence of the belief that Osiris was enabled to travel safely through the Ṭuat by means of the spells, and incantations, and magical formulae, and words of power which were uttered by ḤERU-UR. The Twelve gods who are in front of the shrine ascribe praise and dominion to KHENTI-ÅMENTI, and declare that his son Horus has restored to him his crown, and crushed his enemies, and made strong OSIRIS-KHENTI-ÀMENTI. To these ÀFU-RĀ makes no answer, but he calls upon Horus to avenge him on those who work against him, and to cast them to the Master of the lords of the pits, so that they may be destroyed. Now the pits here referred to are four in number (vol. ii., p. 137), and they are filled with fire; into these the enemies of the god are cast, and the keepers of them are adjured by Horus to watch and tend the fires. Who the plotters against the god may be it is impossible to say, but it is quite clear that one portion of the FOURTH DIVISION OF THE ṬUAT was a fiery hell wherein all the wicked were consumed. It is interesting to note that of the beings who are to the left of the Boat of ÀFU-RĀ Horus is the only one whom the god addresses.

FIFTH DIVISION OF THE ṬUAT.

II. THE KINGDOM OF KHENTI-ÀMENTI-OSIRIS ACCORDING TO THE BOOK OF GATES.

The FIFTH, like the FOURTH DIVISION of the BOOK OF GATES, in no way resembles that in the BOOK ÀM-ṬUAT, and it has nothing whatsoever to do with the kingdom of SEKER. The god ÀFU-RĀ, having passed through the Gate of the DIVISION or HOUR, which is called ÀRIT, and which has been opened by the monster serpent TEKA-HRÀ that guarded it, is towed along by four of the gods of this section of the

Ṭuat. The ministers of the god consist of nine gods whose hands and arms are covered, and twelve gods who are under the direction of ḤERI-QENBET-F; the nine gods are called KHERU-ENNUTCHI, i.e., "those who hold the serpent ENNUTCHI," and the twelve gods BAIU RETH ȦMMIU ṬUAT, i.e., the "souls of men who dwell in the Ṭuat" (vol. ii., pp. 144, 145). The exact functions of Ennutchi are not known, but his presence is baleful, and ȦFU-RĀ straightway calls upon the group of gods to destroy him; the god would press on to the next Gate, NEBT-ĀḤĀU, but ENNUTCHI can travel to that point, and he must therefore be removed.

The next group of gods is of peculiar interest, for they represent the souls of those who have spoken "what is right and true upon earth, and who have magnified the forms of the god RĀ." In return for such moral rectitude and piety, ȦFU-RĀ orders ḤERI-QENBET-F to invite them to "sit at peace in their habitations in the corner of those who are with myself," where praises shall be sung to their souls, and where they shall have air in abundance to breathe; they shall, moreover, have joints of meat to eat in SEKHET-ȦARU. Besides this, offerings shall be made to them upon earth, even as they are to the god ḤETEPI, the lord of SEKHET-ḤETEPET (vol. ii., pp. 145, 146). Now from these statements some very interesting deductions may be made. In the first place, it is now certain that there was a place specially set apart for the souls of men in the Ṭuat, and that those who were allowed to enter it had lived a life of moral rectitude, and had followed after righteousness and integrity when they were upon earth. Secondly, they were allowed to live in the corner of the SEKHET-ḤETEPET with the great god himself, in the place where, as we know from the Papyrus of Ȧni (see above, p. 44), most wonderful grain grew. Thirdly, an everlasting supply of offerings made upon earth was assured them, and in this respect they were coequal with ḤETEPI, the chief god of the Field of Peace (or, Field of Offerings). Thus the religion of Osiris undoubtedly taught that those who were good on this earth were rewarded in the next world.

On the right of ȦFU-RĀ are the twelve gods called HENIU-ȦMMIU-ṬUAT, i.e., "those who sing praises in the Ṭuat," and the twelve gods called KHERU-ENNUḤU-EM-ṬUAT, i.e., "those who hold the cord in the Ṭuat," and the four ḤENBIU gods (vol. ii., pp. 148-150). The first company of gods are, as we learn from the text, engaged in praising ȦFU-RĀ, and they have been rewarded with the exalted office which they hold in Ȧment because they praised Rā at sunrise and sunset when they lived upon earth, and because Rā was "satisfied" with what they did for him. They enjoy, moreover, a share of the offerings which are made to the god. A little beyond the HENIU are the "gods who hold the measuring cord," and by the orders of the great god they go over the fields of Ȧmentet, and measure and mark out the plots of ground which are to be allotted to the KHU, or spirits of the righteous. Every spirit is judged by the god of law and righteousness, and only after a strict examination is he allowed to take possession of his allotment. As there seems to have been only one standard of moral and religious excellence all the allotments were probably of the same size. The food of the spirits who live in the homesteads which have been thus measured in SEKHET-ÅARU comes from the crops which grow in that region, and the four ḤENBIU gods, who superintended the measuring of the fields, are ordered to provide sand, that is to say soil, for the replenishing of the ground.

The beings who are on the left of ÅFU-RĀ in this Division are not less interesting than those on the right. Among these are are four representatives of the four great classes into which the Egyptians divided mankind, namely, the RETH (for REMTH), the NEḤESU, the THEMEḤU, and the ĀAMU (vol. ii., p. 153). Of these the RETH, i.e., the "men" *par excellence*, were Egyptians, who came into being from the tears which fell from the Eye of RĀ. The THEMEḤU, or Libyans, were also descended from the Eye of RĀ. The ĀAMU were the people of the deserts to the north and east of Egypt, Sinai, etc., and the NEḤESU were the black tribes of Nubia and the Sûdân. It is noteworthy that the members of each nation or people keep together. The representatives of the Four Nations are followed by twelve gods who are called KHERU-ĀḤĀU-ÅMENT, i.e., "The Holders of the Time of Life in Åment," and who hold the serpent METERUI. These remarkable beings have in their hands the power to determine the length of life which is to be meted out to the souls who have been doomed to destruction in Ȧmenti, that is to say, they were able to defer the doom which had been decreed for souls, though in the end they were compelled to carry out the edict of destruction. In close connexion with these gods are the TCHATCHAU, or "Great Chiefs," who were believed to write the edicts of destruction against the damned (vol. ii., p. 156), and to record the duration of the lives of those who were in Ȧmentet; in fact, they appear to have kept the registers of Osiris, and to have served in some respects as recording angels. From what has been said above it will be clear that all the scenes and texts which illustrate and describe the Kingdom of Seker have been omitted from the BOOK OF GATES, and that the first five sections of this work describe—1. The Antechamber of the Ṭuat. 2. The Divisions of the Kingdom of KHENTI-ȦMENTI, which extended from Abydos to a region a little to the north of Memphis. We may now proceed to consider the Kingdom of Osiris, the lord of Mendes and Busiris.

CHAPTER X.

SIXTH DIVISION OF THE ṬUAT.

I. KINGDOM OF OSIRIS ACCORDING TO THE BOOK ÅM-ṬUAT.

THIS DIVISION, or HOUR, is the first of four which are devoted to the Kingdom of Osiris; its name is METCHET-MU-NEBT-ṬUAT, its Gate is called SEPṬ-METU, and the Hour-goddess is MESPERIT-ÅR-ĀT-MAĀTU. Here we see at once that the god ÅFU-RĀ has re-entered his boat, and that he has discarded the serpent-boat in which he travelled through the Land of Seker; the boat advances by means of paddling and not by towing. The greater part of the road of ÅFU-RĀ in this DIVISION is occupied by a very long building—or series of houses, or chambers, set close together—which contains the forms of Osiris. Here are four representatives of each of four classes of beings, viz., the SUTENIU, or kings of Upper Egypt, the BÅTIU, or kings of Lower Egypt, the ḤETEPTIU, or those who have been abundantly supplied with offerings, and the KHU, or spirits of the beatified dead. Thus it seems that the first mansion of the House of Osiris contains royal folk, the rich, and the superlatively good (vol. i., p. 117-120); as ÅFU-RĀ passes these by he salutes them, and wishes them an abundant supply of offerings, and entreats them to hack ĀPEP in pieces for him. Immediately beyond these we see represented the transformation of AFU-RĀ into the living Sun-god. Here is the five-headed serpent ĀSHT-ḤRÂU, and on his back lies the dead Sun-god; with his right hand, which is raised above his head, he is drawing to himself the Beetle of KHEPERÅ, which is the type of regeneration,

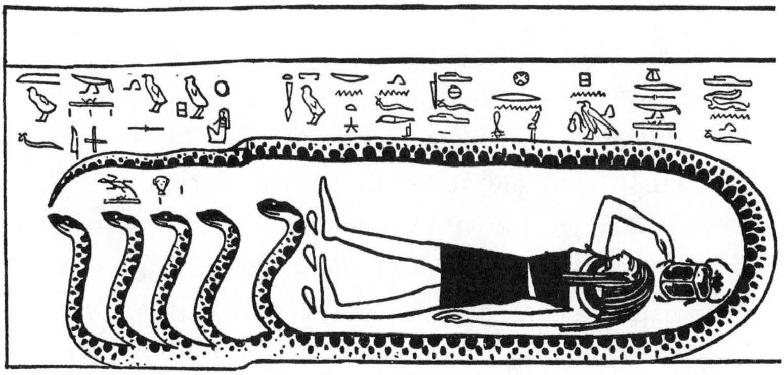

The Serpent Āsht-ḥrâu.

or new birth, or resurrection. This is the equivalent of the scene in the BOOK ÅM-ṬUAT where the Beetle descends from the vault of night, and joining itself to the Boat of ÅFU-RĀ revivifies the dead Sun-god (see vol. i., p. 103). That this revivification of ÅFU-RĀ should take place at the end of the SIXTH DIVISION is quite correct, for at this point the god arrives at the most northerly limit of his course. He has travelled due north from Thebes and Abydos, and has occupied six hours in performing the journey; he must now alter his course and travel towards the East so that he may appear at BAKHAU, , the Mountain of Sunrise. The path over which he now journeys is called the "secret path of Åmentet," and he who knoweth it, and the names of those who are on it, and their forms, shall partake of the offerings made to the gods of Osiris, and receive the gifts which his relatives (, *ābt*)[1] shall make upon earth.

On the right of ÅFU-RĀ are a company of gods and goddesses, and a group of sceptres surmounted by crowns and uraei, and provided with knives; these are the beings who hold and cultivate the territory in this DIVISION, or HOUR, and minister to the wants of the followers of Osiris. Beyond these we have a lion, the two Eyes of Horus, three deities, and three small sepulchres, into each of which, through an opening under the roof, a serpent is belching fire (vol. i., pp. 124-130). In each sepulchre is an "image" of Rā, i.e., a human head, a hawk's wing, and a hind-quarter of a lion, and these appear to be symbols under which the god was worshipped in and around Ånnu, or Heliopolis. On the left of ÅFU-RĀ are eight gods and four goddesses, whose duty it is to accompany his Boat, and to escort the souls and shadows of men through the Division, and to provide the spirits with food and water. Next is the

[1] See above, p. 66.

monster serpent "Am-Khu," i.e., "Eater of the Spirits," whose duty it is to devour the shadows of the dead, and to eat up the spirits of the foes of Rā; from his back spring the heads of the Four Children of Horus, and they come into being when they hear the voice of Ȧfu-Rā. Beyond these are four Osiris forms, "which stand though they are seated, and move though they are motionless," and nine serpents armed with knives, which represent the ancient gods, Ta-thenen, Temu, Kheperȧ, Shu, Seb, Ȧsȧr (Osiris), Ḥeru, Ȧpu, and Ḥetepui. These gods had faces of fire, and lived in the water of Tathenen, and they only came to life by virtue of the words of power of Ȧfu-Rā, who is now to be regarded as Kheperȧ.

SEVENTH DIVISION OF THE ṬUAT.

I. Kingdom of Osiris according to the Book Ȧm-Ṭuat.

The name of this Division, or Hour, is Thepḥet-shetat, the name of the Gate is Ruti-Ȧsȧr, and the goddess of the Hour is Kheftes-Ḥȧu-ḥesq-Neḥa-ḥrȧ. On looking at the "secret path of Ȧmentet" wherein Ȧfu-Rā is still travelling, we note that the face of the god is turned in another direction, that the crew is increased by Isis and by Ser, , whose name has also been read Semsu, and that the canopy under which Ȧfu-Rā stands is formed of the body of the serpent

Meḥen (vol. i., p. 140). There is a good reason for these changes, for the god has now to traverse a region where there is not sufficient water to float his boat or to permit of its being towed; moreover, his way is blocked by a monster serpent called Neḥa-ḥrå, which lies on a sand bank 450 cubits long.[1] In other words, the Boat of Åfu-Rā has arrived at a region of sandbanks and shallows, where serpents and crocodiles live; but the words of power of Isis, the great sorceress, and of Ser, and of the god himself protect him from mishap, and eventually he passes through this division by taking upon himself the form of the serpent Meḥen in which he glides onwards. The region of the Ṭuat where the serpent Āpep or Neḥa-ḥrå lives is called Tchau, , and it is 440 cubits long, and 440 cubits wide; his head and his tail are caught in fetters by Serqet and Ḥer-ṭesu-f respectively, and these gods have transfixed him to the ground with six huge knives (vol. i., p. 142). When the body of the serpent has been removed, Åfu-Rā advances, and, passing four goddesses each armed with a knife, arrives at four rectangular buildings. Inside each building (vol. i., p. 144) is a mound of sand, and at each end of each building is the head of a man. These buildings are the tombs wherein the four chief forms of the Sun-god have been buried, the first containing the "Form of Tem," the second the "Form of Kheperå," the third

[1] This statement is found in the Summary.

the "Form of RĀ," and the fourth the "Form of OSIRIS." The heads which appear at the ends of the tombs are those of the enemies who were slain at the tombs, and were buried in the foundations in order to drive away evil spirits. The texts which refer to these scenes state that the four goddesses join in slaying ĀPEP, that the human heads appear as soon as any one comes to the tombs; and that as soon as they have heard the voice of ȦFU-RĀ, and he has gone by, they "eat their own forms," i.e., they disappear until Rā again comes (vol. i., p. 145).

On the right of the Boat of ȦFU-RĀ, and facing it, are HORUS, and the twelve gods of the hours, who protect the tombs of Osiris, and assist RĀ in his journey (vol. i., pp. 154-156); next come twelve goddesses of the hours, who face in the opposite direction, and are entreated to guide "the god who is on "the horizon to the beautiful Ȧmentet in peace." Beyond these is the great Crocodile, called ĀBSHE-ȦM-ṬUAT, which is stretched out at full length over the tomb of Osiris; as the Boat of ȦFU-RĀ passes it, the god addresses words to Osiris, who for a season puts forth his head, which disappears as soon as the Boat has entered the next DIVISION.

On the left of ȦFU-RĀ we have also a number of gods and goddesses who belong to this DIVISION, and among them may be specially noticed the serpent MEḤEN, the lord of this region; his body is bent in the form of a canopy, and beneath is the "Flesh of Osiris" in the form of a god (ȦFU-ȦSAR) seated on a throne (vol. i., p. 149). In front of it are a number of the enemies of Osiris, some decapitated by the LYNX-GODDESS, and some in fetters which are held in the hands of the god ȦNKU (vol. i., pp. 149, 150). Beyond these are three living souls, representatives of the blessed dead in this region, and the "Flesh of Tem" (ȦFU-TEM) in the form of a god seated on the back of a huge serpent resembling MEḤEN (vol. i., p. 151).

EIGHTH DIVISION OF THE ṬUAT.

I. KINGDOM OF OSIRIS ACCORDING TO THE BOOK ȦM-ṬUAT.

The name of this DIVISION, or HOUR, or CITY, is ṬEBAT-NETERU-S, its Gate is called ĀḤĀ-ȦN-URṬ-NEF, and its Hour-goddess is NEBT-USHAU. The Boat of ȦFU-RĀ now enters one of the most holy places in the Kingdom of Osiris, for in it abide the Four Forms of TATHENEN. Looking at the Boat (vol. i., p. 164) we see that ISIS and SER are no longer in it, a fact which indicates that the dangers incidental to passing through this DIVISION are not great, and that it is towed by a company of gods. Immediately in front of them are nine SHEMSU, or "Followers," i.e., "servants" (of Osiris), each with an object before him (vol. i., p. 167), which indicates that he is a properly bandaged mummy, and leading these are Four Rams, each wearing a different kind of crown, which represent the Four Forms of TATHENEN (vol. i., pp. 168, 169). The heads which are attached to the symbols of the "Followers" only appear when they hear the voice of ȦFU-RĀ, and when he has passed them they disappear; the huge knives which they have are used in slaughtering any of the enemies of Rā who may succeed in entering the City.

On the right and left of the path of ȦFU-RĀ are a number of "Circles" in which dwell the "gods" who have been mummified, and for whom all the prescribed rites and ceremonies have been performed; the greater number of these gods are not well known, and their exact functions are not well understood. The CIRCLES on the right are: 1. ḤETEPET-NEB-S, 2. ḤETEMET-KHEMIU, 3. ḤAPSEMU-S, 4. SEḤERT-BAIU-S, 5. ĀAT-SETEKAU, 6. The door ṬES-AMEM-MIT-EM-SHETA-F. As ȦFU-RĀ passes these gods their doors fly open and those within hear what he says, and they respond with cries which are like unto those of male cats, or the "noise of the confused murmur of the living," or the "sound of those who go down to the battle-field of Nu," or the "sound of the cry of the Divine Hawk of Horus," or the "twittering of the birds in a nest of water-fowl." The CIRCLES on the left are: 1. SESHETA, 2. ṬUAT, 3. ȦS-NETERU, 4. ȦAKEBI, 5. NEBT-SEMU-NIFU, 6. The door ṬES-KHAIBITU-ṬUATIU. The sounds made by the gods in these resemble the "hum of many honey-bees," the "sound of the swathed ones," the "sound of men who lament," the sounds "of bulls and other male animals," and the sound of those "who make supplication through terror" (vol. i., pp. 170 ff.).

NINTH DIVISION OF THE ṬUAT.

I. Kingdom of Osiris according to the Book Ȧm-Ṭuat.

The name of this Division, or Hour, or City, is Best-Ȧru-Ānkhet-kheperu, the Gate is called Saa-em-Ḳeb, and its Hour-goddess is Ṭuatet-Māketet-en-neb-s. The Boat of Ȧfu-Rā now enters the last of the four Divisions of the Kingdom of Osiris, and moves without the aid of towing. Immediately in front of it are twelve sailor-gods, each grasping a short paddle with both hands; they appear to have been depicted in front of the Boat because there was no room for them in it. The god is still under the form of Meḥen, and is still passing over the secret path of Ȧmentet, and his Sailors sing to him, and as they do so they scatter water from the stream with their paddles on the Spirits who dwell in this City (vol. i., pp. 189-191). In front of these are three deities, seated on baskets, and the god Ḥetep-neteru-Ṭuat; they accompany the Boat of Ȧfu-Rā, and it is their duty to provide food, or offerings, for the gods who are in the Division. On the right of the path of the god are twelve uraei, who lighten the darkness by means of the fire which they pour out from their mouths: they rest upon objects which suggest that they have received their places in this DIVISION because all the appointed funeral rites and ceremonies were duly performed for them (vol. i., p. 201). In front of these are the nine gods who represent the field-labourers in the Ṭuat (vol. i., pp. 204, 205), and each holds a heavy stick, similar to that which the peasants in Egypt have always carried to protect themselves. Their "ganger" is ḤERU-ḤER-SHE-ṬUAT, i.e., "He who is over the lakes (or sand) in the Ṭuat."

On the left of the path of the god are twelve gods, each of whom is seated on a weaving instrument (vol. i., p. 195), and twelve goddesses (vol. i., p. 199); the gods are the TCHATCHA, or "Great Chiefs" of Osiris, and their duty is to avenge Osiris each day, and to overthrow the enemies of Osiris, and the goddesses spring into existence when they hear the god's voice, and sing praises to Osiris each day.

CHAPTER XI.

SIXTH DIVISION OF THE ṬUAT.

II. KINGDOM OF OSIRIS ACCORDING TO THE BOOK OF GATES.

THE Boat of ȦFU-RĀ, having passed through the first five DIVISIONS of the Ṭuat, now, according to the BOOK OF GATES, arrives near the southern part of the Delta, and near the kingdom of Osiris, lord of Mendes and Busiris. Before, however, the god can enter it, he must pass through the Gate of the SIXTH DIVISION, which is called NEBT-ĀḤĀ, and which is guarded by the monster serpent SET-EM-MAAT-F. In the Gate or close to it, is the JUDGMENT HALL of OSIRIS, and it is tolerably certain that no soul entered his kingdom without being weighed in the balance of the god. The scene in which the Hall is depicted is of great interest, for it is different in many important particulars from the representations of the Judgment which we find on papyri, even in those which belong to the period of the XVIIIth and XIXth Dynasties. All the texts which describe it are written in hieroglyphics, but in many of them the hieroglyphics have, as Champollion pointed

Nebseni being weighed against his heart.

out, special and very unusual values, and the title "enigmatic writing" given to them by Goodwin is appropriate. In the ordinary Judgment Scenes we find that the heart of the deceased is weighed in the balance against the feather symbolic of Maāt or righteousness, that the operation of weighing is carried out by Thoth and Anubis in the presence of the great gods, the owner of the heart himself sometimes looking on, that the gods accept and ratify the verdict of Thoth, and that the deceased is then led into the presence of Osiris by Horus. Sometimes the heart of the deceased is weighed against his whole body, as in the Papyrus of Nebseni, and at other times the pans of the scales only contain weights. In the scene before us the arrangement is quite different. Osiris is seated on a chair of state, and wears the crowns of the South and North united; in

The Scales of Osiris, with weights.

his hands are the symbols of "life," 𓋹, and "rule," 𓋾. His chair stands on a raised platform, on the nine steps of which stand the nine gods who form his company; beneath the feet of the god, perhaps under his platform, are the dead, i.e., the damned, or his enemies. The top of the Hall is protected with a row of spear heads, and from the ceiling hang four heads of gazelle, or oryges; according to a legend certain enemies of Osiris transformed themselves into these animals, and were slain by the god. On the platform, immediately in front of the god, stands THOTH, in the form of a mummy, and he serves as the standard of the balance; the object in the pan is being weighed against the symbol of "evil," 𓅪, which it seems to counterbalance exactly. This being so, it seems that the wickedness of the deceased did not go beyond a recognized limit. ANUBIS, in the upper corner of the scene, addresses some words to THOTH, who bears the Balance on his shoulders. In the small boat near the Balance is a pig being beaten by an ape;[1] the name of the pig is ĀM-Ā, but neither his functions, nor those of the ape are clearly known. The ape may be the equivalent of the dog-headed ape which sits on the beam of the Balance in the pictures in the Theban papyri, and the pig may represent the Eater of the Dead; but at present these are matters of conjecture. With reference to the pig it is interesting to note that

[1] The boat sometimes contains two apes (see Sharpe, *Eg. Inscriptions*, part ii., pl. 9), and in a tomb at Thebes one ape is in the boat and one outside it (see the illustration opposite).

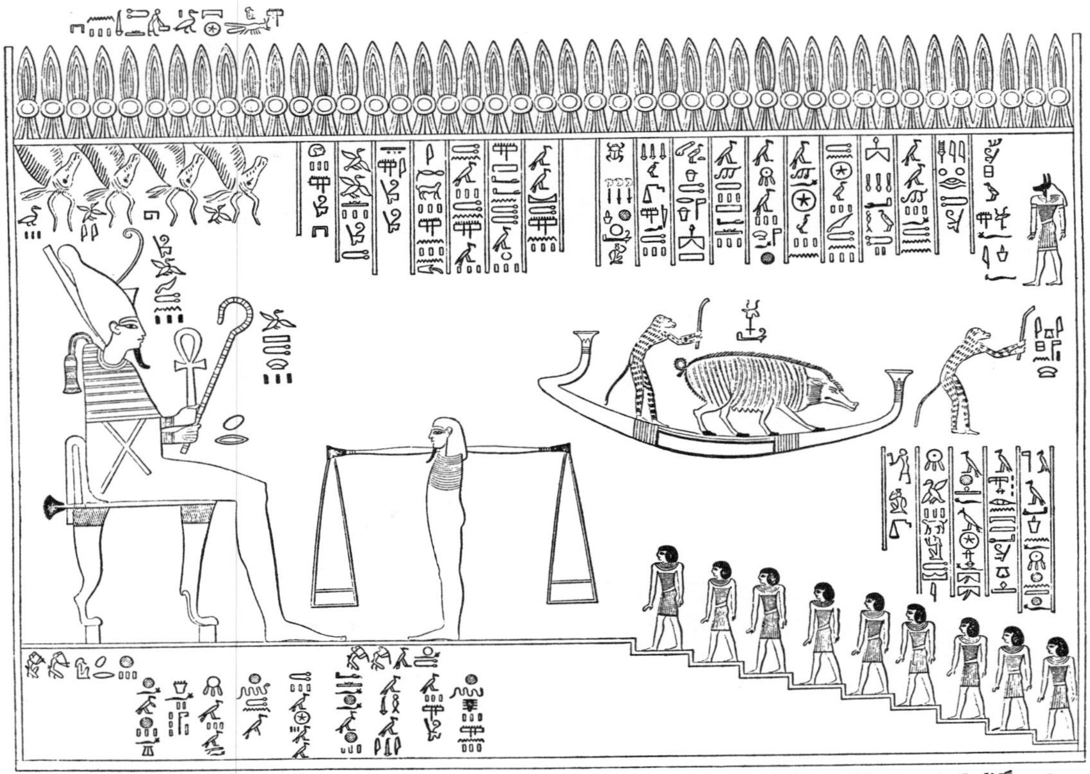

The Judgment Hall of Osiris according to the Book of Gates. (From Champollion, *Monuments de l'Égypte*, tom. iii., pl. cclxxii.)

in the Papyrus of Nekht the deceased is seen grasping a chain by which a serpent is fettered, and spearing a pig. The chief point of interest in the whole scene is the fact that the Judgment here depicted is of a more primitive character than that given in the Book of the Dead.

The Boat of Ȧfu-Rā, having passed through or by the Hall of Osiris, now enters the abode of the blessed, and the pictures of the Sixth Division are intended to show us the occupations of those who have been declared to be "right and true." The Boat is towed through this Division by four gods of the Ṭuat and immediately in front of it is a series of jackal-headed sceptres of Seb, to each of which two enemies are tied; by the side of each sceptre is a god, who takes care that the punishments which have been decreed by Osiris are duly executed. It is noteworthy that the two eyes of Rā, , are placed between the first two sceptres (vol. ii., p. 172). The Egyptian text (vol. ii., p. 183) makes it quite clear that the enemies of Osiris are tied to the standards of Seb according to the god's decree, and preparatory to slaughter in the Hall of Rā.

Nekht spearing the pig of evil.

To the right of the path of Ȧfu-Rā are twelve Maāti gods who carry Maāt, and twelve Ḥeteptiu gods who carry provisions. These are they who offered up incense to the gods, and whose *kau* or "doubles have been washed clean, whose iniquities have been done away, and who were right in the judgment." Therefore has Osiris decreed them to be "Maāt of Maāt," i.e., most "righteous," and he has given them a place of abode in his own presence with peace and the food of Maāt thereon to live (vol. ii., pp. 177, 186).

To the left of the path of ȦFU-Rā are twelve gods, each of whom is tending a colossal ear of wheat, and twelve gods provided with sickles, engaged in reaping. The ears of wheat here growing are the "members of Osiris," (*ḥāt Sar*, ), that is, they are regarded as parts of the god's own body,[1] and the inhabitants of the Kingdom of Osiris and human beings on earth alike ate the body of the god when they ate bread of wheat. The wheat which grew in the kingdom of Osiris was, of course, larger, and finer in every respect than that which grew on earth, and it is expressly said that the "Khu," i.e., beatified spirits, feed upon the divine grain (NEPRȦ) in the land of the Light-god (vol. ii., p. 188). Therefore since the divine grain is here a form of Osiris, the Khu live upon the god himself, and eat him daily; this is exactly the kind of belief which we should expect the primitive Egyptians at one period to possess. The idea of a heaven wherein

[1] Prof. Wiedemann has collected a number of important facts on this subject in his most interesting paper "OSIRIS VÉGÉTANT."

wheat grew luxuriantly, and food made of the same could be had in abundance, was evolved in their mind after the introduction of wheat into Egypt from Asia, and after the Egyptians had settled down to agricultural pursuits. The god of such a heaven was naturally the Corn-god NEPRÀ, but it seems as if Osiris were identified with him at a very early period, and as if, finally, he absorbed all his attributes. The idea of a heaven of this simple character must of necessity be very old, and it presupposes the existence of beliefs concerning the future life which the later Egyptians must often in their secret hearts have repudiated. In the BOOK OF GATES we find NEB-ĀUT-ÀB, i.e., RĀ, decreeing that the wheat of this region should germinate, and that the plants should grow to a large size, and those who are tending the crops beseech him to shine upon them, for when he shines the grain sprouts and the plants grow.

Now, though Osiris was from a material point of view the Grain-god, or Corn-god, and the wheat was his members, which were eaten by his followers, he was also the lord of MAĀT, i.e., "righteousness" and "integrity," and even the personification of those abstract qualities. When, addressing the MAĀTI gods, he declares they are "MAĀT OF MAĀT," he makes it clear that he considers them to be beings of like nature to himself, and that they will live upon MAĀT; in other words, they have become Truth, and they will live upon Truth, and exist as Truth for ever. The MAĀTI gods apparently represent the highest conception of spiritual beings which the Egyptians arrived at in the early period, and which is only paralleled by that of a later period, according to which the followers of the Sun-god, who travelled with him in the Boat of Millions of Years, eventually became beings consisting of nothing but light. It would be useless to contend that either conception was believed in throughout the country generally, for the Egyptians as a nation believed in a heaven wherein happiness of a very material character was to be found; still there must have been among the educated and priestly classes devout men and women whose yearnings for future happiness would not be satisfied with promises of cakes, and ale, and love-making, and to whom the idea of becoming the counterpart of the eternal god of the dead would afford consolation and hope.

SEVENTH DIVISION OF THE ṬUAT.

II. KINGDOM OF OSIRIS ACCORDING TO THE BOOK OF GATES.

The SEVENTH DIVISION, or HOUR, is entered by the Gate PESṬIT, which is guarded by a monster serpent called ĀKHA-EN-MAAT; the pictures and texts are incomplete on the sarcophagus of Seti I., and those which are given in vol. ii., p. 190 ff., are taken from M. E. Lefébure's *Les Hypogées Royaux de Thèbes*, tom. ii., part ii., pl. 11 ff. The Boat of ȦFU-RĀ is, as before, towed by four gods of the Ṭuat. The procession of the ministers of the god consists of twenty-four gods, twelve of whom have their hands and arms hidden; these last "are invisible beings, but those who are in the Ṭuat and the dead can see them," and Rā promises them that they shall be with him in Ḥet-Benben, that is to say, in the heavenly counterpart of one of the temples of the Sun-god of Heliopolis (see vol. ii., p. 194 ff.).

To the right of the path of Ȧfu-Rā are twelve gods armed with clubs having forked ends; they are called Kheru-metauḥ, and their duty is to repulse the serpent Āpep. Immediately in front of them is the serpent Sebȧ, on the head and back of which twelve human heads are seen; these make their appearance (vol. ii., p. 206 ff.) at the coming of Ȧfu-Rā, and the twelve gods who grasp the monster's body are exhorted to destroy them. The serpent is called Sebȧ, and Āpep, and Ḥefau. Beyond these groups of gods are twelve star-gods, who hold in their hands a long rope which is twisted round the neck of a god in mummied form called Qān, or Āqen, or Nāq (vol. ii., pp. 208, 209). To the left of the path of Ȧfu-Rā is the god of the Ṭuat, called Ṭuati, who leans on a staff, and is in charge of the twelve mummies which lie on the back of the serpent Nehep; the serpent has twenty-four lions' legs arranged at intervals (vol. ii., p. 210), and a mummy rests over each pair of them. The mummies are described as "those who are in inertness," and "those who are in the body of Osiris asleep."

As ÅFU-RĀ passes them the god ṬUATI encourages them to loosen their bandages, to untie and take off their wigs, to collect their bones, to gather together their flesh and their members, to open their eyes and look at the light, to get up from their state of inertness, and to take possession of their fields in SEKHET-NEBT-ḤETEPET. Beyond these is another group of gods whose duty it is to live near the pool of a serpent, the water of which is of fire; its flames proceed from the serpent, and they are so fierce that the gods and souls of the earth dare not approach them. On the other hand, the gods of the pool are adjured to give water to KHENTI-ÅUḲERT, i.e., the Governor of Åuḳert. Now Åuḳert is the name of the Other World, or Ṭuat, of HELIOPOLIS, and the mention of it and of ḤET-BENBEN suggests that the Kingdom of Osiris according to the BOOK OF GATES was made to include that of the god TEMU, a form of the Night-sun. The gods who sit round the lake of fire receive their bodies and souls from the serpent NEHEP, and then they journey into SEKHET-ÅARU, which apparently has not yet been reached.

EIGHTH DIVISION OF THE ṬUAT.

II. KINGDOM OF OSIRIS ACCORDING TO THE BOOK OF GATES.

The Boat of ÅFU-RĀ next passes through the Gate of Bekhkhi, which is guarded by the monster serpent

SET-ḤRȦ, and is towed over this DIVISION, or HOUR, by the gods of the Ṭuat. The region is a remarkable one, and it certainly forms part of the Kingdom of the Sun-god of ȦNNU, or Heliopolis. At one end of the long Lake, or Pool, which represents the celestial waters of NU (vol. ii., pp. 225, 226) stands the god "who dwelleth in NU," and in the Lake itself we see four groups of beings in human forms who are called "Bathers" (Herpiu), "Floaters" (Ȧḳiu), "Swimmers" (Nubiu), and "Divers" (Khepau). The gods who tow the Boat call on the dwellers in this DIVISION to praise the soul of RĀ, which is in heaven, and his body, which is on earth; for heaven is made young again by his soul, and earth by his body. Then, addressing the god in the Boat, they declare that they will make his paths straight in ȦḲERT, and that they will make his Boat to pass over the beings who are immersed in the waters of the Lake. The god "who dwelleth in NU" then calls upon the beings in the water to pay homage to RĀ, and he promises that they shall enjoy breath for their nostrils, and peace in their cisterns of water. Their souls, which are upon earth, shall enjoy offerings in abundance and shall never die, and shall be as fully provided with food as is RĀ, whose body is on earth, but whose soul is in heaven.

On the left of the path of ȦFU-RĀ are twelve TCHATCHA, or "Great Chiefs," and nine SOULS, who are adoring a god (vol. ii., pp. 227, 231); before each Soul are a loaf of bread and some *sekemu* herbs. The TCHATCHA perform a very important duty in this DIVISION, for they distribute to the SOULS who have been ordered by RĀ to live by the fiery Lake SERSER the food which has been allotted to them; in other words, they give the SOULS the portion of food which it has been decreed they should receive daily, and no more and no less, and the SOULS receive their destined allowance, and have to be content therewith. Judging from the texts here and elsewhere in the BOOK OF GATES it seems that there was some power in the Ṭuat, probably KHENTI-ÅMENTI, or OSIRIS KHENTI-ÅMENTI, who decreed that the beings therein should receive a regular, fixed, and unalterable allowance of food each day, and who appointed ministers, who are here called TCHATCHA, to see that each being received his "ration," without addition, and without diminution. The Sun-god in passing through the Ṭuat confirms the "ration," and orders its continuance to each being therein.

On the right of the path of ÅFU-RĀ is HORUS THE AGED, leaning on a staff, and addressing a company of twelve of the enemies of Osiris (vol. ii., pp. 232-234), who stand with their arms tied together behind their backs in very painful attitudes. Before these is a huge serpent called KHETI, belching fire into the faces of the enemies of Osiris; in each of the seven undulations of the serpent stands a god, who is adjured by Horus to aid in the work of destruction. From the text we learn that the chief offences with which these enemies are charged is the "putting of secret things behind them, the dragging forth of the sacred object *sekem* from the secret place, or sanctuary, and the profanation of certain of the hidden things of the Ṭuat"; because of these things they are doomed to have their bodies first hacked in pieces, and then burned, and their souls utterly annihilated.

CHAPTER XII.

TENTH DIVISION OF THE ṬUAT.

I. Kingdom of Temu-Kheperȧ-Rā according to the Book Ȧm-Ṭuat.

The Tenth and Eleventh Divisions, or Hours, are intended to illustrate the passage of Ȧfu-Rā through the region of Ȧḳert, or Ȧuḳert, that is to say, the Kingdom of the Sun-god of Ȧnnu, or Heliopolis. The name of the Tenth Division is Metchet-qat-utchebu, its gate is called Āa-kherpu-mes-ȧru, and the Hour-goddess is Ṭenṭenit-uḥeset-khak-ȧb. The pictures and texts which illustrate and describe this region are of peculiar interest, for they refer to the union of Kheperȧ with Rā, i.e., the introduction of the germ of new life into the body of the dead Sun-god, whereby Ȧfu-Rā regains his powers as a living god, and becomes ready to emerge into the light of a new day with glory and splendour. It must be understood that the constitution of this Division is quite different from that of any which we have seen hitherto, and that the gods who are in it are peculiar to the region of Ȧḳert. It is impossible to say where Ȧḳert began or ended, but as the Ṭuat of the inhabitants of Heliopolis was represented by it, it follows, perhaps, that it was believed to be situated quite near that city. It is pretty certain that it comprised a part of the Eastern Delta, and that it extended along the eastern bank of the Nile some considerable distance to the south of Memphis, in fact, so far as BAKHAU, the Mountain of Sunrise; if this be so, it follows that when the Boat of ȦFU-RĀ entered this DIVISION the god would have to alter his course from east to south. As the Kingdom of Osiris marked the limit of his journey northwards, and the Boat then turned eastwards, so the northern end of ȦḲERT marked the limit of his journey eastwards, and the Boat then turned southwards.

A glance at the Boat of ȦFU-RĀ as it enters this DIVISION shows us that it is neither being towed nor rowed along. Immediately in front of it (vol. i., p. 209) is the serpent THES-ḤRȦU, with ḤERU-KHENTI, in the form of a black hawk, sitting on its back; on one side is a goddess of the North, and on the other a goddess of the South. Next we have the serpent ĀNKH-TA, (vol. i., p. 210), and then a group of twelve gods, four having disks for heads, and carrying arrows, four carrying javelins, and four carrying bows (vol. i., p. 210, 211). The serpent is the "watcher of the Ṭuat in the holy place of Khenti-Ȧmenti," and the weapons carried by the twelve gods are to enable them to protect ȦFU-RĀ against his enemies in this region. To the right of the path of ÅFU-RĀ are twelve lakes of water, which are intended to represent the celestial watery abyss of NU, from which the Nile on earth was supposed to obtain its supply. At one end of the scene is Horus, who leans on a staff, and addresses the beings who are seen plunging, and swimming, and floating in the various lakes (vol. i., pp. 226, 227), and bids them to come to ḤĀP-UR, and promises them that their members shall not perish, nor their flesh decay. Who the beings in the water are it is impossible exactly to say, but it is clear that they were supposed to have the power to hinder the progress of the Boat of ÅFU-RĀ, for Horus propitiates them with promises of health and strength, as we have seen above. A little beyond the lakes are four goddesses who "shed light upon the road of RĀ in the thick darkness," and in front of them is the mystic sceptre which represents "SET the Watcher," who "waketh up and travelleth with the god."

To the left of the path of ÅFU-RĀ we see first the god P-ĀNKHI, i.e., "he who is endowed with the property of life," and KHEPER-ĀNKH, in the form of a beetle, who is pushing before him an oval of sand, which either contains his germ, or is intended to represent the ball of eggs which the *Scarabaeus sacer* rolls before him, and which he wishes to take through the DIVISION into the Eastern Horizon of the sky (vol. i., p. 216). Then we have the two serpents Menenui supporting a disk, and goddesses of the North and South (vol. i., p. 217). To the right of these are the goddesses NETHETH and KENȦT, who spring from the axe SEṬFIT, which supports a disk. These four goddesses gather together souls on earth, and they purify the mighty spirits in the Ṭuat; they only become visible when ȦFU-RĀ appears, and so soon as he has passed them by they vanish. Beyond these is a long procession of deities who assist ȦFU-RĀ in his journey. The first eight, who are goddesses, stand before the Ape-god called ȦF-ERMEN-MAAT-F, who holds the Eye of Horus, and it is their duty to recite the words of power which shall cause splendour to issue from the Eye of Horus each day, and to sing praises to it (vol. i., pp. 219-221). The other deities only come into being when ȦFU-RĀ utters their names; they live in the shades which are in the mouth of the great god, and then their souls travel with him. Their work is to strip the dead of their swathings, and to break in pieces the enemies of Rā, and to order their destruction.

ELEVENTH DIVISION OF THE ṬUAT.

I. KINGDOM OF TEMU-KHEPERȦ-RĀ ACCORDING TO THE BOOK ȦM-ṬUAT.

The name of this DIVISION, or HOUR, or CITY, is RE-EN-QERERT-ȦPT-KHATU, i.e., "Mouth of the Circle which judgeth bodies," the name of its Gate is SEKHEN-ṬUATIU, i.e., "Embracer of the gods of the Ṭuat," and the Hour-goddess is SEBIT-NEBT-UȦA-KHESEFET-SEBȦ-EM-PERT-F, i.e., "Star, lady of the Boat which repulseth Sebȧ at his appearance." This DIVISION of the ṬUAT was very near the Mountain of the Sunrise, from which the newly-born Sun-god would appear soon after day-break, and the knowledge of the gods in it, and of their forms and names, was believed to ensure to its possessor the power to emerge from the Ṭuat as a spirit equipped for travelling with the Sun-god over the sky. The Boat of ȦFU-RĀ makes its way through this region, and on looking at it (vol. i., p. 233) we see on its prow a disk of light encircled by a serpent; the disk is that of the star PESṬU, and it "guideth this great god into the ways of the darkness which gradually lighteneth, and illumineth those who are on the earth." The Boat is now towed by twelve gods, who employ as a rope the immensely long serpent MEḤEN, the tail of which is supposed to be fastened to the front of the Boat (vol. i., p. 235); so soon as they have towed the god to the end of this DIVISION, and he has set himself in the horizon, they return to their own places. Immediately in front of these gods are two Crowns, the White and the Red (vol. i., p. 237), which rest each on the back of a uraeus; so soon as ȦFU-RĀ comes three human heads look forth, one from each side of the White Crown, and one from the Red Crown, and they disappear when he has passed by. The leaders of this remarkable procession are four forms of the goddess NEITH of Saïs, who spring into life so soon as the sound of the voice of ȦFU-RĀ is heard; these are Neith the Child, Neith of the White Crown, Neith of the Red Crown, and Neith of the phallus. These goddesses "guard the holy gate of the city of Saïs, which is unknown, and can neither be seen nor looked at."

On the right of the path of ȦFU-RĀ we see the two-headed god ĀPER-ḤRȦ-NEB-TCHETTA, with the Crown of the South on one head, and the Crown of the North on the other. Next come the god TEMU, his body, and his soul, the former in the shape of a serpent with two pairs of human legs and a pair of wings, and the latter in that of a man, with a disk on his head, and his hands stretched out to the wings (vol i., p. 242). In front of these are the body and soul of the Star-god SHEṬU, who follows ȦFU-RĀ and casts the living ones to him every day. All the other deities here represented assist the god in his passage, and help him to arrive on the Horizon of the East.

The region to the left of the Boat is one of fire, and representations of it which we have in the BOOK ȦM-ṬUAT and the BOOK OF GATES may well have suggested the beliefs in a fiery hell that have come down through the centuries to our own time. Quite near the Boat stands Horus, holding in the left hand the snake-headed boomerang, with which he performs deeds of magic; in front of him is the serpent SET-ḤEḤ, i.e., the Everlasting Set, his familiar and messenger (vol. i., p. 249). Horus is watching and directing the destruction of the bodies, souls, shadows, and heads of the enemies of Rā, and of the damned who are in this Division, which is taking place in five pits of fire. A lioness-headed goddess stands by the side of the first pit which contains the enemies of Rā; the fire with which they are consumed is supplied by the goddess, who vomits it into one corner of the pit.

The next four pits contain the bodies, souls, shades, and heads respectively, of the damned, the fire being supplied by the goddesses in charge. In the pit following are four beings who are immersed, head downwards, in the depths of its fires (vol. i., pp. 249-253). The texts which refer to the pits of fire show that the beings who were unfortunate enough to be cast into them were hacked in pieces by the goddesses who were over them, and then burned in the fierce fire provided by Set-Ḥeḥ and the goddesses until they were consumed. The pits of fire were, of course, suggested by the red, fiery clouds which, with lurid splendour, often herald the sunrise in Egypt. As the sun rose, dispersing as he did so the darkness of night, and the mist and haze which appeared to cling to him, it was natural for the primitive peoples of Egypt to declare that his foes were being burned in his pits or lakes of fire. The redder and brighter the fiery glare, the more effective would the burning up of the foes be thought to be, and it is not difficult to conceive the horror which would rise in the minds of superstitious folk when they saw the day open with a dull or cloudy sky, with no evidence in it that the Sun had defeated the powers of darkness, and had suffered no injury during the night.

The presence of the pits of fire in this DIVISION suggests that we have now practically arrived at the end of the Ṭuat, and, according to the views of those who compiled the original description of ÅḲERT, this is indeed the case. We have, in the Boat of ÁFU-RĀ, now passed through the Ṭuat of Khenti-Åmenti, the Ṭuat of Seker, the Ṭuat of Osiris, lord of Mendes and Busiris, and the Ṭuat of TEMU-KHEPERÅ-RĀ, lord of ÅNNU, i.e., the four great Ṭuats which comprised all the great abodes of the dead of all Egypt. Now to enter this group of Ṭuats it was necessary to pass through a forecourt or antechamber, which for purposes of convenience has been called a DIVISION of the Ṭuat, and before ÁFU-RĀ can emerge from the last of the group of Ṭuats into the light of a new day, he must pass through a region which corresponds to the forecourt of the Ṭuats, and serves actually as a forecourt of the world of light. In the forecourt of the Ṭuats the darkness became deeper and deeper the further it was penetrated, but in the forecourt of the world of light the darkness becomes less and less dense as the day is approached. Considered from this point of view, the Four Ṭuats only contain Ten Divisions, or Hours, which corresponded roughly with the Ten GATES of the Kingdom of Osiris, as set forth in many copies of the

Theban Recension of the Book of the Dead. Strictly speaking, the addition of a forecourt to the world of light was unnecessary, but as the Theban priests had added one at the beginning of the Four Ṭuats, symmetry demanded that there should be another supplementary region at their end.

If now we treat the Ten Divisions of the Four Ṭuats as Hours, and assume that the Book of ÀFU-RĀ began its journey through them on an average between six and seven o'clock in the evening, it follows that the god reached the abode of Osiris about midnight, together with those souls who travelled with him. The souls who chose to be judged by Osiris, preferring a heaven full of material delights to spiritual happiness, disembarked, and passed into the Judgment Hall, where they received their sentence, and were made joyful or miserable. For the blessed homesteads were provided, and for the wicked slicings and gashings with knives, and pits of fire, wherein their bodies and souls and shadows were destroyed for ever. The evidence indicates that Osiris passed judgment on souls each day at midnight, and that the righteous were rewarded with good things shortly afterwards; the wicked also were punished with tortures and burnings, probably soon afterwards, or at all events before the Sun rose on the following day. Thus Osiris in the Ṭuat, and Rā in the world of light, would rejoice in freedom from foes until the time arrived for a new "weighing of words" to take place, and, according to one view, the enemies of Osiris, and the foes of Rā, were consumed in fire together, and it was the smoke and fire of their burning which were seen in the heavens at sunrise. We may now consider the vestibule at the end of the Four Ṭuats, and describe the beings who were in it.

CHAPTER XIII.

NINTH DIVISION OF THE ṬUAT.

II. Kingdom of Temu-Kheperȧ-Rā according to the Book of Gates.

The Ninth, Tenth and Eleventh Divisions of the Book of Gates contain series of pictures and texts which are very hard to explain satisfactorily, and the difficulty is further increased by the fact that only one copy of them is known, i.e., that on the sarcophagus of Seti I. It is quite certain that they cannot refer to the Kingdom of Osiris, and we are driven to conclude that they are intended to illustrate and describe the region of Ȧḳert, which, as has already been said, formed the Ṭuat to which the worshippers of the Sun-god of Heliopolis relegated the spirits of their dead. The First Division of this remarkable region, i.e., the Ninth in the Book of Gates, is entered by the Gate called Āat-shefsheft, which is guarded by the monster serpent Āb-ta; a company of gods keep watch outside, and the corridor is swept by flames of fire, and a warder in mummied form stands on guard at each end of it.

When Ȧfu-Ra has passed through, and the Gate is closed, the gods outside set up a wail, for they must abide in darkness until he re-appears. So soon as the god has entered the Division four gods of the

Ṭuat appear and take hold of the tow-line, but they cannot advance until a path is cleared for them. The obstacles in their way take the forms of the huge serpent ĀPEP, and a great crocodile, the tail of which is in the form of a serpent's head and neck ; the name of the latter monster is given both as SESHSESH and SESSI (vol. ii., pp. 242, 244). These have taken up their positions at the end of the DIVISION, in that portion of the Ṭuat which is not very far from the place of sunrise, and a company of beings appear on behalf of ȦFU-RĀ, and proceed to remove the monsters by means of words of power and magical ceremonies.

The company consists of six men, four apes, and four goddesses; in front of these are three men armed with harpoons, and grasping a rope, which passes over the prostrate body and head of the god ȦAI, its end being held fast in his two hands. ȦAI has on his head a small disk, which is set between two objects that resemble the ears of an ass, and these suggest that the figure is intended to represent a form of the Sun-god. The ass is well known as a type of the Sun-god, and "Eater of the Ass" is equally well known as a name for SET or ĀPEP. In an illustration from the Book of the Dead (Chapter XL.; see above, p. 113), the "Eater of the Ass" is seen biting into the back of an ass, which is being delivered by the scribe Nekht in his character of Osiris. That ȦAI is a solar being, and that he opposes ĀPEP on behalf of Rā, is obvious. It seems, however, that he is in need of the help of the men with harpoons, and of their companions behind them, each of whom holds the ends of a pole or rope (of a net), which is bent in the shape of a bow over his or her head. The men are called ḤERU-METU-ḤEKAIU, i.e., "those who are over the words (which have) magical power"; the apes are called SAIU, i.e., producers of magical effects by making knots in ropes, over which they whisper incantations; and the women are called SAIT, and work the same kind of magic as the apes. The object which each member of these three groups holds with both hands above his, or her, head is probably a net and, as M. Lefébure has pointed out, it is actually so represented in the tomb of Rameses VI. (?). In the Babylonian legend of the fight between Marduk and Tiāmat, the great she-monster of the deep, the god is made to provide himself with a net with which to entangle her feet. In the Book of the Dead (Chapter cliii.B.) we read of the net ȦNQET, and in the vignette we see three apes working it, and securing the fish which are caught inside it. As Apep was a monster of the deep, to make use of nets in his capture was a wise decision on the part of the friends of ȦFU-RĀ.

The Apes working the net.

Having taken up their positions for attacking Āpep the men with the harpoons work the rope which is attached to ȦAI, the goddesses and the apes shake out their rope nets over their heads, and recite their spells, and the men who know the proper words of power shake out their nets and recite the formulae which shall have the effect of throwing ĀPEP and SESSI into the state of stupefaction wherein it will be easy to slay them. The spells and words of power have their proper effect, the monsters are fascinated and slain, and the path of ȦFU-RĀ is clear.

On the right of the Boat of ȦFU-RĀ is the huge serpent KHEPRI, with a head and a pair of human legs at each end of his body; one head faces north (*or*, west), and the other south (*or*, east). Behind each head is a uraeus, and between the uraei stands "HORUS OF THE ṬUAT," wearing the crowns of the South and North (vol. ii., p. 257). A rope passes under KHEPRI, and on one side is hauled by Eight Powers (SEKHEMIU), and on the other by the "Souls of Ȧment," who are man-headed; by the "Followers of Thoth," who are ibis-headed; by the "Followers of Horus," who are hawk-headed; and by the "Followers of RĀ," who are ram-headed (vol. ii., pp. 255, 256, 258). It will be noted that the two pairs of legs of KHEPRI face in opposite ways, so that in whichever direction he moves one pair must walk backwards; the Eight Powers have overcome the resistance of the sixteen gods, and the face of Horus of the Ṭuat is towards the rising sun.

On the left of the path of ȦFU-RĀ we see a hawk-headed lion called ḤERU-ȦM-UȦA, i.e., "Horus in the Boat," wearing the Crown of the South; on his back stands the two-headed god Horus-Set (vol. ii., p. 247), whose faces typify Day and Night, and Light and Darkness, and the Sun-gods of the South and North. Above the hind-quarters of the lion is the head of the god Ānā (?), wearing the Crown of the South; on the one side we have four gods of the South assisting in the raising of a column surmounted by the Crown of the South, and on the other four gods of the North assisting in the raising of a column surmounted by the Crown of the North. These ceremonies appear to have some connexion with the magical rites which were performed in Egypt in primitive times in the making ready of the crowns for the Sun-god to wear on his rising. Beyond these gods are: 1. The serpent Shemti, with four heads at each end of his body, and his warder Åpu. 2. The serpent Båta, with a head at each end of his body. 3. The serpent Ṭepi, with four human heads and bodies at each end of his body, and his warder Åbeth. These are faced by two gods who are about to attack these serpents with nets, and who assist Horus by reciting words of power for him.

TENTH DIVISION OF THE ṬUAT.

II. Kingdom of Temu-Kheperå-Rā according to the Book of Gates.

In the Tenth Division, or Hour, which Åfu-Rā enters so soon as he has passed through its Gate, which is called Tcheserit, and is guarded by the monster serpent SETHU, it seems that the reconstitution of the Sun-god took place. The god ÀFU-RĀ is towed by gods of the Ṭuat as before, and in this DIVISION all danger appears to have been removed from his path. First stands UNTI, with two stars, and he lights up the upper heaven; next come four deities of flame and fire, who travel with ÀFU-RĀ and give him light. These are followed by three star-gods, who draw towards them a small boat containing a face which is intended for ÀTEN, or the Sun's Disk. The winged serpent SEMI acts as a guide for the god; BESI, the Flame-god, collects fire to put in the new sun; ĀNKHI, the god of Time, in the form of a serpent, with two faces which look in opposite directions, decrees the length of the new Sun's life; the four goddesses cry "Enter in, O Rā! Hail, come, O Rā!" and the MEḤEN serpent surmounted by the god HORUS-SET, with one bow in the dark, and the other in the light, leads the god into the East of heaven (vol. ii., pp. 266, 267).

On the right of the path of ÀFU-RĀ are the twelve ÀKHEMU-SEKU gods, each with his paddle; they are born each day, and after the new Sun-god has entered his boat they join him, and act as his mariners. Beyond these are twelve goddesses who help to tow the Boat of ÀFU-RĀ just before dawn, and then come a god of the Gates of the Ṭuat, the captain of the gods in the Boat, two gods who order the courses of the stars, a star-god in the form of an ape, the Eye of RĀ, which unites itself to the face of Rā, and the guardian of the

Gate of this Division, who does not leave his place. All the other gods travel onwards to the day with Ȧfu-Rā (vol. ii., pp. 273-278).

On the left of the path of Ȧfu-Rā we again see the serpent Āpep. To his neck is attached a chain, which is grasped by the hands of the Four Seṭefiu gods and the Twelve Tchaṭiu gods, and by the colossal hand Ȧmen-khat, and passing over five serpents, to each of which it is attached by a small chain, it disappears into the ground at the feet of the god Khenti-Ȧmenti. Attached to the five small chains are figures of Seb and of the four children of Horus or Osiris, viz., Mest, Ḥāpi, Ṭuamutef, and Qebḥsennuf. Close to the body of Āpep, and lying by the chain which is tied to him, is the goddess Serq. In front Āpep is attacked by the Ȧntiu and Ḥenātiu gods, who are armed with knives and sticks having curled ends. We have seen that in the Ninth Division Āpep was stupefied by the Saiu and other workers of magic, but here it is clear the defeat of this monster is nearly complete. Now that he has been removed from the path of Ȧfu-Rā, and lies fettered, the great god can continue his journey in peace.

ELEVENTH DIVISION OF THE ṬUAT.

II. Kingdom of Temu-Kheperȧ-Rā according to the Book of Gates.

The gate which leads into the Eleventh Division, or Hour, is called Shetat-Besu, and the name of the monster serpent which guards it is ȦM-NETU-F. Mummied forms guard the corridor between the walls of the outworks, but the place of the company of gods who usually stand outside is occupied by two sceptres, or standards, one of which represents SAR, i.e., Osiris, and the other HORUS. The god ȦFU-RĀ enters this DIVISION in the form in which he has hitherto appeared, and he is towed by four gods who belong to it; we see, however, that ĀPEP has not been wholly removed from the path of the god. The serpent lies here (vol. ii., p. 287) in fetters, and a company of the servants of ȦFU-RĀ who live in this DIVISION stand ready to attack him with the knives which they hold in their hands; their sceptres betoken their position as chiefs in the DIVISION. Next come four apes, each holding a large hand, and these stand, according to the text, two on the right and two on the left of the abode of the god; they hold up the Disk of the god, and sing praises to his soul when it looks upon them. In front of these are the goddesses ȦMENTET and ḤERIT, and the god SEBEKHTI, who presides over the entrance into the vestibule of the world of light.

On the right of the path of the Boat of ȦFU-RĀ are gods and goddesses of the South and North who stablish crowns on the head of Rā when he appears in the sky; gods who give names to Rā and all his forms; gods and goddesses who lament when Rā has gone out from Ȧment, and who drive away Set; and gods with bowed heads who sing praises to Rā and keep guard over the Hidden Door. The souls of these gods follow after Rā, and accompany him on his way, but their bodies stay always where we see them. Their guardian is (vol. ii., pp. 296-299) the god called MȦTI, who has the head of a cat or lion.

On the left of the path of the Boat of ȦFU-RĀ is a company of his ministers who perform various important duties for him. Four of them carry disks, and give the command to the Gate of ȦḲERT so that the god may be allowed to pass through and set himself in the sky. The mention of ȦḲERT in the text which refers to these is interesting, for it shows that the ELEVENTH DIVISION of the BOOK OF GATES represents a portion of the Kingdom of the Sun-god of Heliopolis. Four other gods carry stars, and when ȦFU-RĀ passes out of this DIVISION, and is received into the arms of NU, the Sky-god, they shout hymns of praise.[1] Before these are twelve gods with sceptres, four having human heads, four the heads of rams, and four the heads of hawks. The first four are the lords of the region, and stablish the domains of Rā in the sky; the second four provide offerings of bread and water for the god; and the third four set the shrine of Rā in the Mātet-Seḳtet Boat, and place in it the paddles whereby it is to be paddled across the sky. The eight star-goddesses who sit upon uraei belong to the abode of the great god, four coming from the East and four from the West;

[1] Compare Job xxxviii. 7—"When the morning stars sang together, and all the sons of God shouted for joy."

they invoke the Spirits of the East, and join with them in singing hymns to the god, and in praising him after he has appeared in the sky. At the head of the whole company stands a god with the head of a crocodile (vol. ii., pp. 290-293). The Kingdom of TEMU-KHEPERÅ-RĀ differs from other Ṭuats from the fact that, according to the BOOK OF GATES, it contains no place specially set apart for the punishment of the enemies of Osiris and Rā, and of the damned. The pictures which illustrate it supply us with representations of the enemies of the Sun-god and of the beings who vanquish them, and secure his triumphant progress. Having arrived at the end of the ELEVENTH DIVISION the Boat comes to the end of the Fourth Ṭuat;[1] ÅFU-RĀ has effected his transformation as KHEPERÅ, and is now ready to appear in the sky of this world as RĀ. How he effects this we shall see from the next DIVISION.

[1] The Four Ṭuats are the Kingdoms of Khenti-Åmenti-Osiris, Seker, Osiris of Mendes and Busiris, and Temu-Kheperå-Rā.

CHAPTER XIV.

TWELFTH DIVISION OF THE ṬUAT.

II. EASTERN VESTIBULE OF THE ṬUAT, OR THE ANTE-CHAMBER OF THE WORLD OF LIGHT ACCORDING TO THE BOOK ȦM-ṬUAT.

THE TWELFTH DIVISION, or HOUR, or CITY, is called KHEPER-KEKIU-KHĀU-MESTU, the name of its Gate is THEN-NETERU, and the Hour-goddess is MAA-NEFERT-RĀ; it is the "uttermost limit of thick darkness," i.e., it is not a part of the Ṭuat proper, and it contains the great celestial watery abyss NU, and the goddess NUT. who is here the personification of the "womb of the morning." So soon as the Sun-god passes from the thighs of Nut he will enter the Māṭet Boat, and begin his course in the world of light. We see ȦFU-RĀ in his Boat as before, and in the front of it is the Beetle of Kheperȧ, under whose form the god is to be re-born. The space in front of the Boat is filled by the body of a huge serpent called ĀNKH-NETERU, which lives upon the rumblings of the earth, and from the mouth of which *ȧmakhiu*, or loyal servants, go forth daily. Twelve *ȧmakhiu* of Rā now take hold of the tow-line, and entering in at the tail of the serpent ĀNKH-NETERU draw ÅFU-RĀ and his Boat through its body, and bring him out at its mouth (vol. i., p. 263). During his passage through the serpent, the god transforms himself into Kheperå and the twelve *åmakhiu* who have been with him throughout his journey in the Ṭuat are, after they have passed out of the serpent's body, re-born on the earth each day. They enter the tail of the serpent as loyal servants, but, like their master, are transformed during their passage through its body, and they emerge from its mouth as "rejuvenated forms of RĀ" ( ) each day. They live on the earth during the day, but at sunset they rejoin their lord, and re-enter the Ṭuat; whilst they are upon earth to utter the name of the god is forbidden to them.

The transformation of the dead Sun-god into the living Kheperå having been effected, twelve goddesses step forward when he emerges from the serpent, and tow the great god into the sky, and lead him along the ways of the upper sky. "They bring with them the soft winds and breezes which accompany the dawn, and guide the god to SHU," who is the personification of the atmosphere and of whatever is in the vault of heaven. Of this god are seen (vol. i., p. 277) only the head and arms, and when the Beetle of Kheperå comes to him, he receives him, and places the newly-born Sun-god in the opening in the centre of the semi-circular wall which ends this vestibule of the world of light, where he is seen by the people on earth in the form of a disk. This disk either represents a transformation of the Sun-god effected by Shu, or the celestial ball containing the germs of life, of which the type on earth is the ball of eggs which the sacred beetle is seen rolling along the ground. The mummified form in which the dead Sun-god travelled through the Ṭuat is now useless, and we see it cast aside and lying against the wall which divides the Ṭuat from this world; that there shall be no doubt about this it is described by the words "Image (or, form) of ÅF" ().

Turning now to the beings who are on the right and left of the path of the god, we see in the upper register twelve goddesses, each of whom bears on her shoulders a serpent which produces light by belching fire from its mouth (vol. i., pp. 265, 266); these drive away ĀPEP, and frighten the beings of darkness by their fires. Next to these are twelve gods who sing praises at dawn to the god, whom they assert to be "self-begotten" and the author of his own being, and they rejoice because at his new birth his soul will be in heaven, and his body on earth. These gods are indeed spirits of the East, and they are declared to have jurisdiction over the gods of the "land of the turquoise," i.e., Sinai. In the lower register we have a company of twenty-three gods (vol. i., pp. 271-274) who stand in the sky ready to receive Rā when he appears, and to praise him; some of them drive ĀPEP to "the

back of the sky," some support the Great Disk in the sky, and the duty of one of them, who is called SENMEKHEF and appears in the form of a serpent, is to burn up the enemies of Rā at dawn. Thus the Sun-god passed out of the Ṭuat even as he entered it, with praises, and as he did so he bade farewell to Osiris, the Lord of the Ṭuat, under one of whose forms he had completed successfully his journey, in these words:—
"Life to thee! O thou who art over the darkness! "Life [to thee]! in all thy majesty. Life to thee! O "KHENTI-ȦMENTET-OSIRIS, who art over the beings of "Ȧmentet. Life to thee! Life to thee! O thou who "art over the Ṭuat. The winds of Rā are in thy "nostrils, and the nourishment of Kheperȧ is with "thee. Thou livest, and ye live. Hail to Osiris, the "lord of the living, that is to say, of the gods who are "with Osiris, and who came into being with him the "first time."

TWELFTH DIVISION OF THE ṬUAT.

II. EASTERN VESTIBULE OF THE ṬUAT ACCORDING TO THE BOOK OF GATES.

The last section of the BOOK OF GATES contains representations of the Gate ṬESERT-BAIU, with its two doors (vol. ii., pp. 302, 303), which lead into that portion of the sky wherein the sun rises, and of the stablishing of the Sun-god in his Boat in the sky. This Gate has no company of gods in mummied forms to guard it, and in front of it are two standards, or sceptres, each of which is surrounded by a human head; above that on the left is the Beetle of KHEPERȦ, and over the other is the Disk of TEMU. In other words, the Gate is guarded by symbols of the rising and the setting sun. The corridor between the walls is swept by flames as before, and a warder in mummied form guards each end of it; the one, PAI or BAI, represents the dawn, and the other, ȦKHEKHI, the evening. Within the Gate are two doors, one guarded by the monster serpent SEBI, and the other by the monster serpent RERI. At the threshold is the uraeus of NEPHTHYS, and by the lintel is the uraeus of ISIS, for these goddesses guard this "Secret Gate."

The god ȦFU-RĀ having, as we have seen, transformed himself into KHEPERȦ, and, by the help of the god whose operations have been described, provided himself with a new face, or disk, and new light and fire, passes through the Gate ṬESERT-BAIU, which marks the end of the ṬUAT, into the Vestibule of the world of light. We no longer see him in the form of a ram-headed man, standing under the folds of the serpent MEḤEN, but he appears as KHEPERȦ, i.e., as his Beetle, with the disk in front of him. From the scene which ends the BOOK OF GATES we learn that so soon as the god passes through the Gate of ṬESERT-BAIU he enters the waters of NU, the god of the primeval watery abyss of the sky. The ministers of KHEPERȦ now appear with the MĀṬET-SEKṬET BOAT which they have in readiness, and the god takes his place in it, with the gods who are to guide and propel it. Nu then lifts the Boat up above his head, and the goddess Nut receives the Disk of the sun in her hands. It will be noted that she stands on the head of a god whose body is bent in such a way that it forms a circle: the explanatory text shows that the god is Osiris, and that his body is the Ṭuat. Thus we see that the "womb of Nut," 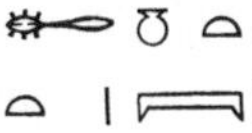, from which the Sun-god is said to be born, lies quite close to the eastern end of the Ṭuat, and that it forms by itself the Vestibule which leads into the world of light.

Close to the high prow of the Boat we see (vol. ii., p. 303) the sun's disk passing through a gap in the mountain which divides the Eastern Vestibule of the Ṭuat from the sky of this world; this disk is the same which we have seen Nut receive from the Beetle of Kheperȧ, and whilst it is traversing the gap dawn is taking place on the earth. When the disk is on the horizon all men know that the monsters of the Ṭuat have failed to destroy Ȧfu-Rā or to obstruct his passage, that the god has, with the aid of Kheperȧ, made all his transformations, that he has appeared in the sky again, full of light, and fire, and life, and that for another day at least all will be well with the world. Meanwhile the souls of the blessed who have travelled through the Ṭuat in the Boat with Ȧfu-Rā have escaped with him from all its dangers, and have made their transformations as he has done, and now they rise with him above this earth, and are able to look once again upon their own homes and haunts, and friends. Their companions are the gods who minister to Rā, and as they live upon the food of Rā, and are arrayed in his apparel, they become in all respects like him.

For the beings who were left in the Ṭuat, i.e., for those who were not provided for by Osiris in SEKHET-ȦARU and SEKHET-ḤETEPET, existence must have been a sad one, for they were obliged to sit in darkness and misery, except for the brief space each night when ȦFU-RĀ passed through their DIVISIONS, when the gods who were in his train lightened the darkness with the fire which proceeded from their bodies, and the god himself, taking pity on those to whom the making of offerings on earth had ceased, spoke the words which procured sustenance for them. Such acts of grace, however, cannot have been sufficient to secure the happiness of those upon whom they were bestowed, for, with every mention in the texts of the closing of the door of a DIVISION after the god has passed through it, we read that the souls who were outside the door uttered cries of lamentation and wailed bitterly.

It must be remembered that views such as are here described were held only by the priests of ȦMEN-RĀ, who, as we have seen, tried to show that their god was lord of all the Ṭuats of Egypt, and that all the gods of the dead, including even Osiris, and all the blessed, depended upon him for light and food, which they received from him in return for the services which they rendered to him as their overlord. Those who held not these views, and were not followers of Osiris, believed, as did all the primitive Egyptians, that the Ṭuat was a place of darkness, hunger, thirst, and misery, and finally of annihilation. They had no belief either in purgatory or in everlasting punishment; the beings in the Ṭuat lived just so long as their friends and relatives on earth made the prescribed funeral offerings on their behalf, and no longer. The shadows, souls, and bodies of those who were without food in the Ṭuat were, together with the fiends and monsters which opposed the progress of the Sun-god, destroyed by fire each day, utterly and finally; but each day brought its own supply of the enemies of Rā, and of the dead, and the beings which were consumed in the pits of fire one day were not the *same*, though they belonged to the *same classes*, as those which had been burnt up the day before.

INDEX

A CATALOG OF SELECTED

DOVER BOOKS

IN ALL FIELDS OF INTEREST

BRASS INSTRUMENTS: Their History and Development, Anthony Baines. Authoritative, updated survey of the evolution of trumpets, trombones, bugles, cornets, French horns, tubas and other brass wind instruments. Over 140 illustrations and 48 music examples. Corrected and updated by author. New preface. Bibliography. 320pp. 5⅜ × 8½. 27574-4 Pa. $9.95

HOLLYWOOD GLAMOR PORTRAITS, John Kobal (ed.). 145 photos from 1926–49. Harlow, Gable, Bogart, Bacall; 94 stars in all. Full background on photographers, technical aspects. 160pp. 8⅜ × 11¼. 23352-9 Pa. $11.95

MAX AND MORITZ, Wilhelm Busch. Great humor classic in both German and English. Also 10 other works: "Cat and Mouse," "Plisch and Plumm," etc. 216pp. 5⅜ × 8½. 20181-3 Pa. $5.95

THE RAVEN AND OTHER FAVORITE POEMS, Edgar Allan Poe. Over 40 of the author's most memorable poems: "The Bells," "Ulalume," "Israfel," "To Helen," "The Conqueror Worm," "Eldorado," "Annabel Lee," many more. Alphabetic lists of titles and first lines. 64pp. 5³⁄₁₆ × 8¼. 26685-0 Pa. $1.00

SEVEN SCIENCE FICTION NOVELS, H. G. Wells. The standard collection of the great novels. Complete, unabridged. First Men in the Moon, Island of Dr. Moreau, War of the Worlds, Food of the Gods, Invisible Man, Time Machine, In the Days of the Comet. Total of 1,015pp. 5⅜ × 8½. (USO) 20264-X Clothbd. $29.95

AMULETS AND SUPERSTITIONS, E. A. Wallis Budge. Comprehensive discourse on origin, powers of amulets in many ancient cultures: Arab, Persian, Babylonian, Assyrian, Egyptian, Gnostic, Hebrew, Phoenician, Syriac, etc. Covers cross, swastika, crucifix, seals, rings, stones, etc. 584pp. 5⅜ × 8½. 23573-4 Pa. $12.95

RUSSIAN STORIES/PYCCKNE PACCKA3bl: A Dual-Language Book, edited by Gleb Struve. Twelve tales by such masters as Chekhov, Tolstoy, Dostoevsky, Pushkin, others. Excellent word-for-word English translations on facing pages, plus teaching and study aids, Russian/English vocabulary, biographical/critical introductions, more. 416pp. 5⅜ × 8½. 26244-8 Pa. $8.95

PHILADELPHIA THEN AND NOW: 60 Sites Photographed in the Past and Present, Kenneth Finkel and Susan Oyama. Rare photographs of City Hall, Logan Square, Independence Hall, Betsy Ross House, other landmarks juxtaposed with contemporary views. Captures changing face of historic city. Introduction. Captions. 128pp. 8¼ × 11. 25790-8 Pa. $9.95

AIA ARCHITECTURAL GUIDE TO NASSAU AND SUFFOLK COUNTIES, LONG ISLAND, The American Institute of Architects, Long Island Chapter, and the Society for the Preservation of Long Island Antiquities. Comprehensive, well-researched and generously illustrated volume brings to life over three centuries of Long Island's great architectural heritage. More than 240 photographs with authoritative, extensively detailed captions. 176pp. 8¼ × 11. 26946-9 Pa. $14.95

NORTH AMERICAN INDIAN LIFE: Customs and Traditions of 23 Tribes, Elsie Clews Parsons (ed.). 27 fictionalized essays by noted anthropologists examine religion, customs, government, additional facets of life among the Winnebago, Crow, Zuni, Eskimo, other tribes. 480pp. 6⅛ × 9¼. 27377-6 Pa. $10.95

FRANK LLOYD WRIGHT'S HOLLYHOCK HOUSE, Donald Hoffmann. Lavishly illustrated, carefully documented study of one of Wright's most controversial residential designs. Over 120 photographs, floor plans, elevations, etc. Detailed perceptive text by noted Wright scholar. Index. 128pp. 9¼ × 10¾.
27133-1 Pa. $11.95

THE MALE AND FEMALE FIGURE IN MOTION: 60 Classic Photographic Sequences, Eadweard Muybridge. 60 true-action photographs of men and women walking, running, climbing, bending, turning, etc., reproduced from rare 19th-century masterpiece. vi + 121pp. 9 × 12. 24745-7 Pa. $10.95

1001 QUESTIONS ANSWERED ABOUT THE SEASHORE, N. J. Berrill and Jacquelyn Berrill. Queries answered about dolphins, sea snails, sponges, starfish, fishes, shore birds, many others. Covers appearance, breeding, growth, feeding, much more. 305pp. 5¼ × 8¼. 23366-9 Pa. $7.95

GUIDE TO OWL WATCHING IN NORTH AMERICA, Donald S. Heintzelman. Superb guide offers complete data and descriptions of 19 species: barn owl, screech owl, snowy owl, many more. Expert coverage of owl-watching equipment, conservation, migrations and invasions, etc. Guide to observing sites. 84 illustrations. xiii + 193pp. 5⅜ × 8½. 27344-X Pa. $8.95

MEDICINAL AND OTHER USES OF NORTH AMERICAN PLANTS: A Historical Survey with Special Reference to the Eastern Indian Tribes, Charlotte Erichsen-Brown. Chronological historical citations document 500 years of usage of plants, trees, shrubs native to eastern Canada, northeastern U.S. Also complete identifying information. 343 illustrations. 544pp. 6½ × 9¼. 25951-X Pa. $12.95

STORYBOOK MAZES, Dave Phillips. 23 stories and mazes on two-page spreads: Wizard of Oz, Treasure Island, Robin Hood, etc. Solutions. 64pp. 8¼ × 11.
23628-5 Pa. $2.95

NEGRO FOLK MUSIC, U.S.A., Harold Courlander. Noted folklorist's scholarly yet readable analysis of rich and varied musical tradition. Includes authentic versions of over 40 folk songs. Valuable bibliography and discography. xi + 324pp. 5⅜ × 8½. 27350-4 Pa. $7.95

MOVIE-STAR PORTRAITS OF THE FORTIES, John Kobal (ed.). 163 glamor, studio photos of 106 stars of the 1940s: Rita Hayworth, Ava Gardner, Marlon Brando, Clark Gable, many more. 176pp. 8⅜ × 11¼. 23546-7 Pa. $11.95

BENCHLEY LOST AND FOUND, Robert Benchley. Finest humor from early 30s, about pet peeves, child psychologists, post office and others. Mostly unavailable elsewhere. 73 illustrations by Peter Arno and others. 183pp. 5⅜ × 8½.
22410-4 Pa. $5.95

YEKL and THE IMPORTED BRIDEGROOM AND OTHER STORIES OF YIDDISH NEW YORK, Abraham Cahan. Film Hester Street based on Yekl (1896). Novel, other stories among first about Jewish immigrants on N.Y.'s East Side. 240pp. 5⅜ × 8½. 22427-9 Pa. $6.95

SELECTED POEMS, Walt Whitman. Generous sampling from *Leaves of Grass*. Twenty-four poems include "I Hear America Singing," "Song of the Open Road," "I Sing the Body Electric," "When Lilacs Last in the Dooryard Bloom'd," "O Captain! My Captain!"—all reprinted from an authoritative edition. Lists of titles and first lines. 128pp. 5³⁄₁₆ × 8¼. 26878-0 Pa. $1.00

THE BEST TALES OF HOFFMANN, E. T. A. Hoffmann. 10 of Hoffmann's most important stories: "Nutcracker and the King of Mice," "The Golden Flowerpot," etc. 458pp. 5⅜ × 8½. 21793-0 Pa. $8.95

FROM FETISH TO GOD IN ANCIENT EGYPT, E. A. Wallis Budge. Rich detailed survey of Egyptian conception of "God" and gods, magic, cult of animals, Osiris, more. Also, superb English translations of hymns and legends. 240 illustrations. 545pp. 5⅜ × 8½. 25803-3 Pa. $11.95

FRENCH STORIES/CONTES FRANÇAIS: A Dual-Language Book, Wallace Fowlie. Ten stories by French masters, Voltaire to Camus: "Micromegas" by Voltaire; "The Atheist's Mass" by Balzac; "Minuet" by de Maupassant; "The Guest" by Camus, six more. Excellent English translations on facing pages. Also French-English vocabulary list, exercises, more. 352pp. 5⅜ × 8½. 26443-2 Pa. $8.95

CHICAGO AT THE TURN OF THE CENTURY IN PHOTOGRAPHS: 122 Historic Views from the Collections of the Chicago Historical Society, Larry A. Viskochil. Rare large-format prints offer detailed views of City Hall, State Street, the Loop, Hull House, Union Station, many other landmarks, circa 1904–1913. Introduction. Captions. Maps. 144pp. 9⅜ × 12¼. 24656-6 Pa. $12.95

OLD BROOKLYN IN EARLY PHOTOGRAPHS, 1865–1929, William Lee Younger. Luna Park, Gravesend race track, construction of Grand Army Plaza, moving of Hotel Brighton, etc. 157 previously unpublished photographs. 165pp. 8⅞ × 11¾. 23587-4 Pa. $13.95

THE MYTHS OF THE NORTH AMERICAN INDIANS, Lewis Spence. Rich anthology of the myths and legends of the Algonquins, Iroquois, Pawnees and Sioux, prefaced by an extensive historical and ethnological commentary. 36 illustrations. 480pp. 5⅜ × 8½. 25967-6 Pa. $8.95

AN ENCYCLOPEDIA OF BATTLES: Accounts of Over 1,560 Battles from 1479 B.C. to the Present, David Eggenberger. Essential details of every major battle in recorded history from the first battle of Megiddo in 1479 B.C. to Grenada in 1984. List of Battle Maps. New Appendix covering the years 1967–1984. Index. 99 illustrations. 544pp. 6½ × 9¼. 24913-1 Pa. $14.95

SAILING ALONE AROUND THE WORLD, Captain Joshua Slocum. First man to sail around the world, alone, in small boat. One of great feats of seamanship told in delightful manner. 67 illustrations. 294pp. 5⅜ × 8½. 20326-3 Pa. $5.95

ANARCHISM AND OTHER ESSAYS, Emma Goldman. Powerful, penetrating, prophetic essays on direct action, role of minorities, prison reform, puritan hypocrisy, violence, etc. 271pp. 5⅜ × 8½. 22484-8 Pa. $5.95

MYTHS OF THE HINDUS AND BUDDHISTS, Ananda K. Coomaraswamy and Sister Nivedita. Great stories of the epics; deeds of Krishna, Shiva, taken from puranas, Vedas, folk tales; etc. 32 illustrations. 400pp. 5⅜ × 8½. 21759-0 Pa. $9.95

BEYOND PSYCHOLOGY, Otto Rank. Fear of death, desire of immortality, nature of sexuality, social organization, creativity, according to Rankian system. 291pp. 5⅜ × 8½. 20485-5 Pa. $8.95

A THEOLOGICO-POLITICAL TREATISE, Benedict Spinoza. Also contains unfinished Political Treatise. Great classic on religious liberty, theory of government on common consent. R. Elwes translation. Total of 421pp. 5⅜ × 8½. 20249-6 Pa. $8.95